1989 1990 1993 **1994** 1997 **2000** **2003** **2005** **2011** **2012**
38 1991 1992 **1996** **1999** 2002 2004 **2007** 2010 **2008** **2013**
1995 1998 **2001** 2006 2009

1963–2013

CHRONICLE

OF

MALAYSIA

FIFTY YEARS OF HEADLINE NEWS

Above: 'Malaysia and You'. A Sarawak tribesman studies a poster explaining the impact of the formation of Malaysia, 1 November 1962.

Page 5: Students of Sekolah Kebangsaan Seri Nilam, Kuala Terengganu display a *Jalur Gemilang* (Malaysian flag) measuring 55m x 4.5m as part of celebrations to mark the 56th anniversary of Merdeka and 50th anniversary of Malaysia, 5 September 2013.

1963–2013
CHRONICLE OF MALAYSIA

FIFTY YEARS OF HEADLINE NEWS

Editor-in-Chief
Philip Mathews

edm EDITIONS DIDIER MILLET

Editorial Committee

Chairman
Tun Mohammed Hanif Omar
• Deputy Chairman, Genting Bhd
• President, Malaysian Branch of the Royal Asiatic Society

Members

Tan Sri Mohamed Jawhar Hassan
• Chairman and Chief Executive Officer,
Institute of Strategic and International Studies (ISIS) Malaysia
• Chairman, The New Straits Times Press (Malaysia) Bhd

Dato' Henry S. Barlow
• Honorary Treasurer, Malaysian Branch of the Royal Asiatic Society
• Honorary Secretary, Badan Warisan Malaysia

Dr Lee Kam Hing
• Senior Research Fellow, Social and Behavioural Sciences Research Cluster,
Universiti Malaya

Tan Sri Dr Visu Sinnadurai
• Former High Court Judge

Datuk Mohammad Nor Khalid (Lat)
• Cartoonist

Dato' Ranita Mohd Hussein
• Chairman, Securities Industry Dispute Resolution Centre

P. C. Shivadas
• Former Group Editor, New Straits Times

Editorial Team

Publisher
Didier Millet

General Manager
Charles Orwin

Editorial Director
Douglas Amrine

Project Manager and Editor
Martin Cross

Editor-in-Chief
Philip Mathews

Editor and Researcher
Joane Sharmila

Sabah Research
Professor Dr Danny Wong

Design
Vani Nadaraju

International and Regional News Editor
Thor Kah Hoong

Sarawak Research
James Ritchie

Marketing
Suresh Sekaran

Copy Editors
Tan Bee Hong
Sharipah Intan Syed Hussein

Production Manager
Sin Kam Cheong

Additional Editorial Team members for *Chronicle of Malaysia 1957–2007*

Editorial Consultant
Michael Maclachlan

Production Editor
Leonard Pasqual

Editors
William Citrin
Kiri Cowie
Nurin Mastura
Nurshafenath Shaharuddin
Sheila Natarajan Rahman

Copy Editors
Cheah Chor Sooi
Gerald Martinez
Patricia Pereira
Christy Yoong

Visual Arts Consultant
Zanita Anuar

News and Picture Researchers
Eleanor Choo
Suzana Kudil (*Sabah*)
Lee Li Lian
Heidi Munan (*Sarawak*)
Yasmin Salsabil binti Masidi

Overseas Researchers
UNITED KINGDOM
Neil Khor

AUSTRALIA
Ed Giles

SINGAPORE
Sng Siok Ai

Studio Manager
Yusri bin Din

Designers
Pascal Chan
Mohd Farid Zainuddin
Muamar Ghadafi
Charles P.E. Yeoh

© Editions Didier Millet, 2013

Editions Didier Millet
25, Jalan Pudu Lama, 50200 Kuala Lumpur, Malaysia
Tel: 03-2031 3805 Fax: 03-2031 6298
E-mail: edmbooks@edmbooks.com.my
Website: www.edmbooks.com

Editions Didier Millet Pte Ltd
121, Telok Ayer Street, #03-01, Singapore 068590
Tel: 65-6324 9260 Fax: 65-6324 9261
E-mail: edm@edmbooks.com.sg

First published in 2013 by Editions Didier Millet

ISBN 978-967-10617-4-9

Colour separation by PICA Digital Pte Ltd
Printed by Tien Wah Press

NOTE TO READERS:
Units of measurement
are those in general use
at the time of the event
reported.

The *Chronicle of Malaysia 1963–2013* was made possible thanks to the generous support of:

The publisher would also like to thank the following organisations for their support of *Chronicle of Malaysia 1957–2007*:
Genting Berhad, Petronas Berhad, CIMB Group,
Ministry of Information, Bernama, Film Negara Malaysia, RTM,
Astro, Maxis, Measat Satellite Systems Sdn Bhd, Tanjong Public Limited Company,
Star Publications, Mandarin Oriental Kuala Lumpur, Media Prima Berhad, Bursa Malaysia.

Acknowledgements

This revised and updated edition of the Chronicle was made possible due to the assistance of a large number of people and organisations.

For advice on the background to the formation of Malaysia:

Dato' Dr Zakaria Haji Ahmad, Deputy Vice Chancellor (Research), HELP University • Tan Sri Peter Lo Su Yin, former Chief Minister of Sabah

For providing access to newspapers, special thanks are due to the management and staff of the following organisations:

Arkib Negara Malaysia: Mohd Nazri Baharuddin, Seksyen Rujukan dan Akses

Jabatan Muzium Sarawak: Ipoi Datan, Director, Sarawak Museum Department

The publisher would also like to thank the following individuals and organisations for providing photographs for the book:

Bernama: Hamdanawal bin Muhamad Sukri

Jabatan Penerangan Malaysia: Staff of the Tan Sri Mubin Sheppard Resource Centre, Putrajaya

New Straits Times Press (Malaysia) Bhd: Mohammad Azlan Abdullah, Chief Executive Officer • Datuk Abdul Jalil Hamid, Group Managing Editor • Ramlan Ramli, Manager, Resource Centre • Mohd Azlee bin Abdul Aziz • Jandariah binti Mohamad • Santha Kumari • Shukor Othman • T. Mahendran • Muhammad Hamizi bin Abdul Hamid • Nik Azwan bin Nik Mustapha

Sin Chew Jit Poh: Low Soo Yoke, Assistant Supervisor (Library)

Star Publications (M) Bhd: Leanne Goh Lee Yen, Deputy Group Chief Editor II • Zaini Amri Abidin, Head Info Centre, Operation • Ravichandran Muniandi • Chan Bibi Gulam Khan and all Staric staff

Utusan Borneo: Francis Chan, Chief Editor • Phyllis Wong

Utusan Melayu (M) Berhad, Information Centre: Fouziah Abd Rahim, Head, Information Centre • Noridzan Kamal, Senior Manager, Information Centre, and all Information staff

Boh Plantations Sdn Bhd • Bukit Merah Laketown Resort • Richard Curtis • John Falconer • David Alan Harvey • Hijjas Kasturi Sdn • James Lee Peek Kuan • Dr Lee Siow Ming • C.Y. Leow • Dato' Seri Lim Chong Keat • M. Magendran • Muzium Negara • Muzium Polis Diraja Malaysia • National Art Gallery, Malaysia • Paramsothy S. • Pelanduk Publications (M) Sdn Bhd Prabakaran Nair • The Tunku Abdul Rahman Memorial • The Tun Abdul Razak Memorial • The Tun Hussein Onn Memorial

For the provision of cartoons, the publisher is grateful to:

Heng Kim Seng • C.W. Kee • Lat • Tan Sri Dato' Lim Kok Wing

The publisher and editor-in-chief would also like to thank Padman Gopal and Unny Krishnan.

Bersekutu Bertambah Mutu (Unity is Strength). An official poster commemorating the formation of Malaysia in 1963 prominently features Prime Minister Tunku Abdul Rahman.

CONTENTS

Prime Minister Dato' Seri Dr Mahathir Mohamad takes the salute at a police function, 4 April 1987. He is flanked by (left) Inspector General of Police Tan Sri Mohammed Hanif Omar and Deputy Home Affairs Minister Dato' Seri Megat Junid.

FOREWORD

In 2007 the original *Chronicle of Malaysia* was published to commemorate and celebrate the 50th anniversary of Merdeka, that is Peninsular Malaysia's independence. In my foreword to that first edition, I expressed my hope that the book would remind Malaysians of all that is dear to us so that we might continue to preserve and protect the well-being and prosperity of the nation.

As the golden anniversary of the formation of Malaysia approached in September 2013, the publishers of the *Chronicle of Malaysia* and I felt it would be appropriate to publish a new edition of the book to bring it up to date and to record this important milestone.

Having decided to do so, we reviewed the news stories that were included in the original edition and made a conscious effort in this new and revised edition to redress the imbalance in news coverage between Peninsular Malaysia and the States of Sabah and Sarawak. On the pages of this edition, you will therefore find newly inserted items on Sabah and Sarawak from 1963 onwards. These stories cover State elections, the development of townships and infrastructure, biodiversity, festivals and the gamut of fires and natural disasters.

We also felt it important that a major feature of the book be a coherent account of the complex and drawn-out process of Malaysia's formation. Uniting the distinct socio-political territories that now comprise Malaysia—with their varied histories, cultures and populations—was far from a simple task and took a great deal of political will and finesse, under the masterly eye of Tunku Abdul Rahman, to achieve. You will find the account of the formation of Malaysia in Professor James Chin's appropriately titled introduction.

It is said that a week is a long time in politics, and for a new nation 50 years might be an eternity. In that time, much has indeed changed; but at the same time, much has stayed the same. The hundreds of news stories in this book together provide a nostalgic insight into how, little by little, the nascent nation of then has been transformed into the Malaysia of today.

Readers should indeed find inside the *Chronicle of Malaysia* interesting reminders of what is important to us Malaysians. If so, then my earlier expressed hope will have been fulfilled.

Tun Mohammed Hanif Omar
Chairman
Editorial Committee

PREFACE

THE CHANGING FACE OF JOURNALISM

Not all stories circulating in newsrooms get into print. Some morph into legends, like the one surrounding veteran newsman P. Krishnan. The story is told of how one day he returned to the *Straits Times* newsroom in Robson House on Kuala Lumpur's Jalan Pudu and sat at the untidy and cluttered table he shared with five others. He bashed out a story on his heavy-duty Royale typewriter.

The year was 1965. The story was a speculative article about how Singapore would soon be expelled from the newly minted Federation of Malaysia. Yet it was rejected by Editor-in-Chief Leslie Hoffman, for two reasons. First, the source of the story was not identified and second, the separation of Singapore was unthinkable, and had been neither discussed nor contemplated, in public or in private.

A few days later however, on 7 August, Prime Minister Tunku Abdul Rahman made the shock announcement that Singapore would soon exit Malaysia. Had Krishan's story been published, it would have qualified as a world 'exclusive'. In those days, a major news scoop was valued as much as a month's salary and rewarded with a thick story byline (set in 18-point Times Roman Bold typeface) and free beer at The Pines in Brickfields.

As news of the Tunku's announcement reached the newsroom, an incensed Krishnan carried his typewriter and walked to Hoffman's room. Krishnan swung it once and then flung it into the room, smashing the glass door but causing no other harm except for a temporary dent in the Editor-in-Chief's infallible judgment.

Krishnan embodied the spirit of journalists of the time, expressed through their dedication to their profession, their search for the facts and their desire to present it to the public fully and truthfully. For Krishnan, like his colleagues, the event was not as important as the story. They knew they had no control over events, but they had full control over how and when the details of the event were presented. They took a detached view of events as they arose and presented them without comment or bias. Their job was first to gather all the facts and then to tell the story as objectively as possible. If all the facts were not available by press-time, the story would be held over until the verification process was completed. That was responsible journalism.

Opposite: The open editorial office at Robson House, Jalan Pudu, Kuala Lumpur in the mid 1960s. The *Malay Mail* newsdesk is in the foreground with those of *Berita Harian* behind them and the *Straits Times* at the far end. Engrossed in various stages of editorial work—news gathering, news writing and news editing— are news editor David Tambyah (extreme left) and reporters Willie Soh, Balachandran (on the phone), Anthony Ng and Jerry Francis. In the background is crime reporter Rudy Beltran. They are surrounded by the tools that defined newsrooms of the era: rotary dial telephones, manual typewriters, improvised ashtrays and cluttered formica-top desks.

But once in a while, this obsession to get the story, at the expense of the event, would be so overpowering that better judgment would take a back seat. On one such occasion, it changed the course of history. In late 1962, there was a breaking story—the powerful Railwaymen's Union of Malaysia (RUM) was agitating over workers' pay, but the railway administration would not give in to their demands. A reporter at the *Malay Mail* followed the unfolding events until negotiations became deadlocked. This meant that there would be no more news from the railwaymen's front, at least for a while. So, one fine day, this reporter wrote an advance story saying that the railway workers had indeed gone on strike. The reporter then called the union leaders and said the story of their strike would appear in the next *Malay Mail* edition that would hit the streets at mid-morning. And indeed the union went on strike immediately, confirming the story that preceded it.

Malaysian journalists also had a strong sense of nationalism, with those from all language streams united in espousing national causes such acting in unison on matters related to national security and racial harmony.

So dedicated to their profession were they that during the riots of 13 May 1969, journalists spent days and nights in their newsrooms, living off sardines and bread flown in by helicopter during the curfew hours and sleeping on bare table tops. Although newspapers were suspended for a few days, reporters stayed on at their posts along with the security forces on duty. The situation was no different in the Television Malaysia newsroom at the Angkasapuri building. For days on end, there was only one newsreader on duty. On the third day, he looked tired, but still appeared before the camera in his jacket and tie. And then it happened. The camera was still rolling when the reader got up from his desk, revealing the embarrassing fact that from the waist down he was still wearing the sarong that he had been sleeping in before he was quickly awakened and rushed to the newsroom to read the news.

In those days, there was a clear tradition of separating facts and comment in the newspaper columns. Reporters on the newsdesk would not include commentary in the news stories that they produced. Newspapers jealously followed the principle enunciated by *The Guardian* editor C.P. Scott half a century earlier. He had said that in his newspaper, comment was free but facts were sacred.

Commenting on current issues was the job of leader writers such as Allington Kennard, Hugh Mabbet, Peter Lim and others who sat cocooned in their cubicles surrounded by library files of newspaper clippings, only making an appearance in the newsroom en route to the washroom. It was for them to pontificate or comment on matters such as the rise and fall of the prices of rubber, tin and palm oil. Street crime, as opposed to communist terrorism, was not a major issue then and therefore rarely merited the attention of leader writers.

Today's news organisations have had to move with the times. Gone are the days of smoke-filled, cluttered open floors where shouts of 'thamby' by the likes of David Tambyah would would see office boys grabbing sub-edited hard copy and shoving them down the chute in cut-out biscuit tins to the production floor downstairs to be typeset and then hauling them upstairs afterwards.

News gathering has been revolutionised. In earlier decades, the only sources of news were interviews conducted face-to-face or by telephone or by witnessing an event first-hand such as watching a football match. If you worked for a news bureau, you would call headquarters (if you were lucky enough to find a working public telephone) and dictate stories to a harassed duty reporter who took it all down in longhand.

News distribution too has changed immeasurably. Back then, the written news was solely distributed by news vendors. Now it is communicated online on websites, apps, via email, SMS, Twitter, Facebook and scores of other electronic platforms. Much has also changed in the presentation of news, in the way it is processed, and in the manner in which one responds to it. There is no denying that the digital age has dramatically changed the way we protect life, liberty and the pursuit of happiness.

With the rise of smartphones, now everyone is a news consumer and everyone is (or has the potential and equipment to be) a news gatherer. They will help redefine journalism, they will set its parameters, they will be their own gatekeepers, and they will write their own stories. Journalism, albeit in a different form, will survive, as it has done since 1608 when the first newsletter was published in Jamestown by Captain John Smith. That's not an opinion. That is a fact, gleaned from the Internet, journalism's new frontier.

This book, *Chronicle of Malaysia: 1963–2013*, like its precedessor *Chronicle of Malaysia: 1957–2007*, is a recognition of the labours of journalists past and present, and of the contribution of the many newspapers published over the years in Peninsular Malaysia, Sabah and Sarawak. It is a gift to all Malaysians who may find in it a slice of their own living history.

Philip Mathews
Editor-in-Chief

A BRIEF HISTORY OF THE MALAY PENINSULA AND NORTHERN BORNEO

Professor James Chin
Head, School of Arts and Social Sciences
Monash University (Malaysia Campus)

The political history of the territories of the Malay Peninsula and northern Borneo that, with the exception of Brunei, went on to form Malaysia is varied and somewhat complex. But the history of each shares a common thread: they were to a large extent shaped by European colonial intervention. As this came to an end after World War II, the states moved towards independence.

The Malay Peninsula

Following Portuguese (1511–1641) and then Dutch (1641–1825) occupation of Malacca, it was the British who ultimately gained the upper hand in the peninsula. Beginning with the East India Company's trading post on the island of Penang, founded in 1786, and then its administration of Malacca (as 'caretaker' from 1795–1818, and then from 1825) the United Kingdom gradually gained de facto control of the peninsular states from 1874. The Federated Malay States (FMS)—comprising Selangor, Perak, Pahang and Negeri Sembilan—was established in 1896. The FMS formed the basis of the Federation of Malaya which was constituted in 1948 after the Japanese Occupation of World War II (1941–1945) and the abortive Malayan Union.

Chief Minister (later Prime Minister) Tunku Abdul Rahman and the Alliance that he led, successfully negotiated independence from the United Kingdom for the Federation of Malaya, or Persekutuan Tanah Melayu as it was termed in the Proclamation of Independence, on 31 August 1957. The Tunku had shown he was able to unite all three main ethnic groups in the country—the Malays, Chinese and Indians—under the umbrella of the Alliance. The Alliance consisted of three political parties, each representing one of the three ethnic groups.

Malaya was an independent country, but it was a nation under threat as the communists had launched an insurgency in 1948. Called the 'Emergency', it lasted until 1960. During this period, large areas of Malaya were under threat of attack by communists hiding in the jungle. Commonwealth forces were deployed to help prevent the country from falling into communist hands and large numbers of Chinese were relocated from the jungle fringe to 'new towns'.

Sarawak

The history of modern Sarawak is closely tied to the adventures of an Englishman, James Brooke. He founded the Brooke dynasty that was to rule Sarawak for a hundred years. Brooke was installed as first Rajah of Sarawak in 1841. James was succeeded by Charles (r. 1868–1917), the second Rajah, and Vyner, the third and last Rajah (r. 1917–1946).

In 1941, a new constitution was established by Vyner, the preamble of which was the Nine Cardinal Principles of the rule of the English Rajah (see p. 25) which paved the way for self-governance by the people. Before the enactment could be effected, however, the Pacific War broke out and the whole of Borneo came under Japanese rule.

After Sarawak was liberated by Allied troops, in 1946 Rajah Vyner ceded Sarawak to Great Britain.[1] Although Sarawak was officially annexed as a Crown Colony, it had a full legislature, the Council Negri[2] (renamed the Dewan Undangan Negeri in 1976), and a Cabinet, the Supreme Council. Nonetheless, real power was always in the hands of the British Governor and all senior administrative positions were held by expatriate British officers. On 22 July 1963, in the shadow of the Malaysia concept, Sarawak moved towards self-government with Stephen Kalong Ningkan as its Chief Minister.

North Borneo

European influence in Sabah extended back even further than it did in Sarawak. In 1761, Alexander Dalrymple, an officer of the British East India Company, concluded an agreement with the Sultan of Sulu to allow him to set up a trading post in North Borneo. In 1846, the island of Labuan off Sabah's west coast was ceded to Britain by the Sultan of Brunei and in 1848 it became a British Crown Colony.

In 1865 the United States Consul General of Brunei, Charles Lee Moses, obtained a 10-year lease over North Borneo from the Sultan of Brunei. The Sultanate of Brunei had at one time controlled the entire region, all the way up to the Southern Philippines. The lease

The first Durbar of the Rulers of the Federated Malay States at Kuala Kangsar, 1897. Seated on chairs from left: Sultan Ahmad of Pahang, Sultan Abdul Samad of Selangor, British High Commissioner Sir Charles Mitchell, Sultan Idris of Perak and Tuanku Muhammad the Yang di-Pertuan of Negeri Sembilan.

Opposite page: Temple Street (Jalan Tokong), Malacca, c. 1930. It is nicknamed the Street of Harmony, as it contains the Sri Poyyatha Vinayagar Moorthi Hindu Temple (in the foreground), the Kampung Kling Mosque (centre) and the Cheng Hoon Teng (just visible beyond the mosque), the oldest functioning Chinese temple in Malaysia.

Artist's impression of the signing of a treaty between James Brooke and the Sultan of Brunei in 1844.

Opposite: Tunku Abdul Rahman proclaims 'Merdeka!' in front of thousands of Malayans at Stadium Negara, Kuala Lumpur, on 31 August 1957.

was then sold several times to different merchants. In 1878, an agreement which overlapped that signed in Brunei was executed between the Sultanate of Sulu and a British commercial syndicate stipulating that North Borneo was to be leased for an annual payment. The rights under this agreement were subsequently transferred to Alfred Dent who in 1881 formed the British North Borneo Company. That same year, the British Government granted the company a royal charter and William Hood Treacher was appointed the first British Governor of North Borneo. In 1903, Sulu Sultan Jamalul Kiram signed another document which ceded additional islands off the coast of Sabah to the British North Borneo Company. In 1888 North Borneo became a British protectorate although, in practice, it was ruled by the British North Borneo Company, which was a private company.

After the Japanese Occupation during World War II, North Borneo became a British Crown Colony from 1946 until 1963. A British Governor was appointed to rule. There was an Executive Council (Cabinet) and a Legislative Council. The Governor was head of both Councils.[3]

Brunei

The history of the Sultanate of Brunei stretches back as far as the 7th century AD. At one time, Brunei was a major power in the region, controlling territories all the way from the southern Philippines, North Borneo and Sarawak to parts of northern Kalimantan. The arrival of European powers in the region, beginning with the Portuguese and Spanish in the 16th century marked the start of the sultanate's decline.

In 1839 the Sultan asked James Brooke to help put down a rebellion and later appointed him Governor of Sarawak (which then comprised a much smaller territory around present-day Kuching). Within a decade, and continuing up to the early 20th century, the Sultan was forced to cede large areas comprising present-day Sarawak to the Brookes. Present-day Sabah was ceded to the North Borneo Company. In 1888, Brunei became a British protectorate.[4]

Singapore

The history of modern Singapore began with the arrival of Sir Stamford Raffles in 1819 and the establishment of a British trading settlement there. Its status as a free port attracted traders and the city's wealth and population grew quickly. In 1826 the East India Company grouped Singapore with Penang and Malacca to form the Straits Settlements which it administered until 1867. In that year, the Straits Settlements became a British Crown Colony.

After the Japanese Occupation of World War II, the Straits Settlements was dissolved and Singapore became a separate Crown Colony. Local participation in the Executive and Legislative Councils increased and in 1955 Singapore achieved self-government. During this time the threat of communism was even greater than in the neighbouring Malay Peninsula as left-wing elements were in control of trade unions and political parties, including the People's Action Party (PAP).[5]

ENDNOTES

1. R.H.W. Reece, *The Name of Brooke. The End of White Rajah Rule in Sarawak* (Kuala Lumpur: Oxford University Press, 1982).
2. Michael B. Leigh, *Council Negri: Dewan Undangan Negeri Sarawak: Malaysia's Oldest Legislature* (Kuching: Sarawak Government, 1992).
3. Ooi Keat Gin, *Post-War Borneo, 1945–1950: Nationalism, Empire, and State-Building* (Abingdon: Routledge, 2013).
4. Graham E. Saunders, *A History of Brunei* (Kuala Lumpur; Singapore: Oxford University Press, 1994).
5. C.M. Turnbull, *A History of Singapore, 1819–2005* (Hawaii: University of Hawaii Press, 2010).

THE FORMATION OF MALAYSIA

Professor James Chin
Head, School of Arts and Social Sciences
Monash University (Malaysia Campus)

Post-War Decolonisation

After the end of World War II, decolonisation became the goal of the Western powers. The United States of America in particular pushed for decolonisation in the United Nations. A Declaration on the Granting of Independence to Colonial Countries and Peoples was adopted by the UN General Assembly in December 1960 and a Special Committee on Decolonisation was established in 1961 by the General Assembly to monitor implementation of the Declaration. British Government policy changed too. With the granting of independence to India in 1947, Whitehall decided that there would be a gradual drawdown of British military and political presence 'East of Suez'. The Suez Crisis in 1956, triggered by Egyptian nationalists led by President Gamal Abdel Nasser seizing control of the Suez Canal, was a reminder that the days when Britain had absolute control over its colonies were past.

Events took place against the backdrop of the Cold War. In Southeast Asia the biggest issue was the rise of communism in China and the threat of communism expanding southwards. China had fallen to the communists in 1949, the United States was already involved in military action in Vietnam and communism was spreading fast in French Indochina. The Americans were especially worried about the 'domino' theory—that if one state in a region came under the influence of communism, then countries surrounding it would too. This theory, together with that of 'containment'—the policy of containing the spread of Soviet communist influence around the world—dominated the thinking of White House policy makers. For the US and the British, Southeast Asia was one of the battlegrounds of the Cold War. Malaya and Singapore were targets for communist takeover while Indonesia was under the influence of left-leaning President Sukarno. The Parti Komunis Indonesia (PKI), at that time, was the second largest communist party after Italy outside the communist bloc.

The Tunku's Malaysia Proposal

The original idea for a merger did not come from Tunku Abdul Rahman. In fact, British colonial policy makers had suggested it several times. During World War II, Whitehall's plans for the region were made on the assumption that the five British-controlled territories—Malaya, Singapore, North Borneo, Sarawak and Brunei—were, more or less, a single political unit.

In 1955, David Marshall, Chief Minister of Singapore, suggested a merger with Malaya. This was rejected by Tunku Abdul Rahman. Four years later, in 1959, Lee Kuan Yew again proposed the idea but it was turned down by the Tunku once more. The Tunku felt the time was not right. Earlier, Malcolm MacDonald, Britain's Secretary of State for the Colonies, had said that 'after the federation of the Borneo territories, a confederation with Malaya and Singapore could have been attempted'.[1]

On 27 May 1961, Tunku Abdul Rahman announced to the Foreign Correspondents' Association of Southeast Asia in Singapore that he would push for a merger of Malaya with Singapore, North Borneo (as Sabah was then called), Sarawak and Brunei. He said that Malaya '...should have an understanding with Britain, and the peoples of the territories of Singapore, North Borneo, Brunei and Sarawak ... it is inevitable that we should look ahead to this objective and think of a plan whereby these territories can be brought closer together in political and economic cooperation'.[2]

The Tunku's decision to merge the four territories can be easily explained. First, Malaya and Singapore were closely integrated

Tunku Abdul Rahman speaking at the Foreign Correspondents Association in Singapore on 27 May 1961. It was here that he proposed what the press referred to as the 'Mighty Malaysia' plan.

Opposite page: Cartoon from the *Straits Times* of 3 June 1961 depicting the state of play among political leaders and observers following the Tunku's announcement

Pages 18–19: The fourth and final meeting of the Malaysia Solidarity Consultative Committee at Victoria Theatre, Singapore, 1 February 1962. The committee was composed of representatives of the five proposed states of Malaysia: the Federation of Malaya, Sarawak, North Borneo, Brunei and Singapore.

Clockwise from top left: Lord Selkirk, Sir Alexander Waddell, Sir William Goode and Sir Dennis White. These four senior colonial officials agreed in June 1961 that the proposed merger to form Malaysia should be supported by the British administration.

politically, culturally and economically. People moved freely across the Strait of Johor on a daily basis. It made economic sense to merge the two entities to promote further economic growth. Second, to curb the spread of communism. Although the Emergency had ended in Malaya in 1960, parts of the peninsula were still under communist influence and sections of the Chinese population were still supportive of communist ideology. The Malayan Communist Party (MCP) was no longer a military threat, but it remained an ideological threat. There were also signs that the communists were gaining influence in Singapore and if Singapore fell to the communists, then the Tunku would have to deal with a communist state in next door Singapore in addition to the Communist Party of Malaya terrorist organisation in South Thailand. Third, the inclusion of the Borneo territories of North Borneo, Sarawak and Brunei made sense given that they were all current or former British colonies or protectorates. Including them would accelerate their independence within a viable entity. Fourth, the merger of Singapore and Malaya alone would upset the racial balance and could not work on its own. The majority of Singapore's population was (and still is) Chinese. If the merger was confined to only Malaya and Singapore, the non-Malays would comprise the majority of the population in the new federation. It was thus imperative that the Borneo territories be included to ensure racial balance. Just under 70 percent of the nearly 1.3 million inhabitants[3] of North Borneo, Brunei and Sarawak comprised Malay-Muslims and non-Muslim indigenous peoples. The native population of these Borneo states combined with the Malay population of Malaya would mean a clear Malay–indigenous majority in the new federation. The racial factor was, however, not publicly emphasised at the time.

Immediate Reactions: the British

In June 1961 Sir Alexander Waddell, Governor of Sarawak (1960–1963), Sir William Goode, Governor of North Borneo (1960–1963), and Sir Dennis White, High Commissioner in Brunei (1959–1963), were summoned for talks in Singapore with Lord Selkirk, Commissioner General for the United Kingdom in Southeast Asia (1959–1963). The meeting agreed that the proposed merger was a sound idea and was to be supported by the British administration. From then onwards, the British used all their influence to ensure that the federation would be a success. This included using the civil service of all the potential component states to promote the Malaysia proposal. British support for the Malaysia proposal was crucial given that the native population usually followed the cue from the colonial administrators.

Immediate Reactions: Singapore

Lee Kuan Yew immediately welcomed the idea—he had been, after all, keen on the merger earlier on. He wanted the merger to go ahead for two main reasons. First, he felt that Singapore was too small to survive as an independent state. Second, he was worried that the communists and leftists in Singapore might gain the upper hand. His People's Action Party (PAP) was already showing signs of losing support to left-wing political parties such as the United People's Party (UPP) and Barisan Sosialis. The PAP had lost two by-elections in 1961. Generally, the left did not support the merger after the failure of the MCP to capture Malaya; they felt they could gain control of Singapore.[4]

Immediate Reactions: Brunei

Initially, the Brunei palace was keen on the merger; Sultan Omar Ali Saifuddin openly expressed support for the Tunku's proposal. On the other hand, Sheikh Azahari bin Sheikh Mahmud, commonly known as A.M. Azahari, and Parti Rakyat Brunei (PRB, the Brunei People's Party) were not keen at all.

Established in 1956, PRB was Brunei's first political party. Azahari was PRB's leader. He was a nationalist whose anti-colonial views were well known to the British[5] and who wanted Brunei to be fully independent. If independence was not possible, Azahari aspired towards the formation of a federation of Brunei, Sabah, Sarawak and Indonesian Borneo to be called Persekutuan Borneo Utara as a first step before deciding on a merger with Malaya and Singapore. PRB had significant support in Brunei as was shown when it won all 16 elected seats in Brunei's 33-seat Legislative Council in the State's first election in 1962.[6]

Immediate Reactions: North Borneo and Sarawak

The initial reactions from North Borneo and Sarawak were mixed. Many could see that the merger was beneficial in some ways: it would mean earlier independence, more rapid economic development, that the threat of communism could be better controlled, and that there would be a better racial balance between the indigenous and non-indigenous populations in the new federation.

However, there were some who rejected Tunku's proposal. They had several concerns including that the Peninsular Malaysians would dominate the new federation. In addition, there were concerns among the non-Malay indigenous population about the status of their own religions, cultures and languages. The majority of the indigenous people in North Borneo and Sarawak were non-Muslims and their cultures and languages were very different from those of the Malays. The Chinese community in both states was worried about economic competition from Malayan and Singaporean Chinese businessmen.

In Sarawak in particular, there was a lot of opposition to the Malaysia proposal. Sarawak's first political party, the Sarawak United People's Party (SUPP), was established in 1959 and, by the time of the Tunku's announcement in 1961, there were three active political parties in the state. The SUPP, led by Ong Kee Hui and Stephen Yong Kuet Tze, was, like many Chinese-based parties in the region, infested with left-wing members who saw the formation of communist states as the only path to independence and progress.[7] Two other parties, the Sarawak National Party (Snap) and Parti Negara Sarawak (Panas), represented the local native population and were more neutral towards the Malaysia proposal. Nonetheless, while Snap, led by Stephen Kalong Ningkan and supported mainly by Ibans, was opposed to the Malaysia proposal, Panas, led by a Sarawak Malay, Datu Bandar Abang Haji Mustapha, supported it. Later, the paramount leader of the Ibans, Temenggong Jugah anak Barieng, was to play a crucial part in mobilising the community to support the Malaysia proposal.

The anti-Malaysia stand taken by the left-wing Chinese in SUPP was moderated by the Sarawak Chinese Association (SCA) led by two timber-tycoon brothers, Ling Beng Siong and Ling Beng Siew. The SCA represented Chinese businessmen who saw the potential of Malaysia and the brothers used their considerable financial resources to gain support from the indigenous population for Malaysia.

In North Borneo, there was less political opposition to the Malaysia proposal than in Sarawak, partly as there were no political parties in the territory when the Tunku made the proposal. The two leading indigenous politicians had both been appointed to the North Borneo Legislative Council by the British. They were Donald Stephens[8] and Mustapha Harun. Both went on to establish political parties in Sabah. Stephens, leader of the indigenous Kadazans, founded the United National Kadazan Organisation (Unko) in August 1961 while Mustapha Harun, leader of the Muslim community in Sabah, went on to establish United Sabah National Organisation (Usno) in the same year.[9]

Early Borneo opposition to Malaysia

On 9 July 1961, less than two months after the Tunku's proposal, three leaders representing Sarawak, North Borneo and Brunei gathered in Jesselton (now Kota Kinabalu) to reject the proposal. They were Ong Kee Hui, chairman of SUPP, A.M. Azahari, chairman of PRB, and Donald Stephens, chairman of the soon-to-be-registered Unko. Calling themselves the United Front, they declared that the 'British Government should be advised that so far as the wishes of the people in the three territories are ascertainable, any plan in accordance with the pronouncements made by Tunku Abdul Rahman … would be totally unacceptable.'[10]

The Tunku's Visit to Brunei and Sarawak

In early July 1961, the Tunku visited the Borneo territories to drum up support for his proposal and to get feedback. He made it clear that he was willing to listen to the concerns of the people of Borneo. He wanted them to understand the concept directly from him. In both Brunei and Sarawak, the Tunku was met by the most senior government officials and was asked to explain his Malaysia proposal. In Kuching he met Governor Sir Alexander Waddell. He gave the assurance that he was willing to listen to the

Above, from left: Ong Kee Hui, chairman of the Sarawak United Peoples Party (SUPP); A.M. Azahari, chairman of Parti Rakyat Brunei (PRB).

Top: Stephen Yong Kuet Tze, secretary-general of SUPP, speaking at an anti-Malaysia rally.

Clockwise from top left: Ling Beng Siew; Temenggong Jugah Anak Barieng; Ling Beng Siong; Stephen Kalong Ningkan.

Protest against the Malaysia concept, Kuching, 1962.

The chief delegates of the proposed states who attended the MSCC (Malaysia Solidarity Consultative Committee) chaired by Donald Stephens (seated centre) sign the Memorandum on Malaysia, 3 February 1962. From left: Yeo Cheng Hoe (Sarawak), Datu Mustapha bin Dato Harun (North Borneo), Mohamed Khir Johari (Malaya), Dato Setia Pengiran Ali (Brunei) and Lee Kuan Yew (Singapore).

concerns of the Borneo people over his proposal and was happy to give autonomy to the Borneo states to get their support for the proposal.[11] While in Sarawak, the Tunku learnt that the SUPP and Snap were against the Malaysia Proposal while the other political parties were supportive. In Brunei he learnt that A.M. Azahari and the PRB were against the merger. They wanted a federation of Brunei, North Borneo and Sarawak. The Sultan of Brunei, on the other hand, promised to form a special committee to assess the public's opinion on the proposal. In North Borneo, Unko's leader Donald Stephens rejected the idea of Malaysia. The Tunku countered by stating that he would grant autonomy to all the Borneo states.

The Malaysian Solidarity Consultative Committee

The British arranged for local Sarawak and North Borneo leaders to attend a Commonwealth Parliamentary Association (CPA) Meeting in Singapore on 21 July 1961. Malayan and Singapore leaders led by Lee Kuan Yew used the opportunity to speak to the Borneo leaders and convince them that Malaysia was viable. It was during this period that Donald Stephens changed his stance from anti-Malaysia to pro-Malaysia. At the CPA meeting, the Borneo delegates decided that the way forward was to establish the Malaysian Solidarity Consultative Committee (MSCC) to study the Malaysia proposal in detail and to drum up support for it. Lee Kuan Yew played a critical role in the MSCC meetings. To encourage support from North Borneo, Donald Stephens was made chairman of the MSCC.

Between 24 August 1961 and 1 February 1962, the MSCC held four meetings, in Jesselton (now Kota Kinabalu), Kuching, Kuala Lumpur and Singapore. The fears of the Borneo territories were discussed in detail at these meetings and promises were made regarding the territories' autonomy in key areas such as religion, culture and language, administration and development.

Interestingly, SUPP Chairman Ong Kee Hui participated in the MSCC as, even though his party was officially against the Malaysia proposal, he himself had become supportive of it. The difference in opinion between him and his party can be explained by the fact that, while the mass membership of SUPP was largely

controlled by leftists, the top leadership of SUPP was in the hands of moderates comprising mostly businessmen.

Soon after the MSCC meetings had concluded, the North Borneo and Sarawak governments each published a pro-Malaysia White Paper. These White Papers stated that the obvious advantage of the Malaysia proposal would be the way in which North Borneo and Sarawak could easily 'fit in' with Malaya because of existing cultural, economic and historical ties.

The most important outcome of the MSCC was an agreement to establish a commission to ascertain the 'wishes' of the peoples of North Borneo and Sarawak on the proposed federation.

The Cobbold Commission

On 23 November 1961, a joint statement was issued by the British and Malayan governments to the effect that the proposed Federation of Malaysia was desirable, and that a commission would be set up to ascertain the views of the peoples of Sarawak and North Borneo. Brunei was excluded from the process as it had not played much of a role in the MSCC.

The Commission of Enquiry, North Borneo and Sarawak, headed by Lord Cobbold, a former Governor of the Bank of England, had four members. The two appointees of the Malayan Government were Wong Pow Nee, the MCA Chief Minister of Penang, and Mohammad Ghazali bin Shafie, Permanent Secretary to the Malayan Ministry of Foreign Affairs. The British side also appointed two members: Anthony Abell, the former Governor of Sarawak, and David Watherston, the former British Chief Secretary of Malaya.[12]

The Commission sat from 19 February to 17 April 1962, a period of eight weeks. It held a total of 35 public hearings—20 in Sarawak and 15 in North Borneo. The Commission also received more than 600 written submissions in North Borneo and more than 1,600 written submissions in Sarawak.

On the whole, the Commission did not encounter any problems in North Borneo; the two major political parties there—Donald Stephen's Unko and Mustapha Harun's Usno—were clearly in favour of the federation. In Sarawak, however, it did. SUPP organised a series of anti-Malaysia rallies in towns and places where the Commission held its hearings.[13] In addition, SUPP submitted a memorandum to the Commission containing seven resolutions. The main points of which were that:[14]

1. Sarawak should be granted independence in accordance with the Nine Cardinal Principles set out by the Brookes and Britain should honour its pledge of giving independence to Sarawak should it decide to withdraw from the territory.
2. SUPP objected to the inclusion of constitutional amendments which would discriminate against the non-indigenous, i.e. Chinese, population and was worried that they would become second-class citizens.
3. Economically and financially, Sarawak was more stable and had better prospects as an independent concern than through any merger with Malaya.
4. Islam and Malay were unacceptable as the national religion and language respectively.

The submission also called for a referendum to be held on Sarawak's future and stated that the majority of Sarawakians were against the Malaysia Plan.

The Cobbold Commission released its report in mid-August 1962.[15] It concluded that about one third of the population in each territory strongly favoured early realisation of Malaysia without too much concern about terms and conditions. Another third, many of them favourable to the Malaysia project, asked with varying degrees of emphasis for a range of conditions and safeguards. The remaining third was divided between those who insisted on independence before Malaysia was considered and those who would strongly prefer to see British rule continue for some years to come, including a 'hard core, vocal and politically active' segment comprising nearly 20 percent of the population of Sarawak and somewhat less in Sabah 'which oppose "Malaysia" on any terms unless it is preceded by independence and self-government'.

The key recommendations made by the Commission on safeguards for Sarawak and North Borneo were broadly similar to the concerns raised in the four MSCC meetings. The Commission recommended that a Working Party be established to work out in detail the agreement on North Borneo and Sarawak's terms

The Nine Cardinal Principles of the rule of the English Rajah in Sarawak

These formed the Preamble of the 1941 Sarawak Constitution.

- That Sarawak is the heritage of Our Subjects and is held in trust by Ourselves for them.

- That social and education services shall be developed and improved and the standard of living of the people of Sarawak shall steadily be raised.

- That never shall any person or persons be granted rights inconsistent with those of the people of this country or be in any way permitted to exploit Our Subjects or those who have sought Our protection and care.

- That justice shall be freely obtainable and that the Rajah and every public servant shall be easily accessible to the public.

- That freedom of expression both in speech and in writing shall be permitted and encouraged and that everyone shall be entitled to worship as he pleases.

- That public servants shall ever remember that they are but the servants of the people on whose goodwill and cooperation they are entirely dependent.

- That so far as may be Our Subjects of whatever race or creed shall be freely and impartially admitted to offices in Our Service, the duties of which they may be qualified by their education, ability and integrity duly to discharge.

- That the goal of self-government shall always be kept in mind, that the people of Sarawak shall be entrusted in due course with the governance of themselves, and that continuous efforts shall be made to hasten the reaching of this goal by educating them in the obligations, the responsibilities, and the privileges of citizenship.

- That the general policy of Our predecessors and Ourselves whereby the various races of the State have been enabled to live in happiness and harmony together shall be adhered to by Our successors and Our servants and all who may follow them hereafter.

The Commission of Enquiry, popularly known as the Cobbold Commission after its Chairman, Lord Cobbold (centre). Standing with him are the other members of the Commission (from left): Sir Anthony Abell (former Governor of Sarawak), Ghazali Shafie (Permanent Secretary for External Affairs), Dato' Wong Pow Nee (Chief Minster of Penang), and Sir David Watherston (former Chief Secretary of Malaya).

of entry to the proposed federation. This Working Party became known as the Inter-Governmental Committee.

It has been suggested that the Cobbold Commission's findings were flawed as it 'failed to question the representative character of the meetings of chiefs who purported to speak for 112,000 Ibans' and 'did not concern itself with the depth of understanding of those supporting Malaysia'.[16] The Commission itself acknowledged this when it stated that 'there are large sections of the population in the interior who have no real appreciation of the Malaysia proposal'.[17] It has also been argued that members of the Cobbold Commission were selected with a view to ensuring pro-Malaysia findings.[18]

Lord Lansdowne (right), who represented the United Kingdom on the Inter-Governmental Committee, with British High Commissioner to Malaysia, Sir Geofroy Tory.

Inter-Governmental Committee

The Inter-Governmental Committee (IGC), sometimes referred to as the Lansdowne Committee, was formed to plan the legislative framework of the Malaysia Agreement. Lord Lansdowne represented the United Kingdom and Tun Abdul Razak, Deputy Prime Minister of the Federation of Malaya, represented Malaya. The IGC held meetings from August to December 1962. It was divided into five sub-committees: constitutional, fiscal, legal and judicial, public service, and departmental organisation.

On 12 September 1962, the North Borneo Legislative Council and the Council Negri of Sarawak both unanimously adopted an identical motion which stated that each of them 'welcomes the decision in principle of the British and Malayan Governments to establish Malaysia by the 31st August 1963, on the understanding that the special interests of [Sarawak/North Borneo] will be safeguarded'[19]. The same motion also named those who would represent their respective states on the IGC.

It was clear that both legislative houses had agreed 'in principle' to the Malaysia proposal and wanted safeguards before proceeding further. The purpose of the IGC was to document the necessary safeguards to be inserted into the new Constitution of the proposed federation.

The final IGC report published in February 1963 contained the safeguards demanded by the leaders and peoples of North Borneo and Sarawak at the MSCC. The demands by North Borneo comprised 20 points and those by Sarawak, 18 points. Collectively the safeguards are known as the '20 Points'. They were deliberated extensively by the five sub-committees with full participation from the North Borneo and Sarawak representatives; some were modified and others were amended before they were agreed upon in the final report.

With the safeguards in place, on 8 March 1963 Sarawak's Council Negri unanimously adopted the recommendations of the IGC report. The North Borneo Legislative Council followed suit on 13 March.

Successful London Delegation

In July 1962, Tunku Abdul Rahman flew to London for talks with British Prime Minister Harold Macmillan on Malaysia. Deputy Prime Minister Tun Abdul Razak and Finance Minister Tan Siew Sin flew ahead of him for preliminary talks with Duncan Sandys, Commonwealth and Colonial Secretary, at the Commonwealth Office. Singapore's Prime Minister Lee Kuan Yew also attended.

The talks were successfully concluded on 31 July. It was agreed that Malaysia would come into permanent being on 31 August 1963, when the British would hand over sovereignty of North Borneo, Sarawak and Singapore to the Malaysian Government, and that a transitional period would begin from 31 August 1962.

Commonwealth and Colonial Secretary Duncan Sandys (left) shakes hands with Tun Abdul Razak as Tan Siew Sin and Lee Kuan Yew look on. They were members of the delegation in London to discuss the Malaysia Plan, 29 July 1962.

The 20 Points

Point 1: Religion

While there was no objection to Islam being the national religion of Malaysia, there should be no State religion in North Borneo, and the provisions relating to Islam in the present Constitution of Malaya should not apply to North Borneo.

Point 2: Language

a. Malay should be the national language of the Federation
b. English should continue to be used for a period of 10 years after Malaysia Day
c. English should be an official language of North Borneo for all purposes, State or Federal, without limitation of time.

Point 3: Constitution

Whilst accepting that the present Constitution of the Federation of Malaya should form the basis of the Constitution of Malaysia, the Constitution of Malaysia should be a completely new document drafted and agreed in the light of a free association of states and should not be a series of amendments to a Constitution drafted and agreed by different states in totally different circumstances. A new Constitution for North Borneo was of course essential.

Point 4: Head of Federation

The Head of State in North Borneo should not be eligible for election as Head of the Federation.

Point 5: Name of Federation

'Malaysia' but not 'Melayu Raya'.

Point 6: Immigration

Control over immigration into any part of Malaysia from outside should rest with the Federal Government but entry into North Borneo should also require the approval of the State Government. The Federal Government should not be able to veto the entry of persons into North Borneo for State Government purposes except on strictly security grounds. North Borneo should have unfettered control over the movements of persons other than those in Federal Government employ from other parts of Malaysia into North Borneo.

Point 7: Right of Secession

There should be no right to secede from the Federation.

Point 8: Borneanisation

Borneanisation of the public service should proceed as quickly as possible.

Point 9: British Officers

Every effort should be made to encourage British Officers to remain in the public service until their places could be taken by suitably qualified people from North Borneo.

Point 10: Citizenship

The recommendation in paragraph 148(k) of the Report of the Cobbold Commission should govern the citizenship rights in the Federation of North Borneo subject to the following amendments:
a. sub-paragraph (i) should not contain the proviso as to five years residence
b. in order to tie up with our law, sub-paragraph (ii)(a) should read '7 out of 10 years' instead of '8 out of 10 years'
c. sub-paragraph (iii) should not contain any restriction tied to the citizenship of parents—a person born in North Borneo after Malaysia must be a federal citizen.

Point 11: Tariffs and Finance

North Borneo should retain control of its own finance, development and tariff, and should have the right to work out its own taxation and to raise loans on its own credit.

Point 12: Special position of indigenous races

In principle the indigenous races of North Borneo should enjoy special rights analogous to those enjoyed by Malays in Malaya, but the present Malaya formula in this regard is not necessarily applicable in North Borneo.

Point 13: State Government

a. the Chief Minister should be elected by unofficial members of Legislative Council
b. There should be a proper Ministerial system in North Borneo.

Point 14: Transitional period

This should be seven years and during such period legislative power must be left with the State of North Borneo by the Constitution and not be merely delegated to the State Government by the Federal Government.

Point 15: Education

The existing educational system of North Borneo should be maintained and for this reason it should be under State control.

Point 16: Constitutional safeguards

No amendment, modification or withdrawal of any special safeguard granted to North Borneo should be made by the Federal Government without the positive concurrence of the Government of the State of North Borneo
The power of amending the Constitution of the State of North Borneo should belong exclusively to the people in the State.

[*Note*: The United Party, the Democratic Party and the Pasok Momogun Party considered that a three-quarters majority would be required in order to effect any amendment to the Federal and State Constitutions whereas Unko and Usno considered a two-thirds majority would be sufficient.]

Point 17: Representation in Federal Parliament

This should take account not only of the population of North Borneo but also of its size and potentialities and in any case should not be less than that of Singapore.

Point 18: Name of Head of State

Yang di-Pertua Negara.

Point 19: Name of State

Sabah.

Point 20: Land, Forests, Local Government, etc.

The provisions in the Constitution of the Federation in respect of the powers of the National Land Council should not apply in North Borneo. Likewise, the National Council for Local Government should not apply in North Borneo.

[*Note*: The 20 Points (in Sabah), and the similar 18 Points in Sarawak, were referred to in the original documents as 'safeguards'. They are a summary of the issues and concerns raised with the Cobbold Commission by interest groups and political parties in North Borneo and Sarawak. The safeguards were then deliberated upon by the Inter-Governmental Committee (IGC) for possible incorporation into the new Malaysian Constitution. Not all the safeguards were inserted into the Constitution. The North Borneo safeguards were submitted jointly by five political parties: United National Kadazan Organisation (Unko), United Sabah National Organisation (Usno), United Party, Democratic Party and National Pasok Momogun Organisation (Pasok).]

The Brunei Revolt and Singapore's Referendum

In Brunei, A.M. Azahari and his PRB launched an armed insurrection against the Brunei Sultanate on 8 December 1962. With help from British troops, the rebellion was put down in less than a fortnight, although mopping up operations continued for several months, and the country was placed under emergency rule by the Sultan. Azahari, who was in the Philippines when the rebellion broke out, was left stranded as his supporters were all arrested or killed in Brunei and Limbang. From then on, Brunei lost interest in the Malaysia proposal.

Earlier, on 1 September 1962, in Singapore, Lee Kuan Yew arranged for a referendum on the Malaysia proposal. Although it was termed a referendum, all three choices given to the people of Singapore meant merging into the new entity of Malaysia. Only the conditions of merger differed. Amidst opposition from left-wing parties grouped under Barisan Sosialis, Lee promised that if the merger were to go ahead, Singapore would retain autonomy in language, educational and labour issues, that it would be guaranteed 15 seats in the new 159-seat Malaysian Federal Parliament, and that all Singapore citizens would automatically become citizens of Malaysia. Lee also campaigned heavily on the fact that the merger in Malaysia would bring about better economic prospects for Malaysia as a whole, and make it easier

December 1962: In Manila, Brunei revolutionary leaders A.M. Azahari (left) and his economic minister Zaini Haji Ahmad read the latest news reports on the situation in Brunei, as they safely sat out the insurrection there. Azahari, who proclaimed himself revolutionary prime minister of Brunei, North Borneo and Sarawak, appealed to the UN to allow him to plead his cause. However, he was refused a US visa for the journey to the United States.

Options given to voters in Singapore's referendum on the terms of integration into Malaysia, 1962

A. 'I support merger giving Singapore autonomy in labour, education and other agreed matters as set out in Command Paper No. 33 of 1961, with Singapore citizens automatically becoming citizens of Malaysia.'

B. 'I support complete and unconditional merger for Singapore as a state on an equal basis with the other 11 states in accordance with the Constitutional documents of the Federation of Malaya.'

C. 'I support Singapore entering Malaysia on terms no less favourable than those given to the Borneo territories.'

Note: Those who rejected the proposal for merger had to leave the form blank.

Source: Singapore Select Committee on the Singapore National Referendum Bill (1962).

---

to curb the communist threat. Lee won the referendum with about 71 percent of the vote.[20]

External Opposition to Malaysia

As well as opposition to the formation of Malaysia from within its potential component territories, the Philippines and Indonesia were also opposed to it. Filipino opposition stemmed from its claim to North Borneo (Sabah) based on the argument that the territory was once part of the Sulu Sultanate and that the Sulu Sultan had only leased rather than ceded it.

On 11 September 1962, the self-appointed 'Sultan of Sulu'[21], Muhammad Esmail E. Kiram, purported to 'cede' the 'Territory of North Borneo' to the Philippines. Filipino President Diosdado Macapagal then started to revive the long-dormant Filipino claim to Sabah. Manila saw the proposed Federation of Malaysia as a plot to remove its sovereignty over North Borneo and charged that Malaysia was a 'continuation of colonialism'[22]. In early 1963 the Philippines broke off diplomatic relations with Malaysia.

Indonesia's opposition to Malaysia was largely due to President Sukarno's grand plan to merge the whole of the Malay Archipelago to be controlled from Jakarta. Under this plan, Indonesia and Malaya, including the whole island of Borneo as well as Singapore and East Timor, would form a new country called Indonesia Raya (Greater Indonesia). Sukarno was especially unhappy that Brunei, Sarawak and North Borneo would be part of Malaysia, since he saw them as a core part of the Malay Archipelago.[23] In public, however, Sukarno said his opposition was due to the fact that the new state, Malaysia, was nothing more than a puppet state of the British, and the proposal was merely a cover to increase colonial control over the region.

On 20 January 1963, Indonesian Foreign Minister Subandrio announced that Indonesia would pursue a policy of Konfrontasi (Confrontation) against Malaysia. On 12 April, Indonesian Army personnel wearing civilian clothing began guerrilla raids in Sarawak and North Borneo. A few months later, Sukarno declared that he was going to *ganyang* (crush) Malaysia.[24] The military attacks escalated, reaching the Malay Peninsula and Singapore, and did not cease until 1965.

Signing of the Malaysia Agreement

The Malaysia Agreement was formally signed in London on 9 July 1963 ahead of the Malaysia Bill being passed by the British House of Commons on 22 July 1963, paving the way for the new federation to be created on the stipulated date of 31 August 1963.

Brunei did not sign the agreement although there was a Brunei delegation. In the end, Brunei decided not to join Malaysia as the issue of the Sultan of Brunei's standing among the nine other Malay Rulers could not be resolved. The Sultan of Brunei wanted to be recognised as the most senior Malay Ruler and was probably expecting to be appointed the first Yang di-Pertuan Agong (King) of the new federation.

The Final Hurdles

To try and resolve the objections from Manila and Jakarta, Tunku Abdul Rahman accepted an invitation from President Macapagal to attend a summit in Manila on 31 July 1963. President Sukarno was invited as well.[25] The main item on the agenda was President Macapagal's idea of Maphilindo—a proposed confederation of Malaysia, Philippines and Indonesia, hence the name. Nevertheless, at the summit the three leaders agreed to send a joint letter to United Nations Secretary-General U Thant. In it, they requested that a UN mission be sent to North Borneo and Sarawak to ascertain the wishes of the people. U Thant agreed.

The nine-member UN team, led by the secretary-general's representative Laurence Michelmore, visited North Borneo and Sarawak from 15 August to 5 September 1963. The report was released on 14 September. Its conclusion was largely similar to the Cobbold Report: that the majority of people in both states wanted to merge to create the new state of Malaysia.

Four days before the release of the UN report, on 10 September 1963, the Government of the State of Kelantan sought a High Court declaration that the Malaysia Agreement and Malaysia Act were null and void. It cited several grounds for the declaration:[26]

- The Malaysia Act would violate the Federation of Malaya agreement 1957 by abolishing the Federation of Malaya.
- The proposed changes needed the consent of each of the constituent States including Kelantan, and this had not been obtained.
- The Sultan of Kelantan should have been made a party to the Malaysia Agreement.
- Constitutional convention dictated that consultation with rulers of individual states was required before substantial changes could be made to the Constitution.
- The Federal Parliament had no power to legislate for Kelantan in matters that the state could legislate for on its own.

Chief Justice of Malaya James Thomson summarised that these grounds raised the question 'whether Parliament or the executive Government has trespassed in any way the limits placed on their powers by the Constitution'. He ruled that the proposed Malaysia did not. The judgement was delivered two days before the new federation was proclaimed.

With no further political or legal hurdles to overcome, the Proclamation of Malaysia was read in public on 16 September 1963 in Jesselton, Kuching, Kuala Lumpur and Singapore (see pp. 40–41). On the same day, North Borneo was renamed Sabah and, together with Sarawak, Singapore and Malaya, became the Federation of Malaysia.

The position of Sabah and Sarawak in the Federation

A matter of contention after the formation of the Malaysian federation has been the question of whether Sabah and Sarawak became part of Malaysia as equals of the individual peninsular states or of the peninsula—the Federation of Malaya—as a whole. James Wong Kim Min, one of the founding fathers of the federation was of the view 'that Malaysia is a Nation formed as equal partners. Sarawak did not join; but Sarawak formed Malaysia together with Malaya, Sabah and Singapore'.[27] James Wong was well-placed to know. He was involved in the entire formation process, as a member of the Sarawak delegation to the MSCC, a member of the Council Negri (he served for close to 50 years) and as Sarawak's first deputy Chief Minister in the Snap-led Government in 1963. He was also briefly leader of the Opposition in the Malaysian Parliament

United Nations Secretary-General U Thant (fourth from left) photographed in New York on 10 September 1963 with some of the members of the United Nations Malaysian Mission. They are (from left): George Howard, Kenneth Dadzie, Laurence Michelmore (Representative of the secretary-general and Head of Mission), George Janecek (Deputy Representative of the secretary-general) and Neville Kanakaratne. Members of the Mission included members of the UN Secretariat from Argentina, Brazil, Ceylon, Czechoslovakia, Ghana, Pakistan, Japan and Jordan.

In Jesselton, North Borneo, crowds greeted the UN's fact-finding mission, 19 August 1961. Banners urged the mission to complete their work quickly so that the State could gain its independence without delay on 31 August.

The Malaysia Agreement

The United Kingdom of Great Britain and Northern Ireland, the Federation of Malaya, North Borneo, Sarawak and Singapore;

Desiring to conclude an agreement relating to Malaysia;

Agree as follows:

Article I

The Colonies of North Borneo and Sarawak and the State of Singapore shall be federated with the existing States of the Federation of Malaya as the States of Sabah, Sarawak and Singapore in accordance with the constitutional instruments annexed to this Agreement and the Federation shall thereafter be called 'Malaysia'.

Article II

The Government of the Federation of Malaya will take such steps as may be appropriate and available to them to secure the enactment by the Parliament of the Federation of Malaya of an Act in the form set out in Annex A to this Agreement and that it is brought into operation on 31st August 1963 (and the date on which the said Act is brought into operation is hereinafter referred to as 'Malaysia Day'). [*Note:* Came into force on 16 September 1963 in accordance with Article II, as amended by the Agreement of 28 August 1963.]

Article III

The Government of the United Kingdom will submit to Her Britannic Majesty before Malaysia Day Orders in Council for the purpose of giving the force of law to the Constitutions of Sabah, Sarawak and Singapore as States of Malaysia which are set out in Annexes B, C and D to this Agreement.

Article IV

The Government of the United Kingdom will take such steps as may be appropriate and available to them to secure the enactment by the Parliament of the United Kingdom of an Act providing for the relinquishment, as from Malaysia Day, of Her Britannic Majesty's sovereignty and jurisdiction in respect of North Borneo, Sarawak and Singapore so that the said sovereignty and jurisdiction shal on such relinquishment vest in accordance with this Agreement and the constitutional instruments annexed to this Agreement.

Article V

The Government of the Federation of Malaya will take such steps as may be appropriate and available to them to secure the enactment before Malaysia Day by the Parliament of the Federation of Malaya of an Act in the form set out in Annex E to this Agreement for the purpose of extending and adapting the Immigration Ordinance, 1959, of the Federation of Malaya to Malaysia and of making additional provision with respect to entry into the States of Sabah and Sarawak; and the other provisons of this Agreement shall be conditional upon the enactment of the said Act.

Article VI

The Agreement on External Defence and Mutual Assistance between the Government of the United Kingdom and the Government of the Federation of Malaya of 12th October, 1957, and its annexes shall apply to all territories of Malaysia, and any reference in that Agreement to the Federation of Malaya shall be deemed to apply to Malaysia, subject to the proviso that the Government of Malaysia will afford to the Government of the United Kingdom the right to continue to maintain the bases and other facilities at present occupied by their Service authorities within the State of Singapore and will permit the Government of the United Kingdom to make such use of these bases and facilities as that Government may consider necessary for the purpose of assisting in the defence of Malaysia, and for Commonwealth defence and for the preservation of peace in South-East Asia. The application of the said Agreement shall be subject to the provisions of Annex F to this Agreement (relating primarily to Service lands in Singapore).

Article VII

(1) The Federation of Malaya agrees that Her Britannic Majesty may make before Malaysia Day Orders in Council in the form set out in Annex G to this Agreement for the purpose of making provision for the payment of compensation and retirement benefits to certain overseas officers serving, immediately before Malaysia Day, in the public service of the Colony of North Borneo or the Colony of Sarawak.

(2) On or as soon as practicable after Malaysia Day, Public Officers' Agreements in the forms set out in Annexes H and I of this Agreement shall be signed on behalf of the Government of the United Kingdom and the Government of Malaysia; and the Government of Malaysia shall obtain the concurrence of the Government of the State of Sabah, Sarawak or Singapore, as the case may require, to the signature of the Agreement by the Government of Malaysia so far as its terms may affect the responsibilities or interests of the Government of the State.

Article VIII

The Governments of the Federation of Malaya, North Borneo and Sarawak will take such legislative, executive or other action as may be required to implement the assurances, undertakings and recommendations contained in Chapter 3 of, and Annexes A and B to, the Report of the Inter-Governmental Committee signed on 27th February, 1963, in so far as they are not implemented by express provision of the Constitution of Malaysia.

Article IX

The provisions of Annex J to this Agreement relating to Common Market and financial arrangements shall constitute an Agreement between the Government of the Federation of Malaya and the Government of Singapore.

Article X

The Governments of the Federation of Malaya and of Singapore will take such legislative, executive or other action as may be required to imple- ment the arrangements with respect to broadcasting and television set out in Annex K to this Agreement in so far as they are not implemented by express provision of the Constitution of Malaysia.

Article XI

This Agreement shall be signed in the English and Malay languages except that the Annexes shall be in the English language only. In case of doubt the English text of the Agreement shall prevail.

IN WITNESS WHEREOF the undersigned, being duly authorized thereto, have signed this Agreement.

DONE at London this Ninth day of July, 1963, in five copies of which one shall be deposited with each of the Parties.

For the United Kingdom:	*For North Borneo:*	*For Sarawak:*
HAROLD MACMILLAN	DATU MUSTAPHA BIN DATU	P.E.H. PIKE
DUNCAN SANDYS	HARUN	T. JUGAH
LANSDOWNE	D.A. STEPHENS	ABANG HAJI MUSTAPHA
	W.K.H. JONES	LING BENG SIEW
For the Federation of Malaya:	KHOO SIAK CHIEW	ABANG HAJi OPENG
T. A. RAHMAN	W.S. HOLLEY	
ABDUL RAZAK	G.S. SUNDANG	*For Singapore:*
TAN SIEW SIN		LEE KUAN YEW
V. T. SAMBANTHAN		GOH KENG SWEE
ONG YOKE LIN		
S.A. LIM		

in 1974 as well as president of Snap. Wong's strong stand is supported by the original Article 1 of the Federal Constitution of Malaysia which read:

1. The Federation shall be known, in Malay and in English, by the name Malaysia
2. The States of the Federation shall be –
   a. the States of Malaya, namely, Johore, Kedah, Kelantan, Malacca, Negeri Sembilan, Pahang, Penang, Perak, Perlis, Selangor and Trengganu;
   b. the Borneo States, namely, Sabah and Sarawak; and
   c. the State of Singapore.

The Federal Constitution was later amended to read:

1. The Federation shall be known, in Malay and in English, by the name Malaysia.
2. The States of the Federation shall be Johore, Kedah, Kelantan, Malacca, Negeri Sembilan, Pahang, Penang, Perak, Perlis, Sabah, Sarawak, Selangor and Trengganu.
3. Subject to Clause (4), the territories of each of the States mentioned in Clause (2) are the territories comprised therein immediately before Malaysia Day.

However, there are those who disagree with James Wong's assessment. Their argument is that, if the original intention was to give Sabah and Sarawak a higher status than mere States in the federation, then the original Article 1(2)(a) should have read:

2. The States of the Federation shall be –
   a. the State of Malaya
   b. the Borneo States, namely, Sabah and Sarawak; and
   c. the State of Singapore

This issue has never been tested in court because the Constitution was subsequently amended to state clearly that Sabah and Sarawak were two of the 13 states in the federation.

ENDNOTES

1. James P. Ongliki, *Nation-building in Malaysia 1946–1974* (Singapore: Oxford University Press), 151.
2. *Straits Times*, 29 May 1961.
3. 1960 census.
4. Leon Comber, *Singapore Correspondent: Political Dispatches from Singapore (1958–1962)* (Singapore: Marshall Cavendish, 2012).
5. B.A. Hussainmiya, *Sultan Omar Ali Saifuddin III and Britain: The Making of Brunei Darussalam* (Kuala Lumpur: Oxford University Press, 1995).
6. Harun Abdul Majid, *Rebellion in Brunei: The 1962 Revolt, Imperialism, Confrontation and Oil* (London; New York: I.B. Tauris, 2007).
7. Chin Ung Ho, *Chinese Politics in Sarawak: A Study of the Sarawak United People's Party (SUPP)* (New York: Oxford University Press, 1997).
8. Later in life, Donald Stephens converted to Islam and took the name Mohammad Fuad Stephens.
9. R.S. Milne and Ratnam, K.J., *Malaysia: New States in a New Bation: Political Development of Sarawak and Sabah in Malaysia* (London: Frank Cass, 1974).
10. *Straits Times*, 10 July 1961.
11. *Sarawak Tribune*, 7 and 8 July 1961.
12. See *Sarawak Tribune*, 19 January 1962.
13. SUPP distributed leaflets with anti-Malaysia slogans such as 'Condemn reactionary Malaysia Plan' to its members, with instructions to repeat such slogans in front of the Cobbold Commission. See *Sarawak Tribune*, 3, 23 and 26 February and 17 and 19 March 1962.
14. *Report of the Commission of Enquiry, North Borneo and Sarawak* (Kuala Lumpur: Government Printer, 1962), 20–21.
15. *Report of the Commission of Enquiry*.
16. Michael Leigh, *Rising Moon: Political Change in Sarawak* (Sydney University Press, 1974), 41.
17. *Report of the Commission of Enquiry*, 13.
18. James P. Ongkili, *The Borneo Response to Malaysia*, (Singapore: Donald Moore Press, 1967), 67.
19. *Report of the Commission of Enquiry*, 7–8.
20. Ser Hwee Quek, *The Singapore Referendum on the Merger Question 1962* (Singapore: University of Singapore, 1975).
21. It should be noted that the position of Sultan of Sulu is disputed and there are at least a half a dozen active claimants to the throne, including several living in present day Sabah.
22. *Straits Times*, 12 March 1963.
23. Garth N. Jones, 'Soekarno's early views upon the territorial boundaries of Indonesia', *Australian Outlook* Volume 18, Issue 1 (1964), 30–39.
24. J.A.C. Mackie, *Konfrontasi: The Indonesia–Malaysia Dispute 1963–1966* (Kuala Lumpur: Oxford University Press, 1974).
25. Prior to the Manila meeting, Sukarno and the Tunku met unofficially in Tokyo. At this meeting, Sukarno agreed to attend the Manila meeting.
26. *Government of the State of Kelantan v The Government of the Federation of Malaya and Tunku Abdul Rahman Putra Al-Haj* [1963] MLJ 355 HC. See also Johan S. Sabaruddin, 'The Kelantan Challenge' in Andrew Harding and Lee, H.P. (ed.), *Constitutional Landmarks in Malaysia: The First 50 Years* (Kuala Lumpur: LexisNexis Malaysia, 2007).
27. James Wong Kim Min, *The Birth of Malaysia: A reprint of the Cobbold Report, the I.G.C. Report and the Malaysia Agreement* (Petaling Jaya: Sweet & Maxwell Asia, 2008), 9.

Yang di-Pertuan Agong Tuanku Putra Jamalullail proclaiming the formation of Malaysia, Stadium Merdeka, Kuala Lumpur, 16 September 1963.

The Proclamation of Malaysia, signed by Prime Minister Tunku Abdul Rahman and dated 16 September 1963.

AVERAGE DAILY CERTIFIED SALE EXCEEDS 100,000

The Straits Times

Estd. 1845.   TUESDAY, JANUARY 1, 1963.   ★ ★   15 CENTS   KDN 371

The Tengku's 'blunt' warning

'Enemies outside—fifth-columnists inside'

PERILS OF 1963

Hunt for Jakarta rebel leaders

JAKARTA, Mon.—Military authorities here were yesterday reported to be holding a full-scale search for the leaders of an anti-government movement who escaped arrest on Friday night.

Indonesian sources said the leaders were still at large, despite the arrest of several hundred people at a meeting and the seizure of arms and explosives.

They include Major Suyitaran, commander of the "Pembela Volunteer Army Command," former Chief RAR Amiruddiena and Captain A. Sudiono.

Wanted men

Major Amiruddiena and Captain Sudiono are said to be the leaders of the "team for reactivating the 16th Brigade," which is associated with the PVAC.

Jakarta Army Garrison said yesterday those three were wanted men. Their organisations were illegal.

The garrison commander, Brigadier General Umar Wirahadi-Kusumah, claimed to have arrested "a number of leaders" at the meeting on Friday.

Troops supported by armoured cars and tanks surrounded a Jakarta cinema where the meeting was in progress and arrested several hundred people, most of whom were released previously after questioning.—Reuter.

Even 'volunteers' cannot stop Malaysia—Lee

SINGAPORE, Mon.—In a New Year message today, the Prime Minister, Mr. Lee Kuan Yew, said 1963 would be "our year of fulfilment."

He said: "Malaysia comes of age. Amidst the jubilation and festivities there has been some sober realisation of the problems we face.

"We want to be friends with all in Asia. We know we cannot afford a power vacuum in South-East Asia. And it is better we know these things now than later."

Security

"Malaysia gives us more security internally. But there are new and other problems, to be faced. Coming of age is a necessary if challenging experience."

Looking back on the past year, the Prime Minister said 1962 would always be a memorable year in the history of Malaysia.

A year before, it was popularly believed that Singapore was a troublesome place and Brunei a peaceful and prosperous kingdom.

"It was said Singapore, mainly Chinese, would oppose Malaysia, and Brunei, mainly Malay, and ruled by a benign Sultan, would fit so well into the Federation.

"But the prospects were proved wrong. In 1962, like one of Kipling's 'Believe it or not,' it has all peace and tranquility in Singapore and people got down to working and planning for more prosperity in Malaysia.

Solidarity

"A bare three months sufficiently recently for events, perhaps just as well. For even before West Irian is liberated and Malaysia established, events have moved to show that nations in Asia are just like nations in Europe, they all like to grow bigger and more important and more prosperous.

"The solidarity of Asia was and has a solidarity against European colonialism. Once this common enemy is pushed out of the ring, the people of the kingdom.

'They will strike' says the Premier

KUALA LUMPUR, Mon.

TENGKU Abdul Rahman warned tonight that the enemies of Malaysia will "strike" not only from outside, but through fifth columnists within the country.

To meet this threat, the Prime Minister stressed that "every available force at our command will be needed."

The Tengku, who was making a New Year's Eve broadcast, regretted having to be "blunt and forthright" during the festive season, but, he added:

"I would fail in my duty to you and to our country if I did not give you a picture of what may come."

'Children in the sun'

He stressed that everyone in Malaya was free to live without interference—"like carefree children in the sun"—and then reiterated that the policy of his Government was to provide the people with:

FOOD instead of bullets;
CLOTHING instead of uniforms; and
HOUSES instead of barracks.

Turning to Malaysia, the Tengku spoke of how "certain people in Indonesia" had at one stage suggested that Malaya should back out from the plan.

— TEXT —
of the Prime Minister's New Year broadcast in Page 6

To this suggestion, the Tengku replied "Never"—and he added:

"Our Federation of Malaya was born in independence under stress and strain of Communist insurrection. The birth of Malaysia under similar conditions will not deter us from going ahead with it.

"The threat from the Indonesian Communists is very great indeed. We must meet it."

As a nation, the triumphs and trials of 1962 showed that the people had a deep and abiding faith and confidence in themselves and in their future. The only "note of discord" was the railway strike.

'I've not been asked'

He said that this was the first "big" strike in the country for many years — a strike which could have been averted.

"Unlike other strike situations in the past when my good offices were sought, on this occasion no approach was made to me except a request to give in to what the railwaymen demand and to seek a guarantee that there will be no interference in the strike from the Government," he said.

"Moreover, I have been keeping in close touch with officials and offering advice."

The Tengku then spoke about the coming year, which presented a special challenge.

"Before the year is out the Federation of Malaya will expand to take in new members of the family in a brand-new nation with a larger area and wider responsibilities and duties — the Federation of Malaysia," he added.

SULTAN OF PERAK GRAVELY ILL

KUALA KANGSAR, Mon.— The condition of the Sultan of Perak, 72, who has been ailing since October, is giving cause for anxiety.

A brief Government bulletin issued this evening said: "His Highness the Sultan has been ill for some time. His condition has suddenly deteriorated and there is cause for anxiety."

The Sultan, who has suffered a partial stroke in late October, developed paralysis of both legs. He has been receiving treatment at the Istana Iskandariah.

His condition apparently sufficiently recently for him to be taken out for evening drives.

A few days ago his condition began to deteriorate.

Holyoake is honoured

LONDON, Mon.— Queen Elizabeth has named Mr. Keith Holyoake, 58, Prime Minister of New Zealand, a Companion of Honour, an order of chivalry, appointment to which is in the Sovereign's own gift.

The Queen and her husband the Duke of Edinburgh will be seeing Mr. Holyoake early this year during their tour of New Zealand and Australia.—Reuter.

Peking welcome

TOKYO, Mon.—The Ceylon Prime Minister, Mrs. Sirimavo Dias Bandaranaike, arrived in Peking on her peace mission and received a rousing welcome from "hundreds of thousands of people," the New China News Agency reported.—UPI.

Grimond poll call

LONDON, Mon. — In a New Year message to the Liberals, Mr. Jo Grimond tells them today that their task is to prepare for a General Election, to harness the forces of being "pushed behind no other side and to return to office."

Rail strike: 'Govt can't stay idle' warning

KUALA LUMPUR, Monday.

TENGKU Abdul Rahman warned tonight that the Government could not remain idle if the railway strike reached a situation where the economy and life of the country was seriously threatened.

In a statement, the Prime Minister said that recent utterances by trade union leaders had aggravated the situation, and if the situation deteriorated the Government might be "compelled to act" to remedy the situation.

The Tengku's warning came after a series of meetings by the Railwaymen's Union of Malaya, MTUC, CUPPACS and other workers organisations.

It also followed announcements by unions pledging support for the strikers.

This afternoon RUM's president Mr. Donald Uren and his secretary Mr. R. Packhurany, went to the Labour Ministry, but the result of the meeting was not revealed.

Appeals

This is the Tengku's statement:

"I have during the last few days received messages and appeals asking me to intervene in the railway dispute and also requesting the Government not to interfere with the legitimate right of a trade union to conduct a strike.

"I have been constantly following the developments in the railway dispute and am fully aware of the circumstances of the dispute.

"I had hoped until now that this being purely a trade dispute, the parties would be able, with the assistance of the Minister of Labour, to settle their problems and bring about an end to the present crisis.

Concern

"However, events and utterances of leading trade union officials since the strike have given me great cause for concern.

"The situation today appears to be that the trade union movement as a whole is bent on continuing the crisis and thereby causing irreparable damage not only to the economy of this country but also to the industrial peace and understanding that has prevailed in this country so far.

"While I appreciate that the trade union movement is in general sympathy with the strikes of RUM, I find it difficult to understand how the trade union movement, which has been regarded as a reasonable body, could now press for the settlement of the present crisis

● Back Page Col. 3

Pirates take tongkang with $100,000 cargo

JOHORE BAHRU, Mon.—Pirates captured a Malayan tongkang laden with a cargo estimated at $100,000 in Pulau Pisang, near Pontian, yesterday morning.

The tongkang's crew of six told Pontian police they were chased by an armed motor-boat, believed to be Indonesian. It fired on them.

The crew lowered a motor-boat and made to it, landing on Pontian beach. The pirates boarded the tongkang and sailed away. The cargo was mainly rubber.

SIMONIZ SILICONE SPEEDWAX

CLEANS
WAXES
POLISHES
PROTECTS
YOUR CAR
FAR MORE EFFICIENTLY

SIMONIZ SPEEDWAX FOR CARS
SIMONIZ SILICONE SPEEDWAX FOR CARS
MALAYA   JACKA   BRAND   SINGAPORE

Brunei force to be cut

SINGAPORE, Mon.— The British military strength in Brunei is to be cut Admiral Sir David Luce, Commander - in - Chief Far East, said today.

The requirement for British military support of the civil power in Brunei" had diminished, he said.

"The first unit to be withdrawn will be the 42 Commando Royal Marines, who are due back here in early January.

STOP PRESS

14 DETAINED

KUCHING, Mon.— Fourteen people — 13 Malays and one Dyak—detained by police last night under Preservation of Public Security Ordinance.
—Reuter.

FOR 4 GENERATIONS

白蘭氏

BRAND'S ESSENCE OF CHICKEN

BRAND'S
essence of strength—since 1835

A Happy New Year to all our readers!

1963

A new nation is born. North Borneo, Sarawak, and Singapore joined the Federation of Malaya to form Malaysia. Its arrival was however not without birth pangs, the date of formation being postponed from 31 August (to coincide with Hari Merdeka) to 16 September to enable the United Nations to conduct referendums in North Borneo and Sarawak. Amid widespread rejoicing, there were fears of troubles ahead due to opposition to the new nation by the Philippines and Indonesia, leading to Malaysia severing diplomatic ties with the two countries. Towards the end of the year Malaysians stayed glued to television sets in radio shops as Television Malaysia made its debut in Kuala Lumpur.

MAY
The Brooke legacy in Sarawak ends with the passing of the last White Rajah of Sarawak.

AUGUST
The UN despatch a team to Borneo to assess public opinion on the formation of Malaysia.

SEPTEMBER
The birth of Malaysia is celebrated in Malaya, Sabah, Sarawak and Singapore.

DECEMBER
Tunku Abdul Rahman launches Television Malaysia's pilot service.

November: An aerial view of Parliament House under construction shortly before it was opened by the Yang di-Pertuan Agong.

Malaysia Facts		
8.9 million	Population	
$8.3 billion	Gross Domestic Product	
$904	Gross National Income (per capita)	
38.1	Crude Birth Rate (per 1,000 persons)	
55.5	Infant Mortality (per 1,000 live births)	
21.7	Consumer Price Index (base 2010=100)	

'We are determined to defend the sovereignty and independence of Malaysia ... for all time.'

Tunku Abdul Rahman, after the Malaysian flag was raised for the first time, 17 September 1963.

1963

world news

29 January
President de Gaulle vetoes the entry of the UK into the EEC.

29 January
Death of American poet Robert Frost, 89. President Kennedy had him read a poem at his inauguration.

16 March
Mt Agung in Bali erupts, killing 11,000.

22 March
British Minister of War John Profumo denies sexual liaison with prostitute Christine Keeler. He later resigns for lying.

10 April
The nuclear submarine USS *Thresher* sinks off Cape Cod, killing all 129 crew.

8 May
'The name is Bond, James Bond.' *Dr No* premieres.

28 May
A cyclone in the Bay of Bengal drowns an estimated 22,000 people.

5 June
A state of siege is proclaimed in Iran after a bloody uprising against the Shah.

Daily-rated workers get monthly wages

19 January Kuala Lumpur

Monthly pay packets were agreed for the Government's 56,000 daily-rated workers. The conversion was to be at 27 times the basic daily wage. Malaya's No. 1 civil servant, Datuk Abdul Aziz bin Majid, made the surprise announcement to loud applause from delegates of 25 daily-rated workers' organisations affiliated to the Daily-Rated Services Staff Council at the opening of its seventh annual general meeting.

Floored by the decision, the council's secretary, Mr V. Thambiah, tore up a prepared speech which condemned the daily wage system that had been in practice for many years. 'I don't know what to say now…I can only thank the Datuk and the Government for this decision,' he said.

Supermarket merger

1 February Kuala Lumpur

Cold Storage (M) Limited and Fitzpatrick's merged, creating the largest supermarket chain in Malaya. The new company, Supermarkets Malaysia Ltd, had already taken over the Cold Storage supermarket in Mountbatten Road. Under the merger, Cold Storage was slated 'to take a half share in the Fitzpatrick's supermarket project in Weld Road, rather than proceed with a second, independent supermarket in Circular Road.'

Exposed: Communist plot to create unrest

2 February Singapore

Under orders from the Internal Security Council, Singapore police arrested 107 left-wing politicians and trade unionists in a massive swoop that began at 3am.

The operation, in the wake of Indonesia's Confrontation policy and military alert, was aimed at preventing subversives from establishing a Cuba-style base in Singapore and using violence to disrupt the formation of Malaysia.

The council revealed this in a document, *The Communist Conspiracy*, detailing a plot against Malaysia.

Umno expels ex-Minister

12 February Kuala Lumpur

Former Minister of Agriculture and Co-operatives Abdul Aziz Ishak had been 'telling lies' about the country's political, economic and social policies, declared the Alliance Government. Tunku Abdul Rahman said Abdul Aziz should be expelled from the United Malays National Organisation.

Subsequently, acting Umno secretary-general Syed Jaafar Albar announced Abdul Aziz's expulsion, saying all 27 members of the party's central executive council backed the move.

Abdul Aziz was for four years one of three Umno national vice-presidents, until the middle of 1962 when the Umno general assembly rejected his nomination.

He was, however, returned to the central executive council.

For 20 years he saved 10 cents a day…

27 February Port Swettenham

Labourer Muhamed Rashid Muhamed Salleh, 65, had been steadfastly saving 10 cents a day for 20 years to fulfil his religious obligation of performing the Haj. Today he set sail for the holy city of Mecca. Passage on the 12,000-ton liner *Kuala Lumpur* cost $661. 'I did all sorts of odd jobs… It took a long time—but it was worth it,' said Muhamed Rashid, from Hulu Langat, who left with $100 in his pocket.

One union for all Government servants

12 March Kuala Lumpur

The Congress of Unions of Employees in the Public and Civil Service joined forces with the Civil Service Clerical Federation (CSCF) to form a single national union for all Government workers.

CSCF president Mas Junid Mas Amin was elected pro-tem chairman of the proposed union.

'The formation of a national union is long overdue,' said Mas Junid.

'If we do not at this juncture resolve to form a common union for all categories of clerks, I am positive the existing Government clerical unions will dissolve into nonentities.'

Remembering our war dead…

30 March Kuala Lumpur

All those who fell in defence of Malaya during World War II and the 12-year Emergency would be given a 'special place' at the National Monument in the Lake Gardens, sculptor Felix W. de Weldon said. Their names would be recorded in books of honour in the monument's Hall of Memory.

Cement work on the foundation had started and the tableau, comprising seven figures, would be shipped from Rome in July.

Mr Weldon was supervising delivery of 242 tons of stone and granite for the plinth of the 75ft memorial, which were arriving from Singapore.

'Made-in-Malaya' cars?

2 March Petaling Jaya

It should not be long before 'we shall have our first car manufactured in Malaya,' Minister of Commerce and Industry Dr Lim Swee Aun said at the official opening of the Dunlop tyre factory by Prime Minister Tunku Abdul Rahman. 'By starting as a car assembly plant, using tyres made by Dunlop, cushions from Dunlopillo, and with electric cables, batteries and paints already manufactured in Malaya, it should not be long before a truly made-in-Malaya car is a reality,' he added.

The $25-million factory—Dunlop's 109th in the world—takes up 145,000 square feet of a 36-acre site and is equipped with machinery worth over $9 million. In his speech, the Prime Minister remarked that 'it makes good economic sense—I might even say good common sense—to establish a manufacturing industry for tyres right in the home of rubber.'

Young princess gets engaged

9 March Ipoh

Ancient traditional rites were observed at an engagement ceremony that further cemented ties between the royal families of Perak and Pahang.

The bride-to-be is Raja Amina, 17, second daughter of the Raja Muda of Perak, Raja Musa ibni Sultan Abdul Aziz.

The groom-to-be is Sandhurst-trained Lt Tengku Ibrahim, 25, second son of the Sultan of Pahang, who is with the 5th Battalion, Royal Malay Regiment, based in Batu Gajah. The young couple first met on 30 November at a dance.

The April 1963 issue of *Time* magazine.

Tunku on cover of 'Time' magazine

13 April Kuala Lumpur

Tunku Abdul Rahman has described his portrait on the cover of the latest issue of Time magazine as 'more of a Ghanaian that a Malayan…the songkok is rather small and my lips look rather thick.' Asked if he was pleased about the portrait, the Prime Minister replied: 'It is very difficult to say but truthfully speaking, I'm not very pleased with it.' In the story itself, which also covered the proposed Federation of Malaysia, *Time* magazine said the Tunku had 'the charisma of a really successful politician', and also, 'Under his leadership, Malaysia can be, as John F. Kennedy has said, the best hope for security in that vital part of the world.'

40,000 at National Language parade

7 April Kuala Lumpur

Actions speak loud—and more than 40,000 people from all walks of life, including 15,000 schoolchildren showed their support at a Selangor Club padang rally for the first phase of National Language month. Stating that the Government would not budge from its decision to make Malay the official language by 1967, Health and former Minister of Education Inche Abdul Rahman bin Haji Talib said that 'when the time comes, the Government does not wish to see people facing difficulties just because of their neglect to learn the national language.'

Malayans are 'in the money'

13 April Kuala Lumpur

Public offers of shares, 'all hopelessly oversubscribed', were an indication that Malaya was in the money—and in no small way. *The Straits Times*, in a front-page analysis, reported that no less than $600 million in hard cash had been paid in less than 20 months for eight new issues—Esso ($226 million for 8.75 million $2 shares); Hotel Singapura ($24 million for one million $1 shares); Shell ($142 million for 7.5 million $1 shares); Containers ($53 million for 5.75 million $1 shares); Malayan Tobacco ($72 million for 7.2 million $1.90 shares); Eastern Smelting ($20 million for 4.5 million $2.25 shares); Rothmans ($23 million for 6.375 million $1 shares); and Dunlops ($17.5 million for 4.68 million $1 shares).

The Straits Times described this as 'nothing short of dramatic considering half the population is under 21'.

More people, the report said, also owned homes, cars, motorcycles and radios—'much to the envy of Asian tourists bewildered at our prosperity.'

Ice from the sky smashes attap homes

21 April Kangar

Hailstones fell in five kampongs in the Beseri area for about 40 minutes, damaging 21 attap houses and injuring a woman. Damage was estimated at $10,000.

The hailstones, described by some villagers as 'tennis balls from the sky', were followed by an hour of heavy rain. It was the first downpour in the area after a four-month drought.

It brought joy to 20,000 residents in the five kampongs. Many families put out buckets to collect water.

The victims spent the night in the homes of friends and relatives.

Stay clear of politics, Sultans are warned

11 May Kuala Lumpur

Chiding the Sultan of Perak for a Hari Raya Haji speech in which he allegedly criticised Umno and the Alliance Government, Prime Minister Tunku Abdul Rahman said that Rulers 'would do more harm than good if they took part in politics.'

The Sultan had taken to task elected representatives who, he said, were not carrying out their responsibilities. 'The Malay Rulers are symbols. They must steer clear of politics,' said the Tunku. 'It is not that I don't like criticism or cannot take it—criticism coming from a Ruler is a different thing.'

Sir Charles Vyner in retirement at his home in Bayswater, London, which was described as a 'museum'.

Another first for Nik Ahmad

2 May Kuala Lumpur

Datuk Nik Ahmad Kamil was made chairman of the board of a $5-million Malay finance company, the Sharikat Kewangan Melayu Raya Ltd.

Among the company's objectives were to act as financiers and bankers and commercial agents, and to become builders and property developers.

Datuk Nik Ahmad, who retired from public service the previous year, was also the first Malayan executive director of Rothmans of Pall Mall and was connected with about a dozen other businesses.

He was Malaya's youngest Menteri Besar when, in 1948 at the age of 38, he was appointed to the job in Kelantan.

He was the country's first High Commissioner to Australia, and was later posted to London.

Datuk Nik Ahmad was also Ambassador to Washington for three years and leader of the Malayan delegation to the United Nations.

Last White Rajah of Sarawak dies

9 May London

Sir Charles Vyner Brooke, 88, the third and last White Rajah of Sarawak (from 1917 to 1946), died at his home in Bayswater here after a prolonged illness. Sir Charles ruled Sarawak as Rajah until he ceded it to the British Government in 1946.

The territory came into the possession of his great-uncle Sir James Brooke, a 19th-century English adventurer, after the Sultan of Brunei presented it to him in 1840 as a reward for rendering aid in crushing insurgent tribesmen.

Sir James was succeeded in 1864 by his nephew and Sir Charles' father Sir Charles Anthony Johnson-Brooke. Sir Charles Vyner took over when his father died in 1917.

Straits Times Annual

Bukit Besi is truly an iron mountain

Bukit Besi, the 1,100ft-high 'hill of iron' thrusting up from the coastal plain near Dungun, supplied more than half of Terengganu's local revenue. Asia's biggest iron mine poured out an endless 20,000-ton stream of ore. The nearby township had a population of 6,000 with its own schools, clubs, shopping centre and fire brigade.

The Bukit Besi vicinity which has a 6,000 population and amenities for its inhabitants. In short, a town of its own.

'Friends again' with Indonesia

1 June Tokyo

After a two-day meeting here, Tunku Abdul Rahman and President Sukarno of Indonesia reaffirmed their adherence to the 1959 treaty of friendship between their countries. Malaya accepted that the concept of Malaysia should initially have been discussed with Indonesia; Sukarno agreed to end the confrontation and verbal war which Indonesia claimed had arisen due to a lack of discussion about Malaysia; and both parties accepted they should be friendly neighbours. It was also agreed that they should hold a summit with another neighbour, the Philippines, to strengthen relations among all three.

Promotion for Malay woman barrister

18 June Kuala Lumpur

Malaya's first Malay woman barrister Siti Norma Yaakob, 24, was appointed senior assistant registrar in the Federation Registry at the Supreme Court in Kuala Lumpur

She was the first woman to hold an executive post in the Government legal service. On 19 October, Siti Norma was gazetted acting president of the Sessions Court to enable her to preside over Juvenile Court cases every Saturday, in addition to her duties as senior assistant registrar.

1963

world news

11 June
A Buddhist monk immolates himself in protest against the South Vietnamese Diem regime.

16 June
Russian Cosmonaut Valentina Tereshkova becomes the first woman in space.

24 June
First demonstration of a home video recorder at the BBC studios, London.

26 July
An earthquake in Yugoslavia kills 1,800.

27 July
President Sukarno declares he will crush Malaysia.

5 August
A nuclear test ban treaty is signed by the US, the Soviet Union and the UK.

8 August
A robbery on the night mail train from Glasgow to London nets £2,500,000.

27 August
Cambodia severs ties with South Vietnam.

28 August
Martin Luther King delivers his 'I Have a Dream' speech to 250,000 people in Washington.

Malaysia Agreement signed in London

9 July London

The final round of negotiations on the proposal to form Malaysia was successfully conducted with the signing of the agreement at Marlborough House here. Signatories to the Malaysia Agreement were representatives of the Federation of Malaya, Singapore, Sarawak and North Borneo (now Sabah). Among those present at the signing were Prime Minister Tunku Abdul Rahman, Deputy Prime Minister Tun Abdul Razak and Sarawak delegate Temenggong Jugah.

The Tunku and Tun Razak (right) after the signing of the Malaysia Agreement at Marlborough House. With them are Temenggong Jugah (left) and British Prime Minister Harold Macmillan.

Stephen Kalong Ningkan, first Sarawak CM

22 July Kuching

His Excellency the Governor of Sarawak, being satisfied that Mr Stephen Kalong Ningkan was likely to command the confidence of the majority of the members of the Council Negeri, appointed him Chief Minister of Sarawak. Mr Ningkan, born in 1920 at Betong in the Saribas District, was one of the founders of the Sarawak National Party (Snap) which was formed in April 1961.

Protest march by amahs seeking better wages

11 August Kuala Lumpur

More than 1,000 amahs employed by the British Commonwealth Armed Forces throughout Malaya staged a protest march through Kuala Lumpur over their working conditions. The amahs, who were asking Queen Elizabeth to intervene on their behalf, were members of the War Department Civilian Staff Association, which represented more than 10,000 workers of various categories. Association president S.J.H. Zaidi said this was 'the first time a trade union is staging a protest march in Kuala Lumpur.' An amah's pay was $125 a month and a cook-amah's $180–$200 (*see 9 June 1964*).

King opens $125m hydro project

26 June Cameron Highlands

Malaya's largest single engineering feat, the Cameron Highlands hydroelectric power project, was officially opened by the Yang di-Pertuan Agong. The $125-million project included a 130-acre artificial lake holding 1,670 million gallons of water and a 375ft-wide dam. Work on this first of a two-phase Central Electricity Board project to meet Malaya's increasing demand for power began in March 1959.

When completed, the project would be the country's largest source of power. The project was financed with loans from the Federation Government ($38 million), the International Bank for Reconstruction and Development ($84 million) and the Commonwealth Development Finance Corporation (£500,000).

Maphilindo the first regional organisation

5 August Manila

A new chapter in Southeast Asian history began with the signing of summit agreements to launch Malaysia and to establish the regional association of Maphilindo (Malaya, the Philippines and Indonesia)—with the objective of approaching issues of common concern in a spirit of consensus.

Prime Minister Tunku Abdul Rahman, President Sukarno of Indonesia and President Macapagal of the Philippines also decided that a letter should be sent to United Nations Secretary-General U Thant to ascertain the wishes of the peoples of Borneo prior to the establishment of Malaysia.

Tunku Abdul Rahman, President Sukarno of Indonesia and President Macapagal of the Philippines sign the Manila Declaration Accord and Joint Statement on 5 August after their Manila summit meeting.

Preserving the delicate balance of nature

Asia Magazine

Man can sometimes be the most destructive of animals, *Asia Magazine* said in an article headlined 'Men and animals: the case for conservation.' In Malaya, it said, the two-horned rhinoceros had been reduced to 'a pathetic few' by hunters. The same fate threatened the orang utan.

Wild cattle roam on the cover of Asia Magazine.

'Species in any habitat are interdependent. Eliminating one will adversely affect their delicate harmony,' the article said. It pointed out that tigers kept the number of deer and wild pigs in check so 'excessive shooting of the big cats results in greater damage to rubber plantations and tea estates from the deer. Conversely, wiping out deer and wild pig turns the carnivores into cattle killers and a threat to man.' The article praised a pilot scheme to save the giant leathery turtle, which had been almost wiped out due to egg collection.

'As a conservation consciousness is fostered in Malaya measures are being taken to preserve the few remaining two-horned rhinoceros. The game department has also banned export of the orang utan.'

Pahang Sultan names giant Highlands dam

11 August Tanah Rata

The giant dam at Ringlet, six miles south of Tanah Rata, has been named the Sultan Abu Bakar Dam by the Sultan of Pahang. The giant dam is one of the main features of the Cameron Highlands hydroelectric power project. After the naming ceremony, the Sultan and his consort were presented bouquets of flowers and entertained to a water display at the 130ft dam.

A view of the National Museum under construction. Right: Tunku Abdul Rahman visits the site, accompanied by the museum director Mubin Sheppard, architects, and senior officials of the museum.

Muzium Negara opens

31 August | **Kuala Lumpur**

Muzium Negara, designed by architect Charles Ho and built in the style of a Minangkabau palace, was opened by the Yang di-Pertuan Agong. It consists of a large central main entrance hall flanked by two exhibition wings. Two large murals on the exterior of the wings depict the rich past and culture of the country.

'Hungry' Perak River

11 August | **Teluk Anson**

The 'ravenous' Perak River once again claimed another slice of Telok Anson (now Teluk Intan), a 50ft stretch of land off Denison Road. The affected area contained 10 wooden structures which housed some 75 people. Fortunately, no lives were lost. The area was declared a danger zone but residents had no plans to move. 'We know it is dangerous to live here, but where are we to move to?' they asked.

UN sends assessment teams

20 August | **Kuala Lumpur**

UN Secretary General U Thant has sent a letter to the Foreign Ministers of the Philippines, Indonesia and Malaya stating that he plans to send two teams of five men each to Sarawak and North Borneo to sample the 'Malaysia sentiment' in these British-held territories.

The teams arrived on 1 September. They were given an additional three days to complete their task of assessing the views of the people of Sarawak and North Borneo on Malaysia's formation.

Racing driver killed in Johor GP crash

1 September | **Johor Bahru**

'Fatso' Yong Nam Kee, a popular racing driver who won the first Malaysia Grand Prix last year, was killed when his D-type Jaguar crashed at more than 100mph at the Zoo corner on the 58th lap of the Johor Grand Prix. Yong, lying second behind eventual winner Albert Poon of Hong Kong, was thrown out of his car. He was apparently attempting to overtake two cars when he crashed.

Poon said: 'I am most unhappy that this should happen to Nam Kee. He was a good, tough rival.'

Circuit crew at the crash scene attempting to extricate Yong from his mangled vehicle.

What the foreign press said

Malayan women's lives explained for British readers

16 September | **London**

A feature in *The Times* of London asked: 'What then of the woman of Malaya?' Answering the question, writer Katharine Sim went on: 'There are now women representatives of the three main races in politics. Independence brought many Malay women, at first shyly, from their quiet family lives. Now as the wives of Ministers and ambassadors, Government and court officials, they are more constantly at their husbands' side.

'Many educated Malay women are teachers, nurses or work in offices and shops. There is no caste system among Malays, they have been for the last 55 years a democratic people. It has often been said that the humblest kampong boy may aspire to be a Minister, and you might well find a prince's son working as an office boy. This may not yet be true of Malay women but they are becoming more emancipated.

'The Malay peasant woman still lives her quiet semi-matriarchal existence in the kampong, making her coconut oil for cooking, rearing her chickens, and caring for her little brood of golden-skinned children.

'Chinese women labourers, particularly the Hakkas, work with the men on the roads, at house building, on tin mines and on rubber estates, but however hard they work in the sun they take care always to protect their skins. Chinese girls have a flair for chic, they are invariably well turned out in a way that makes most of their English counterparts look dowdy. They have none of the Malay woman's natural shyness.

Kelantan dancers perform a wedding dance during a cultural show at Stadium Negara on 31 August.

'Among educated Chinese women some are highly trained, clever and charming too, and intense about their work in schools, or as lawyers; many are nuns. Others are running homes, perhaps one of the old-fashioned mansions of their tin or rubber dollar millionaire fathers. They employ servants of their own clan and often provide a home and a livelihood for poor relatives. Many Tamil women, like the Chinese, labour beside their men on the roads and in the rubber estates. Some educated Indian women are teachers, and many, wives of ministers and prominent citizens, take part in public life and entertain formally for their husbands. There are a number of keen amateur dancers and musicians who practise and sometimes teach the ancient classical dances of India.

'Girls of the Eurasian community are keen sportsmen. Many Eurasians are members of the churches, some are teachers, typists, nurses and often beauty queens. Today there is another increasing little group: English girls, young wives of Malays met in London.'

MALAYSIA!

The Malaysia Proclamation is read by Prime Minister Tunku Abdul Rahman, witnessed by the Malay Rulers (right).

16 September | **Kuala Lumpur**

Across the nation, the new Malaysian flag with its 14 stripes was ceremonially unfurled for the first time. Thousands jammed the gaily-decorated streets of all 14 States to greet the new-minted nation of 10 million. In all States, colourful parades were held.

The high point for Singapore was a 5pm reading of the Proclamation on the steps of City Hall. In Kuala Lumpur, an inaugural ceremony took place at 8.20am. In Jesselton (Kota Kinabalu), Sabah's main city, and Kuching in Sarawak, official festivities began at 7.30am.

More than 20,000 had been gathering at the Merdeka Stadium in the Federal Capital since the early hours. At the stadium ceremony, Tunku Abdul Rahman said that 'I cannot express how happy and grateful I am' on 'this auspicious and historic day.' But he called on Malaysians to defend the flag of the new nation 'with all our strength, even if necessary with our lives.'

Meanwhile, with Indonesia and the Philippines recalling their envoys in Kuala Lumpur the day before, and announcing that they would not recognise Malaysia, thousands screaming anti-Malaysia slogans stoned the Malaysian and British embassies in Jakarta. In Medan, Sumatra, demonstrators broke into the British consulate and destroyed furniture and fittings. Malaysia's consul was given refuge at the US consulate.

Rioters in Sibu overturn a police van while police (left) hold back a demonstrator during protests when the UN inspection team visited Sarawak on 16 August.

Birth of the nation not without its pains

16 September | Kuala Lumpur

The birth of Malaysia was not without its pains. There was doubt about the commitment of the people of Borneo to the new State as some local leaders in North Borneo (now Sabah) had hoped for an independent State of their own. Also, at one stage Singapore threatened to proclaim independence alone.

The original date set for Malaysia's formation was 31 August, Merdeka Day. But on 24 August it was announced that a new date was to be fixed by British Colonial Secretary Duncan Sandys after consultation with Sabah, Sarawak and Singapore. A few days later he held a 'little summit' in Singapore with the territories' leaders and Malayan Deputy Prime Minister Tun Abdul Razak.

Earlier, United Nations Secretary-General U Thant had announced that two UN teams would go to Sarawak and North Borneo to assess the 'Malaysia sentiment' in the British-held territories. Stating that Malaya would stick to sending four observers with the UN assessment team as planned, Tunku Abdul Rahman said: 'It is a waste of manpower, time and money ... I fail to understand the fuss.' On the postponement of Malaysia Day originally scheduled for 31 August, the Tunku said: 'We are taking it as a matter of course ... The people of Malaya are very cool. This is the attitude of mature people.'

Meanwhile, the Yang di-Pertuan Agong signed a Proclamation declaring 16 September 'Malaysia Day'. The proclamation was made in accordance with the provisions of the Malaysia Act, under which a new date for the formation of Malaysia had to be specified by 31 August. The Government said the agreement reached in London on 9 July was to the effect that Malaysia should come into being on 31 August. However, the Philippines and Indonesia wanted the wishes of the peoples of the Borneo territories to be ascertained by the UN.

When the UN inspection team arrived in Kuching on 16 August it was greeted by crowds shouting anti-Malaysia slogans. The team's motorcade was halted several times by protesting crowds. At one stage police had difficulty dispersing the demonstrators and SUPP leaders were called in to help; but they refused to leave until people already arrested by the police were released. SUPP secretary-general Stephen Yong addressed the crowds and urged them to return to their homes, saying they should not go against police orders.

In Sibu, which the team also visited, there were also clashes with the police. Communist elements were suspected of organising the violence.

Barely a week before the new federation was to be declared, the northern state of Kelantan tried to block the formation of Malaysia.

The State Government started legal proceedings against the Federal Government and Prime Minister Tunku Abdul Rahman, declaring that the Malaysia Act was illegal and not binding on the State.

One of its arguments was that the resultant changes to the Federation of Malaya Agreement of 1957 needed the consent of each of the constituent States including Kelantan, and this had not been obtained. It also contended that the Federal Parliament had no power to legislate for Kelantan in matters that the State could legislate for on its own.

Chief Justice James Thomson delivered his decision just 30 hours before Malaysia was to be declared. Before dismissing Kelantan's claims, he said: 'Never, I think, has a judge had to pronounce on an issue of such magnitude on so little notice and with so little time for consideration.'

Malaysia cuts links with Jakarta, Manila

17 September | Kuala Lumpur

Malaysia severed diplomatic relations with Indonesia and the Philippines. 'In view of the fact that the Indonesian Government has broken off diplomatic relations with Malaysia without any apparent reason, we have no choice but to do likewise,' said Prime Minister Tunku Abdul Rahman.

'The fact that the Federation has admitted new States does not in any way change the status and identity of the nation, and therefore no fresh recognition is necessary...the Government of the Philippines has asked that the status of its embassy in Kuala Lumpur be reduced to that of a consulate.

This proposal is not acceptable to the Malaysian Government. There is, therefore, no choice for this Government but to recall its Ambassador,' the Prime Minister said.

Thailand was asked to represent Malaysia's interests in both Maphilindo countries.

Malaysia, Indonesia and the Philippines—silent discord led to severance of links.

Tunku warns political parties

7 November | Kuala Lumpur

Political parties or individuals who persist in siding with Indonesia or the Communist Party against Malaysia have been warned of dire consequences. Speaking at the annual delegates' meeting of the MCA Youth section, Prime Minister Tunku Abdul Rahman accused the Socialist Front and the Pan-Malayan Islamic Party of trying to create chaos in the country. Socialist Front leader Inche Ahmad Boestamam, who was under detention, had tried to cause a split within the armed forces at the instigation of Indonesian leaders, the Tunku said.

The PMIP, he said, had been trying to create trouble between the Malays and the Chinese by saying that Muslims should not associate with non-Muslims, and was using religion to create 'chaos' in the country.

The Malaysia Proclamation was read out in all four territories of the new nation. In addition to the reading in Kuala Lumpur by Prime Minister Tunku Abdul Rahman, there was a ceremony in Singapore, led by Prime Minister Lee Kuan Yew (far left). In Sarawak's capital Kuching, the proclamation was made by Federal Government representative Mohamad Khir Johari, with Governor Datu Abang Haji Openg and Chief Minister Stephen Kalong Ningkan (centre), and in Jesselton by Sabah Chief Minister Datuk Donald Stephens with Governor Tun Mustapha Harun and Deputy Prime Minister Tun Abdul Razak (above).

Snapshots of a new nation

Clockwise from top left: Singapore's teeming maze lies at an Asian crossroads; George Town, which the article said was pervaded by 'blaring signs of a boom', as tourists throng Penang to shop for duty-free bargains; Deputy Prime Minister Tun Abdul Razak discusses with officials plans for a new rural settlement; and a dash to shelter from the rain in Singapore.

A special feature in *National Geographic* magazine gave a pen-portrait of Malaysia and a wealth of photographs of the newly born nation.

New Zealand travel writer Maurice Shadbolt and staff photographer Winfield Parks roamed for months through 'tin-and-rubber-rich Malaya, teeming Singapore and their wild, romantic neighbours, Sarawak and North Borneo.' Shadbolt wrote that Prime Minister Tunku Abdul Rahman 'described these far-flung lands to me as a crescent of freedom'.

He travelled nearly 9,000 miles, watching 'fascinated' as the foundations of 'a nation which its builders hope will be an example to all Asia' were laid. It was a keenly sought prize in the battle between East and West, he wrote, and 'in Malaya genuine democracy has won a decisive victory over militant Communism'. His travels took him from the logging settlement of Kalabakan, where Dai Rees, a trading company manager, told him 'We've got 20 different nationalities including one Welshman', to bustling George Town, Penang, where 'shuttered colonial homes soon gave way to the flashing neon and busy traffic.' From the West Coast of the Peninsula he journeyed to the East, to Kelantan and Kota Bharu, and back to Kuala Lumpur, where he interviewed the Tunku, and to Singapore. 'Now, in all their diversity, I have seen the faces of Malaysia,' he concluded. 'Can people of so many races, so many beliefs, find true harmony? The answer affects us all. Because Malaysia is not simply a test for Asians. It is a test for the human race itself'.

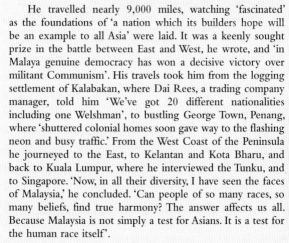

Clockwise from top left: 'Age-old transport, the human back,' in Kuala Lumpur; Orang Asli train as home guards near Kuala Lumpur; Fort Legap, once an outpost against the Communists, now a trading and educational centre for Orang Asli; Mengkabong, a Bajau village near Tuaran, Sabah, ; handloom silk on sale at Raffles Hotel, Singapore; European and Chinese dance together in swinging Singapore; loggers, whipping rope slings ever higher, climb a 150ft hardwood tree near Kalabakan, Sabah; the Sunday market at Kota Belud 'offers a harvest from home industries'.

1963

Parliament House— beacon of democracy

2 November Kuala Lumpur

Malaysian democracy took a step forward with the opening of the $17-million Parliament House in the Lake Gardens by the Yang di-Pertuan Agong. He reminded assembled guests that the first King had described the country's Senate and Lower House as 'twin dynamos' of democracy. 'The new Parliament, operating under a new Constitution, will be newer and larger dynamos of democracy', he said.

Fifty-five new MPs—24 from Sarawak, 16 from Singapore and 15 from Sabah—were sworn in at the oak-panelled, plush 159-seat chamber of the House of Representatives. Design of the Parliament House began in 1960 headed by Public Works Department architect Ivor Shipley.

Cholera alert

20 November Kuala Lumpur

It was anti-cholera jabs for all. In Singapore, five new cases were reported in 24 hours, bringing to 10 the number of confirmed cases. The Health Ministry advised those who had not been immunised within the past six months to get their inoculations from health offices and hospitals as soon as possible. As an added precautionary measure, all travellers to and from Malaysia and Singapore were required to possess a valid certificate of inoculation against cholera. The first case in Kuala Lumpur was detected on 27 November.

This was the queue at the inoculation centre in Meyappachetty Road in Potong Pasir, Singapore, where the first case of cholera was reported on 17 May.

First border incident

24 September Kuching

In the first serious border incident since the formation of Malaysia, four mortar bombs were fired from the direction of the Indonesian border towards Kampong Serabak, about three miles from the Sarawak–Kalimantan border. There were no casualties other than a dog, which was killed by shrapnel.

All eager to serve their country, recruits including a woman, queue to sign up in Penang.

Call to National Service

18 November Kuala Lumpur

The Yang di-Pertuan Agong signed a proclamation invoking the National Service Ordinance 1952, the first step to a call-up. It empowered the Government to call on the 600,000 male Federal citizens aged 21 to 28 to register for National Service. Those outside this age group, and women over 21, could volunteer. The proclamation applied only to Malaya, as the Ordinance did not at the time cover Singapore or the Borneo States. This was the second time the ordinance had been invoked since independence. The first, in March 1958, was when the Government went flat out to end the Emergency (see 16 July 1964).

Sabotage plot uncovered

18 December Kuala Lumpur

Tunku Abdul Rahman exposed an Indonesian plot to blow up the water mains between Singapore and Johor, the Pasir Panjang power station and other vital installations in the State. Thirty-seven people had been arrested, and a large quantity of 'sabotage equipment' confiscated.

In the long term, the Tunku told a stunned House of Representatives, the Indonesians had in mind the establishment of 'battalions' in Singapore, Johor and Kelantan, with which to launch armed revolution, in an attempt to destroy Malaysia by violent means.

Television comes to Malaysia.

TV comes to life in KL

28 December Kuala Lumpur

Tunku Abdul Rahman launched Television Malaysia's pilot service to Kuala Lumpur. Those without TV sets jammed radio shops to watch the 30-minute ceremony on display sets. 'Before next year is out, the TV service will cater for people in Ipoh, Taiping, Penang, Alor Star, Seremban, Tampin, Malacca and Johor Bahru,' said the Tunku.

From swampland to modern port

27 December Port Swettenham

From swampland, inaccessible even by foot, it took more than three years—and $40 million—to build the North Klang port. At the opening ceremony in the afternoon, the Yang di-Pertuan Agong commended the Central Government for its 'significant and far-sighted' decision to build the port. With four deepwater wharves, the port was able to deal with 17 ships simultaneously.

1964

Indonesia launched its violent campaign to crush Malaysia, leading to skirmishes along parts of the Peninsula's west coast. Scores of Indonesian commandos and guerrillas were captured on Malaysian soil and Malaysia protested to the United Nations over the Indonesian aggression. At home, postal workers went on strike for better pay. The ruling Alliance Party was returned to power, winning 89 of 104 seats in Parliament. This victory and the rise in spirit of nationalism provided the impetus for the introduction of the National Service Bill and paved the way for the first batch of women to join the Territorial Army and volunteer for combat training. Also, a National Solidarity Week showcased Malaysians' unity and 'heroic spirit and patriotism'.

FEBRUARY
Malaysia, Indonesia and the Philippines discuss the Borneo ceasefire at the tripartite peace talks in Bangkok.

APRIL
The Alliance wins comfortably in the 1964 general election.

AUGUST
Malaysia is on security alert as Indonesians attempt to infiltrate the country.

NOVEMBER
The National Solidarity Week to celebrate Malaysian unity in the face of foreign aggression is marked with rallies and processions.

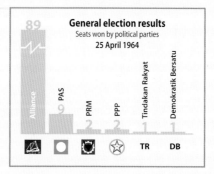

May: Postal workers go on strike to demand a separate salary scale from the rest of the civil service.

General election results
Seats won by political parties
25 April 1964

Alliance	PAS	PRM	PPP	Tindakan Rakyat	Demokratik Bersatu
89	9	2	2	1	1
				TR	DB

'We are defending not only our own independence, but also democracy.'

Tun Abdul Razak, in Parliament, speaking on Malaysia's rejection of a defence loan offer by the United States, 30 December 1964.

1964

world news

Indonesian aggression: Protest to UN

1 January | **Kuala Lumpur** ▶ Malaysia officially lodged a protest to United Nations Secretary-General U Thant over Indonesian aggression in the Borneo States. The note followed news of further Malaysian casualties as an officer and seven soldiers were killed in a major clash in East Sabah two nights before. Nineteen men of the 3rd Battalion Royal Malay Regiment were wounded and were being treated in the Tawau hospital, with several of them in critical condition.

In his New Year's message to the nation, Prime Minister Tunku Abdul Rahman paid tribute to the defenders against the Sunday night attack on the defence post in the timber village of Kalabakan, praising their gallantry and courageous fight 'to uphold democracy and freedom in our country'.

Little Kaman's Thaipusam surprise

28 January | **Kuala Lumpur**

Two-year-old Kaman suddenly found himself high above the crowds when his mother handed him to a man on stilts during the Thaipusam celebrations at Batu Caves.

Islamic studies for Penang Catholic seminary

2 February | **Penang**

The Pulau Tikus College General introduced the study of Islam into its scripture course. For the first time in its 155-year history, the major Catholic seminary in Penang made Islam a compulsory subject. It was being introduced to give non-Muslims a better understanding of religion, and it is felt that it would be one way to build racial tolerance between the two faiths. The college's professor of scripture also felt that there should also be spiritual contacts and exchange of views on theology between Muslims and Christians.

Ceasefire!

23 January | **Kuala Lumpur**

The Malaysian Government pledged to extend its 'full cooperation' to facilitate a ceasefire in the Borneo States.

Tunku Abdul Rahman made the announcement a few hours after President Sukarno of Indonesia said that Malaysia, the Philippines and Indonesia had agreed to a truce and a tripartite meeting at Ministerial level for peace talks.

Indonesia's Information Minister, Roslan Abdulgani, said this did not mean the end of Confrontation. The ceasefire order to Indonesian troops was due to take effect at midnight the following day.

Indonesian bombers over Sibu, Kuching

1 February | **Kuala Lumpur**

Thousands of leaflets in red and white —Indonesia's national colours—were dropped from Indonesian bombers, containing orders for Indonesian troops and North Kalimantan volunteers to 'keep your weapons always in your hands and defend your present position', even as they observe the ceasefire announced earlier. They were signed 'President, Supreme Commander and Supreme Leader of the Republic of Indonesia, Soekarno'.

First-day accord

6 February | **Bangkok**

The first day of tripartite peace talks started well when Malaysia, Indonesia and the Philippines reached agreement on the 'guiding principles' of how to make the ceasefire in Borneo effective. However, no one was willing to predict whether this positive mood would last until the meeting adjourned on Saturday.

Tun Thanat Khoman of Thailand garlanding Deputy Prime Minister Tun Razak on his arrival in Bangkok.

Talks broken off

4 March | **Bangkok**

The Borneo ceasefire was called off after the collapse of tripartite Ministerial talks. The Malaysian delegation said in a statement: 'The refusal of the Indonesians to give an assurance on the withdrawal of their armed forces from Malaysian territory brought the talks to an end.' Tunku Abdul Rahman commented that the breakdown of the Bangkok meeting was inevitable due to Indonesia's uncompromising attitude towards the ceasefire.

New school system

6 March | **Kuala Lumpur**

The Malayan secondary school entrance examination, introduced in 1957 for the 11-plus, was scrapped. This meant that Standard Six pupils would be automatically promoted to secondary Form One. The present secondary continuation school system was also to be scrapped. The decision was to ensure that all children received nine years of general education— six years at primary level and three years at lower secondary level.

Why I will retire in 1969—Tunku

4 April | **Langkawi**

Prime Minister Tunku Abdul Rahman said he had decided not to seek re-election in 1969 because 'I wish to devote my remaining years to working for the Alliance Party'.

'I prefer to let a younger man take my place, but I will be behind the party all the time,' he told *The Straits Times* at the Langkawi Island rest house where he was staying. He also planned to devote his time to promoting Islam, setting up Muslim welfare societies 'everywhere'.

He added: 'There are many Chinese very keen to embrace the religion and these societies will be very helpful to them.'

The battle of the bulls

4 April | **Kuala Lumpur**

Mr Dara Singh, a game warden, found himself playing referee over the question of whether the bull in the Socialist Front's symbol was a Malayan seladang or an Indonesian animal. It all started when Minister of Commerce and Industry Dr Lim Swee Aun said the bull was another indication of the Front's connections with Indonesia. In response, the Front held a special news conference, where Miss P.G. Lim, the Front's candidate for the Sentul state constituency, denied the charge.

Dr Lim riposted, with Mr Singh's opinion to back him up. 'I'm surprised,' Dr Lim said, 'that Miss Lim cannot distinguish between the seladang's head and that of the symbol of the Socialist Front.'

The People's Action Party (PAP) came out in support of Dr Lim and refuted the Front's suggestion that the red and white of Singapore's flag were connected to the colours of the Indonesian flag.

Tuberculosis kills 5,000 every year

6 April Kuala Lumpur

Tuberculosis was still the biggest killer in the country, according to a report by the senior tuberculosis specialist and director of the National Tuberculosis Control Campaign, Dr J.S. Sodhy. More than 5,000 died from tuberculosis every year. Almost one-tenth of the country's health budget was spent on fighting and treating TB. The prevalence of the disease was such that by the age of 15, three out of four children were infected, although not all developed the disease.

Postal workers demonstrating in the streets demanding better pay.

Postal service strike goes on

17 May Kuala Lumpur ▶ The Union of Post Office Workers decided to continue indefinitely a strike which began this morning and rejected calls for arbitration. They had rejected an appeal by Minister of Labour V. Manickavasagam not to resort to industrial action. The strike was to demand a salary scale for the postal service separate from the rest of the civil service.

Women teachers to get equal pay

18 June Kuala Lumpur

After four years of active agitation, the Women Teachers' Union finally succeeded in achieving equal pay for women teachers. Among the many congratulatory telegrams that Mrs F.R. Bhupalan, the union president, received was one from Inche Ahmad bin Abdul Rahman, president of the National Union of National School Teachers, who also invited her to join a single national teachers' union.

He said: 'There are many things like pension rights, housing allowances, leave and other conditions of service which have yet to be improved.' In August, Australian teachers studied the tactics used by the Malaysian women in their 20-year fight for equal pay.

Mrs F.R. Bhupalan, president of the Women Teachers' Union.

16 killed in lorry crash

11 May Kajang

In one of the nation's worst road accidents, 16 rubber tappers were killed and 10 injured when the lorry carrying them collided with a military truck at the 13th Mile, Serdang–Kuala Lumpur Road.

The accident occurred at 3pm when the tappers were returning from the Prang Besar Estate. Fourteen of them died on the spot. All 13 soldiers in the truck escaped unhurt. Many of the bodies were so badly mangled that it took a considerable time to identify them. A mass burial was held the next day.

$2m benefits for amahs

9 June Kuala Lumpur

The British War Department said it would pay gratuities to the 3,000 amahs due to leave the employment of the British, Australian and New Zealand Forces in Malaya at the end of June. It would cost the three services $2 million, with the amahs receiving an average of $700 each depending on their length of service. This followed strike threats in October 1963 in protest against a move to delegate the responsibility of employment to individual soldiers.

Hope of troop pullout comes to nothing

17 June Tokyo

A special envoy of President Macapagal of the Philippines told Deputy Prime Minister Tun Razak that President Sukarno had ordered Indonesian forces to withdraw from Sabah and Sarawak and would establish a checkpoint on the Indonesian side of the border to monitor returning guerrillas.

It also appeared that the Indonesians were prepared to start the ministerial talks on the Malaysia issue that night. The Foreign Ministers of the three countries were due to meet the following day.

Five days later, it was revealed that the withdrawal order was a fake. Summit talks in Tokyo collapsed as Sukarno declared unequivocally that he could not accept Malaysia and it was a British act and must be crushed. The Confrontation continues.

Rail sabotage

25 June Tampin

Terrorists derailed a 50-wagon goods train last night with a dynamite charge on the line, four miles north of here. The first explosion—which threw 15 wagons of the Kuala Lumpur–Singapore goods train off the track—was followed by another one two hours later that was caused by a time bomb placed near the line. They took place a quarter-mile north of the railroad crossing on the Seremban–Malacca Road.

Though no one was injured, the damage was estimated to be at about $250,000. The Minister of Transport, Datuk Sardon Haji Jubir, blamed saboteurs from Indonesia for the explosions.

Datuk Loke with Prime Minister Tunku Abdul Rahman in 1963, during a demonstration flight on Malayan Airways' new Fokker F-27 Friendship.

Loke Wan Tho killed in air crash

20 June Taipeh

Cinema magnate and chairman of Malayan Airways Datuk Loke Wan Tho and his wife were among 53 people killed when a Civil Air Transport airliner crashed in flames shortly after take-off from Taichung in central Formosa (now Taiwan).

Datuk Loke had been leading the Malaysian delegation to the 11th Asian Film Festival which ended on 19 June. He was a respected philanthropist and his interest in ornithology and photography made him the one of the foremost experts in documenting Malayan birds. There were no survivors of the crash.

The scoreboard on the Selangor Club field showing the results of the general election as they came in from all around the country.

I am so happy, says Tunku

24 April Kuala Lumpur

The Alliance won 89 out of 104 seats in Parliament, comfortably returning to power once again. Tunku Abdul Rahman described himself as 'very, very happy' and announced that his first task would be to appoint a new Minister to look after operations in the Borneo area. The Tunku saw the result as a show of confidence in the Alliance and the people's endorsement of its policies over the past few years. The victory gave 'added strength' to counter President Sukarno's 'Crush Malaysia' campaign.

1964

Confrontation

US to stand by Malaysia

11 July Kuala Lumpur

The United States would not sacrifice Malaysia's interests to placate President Sukarno and so save Indonesia from Communism, said Mr James D. Bell, the US Ambassador to Malaysia. He made the promise while on his way to Washington to prepare for the visit to the US by Prime Minister Tunku Abdul Rahman.

The Tunku was scheduled to arrive on 22 July at the invitation of President Lyndon B. Johnson.

Two Indonesian paratroopers who were captured on 15 September are seen here roped together and being led to the Labis police station in Johor for interrogation.

Two of the captured Indonesians in Singapore, with their hands up, crossing a muddy stream.

National Service Bill passed

16 July Kuala Lumpur

The National Service Bill was passed, providing for the establishment of a National Service Reserve in which trained youths would serve for five years. It amended the 12-year-old National Service Ordinance. Only one Opposition MP spoke out against the Bill in the House of Representatives, Mr Lim Huan Boon of the Barisan Sosialis.

The first batch of 400 recruits would arrive in Port Dickson on 1 August to begin their two-month training there at the Seginting training camp. The call-up plan affected Malaysians aged between 21 and 29.

Singapore plot exposed, arrests made

8 September Singapore

Deputy Prime Minister Tun Abdul Razak disclosed that the police had uncovered an Indonesian plot responsible for disturbances in Singapore and had arrested several of its leaders. Further arrests of people involved would be made.

'They have been responsible for all the present trouble, including the first stabbing case,' said Tun Razak. He also said Communists were working with Indonesian agents. But he was satisfied that the situation was under control.

Shock report on traitors by Tunku

10 September Kuala Lumpur

In a special session of Parliament, Prime Minister Tunku Abdul Rahman revealed that some 2,500 Malaysian traitors had crossed over to Indonesia from Sabah, Sarawak, Singapore and Malaya in the last two years.

He said this as he tabled a resolution calling on all members to endorse the proclamation of a State of Emergency that was issued last week.

He also said if the distribution of unpatriotic, un-Malaysian pamphlets by a certain political party went unchecked, 'it would not be possible to defend Malaysia from the traitors within'.

Five Malaysians among guerrillas captured

29 October Malacca

Five Malaysian traitors were among 25 Indonesian commandos and guerrillas captured in the Kesang area, seven miles north of Muar, by security forces.

They were from a larger group of 52, who landed early in the morning of the same day on the Johor–Malacca border. Large quantities of arms, ammunition and equipment were found, as well as large sums of money.

They landed using previously seized fishing boats. A curfew in the area was lifted a day later when all but two of the Indonesians had been captured.

On 22 December, a group of Indonesians landed in Sungai Buntu, eight miles south of Pontian Kecil. Fourteen were quickly captured, including three killed, while 13 more surrendered five days later, after taking refuge knee deep in a swamp in Sungai Kerang.

With 23 of them accounted for, the military operations in the Pontian area were called off. Later, on 28 December, nine starving Indonesian guerrillas turned themselves in after hiding in the swamps of Singapore's west coast for four days. They had been sent to destroy specific targets in the Pasir Panjang area.

Nation on security alert

17 August Pontian

As Malaysian forces stood on alert today—Indonesia's National Day, a time when nationalist feelings were expected to run high—armed Indonesians landed in Pontian, Johor. Security forces had captured at least 21 raiders and the sampans they had arrived in within three days. A round-the-clock watch on the coast area also indicated an increasing number of Indonesian boats defying the barter trade ban.

On 5 September, the Yang di-Pertuan Agong proclaimed the whole of Malaysia a security area. This was intended to give police and security forces wider powers to deal with any situation that might arise following the Pontian landings and others in Labis on 3 September.

Security forces leading two captured Indonesians to the Pontian Kechil police station.

Fishermen hijacked

5 October Port Swettenham

In the biggest act of piracy of the Confrontation, an Indonesian naval vessel hijacked 25 Malaysian fishing boats in the Straits of Malacca during the weekend. The boats contained fish, nets, other fishing apparatus, food and cooking utensils, their value totalling $150,000.

Twelve fishermen, all from Ketam Island, were held hostage, while the remaining 43 were released and sent back in four boats.

The incident, which occurred at 8am, involved an Indonesian naval craft later identified as a frigate or destroyer.

Malaysia to 'pursue' enemy

24 December Kuala Lumpur

In the event of more massive attacks by Indonesia, Malaysia may be forced to 'pursue' the enemy, said Minister of Home Affairs Datuk Dr Ismail bin Dato' Abdul Rahman. He made the statement at a press conference following the disclosure by Deputy Prime Minister and Defence Minister Tun Abdul Razak of a military build-up in Sumatra and along the Borneo border.

Tun Abdul Razak added that the United Nations Security Council would be informed of this steady build-up, including a fresh landing by Indonesian guerrillas at Pontian on 23 December. Datuk Ismail declared: 'In the event of more massive attacks, we will have to take defensive measures in conformity with the provisions of the UN Charter. Under the Charter, the party that is attacked is allowed to pursue the enemy'. He said: 'We want to serve notice to the UN and the whole world that we are not going to take it lying down.'

Farmer outwits guerrilla leader

17 November Singapore

Quick thinking led farmer Tan Tian Oo, 27, to deliver the leader of Indonesian infiltrators straight into the arms of the law. The leader was literally taken for a ride, when he was carried six miles on Tan's bicycle crossbar to a police station in Jurong. Tan was approached by the man, who was asking for food, at 8.30pm. Though frightened, his presence of mind meant that within the hour, hundreds of policemen were on the hunt for the rest of the infiltrators.

Rulers give to fund

15 October Kuala Lumpur

Tunku Abdul Rahman's proposal to launch a National Defence Fund soon to meet Indonesian aggression was 'gladly accepted'. It was submitted on the last day of the Conference of Rulers here. As a start, the Rulers, the Governors of Penang, Malacca and Sarawak and the Heads of State of Singapore and Sabah decided to donate $1,000 each.

200 doctors offer aid in crisis

14 October Kuala Lumpur

Following nationwide appeals by the Yang di-Pertuan Agong and Prime Minister Tunku Abdul Rahman, more than 200 private doctors quickly responded to a call to render voluntary service during the emergency.

The Malayan Medical Association had decided to organise the profession to meet medical problems associated with the emergency, and was pleased with the response. It expected more to come forward. The types of voluntary service being organised include assisting in under-staffed government facilities.

Women show they are ready for combat

6 November Johor Bahru

These women were the first to volunteer for combat training. Dressed in the Territorial Army uniform, they attended training sessions for two hours per week and were soon learning how to use small arms.

What the foreign press said

Confrontation at the ballot box

'The momentous victory gives us very much courage,' *Time* magazine quoted Prime Minister Tunku Abdul Rahman as saying after the May general election. 'I pray that God will give us help and shelter from adversity and that Malaysia will continue to flourish and prosper in peace. To hell with Sukarno.'

The magazine commented: 'It was quite a post-election statement, but justified in the sense that the big issue at the polls had indeed been Sukarno and his vicious guerrilla and propaganda offensives against the new Federation of Malaysia.'

It said 'a lively five-week campaign' was marked by claims that politicians were luring women voters with love potions.

'More serious were charges that some of the parties were playing into the hands of the Indonesians by opposing the Prime Minister's stand against Sukarno,' it added.

The Tunku aimed his sharpest shots at the Socialists, alleging that they were cooperating with the Indonesian Communist Party, it said, adding that he also condemned the right-wing, fanatical Muslim groups, who might be receptive to Indonesian arguments because of their distaste for the multiracial, multireligious character of the Federation.

In September the magazine reported on Malaysia's 'dramatic' appeal to the United Nations for help in ending Confrontation 'after more than a year of harassment by Indonesia', saying: 'Onto the polished horseshoe-shaped table plopped a miniature arsenal, an automatic rifle and a light mortar, a helmet, a backpack, an opened parachute, a camouflage suit.'

The equipment, it said, had been captured from the '40-odd paratroopers dropped into mainland Malaya two weeks ago'.

Malaysian political poster.

1964

Straits Times Annual feature

Malayan students in Britain

In terms of numbers, Malaya may be second to Nigeria among the countries with a large number of students abroad, but in terms of population ratio Malaya has the highest percentage of students studying in the United Kingdom. There was a sharp increase, from fewer than 1,500 students in 1958 to more than 4,000 in the United Kingdom and the Republic of Ireland in the early part of 1963.

A feature in the *Straits Times Annual* commented that perhaps parents now placed a greater importance on education, or perhaps sending children overseas to study was a sign of status. But the shortage of qualified teachers in Malaysia had led to an insufficient number of places in the Sixth Form. As a result, many students who failed to gain places went to Britain, to either boarding school or technical college, to study for the General Certificate of Education Advanced-level examination, in order to qualify for university admission. The curriculum there also has a wider

range of subjects. But sending their children to Britain to study was no guarantee of gaining a place in the universities, as the competition is extremely fierce, and the young Malayans would have to compete with the best from all over the world.

The reception room at the Malayan Students' Department in Malaya Hall, London.

$2m cargo seized from Indonesian ship

2 November Port Swettenham

A 140-ton Indonesian vessel from Sumatra was detained by the Royal Malaysian Navy. The ship was carrying a 100-ton cargo valued at $2 million that included smelted tin slabs, barrels of vegetable oil for soap manufacturers, and bags of onions and garlic.

It was the biggest vessel detained since barter trade between Malaysia and Indonesia was banned on 13 August. The ship was intercepted by a Royal Malaysian Navy craft patrolling the Straits of Malacca as it was approaching Port Swettenham.

Its crew of 21 Indonesian men, who did not resist capture, were taken to Kuala Lumpur for interrogation.

'Berjaya Malaysia!'

10 November Kuala Lumpur

National Solidarity Week began with shouts of 'Berjaya!' ('Success!') ringing throughout the country in all 14 States. The day was marked with mass rallies, processions and exhibitions spotlighting Indonesian aggression and the unity of the Malaysian people.

'Berjaya' flags and stickers had brisk sales. The proceeds from the sales, as well as donations, went towards the newly created National Defence Fund.

Tunku Abdul Rahman addressing a mass solidarity rally at Merdeka Stadium.

In inaugurating National Solidarity Week, Yang di-Pertuan Agong Tuanku Syed Putra said he was proud of the heroic spirit and patriotism of Malaysians.

Straits Times Annual feature

Malay dictionaries

With Malay becoming the national language of Malaya, used in schools and businesses, the demand for Malay language dictionaries was growing, said the *Straits Times Annual*. The first known English–Malay dictionary was published in 1614, but the 'father' of every modern Malay–English and English–Malay dictionary was one complied by British civil servant R.J. Wilkinson, first published in 1903. Now another former civil servant, Charles C. Brown (above), hoped to add to the legacy, with the modern English–Malay counterpart of Wilkinson's dictionary. He expected to finish the project later in the year.

Rahman Talib with his wife leaving the courtroom after losing his libel and slander case.

Rahman Talib resigns

7 December Kuala Lumpur

Minister of Education Inche Abdul Rahman bin Haji Talib resigned from the Cabinet. His resignation was accepted 'with regret' by Tunku Abdul Rahman. Inche Rahman's resignation came after losing a libel and slander action against Mr D.R. Seenivasagam, the PPP leader, and a company director, Inche Abu Bakar bin Ismail. In a letter, the Tunku told Inche Rahman: 'Your colleagues and I are convinced of your innocence, having known you for this number of years.'

Barter traders turned back, minus cargo

11 December Kuala Lumpur

Tunku Abdul Rahman ordered the return of about 950 Indonesian barter traders held in Singapore and Peninsular Malaysia back to their country in their own boats but without their cargoes.

Those affected were traders who have entered Malaysian territorial waters since the ban on unofficial barter trade with Indonesia was imposed on 13 August. In future Indonesian barter traders caught sneaking in would not be prosecuted. Instead, they would be escorted out of Malaysian waters after their cargoes were confiscated.

The new orders were meant to save the Government money and time.

Manila's surprise move

15 December Kuala Lumpur

The Philippines broke the deadlock on its claim to sovereignty over Sabah with a surprise announcement that it would discuss legal aspects of the claim with the Malaysian permanent representative to the United Nations, Mr R. Ramani. Previously Manila had insisted that the claim should go to the World Court without preliminary discussions on its legality. The announcement came from the Philippine Foreign Secretary Mauro Mendez, who was back from the United Nations General Assembly.

Malaysia turns down US defence loan

28 December Kuala Lumpur

Malaysia had rejected a defence loan offer by the United States, Deputy Prime Minister and Defence Minister Tun Abdul Razak told the House of Representatives. The loan was for five to seven years, carried 2½ per cent interest, and was intended for the purchase of military equipment. Saying that he was 'disappointed' with the terms, Tun Razak said: 'Since we are defending not only ourselves, but also democracy in this part of the world, our friends ought to look at us with more sympathy and give us more aid'. Though Malaysia needed help, she would not go begging for it, he said (*see 25 January 1965*).

1965

Exit Singapore. Finding 'no hope for peace' if Singapore continued to be in Malaysia, Prime Minister Tunku Abdul Rahman suggested that Singapore should withdraw from the Federation. And, on 9 August, it left. Indonesian President Sukarno stepped up the war against Malaysia on land and sea, deploying an estimated 10,000 troops. This did not deter the nation from forging ahead with its development plans. In quick succession, three iconic buildings were opened by the Yang di-Pertuan Agong—the new studios of Filem Negara Malaysia, the National Mosque (the biggest in Southeast Asia and financed by many non-Muslims) and the new 'space age' airport in Subang (the costliest single construction project in the country).

FEBRUARY
Britain's Chief of Defence Staff and Admiral of the Fleet Lord Mountbatten and Prince Philip visit Malaysia.

JULY
Malaysians react overwhelmingly to the sale of National Defence Bonds, buying at least $1.5 million on the first day of sale.

AUGUST
Singapore withdraws from Malaysia and becomes an independent sovereign State.

DECEMBER
The Third SEAP Games opens at Merdeka Stadium.

August: The state-of-the-art international airport in Subang opens.

Malaysia Facts		
9.4 million	Population	
$9.8 billion	Gross Domestic Product	
$994	Gross National Income (per capita)	
36.1	Crude Birth Rate (per 1,000 persons)	
48.5	Infant Mortality (per 1,000 live births)	
21.5	Consumer Price Index (base 2010=100)	

'If you marry a pretty girl and don't get on well with her, you've got to divorce her.'

Tunku Abdul Rahman, speech in Parliament on Singapore's separation, 10 August 1965.

1965

2 January
Indonesia withdraws from the UN over lack of support for Confrontation.

24 January
Death of Sir Winston Churchill, 90.

27 January
Military leaders oust the civilian Government in South Vietnam. Air Marshal Nguyen Cao Ky becomes PM and General Nguyen Van Thieu head of State.

7 February
The US begins regular bombing of North Vietnam.

7 February
Cassius Clay converts to Islam under the name Muhammad Ali.

2 March
Premiere of the film *The Sound of Music*.

8 March
The first US combat troops, 3,500 Marines, land in South Vietnam.

18 March
Cosmonaut Aleksei Leonov is the first man to be really spaced out, leaving his craft to 'walk' for about 20 minutes.

Peter Lo is 2nd Chief Minister of Sabah

1 January Jesselton

In his special New Year address, retiring Chief Minister Datuk Donald Stephens urged the people to give their total support to incoming CM Peter Lo Sui Yin. Stephens was to take up the Federal portfolio of Minister For Sabah Affairs.

Never too old for school

5 January Kuala Lumpur

More than 50 illiterate women in Kampung Baru, including 75-year-old Marian binte Awal, had signed up for adult education classes run by Senator Aishah Ghani, vice-president of the Umno Women's Section. Classes were held in the living room of the senator's house where teacher Rohana binte Narawi gave one-hour lessons three times a week.

$12m defence gift from Canada

25 January Kuala Lumpur

A month after Malaysia rejected an American defence loan, Canada made the nation an outright gift of $12 million in defence equipment and training facilities. The offer was the result of a request for assistance from Prime Minister Tunku Abdul Rahman the previous year.

What the foreign press said

'Confrontation does not mean nation is united'

On 23 January the British magazine *The Economist* commented: 'Romantics have tended to argue that Confrontation has helped to weld the ... communal groups into a united nation. While it is true that a common danger has been recognised, it would be prudent to consider the possibility that it is abhorrence of Sukarno rather than new-found blood brotherhood that has closed the Malaysian ranks.'

Unionist held after disturbances

14 February Kuala Lumpur

Trade unionist V. David walked into a police station to inquire about Socialist Front colleagues arrested in connection with disturbances outside the party's headquarters the previous day—and was himself arrested.

A Selangor State Assemblyman and former MP, David, who had styled himself secretary of the Detainees' Day Organising Committee, was among five Socialist Front leaders detained in the past 24 hours. A total of 249 people had been arrested so far in connection with the disturbances.

Meanwhile, at a first-ever Sessions Court sitting on a Sunday, 166 people were charged before the senior president of the court, Syed Hassan Al Jeffri, with taking part in the previous day's disturbances.

Serious view of industrial action

4 February Kuala Lumpur

After a two-hour emergency session the Cabinet announced that it was taking a 'serious view' of a threat of industrial action by Government servants at a time when the country's security was at stake.

Prime Minister Tunku Abdul Rahman said: 'It is really harassing. We are in a state of emergency.' He also warned 135 firemen on a work-to-rule not to neglect their duties.

As the Cabinet was in session, the executive council of the Union of Post Office Workers met and announced plans to discuss strike action.

Post workers begin Operation Clean-up

8 February Kuala Lumpur

After 12 days of work-to-rule, postal workers began a massive Operation Clean-up to clear the backlog of mail. Staff volunteered to work overtime throughout this week to ensure immediate delivery of letters and parcels that had been sent over a week ago. The General Post Office and the parcel office in Brickfields were bustling with activity as hundred of mailbags were quickly dispatched to sub-post offices. Controller of Posts R. Murugiah said it would take two to three days to clear ordinary mail and another day for parcels.

Volunteers help firemen in Chinatown

17 February Kuala Lumpur

In a show of true public spirit, hundreds of volunteers helped firemen put out a fire in Petaling Street, Chinatown. The fire destroyed three shops before it was brought under control. Passers-by helped firemen by lifting the hose over their heads to prevent curious crowds trampling it.

The Tunku introduces Prince Philip to members of the Cabinet on his arrival in Kuala Lumpur in March.

Lord Mountbatten and Prince Philip on visits

4 February Kuala Lumpur

The British Chief of Defence Staff, Admiral of the Fleet Earl Mountbatten of Burma, arrived for a two-day visit to Malaysia.

He was due to meet Federal Government leaders and hold talks with service chiefs. After a brief visit to Singapore he was to move on to East Malaysia for four days.

The following month, on 4 March, Prince Philip, husband of Queen Elizabeth II (and Lord Mountbatten's nephew) arrived on a two-day official visit.

He was welcomed by Prime Minister Tunku Abdul Rahman and British High Commissioner Lord Head.

Lion of Malaya dies

7 March Kuala Lumpur

A last-minute decision not to fly to Singapore proved fatal for the *Singa* (Lion) of Malaya, Mr Gurchan Singh (right), when his Borgward coupe went off the road near Batu Pahat. He was admitted to the Batu Pahat hospital and died two hours later. Gurchan,  nicknamed 'Singa' because of his book, *Singa, Lion of Malaya*, recounting his anti-Japanese activities during the Occupation, was on his way to Singapore to look into security measures in anticipation of Prime Minister Tunku Abdul Rahman's visit.

No undress for Andress

17 March Kuala Lumpur

Reports that she would appear in the nude in her latest film were news to her, said Ursula Andress, the sexpot who played secret agent James Bond's girlfriend in *Dr No*.

Ursula Andress talks to reporters.

She arrived today for a 10-day shoot of her new film, *That Man From Hong Kong*, in Langkawi Island. 'We don't do such things. It is not needed,' she said. 'I play the role of a nice girl.' When asked what her vital statistics were, she said she didn't know.

Sepak raga takes its place in SEAP Games

26 March Kuala Lumpur

At Malaysia's request, and with support from Laos and Thailand, sepak raga was set to be included in the Third SEAP Games in December.

Malaysia's delegate to the executive committee of the SEAP Games Federation, Datuk Ghazali Shafie, said: 'Sepak raga does not only belong to Malaysia or Thailand. It belongs to the Southeast Asia peninsula. We will be fulfilling our objectives if we make it belong to the rest of the world.'

Hockey and wrestling were taken off the list as they did not get the minimum entry of three. Fencing was also not accepted, leaving only 14 events for the Games in Kuala Lumpur.

Malaysia ready to dial the world

30 March Kuala Lumpur

Malaysians were on the way to dialling the world with the official opening of the Jesselton–Hong Kong telecommunications link, part of the $201-million Southeast Asia Commonwealth cable system (Seacom).

The link, traversing 1,050 nautical miles along the seabed, was launched when Hong Kong Governor Sir David Trench made a direct telephone call to Sabah Head of State Tun Mustapha bin Datu Harun in Jesselton (now Kota Kinabalu). Simultaneously, in Kuala Lumpur, Minister of Works, Posts and Telecommunications Datuk V.T. Sambanthan received a call from the chairman of Cable and Wireless Ltd, Sir John MacPherson, in Hong Kong.

This is a long way from the first telegraph circuit, a submarine cable linking London with Penang and Singapore in 1870. The first internal telegraph circuit in Malaya, in 1876, consisted of a single copper wire hung on jungle trees between Kuala Kangsar, Taiping and Matang, a distance of 27 miles.

Man hurt in train blast

2 April Kuala Lumpur

An explosion ripped a hole in a crowded second-class coach of the Penang-bound night mail train soon after it left the station in Kuala Lumpur. Only one man was injured. Travelling in the train were several VIPs, among them the Regent of Perlis and the State's Menteri Besar who were on their way home after seeing the Yang di-Pertuan Agong off on a tour of four Arab countries.

First record for youngest pop band

2 May Kuala Lumpur

Malaysia's youngest pop band, the Falcons, cut their first record, of tunes they composed themselves. The students of St John's Institution, led by 13-year-old guitarist Brian Felix, released *Baby Barefoot Walk* and *Nightmare*.

In December 1963, the Falcons were the first local band to appear on TV Malaysia. The other members were Jerry Ventura, 13 (bass guitar), Francis Samuel, 12 (rhythm guitar), and drummer Gerry Felix.

Sunny Ang is led away after the court hearing.

Ex-Grand Prix driver Sunny Ang to hang

18 May Singapore

The High Court sentenced former Singapore Grand Prix driver Sunny Ang, 27, to death for the insurance murder at sea of Jenny Cheok Cheng Kid 21 months before. After a 13-day trial, the jury took two hours to return a unanimous verdict of guilty. Ang showed no emotion as sentence was passed.

The court was told how Ang had renewed a $150,000 policy three hours before he and Jenny, a former bar-girl, took off for Sisters Island to scuba-dive. Less than 24 hours after Jenny's disappearance, Ang made claims against the insurance companies concerned.

Ramani is Security Council president

30 April New York

The Malaysian Ambassador to the United Nations, Mr R. Ramani, was appointed to serve as president of the Security Council in May, taking over under an alphabetical rotation system from Mr Abdul Monem Rifai of Jordan.

Lee Kuan Yew warned

3 June Kuala Lumpur

Deputy Prime Minister Tun Abdul Razak warned Singapore Prime Minister Lee Kuan Yew that while the Central Government did not consider him a threat to the Alliance, he would be held responsible 'if trouble should break out as a result of his adventures'.

Tun Razak told Parliament Lee was 'a great expert' in creating situations which did not exist. He blamed Lee for spreading stories among the diplomatic corps that Tunku Abdul Rahman did not like him and twisted facts to cast doubt in the minds of the people. He said Lee hoped that out of 'chaos and trouble', he would emerge as a leader who could save the country.

Lee attempted to interrupt Tun Razak several times in order to clarify certain points but each time he was shouted down by backbenchers. Eventually the Speaker told Lee: 'Would you please sit down. The Honourable Deputy Prime Minister has the right to be heard in silence.' Lee claimed that he had been misquoted.

New bank to be set up with Government capital

7 June Kuala Lumpur

The Government would soon set up Bank Bumiputra as recommended by the Economic Congress of Indigenous People, Deputy Prime Minister Tun Abdul Razak announced. The initial capital of $5 million would be provided by the Government.

At the closing ceremony of the congress, he said the bank, with its headquarters in Kuala Lumpur, would be run on strictly commercial lines and would have branches in mainland States and in Sabah and Sarawak.

Triple wedding joy for Orang Asli

16 May Seremban

Three Orang Asli couples were married over the weekend in Tanjung Langkap near here. The two-day ceremony was held according to Orang Asli customs and rites with elements of a typical Malay wedding such as bathing and teeth sharpening. All three brides were daughters of

mentris. More than 350 guests, including tribal chiefs from nearby communities, turned up for the event, which was marked by much merriment.

1965

world news

Yes to topless dancers of 'Les Ballets Africains'

7 June Kuala Lumpur

The women of 'Les Ballets Africains' were given the green light to dance topless after a special preview for the police.

After the two-hour show, in which the women appeared bare-bosomed, the police were satisfied there was nothing obscene about the native dances. They imposed only one condition. Before the start of each performance, it must be announced that 'this is a cultural show from Africa'.

Sounds of the jungle

22 June Kuala Lumpur

A Dayak and his violin. Australian infantrymen on border security patrol in the jungles of Sarawak couldn't believe their eyes when they passed through a kampong and heard the strains of violin music.

Sergeant Jim Clarke, of the 3rd Bn Royal Australian Regiment, took a closer look to make sure it wasn't a gun in disguise.

Extremists in control of Sarawak party

28 June Kuching

The entire moderate leadership of the opposition Sarawak United People's Party (SUPP) resigned their positions and walked out of the party's annual central committee meeting here.

Earlier the meeting had decided by a majority vote to withdraw the party from the Malaysian Solidarity Convention. The resignations brought the SUPP under the control of anti-Malaysia extremists with close links to the Barisan Sosialis of Singapore.

Leading the walkout at the meeting were the chairman Ong Kee Hui, secretary-general Stephen Yong and treasurer Ho Ho Lim.

Mr Ong and Mr Yong had held their positions since the formation of the SUPP as Sarawak's first political party in 1957.

Rush to invest in new defence bonds

16 July Kuala Lumpur

More than $1.5 million worth of national defence bonds were bought by Malaysians from Bank Negara alone on the first day they were on sale. The figure was expected to double or even triple when the influx of application forms from banks, post offices, stockbrokers and branches of Bank Negara throughout the country was sorted. The biggest single sale to date for the bonds was $39,600 bought by 124 employees of Bank Negara. Government sources described the response as 'magnificent' and 'truly patriotic'.

University faculty is medical milestone

1 August Kuala Lumpur

Acting Prime Minister Tun Abdul Razak opened the $20-million Faculty of Medicine at the University of Malaya and laid the foundation stone of a $50-million teaching hospital.

The faculty would be the first medical school in the country and the hospital the first built in the country since World War II. It would also be the first teaching hospital in Southeast Asia. The medical centre would provide undergraduate and post-graduate courses and was developed after intensive study of such facilities overseas, particularly in the United States.

Exit Singapore

9 August Kuala Lumpur

Singapore became an independent sovereign State, separate from Malaysia, following an amendment to the Constitution, approved unanimously by both Houses of Parliament under a certificate of urgency. This dramatic event followed the secret signing of the Independence of Singapore Agreement on 7 August by leaders of the two Governments.

Prime Minister Tunku Abdul Rahman told a special press conference that there was 'no hope for peace' and that Malaysia would sponsor Singapore's admission to the United Nations and as a member of the Commonwealth. The Tunku said it was his idea that Singapore should withdraw from Malaysia. While in hospital in London he had asked Deputy Prime Minister Tun Abdul Razak to have talks with Lee Kuan Yew (above, right). Tun Razak reported back that 'our minds did not meet on most points'. After receiving a full report from Tun Razak, the Tunku saw Lee and 'made things clear to him'. He added: 'There was no hope of compromise.'

In Singapore, Lee told a press conference, his eyes brimming with tears: 'What has happened has happened.' He called on his people to remain firm and calm and said: 'Everyone will have a place in Singapore.' In the next few days it was reported that independence had resulted in a boom on the island's stock market, with the highest volumes of business ever; that Indonesia's Foreign Minister Dr Subandrio said his Government would find it difficult to recognise Singapore because of the presence of British troops there, and that Singapore was likely to become a republic.

Sabah, Sarawak pledge to stay in Malaysia

10 August Kuala Lumpur

The Chief Ministers of Sabah and Sarawak gave their full backing to the Central Government in the wake of rumblings that they were having second thoughts about Malaysia's future. On 16 August, the United National Pasokmomogun Kadazan Organisation (Upko) called for a re-examination of the arrangements made in respect of Sabah's joining Malaysia in view of Singapore's separation from the Federation.

Tun Razak chairs a meeting on rural development.

Umno chief resigns

11 August Kuala Lumpur

Umno secretary-general Datuk Syed Jaafar Albar resigned following disagreement with Prime Minister Tunku Abdul Rahman over the separation of Singapore from Malaysia. He would continue to serve on the Umno executive council.

The resignation came after what was reported to be a long discussion between the two of them.

Datuk Syed Jaafar said Malaysia could not afford to have a close neighbour ruled by a party hostile to the Central Government and that 'Malaysia without Singapore has become illogical.'

Sukarno steps up the war

Along the border in Borneo, the Federation's far-flung security force—Malaysian, British and Australian—now faced an estimated 10,000 Indonesian troops, *Time* magazine reported in July.

'In the Riau Archipelago, just across from Singapore, Indonesia's crack Siliwangi Division awaits President Sukarno's irredentist orders,' it said. 'Since late April, Malaysian patrols have annihilated four major raiding parties from the Indonesian side, and severely mauled a fifth. And Sukarno's increasingly desperate Crush Malaysia campaign has spawned ugly new tactics.'

At sea, the Indonesians were now using kamikaze tactics to frustrate Malaysian patrol boats which had intercepted scores of boats carrying infiltrators. 'Suicide sampans are rigged with explosives so that they blow up when halted or hit by naval guns' thus deterring attack and giving other insurgent craft a chance to escape in the confusion.

On land, 'last week a band of some 40 Indonesians in berets and tennis shoes surprised a police outpost, chopped down six Malaysian cops with a burst from a Czech burp gun. Led by a pair of Malaysian exiles, both Chinese Communists, the guerrillas went searching for Chinese peasants loyal to the Government. They killed three in one family, stabbed three men near a bridge on the road to Kuching, and reportedly hanged a Chinese patriarch, in an attempt to scare others into turning against the Government.'

Tunku visits war memorial site

6 August Kuala Lumpur

Prime Minister Tunku Abdul Rahman checked on the progress of work on the National Monument taking shape at the Lake Gardens.

He and Minister of Works, Posts and Telecommunications Datuk V.T. Sambanthan, were shown around the site by Mr Felix de Weldon, the designer and sculptor of the monument.

The National Monument, made up of seven 24ft-high statues, was the biggest bronze monument grouping in the world.

Buy Malaysian, even if it costs more

10 August Kuala Lumpur

All Government departments have been told to buy Malaysian goods even if they cost 10 per cent more than imports, Finance Minister Tan Siew Sin said. The previous margin allowed was only five per cent. This was one of the steps being taken to protect the interests of manufacturers in difficulty as a result of Singapore's imposition of import restrictions aimed at Malaysian manufacturers, he said.

'Do or die together'

18 August Kuala Lumpur

Singapore and Malaysia agreed to form a combined operations committee for the defence of the two territories. Singapore's Defence Minister Dr Goh Keng Swee, who flew here for the inaugural meeting, told reporters: 'Our defence is indivisible.'

He also announced that the Singapore Infantry Regiment would be ready for action against the Indonesians along the Borneo border. After the meeting, a happy Tunku Abdul Rahman patted Dr Goh on the back and said: 'We will do or die together.'

Filem Negara Malaysia opens new studios

25 August Kuala Lumpur

The Yang di-Pertuan Agong opened the $4.1-million studios and offices of Filem Negara Malaysia on a hill in Petaling Jaya. The King and Queen were welcomed by Minister of Information and Broadcasting Inche Senu bin Abdul Rahman, and the head of Filem Negara, Mohamed Zain bin Hussein.

Complete facilities were available at the studios for the production of 35mm and standard cinematographic films. There were up-to-date laboratories to process and print 35mm and 16mm black-and-white films. The studios were set to process colour films the following year.

50 homeless after fire

25 August Kuala Lumpur

Fire swept through a row of terrace houses off Ipoh Road here, making 50 people, including 28 children, homeless.

The blaze damaged the roofs of at least 13 houses, a Chinese temple and a coffee factory. Nine of them suffered damage estimated at $50,000.

Most of those made homeless managed to salvage their belongings with the help of neighbours. Mainly women and children were at home when the fire, believed to have started in the coffee factory, broke out. Within minutes, it had spread to at least 30 houses. Firemen fought the blaze for more than an hour before they had it under control.

Rallies for Women's Day

26 August Kuala Lumpur

Women's Day was celebrated with a rally attended by about 500 women at the Girl Guides' headquarters, opened by the Raja Permaisuri Agong, who also visited an exhibition in the British Council Hall on the theme of 'Women's Role in National Development'.

In the evening, the Queen was guest-of-honour at a women-only dinner at Parliament building, the first of its kind. The celebration was the biggest since Women's Day was inaugurated in 1962.

Rallies as well as other activities were also held in the other States to mark the occasion.

National Mosque opens

26 August Kuala Lumpur

The Yang di-Pertuan Agong opened the $10-million National Mosque. The biggest mosque in Southeast Asia, it was originally conceived as a gift to Prime Minister Tunku Abdul Rahman. However, he said that instead it should be a memorial of independence and should be named Masjid Negara. Commemorative stamps to mark its opening went on sale. Meanwhile, the Government of India presented a $30,000 silver chair to be used by the imam of the mosque.

On 27 February 1963, Deputy Prime Minister Tun Abdul Razak had said that many non-Muslims contributed generously to the National Mosque Fund. 'This mosque is the symbol of the unity of the diverse peoples and religions in our country,' he said, adding that the $10-million building was a testament to cooperation and harmonious relations.

What the foreign press said

'Uneasiness' over national language

'Every country that bravely sets a date for a language to be adopted as official will usually find objectors springing up as the time approaches,' *The Times* of London commented on 17 September.

In 1957, the newspaper said, 10 years seemed a long time to allow before Malay became the medium for all Government business. 'However, there are signs already of uneasiness. A delegation representing Chinese guilds now wants to convince Tunku Abdul Rahman that Chinese is after all no less feasible as an official language.'

The Times pointed out that written Chinese presents difficulties and that the standard spoken Chinese taught in Chinese schools in Malaya was 'rarely the native tongue of immigrants. With not a Malay or an Indian to support them the Chinese thus have small chance of making their case.'

Space-age Subang Airport opens

30 August Kuala Lumpur

A new gateway to Malaysia opened when the King unveiled a commemorative plaque at the new $52-million international airport in Subang.

The space-age airport was the costliest single construction project completed in the country. The 11,400ft runway was the longest in Southeast Asia and was capable of accommodating any type of aircraft.

1965

world news

2 September
Pakistani troops enter the Indian sector of Kashmir, sparking war.

4 September
Death of Nobel laureate theologian/doctor Albert Schweitzer, 90.

23 September
End of the India–Pakistan war with a ceasefire to be enforced by the UN.

30 September
A group of President Sukarno's guards kidnap and kill six right-wing generals. The army, led by General Suharto, calls it a Communist coup and moves to crush it.

16 October
Death of writer Somerset Maugham, 91.

11 November
Rhodesia proclaims its independence.

21 December
The Soviet Union announces it has shipped missiles to North Vietnam.

30 December
Ferdinand Marcos is sworn in as President of the Philippines.

Tariffs on Malaysian goods in Singapore

11 October | Singapore

The Singapore Government slapped tariffs on 154 Malaysian-made products. Its Finance Minister, Lim Kim San, said the move would provide Singapore manufacturers with a market protected from Malaysian goods.

The list of goods ranged from rubber tyres and tubes, dairy produce, sweets and chocolates to insecticides, fungicide, dental products, household articles and building materials. The new tariff rates were the same as those imposed by the Malaysian Government two days earlier, except for two which were lower.

Hospital workers strike

12 October | Kuala Lumpur

Patients were left unattended at the Kuala Lumpur General Hospital as some 300 workers staged a lightning strike which caught the hospital authorities by surprise.

The protest was over the allotment of new quarters at the maternity ward. The strikers—hospital attendants, cooks and ayahs—were members of the Government Medical and Health Union. They returned to work six hours later.

Boy who trapped Indonesians honoured

4 October | Kuala Lumpur

A special award for patriotism was given at a Universal Children's Day rally at Stadium Negara to Karim bin Harun, 8, of Kuala Benut, Batu Pahat. On a fishing trip with his uncle, he helped capture three boatloads of armed Indonesians by misdirecting them, then telling police where they were going. The Indonesians had stopped his uncle's boat and asked them for directions to Sungai Benut. Instead he told them the way to Sungai Sangkang, then hurried back to Sungai Benut and told police what had happened.

Chang Har acknowledges the cheers at Stadium Negara after receiving the Hang Tuah Medal

As a result of his actions, the Indonesians had a rude reception when they landed, stepping right into the hands of waiting Malaysian troops.

Also at the rally, Chang Har, 13, of Chenderlang, Tapah, received the coveted Hang Tuah Medal for child heroism after rescuing his younger brother Chang Cheong, 11, and a 13-year-old friend, Low Wai Kit, from a fast-flowing river near his home. Low, who could not swim, was swept away by the strong current, and dragged Chang Cheong with him. Chang Har dived in and saved both boys, who were by then unconscious.

Flaming flamingoes for National Zoo

1 November | Kuala Lumpur

A pair of American flamingoes came to stay at the National Zoo. The gift from the people of Dade County in Florida was presented to the zoo by US Ambassador to Malaysia, Mr James D. Bell. The two pink-plumaged birds are the first flamingoes in the country.

Mr James D. Bell (in jacket) watches the flamingoes flap their wings on their release in the zoo.

Malaysia Five-Year Plan 'for all'

9 December | Kuala Lumpur

Deputy Prime Minister Tun Abdul Razak announced that the first Malaysia Five-Year Plan would provide plenty for all Malaysians, irrespective of race, creed or political affiliation.

The newly published plan would see 360,000 new jobs created in Peninsular Malaysia and 80,000 in Sabah and Sarawak over five years.

The main objectives were to promote integration; provide a steady increase in levels of income and consumption; generate employment opportunities at a rate sufficient to provide productive work for new entrants to the labour force; stimulate new kinds of economic activity, both agricultural and industrial, to reduce the nation's dependence on rubber and tin; open new land for development; and reduce the number of landless requiring plots for agricultural purposes.

Health and social welfare developments, low-cost housing and other projects would also be undertaken.

Third SEAP Games opens

14 December | Kuala Lumpur ▶ The Third SEAP Games was declared open by the Yang di-Pertuan Agong, watched by athletes from seven nations and a crowd of 15,000 at the Merdeka Stadium. Earlier, athletes from the participating countries Burma, Cambodia, Laos, Singapore, Thailand, South Vietnam and finally Malaysia marched past in a colourful parade.

Then, at precisely 5.58pm, torch bearer Rahim Ahmad entered the stadium and, to the beat of drums, mounted red-carpeted steps to dip the torch into the cauldron which burst into flames. Hundreds of pigeons and multi-coloured balloons were released to mark the event.

Before the opening, the Tunku lights a torch at Parliament House to be carried in relays to the stadium.

Tin pact ratified

29 December | London

Malaysia's High Commissioner in London, Tunku Ya'acob Ibni Sultan Abdul Hamid Halim Shah, signed the Third International Tin Agreement at Clive House.

It was his last official duty before leaving for Paris as ambassador. The signing was 'the most important task I have undertaken this year,' he said. Malaysia's participation in the pact was 'received with joy by all member countries.'

1966

Following the ouster of Sukarno, Indonesia ended Confrontation. Cheers greeted the signatories of the peace treaty—Deputy Prime Minister Tun Abdul Razak and Indonesian Foreign Minister Adam Malik—as they arrived at Subang Airport from Bangkok where the accord was reached. Malaysians also gave a rousing welcome to Lyndon B Johnson, the first US President to visit Malaysia. The Tunku named Tun Razak as his eventual successor while the latter called on the civil service to stamp out corruption. Malaysians also won accolades—javelin ace Natashar Singh won a gold medal at the Asian Games in Bangkok and Malaysian women won praise from fashion designer Pierre Balmain for their 'graceful walk and for knowing how to dress correctly'.

FEBRUARY
Tunku Abdul Rahman names Tun Abdul Razak as his successor.

AUGUST
Malaysia–Indonesia treaty signed in Bangkok, marking the end of Confrontation.

SEPTEMBER
Sarawak Chief Minister Stephen Kalong Ningkan is ousted by a no-confidence vote in the State Assembly.

OCTOBER
US President Lyndon B. Johnson is the first US President to visit Malaysia.

February: The official unveiling of the National Monument was attended by South Korean president Park Chung Hee (front, in suit) and his wife (extreme right, clad in *hanbok*).

'The people of Malaysia and Indonesia want peace, not war, friendship, not hostility.'

Tun Abdul Razak, at the end of Confrontation, 12 August 1966.

1966

world news

10 January
Peace talks between India and Pakistan are successfully concluded with the Tashkent Agreement.

11 January
Indian Prime Minister Lal Bahadur Shastri dies of a heart attack in Tashkent.

17 January
A mid-air collision between a B-52 bomber and a tanker results in three unarmed hydrogen bombs dropping onto Spanish territory and one into the sea. 7 April: One hydrogen bomb is recovered from the sea.

24 January
Indira Gandhi, the daughter of Nehru, is sworn in as Prime Minister of India.

1 February
President Sukarno promotes Suharto to Lt-General in an effort to play him off against General Nasution, who is forced out of the Defence Ministry later in the month.

3 February
Luna 9 is the first spacecraft to land on the moon.

24 February
A military coup ousts Ghana's President Kwame Nkrumah.

Detained political figures freed

20 January | Kuala Lumpur

The Government released three politicians who were involved in a conspiracy with Indonesia to establish a government in exile. Inche Abdul Aziz Ishak was a former Agriculture and Cooperatives Minister, and was also a leader of the National Assembly Party. Inche Ishak bin Haji Muhammad was a former chairman of the Labour Party, while Inche Abu Hanifah bin Haji Abdul Ghani was a former vice-president of Pas and a former MP. Prime Minister Tunku Abdul Rahman said the Cabinet had decided to release them as they were no longer considered a threat to the nation's security. All three, who were detained for two years, announced their retirement from politics.

Costly crop: Price rise 'would not affect farmers'.

The price of rice

26 January | Kuala Lumpur

Minister of Agriculture and Cooperatives Haji Ghazali Haji Jawi announced that the price of padi, irrespective of type, would be $16 a picul (about 60kg) for the first season of the year. But in the second season, only the Malinja and Mahsuri padi types would be priced at $16, while the other types would be $14. Haji Ghazali explained that the price issue would not affect farmers in Perlis, Kedah, Kelantan and Terengganu as they do not plant padi in the second season.

He said his Ministry was not responsible for the supply and sale of padi in this country. Its role was to encourage farmers to plant sufficient padi and other types of crops. The prices and sales were determined by the Ministry of Trade and Industry.

Tun Razak named as Tunku's successor

1 February | Kuala Lumpur

'Tun Razak will be the Prime Minister if anything befalls me,' Prime Minister Tunku Abdul Rahman said in a speech, adding that 'certain quarters' had been spreading rumours about Tun Razak. He described Tun Razak as a proficient, honest and earnest person and urged Malaysians not to doubt him. The Tunku also called for the MCA and MIC to help uphold the good image of Tun Razak.

Malaysian to lead police force

26 January | Kuala Lumpur

For the first time a Malaysian will head the police force. Retiring Inspector General of Police Datuk Sir Claude Fenner will be replaced by Commissioner Datuk Mohamed Salleh bin Ismael. Datuk Salleh, 49, joined the force in 1935 and became the first Asian to be appointed a police commissioner.

Setting out to win

12 February | Kuala Lumpur

Deputy Prime Minister Tun Abdul Razak announced the setting up of the National Sports Foundation of Malaysia in an effort to improve the quality of sport in the nation. Among other ventures the foundation is to improve standards by employing foreign coaches and making an evaluation of amateur sports activities.

Cherished gift for Tunku and his wife

6 February | Kuala Lumpur

Prime Minister Tunku Abdul Rahman received a very unusual gift for his 63rd birthday, which fell on 8 February. Mrs Saw Poh Choo and her husband, who had known the Tunku and his wife Puan Sharifah Rodziah for a long time, gave their year-old daughter to the Prime Minister and the first lady as a 'gesture of their love and friendship.' The child was named Faridah by her new parents, who were reported to be completely surprised and delighted by the unexpected gesture.

The Tunku gives Faridah a cuddle in this July 1968 picture.

Monument symbol of the people's victory

9 February | Kuala Lumpur

The National Monument at Bukit Perwira was officially unveiled by the Yang di-Pertuan Agong. Prime Minister Tunku Abdul Rahman described the monument as a symbol of a double victory for the people of Malaysia.

The first victory, said the Tunku, was the triumph of good over evil, while the second was the unwavering faith of the people towards the country. The Tunku went on to say that thousands of lives had been sacrificed in order for these victories to be achieved. This sacrifice, he said, would forever be etched in the hearts of Malaysians for time immemorial.

Present at the unveiling ceremony were South Korean President Park Chung Hee and family members of soldiers killed during the Emergency.

The National Monument: 'Triumph over evil'.

Chinese urged to accept national language

27 February | Kuala Lumpur

Finance Minister and MCA president Tan Siew Sin urged the Chinese to accept Malay as the national language and to help rural people achieve a better standard of living.

He said if the matter of the national language could be resolved, petty disagreements and disputes would be a thing of the past. Mr Tan also said economic development had to be undertaken in rural areas and stressed that no one would benefit if half the Malaysian population were living in poverty.

Satisfaction at anti-Communist ops

1 March | Kuala Lumpur

Chief of the Malaysian Armed Forces Lt-General Tengku Osman bin Tengku Mohamed Jewa expressed satisfaction at operations to eradicate remnants of Communist terrorists along the Malaysia–Thailand border. According to Tengku Osman, the Armed Forces Chief of Thailand General Prapas Charusathiara had personally ordered operations at the border.

The intensified operations were a result of negotiations between defence officials of Malaysia and Thailand.

Aida best of them all

4 March | Kuala Lumpur

Seventeen-year-old Aida binte Aladad Khan obtained the best result among her Malay peers in the Senior Cambridge examination in Johor, scoring distinctions in all her six subjects. A student of the Sultan Ibrahim Girls' School, she also obtained first class in the examination and first class in the Malaysian Certificate of Education. Aida, who was continuing her studies in the Sixth Form, hoped to enter the Science stream and eventually qualify as a doctor.

Youths stage lightning
Vietnam War protest

9 March Kuala Lumpur

More than 200 Chinese youths staged a lightning anti-America demonstration at Ampang Road in opposition to US intervention in Vietnam. In a protest lasting only five minutes, the youths also demonstrated against the visit of the US Assistant Secretary of State for East Asian and Pacific Affairs, William P. Bundy.

The demonstrators shouted anti-America slogans, carried anti-America placards and smashed the windows of the First National City Bank premises. Mr Bundy was in Kuala Lumpur for talks with Prime Minister Tunku Abdul Rahman after meeting Singapore's Prime Minister Lee Kuan Yew. Deputy Prime Minister Tun Razak expressed disgust at the incident and said that the violent actions of the demonstrators marred Malaysia's image.

Later in the year, some 200 demonstrators hurled bottles and broke windows at the United States Information Service building.

Crown Prince pulls out
of tennis tournament

9 March Kuala Lumpur

The 16th Malaysian Malay Tennis Tournament, held at the Selangor Club, began with the first round of the men's singles.

Star national player S.A. Azman easily defeated Mohamed Ali Salleh 6–0, 6–2. Azman, last year's runner-up, was expected to meet last year's men's singles champion and King's Cup holder Shahrin Osman in the finals. Zulkifli Abdul beat Aziz Osman 6–1, 6–3 and Rahim Bakar was given a walk-over by Zahari Bakar.

The Crown Prince of Pahang, Tengku Ahmad Shah, pulled out of the tournament as he had to return to Pekan.

Mara moves to end 'Ali Baba' schemes

26 April Kuala Lumpur

Mara would undertake to buy shares allotted to Malays by companies which have joint capital, it was announced. Acting Prime Minister Tun Razak said the move was necessary to ensure that the shares were genuinely being bought by Malays and not end up as 'Ali Baba' investment schemes in which sleeping partners are taken on merely because they are Malays. Mara would sell shares to Malays who were genuine in wanting to invest and could afford it, he said.

Fourth King installed

12 April Kuala Lumpur

Tuanku Ismail Nasiruddin Shah was installed as the country's fourth Yang di-Pertuan Agong. In a ceremony full of pomp and splendour, the new King took an oath to uphold the Constitution and the country's official religion, Islam. Present at the installation ceremony were the State Rulers and their consorts.

Prime Minister Tunku Abdul Rahman expressed confidence that the reign of the new King would be an era of glory, peace and tranquillity for the nation and the country.

More than 10,000 schoolchildren lined the streets leading to the palace chanting 'Daulat Tuanku' as the royal motorcade made its way from Dewan Tunku Abdul Rahman through Jalan Ampang, Jalan Melaka, Medan Pasar and Jalan Sultan Hishamuddin to Istana Negara. The children came from various schools in Kuala Lumpur. Members of the public also arrived in droves to catch a glimpse of the royal couple.

At the Mountbatten Road–Melaka Road junction, police had to hold back people who swarmed to have a closer look at the King.

A flight for sight

4 May Kuching

The Royal Malaysian Air Force offered to fly Martin anak Ngaib, 4, from Kuching to Kuala Lumpur for treatment by eye specialists. Martin was in danger of losing his sight unless he received immediate treatment.

Australian PM arrives
for talks on aid

28 April Kuala Lumpur

Australian Prime Minister Harold Holt arrived for a four-day visit during which he was to hold talks to discuss how Australia can aid Malaysia in developing its economy and defence.

Mr Holt was greeted on arrival at Subang Airport by acting Prime Minister Tun Abdul Razak and the Australian High Commissioner, Mr A.J. Eastman.

After inspecting a guard-of-honour comprising 50 members of the Royal Malay Regiment, the premier was taken to Istana Negara for a royal audience with the King. Later, Mr Holt met Cabinet Ministers and was given a briefing on the development of the country.

Mr Holt inspecting the guard-of-honour.

School bus crash: 4 killed, 52 hurt

10 May Petaling Jaya

Four people including two schoolchildren were killed and 52 other schoolchildren were injured in probably the worst accident to occur in Petaling Jaya. In the accident which happened in the afternoon, the school bus they were travelling in was thrown into a drain and turned turtle after colliding with a car at Templer Road. The boys and girls, who were trapped in the bus, were on their way to Kuen Cheng Girls' School at Lornie Road.

Police and a fire-and-rescue team rushed to the scene to help the trapped victims, who included the conductress and driver. Hundreds of passers-by also gave help. It took half an hour for the rescue team to lift the bus and extricate victims pinned under the wreckage. Two schoolchildren, a 50-year-old female teacher and the 18-year old conductress died on the spot. The injured were taken to the Assunta Hospital.

1966

world news

5 March
A BOAC flight crashes into Mt Fuji, killing 124.

11 March
In a letter, President Sukarno hands over most executive powers to Suharto, and declares a state of emergency.

21 March
The US Supreme Court rules that the bawdy English classic *Fanny Hill* is not obscene.

23 March
First official talks between the Catholic and Anglican churches after 400 years of non-communication.

21 April
A Houston, Texas, hospital installs an artificial heart in a patient.

16 May
Chairman Mao raises the curtain on China's Great Proletarian Cultural Revolution. The declared aim is to continue the revolutionary struggle and to remove the 'liberal bourgeoisie'.

25 May
Peruvian and Argentinian football fans fight in Lima. Score: 248 dead.

Five-country association under consideration

5 June Kuala Lumpur

The formation of an association made up of five Southeast Asian countries, Indonesia, Singapore, the Philippines, Malaysia and Thailand, was perhaps the ideal solution towards ensuring peace and prosperity in the region, said Finance Minister Tan Siew Sin in a statement in the MCA newsletter *The Guardian*. He said such an association could serve as the foundation for an organisation for all Southeast Asian countries which share the same aspirations for peace and prosperity.

Historian Winstedt dies

5 June London

Sir Richard Winstedt, one of the foremost experts on Malayan culture and history, passed away at his home in London. He was 87. Sir Richard contributed many writings on Malaya, its peoples, the Malay language and the history and culture of Malaya.

He joined the Malayan Civil Service in 1902 and was district officer for 19 years. From 1924 until 1931 he was Straits Settlements and Federation of Malay States Education Director. In 1931, he was appointed British Adviser in Johor and served in that capacity until he retired in 1935. Sir Richard spoke fluent Malay.

Demo over pay

7 July Kuala Lumpur

More than 500 teachers who graduated from the Day Training College (DTC) took part in a demonstration at Dewan Bahasa dan Pustaka. It was organised by the National Union of Teachers to highlight the salary and medical benefit claims of the DTC teachers. They were demanding that they be placed in the same salary scale as that of School Certificate graduate teachers.

Sport for the disabled

29 June Kuala Lumpur

The first national sports event for disabled people was held in Stadium Merdeka. There were 237 participants comprising paraplegics, blind, deaf and the mentally disabled, ranging in age from five to 32. Among the interesting highlights were a gymnastics performance by the blind from Penang and a blind marching band competition.

Brother Henry, a champion archer, lit the tournament torch by shooting an arrow at the target.

Army, navy and air force to be strengthened

31 July Kuala Lumpur

Steps were being taken to reinforce the Army and increase its size to 20 battalions, Prime Minister Tunku Abdul Rahman said. The army would be assisted by the Territorial Army battalions to double its current numbers. The Tunku said that steps were also being taken to increase the size of the navy and air force. He said this move would augment the strength of the Malaysian Armed Forces to ensure their readiness and capability of defending the nation's sovereignty and security.

'15 years for Malaysia to be a developed nation'

1 August Kuala Lumpur

Malaysia would achieve developed nation status by 1981 with the implementation of three Malaysia Plans, said Deputy Prime Minister Tun Abdul Razak.

This meant Malaysia would achieve that status in only 15 years compared to centuries as required by European nations. He said current development plans were in 'second gear' and would only achieve complete success that would satisfy every Malaysian in another 15 years.

He gave an assurance that the Government would take any means necessary to improve the economic status of Bumiputras and ensure that they would take their place economically on a par with the other races in Malaysia.

Malaysia–Indonesia treaty

12 August Bangkok

Deputy Prime Minister Tun Abdul Razak and Indonesian Foreign Minister Adam Malik signed a treaty ending the undeclared war between the two nations. About 700 had been killed, mostly in the virgin jungles of East Malaysia, since 1963. Tun Razak, who was accompanied by a 50-member delegation, said the occasion opened up a new chapter of relations between the countries which had been closely linked for centuries.

The treaty, agreed on 2 June after a 2½-day discussion in Bangkok, recognised Malaysia's sovereignty over Sabah and Sarawak, thus ending Indonesia's claim over the East Malaysian States.

Mr Malik said the treaty proved true the doctrine that problems in Asia must be resolved by Asians themselves.

The following day, the Deputy Prime Minister was greeted on arrival at the Subang Airport with shouts of 'Merdeka' and 'Berjaya' by more than 30,000 people. Receiving an equally warm and enthusiastic welcome was Mr Malik, who arrived about half an hour later.

Tears flowed as Indonesia's national anthem, *Indonesia Raya*, was played in Malaysia for the first time in three years. Never before had a foreign dignitary been so overwhelmingly and passionately received. Malaysia had not seen such emotional outpouring since independence.

What the foreign press said

Australia 'relieved' at end of Confrontation

The *Sydney Morning Herald* commented: 'No country will welcome the end of the undeclared war between Indonesia and Malaysia with more heartfelt relief than Australia.' It said Confrontation 'threatened Australia's whole future by embroiling her with her nearest and most powerful neighbour.'

According to *Time* magazine, 'champagne glasses clinked in Bangkok last week. At long last, Indonesia's konfrontasi with Malaysia was over.' It commented that the two nations had taken 'only three glowing days together to resolve most of their differences'. But it went on: 'What Indonesia's Adam Malik and Malaysia's Abdul Razak actually signed [pictured below] fell considerably short of the official peace treaty for which Malaysia had hoped. It was, rather, a limited declaration of intent.'

Riddle of 'missing' diplomat is solved

1 July Canberra

There was gossip in the Australian capital Canberra when the Malaysian High Commissioner, Tun Lim Yew Hock, was not to be seen anywhere, *Time* magazine reported. Police and the local press began a search, it said. His wife and two daughters went on TV with a tearful plea for him to return. Even Prime Minister Tunku Abdul Rahman made a personal appeal to 'come back, my dear friend'.

Then a Sydney newspaperman discovered that Lim had been flying to Sydney under the assumed name of 'Hawk' and meeting with a stripper, Sandra Nelson (43-24-36), in the notorious King's Cross district. After three days Lim reappeared, driven by car from Sydney by a mysterious benefactor described as a 'good Samaritan' who was said to have found him ill in the city. There was no comment from Sandra apart from the fact that they were 'just good friends' who chatted between shows.

Toddler earns spot at art exhibition

6 September Kuala Lumpur

Two-and-a-half-year-old Patrick Lee was the youngest artist whose work was put on display among the 322 exhibits at the AIA Building in Jalan Ampang.

Patrick's drawing was one of those chosen from the 15,000 entries received for an art competition open to Malaysian schoolchildren. Patrick's parents, Mr and Mrs Lee Cheng Yan, said their nine-year-old daughter Vivian was keen on drawing and every time she finished one, Patrick would insist on drawing one himself.

Sarawak Governor sacks Chief Minister

25 September Kuching

The Governor of Sarawak, Tun Abang Haji Openg, invoked Federal powers to dismiss Chief Minister Datuk Stephen Kalong Ningkan. The move was deemed necessary by the Federal Government as the political situation in the State had deteriorated to the extent that it posed a serious threat to the security of Sarawak and Malaysia.

On 15 September, the King, on advice from the Cabinet, declared a state of emergency in Sarawak. The Federal Government also amended the Sarawak Constitution to allow the Governor to summon the Assembly and dismiss a Chief Minister who failed to get majority support. Datuk Ningkan had earlier refused an invitation from the Governor to resign.

The haunted embassy of Jalan Ampang?

9 September Kuala Lumpur

The unoccupied two-storey Pakistani Embassy in Jalan Ampang was reported to be haunted. The caretaker, Inche Yahya bin Ahmad, who had been looking after the building for the past three years, said the haunting first hit him four months after he started work with the embassy in 1963.

One night, the former police detective sergeant said, he heard the spine-chilling scream of a woman but on investigation could not find anyone. The same thing happened a week later and since then he has heard screaming very regularly but only after 2am. Sometimes there would be loud bangs as though someone was thumping on the floor. Inche Yahya said he was quite used to it now but challenged people who did not believe to 'come and witness it personally'.

Ancient stone carvings to go on display

12 September Kuala Lumpur

Five-hundred-year-old stone carvings discovered in a village near Port Dickson would go on display at the National Museum by the end of the month, said the museum's curator of archaeology, Inche Abdul Aziz bin Yahya.

The museum so far had never had megaliths on display. The megaliths, which are only known to exist in Malacca and Negeri Sembilan, were discovered at Kramat Sungai Udang, about a quarter of a mile from the village of Pengkalan Kempas near Port Dickson.

Time Magazine

Looking for an angel

4 November

Malaysia was what South Vietnam hoped to be a decade in the future, according to *Time* magazine: a bustling little land that survived twelve vicious years of internal assault by Communist guerrillas and has gone on to achieve one of the highest standards of living in Asia.

Until recently, Malaysians could look forward to continued progress. Now a cloud had fallen over their future. The reason was the sudden reduction in Britain's role as Malaysia's longtime financial angel and protector.

With the end of the external threat from nearby Indonesia, Britain was withdrawing its 10,000-man military force, and had put Malaysia on notice that some $200 million in economic and military aid would not be forthcoming.

As Malaysians prepared last week to greet President Johnson, they were hoping that the US would fill the gap left by the departing British. Even before leaving on his trip, the President took measures to reassure the Malaysians.

He ordered a reduction in US sales of stockpiled rubber in order to bolster the price and thus help Malaysia, which supplied one-third of the world's rubber. US aid officials were also studying requests for at least a modest amount of economic aid to support Malaysia's ambitious five-year development programme, which would suffer if funds were diverted to a defence buildup to replace departing British troops.

Security threat to East Malaysia

5 October Tawau

In the preceding month, 66 volunteers of the so-called Tentera Nasional Kalimantan Utara (TNKU) had been captured and one killed in East Malaysia, according to Prime Minister Tunku Abdul Rahman. The previous day alone, 19 had been captured.

The Tunku said the TNKU posed a security threat to East Malaysia as they had regrouped along the Sabah–Sarawak border but assured that security forces would deal with the situation, adding that there was 'no need to request Britain for help'.

Asia Magazine, July issue

Longest bridge opened

28 October Kuching

The Batu Kitang Bridge was officially declared open by Sarawak Governor Tun Abang Haji Openg. Spanning 380ft over Sungai Sarawak Kiri, it was the longest bridge in the State and linked Kuching and the Bau district.

188 set for Asian Games

13 November Kuala Lumpur

The Malaysian contingent to the Fifth Asian Games in Bangkok was expected to be the biggest to leave the country for an international meet.

The contingent was currently numbered 188, with the possibility of further additions. Of the total so far, 152 were competitors and 36 were officials.

The contingent would be the fourth largest among the 18 nations taking part in the Games from 9 to 20 December.

Designer Balmain praises Malaysian women

16 November Kuala Lumpur

Fashion designer Pierre Balmain said that Malaysian women have a graceful walk and know how to dress correctly.

Balmain, who was designing a new uniform for Malaysian Airways hostesses, said that the fitting dresses Malaysian women wore allowed them to walk elegantly.

Here on his first visit to Malaysia, the Paris-based designer also described the sarong kebaya, cheongsam and sari as beautiful. He said that the new uniform for the airline hostesses would have an Eastern flavour and be made from batik. 'It will be specially designed so as to attract more tourists to this part of the world,' he added.

1966

26 May
A Buddhist monk is engulfed in flames at the US consulate in Hue, South Vietnam.

30 June
England beats West Germany 4–2, after extra-time, at Wembley Stadium to win the World Cup.

27 August
Sir Francis Chichester sets sail on the first solo voyage round the world.

6 September
South African Prime Minister Hendrik Verwoerd is stabbed to death in Parliament by a deranged page.

8 September
The first flight of Star Trek's *The Enterprise* is launched to boldly go where no man has gone before.

20 November
Men in Zurich say no to women having the vote.

15 December
Death from lung cancer— Walt Disney, 65.

Historic presidential visit

30 October | **Kuala Lumpur**

US President Lyndon Johnson arrived in Kuala Lumpur, the first American President to set foot on Malaysian soil. Mr Johnson and his wife Ladybird were greeted at Subang International Airport by the Yang di-Pertuan Agong and the Raja Permaisuri Agong, Prime Minister Tunku Abdul Rahman, Cabinet Ministers and heads of diplomatic missions.

During their 21-hour visit, the presidential couple had a royal audience and luncheon with their majesties at Istana Negara and attended a State banquet at Parliament House. Mr Johnson also had talks with the Prime Minister and Cabinet Ministers and visited a Federal Land Development Authority scheme where he was given a demonstration of rubber-tapping techniques.

In Washington before his visit, Mr Johnson gave an assurance that he would fully consider Malaysia's interests when carrying out the US rubber disposal programme. The Deputy Prime Minister Tun Abdul Razak said the US President expressed appreciation for Malaysia's friendship towards America and would do everything possible to make life peaceful and comfortable for the Malaysians.

Mr Johnson meets the citizens of tomorrow during his whirlwind 21-hour visit to Malaysia.

Siam Death Railway link is fading fast

21 November | **Kuala Lumpur**

Eighty-three names in Government records were the only remaining tangible link with the Burma–Siam 'Death Railway'. The names were of dependants of Malaysians who died building the railway and were on Government relief.

After the war, the Burma–Siam Relief Scheme had 1,175 registered dependants. The number was reduced over the years with remarriage of widows, departures from the country, employment and dependants' children becoming old enough to fend for themselves.

New stamps to mark First Malaysia Plan

5 December | **Kuala Lumpur**

Five commemorative stamps were issued to mark the First Malaysia Plan. The 15-cent stamps depicted five themes: irrigation, agriculture, rural health, communications and education. Each has the word Malaysia in black on a coloured band down the left of the stamp, and the legend *Ranchangan Pembangunan 1966-70 Kema'moran Negara* (National Development and Prosperity Plan 1966-70) at the top of the design.

$60 million for ADB

22 November | **Kuala Lumpur**

Malaysia contributed $60 million to the Asian Development Bank, Finance Minister Tan Siew Sin said. Tan was to lead a four-man delegation, which included Bank Negara Governor Tan Sri Ismail Mohamed Ali and Treasury officials Rastam Abdul Hadi and Badaruddin Samad, to the bank's inauguration in Tokyo.

A total of 31 countries had contributed $3 billion towards the establishment of the bank, which would be based in Manila. The bank would be fully operational by June 1967 and would, among other aims, seek to promote investments in the Economic Commission for Asia and the Far East region and provide technical assistance for development projects.

Wipe out corruption, Tun Razak urges

4 December | **Tapah**

Deputy Prime Minister Tun Abdul Razak called for the stamping out of corruption in the civil service. Speaking at the Operations Room here, Tun Razak said that although corruption could not be eradicated, heads of departments could keep it to a minimum by making regular checks.

'The good name of the Government must be maintained,' he added. Tun Razak also urged Government officers to change their 'colonial days' attitude by going to the people, asking what they needed and ensuring that their requirements are met. On the other hand, he said the people should not make unreasonable demands of the Government.

Sparrows at breakfast upset UM students

4 December | **Tapah**

Students at the University of Malaya had an unusual protest, not about education or politics but about sparrows. The buildings were overrun by the birds, students complained. 'Nobody minds a cheep or two or a flutter here and there,' said one student, M.K. Lee. 'But the sparrows descend on us during mealtimes in the canteen. Now you try having breakfast or lunch with scores of sparrows flitting about above you. They have not even been house-trained.'

Kuala Lumpur's grand old man dies at 107

23 November | **Kuala Lumpur**

One of Kuala Lumpur's oldest residents, Mr Mihan Singh, died at the age of 107. He was the father of the late Mr Gurcharan Singh, author of the book *Singa, Lion of Malaya*. Mr Mihan Singh arrived in Malaya in 1898 and worked as a ticket agent for Boustead and Co. before going into business. According to his son, Mr G.S. Gill, he walked almost daily from his house in the Lake Gardens to Jalan Tuanku Abdul Rahman, about 2½ miles away, and remained very active and vigorous until two years ago.

Nashatar's golden thrust marks a first for nation

13 December | **Bangkok**

Javelin ace Nashatar Singh won the country's first-ever Asian Games gold medal for a field event. The 26-year-old police inspector's win, with a throw of 72.93m, gave Malaysia its fourth gold medal of the Games.

Malaysia sent its biggest ever team to the Games, which ran from 9 to 20 December in Bangkok, with at least 152 competitors and 36 officials. There was also a 12-man cultural troupe. The contingent was the fourth-largest among the 18 nations taking part. It took part in all listed events at the Games except wrestling. The first team sent abroad by the country's Olympic Council consisted of 10 athletes for the second Asian Games in Manila in 1954.

Going for gold: Nashatar Singh in action.

1967

Boost for the national language: with the passing of the National Language Act, Malay became the sole national language which was also to become the language of instruction of selected subjects in schools. Boost for athletics: sprinters M. Rajamani and M. Jegathesan became Sportswoman and Sportsman of the Year respectively. Boost needed for rubber: Malaysia told the United Nations General Assembly that developed nations must help less-developed countries by offering fair recompense for primary commodities, especially rubber, the price of which had slumped. As the nation celebrated 10 years of independence, Tunku told *Time* magazine that his hope was not for a 'mighty Malaysia but a happy one'.

JANUARY
A state of emergency is declared in flood-hit Kelantan and Terengganu.

MARCH
'Thai Silk King' Jim Thompson vanishes without a trace in Cameron Highlands.

JULY
The fastest man in Asia, M. Jegathesan is named Sportsman of the Year.

OCTOBER
Police arrest squatter leader Hamid Tuah and his deputy at Teluk Gong, Klang. Their illegal settlement housing their 530 followers was then demolished.

January: Tunku Abdul Rahman directing a scene from the epic *Raja Bersiong* (*The Fanged King*) for which he wrote the script. He took over from director Jamil Sulong for an hour.

'Our people have the will and determination to stand together in defence of our nation.'

Tunku Abdul Rahman, in his Radio Malaysia broadcast to the nation on the 10th anniversary of independence, 31 August 1967.

1967

world news

27 January
Three US astronauts are killed when their Apollo spacecraft catches fire on the launch pad.

9 March
Stalin's daughter Svetlana Alliluyeva defects to the US.

12 March
The Indonesian Assembly removes all presidential powers from Sukarno and names Suharto as acting President.

19 April
Death of former German Chancellor Konrad Adenauer, 91.

21 April
A military dictatorship seizes power in Greece.

24 April
Cosmonaut Komarov dies during re-entry when parachutes fail to deploy.

28 April
Boxer Muhammad Ali refuses military service and is banned from boxing in the US.

1 May
Elvis Presley and Priscilla Beaulieu marry in Las Vegas.

The floods cannot keep this woman from dressing up, hailing a sampan and going to work.

Flood worsens

5 January | **Kuala Lumpur**

A state of emergency was declared in Kelantan and Terengganu as floods rose in four States, including Perak and Kedah. A further 9,300 people were moved to safety. Land and telecommunications links with the East Coast were disrupted. A national committee to help the victims of the flood was formed.

Mystery of missing 'Silk King'

26 March | **Tanah Rata**

The 'Thai Silk King', American Jim Thompson, was reported missing after he went for an afternoon stroll in Cameron Highlands. Thompson, the millionaire founder of the Thai Silk Co. of Bangkok, had been staying at 'Moonlight', a cottage owned by a friend.

A police search started, joined by Orang Asli trackers the next day. A helicopter joined the

Without a trace: Jim Thompson picnics hours before he went for an afternoon stroll and was never seen again.

hunt which by 28 March involved more than 300 Police Field Force, British soldiers and others. Even a temple medium was called in and on 31 March, Brig-Gen Edwin Black, commander of US support forces in Thailand and a friend of Thompson, arrived. An aerial tower was set up near the bungalow to give a radar picture of the area. However, on 3 April, Gen Black returned to Bangkok, saying: 'There is no clue, not a bit of torn clothing or even a shoe.' Then on 26 April, another friend, Richard Noone, a SEATO planning officer, said he thought Thompson was not lost in the jungle.

It had been suggested, he said, that he was abducted by Communist terrorists. During World War II Thompson was in the US Office of Strategic Services, the forerunner of the CIA, and it was rumoured that he had maintained intelligence links. No trace of him was ever found.

PRM leader freed

10 January | **Kuala Lumpur**

Ahmad Boestamam, president of the People's Party of Malaya (PRM), was freed one day before Hari Raya Aidilfitri. However, he was prohibited from leaving Kuala Lumpur without police permission.

Inche Boestamam had been arrested under the Internal Security Act on 13 February 1963 for engaging in subversive activities and having Communist links. While in detention at the Batu Gajah detention centre, Perak, he had written five novels, the first four of which had been published.

Sulaiman Club to be demolished

10 February | **Kuala Lumpur**

The 62-year-old Sulaiman Club building, the birthplace of Umno, was due for demolition to make way for two buildings, one to replace the club's present building and the other to serve as the Kampung Baru Civic Hall, it was announced. The club was built as a gift to the people of Kampung Baru from the late Sultan Sulaiman of Selangor.

Tunku's Chinese New Year message

8 February | **Kuala Lumpur**

In a Chinese New Year message to the nation, Prime Minister Tunku Abdul Rahman said: 'As I speak to you, Chinese families all over the country will be gathered together for their traditional family reunion dinner. There will be much firing of crackers as an expression of their joy and those who live in the urban areas will no doubt be disturbed and perhaps lose a few hours of sleep. But what does it matter so long as it makes others happy.

'As I said before, it is better to lose a little sleep through the firing of crackers than lose many lives through the firing of guns. Let everyone, therefore take this noisy cracker-firing in the happy spirit of the joyous occasion. Chinese New Year, like our other great festivals, comes but once a year'.

At the same time, he said, he did not think anyone would begrudge the protection afforded to the indigenous people of his country 'who know no other country but this as their home'.

FLDA project to be bigger

10 February | **Bentong**

Five more FLDA plantation schemes would be opened during the year, adding to the existing 62 covering 150,000 acres, Deputy Prime Minister Tun Abdul Razak announced. The new schemes were expected to benefit 60,000 previously landless families.

Tun Razak also said the Jengka Tiga FLDA land scheme in Pahang would be opened to accommodate another 60,000 families, especially from States that no longer had enough land to develop, such as Perlis, Penang and Malacca.

Menteri Besar resigns

3 March | **Johor Bahru**

Datuk Haji Hasan Yunus tendered his resignation as the Menteri Besar of Johor. He was succeeded by the chairman of the Local Authority Committee, Datuk Haji Othman Sa'ad.

Tunku turns film director

30 January | **Singapore**

Once again the Prime Minister stepped into the world of filmmaking, writing the script of *Raja Bersiong* (*The Fanged King*).

Based on a local legend of a bloodthirsty king, the film was being filmed under the direction of Jamil Sulong.

Today, Tunku Abdul Rahman himself was in the director's chair for an hour.

The Tunku gives instructions to cast members on the set.

Tun Ismail to retire next month

23 February | **Johor Bahru**

Minister of Home Affairs Tun Dr Ismail Abdul Rahman would retire on 14 March due to ill health, said Prime Minister Tunku Abdul Rahman.

The Tunku praised Tun Dr Ismail as a Minister who worked tirelessly in the service of the nation. Later, in Kuala Lumpur, Tun Dr Ismail said he would have wanted to retire much earlier but had stayed on due to Confrontation. Tun Dr Ismail had a long and proud record of service. He was in the delegation that travelled to London in 1956 to discuss independence for Malaya.

Language Bill passed

3 March | **Kuala Lumpur**

The Dewan Rakyat passed the National Language Bill with 95 votes for and 11 against. In his closing address, Prime Minister Tunku Abdul Rahman said it would pave the way to make the Malay language the sole national language of the country. The Act became official on 1 September.

Peninsula hit by typhoon and tremors

13 April | Kuala Lumpur

A typhoon with wind speeds of 80mph swept through parts of Kedah, destroying 143 homes in Kubang Pasu, Kota Star, Yan and Baling. No deaths were reported. The worst-hit was Kubang Pasu, where 60 families from six villages lost their homes.

Tremors were also reported on the west coast of the Peninsula especially in Penang where hundreds of tenants of high-rise buildings left in a hurry. A part of the old market building in Victoria Road collapsed. No casualties were reported.

Collapse of part of the old market building in Victoria Road, Penang during the tremors.

Kuching–Sibu road completed

22 March | Kuching

Finally, folks from Kuching could travel from the State capital to Sibu by road and vice versa. Deputy Prime Minister and Minister for National and Rural Development Tun Abdul Razak performed the opening ceremony for the road by cutting a ribbon at Durin, 260 miles from Kuching.

The $50 million new road was the result of the Government's efforts to link Kuching, Sibu and Simanggang with the outlying districts by road.

Karam Singh arrested

20 April | Kuala Lumpur

A spokesperson for the Kuala Lumpur police headquarters confirmed that Mr Karam Singh had been arrested under the Internal Security Act.

The lawyer, former MP and State Assemblyman was unexpectedly arrested at the Kajang police station, where he was meeting strikers from the Bukit Asohan Estate detained for holding a rally without a police permit.

Perlis Raja pleads for more Federal aid

30 May | Kangar

Former Yang di-Pertuan Agong the Raja of Perlis today appealed to the Central Government for sympathy and continued aid until his State could stand on its own feet. The State, which had undertaken projects under the Five-Year Development Plan for the benefit of its people, had faced deficits every year since 1961.

At the opening of the State Assembly, the Raja of Perlis reiterated that the state was not a burden to the Central Government as it had helped to save $20 million a year in foreign exchange by producing more rice. He said he hoped the people of Perlis would understand the situation and urged wealthy Malays to take advantage of the encouragement given to them by the Government to set up new businesses.

Sabah election results

27 April | Sipitang

State Minister of Finance Encik Harris Salleh won the last seat to be declared in the State Assembly elections, beating his UPKO opponent Sudum bin Agong by 1,112 votes.

The final state of parties was: USNO (14), UPKO (12), SCA plus Alliance (5) and Independent (1). The three Sabah Alliance parties, which won 31 of the 32 seats, all subscribed to the three-point manifesto: reiteration of the people's unshakeable faith in Malaysia, rejection of the Philippine claim to Sabah and a 'revolution for progress'.

Stolen idol costs businessman dear

3 June | Kuala Lumpur

A Chinese businessman in Kuala Lumpur found to his cost that trifling with deities does not pay. The businessman, who unsurprisingly preferred to remain anonymous, had always hankered after an image of the Chinese warrrior-cum-scholar god of health Kwan Ti Kong.

So when a friend offered him one for $150 he grabbed at the chance and placed it on the family altar, not realising that it was stolen from a temple. Not only that, but it was the patron of the village of Kepong. From that time on, the businessman was plagued with crisis after crisis. His business tottered and his family was torn with strife.

It was only after consulting a medium that he realised the idol had been stolen. It has since been returned to its rightful place in the temple.

University College of Penang

10 June | Kuala Lumpur

The University College of Penang, to be established in 1968, would be the first of many such projects, said Prime Minister Tunku Abdul Rahman as he conferred degrees on 1,083 graduates in his capacity as Chancellor of the University of Malaya.

New university colleges were needed, he said, to meet an increasing demand for higher education. The university had grown in only nine years from an enrolment of 100 to 4,500.

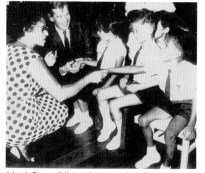

Johnnie Ray, a wildly popular singer of soulful ballads, visited Malaysia on a concert tour in May. He took time off to visit a school for the deaf in Kuala Lumpur. He is seen here with the children and the school's principal, Mrs A.L. Perera.

New notes for old in Bank Negara switch

5 June | Kuala Lumpur ▶ From 12 June, Malaysians could exchange old notes and coins for new ones being issued by Bank Negara, it was announced. The exchanges could be made at any Bank Negara branch or at any commercial bank.

Bank Negara said the old and new currencies would be circulated side by side for a period when both would be legal tender. When the major part of the old money had been withdrawn from circulation, it would cease to be legal tender after adequate notice was given.

People queue at Bank Negara to get their new notes.

Malaysia and Russia to set up embassies

15 June | Kuala Lumpur

Malaysia and Russia agreed to set up embassies in each other's capitals. The agreement was reached after an exchange of correspondence between Kuala Lumpur and Moscow.

The two countries discussed setting up diplomatic missions at consulate level when a Russian delegation led by Mr V.B. Spandarian, a head of department in the Soviet Foreign Trade Ministry, visited Malaysia in April. The one-week visit ended with the signing of a trade pact between Russia and Malaysia.

The modern male steps out in style

7 July | Kuala Lumpur

Stand aside ladies! The modern male stepped out in style in a bandana-style outfit for a romp on the beach. The red and brown batik bare-midriff bolero came with caftan-like sleeves, and a matching belt of the same batik material distinguished the plain, black mini-hipster. Giving a preview of the outfit was Ariff, a student of Mara College and menswear model for a Mara fashion show to be held at the Ideal Homes Exhibition in Stadium Negara on 12 July.

1967

6 May
Dr Zakir Hussain becomes the first Muslim President of India.

7 May
Riots begin in Hong Kong, inspired by the Cultural Revolution and fuelled by leftists.

17 May
Egyptian President Gamal Nasser demands withdrawal of UN peacekeeping forces in the Sinai.

19 May
The Soviet Union, the US and the UK ratify a treaty banning nuclear weapons in space.

23 May
Egypt closes the Straits of Tiran to Israeli shipping, blockading the Israeli port of Eilat.

30 May
Biafra announces independence and secedes from Nigeria.

5–10 June
The Six-Day War: Israel launches a pre-emptive strike against the Egyptian air force, and occupies the West Bank, the Gaza Strip, Sinai and the Golan Heights.

Relations with Singapore

Full immigration controls imposed

1 July Singapore

Hundreds of travellers were caught unawares as Singapore imposed full immigration control at Woodlands for the first time. Previously any Malaysian entering Singapore via the Causeway could stay on indefinitely. Also caught in the immigration net, due to last for two weeks, were some non-citizen permanent residents of Singapore who had gone to West Malaysia with their national passports but without obtaining re-entry permits. They were treated as new arrivals and given only a two-week stay.

Malaysia will not interfere with republic

14 October Kuala Lumpur

Malaysia would not enter Singapore and rule the republic when the British pulled out of the region in the mid-1970s, Tunku Abdul Rahman declared. The Prime Minister gave the assurance to his Singapore counterpart, Mr Lee Kuan Yew, when he opened the two-day Umno general assembly here.

The Tunku said he wanted to dismiss widespread propaganda that Singapore 'is within our clutches and when the British withdraw their troops we would enter to rule the republic'. The Tunku wanted to give Mr Lee the assurance that he has no cause to worry for Malaysia had not the slightest intention to interfere with the sovereignty of the republic. 'Far from it, we will cooperate with Singapore,' the Tunku pledged. It was impossible for Malaysia to dominate Singapore, he added, as it was Malaysia that allowed the republic to break away from the Federation against the wishes of the British Government.

'Charlie Chaplin' shoes are no joke, say nurses

5 July Kuala Lumpur

About 300 nurses and midwives in Pahang protested over the 'Charlie Chaplin' shoes they had been given. They said the shoes when washed 'go flat and spread out like the shoes of Charlie Chaplin in a comedy film'.

They asked the Malayan Nurses' Union to urge the Health Ministry to stop supplying the shoes.

Operation Good Citizen

23 July Kuala Lumpur

Acting Prime Minister Tun Abdul Razak launched Operation Good Citizen at the Dewan Tunku Abdul Rahman. More than 600 people, including Cabinet Ministers and leaders of Umno, MCA and MIC and voluntary organisations attended the launch, organised by the MCA.

The aims of the campaign were to foster a deeper sense and feeling of pride in the nation; and to inculcate a greater sense of respect for national symbols, especially the flag and anthem.

It also aimed to promote an active sense of civic consciousness among citizens and residents; and to cement the bonds of friendship, goodwill, harmony and cooperation among the different communities.

'Tiger Generals' caged

22 July Kuala Lumpur

Several 'Tiger Generals' were among 320 gangsters arrested by police in their fight against the underworld in Selangor. With their capture, the police smashed 10 secret societies and several other small-time gangs and seized 20 revolvers. The success, following the arrest of 200 extortionists in Selangor in January, was the result of months of planning. Police said crime had since decreased to 20 cases a month.

Rajamani named Sportswoman of 1966

22 July Kuala Lumpur

Malaysia's champion woman athlete, runner M. Rajamani, was named the Sportswoman of 1966 during a dinner at Rothman's Pavilion.

She received her trophy from acting Prime Minister Tun Abdul Razak. The Sportsman of the Year Trophy was won by M. Jegathesan.

Sabah opposition given warning

22 July Jesselton

Acting Prime Minister Tun Abdul Razak issued a stern warning that the Central Government would not tolerate any attempt by any opposition party to sour relations between the Centre and the State.

Speaking over Radio Malaysia Sabah before returning to Kuala Lumpur, Tun Razak said that while the Federal Government was alive to the legitimate aspirations of the people of Sabah to maintain a state identity within the context of the larger loyalty to the nation, it was keen to ensure that Sabah played its full role in realising its vast potential, contributing to the prosperity of the State and the nation. He was responding to allegations and criticisms by the United Pasok-Momogun Kadazan Organisation.

Big development in national language

24 August Kuala Lumpur

The national language had developed over the past 10 years and could boast an additional 71,000 new terms. The new terms were 'loan-words', 'loan-translations' and the coining of new words combining several others.

The director of the Dewan Bahasa dan Pustaka, Syed Nasir bin Ismail, said more than 60 per cent of the words were from the existing vocabulary. They were popular words which had received new meanings either singly or in combination with other words. From the 71,000 new words, a modern and specialised language which could be used in the teaching and study of science and technology at places of higher learning was slowly emerging.

The process, however, would take time to be effective as the need to use the language would increase proportionately with the growing modernisation of the language.

Selangor Sultan bans seven from Istana

26 August Kuala Lumpur

Seven State Assemblymen were banned by the Sultan of Selangor from all official functions at his palace, Istana Shah Alam in Klang, for two years. The Sultan announced the ban at a press conference in Istana Selangor here.

The ban was to express his displeasure at the failure of the seven assemblymen, six Alliance and one Labour, to attend a State banquet for the Yang di-Pertuan Agong and Raja Permaisuri Agong at Istana Shah Alam three days earlier.

10 unforgettable years of progress

31 August Kuala Lumpur

Malaysia celebrated 10 years of Merdeka in a wave of unprecedented joy and confidence. Prime Minister Tunku Abdul Rahman in a broadcast over Radio Malaysia expressed a feeling of elation over the positive changes that had taken place in the country over the years.

'When I was in London recently, I was asked what I think is the real achievement of this country in these 10 years of Merdeka, and without hesitation I said that the best, I think, is the way we have worked together, the way we have respected one another's way of life, the way we have really been united,' he said.

The Tunku had every reason to be pleased, *Time* magazine commented. Since he took office in 1957 his ambition had been 'not a mighty Malaysia but a happy one; not bullets but food; not uniforms but clothing.'

Security passes for students suspended

2 September Kuala Lumpur

The Government suspended for two years the requirement that suitability certificates should be held by students seeking admission to the University of Malaya. Education Minister Inche Mohamed Khir Johari said the position would then be reviewed and he hoped it would be possible to dispense with the certificates altogether. He added that only two students had been denied admission on security grounds since the Internal Security Act was amended to demand a suitability certificate.

Journalists call for special commission

7 October Kuala Lumpur

Prime Minister Tunku Abdul Rahman said he was willing to consider a call by the National Union of Journalists for Asean to set up a specialised commission of news media representatives. Its role would be to help promote national and regional development and raise media management and journalism standards in Southeast Asia.

'Rebel' Hamid Tuah and deputy held

12 October Klang

Police raided the illegal settlement of squatter leader Hamid Tuah and his 530 followers at Teluk Gong early in the morning and arrested his deputy leader Haji Yahaya bin Zainuddin. The swoop followed the re-arrest of Hamid Tuah at his home in Batu Tiga at 1.50am. He and his followers had defied the order of Selangor Menteri Besar Datuk Harun bin Haji Idris to clear out of the settlement yesterday.

It was Hamid Tuah's second arrest in two weeks. He was released on 30 September after negotiations between him and Datuk Harun, on condition that he leave the settlement within three days. This order was later extended twice but finally expired. Immediately after the raid, about 250 steel-helmeted policemen stood by as demolition squads pulled down the houses in the settlement.

University of Malaya students collect donations for Hamid Tuah and his followers.

6m go by train

18 September Kuala Lumpur

More than six million people paid $19,404,007 to travel by train during 1965. The Malayan Railway Administration's annual report said passenger numbers totalled 6,104,535 compared with 6,049,839 in 1964. Passenger revenue was $19,404,007 against $18,692,052 for 1964.

Malaysia pleads for fair price for rubber

5 October New York ▶ Industrialised nations needed to cooperate with the less-developed in an effort to establish fair prices for primary products, in Malaysia's case particularly for rubber, the UN General Assembly was told. The price of rubber had fallen to its lowest level since 1950.

Labour Minister V. Manickavasagam told the Assembly that Malaysia needed sympathetic and real friends not synthetic ones. Reviewing the economic and political policies of Malaysia in his speech to the Assembly, Mr Manickavasagam said a conference of natural-rubber-producing countries in Kuala Lumpur had on 2 October decided to adopt a 'common front' to stabilise the price of rubber. It also agreed that joint international action should be taken to rehabilitate the rubber industry to benefit all producers.

The Minister said the question now was whether industrialised countries would give their cooperation to producing countries to obtain fair prices and stability of demand for natural rubber.

Meanwhile, Finance Minister Tun Tan Siew Sin opened talks in Washington with US State Department officials on ways of holding up falling rubber prices. Tun Tan reportedly presented US officials with 'a realistic, constructive and reasonable' plan.

'Super' gang smashed as leaders are held

13 October Kuala Lumpur

A 'super' gang comprising notorious leaders of nine secret societies in various parts of West Malaysia had been smashed by the police in Selangor, it was announced.

The gang, formed as the result of 'peace talks' among the nine, was responsible for a variety of crimes from armed robbery to housebreaking.

Selangor CID chief Assistant Commissioner Ko Kim Cheng said this was the first time the police here had encountered such a criminal organisation.

He was surprised at the 'unique cooperation' of the once-rival leaders. The overall leader was a professional pickpocket. Ko said all members of the gang, some from as far away as Penang and Alor Star, were rounded up within a month.

Ombudsman on way

24 October Kuala Lumpur

New Zealand's Ombudsman, Sir Guy Powles, was expected to visit Malaysia in 1968 in an advisory capacity to help the country set up an ombudsman system, said the New Zealand Deputy High Commissioner in Kuala Lumpur, Mr D.B.G. McLean. New Zealand was the first Commonwealth country to adopt the Swedish ombudsman system to investigate injustices arising from faulty Government administration.

Straits Times Annual feature

Baram regatta, the races born out of war

The annual regatta on Sarawak's second largest river, the Baram, had its origins in the fighting instincts of the indigenous people, said an article in the *Straits Times Annual*.

It began at the end of the 19th century 'at a meeting of an overwhelming force of tribes loyal to Rajah Brooke's Government, of all those tribes whose allegiance was still doubtful and all those who were still at variance with each other' as a way of abolishing blood feuds. Instead of head-hunting the tribes would fight it out in war canoes on the river.

As well as racing in the huge canoes, with up to 60 oarsmen each, the modern regatta included races for longboats and hydroplanes driven by powerful outboard motors 'and aircraft and launches bring a stream of camera-packing visitors.'

The modern version also included displays of tribal dancing.

The article noted that 'it is a rare event to see people apart from the entertainers in their traditional costume.'

A team of oarsmen comes to grief during the regatta.

1967

world news

8 June
Israeli planes and warships attack the USS *Liberty*, killing 34.

10 June
Israel and Syria agree to a UN-mediated ceasefire.

1 August
Israel annexes East Jerusalem.

8 August
The Association of Southeast Asian Nations (Asean) is formed in Bangkok. The founding members are Malaysia, Indonesia, the Philippines, Singapore and Thailand.

4 October
Sultan Omar Ali Saifuddin III of Brunei abdicates in favour of his son Hassanal Bolkiah.

26 October
Mohammad Reza Pahlavi is crowned Shah of Iran.

11 December
The supersonic Concorde is unveiled in Toulouse, France.

19 December
Professor John Wheeler uses the term 'black hole' for the first time.

'True Malaysians' on the way

2 November | Kuala Lumpur

The generation of 1977 would be the true Malaysians, Tun Abdul Razak said, because the country's education policy pointed towards the making of a united race owing loyalty to the nation. The Deputy Premier was confident that the next 10 years would see a more dynamic nation with the people, especially the poor, playing important roles in the fields of business and profession. His prediction was based on the progress and achievements of the nation over the previous 10 years. The most important achievement had been the harmony established among the diverse races in the country, he said.

Switch to Malay in schools

15 October | Kuala Lumpur

The national language would become the medium of instruction for selected subjects in fully-assisted national-type English schools in 1968, Prime Minister Tunku Abdul Rahman announced. He said the effort to strengthen the foundations of the language should be carried out not only in national schools but also national-type ones.

He made it clear, however, that this process must take some time because the Government could not afford to let anything hamper the steady progress of children's education.

The Tunku said that although Malay had become the sole official language, full implementation must be carried out wisely in order to avoid trouble. He gave an assurance that in national-type Chinese and Tamil schools, those languages would continue to be the medium of instruction.

US Vice-President in talks with Tunku

2 November | Kuala Lumpur

United States Vice-President Hubert Humphrey held talks with Prime Minister Tunku Abdul Rahman on world affairs, particularly the stability of Asia.

The hour-long meeting, which covered a wide range of topics including Malaysia's concern about the falling price of rubber, the Vietnam War and the Middle East situation, took place at the Cabinet Room of the Prime Minister's new office in Jalan Dato Onn. Mr Humphrey was on a four-day visit to Malaysia. He also had an audience with the Yang di-Pertuan Agong and laid a wreath at the National Monument.

'Everyone loses' in sterling devaluation

26 November | Kuala Lumpur

The local press reported that nearly the entire nation, from the Goverment to the beggar, had been involved in the loss which Malaysia suffered, directly or indirectly, as a result of the devaluation of sterling.

In July, the Minister of Finance, Tun Tan Siew Sin, said about 90 per cent of Malaysia's total reserves of $2,289 million were in sterling, making her the second largest holder of sterling outside Britain, the biggest being Australia.

The 11.3 per cent devaluation would mean a loss of $327 million to the nation. Since then the country had been converting reserves to other currencies, he said.

Curfew after clashes in Nibong Tebal

28 November | Penang

Police imposed a 24-hour curfew in Nibong Tebal in Penang after disturbances and violence in which four people were killed.

The death toll as a result of the hartal riots reached 16. The number of casualties in the previous night's incidents was not known yet.

The day before, more than 100 people were arrested in a pre-dawn swoop on anti-Government elements and known criminals in and around Kuala Lumpur. Among those arrested were several active members of the Labour Party in Penang. Others included gangsters wanted by the police.

Communist documents and song books, Mao's quotations, pictures of Red Guards and slogans urging the people to follow Mao were seized.

Jesselton is now Kota Kinabalu

22 December | Jesselton

The Sabah State Legislative Assembly passed a Bill allowing the State capital, Jesselton, to be renamed Kota Kinabalu. Chief Minister Tun Datu Mustapha Harun said he first proposed the name change in 1966 at Tambunan. He said 'the opinions expressed indicate very persuasively that the majority of people in Sabah are in favour of the proposal'. Quoting the speech he had given at Tambunan, he said that with each mention of the capital Sabahans honoured a foreigner, Sir Charles Jessel. The new name, said Datu Mustapha, was inspired by the sacred Mount Kinabalu which was revered by the indigenous Dusun.

Straits Times Annual feature

Pipe smoking: A symbol of maturity?

30 December | Kuala Lumpur

In the 1900s, pipe smokers outnumbered cigarette smokers. By the 1960s, most smokers had switched to cigarettes but pipes were again coming back into favour especially with the younger generation, according to an article in *The Malay Mail*.

Pipe smoking had acquired an aura of mystery, and the impression of dead seriousness which it gave to a smoker had turned many an executive from cigarettes to pipes, it said.

The pipe 'has become a symbol of maturity and the creator of a new image—that of the confident and successful executive.'

Niah caves a treasure house of prehistory

Remarkable finds had been made in the great caves at Niah in Sarawak, said an article in the *Straits Times Annual* by Tom Harrisson, curator of the Sarawak Museum. Excavations that had gone on since 1954 had revealed the longest continuous record of human culture in the region, he wrote.

Human remains and tools had been uncovered, showing that modern man was active in Niah more than 40,000 years ago. There were also clear signs of evolution in terms of improvements in tools and other craftwork as well as burial rituals. By 'around 4,000 or 3,000 BC burials are abundant and beautifully done,' he wrote, with bodies laid out on rush mats still preserved today.

An archaeologist at work in the caves where man has been active for 40,000 years.

A general view of the caves and (inset) a beautifully decorated pot.

1968

Games took centre stage: the Thomas Cup, the icon of badminton supremacy, returned to Malaysia; Malaysia's Merdeka football tournament victory earned a half-day holiday for schools; and the first ball flew at the Subang National Golf Course. On the diplomatic front Malaysia welcomed VIP visitors—General Ne Win of Burma, Emperor Haile Selassie of Ethiopia and Indira Gandhi from India—and rebuffed the Philippines' territorial claim to Sabah. On the home front, vast tracts of jungle were slated for clearance for the world's largest land scheme, the Jengka Triangle. Eventually, a total of 150,000 acres of jungle would be transformed for homes for 60,000 people and for the establishment of rubber small holdings.

JANUARY
The Angkasapuri broadcasting centre is opened by Prime Minister Tunku Abdul Rahman.

MAY
Indian Premier Indira Gandhi arrives in Malaysia to a rousing reception.

AUGUST
University Hospital officially opens in a lavish ceremony attended by 500 distinguished guests.

SEPTEMBER
The Philippines House of Representatives passes a Bill declaring three-fifths of Sabah to be Philippine territory.

March: Inche Mohamed Khir Johari, president of the Badminton Association of Malaysia, with the victorious Thomas Cup team.

'What we now have, we must hold.'

Mohamed Khir Johari, Badminton Association of Malaysia president, on defending the Thomas Cup, 28 March 1968.

1968

world news

6 January
First heart transplant in the US. The patient, Mike Kasperak, 54, lives for two weeks.

23 January
North Korea seizes the USS *Pueblo*, claiming it was spying in North Korean waters.

25 January
Sixty-nine crew go down with the Israeli submarine *Dakar* in the Mediterranean.

30 January–24 February
The Vietcong Tet offensive during the lunar new year catches the South Vietnam regime by surprise.

31 January
Thirty-one North Korean commandos infiltrate Seoul and head for the presidential palace before 28 of them are detected and killed.

1 February
A Pulitzer-winning photograph of South Vietnam's national police chief blowing out the brains of a Vietcong prisoner adds fuel to the anti-war movement

No money for school fees? Don't worry...

6 January | **Kuala Lumpur**

No deserving child should be deprived of schooling due to poverty. Education Minister Mohamed Khir Johari directed all State Chief Education Officers in West Malaysia to implement the policy of providing free education for at least 10 per cent of all secondary pupils, stating that the practice of leaving the implementation to school heads was unsatisfactory. State-level reservations would enable Chief Education Officers to fill free places.

Straits Times Annual feature

Kelantanese dancers propitiate the sea spirits.

A feast for the sea spirits

When they went long without a catch, older fishermen in Kelantan were known to revive an ancient ritual and make offerings to the spirits of the sea, an article in the *Straits Times Annual* recalled.

Datuk (later Tan Sri) Mubin Sheppard, an authority on Malay customs, wrote that in earlier times, in a ceremony known as puja pantai, an albino buffalo was offered to the sea spirits. The local people would also entertain the spirits with public performances of the wayang kulit (shadow play) and traditional dances.

In lean times older fishermen continued to make offerings to propitiate the sea spirits and claimed that it was by this means that the annual catch was maintained.

'Most beautiful' broadcasting centre

17 January | **Kuala Lumpur**

The $20-million new broadcasting centre Angkasapuri, described as the 'most beautiful of all Ministry buildings' by Tunku Abdul Rahman, was opened by the Prime Minister. It was planned by him when the Information and Broadcasting Ministry was under his charge. The Tunku also announced plans for a second television channel that would bring 'greater viewing pleasure'. In the past, he said, the Ministry had telecast special programmes, such as the Qur'an-reading competition.

'As a result, non-Muslims have not been able to use their sets. That is why it is essential to have another channel...people will then have a choice,' he explained.

Architecturally designed utilising the same concept as Parliament House, this is an artist's impression of the 'most beautiful' Angkasapuri.

$10,000 for reporting textbook pirates

7 January | **Kuala Lumpur**

Please judge school textbooks by their covers—that's the strategy that infuriated publishers have adopted in an effort to stem the tide of pirated copies flooding the market.

Besides offering a $10,000 reward for information leading to the successful prosecution of those involved in the printing and distribution of the 'fakes', publishers have redesigned book covers in full colour, which hopefully will make the books more difficult and expensive for pirates to reproduce. So far, two persons had been charged in court under the copyright laws for possession of such pirated texts.

WARNING

PIRATED TEXTBOOKS

PARENTS, PRINCIPALS, TEACHERS AND BOOKSELLERS ARE WARNED THAT PIRATED EDITIONS OF TEXTBOOKS OFTEN OF INFERIOR QUALITY ARE BEING OFFERED FOR SALE AT THE SAME PRICES AS THE ORIGINAL EDITIONS. THIS IS ILLEGAL. ANYONE CAUGHT SELLING OR PRINTING PIRATED EDITIONS WILL BE PROSECUTED.

$10,000 REWARD

WE, THE UNDERSIGNED PUBLISHERS ARE PREPARED TO OFFER A TOTAL OF $10,000 FOR INFORMATION WHICH WILL LEAD TO THE ARREST AND SUCCESSFUL PROSECUTIONS OF THE GROUP OR GROUPS ENGAGED IN THE PRINTING

British troops to leave region by end of 1971

16 January | **London**

British Prime Minister Harold Wilson announced the withdrawal of forces from Southeast Asia by the end of 1971, four years earlier than originally envisaged by Malaysia and Singapore. Apart from 'remaining dependencies and certain other necessary exceptions' Britain would not maintain bases east of Suez, he said. 'Our security lies fundamentally in Europe, and must be based on the North Atlantic Treaty Organisation.'

He, however, pledged that Britain will contribute to alliances of which she is a member.

Commenting on the decision, Prime Minister Tunku Abdul Rahman said Malaysia must try to 'depend not only on Britain, but on countries interested in the freedom of small countries and small nations such as we are'.

Old bombs located

January | **Penang**

A Royal Engineers bomb-disposal team recently located 1,300 old Japanese bombs in tunnels on Bukit Gedong, Penang. The tunnels had caved in with the passage of time, and this presented the bomb disposal team with the tedious job of detecting and digging the bombs out.

The bombs were taken 25 miles out to sea to be dumped, an operation that took 10 hours to complete.

Stand for 'Negaraku'!

1 March | **Kuala Lumpur**

A Bill making it an offence punishable by law to fail to stand when the *Negaraku* is played was passed today. But on 4 April the Government announced that the national anthem will no longer be played in cinemas, nightclubs and similar venues but only at some official functions and those attended by royalty.

Alatas: Let's discuss communal tension

4 March | **Penang**

Citing the disturbances in Penang in November 1967, Professor Syed Hussein Alatas, head of Malay studies at the University of Malaya, called for the setting up of a special committee to conduct research into communal tension in the country. 'Communalism in Malaysia is relatively mild and is not associated with colour or racial prejudice,' Dr Alatas said.

Clarifying that he was not suggesting the Government was not earnest in its desire to avoid communal conflicts, he explained that 'the non-violent behaviourist expression of a communal attitude in this country is not in the form of social discrimination between groups but of distorted images about each other'.

$142-million hydro project commissioned

10 February | **Tapah**

The Sultan of Perak commissioned the country's largest hydroelectric scheme—the $142-million Batang Padang project which was named the Sultan Idris II Station, after him. The new source of power was able to light up over a million homes and was expected to accelerate the pace of rural electrification.

Coupled with the production capacity of the $125-million Cameron Highlands hydro project, there was now ample power for factories on the western grid of the Peninsula.

'Electricity is now no longer a luxury,' the Sultan said. 'It has become a necessity. Even the kampong people are no longer satisfied with flickering kerosene lamps.' This was as it should be, he said, 'otherwise the seeds of discontent may spring up.'

Currency exchange suspended

14 March Kuala Lumpur

A gold-buying rush of record proportions on the European markets extended to South Africa and the Far East with bullion dealers in London, Paris and Zurich reporting a huge demand for bars and ingots—resulting in severe pressure on sterling and the dollar. The London foreign exchange market closed in a bid to halt the stampede.

On the local front, confusion reigned with the non-acceptance by many business establishments of the inter-changeable Malaysian, Singapore and Brunei dollars. After consultations between Bank Negara Malaysia and the Singapore Commissioner of Banks, all foreign exchange transactions in Malaysia and Singapore were suspended the following day. On 17 March, the International Gold Conference announced a sweeping reorganisation of the existing system to restore public confidence in the global monetary exchange system. Commercial banking transactions between Malaysia and Singapore resumed the next day.

Batik Saturday

16 March Kuala Lumpur

It was like a fashion house at Angkasapuri, where all staff members—from office boys to the Minister himself—turned up for work in batik. All Information and Broadcast Ministry staff throughout the country were encouraged to incorporate batik as a feature of their office wear every Saturday to support the local batik industry.

Operation Swop begins

20 March Kuala Lumpur

'Operation Swop'—aimed at switching thousands of Malaysian and Singaporean workers back to their own countries—began. The Government hoped to replace 60,000 Singapore workers in the capital with the 50,000 Malaysians in Singapore, following Singapore's decision to withdraw non-citizens' work permits.

Lightning kills athlete, injures sprinters

20 March Kuala Lumpur

National runners M. Rajamani and Cheryl Dorall, and newcomer P.N. Govindan, were struck by lightning while training at the Jalan Gurney Police Depot ground. Govindan, 22, a police recruit, died on the way to hospital.

Sportswoman of the Year Rajamani, who was knocked out, regained consciousness an hour later at the KL General Hospital. Cheryl was admitted with a leg injury. Rajamani, Cheryl and Govindan were among nine athletes who were running around the track in a slight drizzle about 5.30pm. They were in front of a large group of runners when, another runner said, 'there was a flash of lighting and the three dropped.'

On 26 March, Rajamani received a bouquet of flowers from Tunku Abdul Rahman. She said it was her 'best tonic'.

Secret Philippine training camp

23 March Kuala Lumpur ▶ Malaysia lodged a formal protest with the Philippine Government. It claimed that Special Forces were being trained on Corregidor Island to 'infiltrate, subvert and sabotage Sabah'. The Foreign Ministry said the Malaysian Government took a serious view of events, especially in light of the recent arrest of 20 Filipinos in Sabah in possession of arms of the same make as those of the Corregidor force, who could not explain their presence in Sabah.

Philippine Foreign Secretary Ramos claimed training at the Corregidor Camp was not aimed at Sabah but was for 'counter-insurgency operations in Sulu.' However, chief of the military-run Civil Affairs Office and commander of the camp, Air Force Major Eduardo (Abdul Latiff) Martelino, was put under 'technical arrest' and on 28 March told a congressional investigating committee in Manila of a top-secret project codenamed 'Merdeka'. Major Martelino had said that it was strongly felt in southern Philippines that decisive action should be taken concerning the claim to Sabah. The next day, he denied his claims.

In Penang, thousands turn up for a glimpse of the Thomas Cup and champion badminton players.

Thomas Cup is back!

27 March Kuala Lumpur

Amid shouts of 'Syabas!', the coveted Thomas Cup returned to an uproarious welcome from thousands at Subang Airport. The Malaysian badminton team escorted the Cup fought for in Jakarta last June, where play was halted due to hostile crowd behaviour. In August the International Badminton Federation awarded the Cup—after a decade in Indonesian hands—to Malaysia. The Cup was taken on a tour of the capital in a motorcade.

Gerakan Ra'ayat Malaysia formed

25 March Kuala Lumpur

Three doctors, two professors and a lawyer announced the birth of a new political party, Gerakan Ra'ayat Malaysia (Malaysian People's Movement).

They were Dr Tan Chee Khoon, MP (formerly Labour); Dr Lim Chong Eu, MP (United Democratic Party); Dr J.B.A. Peter (president of the Malayan Medical Association); Dr Wang Gungwu (head of the University of Malaya history department); Dr Syed Hussein Alatas (head of the University of Malaya's department of Malay studies); and V. Veerappen, former MP for Seberang Selatan.

Royal tax challenge

12 April Kuantan

Tengku Arif Temenggong, younger brother of the Sultan of Pahang, was expected to use an 84-year-old will to challenge the State Government over the right to collect taxes from the mineral-rich sub-district of Rompin. The will was written in 1884 and bears the seal of Sultan Ahmad, Ruler from 1863 to 1914. It gave his sons power to collect revenues and taxes.

14 potential padi areas identified

23 March Kuching

Federal Minister for Agriculture And Cooperatives Tuan Haji Ghazali Jawi said the Government had identified 14 potential padi planting areas in Sarawak, totalling 38,000 acres. Two of these areas—20,000 acres between Sungai Santubong and Sungai Sarawak, and 2,000 acres in Bating in the Second Division—would be given priority with the aim of double-cropping, he added. In order to increase yield per acre in existing padi areas, a subsidy would be given to farmers worth $45 per acre.

Lever Brothers Malaysianised

19 April Kuala Lumpur

With the appointment of Mr R. Dharmarajah as technical director, Lever Brothers (Malaysia) Sdn Bhd now had a Malaysian majority on its board of directors; Malaysianisation had extended to its top technical posts. Mr Dharmarajah succeeded Mr A. Boyd, who returned to England on retirement. He joined Lever Brothers as an assistant engineer in 1959. The other two Malaysians on the five-man board of directors were Raja Kamarudin bin Raja Tun Uda (personnel) and Mr Yuen Hon Chong (commercial).

Three killed and 50 hurt in express rail crash

23 April Layang-Layang

Three people died when a railcar express carrying 90 passengers from Kuala Lumpur to Singapore rammed a stationary passenger-goods train. The front railcar coach plunged into a ravine and burst into flames, killing the railcar driver, the train fireman and a seven-year-old boy. The crash was the worst in Malaysian railway history.

1968

world news

26 February
Thirty-two African nations agree to boycott the Olympics because of the participation of South Africa.

16 March
US troops massacre over 100 villagers in My Lai, South Vietnam.

27 March
Death of space pioneer Yuri Gagarin in a plane crash.

4 April
Martin Luther King is assassinated in Memphis, Tennessee. Riots erupt in major American cities.

3–17 May
France is hit by student riots and strikes by 10 million workers.

22 May
US nuclear sub *Scorpion* sinks with 99 crew south of the Azores.

5 June
Robert Kennedy, on the US presidential campaign trail, is shot in Los Angeles by Sirhan Sirhan.

6 June
Robert Kennedy dies.

8 June
James Earl Ray is arrested for the murder of Martin Luther King.

Bernama makes news

20 May Kuala Lumpur

The first story from Malaysia's national news agency Bernama was clattered out to subscribers on teleprinters—and it was a report on the launching of its own service. Watched by representatives of overseas news agencies as well as press and information attachés from various embassies, Information and Broadcasting Minister Senu Abdul Rahman released 13 doves representing Malaysia's 13 States—and literally launched Bernama with a flying start. Bernama is an acronym for Pertubuhan Berita Nasional Malaysia and was first mooted seven years ago.

Senu gets Bernama off to a flying start.

VIP Visitors

Military welcome for General Ne Win

23 April Kuala Lumpur

General Ne Win, chairman of Burma's Revolutionary Council, was greeted with full military honours upon arrival at Subang Airport for a six-day State visit. A 21-gun salute greeted the general and Madame Ne Win as the door to the special Viscount opened. First to greet them were the King and Queen, Prime Minister Tunku Abdul Rahman and his wife, and the Burmese ambassador to Malaysia, U Pe Kin.

General Ne Win inspecting the guard-of-honour.

Haile Selassie flies in

21 May Kuala Lumpur

Emperor Selassie with the King on arrival at Subang.

The almost legendary Emperor Haile Selassie of Ethiopia and a retinue of 34 arrived for a State visit. Upon arrival at Subang Airport, the bearded imperial figure, who claims lineage from King Solomon and the Queen of Sheba, was greeted by a 21-gun salute.

On a dais, the Emperor wearing the headgear of a lion's mane, took the royal salute with the Yang di-Pertuan Agong.

A handshake in the Kremlin

25 May Moscow

Deputy Prime Minister Tun Abdul Razak, the first Malaysian Minister to visit the Soviet Union, met President Podgorny and other Russian leaders in the Kremlin. His message was: 'Malaysia wants to be friends with all those who want to be friends with her and who will respect her territorial integrity and not interfere in her internal affairs.'

He added that the big powers have an important role to play towards peace and stability in Southeast Asia.

In reply, the Vice-Chairman of the Council of Ministers, Mr Vladmir Novikov, said: 'There is every opportunity for the two countries to cooperate in the political field in an attempt to reduce international tension.'

Jungle cleared for world's largest land scheme

25 May Temerloh

Jengka had probably never seen such extensive development. The Jengka Triangle, comprising 150,000 acres of jungle between Temerloh, Maran and Jerantut, was being transformed into homes for 60,000 people or more. Since work started in January 1967, about 8,000 acres of jungle had been cleared. In 1969, another 9,000 acres were due to be cleared and the first settlers move in.

However, it had its share of setbacks, especially the drop in rubber prices, causing rubber planting to be scaled down.

Rousing welcome for Indira

29 May Kuala Lumpur

Indira Gandhi, overcome by a rousing reception by more than 10,000 people at Subang Airport, broke protocol to step off the red carpet to get closer to them.

The Indian Prime Minister responded time and again with the traditional 'namaste', and policemen with arms linked ringing her had a hard time keeping the surging sea of people—most of them of Indian origin—away.

Although it was already nightfall, crowds lined the roads to the Istana Tetamu, where she was staying, for a glimpse of her. And the next day, she addressed a 'full-house' mass rally at 5pm at the Stadium Merdeka—where there was hardly any standing room, even outside the stadium.

Prime Minister Indira Gandhi was overwhelmed by the crowds that turned out to greet her.

Arsenal go great guns to hit half a dozen

2 June Kuala Lumpur

Arsenal unleashed themselves, leapt into action and smashed the FAM President's Asian All-Stars 6–2 at Merdeka Stadium last night. The first half saw Arsenal and Asian players foraging for the ball in the Stars' half of the field. After Arsenal's first goal, the Stars equalised two minutes into the second half, courtesy of their Malaysian captain Chandran. The 35-yard shot stirred the sleeping giant and let Arsenal regain the lead in four minutes and left the Stars' groping for another equaliser.

The Stars did equalise with a second goal, but it was Arsenal's night. At least the Stars, with top players from all over Asia, could be proud that they went down fighting until the very end.

Vroom! Vroom! at Vespa plant

24 May Petaling Jaya

Every 20 minutes a Vespa was born in Petaling Jaya. The East Asiatic Company's new Vespa assembly plant was opened by Minister of Commerce and Industry Dr Lim Swee Aun, 'marking another milestone in the industrial expansion of modern Malaysia.' The plant initially employed 50 people.

Capital Issues Committee formed

22 June Kuala Lumpur

A Capital Issues Committee to approve new share issues was formed to prevent unscrupulous company promoters from exploiting the public, and to ensure the public was given adequate information.

Firms wishing to offer shares for subscription through public issue or private placement had now to seek approval of the committee, which was headed by Bank Negara Governor Tan Sri Ismail Mohamed Ali. In the past, no Government authority was consulted when a public issue was made although an informal arrangement existed—a company wishing to issue shares to the public approached Bank Negara.

'The Government,' said Finance Minister Tun Tan Siew Sin, 'has decided this arrangement should be formalised.'

Artist who brushed off death…

8 July | **Kuala Lumpur**

Despite being terminally ill, Lee Hoon Leng, 24, was bent on finishing 20 paintings for a pre-planned joint exhibition with four friends. Lee, a graduate of the Nanyang Academy of Fine Arts, died of a kidney ailment exactly six weeks ago, on 20 May—but not before achieving his goal. At the British Council, his 20 works were displayed with those of his friends at the 'Quintet Art Exhibition'.

'Even though he was very ill and knew he was dying, he carried on with his work,' said fellow artist and one of the 'quintet' Li Chong Chuan. 'He wanted to leave something to be remembered,' said Li, 'and we always will.' Lee, according to his friends, was fond of painting local scenery, especially kampongs. He was also noted for his Chinese style of painting. As a mark of respect, old boys of the Nanyang Academy decided to buy some of his paintings for presentation to the National Art Gallery.

King opens University Hospital

5 August | **Petaling Jaya** ▶ The $50-million University Hospital was officially opened by the Yang di-Pertuan Agong in a ceremony witnessed by 500 distinguished guests including Cabinet Ministers, heads of the diplomatic corps and 34 professors and doctors from similar institutions all over the world. In an earlier speech, Tunku Abdul Rahman, who was also University of Malaya Chancellor, described the new hospital as the answer to 'far too much ill-health in Malaysia, about which little is known'. He recalled: 'Personally, I must confess to a thrill of pride today as one of my first acts as Prime Minister was to choose this site as campus of the University of Malaya. In doing so, I actually earmarked the whole of this immediate sector as the land for the future development of a Medical Faculty and University Hospital—ideals we already had in those early days of independence.'

University Hospital's 15-storey tower block houses 20 wards for 756 patients. The equipment at the hospital is unrivalled in Southeast Asia.

14 killed in border ambush

17 June | **Penang**

Communist bandits ambushed a 50-strong Police Field Force patrol along the Malaysian–Thai border at 4pm and heavy fighting, with automatic weapons and grenades, ensued. It was all over in six minutes—leaving 14 of the police squad dead and 16 seriously injured—and a trail of blood leading into the thick jungle where the bandits retreated, carrying their wounded and dead. This was the worst attack the Police Field Force had suffered in years. More than 1,000 reinforcements were sent to the area for follow-up operations.

It's a Renault to the finish!

12 June | **Batu Tiga**

The first car—a Renault R10—came off the assembly line at the Associated Motor Industries Malaysia's $8-million motor assembly plant.

'We shall shortly produce between 30 and 40 R10s a month,' said plant manager Paul Brown, adding that the plant was better equipped than most similar-sized ones overseas. When in full production, the AMIM plant was planned to have a capacity for 7,500 cars a year, which would include vehicles for BMC, Ford, General Motors, Holden, Renault and Rootes.

Sabah: Malaysia rejects Manila claim

16 July | **Bangkok**

After a meeting lasting four weeks, Malaysia rejected Manila's claim to Sabah, saying there was no political or legal foundation for it. In a 17-page statement read by the chief Malaysian delegate, Tan Sri Ghazali Shafie, the Philippines' delegates were told that as far as Malaysia was concerned, the talks were 'over and done with'. Referring to Manila's claim that Sabah was vital to the security of the Philippines, Tan Sri Ghazali said: 'Do not pursue your claim to Sabah in order to satisfy your economic and security needs. These can be filled only through cooperation with us.' Philippine officials expressed shock and disbelief at Malaysia's formal rejection, calling it a 'bitter disappointment'.

Tunku Abdul Rahman College

11 August | **Kuala Lumpur**

The higher education institution initiated by the MCA is to be known as the Tunku Abdul Rahman College. At an MCA meeting attended by more than 500 party leaders, MPs and State Assemblymen to learn about the objectives of the college, more than $1 million was donated towards its building fund, making a total of $1.6 million.

MCA president Tun Tan Siew Sin, in a message read out by Commerce and Industry Minister Tan Sri Dr Lim Swee Aun, said the Government's acceptance of the idea was a considerable achievement. It would cater to the needs of all Malaysians of all racial groups, as was right, said Tun Tan, calling on all communities to 'respond to the spirit' in which the Government had acted.

According to a prospectus, the college would offer both academic and professional courses. There would be 21 professional courses available, ranging from automotive engineering to surveying.

In his message Tun Tan said the standards of the college would compare favourably with similar institutions of higher learning in Malaysia and its diplomas would be recognised.

Dizzying heights with revolving restaurant

8 July | **Kuala Lumpur**

It was a moving sight—a bird's eye view of the capital at 350ft. And one could see it comfortably seated, with a cup of coffee or a drink at the new revolving restaurant, the Bintang Lounge, in the newly opened Federal Hotel in Jalan Bukit Bintang. All landmarks of Kuala Lumpur could be viewed in the hour it took to make a complete revolution. This was the second revolving restaurant in Southeast Asia—the first was in Manila.

An advertisement for the Federal Hotel's facilities, including its revolving Bintang Lounge.

Tunku Abdul Rahman visits the shipyard in Glasgow, Scotland, where the KD *Hang Jebat* is being built for the Royal Malaysian Navy. With him is the chairman of the company, Sir Eric Yarrow.

Longest bridge opened

14 August | **Kuching**

Sarawak Chief Minister Penghulu Tawi Sli declared open the $1.15 million Batang Lupar Bridge on the Kuching–Sibu trunk road about 25 miles from Simanggang Town. At 384ft, it was the longest vehicular bridge in Sarawak built under the First Malaysia Development Plan. It was the third of the permanent bridges provided under the Colombo Plan by the Australian Government.

Holiday to celebrate football victory

25 August | **Kuala Lumpur**

Three splendid goals in a span of 15 minutes in the second half saw Malaysia hammering home a 3–0 victory over Burma in the final of the Merdeka football tournament. Watched by a record 38,000 crowd, euphoric Education Minister Khir Johari announced a half-day holiday for all schools to celebrate Malaysia's triumph.

1968

28 August
Warsaw Pact troops
and tanks invade
Czechoslovakia.

2 October
Mexican soldiers
machine-gun
hundreds of student
demonstrators in
Mexico City.

12–27 October
XIX Olympiad is held
in Mexico City.

20 October
Greek shipping
magnate Aristotle
Onassis marries
Jacqueline Kennedy.

5 November
Richard M. Nixon
defeats Vice-President
Hubert Humphrey in
the US presidential
elections.

24 December
Apollo 8 carries
astronauts Borman,
Lovell and Anders
into orbit round
the moon.

Ungku Aziz becomes first Malaysian V-C

19 September | **Kuala Lumpur**

Professor Ungku Aziz, dean of the Economics and Administration Faculty, was appointed the University of Malaya's first Malaysian Vice-Chancellor. Academic circles expressed no surprise at the choice, generally agreeing that the internationally renowned figure in economics was 'the most suitable man for the job'. The 46-year-old professor held a first-class honours in economics from the University of Malaya (in Singapore) and a PhD from Waseda University in Tokyo.

Fore! The first ball flies at Subang golf course

1 September | **Kuala Lumpur**

The Yang di-Pertuan Agong drove the first ball—and there was a mad scramble among caddies at the Subang National Golf Course to recover the historic piece, which was to be mounted to mark the occasion. The Sultan of Selangor, the Prime Minister and his deputy and other VIPs took part in the inaugural game.

Tunku Abdul Rahman, who was chairman of the new course, clarified that a loan granted to the Subang Golf Course Corporation would be repaid when 108 acres set aside for a housing and hotel scheme were sold for $4.5 million. The course, he said, was not costing the Government a cent.

The King hits the first ball on the new golf course.

Philippines 'annexes' Sabah

18 September | **Manila**

The Philippines House of Representatives passed a Bill reportedly declaring 'three-fifths of Sabah and a sliver of Indonesian Borneo' as Philippine territory. The following day in Kuala Lumpur, Tunku Abdul Rahman rejected this 'highly improper' Bill without reservation.

The next day, diplomatic relations with the Philippines were suspended. Thousands of angry youths from political parties and trade unions marched from the Selangor Club Padang to the Residency and pledged to defend Malaysia 'to the last drop of blood'. In Manila, Foreign Secretary Narciso Ramos said the Philippines would not go to war to seize Sabah.

Angry youths outside the Residency pledge to defend Malaysia 'to the last drop of blood'.

Foreign planes 'buzz' navy boats

3 October | **Kuala Lumpur**

Tunku Abdul Rahman disclosed that foreign planes had 'buzzed' Royal Malaysia Navy boats in Sabah waters several times, flying as low as 200ft—'but we are not afraid at all.' Returning after a three-day visit to Sabah, the Tunku declined to identify the aircraft but, when asked the purpose of the 'buzzing', the Tunku replied: 'Go ask President Marcos.' Of his Sabah trip, the Tunku said: 'I was very impressed with the people's show of determination to defend their State ... and they mean to stay in Malaysia, come what may.' Deputy Prime Minister Tun Abdul Razak said that sea patrols off the coast of Sabah had been increased to check possible infiltration.

More troops were alerted to move to Sabah, Ministry of Defence sources said. But the Tunku welcomed an offer by President Marcos to hold summit talks without preconditions. Two weeks later it was announced that Tun Razak would meet Philippine Foreign Secretary Narciso Ramos in Tokyo.

Flats disaster: Cabinet to discuss and investigate

23 October | **Kuala Lumpur**

The Cabinet was scheduled to discuss a report by the Commissioner of the Federal Capital on the Jalan Raja Laut disaster. The collapse, which buried alive more than five people and injured more than 15 others, was still being investigated. Deputy Premier Tun Abdul Razak spent some 25 minutes at the scene of the disaster. Early in the morning, rescue workers had dragged out the body of a woman.

There were concerns that people might be trapped between huge beams under the rubble but the beams could not be removed for fear of jeopardising the work of rescue workers.

Meanwhile, the Malaysian Institute of Architects called on the Government to set up a commission to review the whole building industry to ensure such incidents did not recur.

On 24 October, the Government set up a four-man committee of inquiry to investigate the causes and those responsible for the collapse of the four-storey flats building in Jalan Raja Laut. The incident claimed five lives.

Jaywalkers warned

26 October | **Kuala Lumpur**

Forty-five pedestrians who ignored the overhead bridge in Jalan Foch (*now Jalan Tun Tan Cheng Lock*) were stopped by the traffic police and given a stern warning. Selangor traffic police chief Supt Mansor bin Mohamed Noor lectured them on crossing the road the proper way. Since the bridge opened on 14 September, the traffic police guided pedestrians to use the overhead bridge.

116 arrested in Red swoop

9 November | **Kuala Lumpur**

Police arrested 116 Communist militants including 11 women in surprise early-morning swoops throughout the Peninsula.

The mass arrests, among the largest in recent years, marked the start of an intensive crackdown on subversive elements.

The arrests coincided with the release of a 32-page White Paper entitled *The Path of Violence to Absolute Power* dealing with the Communist threat and the public renunciation by Labour Party national chairman Koh Kay Cham of his Communist past. Mr Koh was set free after six months' detention.

In a foreword to the White Paper, which quoted extensively from seized documents, Deputy Prime Minster Tun Abdul Razak warned of the threat that cast its 'sinister shadow' over the nation.

'The Government,' he said, 'has never hesitated in acting firmly against those who knowingly seek to subvert and destroy the democratic way of life people have chosen for themselves. It will not hesitate now.'

New Chief Justice

8 November | **Kuala Lumpur**

Justice Tan Sri H.T. Ong (right), the first Chinese to become a Supreme Court judge in Malaysia, was appointed Chief Justice. Tan Sri Ong succeeded Tan Sri Azmi bin Haji Mohamed, who was appointed Lord President.

1969

A nation in crisis. In the worst racial riots in the nation's history, over 100 people lost their lives in violent clashes that broke out following the closely fought election in Selangor and Perak. Among the measures imposed in an attempt to return to normalcy were the declaration of a state of emergency, suspension of newspapers, banning of political party publications, clamping down on political campaigning, tightening of labour laws to prevent politicians from holding office in trade unions and the formation of the National Operations Council. Other unfolding events included the dismissal from Umno of Dr Mahathir Mohamad. Despite the gloom and doom, Malaysia's GNP rose by nine per cent, the highest in five years.

MAY
The Alliance emerges a battered winner in the 1969 general election.

AUGUST
The FRU uses force to quash a student protest at the University of Malaya, while its vice-chancellor Ungku Aziz tries to restore order.

OCTOBER
Tunku Abdul Rahman visits President Richard Nixon in the US.

DECEMBER
Legendary warrior Mat Kilau emerges after 70 years in hiding.

May: The aftermath of the 13 May riots that had erupted in Kuala Lumpur and some other towns in Peninsular Malaysia following the general election.

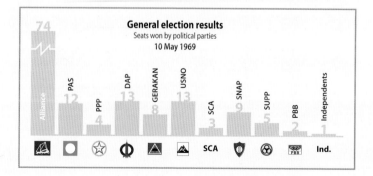

General election results
Seats won by political parties
10 May 1969

Alliance 74
PAS 12
PPP 4
DAP 13
GERAKAN 8
USNO 13
SCA 3
SNAP 9
SUPP 5
PBB 2
Independents 1

'In my estimation, the whole country is now in a chaotic state.'

Tun Dr Ismail bin Datuk Abdul Rahman, Minister of Home Affairs, 26 May 1969.

1969

world news

Double-double delight!

23 January Klang

Sabri Manijo and his wife Che Sarton Ma'arof were expecting twins. When the stork came this morning, however, it overstayed and quadruplets—believed to be Malaysia's first—were delivered. The three boys and a girl weighed 4lb 5oz, 4lb, 3lb 15oz, and 3lb 2oz, with the girl being the smallest. They were born at the Klang District Hospital, with the first at 5.38am. and the fourth at 6.06am. Che Sarton, beaming proudly, said: 'Saya suka hati (I'm very happy)', while Inche Sabri, a Kuala Langat vegetable seller earning about $120 a month, said he considered himself a lucky man, even with the extra mouths to feed. The couple had four other children, two boys and two girls.

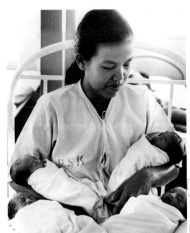

Proud mother Che Sarton with her quadruplets.

Razak: Nothing will stop us buying jets

25 January Kuala Lumpur

The US was being 'unfair and discriminatory' in urging Britain and France not to provide Malaysia with supersonic jet fighters when it had given planes and arms to the Philippines and other Asian countries, said Deputy Prime Minister Tun Abdul Razak, adding that 'nothing will stop us from buying the planes'. Confirming that the matter was discussed in London, a State Department official in Washington said the US would request Britain and France to dissuade Malaysia from buying fighter planes as it would start an arms race.

Road is a river after rain

12 January Kuala Lumpur

Flooding in Kuala Lumpur brought the 'Sungai Bangsar' into existence, leaving thousands of commuters stranded. A two-hour thunderstorm at 4pm flooded the main carriageway of Jalan Bangsar and in many places, water rose to four feet. When it subsided a couple of hours later, the road was almost knee-deep in mud. Long after the rain stopped, vehicles continued to jam the road, and traffic was at a standstill until 6.30pm. In Kampung Baru, the Sungai Bunus overflowed its banks and residents experienced the worst floods in years. In some areas, the water rose to five feet. A month later, the Federal Capital Commission allocated $1.2 million for a flood-alleviation scheme in Bangsar which included raising certain stretches of road and diverting a stream.

A father, like hundreds of other commuters, fails to get his motorcycle—and his children—across 'Sungai Bangsar'.

Reading one million documents a month

31 January Kuala Lumpur

How many people does it take to read 9,651,014 publications in nine months? That's the amount of literature Chew Chon Pin, his assistant Chan Swee Lin and 22 readers had sieved through from January to September last year. This works out to nearly 1,500 articles per day per reader. Mr Chew, head of the Chinese Publications Section of the Home Affairs Ministry, was in charge of scrutinising—and confiscating—Chinese publications brought into the country. Of the more than nine million publications his team went through in 1968, 68,368, mainly Communist propaganda including writings of Mao Zedong, were prohibited.

'Madhouse' Ministry

15 February Penang

Describing his Ministry as a 'madhouse where there is no end to the problems you have to face', Mohamed Khir Johari said his seven years as Education Minister were too long and he would like to have a rest.

He would like to continue his service to the people, he said, but not as Education Minister 'unless, of course, schools stop asking me for money and teachers refrain from asking for transfers'. The transfer of teachers was a continuous problem, he said, and the reasons given were varied, with some bordering on the absurd.

Singapore's fine gesture of friendship

16 February Kuala Lumpur

Singapore promised to send a detachment of its infantry regiment to help Malaysia, should the need ever arise. Its Prime Minister Lee Kuan Yew made the offer of assistance during January's defence pact talks in London, said Tunku Abdul Rahman, adding: 'It is more than an assurance—it is a direct help as a gesture of friendship on his part, which I appreciate very much.'

The Tunku also promised Mr Lee that 'all the irresponsible insinuations that Malaysia had an eye on Singapore' were false. 'We have to work and cooperate with each other,' he said.

Shattering moment captured on camera

14 February Kota Kinabalu

This picture was taken the moment the suspension bridge over the Tuaran River near Kota Kinabalu snapped—and with it more than 20 screaming schoolchildren fell 30 feet into the water. The four steel cables of the bridge broke as the children were on their way to a Solidarity Week gotong-royong project. All the children were safe. Jumat bin Said, who saved a fellow student from drowning, was recommended for a lifesaving medal.

This is National Rice Year

1 March Kerian

Deputy Prime Minister Tun Abdul Razak's launching of the National Rice Campaign marked the first time the Government had singled out a particular commodity for special treatment. This was because rice is the population's staple and there was a great need to aim for self-sufficiency in view of severe shortages in world markets the previous few years. Plans for this National Rice Year were aimed at boosting rice production through mechanisation and conservation at all stages to reduce wastage.

Malaysia's tallest building

5 March Kuala Lumpur

Work started on Malaysia's tallest building, a $10.5-million 26-storey skyscraper, the International Centre, in Jalan Suleiman, adjacent to Shell House and the Police Cooperative Building. It comprised a bank, shopping arcade and offices including diplomatic missions, a supermarket, art centres and restaurants.

PPP leader Seeni dies

15 March Ipoh

People's Progressive Party (PPP) president and Ipoh MP Darma Raja Seenivasagam, 48, died at the Ipoh General Hospital after a heart attack. D.R., as he was popularly known, began his political career in 1953 when he was elected vice-president of the Perak Labour Party.

He was a leading advocate for a joint opposition and played a leading role in the 'Don't fight among ourselves' electoral pact.

UM professor heads Penang University

8 April Kuala Lumpur

University of Malaya's Arts Faculty dean Prof Hamzah Sendut (right), 42, was appointed Vice-Chancellor-designate of Penang University. His appointment was approved by the Yang di-Pertuan Agong. Prof Hamzah, who graduated from the University of Malaya in Singapore with a Bachelor of Arts degree, also held a Master of Civic Design degree from Liverpool University and was a United Nations special consultant on urbanisation between 1963 and 1964.

Stampede at beach show

16 March Penang

Penang's first beach beauty contest nearly didn't take place as the crowd which gathered to watch the filming of Shaw Brothers' *Moon Over The Coconut Grove* became riotous. The winner and runners-up however each received a big kiss from Jimmy Lin Tsung, lead actor in the film.

Genting Highlands boss Lim Goh Tong (centre) briefs the Tunku on plans for the resort.

High note on Highlands

31 March Karak

The foundation stone for the pioneer Highlands Hotel was laid by Prime Minister Tunku Abdul Rahman, marking the completion of the access road to Genting Highlands Resort.

Saying that he was impressed that the private sector, without the assistance of the Government, could develop a mountain resort for the enjoyment of all Malaysians, the Prime Minister suggested a gaming licence to help accelerate the progress and development of the area.

Alliance in rough seas

10–12 May Kuala Lumpur

Malaysians went to the polls with the betting 10-to-1 on another Alliance sweep. The sailboat symbol of the Alliance faced rough seas but managed to find safe harbour at the end of the count for parliamentary seats, and was assured of another five years in office. At State level, however, the Alliance lost Penang to Gerakan which captured 16 of 24 seats; failed to wrest Kelantan from PMIP which won 19 of 30 seats; and was deadlocked in Selangor, where the combined Opposition strength equalled its own at 14–14.

In Perak, the Opposition secured 21 of the 40 seats led by the PPP which won 12 seats, DAP six, Gerakan two and PMIP one. PPP president Dato S.P. Seenivasagam announced the party's intention to form a coalition with the DAP and Gerakan. Selangor Menteri Besar Datuk Harun bin Haji Idris said he would start forming the State Government but would consider a coalition 'especially with Gerakan'.

Three Alliance Ministers lost their seats. They were Minister of Information and Broadcasting Senu Abdul Rahman, Minister of Commerce and Industry Tan Sri Dr Lim Swee Aun and Welfare Services Minister Dr Ng Kam Poh.

'No' to one-race Government

11 April Kota Bharu

The formation of a 'one-race' Government will only bring chaos and destroy the country, Deputy Prime Minister Tun Abdul Razak told an election rally.

'This is why the Alliance totally rejects the PMIP concept of an all-Malay Government, just as we reject the DAP and PPP concept of a non-Malay Government', he said.

Describing the PMIP ideal of forming a Malay Government as a grand illusion like the Melayu Raya and Nusantara concept of deposed Indonesian President Sukarno, he accused the PMIP of trying to cover up its failure to develop the state of Kelantan.

Code to ensure clean and fair elections

14 April Kuching

Supervisor of the Election Commission in Sarawak, Mr Augustine Chong, outlined an 11-point Election Behaviour Code to political parties in the State, their agents, Independents and Election officials. He said the commission was impartial and assured that ballot boxes would be secured when transported from one polling station to another as they would be in the custody of the police and returning officials.

At last—equal pay for women

7 May Kuala Lumpur

It was to be equal pay for women, effective 1 August. Deputy Prime Minister Tun Abdul Razak explained that the principle of equal pay had been accepted in 1964 but due to financial difficulties could not be implemented. 'But the Government wants to be fair to women workers,' he said, adding that implementation from August would initially cost $4.2 million. The full implementation of equal pay in three years' time was expected to cost the Government an additional $11.4 million annually. In December 1968, Parliament had passed a Bill providing pension rights for women and in March 1969, the Teachers' Salary Commission did not recommend a separate salary scheme for women teachers.

The King acts to end mob violence in the nation's capital

Crisis laws after 39 die in riots

Penang quiet: 'Keep calm' appeal by Chief Minister

Decision today on S'pore trading room

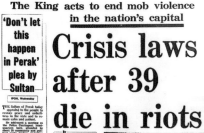

He's smiling and so he should be

TWO BURNT-OUT CARS in Bangsar Road near the Straits Times Kuala Lumpur office yesterday.

The foe—by the Tengku

He's looking forward to a happy future.

NECCHI 544

May 13 Riots

Clashes and curfew in Selangor

13 May | Kuala Lumpur

A curfew was imposed in several areas following clashes between groups of youths in the Federal Capital and Petaling Jaya. The areas under dawn-to-dusk curfew were Kepong, Sungei Buloh, Sungai Pelong, Sungai Besi, Serdang, Serdang Baru, Salak South Baru, Ampang, Ampang New Village, Travers Road, Jalan Pekeliling, Brickfields, the centre of Kuala Lumpur and the Petaling Jaya district. Curfews were also imposed in Penang and Perak (Telok Anson, Taiping, Sitiawan, Kerian, Batu Gajah, Parit and Kampar districts).

Prime Minister Tunku Abdul Rahman appealed for support and cooperation with the security forces in maintaining security. 'I am aggrieved at what has taken place,' he said, warning of the dangers of such occurrences in future.

The Federal Reserve Unit in action.

MCA pulls out of Cabinet

13 May | Kuala Lumpur

The Malaysian Chinese Association (MCA) announced it was pulling out of the Government because of the setback the party suffered in the weekend election when 20 of its 33 candidates were defeated. The MCA would remain part of the Alliance.

Emergency declared

14 May | Kuala Lumpur

The Yang di-Pertuan Agong issued a proclamation of Emergency under Clause 2 of Article 150 of the Constitution—to secure public safety and to 'end mob violence in the nation'. This was announced by Tunku Abdul Rahman over Radio Television Malaysia.

Above: *The Straits Times* reports on the riots.

Right and below: Deserted streets in Kuala Lumpur after a curfew is imposed.

Left: People shopping at Central Market—a sign of the return to normality in the Federal Capital.

Situation improves, NOC formed

17 May Kuala Lumpur

The situation in and around the Federal Capital was improving. Except for one case of arson, no major incident was reported.

Prime Minister Tunku Abdul Rahman announced the formation of the National Operations Council (NOC) with Tun Abdul Razak as the Director of Operations.

The main function of the NOC would be to coordinate the work of the Government, police and military. All executive action would be centred on this new arrangement. Tun Razak immediately announced the composition of the NOC, adding that steps were being taken to set up State Operations Committees comprising army and police officers, under the Menteris Besar or Chief Ministers.

A three-hour curfew relaxation in the Federal Capital saw thousands of people coming out of their homes.

MCA president and NOC member Tun Tan Siew Sin said the Government had worked out a plan to ensure adequate food supply for the public in curfew areas after a meeting with representatives of chambers of commerce and security forces.

Jalan Raja Abdullah in Kuala Lumpur, strewn with debris.

Another tense day with casualties in the midst of the continuing violence.

Newspapers suspended

15 May Kuala Lumpur

The Government suspended the publication of all Malaysian newspapers. No explanation was offered, and attempts on the part of newspaper representatives to communicate with Government officials were fruitless.

The situation in affected areas was reported as 'still tense'. The official casualty toll listed 75 dead and 277 injured, many seriously. On 17 May, the newspaper ban was lifted.

Caretaker Cabinet formed

16 May Kuala Lumpur

Amid an announcement that the MCA would join an emergency caretaker Cabinet, former Home Affairs Minister Tun Dr Ismail bin Datuk Abdul Rahman was recalled to join the Government. It was reported that some Opposition MPs and Assemblymen were arrested following the riots.

'Paid saboteurs' at work

17 May Kuala Lumpur

Paid saboteurs were responsible for some of the violence in Selangor, said Prime Minister Tunku Abdul Rahman. 'Secret society members were involved too,' he said on Television Malaysia.

Left: Tunku Abdul Rahman meeting community leaders at a relief centre in Kuala Lumpur on 17 May.

Below: Tun Abdul Razak and Ghazali Shafie (in dark jacket) observe food distribution at Kampung Datuk Keramat.

1969

world news

17 May
Tom McClean completes the first solo trans-Atlantic crossing—in a rowing-boat.

22 June
Oscar-nominated American film actress and singer, Judy Garland, dies at 47.

8 July
The first withdrawal of US troops from South Vietnam.

8 July
Edward Kennedy drives his car off a bridge after a party. His passenger, Mary Jo Kopechne, does not make it to shore.

14 July
Honduras loses a soccer match to El Salvador resulting in Salvadoran migrant workers being attacked and expelled from the country.

20 July
'The Eagle has landed'. Neil Armstrong takes the first step on the moon.

25 July
President Nixon announces the 'Nixon Doctrine' that Asian allies of the US must take care of their own military defence.

A rare picture and a reassuring signal

26 May | Kuala Lumpur

The Federal Court resumes sitting—and it is a reassuring sign that life in the capital is returning to normal. Although it is strictly forbidden to photograph a court in session, this historic picture was taken with the special permission of the Lord President Tan Sri Azmi bin Mohamed (on the bench, centre) and the Chief Justice Tan Sri H.T. Ong (on the bench, left). Also seated on the bench is Mr Justice Tan Sri Suffian (right). Below the Lord President is High Court Chief Registrar Au Ah Wah. The court dealt mainly with civil appeals.

First woman Minister appointed

20 May | Kuala Lumpur

Tan Sri Fatimah Hashim became the country's first woman Minister. She was appointed the Minister of Social Welfare in the new Cabinet comprising 14 Ministers (three of whom were MCA members) and five Assistant Ministers.

One of Tan Sri Fatimah's very first duties as Minister for Welfare Services was to receive donations for riot victims.

Stock market back in action

27 May | Kuala Lumpur

The Kuala Lumpur trading room of the Stock Exchange of Malaysia and Singapore reopened after a two-week shutdown. A spokesman said 738,000 shares changed hands in the 2½ hours of operation.

Political party publications banned

22 May | Kuala Lumpur

The National Operations Council banned all political party publications. This followed a call by Prime Minister Tunku Abdul Rahman to 'stop all political talk'.

Political party publications that had been in circulation were *The Alliance* (published by the Alliance Party), *Merdeka* (Umno), *The Guardian* (MCA), *The Rocket* (DAP) and *Gerakan* (Gerakan Ra'ayat Malaysia).

GNP up 9% despite riots

31 December | Kuala Lumpur

Malaysia's GNP for the year rose by about nine per cent to $11.3 billion—the highest since 1965—despite the riots.

What the foreign press said:

The Times of London said on 14 May:
'Malaysia's multi-communal Government abruptly fell apart today with the certainty that there is no longer to be Chinese representation in the Cabinet, nor in the State Government controlled by the ruling Alliance Party.

Tun Abdul Razak, the Deputy Prime Minister, brusquely announced this, saying that the Chinese had brought it on themselves by preferring Opposition parties.

Anxieties had been aroused by reliable reports of all-day meetings between Tun Razak and military and police chiefs.'

The *Sydney Morning Herald* said on 14 May:
'Malaysia, especially Kuala Lumpur, has probably never seen such violence and bloodshed before—bodies strewn across the street, vehicles and shops on fire, security forces patrolling the road. Battles flared throughout the night as Chinese and Malays, as well as mobs that comprised up to 700 people, and armed with long knives, poles and other weapons, roamed the streets. The Indians were largely uninvolved.

In Day Two of the horrendous May 13 riots, it is estimated that 39 people died.

The riots were caused by the Opposition's overwhelming win in the general election. Supporters of both the Alliance, comprising mostly Malays, and the mainly-Chinese Opposition parties flooded into the capital from rural areas. The Chinese wanted to celebrate election victories while the Malays came to demand new safeguards for Malay rights.

Tunku Abdul Rahman sobbed as he went on nationwide television to plead with rioters to end fighting. His voice breaking even as he spoke, the Tunku pleaded for the nation to obey military and police orders 'for the love of the country and the love of one another and the racial harmony enjoyed in the past'.

Deputy Prime Minister Tun Abdul Razak was placed in charge of the situation and he has repeatedly broadcast regular warnings to stay calm and observe the curfew, at the risk of being shot.'

The Age said on 15 May:
'A round-the-clock curfew was imposed in Selangor and later extended to parts of Perak and Penang. This was the second time since the Emergency that such a curfew has been imposed.

The Federal Capital's regular police force, army units and the police field force were deployed and a state of emergency was declared in Kuala Lumpur.'

Time magazine said on 23 May:
'Malaysia's proud experiment in constructing a multiracial society exploded in the streets of Kuala Lumpur last week. Malay mobs wearing white headbands signifying an alliance with death and brandishing swords and daggers surged into Chinese areas in the capital, looting and killing. In retaliation, Chinese, sometimes aided by Indians, armed themselves with pistols and shotguns and struck at Malay kampongs.

Government officials, attempting to play down the extent of the disaster, insisted that the death toll was only 104. Western diplomatic sources put the toll closer to 600, with most of the victims Chinese.'

The Times of London said on 6 June:
'Immediate actions that could help revive drained confidence must include the deliberate recruitment of multiracial units in the new battalions to be formed. The old argument of Chinese refusing the call to arms is legend. Young Chinese of Malaysian birth, facing shrinking opportunities for gainful employment, would come forward by the thousands.'

Clampdown on campaigning

11 June Kuala Lumpur

A ban on election campaigns was imposed. The new regulation prohibited organising or convening public meetings, processions or demonstrations, canvassing, using loudspeakers or using the mass media for making statements. The printing, distribution of pamphlets, putting up of posters and banners and the removal or damaging of such items already put up were also barred. There was to be no soliciting of votes—for or against a candidate.

New-look uniforms

1 July Kuala Lumpur

Pupils in Government-aided schools in West Malaysia would be required to wear newly designed uniforms from 1970, said Minister of Education Datuk Abdul Rahman Yaakub. However, he made it clear that only pupils entering Standard One, Form One and Form Six would wear the new uniforms immediately.

Mahathir expelled from Umno executive council

12 July Kuala Lumpur

The Umno executive council dropped the defeated parliamentary candidate for Kota Star Selatan, Dr Mahathir Mohamad, for a 'serious breach of party discipline and regulations which, if unchecked, will destroy unity within the party and the Government which is supported by the party'. The decision was taken after a three-hour emergency meeting at the Deputy Prime Minister's residence amid tight security by armed police personnel. Dr Mahathir, 42, a private medical practitioner, attended the meeting. A statement issued said Dr Mahathir had made public copies of correspondence between himself and Umno president Tunku Abdul Rahman that 'contained vitally important party matters and details which—in view of the present situation in the country—should have been first discussed by the Umno executive council'. The statement added: 'The Tunku was not present at the meeting.' Two days later, on 14 July, the letter by Dr Mahathir to the Tunku on 17 June was among six documents banned by the Government.

All school subjects to be taught in Malay

10 July Kuala Lumpur

All subjects except English, and the pupil's mother tongue, would be taught in Malay in Standard One at national-type English primary schools beginning next year, it was announced.

Four subjects were previously taught in Malay in Standards One, Two and Three: local studies, physical health education, music, and art & crafts.

Education Minister Datuk Abdul Rahman Yaakub also expressed the hope that the new spelling system agreed upon by Malaysia and Indonesia would be speedily implemented.

Against the odds...

14 July Kuala Lumpur

Against astronomical odds, two horses in the big sweep drew exactly the same number—155903. The number was drawn on *Stable Currency* and, subsequently, on *Bernadette Bunty,* the hot favourite. As lottery rules stipulate the same number cannot be drawn on more than one horse, a new one was drawn for *Bernadette Bunty*—152981, which turned out to be the first-prize winner. *Stable Currency* came in fourth.

Tear gas is fired at demonstrating University of Malaya students, sending them fleeing to the Great Hall for refuge.

Police fire tear gas at UM undergrads

28 August Kuala Lumpur

Members of the Federal Reserve Unit took up position at the Speakers' Corner of University of Malaya where students were gathering for a protest. It was timed as foreign delegates were at the university to attend a conference on traditional Southeast Asian music and drama. Calling upon Prime Minister Tunku Abdul Rahman to resign, the students ignored an order to disperse—and the 50-member FRU squad fired two volleys of tear gas, sending them fleeing to the Great Hall for refuge. Vice-Chancellor Professor Ungku Abdul Aziz said: 'This is the first time the FRU has entered the university...either I maintain the law as Vice-Chancellor, or I vacate the seat. I do not wish to be Vice-Chancellor without autonomy.'

Following a 50-minute meeting between the Vice-Chancellor and Minister of Home Affairs Tun Dr Ismail Abdul Rahman, the latter made it clear that the preservation of law and order was the purview of the Minister of Home Affairs, and not of the Vice-Chancellor. 'University autonomy does not mean immunity from the laws of the country. If a student commits an offence, this autonomy does not give him immunity from the police,' Tun Dr Ismail said.

The pride of MSA—Boeing 737.

B-737 flies in from US

30 July Kuala Lumpur

Malaysia-Singapore Airlines (MSA) received its first Boeing 737. Flying into Paya Lebar Airport, Singapore, from Seattle in the United States, the jetliner was the first of five 737s ordered by MSA. The $14-million aircraft, which seats 85 people, touched down to thunderous applause from more than 100 pilots. The new Boeings will replace MSA's fleet of Comet aircraft.

Malaysians watch moon walk

21 July Kuala Lumpur

Large crowds gathered at the Muzium Negara to listen to a live broadcast as *Apollo 11* astronauts Neil Armstrong and Edwin Aldrin took their first steps on the moon. The museum was holding a 'Man on the Moon' exhibition in conjunction with the historic occasion.

In offices, workers had their ears glued to transistor radios and schools allowed the transmission to be aired over the public address systems. In Penang, the St Xavier's Institution hoisted the Malaysian flag at the moment of the walk in salute to the astronauts.

At exactly 2018 GMT on 20 July (3.48am 21 July Malaysian time), the US lunar module 'Eagle' touched down on the moon's Tranquillity Bay, with the famous words: 'The Eagle has landed.'

1969

world news

Musa resumes studies in Britain

11 September Kuala Lumpur

Inche Musa Hitam, former Assistant Minister to the Deputy Prime Minister, left for Britain to take a course in race relations at the University of Sussex.

He said that since his dismissal from his position as Assistant Minister, he had decided to continue his studies in the wake of the state of emergency and suspension of the Malaysian Parliament. His decision was approved by Umno and his constituents in Segamat.

Tunku Abdul Rahman chatting with US President Nixon at the White House, Washington DC on 13 October.

Inter-dependence Day

28 September Kuala Lumpur

Deputy Prime Minister Tun Abdul Razak suggested an Inter-dependence Day 'because we, as a multiracial nation, owe our independence to the inter-dependence of each and every Malaysian, irrespective of racial origin'.

New anti-litter laws signed

14 November Kuala Lumpur

Litterbugs, watch out. Littering became an offence in the Federal Capital under stringent laws approved by the National Operations Council.

Under the law litterbugs would be fined $500 for the first offence and $1,000 for the second or subsequent offences. The laws were signed by Tun Abdul Razak, who was also Director of Operations. The laws came into effect on 1 December.

Amendments to labour laws

9 October Kuala Lumpur

Officers of political parties can no longer hold office in trade unions under amendments to labour laws which come into immediate effect. Additionally, employers may dismiss labourers for misconduct or suspend them for one week without pay.

In a statement, the National Operations Council said these new amendments were to 'maintain a manageable labour force, attract new investments, create employment and to make possible a more rapid pace of industrialisation.'

Islamic party leader dies

25 October Taiping

The national leader of the Pan-Malaysian Islamic Party, Dr Burhanuddin Al-Helmy (below), 58, died in hospital.

He had been in poor health since his release from detention in 1966 and received medical treatment in Australia in 1967. Top PMIP officials and the Menteris Besar of Kelantan and Perlis, Datuk Mohamed Asri bin Haji Muda and Dato Haji Ahmad Said, attended the funeral at the Malay cemetery in Kota Road.

There's nothing like a chair on a raft to provide some comfort in such dismal surroundings. This is the scene two miles out of Kota Tinggi.

30 killed in Johor flooding

12 December Johor Bahru

Floods which cut a swathe of destruction across Johor—from Segamat in the north to Johor Bahru in the south, and from Mersing in the east to Batu Pahat on the west coast—were among the worst recorded in the State. At the end of the day, the death toll was 30—Kluang, 21 drowned including six children; Segamat, four including a child; Mersing, four and Batu Pahat, a boy.

While flood waters were receding in most parts of Johor, the entire town of Kota Tinggi remained under 8 to 10 feet of water. More than 1,500 residents were forced to flee their homes for relief centres on higher ground.

Meanwhile, in the States of Pahang, Kelantan and Terengganu, the situation was reported to be under control and returning to normal with flood waters subsiding.

Airlines reported heavy bookings for flights from Singapore to Kuala Lumpur owing to disruption of rail services and roads being impassable.

Malay warrior returns—after 70 years

13 December Kuantan

A man claiming to be the legendary warrior Mat Kilau, who defended Pahang against the British at the turn of the century, came out of hiding—at the age of 122. Stating that he had made a vow to the late Sultan Abdullah not to reveal his identity, the man had been living at the 5th Mile Gambang–Kuantan Road all this while under the name of Mat Siam until his grandchildren traced him.

He returned to his kampong, Air Tawar, earlier in the month and was staying with his son Omar, 78, who said that although he was very young when his father fled Pahang, he had been told how to identify him—through a birthmark on his left temple, a mole on his right shoulder and a corn on one of his toes. A week later, Hajjah Wan Yang binte To' Rendah, said to be 118 years old, positively identified the man as Mat Kilau. The daughter of a penghulu (village headman) in Pahang, she claimed to have known Mat Kilau from childhood.

The man who claimed to be Mat Kilau. He was identified by two people.

10,000 estate workers return to India

5 December Taiping

At least 10,000 Indian estate workers applied to return to India. Work permits were to expire on 31 December for unskilled workers and in March for skilled workers. Meanwhile, the secretary-general of the National Union of Plantation Workers, P.P. Narayanan, announced that 52,000 of the 55,000 estate workers had been 'saved by the Government's decision to allow the local born to continue working if they apply for citizenship'. He denied that workers were 'packing up and running away because of work permits', saying some of them were going to India to visit relatives, as was normal at the end of the year.

1970

Tunku Abdul Rahman resigned and Tun Abdul Razak took over as Prime Minister. Tun Razak stressed the need for Malaysia to develop its own identity and adopt an independent international stance. The Government made strides in agriculture and technology: it commissioned the $228-million Muda irrigation scheme (to achieve self-sufficiency in rice), and launched the $9 million Kuantan Satellite Station. The private sector did its part by planning to export 20,000 made-in-Malaysia transistor radios every month. To strengthen national unity the King proclaimed the Rukunegara (National Ideology). Efforts to dig up the past resulted in the discovery of structural remains of an ancient civilisation in Kedah.

FEBRUARY
Japanese Crown Prince Akihito and Crown Princess Michiko visit Malaysia for a seven-day goodwill visit.

APRIL
Malaysia joins the space communications club with the opening of the Kuantan Satellite Station.

JUNE
Fire in Saratok, Sarawak destroys 28 shophouses leaving 250 people homeless.

SEPTEMBER
Tunku Abdul Rahman officially resigns as Prime Minister in a brief and poignant ceremony at the Istana Negara.

June: Troops on river patrol as part of the Bersatu Padu exercise which saw the participation of the armed forces of Malaysia, Singapore, the United Kingdom, Australia and New Zealand.

Malaysia Facts		
10.9 million	Population
$13.1 billion	Gross Domestic Product
$1,169	Gross National Income (per capita)
32.4	Crude Birth Rate (per 1,000 persons)
39.4	Infant Mortality (per 1,000 live births)
61.6 / 65.6	Life Expectancy (male / female)
23.2	Consumer Price Index (base 2010=100)

'The unity we aspire to is not only the unity between races, but unity between economic and social groups.'

Tun Abdul Razak, 26 January 1970.

1970

28 January
Israeli jets attack Cairo.

2 February
Death of philosopher
Bertrand Russell, 98.

1 March
Rhodesia severs its
last ties with the UK,
declaring itself
a racially segregated
country.

5 March
The Nuclear Non-
Proliferation Treaty,
ratified by 43 nations,
takes effect.

6 March
A Japanese, Yuchiro
Miura, skies down
Mount Everest.

18 March
Cambodian PM and
Defence Minister
General Lon Nol ousts
Prince Norodom
Sihanouk of Cambodia
while the latter is on
a visit to Moscow.
Lon Nol begins a terror
campaign against the
400,000 Vietnamese
residents of the
country, and asks for
US aid against the
North Vietnamese.

25 March
The Concorde makes
its first supersonic
flight, reaching
700mph (1,127km/h).

New Year, new uniforms

1 January | **Kuala Lumpur**

Police marched into the New Year with a new look. Gone were the heavily starched khaki shorts, stiff khaki shirts and knee-length socks. They were replaced by more colourful and comfortable uniforms of blue-grey shirts made of more appropriate material and non-crease khaki long trousers. Four days later, on the first day of the new school term, Primary One, Forms One and Lower Six pupils throughout the nation were also to don new uniforms.

Policemen in Kuala Lumpur with the new-look uniform (left) and the old that had been in use since pre-independence days.

Crew jump clear as gas blast rocks drillship

5 January | **Kuala Terengganu**

They went to sea in search of gas, but gas found them instead. The 11,000-ton drillship *Discoverer II*, led by a German captain and an international crew, was prospecting in the sea off Terengganu when a loud explosion, caused by a leaking undersea well, rocked the vessel. The crew jumped ship and were rescued by a supply boat in the choppy waters of the South China Sea. In the best seafarers' tradition, Captain R. Olahagan was the last to abandon ship which was quickly taking in water. He swam quite a distance until he was picked up by a boat and later was airlifted by an RMAF helicopter to the Terengganu Hospital where he was treated for exhaustion.

Vice-President Agnew trying his hand at tapping a rubber tree, watched by (from left) tapper V. Lechumy, Commerce and Industry Minister Inche Mohd Khir Johari and Minister-in-Attendance Tan Sri Khaw Kai Boh (right).

VIP visitors

7 January | **Kuala Lumpur**

US Vice-President Spiro Agnew flew into Subang Airport today on his official aircraft, Air Force Two, for three days as part of a tour of countries in the region. In his entourage were *Apollo 10* astronauts Thomas Stafford and Eugene Cernan. Security precautions for the Vice-President were said to be the tightest that Kuala Lumpur had ever seen. A US Secret Service task force of 70 was complemented by an additional 3,500 men of the Royal Malaysian Police for deployment in the capital.

On 7 May, West German Vice-Chancellor Walter Scheel—also visiting for three days—received a quiet but warm welcome at the Subang Airport led by Deputy Prime Minister Tun Abdul Razak.

The monarch of Saudi Arabia, King Faisal ibn Abdul Aziz al Saud, arrived at Subang Airport on 7 June for a four-day State visit. Malaysia was the first leg of a three-nation tour that took him also to Indonesia and Afghanistan. He later opened the $240,000 Muslim College in Petaling Jaya which was named after him—he had donated $170,000 towards the building cost. The King held informal talks on the setting up of a permanent secretariat for the Conference of Islamic Nations.

A *payung* (umbrella) welcome greeted Canada's Prime Minister Pierre Trudeau on 20 May as he stepped off a Canadian Air Force Boeing 707 at Subang Airport. Met by Prime Minister Tunku Abdul Rahman and other Ministers, Mr Trudeau later held talks with the Tunku on China's security role in the region.

King Faisal with Tunku Abdul Rahman at the Muslim College.

Mr Scheel with Tun Abdul Razak at the Subang Airport VIP room.

Japanese royal couple on goodwill visit

19 February | **Kuala Lumpur**

Crown Prince Akihito and Princess Michiko arrived at Subang Airport for a seven-day goodwill visit to Malaysia. They were received by the Timbalan Yang di-Pertuan Agong and his consort, Prime Minister Tunku Abdul Rahman and Puan Sharifah Rodziah as well as Cabinet Ministers. After inspecting the guard-of-honour, the royal couple bowed and shook hands with one of the longest lines of dignitaries ever to assemble at the airport. That night, the royal couple drove to Istana Negara for an exchange of decorations.

Crown Prince Akihito and Princess Michiko on arrival at Subang Airport.

Mr Trudeau being greeted by Tunku Abdul Rahman—with umbrellas—at Subang Airport.

Ministry takes second look at history

20 January Kuala Lumpur

Was Mat Kilau, who led the Pahang revolt against the British, a hero or a villain? It depends on whom you ask. According to past documentation, he was a traitor. But the Culture, Youth and Sport Ministry thought otherwise.

It felt that Malaysia's history was documented by foreigners 'who did not fully understand the country's historical and cultural backgrounds'. It therefore set up a committee, comprising the Archives Department, Dewan Bahasa dan Pustaka, University of Malaya and the National Museum, to coordinate and review research into Malaysia's past.

Malaysia's first soccer pro

28 January Kuala Lumpur

Malaysia's soccer goalkeeper Chow Chee Keong, 21, turned professional. He signed to play for Hong Kong First Division club Jardine for a monthly salary of HK$2,500 (about $1,300). The contract also included employment with Jardine Trading Company's import department for which he was paid separately.

Goalkeeper Chow leaving for Hong Kong from Subang Airport.

Gift 'dragons' from Jakarta

5 March Kuala Lumpur

A pair of Komodo dragons, presented by Indonesia to the people of Malaysia as a gesture of goodwill, made Zoo Negara the fourth in the world to possess these rare, ferocious and carnivorous reptiles.

Indonesia's gift of Komodo dragons to Zoo Negara.

Think afresh, Malaysians told

27 January Kuala Lumpur

Think afresh, said Prime Minister Tunku Abdul Rahman and Director of Operations of the National Operations Council Tun Abdul Razak, to the 66 members of the newly constituted National Consultative Council. The joint plea was for the purpose of constructing 'a political framework on an unshakeable and sound foundation'. Ignoring his physician's advice to stay in bed because of a leg ailment, the Tunku remained seated while making his historic 15-minute speech in which he gave an assurance that the country would return to parliamentary democracy as soon as tensions among the different races were eliminated.

Tun Razak, in appealing to people to rededicate themselves to certain ideals that transcended race, religion, culture, class and political affiliations, stated that racial issues could no longer be swept under the carpet but must be confronted. 'Secret' meetings, he added, would enable all to express their view freely and 'only by expressing our views frankly and fully can we ever hope to arrive at any solution to these difficult and complex problems.'

$228m Muda irrigation project

17 January Alor Star ▶ Boasting a string of superlatives, Malaysia's largest engineering project had come into operation, the *Straits Times Annual* said. Controlled by computer, the Muda irrigation project brought water to 250,000 acres of rice fields, changing the lives of 60,000 farming families. Two dams, on the Pedu River and the Muda River, were built to create lakes of 25 square miles and 10 square miles respectively.

The Muda project, which enabled double cropping for the first time in the area, was one of several designed to make Malaysia self-sufficient in rice. In November, it was announced that West Malaysian farmers were already producing about 190,000 of the 1,034,000 tons of rice required for consumption this year.

Giant pipe being installed for the Muda irrigation scheme.

Baby born on Thai Airways plane

22 January Kuala Lumpur

There were 89 passengers on board the Thai Airways flight that took off from Bangkok, but there were 90 when it landed in Kuala Lumpur.

The extra passenger was a bouncy baby boy born to Gochan Kaur and delivered 29,000 feet above Songkhla.

The extra passenger, who was named Tharminder Singh, was the toast of the crew and the passengers.

For many years afterwards, Thai Airways staff threw a birthday party for Tharminder, his parents and their friends.

Border shoot-out with terrorists

7 February Alor Star

A group of 14 Communist terrorists in the Weng district of Southern Thailand fled into the jungle after a gun battle with a joint Malaysian–Thai police patrol.

Security forces recovered a radio and some food left behind by the terrorists, two of whom were women. More troops were being sent to 'sensitive' border areas that were being threatened by the terrorists.

Three days later Communist slogans were found on the walls and blackboards of an English-medium school here.

1970

world news

10 April
Paul McCartney announces the break-up of the Beatles, and the release of his solo album.

13 April
An oxygen tank explodes during *Apollo 13*'s flight to the moon, forcing the mission to abort. The crew and ship return to earth safely after completing makeshift repairs guided by Houston.

24 April
China launches its first satellite.

29 April
US and South Vietnamese forces invade Cambodia to hunt for the Vietcong.

15 May
South Africa is excluded from the Olympics.

17 May
Thor Heyerdahl sets sail from Morocco across the Atlantic in a papyrus boat *Ra II*.

31 May
An earthquake triggers a landslide that buries more than 47,000 inhabitants of the town of Yungay, Peru.

21 June
Death of former Indonesian President Sukarno, 69.

Sultan slams striptease shows

2 February Petaling Jaya

The Sultan of Selangor, acting on numerous complaints over 'very daring' strip shows in nightclubs, said he had witnessed some of them first-hand and concluded that such 'indecent performances would ruin the outlook or the image of the country where the official religion is Islam'.

He suggested that such shows either be held at other venues and not at leading hotels whose guests included Muslims, or be replaced with cultural dances for foreign tourists who frequent nightclubs.

Two weeks later, after a meeting of representatives from leading hotels and Government departments, licensing conditions for such acts were tightened. New regulations prohibited provocative gestures and under-21s were barred from strip joints.

Singer Susan Lim and members of the well-known Singapore band, The Crescendos.

Crescendos singer still missing at sea

8 February Kemaman

One of Singapore's top recording artistes and lead singer of The Crescendos, Susan Lim, 22, was believed to have drowned after being swept away by huge waves while on Chinese New Year holiday here.

The body of Lau Kheng Khuang, 49, the uncle of her fiancé, was recovered. The five other holiday-makers in the party were safe.

On 13 March, it was announced that Susan, whose body had still not been found, had gained an honours degree in social science from the University of Singapore.

Goodwill Council named

12 February Kuala Lumpur

Tunku Abdul Rahman named the 51 members of the National Goodwill Council of which he was chairman. Among the members 'from all walks of life' were representatives of political parties, Menteris Besar or Chief Ministers (State Goodwill Council chairmen) and Ministers. Pressmen named included former *Straits Times* editor-in-chief Tan Sri L.C. Hoffman, *Straits Times* news editor Felix Abisheganaden and *Utusan Melayu* editor-in-chief Melan Abdullah.

The Labour Party and Party Rakyat, which were not represented, announced that they would boycott the council. The next day, the Malaysian Trades Union Congress and Malaysian Youth Council expressed 'extreme disappointment' over the exclusion of trade union and youth representatives.

'Gentleman' thug gets 35 years' jail, caning

13 March Kuala Lumpur

Described as one of the best-dressed criminals in the region, 'Gentleman' thug Lai See Kiow was jailed for a total of 35 years and given three strokes of the rotan after pleading guilty to three charges of armed robbery, one with a grenade. Lai, apparently, always wore a tie and jacket when 'not on the job'.

Malay businessmen 'do not want sympathy'

26 February Ipoh

Malay businessmen need no mollycoddling, said the Perak Malay Chamber of Commerce. What they needed instead was cooperation and understanding from their non-Malay counterparts, said its president Ismail bin Abdul Majid, adding that the Malays, in their quest to play a more active role in the economic development of the country, did not want sympathy or to be spoon-fed.

He was speaking at the inaugural meeting of the Perak Sino-Malay cooperative economic advisory board. The board was seen as a milestone in the history of the Chinese and Malay chambers of commerce in Perak for its role in forging racial unity.

Inche Ismail also expressed the hope that the board would carry out its duty to promote unity via economic cooperation.

Anita Serawak

1 February

Anita Serawak, the daughter of the famed Malay actress Siput Sarawak, was achieving fame as a nightclub singer.

The husky-voiced songstress, who later changed the spelling of her name to Sarawak like her mother, performed her songs in English, Japanese, Chinese and French, as well as Malay.

More bite for ACA

23 February Kuala Lumpur

New laws came into force empowering the Anti-Corruption Agency (ACA) to freeze any ill-gotten gains of MPs, State Assemblymen and civil servants. The ordinance gave the ACA director the authority to demand a declaration of assets if it was believed they were obtained by corrupt means. Minister of Home Affairs Tun Dr Ismail bin Abdul Rahman explained that the new laws were necessary because 'the ACA was severely handicapped by loopholes in the Prevention of Corruption Act, 1961.' The penalty for corruption was doubled to a maximum of 14 years' jail.

Border treaty puts more heat on Reds

7 March Bangkok

A new Thai–Malaysian border agreement allowing greater military participation in efforts to eliminate Communist terrorists was signed by Deputy Prime Minister Tun Abdul Razak and Thai Armed Forces Chief-of-Staff Air Chief Marshal Tun Dawee Chullasapya.

The new agreement, while retaining the existing limit of five miles on 'hot pursuit' of the enemy into each other's territory, extended the length of time forces could remain in foreign territory from 24 hours to 72. The two countries hitherto had depended mainly on their own police forces for suppression of Communist terrorism.

Teachers rush to brush up on BM

17 March Kuala Lumpur

Teachers were rushing to re-learn Bahasa Malaysia, with some being turned away from special classes being conducted by the National Union of Teachers (NUT) owing to the lack of places.

Under the New Education Policy in force this year, all subjects in Standard One were being taught completely in Bahasa Malaysia while more subjects in Standard Four were being taught in the language. In January, 360 teachers from West Malaysia attended a three-month course at the Language Institute in Pantai Valley.

The NUT president, Mr Gurnam Singh, was taking the course 'to prepare myself for further changes in the coming years.'

Protest at US rubber dumping

5 March Kuala Lumpur

Natural rubber-producing countries, including Malaysia, agreed to make a joint protest to the US Government over its intended release of 169,000 tons of its rubber stockpile. The Malaysian rubber market became erratic, falling to 60¾ cents but recovering slightly to close at 61¾, a quarter cent over the previous day's close. Dealers felt a strong market had helped to cushion the initial effects of the US announcement. On 3 September, a Customs duties order on forward contracts was revoked to boost rubber export earnings and minimise market speculation. National Operations Council Director of Operations Tun Abdul Razak explained that a fall of one cent in the price of rubber would lead to a considerable loss in foreign exchange. This step, recommended by the Finance Ministry, was designed to ensure rubber prices remain stable at a 'fairly reasonable level'.

Treaty of Friendship with Indonesia

16 March Kuala Lumpur

Indonesia's President Suharto, in Malaysia for a three-day State visit, was given an assurance by the Timbalan Yang di-Pertuan Agong, the Sultan of Kedah, that 'no force on earth can disrupt our existing relations'.

The next day, in a brief ceremony in the Cabinet Room of the Prime Minister's Department, a Treaty of Friendship between the two countries was signed by Deputy Prime Minister Tun Abdul Razak, and Indonesia's Foreign Minister Adam Malik.

The treaty of economic, cultural and social cooperation replaced one signed in 1959. Also signed was an agreement concerning the demarcation of the territorial seas of the two nations with Tun Abdul Razak stating: 'The Straits [of Malacca] are historic, and embody the eternal link between our two nations which has never been and will never be severed by sea or history.'

Prime Minister Tunku Abdul Rahman shaking hands with President Suharto of Indonesia after the signing of a treaty by Tun Abdul Razak and Mr Adam Malik.

Forfeited: Part of MB's $1m assets

17 March Kuala Lumpur

The High Court ordered the forfeiture of assets worth $324,979—out of a total of $1,138,403—belonging to Perak Menteri Besar Datuk Sri Haji Ahmad bin Said under the Emergency (Essential Powers) Ordinance No. 22, 1970. Mr Justice Raja Azlan Shah ruled that the assets, in the form of fees, shares and dividends, were acquired in connection with corrupt practices, adding that the respondent was guilty of 'most atrociously dishonest conduct.' Two days later, Datuk Sri Haji Ahmad resigned as Menteri Besar.

Magazine

Beauties and the bra-less rumour

5 April Ipoh

Only six girls turned up for the Miss Perak-Universe contest after rumours that contestants would have to parade in dresses without brassières.

'Inadequate' prizes were also blamed for the poor turn-out. Miss Josephine Lena Wong, 18, a 36-24-36½ car sales representative, won the title.

She later won the Miss Malaysia-Universe contest and became the first Malaysian beauty to reach the semi-final stage of the world competition.

Miss Perak-Universe Josephine Lena Wong flanked by runners-up Jenny Cubinar (left) and Nancy Cheah.

New Zealander retains Selangor Grand Prix title

5 April Batu Tiga

New Zealand's Graeme Lawrence, 29, won the Selangor Grand Prix for the second successive year at the Batu Tiga Circuit. This was a second triumph after winning the Singapore Grand Prix, also for the second time, last week. Lawrence in his red 2.4-litre Ferrari Dino V6 covered the 60 laps (about 126 miles) in 1hr 45:5 on a wet track, two laps ahead of Hong Kong's John MacDonald in a Brabham FVA.

Bonanza for barbers from 'hippies'

10 April Johor Bahru

Barbers here were reaping the benefits of Singapore's clampdown on foreign hippies. Long-haired, unshaven tourists were making stops at barber shops in town before proceeding to the Causeway.

The previous day immigration officials in Singapore began denying entry to people with beards or long hair, saying they looked like hippies and were deemed 'a danger to the social environment'.

The tourists were turned away despite having the necessary documents. Although the barbers were pleased by the new policy, the tourists were not. One, initially turned away at the border, returned shaven and shorn and was greeted with a broad smile, he said.

Undercover fashion

2 April Kuala Lumpur

In what was described as one of the most extravagant shows seen in the country, 14 models and seven dancers emphasised the 'near-nude' look at the Triumph '70 international underwear fashion show. Flesh-tone undergarments were introduced at the show, including clingy brassière and girdle sets which looked sprayed on.

The batik art of Khalil Ibrahim

Batik painting remains a strong challenge to the talents of any artist. Some painters, sensing the difficulties, have not even tried. One painter who faced up to the problems and declined to be daunted in wrestling with the medium is Khalil Ibrahim, 35, according to an article in the *Straits Times Annual*.

His contribution to batik art is a personal achievement. Marked by distinctive style, independence and individuality of approach, and an ever-widening experimentation with colour, the great variety and interest of his themes has extended the whole range of batik painting.

He broke new ground in local art when he attempted pieces with religious themes, which caused a mild sensation with several art patrons who clamoured to buy them.

Khalil broke new ground in local art.

Below: The art innovation that broke new ground in Malaysia with its religious theme. The picture is 'The Last Supper' rendered in batik.

1970

world news

21 June
Brazil defeats Italy 4–1 to win the World Cup in Mexico City.

28 June
US troops withdraw from Cambodia.

7 September
After an assassination attempt against him, King Hussein of Jordan orders the expulsion of the PLO and Palestinians to Lebanon. Syria invades on 20 September, but withdraws after threats from the US and Israel.

18 September
Guitarist Jimi Hendrix dies in London from an overdose of barbiturates.

28 September
Egyptian President Gamal Abdul Nasser, 52, dies from a heart attack. An estimated five million people attend his funeral. Anwar Sadat is named the acting President.

8 October
Russian Alexander Solzhenitsyn is awarded the Nobel Prize for Literature.

9 October
Cambodia changes its name to the Khmer Republic.

Reds booby trap flags

23 April Kuala Lumpur

Seven people, including five police and a forest ranger, were injured when they tore down booby-trapped flags put up in various towns by the Malayan Communist Party (MCP).

Police launched operations against the Communist terrorists in seven States—Selangor, Negeri Sembilan, Malacca, Johor, Pahang, Perak and Kedah—and picked up large quantities of Red pamphlets, hammer-and-sickle flags and Mao Zedong banners.

The 1,000 who can't go home

5 May Sungai Buloh

About 1,000 people, completely cured of leprosy, were still at the National Leprosy Control Centre here—just because of prejudice. Members of the public were apparently slow to accept the rapid advances being made in the treatment of leprosy patients. Permanent secretary to the Ministry of Health Raja Zainal Abidin bin Raja Haji Tachik said that the cured patients would return home if only a welcome hand were stretched out to them.

First woman engineering student

11 May Kuala Lumpur

The University of Malaya Engineering Faculty received its very first female undergraduate. Miss Tan Lee, 20, was the only girl among the 128 freshmen who joined the faculty today.

Some males appeared not keen to have their domain invaded. Miss Tan said they tried to scare her away by drawing a tough picture about the course. And her brave retaliation was: 'What a man can do, a woman can do—perhaps better.'

Malaysia joins the satellite 'club'

6 April Kuantan

The launching of the $9 million Kuantan Satellite Station in Beserah heralded Malaysia's entry into the space communications club. The satellite initially linked the country with India, Ceylon, Pakistan, Indonesia, Australia, Japan, Europe and the United Kingdom. Kuantan was chosen as the site as it provided a favourable 'look angle' towards the Pacific as well as towards the Indian Ocean (*Intelsat III*) satellite.

At the launch, Malaysian television viewers saw the country's first live telecast—a 25-minute broadcast of the Expo 70 in Osaka relayed by the Japan Broadcasting Corporation. Malaysia in turn telecast a 15-minute cultural and musical programme to Japan through the Kuantan ground station. Minister of Works, Posts and Telecommunications Tun V.T. Sambanthan said gross revenue from external telecommunications services had grown from almost $6 million in 1964 to $14 million.

Tunku Abdul Rahman officiates at the launching of the station.

Magazine

Tengku Bahiyah, daughter of the first Yang di-Pertuan Agong, Tuanku Abdul Rahman, adorns the cover of the October 1970 *Wanita* magazine.

Thomas Cup draws the crowds

18 May Kuala Lumpur

The Thomas Cup, insured for $12,000, attracted large crowds at the Royal Selangor Golf Club where it was on display to publicise the finals at Stadium Negara from 28 May to 6 June. Under constant watch by two security guards, the 31-year-old trophy was also to be exhibited at the Selangor Club, Subang Airport and Stadium Negara. Malaysia entered the finals on 5 June but lost to Indonesia 7–2. Indonesian Minister of Information Dr Budiardjo said the Cup would be deposited with the Indonesian Central Bank as a national treasure.

Badminton's 1-1-1 tally for Malaysia

21 July Edinburgh

Badminton was the only sport to deliver medals for Malaysia at the 1970 Commonwealth Games—one gold, silver and bronze. Ng Boon Bee and Punch Gunalan won Malaysia's only gold, beating compatriots Tan Soon Hooi and Ng Tat Wei 15–3, 15–3 in the men's doubles badminton final. Rosalind Ang and Teoh Siew Yong won the women's doubles bronze medal when they beat fellow Malaysians Sylvia Ng and Sylvia Tan 15–2, 12–15, 15–10.

Some fishy business in jungle 'battles'

16 June Kuala Lumpur

Troops taking part in the Bersatu Padu ('Solid Unity') military exercise were beginning to learn about jungle warfare as they started patrols into the Terengganu jungles.

The much-publicised exercise was meant to demonstrate that Commonwealth nations would give military support to Malaysia and Singapore in the event of an attack by foreign forces, in the light of the British pullout from Singapore next year. The armed forces of Malaysia, Singapore, the United Kingdom, Australia and New Zealand were involved.

They were meant to be pursuing soldiers from the fictitious country of Ganasia infiltrating Malaysia through Terengganu. Thus much of the hunt took place in the jungle, in a Vietnam-like scenario created by the battle planners.

Serious business this may be, but as a letter to the editor of *The Straits Times* indicated, something fishy was going on, aside from the Ganasians: rations meant for the British troops in Bersatu Padu were being sold in the black market.

These presumably tax-free goods were being sold for profit in Kuala Terengganu, the letter writer claimed.

A tin of biscuits was going for $5, he wrote, and other tinned foods, as well as cocoa and chocolate, were also available.

The troops on river patrol.

Made-in-Penang radios for export

19 June Penang

More than 20,000 Penang-made transistor radios were scheduled for export every month. Aimed at the US market, the radios were being manufactured and assembled by Penang Electronics Sdn Bhd, a company wholly owned by the Penang State Development Corporation.

Abusive word that led to murder

8 June Klang

Calling someone a 'bastard' constitutes 'grave and sudden provocation', Mr Justice Datuk Abdul Hamid ruled.

Teacher Boran Suleiman was sentenced to 33 months' in jail after pleading guilty to killing his brother-in-law Othman Musa for using the 'abusive' term in reference to him.

Othman died of his injuries three days after he was stabbed in the stomach by Boran during an argument.

A plaque depicting the Malaysian tin industry. It was worked in high tin-content pewter by artist Yan Sook Leong and presented to the Malaysian Embassy in Washington for display in its new building.

Remains of ancient civilisation uncovered

25 July Kuala Lumpur

Structural remains of an ancient civilisation that existed in Kedah from the 6th century to the 14th century were found by a team from the National Museum. The site, located near the foot of Gunung Jerai, was named Chandi (Tomb Temple) Telaga Sembilan.

It was outside the Bujang Valley where more than 30 other 'chandi' had been discovered over the past few years.

Saratok shophouses razed

11 June Kuching

A pre-dawn fire destroyed 28 wooden shophouses in the Sarawak town of Saratok, leaving 250 people homeless. No casualties were reported and the cause of the fire was unknown. About 2,000 people turned out to help the PWD douse the fire and prevent it from spreading to two more rows of shophouses. Initial loss was estimated at $784,000.

Rukunegara proclaimed by King

31 August Kuala Lumpur

The five principles of the Rukunegara (National Ideology), intended to help in building a strong and united nation, were proclaimed by the Yang di-Pertuan Agong. In a National Day broadcast, the king listed the five 'musts' as: Belief in God, Loyalty to King and country, Upholding the Constitution, Rule of Law, and Good Behaviour and Morality. The Rukunegara was drafted by the Department of National Unity to balance economic development with good values.

Tunku Abdul Rahman receives the Darjah Utama Seri Mahkota Negara (DMN) from the King.

Nation's highest award for Tunku

2 September Kuala Lumpur

The Darjah Utama Seri Mahkota Negara (DMN), the nation's highest award, was conferred on Prime Minster Tunku Abdul Rahman by the Yang di-Pertuan Agong at Istana Negara. The DMN is normally reserved for Rulers, heads of foreign missions and other distinguished persons.

At the same ceremony, which was witnessed by Cabinet Ministers, the Prime Minister's wife Puan Sharifah Rodziah received the country's second highest award, the Darjah Seri Maharaja Mangku Negara (SMN), which carries the title Tun. She was the third woman to receive the award, the first two being the first and third Rajas Permaisuri Agong.

First nationwide population census

24 August Kuala Lumpur

Travellers, hotel guests and even the homeless and beggars sleeping on five-foot ways were accounted for in the first Malaysia-wide population census.

Besides other particulars, enumerators also noted the details of all individuals who spent the night in each household from midnight to seven in the morning.

More than 22,000 enumerators were scheduled to visit households throughout the country over 12 days during the exercise.

Tunku resigns as PM

22 September Kuala Lumpur

In a brief, poignant ceremony at 9.20am at Istana Negara, Tunku Abdul Rahman handed his letter of resignation as Prime Minister to the new Yang di-Pertuan Agong, Tuanku Abdul Halim Mu'adzam Shah.

This was the first official function of the Agong. He received the letter in the Throne Room of the Istana, where he was sworn in as the Paramount Ruler on 21 September.

Minutes later, Deputy Prime Minister Tun Abdul Razak entered the room escorted by the Grand Chamberlain. The King handed Tun Razak his letter of appointment as the nation's new leader. In his maiden speech to a special Umno meeting at the Dewan Bahasa dan Pustaka barely 20 minutes after receiving his letter of appointment, Tun Razak stressed the need for the nation to develop its own identity and to show an independent stance in its relations with other countries.

Citing the Rukunegara as the 'signpost and guide' to all Malaysians for a genuinely united and progressive nation, he also announced Home Affairs Minister Tun Dr Ismail bin Dato Abdul Rahman as his deputy.

The Tunku chairs his last Cabinet meeting at Parliament House on 21 September.

Saffron rice blessing for new PM

22 September Kuala Lumpur

Minister of Social Welfare and Wanita Umno leader Tan Sri Fatimah Hashim 'showered' Tun Razak with saffron rice to wish him good luck as Prime Minister. The specially-convened Umno meeting at the Dewan Bahasa dan Pustaka after Tun Razak received his letter of appointment was attended by more than 400 Umno leaders, including MPs, State Assemblymen and divisional chairmen from all over the country. They also bade farewell to former Prime Minister Tunku Abdul Rahman, who called on party members to give their fullest support and loyalty to Tun Razak just as they had given to him.

Dr Mahathir Mohamad's landmark book, *The Malay Dilemma*, published in 1970, was banned by the Government. The ban was lifted in 1981 (*see 12 May 1997*).

1970

10 October
Quebec Vice Premier Pierre Laporte is kidnapped by the FLQ (Fédération de Libération de Québec), Canadian French separatists. He is found dead a week later.

24 October
Salvador Allende is elected President of Chile.

9 November
Charles de Gaulle, 80, dies. He was head of the Free French forces during World War II, and President of France from 1958 to 1969.

13 November
A cyclone hits East Pakistan, killing 250,000 people.

7 December
During a visit to Warsaw, West German Chancellor Willy Brandt goes down on his knees in front of the monument to the victims of the Warsaw Ghetto.

UN envoy Ramani dies of heart attack

30 September | New York

Malaysian Ambassador R. Ramani died of a heart attack in his suite at the Waldorf Towers.

Despite his failing health, Mr Ramani, 70, had travelled to the UN General Assembly session in case the Philippines raised the question of sovereignty over Sabah. He was an expert on the subject.

An Indian who became a citizen of Malaysia, Mr Ramani was an internationally renowned lawyer who turned late to diplomacy, partly at the urging of Prime Minister Tunku Abdul Rahman, who appointed him to the United Nations as Malaysia's Permanent Representative. Mr Ramani gained wide acclaim in this role, particularly for his deft handling of the presidency of the Security Council during the Dominican Republic crisis in 1965.

'Rompin town won't die'

16 November | Rompin

Prime Minister Tun Abdul Razak flew in by Nuri helicopter from Kuantan to reassure some 1,200 retrenched workers of the closed Rompin mine that their town would not die. Their mining town, he pledged, would be the nucleus for the giant Pahang Tenggara land scheme, and alternative jobs would be found for them through rehabilitation projects. As an immediate measure, the Government took over the running of Bukit Ibam at the mine site and began a $1-million power supply project.

'Bakat TV' debuts

25 November | Kuala Lumpur

TV Malaysia's first talent contest was aired—and became an instant hit. *Bakat TV* featured 12 contestants each week. More than 1,000 entries were received but only 144 were shortlisted for the 12 heats scheduled. In the grand finale 12 finalists would compete for the top three prizes of $5,000, $3,000 and $1,000.

Town sitting on $20m tin field

19 November | Ipoh

Plans were announced to relocate Papan town, situated on an estimated $20-million tin field, and give compensation and new homes to its 3,000 residents. Rights to about 80 acres, including the town, were given to a mining company. A new town, with modern conveniences for residents, was expected to be built at a cost of $2 million. Papan, a one-street town that came into existence about 100 years earlier was surrounded by several rich mines.

The *Bunga Raya* gets a grand send-off as it leaves for its first voyage to Europe.

Sailing into maritime history

9 December | Kuala Lumpur ▶ The Malaysian International Shipping Corporation (MISC) Berhad swung into full commercial operations with its flagship, the MV *Bunga Raya*, making her maiden voyage for the national shipping line's Far East–European service. Heralding Malaysia's emergence as a maritime nation, the 14,500-ton cargo liner was the first of 11 to be built by Sumitomo Shipbuilding in Japan. The second, the MV *Bunga Melor*, was launched on 25 November at the Uraga dockyard, south of Tokyo. Puan Sharifah Rodziah, wife of Tunku Abdul Rahman, launched the first vessel while Toh Puan Tan Siew Sin, wife of the Finance Minister, launched the second by cracking a bottle of holy water, rather than champagne, on the ship's bows.

Cycling gold at Asian Games

17 December | Bangkok

Malaysia struck gold at last on the eighth day of the Asian Games—and from the least expected source, cycling. Last-minute selection Dawod Ibrahim won the 1,600m massed-start gold medal. Team manager Amerik Singh explained that Dawod had been substituted for Fadzil Ibrahim 'because Dawod was hitting his peak form. We're glad we made the right decision.' Dawod, a Customs officer, said: 'I'm so happy to have won. I had hopes. I'm a little surprised, of course, that it turned out to be a gold.'

Two days later, Malaysia made a sweep of four more golds, led by another cyclist Ng Joo Ngan, who was victorious in the 200km road race. The crowning glory came from Malaysia's badminton team which netted three golds—Punch Gunalan won the singles and doubles partnering Ng Boon Bee, who in turn teamed up with Sylvia Ng for the mixed doubles title.

Jets bomb Red hideouts

26 November | Kuching

Three Royal Malaysian Air Force Tebuan jets begun strikes against Communist terrorist hideouts in Sarawak, dropping more than 8,000lb of bombs.

Rounds of ammunition were also dropped in two areas so that ground forces could mount follow-up operations against weakened Communist resistance.

This was the first time that RMAF jets taking off from the Kuantan base in Peninsular Malaysia had given air support in East Malaysia.

Museum's gift from Swettenham's widow

13 December | Kuala Lumpur

Muzium Negara inherited a valuable collection of gold and silver Malayan objets d'art from the widow of Sir Frank Swettenham.

In her will, Lady Vera Seton Swettenham, who died in September, said she wanted the museum to have 'all my Malayan silver, gold and black enamel chutan objets d'art, my three Malay sarongs, the engraved gold-topped walking stick presented to my late husband by a Sultan during his governorship of the FMS and my silver kris head.'

1971

The nation recorded several 'firsts'—the first free trade zone was set up in Penang, P.G. Lim became the first woman to be appointed ambassador and the first licensed Casino opened its doors in Genting Highlands—and Punch Gunalan and Ng Boon Bee recaptured the men's doubles title at the All England badminton championship. To help build national unity and ensure 'peace, stability and happiness', the Federal Constitution was amended to place beyond challenge several issues of a sensitive nature. These included citizenship rights, the position of the national language and the use of other languages, the special position of the Malays, the legitimate interests of non-Malays, and the sovereignty of the Rulers.

FEBRUARY
Tuanku Abdul Halim Mu'adzam Shah, Sultan of Kedah, is installed as the fifth Yang di-Pertuan Agong.

MAY
Malaysia's only licensed casino opens at Genting Highlands.

JULY
Tun Abdul Razak unveils the $14.35-billion Second Development Plan designed to 'steer Malaysians through a crucial stage in the nation's history'.

HIGHLIGHTS SECOND MALAYSIA PLAN

SEPTEMBER
Nurses picket in front of the Health Ministry for equal pay and to protest against having to pay for their own lodgings.

January: The Secretariat building in Kuala Lumpur at the height of the floods that inundated much of the city.

'This pagoda is a monument of our Government's policy of freedom of religion.'

Alliance party secretary-general Tan Sri T.H. Tan, at the placement of the International Pagoda, 10 May 1971.

1971

world news

13 January
The 1964 Gulf of Tonkin resolution, which amounts to a declaration of war against North Vietnam, is repealed by the US Congress.

22 January
The Khmer Rouge shells Phnom Penh for the first time.

25 January
Idi Amin deposes Milton Obote and becomes President of Uganda.

3 February
OPEC decides to set oil prices without consulting buyers.

6 February
Astronaut Alan Shepard hits a golf ball on the moon.

13 February
Backed by US air and artillery support, South Vietnamese troops invade Laos.

15 February
Pounds, shillings and pence give way to decimal currency in the UK.

20 February
In Athens, youths protest against the Government forcing them to cut their long hair.

Wet, wet Kuala Lumpur

5 January Kuala Lumpur

Non-stop torrential rain brought the Federal Capital to a standstill as large sections of the city were flooded, from Cheras in the south to Segambut in the north. Many places were in several feet of water. Elsewhere, except for Penang, Kedah and Perlis, the entire country was flooded. Nationwide, thousands of people had to leave their homes and at least 22 were killed.

Prime Minister Tun Abdul Razak proclaimed a state of national disaster and ordered the setting up of emergency headquarters to deal with the situation.

All military and police vehicles were deployed to help victims. Singapore offered medical teams and helicopter services and US air force transport planes flew in flood relief equipment from Vietnam.

Public transport was disrupted and electricity supply was cut off. Radio Malaysia's English Service went off the air due to 'technical difficulties'.

In Klang Road, almost 60 crocodiles escaped from a farm in Hock Ann estate at the height of the floods. Ten were caught by youths but the rest remained on the loose.

Central Kuala Lumpur is awash—the Secretariat building, Supreme Court, municipal building and St Mary's church all stand in five to six feet of water.

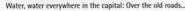

Water, water everywhere in the capital: Over the old roads...

Lat's view: Some flood victims took advantage of the Government's subsequent compensation policy.

Oldest evidence of Islam in Malaysia

19 January Kuala Lumpur

The Terengganu Stone inscription, the oldest evidence of Islam in the country, would be 668 years old on 22 February, according to the calculations of Prof Dr Syed Naguib al-Attas after months of painstaking research.

He was convinced that the date of the inscription was 22 February 1303. The stone inscription was discovered half-buried in the Tersat River near Kuala Berang after a flood in 1887.

The 33-inch-high stone, weighing 400–500lb, was used as a pedestal in a mosque and later in an old Malay fort in Bukit Puteri near the mouth of the river before scholars realised its significance.

The inscription on one face of the 33in stone found in Terengganu.

Quake shock in 12 towns

4 February Kuala Lumpur

Earth tremors caused thousands to panic in at least a dozen towns in West Malaysia and in Singapore. Thousands of people fled outdoors shortly after 11pm in the Federal Capital, Petaling Jaya, Penang, Taiping, Telok Anson, Jasin, Alor Gajah, Malacca, Ulu Kinta, Kuantan, Tanjung Malim and Johor Bahru.

The US National Earthquake Centre reported a major earthquake off the west coast of Sumatra at 11.05pm West Malaysian time.

First free trade zone

16 March Kuala Lumpur

Finance Minister Tun Tan Siew Sin told the Dewan Rakyat, during the debate on the Free Trade Zones Bill 1971, that Penang would get the country's first free trade zone. He said the people of Penang should not lament the end of its free-port status as this was given when entrepôt trade was the island's only means of livelihood.

Constitution amended

3 March Kuala Lumpur

The Dewan Rakyat approved the controversial Constitutional (Amendment) Bill to entrench fundamental guarantees in the Constitution.

The Bill would place beyond challenge several sensitive issues: citizenship, the national language and the use of other languages, the special position of the Malays, legitimate interests of non-Malays and sovereignty of the Rulers. The vote was 125 for to 17 against.

The next day, Penang Chief Minister and Gerakan leader Dr Lim Chong Eu gave his party's emphatic support to the Bill. 'The fundamental question is whether or not we are to have unity and peace, stability and happiness,' he said. After giving 'careful, thorough, responsible and sincere consideration' to the amendments, he said: 'Unless we take firm and resolute action today, the survival of Malaysia will be jeopardised by those who seek to destroy our nation.'

Malaysian teenagers just too shy

20 January Kuala Lumpur

David Cutler, an 18-year-old Australian student who was holidaying in Singapore and Malaysia for six weeks, expressed surprise at how shy Malaysian teenagers were.

'I think the girls here are very pretty but every time I try making conversation with any of them, it's like talking to a blank wall,' he said.

He added that he found girls here, especially those educated locally, narrow-minded and unwilling to explore the way of life of other people.

'Asian girls who are studying overseas are different. They are able to mix well and have a broader outlook,' he said. 'Topics on the Pill, abortion, politics, books, theatre and religion are some of the things discussed freely in our teenage groups.'

Tenders no longer depend only on price

28 February Klang

Only contractors with a labour force reflecting the racial composition of the country would now be awarded tenders for Government projects, said Selangor Menteri Besar Datuk Harun Idris. He said tenders would no longer automatically be given to the contractor with the lowest bid. This was to encourage employers to take in more Malay workers, projecting the multiracial image of Malaysia.

UN post goes to first woman ambassador

17 March Kuala Lumpur

Ms P.G. Lim, a Kuala Lumpur lawyer, was appointed Malaysia's Deputy Permanent Representative at the United Nations, the country's first woman ambassador, Prime Minister Tun Abdul Razak announced.

Ms Lim, a member of the former National Consultative Council, had represented Malaysia in the UN on previous occasions. Tun Razak said her knowledge of the law and experience in politics and diplomacy made her suitable for the post.

$6,000 up in 'Smoke'

15 March Kuala Lumpur

Police booked owners and drivers of 122 motor vehicles and collected a total of $6,000 in fines at the start of Gerakan Asap (Operation Smoke) which was aimed at vehicles emitting excessive exhaust fumes.

Television for Sarawak

15 April Kuching

Information Minister Tan Sri Ghazali Shafie said the Government had given much thought to TV in Sarawak and that an examination was on-going with the Economic Planning Unit. If a definite purpose could be established for introducing TV to the State, the Government would have to find the money for it, he added.

The Minister was in Sarawak for the opening of the Limbang station of Radio Sarawak.

Fifth Agong installed

20 February Kuala Lumpur

Kedah's Sultan Tuanku Abdul Halim Mu'adzam Shah ibni Al-marhum Sultan Badlishah, a nephew of Tunku Abdul Rahman, was installed as the fifth Yang di-Pertuan Agong. About 600 dignitaries witnessed the solemn and stately ceremony.

Danish domination in badminton ends

27 March Wembley

Punch Gunalan and Ng Boon Bee recaptured the men's doubles title for Malaysia after four years of Danish domination when they beat Rudy Hartono and Indra Gunawan of Indonesia in the final of the All England badminton championship.

Increase in accident rate

6 April Kuala Lumpur

About 70 per cent of accidents in Selangor in March took place in the Federal Capital. They were mostly due to motorists jumping red lights, speeding, not keeping to their proper lanes and driving too slowly, said the Selangor traffic police chief Supt Abdul Ghani bin Abdul Rahman.

Tunku Abdul Rahman addressing the Umno general assembly at the Merlin Hotel in Kuala Lumpur on 25 January, with (sitting from left) Tun Abdul Razak, Senu Abdul Rahman and Mohamed Khir Johari.

1971

world news

1 March
A dissident group explodes a bomb in a men's room in the White House to protest against US intrusion into Laos.

1 March
Pakistan President Agha Muhammad Yahya Khan postpones indefinitely sessions of the National Assembly, prompting widespread civil disobedience in East Pakistan.

8 March
Joe Frazier beats Muhammad Ali for the heavyweight boxing title.

25 March
East Pakistan breaks away from West Pakistan.

13 June
The *New York Times* begins publishing the 'Pentagon Papers', a secret history of the Vietnam War, leaked by Daniel Ellsberg.

30 June
The crew of *Soyuz 11* die after their air supply leaks out through a faulty valve.

6 July
Death of a legend: Louis 'Satchmo' Armstrong, 70, sings no more.

Pinnacle of joy for Wesak

9 May Kuala Lumpur

Buddhist devotees gathered at the Brickfields Buddhist temple held their breath as a gleaming pinnacle was placed on top of the new International Pagoda. Then, as bells rang out and prayers were chanted, a bone relic of the Buddha was enshrined in the pagoda.

On its completion in June, the pagoda would display Buddha images and a miniature pagoda presented by 11 Buddhist countries to Asia, giving it the name International Pagoda.

Angry mob sets lorry ablaze

30 May Klang

After a lorry knocked down a woman and an eight-year-old boy, killing the child and injuring the woman, a crowd in Pandamaran set fire to a lorry and overturned six others.

The lorry involved in the accident had driven off after the driver had got out to investigate but, after seeing the large crowd, had panicked. The 100-strong crowd then barricaded the road and stopped seven lorries loaded with sand.

The drivers and attendants abandoned their vehicles and ran. Later, a fire engine and a police party arrived and the police dispersed the mob.

Switch to palm oil

16 May Kuala Lumpur

Malaysia's oil palm industry grew strongly in 1970, spurred on by high prices in the world market. But this was said to be at the expense of rubber, the No. 1 crop.

The industry started the year with 70,000 acres of newly planted or replanted oil palms to bring the total acreage to 665,000. The switch from rubber to oil palm was set to develop further as Malaysia looked to the crop as a complement to rubber.

Overland to Mecca

21 May Kuala Lumpur

Once a soldier, always a soldier. In the case of Col Haji Idrus Abdul Rahman, leading five people to Mecca in a $25,000 motor caravan also satisfied his own wanderlust. Because of the many hazards of such a trip and the possibility that the pilgrimage might be scrapped, there was no announcement of the trip until the group arrived safely.

The four men and two women took four months and 10 days to travel over land and sea and through 11 countries to Mecca, Istanbul and home again.

Hundreds flock to Genting as casino opens

9 May Genting Highlands

Hundreds of people flocked to Casino de Genting, Malaysia's only licensed gambling club, when it opened to the public. The casino, in the still-to-be-completed Genting Highlands Hotel, was packed with people jostling to place chips on the blackjack and roulette tables. Baccarat, fantan and dice games were planned.

Miss Lim Siew Kim, daughter of Mr Lim Goh Tong, managing director of the Genting Highlands project, said: 'All 80 rooms of the partially-completed hotel have been booked in advance.'

New name for PMIP

14 June Kuala Lumpur

The PMIP was to be overhauled and given a new name. The party's 17th congress, which was to open on 18 June at the Dewan Bahasa dan Pustaka, would consider the new name, Parti Islam, to replace the Persatuan Islam Sa-Tanah Melayu.

Six Gerakan leaders quit their posts

13 June Kuala Lumpur

Professor Syed Hussein Alatas resigned as chairman of the Gerakan Ra'ayat Malaysia following a party dispute. He was followed by five other top party officials including Dr Tan Chee Khoon (secretary-general), Mr V. Veerappen (treasurer and member of Penang State Executive Council), Mr Tan Phock Kin (member of Penang State Executive Council), Dr L.H. Tan (of Johor) and Mr Richard Tan Giap Seng (Malacca State Assemblyman). Penang Chief Minister Dr Lim Chong Eu took over the chairmanship but left the door open for Prof. Syed Hussein to return.

On 22 June, the Gerakan crisis took a dramatic turn with the Selangor State Liaison Committee taking over the party headquarters in Jalan Templer. Ten minutes after committee chairman Inche Yunus Nawal announced the 'successful takeover' of the office, former party secretary-general Dr Tan Chee Khoon stormed in fuming and demanding an explanation.

'Who invited the Press? Get them out and lock the gate,' he said before turning to give his colleagues a tongue-lashing. In Penang, Dr Lim Chong Eu said he had no comment on the 'takeover' and Prof. Syed Hussein Alatas said that constitutionally he was still the Gerakan chairman as one month must elapse before his resignation became effective.

'Killer' Kowalski comes to town

13 June Kuala Lumpur

Heavyweight 'Killer' Kowalski (below), 38, of television's World Championship Wrestling fame, arrived with fellow wrestlers 'Bulldog' Bob Brown, 'Tiger' Jeet Singh, Mr Fuji and opponents King Kurtis, Mark Lewin, Spiron Asrion and Dino Lanza for a match at Stadium Negara.

Policemen to learn Mandarin

9 June Kuala Kangsar

Their aim was noble, to create racial harmony and to mix with their Chinese friends more freely. This led to 21 Malay policemen and a daughter of one of them to sacrifice their free time to learn to read and write Mandarin.

The idea came from Assistant OCPD Insp Ismail bin Che Hassan, who said that policemen were always in contact with Chinese members of the public. 'To know another language will always be an advantage in our work,' he said.

Crow shooting holiday

11 June Kuala Lumpur

The Sultan of Selangor decreed that 7 August, the date of a crow-shooting competition and the start of a cleanliness campaign in the royal town of Klang, would be a public holiday. Medals with an engraving of a crow would be awarded to winners of the contest, open to professional shooters and members of shooting clubs.

Degrees of success as 2,423 graduate from UM

26 June Kuala Lumpur

In the biggest and most significant convocation of the University of Malaya on 25 and 26 June, no fewer than 2,423 young Malaysians received their degrees and diplomas. This was the first time more than 2,000 students had received degrees from the university at the same convocation.

Flats 'aid integration'

17 June Kuala Lumpur

Deputy Prime Minister Tun Dr Ismail said a willingness to live in flats would help to integrate Malays and non-Malays in urban areas. He said he was pleased to hear that Malay families living in flats were happy as it proved wrong the belief that Malays could not live in such housing.

He was speaking after a tour of the Selangor State

Tun Dr Ismail (centre) looking at a model of a housing project.

Development Corporation flats at Jalan Pekililing, housing areas in Kampung Datuk Keramat Tambahan and Shah Alam and the corporation's headquarters in Petaling Jaya.

A new flat occupant, Che Aminah Puteh, told Tun Dr Ismail that the sense of security and better sanitation more than made up for not being able to plant tapioca and bananas and rear chickens.

2,600 tons of rubber bound for China

8 July Port Swettenham

A British ship, *Franford*, arrived to pick up 2,600 tons of bale rubber destined for China. The ship loaded 1,100 tons here, then sailed for Penang to collect another 1,500 tons before heading for the port of Dairen in China.

China promised an unofficial Malaysian trade mission earlier that she would buy all the stockpile held by the Malaysian Rubber Exchange and would consider buying 150,000 tons of Malaysian rubber a year.

Mid-air bomb scare

8 July Kuching

Eighteen minutes after take-off, an MSA Boeing 737 bound for Singapore and Kuala Lumpur turned back to Kuching after the pilot received an emergency radio message that there was a bomb on board. Army bomb disposal experts searched the plane but found nothing.

Among the 51 passengers were the General Officer Commanding-in-Chief, East Malaysia, Major-General Ismail Ibrahim, Singapore millionaire banker Wee Cho Yaw and several Sarawak State officials.

Red-carpet welcome for Tun Thanom

13 June Kuala Lumpur

Malaysia gave a warm welcome to Thai Premier Field Marshal Tun Thanom Kittikachorn, who was here on a three-day goodwill and business mission. He was accompanied by his wife and Thai Foreign Minister Tun Thanat Khoman.

Prime Minister Tun Abdul Razak said the visit

Tun Thanom and his Foreign Minister meet Tun Abdul Razak and other Ministers and officials at the Prime Minister's office.

had come at an opportune moment as it would enable him to have talks with the Thai Premier on matters of common interest affecting the stability of the region.

Police Museum at Fort Margherita

30 August Kuching

After nine decades, Fort Margherita will be turned into a Police Museum from tomorrow. The fort was founded in 1880, during the administration of the Second Rajah. Final touches are being carried out at the fort. Cannons and other weapons used by the three Rajahs, on loan from the Sarawak Museum, have been moved to the fort.

Woman Red surrenders

22 June Kota Bharu

After four years spent in the jungle on the Malaysia–Thai border, a woman Communist quietly surrendered on 13 May, it was announced. Che Meriam binte Awang, 33, walked into the police station at Batu Melintang, a border village in the Tanah Merah district, and gave herself up.

She said: 'From the day I joined the Communists, I had no proper food or a place to sleep. Most of the time, I ate bamboo shoots, jungle fruit and sap from banana trees or sought food from nearby kampongs.'

Miss Malaysia

19 August Kuala Lumpur

Miss Selangor, air-stewardess Daphne Munro, 24, won the Miss Malaysia/Miss World title at Stadium Negara. First runner-up was teacher Jean Perera (Miss Negeri Sembilan) while in third place was typist Catherine Tan (Miss Johor). Miss Munro would go to London for the Miss World contest scheduled for 14–21 November.

Hailstones hit KL and PJ

26 September Kuala Lumpur

Hailstones hit the Federal Capital, Subang and Petaling Jaya during a thunderstorm this afternoon, taking the people by surprise. A few roofs were damaged in the 30-minute deluge.

A meteorological station spokesman said hailstorms were not uncommon during the inter-monsoon months of August, September and October. 'Hailstones are caused by thunderstorm clouds which build up to great heights,' he explained.

Kelantan kite is airline symbol

19 August Kuala Lumpur

A giant Kelantan bird kite was chosen to take to the skies as the symbol of

Malaysia Airlines Ltd. The symbol, in red, would be painted on the tails of all its aircraft and would appear on brochures and advertisements. The airline's general manager, Mr Saw Huat Lye, explained that the kite was chosen as it was exclusively Malaysian and he hoped it would conjure up a favourable image of the airline.

Tun Razak unveils Second Malaysia Plan

11 July Kuala Lumpur

With national unity as its overriding objective, the $14.35-billion Second Development Plan was designed to steer Malaysians through a crucial stage in the nation's history, Prime Minister Tun Abdul Razak, its architect, said. It 'aims at creating a viable and dynamic commercial and industrial community of Malays and other indigenous people', he added.

'It will also see the emergence of a new breed of Malaysians—living and working in unity to serve the nation.'

He said the people would see a transformation of the social framework of production and distribution. This would lead to more equitable distribution of income and wealth, and to more balanced regional development. It would also provide expanded opportunities and enduring economic stability.

In a foreword to the Plan, Tun Razak stressed the need to be fully committed to meeting the challenges of the times and to forge a strong, united Malaysian nation with continued progress and prosperity.

Two issues of the *Far Eastern Economic Review* magazine looked to the future of Malaysia. In the first (top), the magazine commented that, while taking over from Tunku Abdul Rahman was no easy task, the emergence of Tun Razak as a leader 'might be more rapid and impressive than many expected'. Later, in a special Focus section on the national development plan, it said 'considerable care' had been taken to make Malays 'feel a decent slice of the cake is coming their way'.

Nurses claim equal pay

7 September Kuala Lumpur

A claim for equal pay by nurses and their protests over having to pay for their accommodation would be referred to the Cabinet, it was decided at a meeting between officials of Health and Labour Ministries, the Public Services Department and the Malaysian Nurses' Union following a mass demonstration by more than 500 nurses. The

Nurses picketing in front of the Health Ministry.

Government agreed to provide nursing sisters and matrons with free uniforms. Payment of allowances for attending courses would also be made soon.

1971

10 July
An attempted military coup against King Hassan of Morocco in his palace leaves nearly 100 of his guests dead.

16 July
Somewhere in the world, some time this day, the world's population reaches four billion.

11 September
Death of former Soviet Chairman of the Council of Ministers (1958–64), Nikita Krushchev, 77.

25 October
The UN General Assembly admits the People's Republic of China and expels Taiwan.

10 November
In Cambodia, the Khmer Rouge attacks Phnom Penh and the city's airport.

15 November
Intel releases the first microprocessor.

2 December
Six Gulf sheikdoms become one as the United Arab Emirates.

3 December
Pakistan jets attack Indian airbases. Indian forces move into East Pakistan the next day. An Indian destroyer sinks a Pakistani submarine.

Malaysia to vote for Peking as UN member

23 September | **Kuala Lumpur**

Tun Abdul Razak announced that Malaysia would support the Albanian resolution to seat China in the United Nations but would explain her stand on the problem of Taiwan. He was leaving for New York on 24 September for the 26th session of the United Nations General Assembly.

The Prime Minister said it was 'beyond doubt' that the Peking Government was the Government of China and it should have the China seat.

The question of Taiwan was a separate issue which would have to be resolved by the parties concerned. 'If the people of Taiwan decide to remain a separate political entity, then they should be given a seat in the United Nations,' he said.

BB Park lit up for the last time on 30 June 1972.

End of a landmark

29 September | **Kuala Lumpur**

A Federal Capital landmark, the Bukit Bintang Park, was to be torn down to make way for a multi-million-dollar shopping complex, it was announced. A syndicate headed by Ipoh tin-miner tycoon Datuk Chong Kok Lim bought the land on which the park stood for $5 million. Work on the project—which would include a supermarket, cinema and nightclub—was due to begin late in 1972.

Bukit Bintang Park, built in 1932, was originally called Hollywood Park. It was renamed during a change in ownership in 1936. The park had restaurants, theatres and dance halls. Chinese wayang and boxing and wrestling matches were big attractions in the '40s and '50s. The BB Cabaret, almost an institution among older KL folk, closed down in early 1971.

Cheering, flag-waving crowds greeted the Malaysian football team.

Home in triumph

7 October | **Kuala Lumpur**

Thousands welcomed home the victorious Malaysian football team which had earned a place in the Munich Olympics following a qualifying tournament in Seoul.

National dress gives the right impact

4 October | **Kuala Lumpur**

The best way to project the Malaysian image at international beauty contests is to wear the kebaya, said newly crowned Miss National Day Kathleen Phuah of Penang. Miss Phuah, who was due to compete in the Miss Pacific contest in Melbourne, Australia, next year, said: 'The sarong kebaya is tops and I am glad I shall be wearing it for the contest in March.'

New course charted for Asia

1 October | **New York**

Tun Abdul Razak suggested in the United Nations that the current thaw in the ideological and political confrontation in Southeast Asia should be used to chart a new course of destiny in Asia and the world. In his first speech before the UN since becoming Prime Minister, he said Southeast Asia would have 'great relevance' in the establishment of an Asian equilibrium.

His proposal for the neutralisation of Southeast Asia was unanimously accepted at the consultative meeting of the 53 'non-aligned' nations, which called for its urgent implementation to ensure Southeast Asia would be free of 'big power rivalries and interference'.

Ministers work towards broad Asian summit

2 October | **New York**

Asean Foreign Ministers took the first step towards setting up a broad Asian summit meeting on such things as the new US policy towards China.

At a meeting chaired by Tun Abdul Razak at his Waldorf Astoria Hotel suite, the Ministers decided to meet in Kuala Lumpur in November to discuss international developments as they affected Southeast Asia and to discuss Philippine President Ferdinand Marcos's proposal for an Asian summit and its agenda. Marcos had envisaged that all nations should participate.

Truly Malaysian lah!

3 October | **Kuala Lumpur**

The Malaysian 'lah' is indigenous, said a linguistics lecturer at University of Malaya, Dr Asmah Haji Omar, commenting on a speculation that it may have come from India, Indonesia or Thailand. 'In the process of Malayanisation, it got into all the spoken languages here, including English,' she said.

Hair protest

3 November | **Kuala Lumpur**

It was a hairy protest when some 200 students of the Technical College sat in at the Speakers' Corner to demonstrate against rulings by both the College and the Government against long hair for students. 'We feel that hair style is a matter of personal taste,' said Inche Abu Bakar Sa'ad, chairman of the students' union.

Church goes batik

22 December | **Ipoh**

The Christmas midnight mass at Our Lady of Lourdes Church would see the priest and altar boys wearing a new look—in batik, said parish priest Fr M. Pakiam. Malaysians were eager for a new identity, he added, and the Church welcomed such aspirations. So he would for the first time wear vestments made from batik instead of the more traditional materials.

Miniature Malaysia ready in time for Pata talks

2 December | **Kuala Lumpur**

Carved out of 300 acres of rolling hills at Ulu Gombak, Mimaland (or Malaysia in Miniature) was expected to be ready in time for the Pata conference next year. The almost-completed first phase of the $30-million project included 24 motels and five chalets and a swimming pool fed by a natural stream, said a spokesman for the developers, Malaysia Lakes Sdn Bhd.

24 called to the Bar

24 December | **Kuala Lumpur**

A record number of 24 lawyers were called to the Bar in the shortest-ever ceremony of 24 minutes before Mr Justice Tan Sri Suffian in the High Court today.

1972

The year when the glitterati came a-calling. Queen Elizabeth II made an official visit to Malaysia winning the hearts of the young and old wherever she went. She was accompanied by Prince Philip and Princess Anne. Indian film idol M.G. Ramachandran (MGR) was welcomed by Malaysian movie icon P. Ramlee when the former visited Penang where the duo took part in a show for which tickets were sold for the princely sums of $10 and $20 a seat. Also noteworthy was the visit, the first since Singapore's separation from Malaysia in 1965, of the island republic's Prime Minister Lee Kuan Yew a couple of weeks after Dr Mahathir Mohamad was welcomed back into Umno from which he had been expelled in 1969.

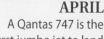

FEBRUARY
Raja Permaisuri Agong Tuanku Bahiyah binti Tuanku Abdul Rahman is appointed Universiti Malaya Chancellor.

APRIL
A Qantas 747 is the first jumbo jet to land at Subang Airport. It is received and inspected by Tan Sri Sardon Jubir, Minister of Communications.

JULY
Indian film fans and P. Ramlee welcome Indian film idol M.G. Ramachandran (MGR) in Penang.

DECEMBER
The trans-Sabah highway nears completion.

February: Queen Elizabeth enjoying a very warm welcome during her nine-day State tour of Malaysia.

'We have left behind the era where political parties placed party politics over the nation.'

Tun Abdul Razak, National Day message, 31 August 1972.

1972

world news

KL becomes a city

1 February Kuala Lumpur

The dazzling ceremony in Parliament House took only eight minutes but it made Kuala Lumpur, the town named 120 years ago after the 'muddy estuary' at the confluence of the Gombak and Klang rivers, officially a city.

Highlights of the ceremony were the presentation of the Royal Proclamation by Tun Abdul Razak to Technology, Research and Local Government Minister Datuk Ong Kee Hui, the reading of the proclamation by Tun Razak (above, right) and the appointment of Tan Sri Lokman Yusof as Datuk Bandar (mayor).

Then a fanfare of trumpets signalled Kuala Lumpur's new status, ending with prayers for the city's prosperity and the mayor's good health.

In the evening fireworks lit up the night sky as City Day celebrations went into full swing. Thousands of people joined in the three-day merrymaking.

On the last day, the highlight was a procession of 25 floats followed by a Mardi Gras. On one of the floats, the first City Queen Lucy Lee waved and smiled to the crowd.

Congratulations, mas

New look for MAS

31 January Kuala Lumpur

MAS air stewardesses donned new uniforms. The crease-proof terylene batik kebaya with an instant Malaysian identity gave a refreshing new look to the airline.

Later in the year, Singapore agreed that its national airline would be called Singapore International Airlines. There had been widespread protests when Singapore announced that, following the break-up of Malaysia–Singapore Airlines, it would use the word 'Mercury' and keep the initials MSA.

Preventing fishing 'war'

6 January Ipoh

The Perak Fisheries Department took steps to prevent further clashes between inshore fishermen and trawler operators. They included arrangements with neighbouring countries to allow fishermen to operate in international waters and having more enforcement officers patrol the coastal waters.

Sales tax confusion

28 January Penang

There was confusion over the introduction of a new five per cent sales tax. 'Basic necessities' were exempt but chambers of commerce and businesses were unsure what constituted a basic necessity.

Operation Hair in schools

2 March Kuala Lumpur

The Selangor Education Department launched Operation Hair to ensure that students and teachers did not sport long hair that was 'painful to the eye'.

Barbers were called to at least two schools to give on-the-spot haircuts.

Chief Education Officer Yap Hong Kuan said Beatle-style haircuts with fringes and long backs were not acceptable.

Drive to contain polio outbreak

4 January Kuala Lumpur

Health authorities launched a massive campaign to contain an outbreak of polio. Health Minister Lee Siok Yew said 46,113 children had been vaccinated in Penang, Negeri Sembilan, Malacca and Selangor.

Malaysians held in US

1 February Honolulu

Malaysians Lee Chee Kong of Penang and Loo Heng Hong of Butterworth arrived here after they were arrested the previous week on charges of smuggling US$8-million worth of heroin into the US. Also in custody were three other Malaysians identified as The Eng Hwa, Wong Ah Soii and Loo Jit Sun, all of Butterworth.

Queen is new UM Chancellor

8 February Kuala Lumpur

The Raja Permaisuri Agong became Chancellor of University of Malaya. She succeeded Tunku Abdul Rahman, who relinquished the post on his 69th birthday today after 10 years. The Queen was the first woman Chancellor in the country.

Romance of the Loke Yew mansion

At the height of his success, mining millionaire Loke Yew, born in poverty in 19th-century China, built for his family a magnificent mansion, Wisma Loke, in Medan Tuanku, Kuala Lumpur. In its time, it was a harmonious architectural blend of East and West, featuring a Chinese moongate and murals but built in an Italianate style.

The last of the family moved out in 1930 and the mansion was unoccupied until the Japanese invasion in 1941. It became a Japanese army headquarters and remained so until the war ended in 1945. During the Emergency it again had a martial air, as a CID and Special Branch training centre. After 1958, it fell into disrepair.

But, wrote Peter Clague in the *Straits Times Annual*, it was being sensitively restored. Partition walls built by the Japanese for offices were torn out to reveal once again

the beautifully proportioned arched doorways. Tiled floors were refurbished and, of course, the moongate and murals were returned to their former glory. It was refurnished with antiques, and pictures by Malaysian artists were installed.

Left: The Italianate facade of the Loke Yew mansion in Kuala Lumpur. Above: The Chinese-style moongate inside the house.

Mahathir rejoins Umno

7 March Kuala Lumpur

Former Alliance MP for Kota Star Selatan Dr Mahathir bin Mohamad, who was expelled from Umno in September 1969, rejoined following a decision by the party's disciplinary committee.

Dr Mahathir, when told of the decision in Alor Star, said: 'I am happy to hear it. I hope to be able to serve Umno in any way that is possible. I hope this means I can play an active role in national politics.'

Cordial welcome for Lee Kuan Yew

22 March Kuala Lumpur

Malaysia gave Singapore Premier Lee Kuan Yew a cordial welcome when he flew in for his first official visit since Separation in 1965. As he stepped from the plane at Subang Airport, he was greeted by Prime Minister Tun Abdul Razak, who was accompanied by more than 30 dignitaries and their wives.

The scene of the train tragedy.

10 die in train crash

30 March Kota Bharu

Ten people were killed and 37 seriously injured in a level-crossing train crash near Pasir Mas, 14 miles from Kota Bharu. Among the dead were seven schoolchildren and the bus driver.

A goods train ploughed into the bus, which was carrying 51 people, and flung it more than 10 feet from the crossing which had no gates.

On seeing the bus just 30ft away, train driver Abu Kassim bin Ishak said he shouted 'Danger!' to his fireman and applied full brakes but was it too late to stop.

A royal welcome for a royal visitor as Queen Elizabeth is escorted by the Yang di-Pertuan Agong at Port Klang.

Playing host to Elizabeth

17 February–5 March Kuala Lumpur

As the *Britannia* steamed slowly into Port Klang, a Royal Navy escort ship fired a 21-gun salute, rousing thousands of Malaysians who had gathered to welcome Queen Elizabeth into a thunderous cheer of welcome. The route from the port to Klang, Shah Alam, Petaling Jaya and Istana Tetamu, where she would stay, was lined with tens of thousands of people, including schoolchildren waving flags, straining for a glimpse of the Queen. At the port, one eager watcher even clambered up the mainmast rigging of a yacht for a clearer view.

On 22 February Queen Elizabeth received Prime Minister Tun Abdul Razak and Toh Puan Rahah at Istana Tetamu. Minister with Special Functions Tan Sri Ghazali Shafie gave a lunch in honour of Lord Mountbatten, uncle of Prince Philip and Supreme Commander of Allied Forces in Southeast Asia during World War II. At a royal banquet in the evening, Queen Elizabeth and the Yang di-Pertuan Agong pledged that Britain and Malaysia would 'continue to enjoy a friendly and productive relationship.'

The following day the Queen visited areas of Kuala Lumpur including Chinatown, shaking hands with the crowd who roared with approval when she told them: 'I am so pleased to be here'. She and Prince Philip also laid a wreath at the National Monument. The Prince opened a $110,000 orang utan enclosure at Zoo Negara. The next day's stop was the East Coast and Kelantan's famous Beach of Passionate Love where a huge kite caught the Queen's fancy. They also watched a giant top-spinning demonstration and chatted with fishermen.

The owners of a humble timber and plaster house were chosen to receive Queen Elizabeth and Princess Anne during the royal visit to Malaysia. The home of factory-hand Inche Mohamed Lot bin Mat and his wife Rohani was the cleanest and best-kept house in the Sungai Buloh rubber experimental station. 'We are very happy to receive Queen Elizabeth in person,' said Inche Lot. His wife said she would spruce up the house and put up new curtains for the occasion.

On 5 March the Yang di-Pertuan Agong bade farewell to the Queen at a reception aboard the royal yacht *Britannia*. After the banquet was over, the *Britannia* sailed for Penang where she was to spend the last of her nine-day State tour of Malaysia.

The Queen had returned that day from Malacca where she made a walkabout. The fishing village of Kampong Pengkalan Perigi stopped work to cheer her.

Crowds see Subang's first jumbo jet land

1 April Kuala Lumpur

A huge crowd arrived at Subang Airport to watch its first jumbo jet, a Qantas 747, touch down. To prepare for jumbo jets, specialised landing equipment worth more than $2.5 million was shipped in and the transit lounge expanded to cope with more travellers. The changes included two large staircases, container loaders, trailers and a vehicle for handling heavy cargo and maintenance equipment. Luggage handling was also upgraded.

Multiracial army unit is awarded 'Royal' title

19 May Kuala Lumpur

The Malaysian Reconnaissance Corps was given the title 'Royal' by the Yang di-Pertuan Agong, marking yet another chapter of achievement in its 10-year history. It was the first multiracial unit of the army to win the honour. The corps was formed in 1960 with the amalgamation of two multiracial units, the 1st Bn Federation Regiment and the Federation Armoured Car Regiment.

Found, 140-year-old coin

11 June Batu Gajah

A dulang washer found a coin, believed to be about 140 years old, in a river near Tronoh, 10 miles from here. The 20-cent coin had a picture of a cockerel and the words Tanah Melayu inscribed in Jawi on one face. On the reverse side, it had a picture of a flower with the date 1250 and an inscription in Arabic. Saidin bin Dahalan, 17, said he intended to keep the coin for luck.

Ace dies in go-kart crash

23 April Ipoh

Indonesian racing ace Hengkie Iriawan, 28, was killed when his go-kart crashed into a tree at the Third BP Kart Prix here. He had just overtaken another kart driven by former Thomas Cup badminton star Eddy Choong at more than 50mph when he crashed. He had head injuries and died without regaining consciousness.

world news

21–28 February
US President Nixon meets Chairman Mao in China. Fearing a Sino–American alliance, the Soviet Union becomes amenable to détente with the US.

30 March
North Vietnamese forces move into the DMZ.

16 April
The US resumes bombing of Hanoi and Haiphong.

16 April
The US sends ping-pong paddlers to China. In return, China sends two pandas to the US.

1 May
South Vietnam abandons Quang Tri City to the North Vietnamese Army.

22 May
Ceylon becomes the Republic of Sri Lanka.

23 May
The Tamil United Front (later renamed the Tamil United Liberation Front) of Sri Lanka is founded.

26 May
Nixon and Brezhnev sign the SALT I Treaty, freezing the number of missile launchers.

Beware spheres of influence

24 May Kuala Lumpur

Prime Minister Tun Abdul Razak said non-aligned nations would have to resist steadfastly any ideas about superpower spheres of influence. He was opening the second meeting of the preparatory committee of non-aligned countries here to prepare the agenda for the non-aligned Foreign Ministers' conference in Georgetown, Guyana, in August.

'As superpowers meet and engage in global diplomacy to resolve outstanding issues between themselves, whether in the field of security, trade or technology, we must remain vigilant that our own interests are not adversely affected,' said Tun Razak.

On 26 May, in a communiqué issued after the three-day meeting, delegates recalled the sense of urgency regarding neutralisation expressed by non-aligned Foreign Ministers at a consultative meeting in New York last October.

It said Foreign Ministers affirmed that Malaysia's proposal for the neutralisation of Southeast Asia would safeguard peace, security, independence and territorial integrity for the region.

The Sultan of Pahang (right) walks with Boh Tea chairman Mr Tristan Russell at the opening of the Sungai Palas Estate.

Sultan opens tea factory

20 June Cameron Highlands

The Sultan of Pahang Sultan Abu Bakar officially opened a new Boh tea factory in the Sungai Palas Estate. The factory would have the capacity to produce one million pounds of tea a year.

Razaleigh is Kelantan Opposition leader

16 July Kota Bharu

Tengku Razaleigh Hamzah, the Alliance chairman in Kelantan, was elected Opposition leader of the State Assembly. Kelantan was the first State to have such a post. Provision was made for the post in a Bill which gave the Opposition leader a $250 monthly allowance. Tengku Razaleigh said the move was a step towards more efficient conduct of House affairs and closer cooperation between the Government and Opposition members.

Education TV switches on

19 June Kuala Lumpur

Tun Abdul Razak launched the education television service. At first, ETV was limited to science and mathematics for Form One, civics for upper primary and lower secondary and general programmes for teachers and adults. The Prime Minister said ETV would be developed and extended to East Malaysia.

Big rush to enrol for MIT courses

30 June Batu Tiga

More than 500 new students turned up, some as early as 7am, when registration opened at the Mara Institute of Technology in Shah Alam.

As the crowd grew, loudspeakers had to be used to direct the students registering for accountancy, administration and law, applied science and mass communications.

Proof of dollar's strength

5 July Kuala Lumpur

The International Tin Council's decision to quote the international tin price range in Malaysian dollars was seen in Government and financial circles as 'world recognition' of the strength and stability of the currency. The council, meeting in London, decided to switch from sterling to offset sterling's reduced value since it was floated.

MGR welcomed by P. Ramlee

20 July Penang

Malaysian movie idol P. Ramlee joined thousands of film fans to welcome Indian film idol M.G. Ramachandran (known as MGR) outside the City Stadium as not all could afford to pay $10 and $20 for tickets to the show after the $3 seats were sold out.

As the star rode around the stadium in a Land Rover, the crowd cheered and shouted: 'Long live MGR'.

The previous day, fans jammed the airport gallery to get a glimpse of their idol, who was accompanied by Indian comedian Nagesh and actress Jayalalitha. Pandemonium broke out at Bangunan Tuanku Syed Putra when MGR arrived to pay a call on Chief Minister Dr Lim Chong Eu. The fans became hysterical and mobbed MGR's car until police were called in to control them.

MGR, in dark glasses and hat, with P. Ramlee.

Town protected by 'floating cannon'

11 July Butterworth

A 120-year-old cannon in a shrine on the beach by the side of Mitchell Pier is said to protect this town from evil. Local residents visit the shrine daily to offer prayers before the famous *meriam timbul* (floating cannon) which is draped with a piece of silk.

The cannon was believed to be a companion of the old Portuguese cannon Si Rambai on the north parapet of Fort Cornwallis, Penang. *Meriam timbul* is said to have fallen into the sea during a battle but miraculously did not sink.

Hermit claims to be 1891 rebel leader

24 July Kuantan

A hermit living in a kampong near here declared that he was Datuk Bahaman, a rebel leader who fought the British at the turn of the century. When asked why he did not reveal his identity earlier, the hermit, known as Tok Guru, said he was afraid of the Sultan but did not reveal which Sultan.

Datuk Bahaman was a Malay chieftain who led a revolt of the Orang Kaya Semantan against the British in Pahang in 1891. In 1895, he fled to Siam but there is no record of what happened to him after that. Tok Guru, who was very ill, was believed to be more than 100 years old.

Supersonic RMAF

19 July Kuala Lumpur

A multi-million-dollar deal reached with Northrop of Los Angeles promised to enable the Royal Malaysian Air Force to go supersonic with a squadron of American F-5E fighters. The jets, with a maximum speed of Mach 1.6 in level flight, would cost about $5 million each and would increase the number of RMAF aircraft to more than 190. Apart from the F-5Es, RMAF jet squadrons consisted of Tebuans and Sabres.

Green light to visit Russia

1 August Kuala Lumpur

The Government relaxed restrictions on Malaysians visiting seven Communist countries. Permission would no longer be needed from the Immigration Department but they must obtain visas. The countries were the USSR, Poland, Czechoslovakia, Hungary, Romania, Yugoslavia and Bulgaria. An Immigration spokesman said restrictions had been relaxed because Malaysia had diplomatic ties with these countries.

Flying cattle

4 August Kuala Lumpur

A total of 125 special breed cattle from the US, costing $10,000, arrived by air. The pure-line cattle were Santa Gertrudis, Brahma, Brahma Hereford cross and Brahma Angus cross from Louisiana and Florida.

Nationalisation ruled out

10 August Kuala Lumpur

Tun Abdul Razak ruled out nationalisation of foreign companies. He told the Dewan Rakyat that the question 'does not arise' in pursuit of the Government's objective of having 30 per cent Bumiputra participation in commerce and industry within the next 20 years. He was replying to Mr Lim Kit Siang (DAP-Bandar Malacca) who asked if the Government would ever consider expropriating foreign companies. Lim said that foreign interests accounted for 62.1 per cent of total share capital.

Bahasa Malaysia musical to be staged

13 August Kuala Lumpur

A musical in Bahasa Malaysia, adapted from the book *Uda dan Dara* by Usman Awang, would be staged at the Experimental Theatre of the University of Malaya in December, it was announced.

The musical, about the love between a kampong girl and a young man of different status, was to be staged by literary group Gema Seni, directed by Inche Rahim Razali.

Volunteer workers remove the bodies of the schoolchildren after the ferry disaster.

33 feared dead in ferry sinking

14 September Parit Buntar

Nineteen bodies were recovered from the swollen Kerian River where the Parit Buntar–Bandar Baru ferry sank in mid-stream. They included 12 children who were trapped inside a school bus. Fourteen others, mostly students, were missing, believed drowned.

A Works and Power Ministry spokesman said the Government planned to build bridges to replace almost all ferry crossings under the Second Malaysia Plan.

Trans-Sabah highway: A road that leads to rural development

Two scenes of work in progress on the mammoth task of building the trans-Sabah highway, featured in an article in the *Straits Times Annual*. The road, being built by Malaysians and Australians, would link the State capital Kota Kinabalu with Sandakan. Work began in 1968 and the road was due for completion in December 1972. It served not only as a link but as a means of opening up the interior. Even before it was finished families were settling along its length.

Russia joins Malaysia in call to ease tensions

5 October Kuala Lumpur

The Soviet Union and Malaysia called for 'urgent elimination' of conflicts and sources of tension in Southeast Asia. A joint communiqué issued at the end of Tun Abdul Razak's week-long visit to Russia laid down principles for strengthening peace and security in Asia and the world. States in their relations with others should strictly adhere to the principles of peaceful co-existence, equality and respect for sovereignty and territorial integrity, it said.

How to spot a hippie

24 August Kuala Lumpur

Hippies were banned from entering the country from 1 September. Those already in Malaysia would be ordered to leave and their visit passes would not be extended. Immigration Department officers were given guidelines on how to identify hippies: people with long, dirty and unkempt hair, untrimmed moustaches or beards and those who were shabbily dressed.

End of the line for station

31 October Kuala Lumpur

Demolition of the 42-year-old railway station at Jalan Sultan started in order to make way for a transport terminal. Malayan Railway had been running the station at a loss for many years.

Spelling changes for Malay language

16 August Kuala Lumpur

Malaysia and Indonesia proclaimed the use of a new common spelling system. The system, with significant changes in the structure of the two closely-related tongues, was agreed earlier in the year.

Tun Abdul Razak gave the go-ahead at the Dewan Bahasa dan Pustaka for the new romanised spelling system to be used nationwide. Directives and manuals on the use of the new system had gone out to all Government departments.

Publications of the Dewan Bahasa, Malay-language (rumi) newspapers such as *Berita Harian* and TV Malaysia in its announcements and subtitles had already made the change.

But the system would not be used in textbooks until sufficient time had been given to schools, parents and publishers, and would not be enforced in school examinations until the Education Ministry was satisfied that schools were ready for the switch-over.

In Jakarta, President Suharto told the nation that common spelling for the Indonesian language would be enforced from tomorrow. Both events signalled the first step towards standardisation of terms and grammar for the 120 million people of the two countries.

Goods without price tags confiscated

30 October Kuala Lumpur

Enforcement officers raided seven shops in Jalan Pekeliling and Jalan Ipoh here and confiscated goods worth several thousand dollars which were not displaying price tags. This was the first crackdown by the Ministry of Trade and Industry's Enforcement Division since the law making the use of price tags mandatory came into force this year.

'We will charge the offenders within the next few days,' said a spokesman for the division, adding that the raid would be the first of many to show that the law enforcing display of price tags must be taken seriously.

First offenders could be fined a maximum of $10,000 or jailed two years or both. For a second offence, the fine was $20,000 or a jail term of five years or both.

1972

world news

18 July
Egyptian President Anwar Sadat expels 20,000 Soviet advisers.

21 July
Twenty-two IRA bombs explode in Belfast, Northern Ireland, killing nine.

4 August
Idi Amin of Uganda expels 50,000 Asians holding British passports.

11 August
The last US ground forces withdraw from South Vietnam.

5–6 September
Eleven Israeli athletes at the Munich Olympics are killed by Arabs who had infiltrated the Olympics Village.

21 September
President Marcos declares martial law in the Philippines.

13 October
A plane transporting a rugby team crashes in the Andes. To survive, 16 eat the flesh of their dead friends.

7 November
President Nixon wins a second term as US President.

29 November
Atari releases PONG, the Adam of computer games.

15 letter bombs found in GPO defused

1 November Kuala Lumpur

Postal authorities found 15 letter bombs containing gelignite at the GPO. They were defused by Army bomb disposal experts at Batu Cantonment. All the letters were posted at Subang Airport and addressed to people mainly in Rome and London.

The investigation started the previous day after the representative in Malaysia of Palestinian group Al-Fatah, Mr Abu Yacoub, received a letter that he did not like the look of. He went to the Saudi Embassy for help and the police were called in. The Army and police began top-level investigations into the letter bombs.

15,000 flee flooded homes in capital

17 November Kuala Lumpur

More than 15,000 people fled their homes as heavy rain caused floods in many low-lying areas in Kuala Lumpur and Petaling Jaya. Areas affected were Klang Road, Puchong, Kampung Baru, Kampung Reddy, Sentul, Kampung Kasipillai, Kampung Raya, Setapak and Campbell Road.

The wet weather was likely to continue for the next two to three days, according to the Meteorological Office at Subang Airport. The National Security Operations Room was prepared for a 24-hour watch on the flood situation. The overdue monsoon was expected soon.

Malaysian Business magazine

An advertisement stresses the rise of the country's recently established businesses.

Work of royal painter goes on display

3 November Kuala Lumpur

A painting of the Istana Negara grounds by the Raja Permaisuri Agong was selected for a landscape art exhibition organised by the National Art Gallery.

This was the first time the Queen had taken part in such an exhibition. A total of 285 paintings were on display.

Razak 'determined' to achieve regional peace

6 November Kuala Lumpur

Prime Minister Tun Abdul Razak said that recent moves towards a peace agreement on Vietnam made Malaysia all the more determined to maintain Southeast Asia as a region of peace, freedom and unity.

In his Hari Raya message, Tun Razak also called on the Malays and Bumiputras to decide whether they wished to march forward to achieve equality with the other communities.

1,900 women apply to join the navy

1 November Kuala Lumpur

About 1,900 women had applied to join the Royal Malaysian Navy Women's Volunteer Section, an RMN spokesman said.

The RMN was the first branch of the armed forces to have women volunteers but the earlier unit was disbanded in 1964.

Out with the dacing

20 November Kuala Lumpur

The Government had decided that traditional weights and measures such as the dacing, gantang and cupak would become obsolete when the metric system was adopted over the next 10 years.

Trade and Industry Minister Mohamed Khir Johari said this when he met officials from the Selangor Consumers' Association and the Negeri Sembilan Consumers' Association.

He said conversion to metric would be a massive operation that would be phased over 10 years (*see 16 February 1980*).

Pas coalition with Alliance

21 December Kuala Lumpur

Pas gave its formal go-ahead to a coalition with the Alliance. Party president Datuk Haji Asri bin Haji Muda said 190 delegates at a special congress were in favour, 94 against and 19 abstained. Thirty delegates were absent when the vote was taken after day-long discussions at the Dewan Bahasa dan Pustaka.

Datuk Asri said the decision was 'satisfying for it is the result of mature thinking'. He added that 'frank views' were expressed at the meeting but he was convinced there would be no division within the party on the issue.

Four rounds of talks had been held with Alliance leaders before agreement was reached. The following day Umno leaders met for a briefing from party president Tun Abdul Razak on the terms of the coalition.

It was left to Pas leaders to work out details of the coalition which was agreed in principle in September.

Malaysian Business magazine

The cover of the November issue of the magazine *Malaysian Business*, focusing on the burgeoning electronics industry.

Exam pep pill peril

28 November Kuala Lumpur

The Education Ministry said a 'shocking number' of students suffered blackouts during recent examinations because of pep pills. The students told teachers they had been taking the pills regularly for two to five weeks before the examinations to help keep awake while studying into the night. They developed symptoms such as trembling, sweating and nervous irritation.

Unity 'the way ahead'

30 November Kuala Lumpur

Tun Abdul Razak said national unity must be achieved through national means. 'The time is now past for achieving national unity through seeking the unity of particular racial groups first,' he told the Unity Advisory Council meeting here. 'It is now our responsibility to see how the various racial groups fit into a cohesive whole.'

62 held in Sarawak

14 December Kuching

Sixty-two people were arrested in 24 hours under Operation Petak III to weed out those involved in subversive activities in Sarawak. Acting Chief Minister Stephen Yong said those arrested were thought to be involved in subversive activities.

10-year tax-free period

15 December Kuala Lumpur

A tax-free period of up to 10 years for certain types of industries in specific areas was approved by the Cabinet.

Trade and Industry Minister Encik Khir Johari said he would introduce a Bill to this effect during the current Parliament session. 'It might cover both old as well as new industries,' he added.

Shares and land prices rise as money pours in

20 December Kuala Lumpur

Finance Minister Tun Tan Siew Sin told the Dewan Rakyat that 'hot money' was pouring in from overseas. Winding up the debate on the Budget, he said: 'It is not just good luck that the Malaysian dollar is today one of the strongest currencies in the world. It is not just good luck that Malaysia is today a haven for hot money from even developed countries, so much so that money is pouring into our stocks, shares and land. The result is that prices of such stocks and shares have risen to unhealthy levels and land prices in certain parts of the country are rocketing.'

1973

Expansion and spiralling prices marked the year. Malaysia's GNP increased by more than 20 percent in what was described as 'miraculous growth', the Federal Highway was to be expanded to cater for increased traffic, and the price of sugar, eggs, bread and clothing went up by 30 percent. Price increases also affected coffee, rice and petrol. It was also a year of tragedies. The nation mourned the deaths of acting Prime Minister Tun Dr Ismail and actor P. Ramlee and, later, more than 50 people who were buried alive when a mountain slope at Gunong Kroh in Perak crashed onto a row of 10 houses. In another accident at the end of the year, 100 people perished when an inter-island passenger boat sank at Kuala Rajang in Sarawak.

MARCH
Motorcyclists and pillion riders are now required by law to wear crash helmets.

MAY
The Malaysia–Singapore currency splits and in June the Malaysian dollar is allowed to float against the US dollar.

AUGUST
Datuk Hussein Onn is sworn in as Deputy Prime Minister following the death of Tun Dr Ismail Abdul Rahman.

OCTOBER
The collapse of a section of mountainside from Gunung Kroh onto a row of houses kills more than 50.

September: The Malaysian contingent at the Southeast Asian Peninsular (SEAP) Games opening ceremony in Singapore.

'A pair of Siamese twins trying to grow together normally.'

Tun Tan Siew Sin, explaining the currency split with Singapore, 9 May 1973.

1973

world news

1 January
Britain joins the EEC.

17 January
Philippine President
Ferdinand Marcos
is named President
for Life.

23 January
Former US
President Lyndon
Johnson, 64, dies.

27 January
Paris Peace Accord
is signed by the US,
North Vietnam,
South Vietnam
and the Vietcong.

21 February
Israeli fighters shoot
down a Libyan
airliner, killing 108.

6 March
Nobel laureate
Pearl S. Buck dies at 81.

27 March
The Godfather wins the
Oscar for Best Film.
Best Actor winner
Marlon Brando refuses
to accept his Oscar as
a protest at the way
Native Americans are
depicted by Hollywood.

3 April
In New York, Martin
Cooper makes the first
call on his invention,
the mobile phone.

4 April
New York City's World
Trade Center is opened.

Dearer New Year

1 January Kuala Lumpur

The year began with Malaysians facing spiralling increases in the price of most foods and other essential items. From the daily cuppa to sugar, eggs, bread, perishables and clothing, prices were up by an average of 30 per cent.

To add to the trouble, there seemed to be a shortage of many essential items, especially sugar and flour. With Chinese New Year approaching, the Government warned shopkeepers that it would not hesitate to increase the penalty on those who deliberately hoarded sugar.

Five days later, the Government pegged the price of sugar at 45 cents a kati (600g) and Trade and Industry Ministry enforcers seized 14 bags of sugar from a shop in Alor Star. The National Padi and Rice Authority gave an assurance that the price of rice would not go up and flour mills were told to rush supplies to areas facing a shortage.

Raja Muda convicted of spraying mace

3 January Johor Bahru

The Raja Muda of Johor was convicted and fined $2,500 by the High Court here on three charges of causing hurt and another charge under the Arms Act. The fines were imposed by Mr Justice Raja Tan Sri Azlan Shah following an appeal by Solicitor General Tan Sri Salleh Abbas.

The Raja Muda was fined $1,000 for spraying mace on Tengku Zakiah binti Tengku Mohamed Yusof at the office of the deputy OCPD (Crime) Johor Bahru. On the three charges of causing hurt, Mr Justice Raja Tan Sri Azlan Shah convicted and fined the Raja Muda $500 for causing hurt to Syed Hassan alias Tengku Zaki bin Syed Zainal Abidin, $500 for causing hurt to Syed Mohsin alias Tengku Mohsin bin Syed Zainal Abidin and $500 for causing hurt to M. Narendran at the Istana Raja Muda.

Shell strikes oil off Sabah

23 January Kota Kinabalu

Sabah Shell struck oil off the Sabah coast and in tests, a well named Erb West had produced 1,800 barrels of oil a day. Minister of Primary Industries Datuk Abdul Taib Mahmud said Shell had applied to convert the area into a mining lease.

Sabah Shell Director Peter Hammacher said the company started drilling in the area three years ago and would continue with its exploration of Sabah. He said signs indicated that the oil was of low sulphur content, a type very much in demand in Japan. The company was given a prospecting licence in 1958.

Tun Razak hails Vietnam Peace Treaty

27 January Kuala Lumpur

Prime Minister Tun Abdul Razak hailed the Vietnam Peace Treaty signed in Paris by the United States, North and South Vietnam and the Vietcong. Tun Razak said it would bring an end to the long years of misery and suffering of the Vietnamese.

IGP Salleh dies

31 January Kuala Lumpur

The Yang di-Pertuan Agong bestowed a posthumous award of Darjah Sri Setia Mahkota on Inspector General of Police Tan Sri Salleh bin Ismael, 55, who died after a stroke. The award carries the title Tun.

Prime Minister Tun Abdul Razak sent his condolences to the bereaved family, saying Tan Sri Salleh was a national warrior whose contribution would be 'carved in gold' in the country's history.

Indian barbers quick to change

8 February Kuala Lumpur

Indian barber shops, especially new ones in Kuala Lumpur and Petaling Jaya, were the most responsive to a request to use Bahasa Malaysia on their signboards.

Chinese shopkeepers showed a reluctance to change due to a superstitious belief that removing a signboard was an indication of difficulties in business.

Royal Thai welcome for King and Queen

1 February Bangkok

On an eight-day State visit to Thailand, the Yang di-Pertuan Agong and the Raja Permaisuri Agong were greeted by King Bhumibol Adulyadej and Queen Sirikit at Don Muang Airport, Bangkok. The King later conferred Thailand's highest awards on the Agong and Permaisuri.

Thursday is Beggars' Day for shopkeepers

8 February Penang

To stop beggars harassing their customers, shopkeepers in the Beach Street area of Penang agreed to observe Beggars' Day every Thursday during which they would give the beggars alms. The beggars gathered at the Clock Tower in King Edward Place each morning and set off at 8am to start begging. Though the amount given by each shopkeeper to each beggar might be only one cent, a stall helper said that up to $3–$4 a day could be paid out.

'Enemies of the State'

22 February Ipoh

Prime Minister Tun Abdul Razak warned that Communist sympathisers and supporters would be treated as 'enemies of the State' and dealt with firmly. 'We have had the Emergency from 1948 and we cannot go on like this,' he said.

Races hit by ban on livestock imports

10 February Singapore

The upcoming Penang race meeting was hit as 77 racehorses could not enter Malaysia. The problem followed a total ban on the import of all livestock and livestock products from Singapore. But a Turf Club spokesman said 10 horses from Singapore had already arrived and the races would go on.

Malaysia imposed the ban after an outbreak of foot-and-mouth disease in cattle from South Thailand in the quarantine station in Singapore. The import of cattle and buffaloes from Thailand was also banned until further notice. Director-general of Veterinary Services Tan Sri Johari bin Haji Mohamad Daud said Malaysia had been free of the disease since 1939.

'Miracle or not, my baby is not for sale'

23 February Penang

Waterfront labourer Lim Ah Bah has turned down all offers to buy his 20-day-old baby boy, said to be the reincarnation of a dead prince. The offers have included $10,000 and a house.

The baby has a blue-black birthmark on his right foot that is said to match that of the dead prince.

A crowd has turned up at his house in Malay Street Ghaut to look at baby Kok Thye though the family has denounced the reincarnation rumours and said that the birthmark had already disappeared.

Playing with fire

18 February Kuala Lumpur

When he got bored while waiting for customers in Jalan Bangsar, goreng pisang (banana fritter) seller Ahmad Ayob, 31, liked nothing better than to play with fire.

He would take a flaming torch and put it in his mouth or run it over his stomach.

Or he would test the temperature of the hot oil by dipping his fingers in it. Ahmad said he could do this only if he rubbed his fingers first with a magic ointment given him by a bomoh, or witch doctor.

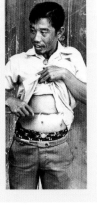

Prime Minister Tun Abdul Razak looks on as Deputy Prime Minister Tun Dr Ismail Abdul Rahman greets Indian President V.V. Giri at an official lunch given by the Prime Minister on 6 March. The Indian leader was on a State visit to Malaysia.

Crash helmet law comes into force

1 March Kuala Lumpur

A law requiring motorcyclists and pillion riders to wear crash helmets came into force. Police stopped those without helmets and gave them a stern warning. The authorities said a few days' grace would be given for all to comply. In Penang and other places, many motorcyclists continued to go about without helmets although motorcycle shops reported a brisk sale in helmets (*see 16 February 1975*).

Stink over plan to move belacan makers

7 March Butterworth

Some 20 belacan (shrimp paste) producers at a fishing village in Bagan Jermal cried foul over plans to relocate them to Kuala Muda after residents of a new housing estate nearby complained of the stink.

The villagers, who produced 1,000 piculs of belacan a month for export to Thailand, said they were there long before the estate was built. As well as belacan the village produced animal feed and exported jellyfish to Thailand and Japan.

Belacan maker Tan Eng Yeow, 60, said the proposed resettlement area was unsuitable. DAP national vice-chairman Yeap Ghim Guan asked the Chief Minister to defer the proposal.

Tun Razak opens $13.9m Wisma Radio

11 March Kuala Lumpur

Opening the $13.9-million headquarters of RTM, Wisma Radio, Prime Minister Tun Abdul Razak said he hoped it would convey the truth of the Government to the people and so win their support and confidence.

He said the radio should be an instrument to help speed up the process of restructuring society to create a united nation, help to oppose anti-national elements, explain foreign policy through its external services and act as a salesman to attract more investment.

'The main issue is unity,' he said. The ceremony was attended by more than 300 guests and was broadcast live by Radio Malaysia.

Aid for families in drought-hit Sabah

20 March Kota Kinabalu

The Sabah Finance Ministry allocated $500,000 for relief work in drought-stricken areas where thousands of families were hit. The Federal Government contributed 1,000 tons of rice and the Royal Malaysian Navy and Army helped to deliver the consignment. The State Disaster Relief Committee met to work out plans to help the victims.

Rubber bounces to a new high

15 March Penang

A new wave of buying sent rubber prices to the highest level for more than three years. The closing price of 140 cents a kg, a rise of more than 20 cents a kg since the beginning of the year, was due to speculative buying and heavy demand from the United States, the Soviet Union, Japan and China.

One broker said the rise could have stemmed from fears of a shortage of rubber due to the annual wintering season. Insiders declined to say how long they expected such price levels to be maintained.

Coffee costs more

15 March Penang

The price of coffee powder was increased by 20 cents a kati. Top-quality coffee powder went up from $1.80 to $2. The increase affected all types and brands of coffee powder as well as processed coffee beans. It was announced in a joint statement by 51 coffee powder dealers in Penang, Kedah and Perak and followed a price rise in raw coffee beans.

Rice is rising

20 March Penang

The price of rice here climbed 15–20 cents a gantang (3.25kg) in a week. The common Mahsuri variety, sold at $1.80 a gantang, rose to $2.

Urging the Government to take action immediately, dealers said the increase was due to a shortage of local supplies and a temporary ban on Thai rice. Also, during the past six months, no rice had been imported from China because of a quota imposed by the Government.

Pricier at the pumps

21 December Kuala Lumpur

Minister of Primary Industries Datuk Taib Mahmud announced an increase in the price of petrol, gas, diesel and fuel.

The price of premium petrol went up by 34 cents a gallon, regular by 24 cents, gas and diesel by 11 cents and fuel by five cents. The retail price of kerosene remained the same at 71 cents.

Currency split

Singapore cash subject to exchange rates

10 May Kuala Lumpur

The Treasury announced that after 19 May, the exchange of Singapore currency for Malaysian dollars would be subject to a charge depending on exchange rates.

On the whole, Malaysians remained cool over the currency split with Singapore and there was no rush for Malaysian currency. But after the split many people had a hard time persuading hawkers to accept the Singapore dollar.

Explaining the currency split, Finance Minister Tun Tan Siew Sin said the Malaysian and Singapore economies were basically different.

Malaysia was mainly a producer of primary commodities while making significant progress in industrialisation but Singapore depended largely on trade and the provision of services.

Tun Tan also announced that the Government had decided to set up a separate Malaysian Stock Exchange.

Dollar will be allowed to float

21 June Kuala Lumpur

Finance Minister Tun Tan Siew Sin announced that the Malaysian dollar would be allowed to float upwards. Bank Negara was no longer bound to buy US dollars at the ceiling rate of $2.4805 for US$1.

Tun Tan said the decision was taken because the Malaysian dollar market rate against the US dollar had been persistently at the ceiling. The Malaysian dollar exchange rate had been at its strongest permissible level under the IMF rules relating to fixed parities and, as a result, Bank Negara had had to absorb a substantial inflow of US dollars in recent weeks.

Fund-raising drive for National Heroes

29 March Kuala Lumpur

Deputy Prime Minister Tun Dr Ismail began a six-month drive to collect at least $1.5 million for the National Heroes' Welfare Trust Fund which gave out $100,000 in aid annually. To date, $500,000 had been raised. He reminded the people not to forget the role played by the security forces in defence of the country.

The trust fund was initiated by the Utusan Melayu group, which launched a fund-raising campaign on 28 June 1968 for families of security forces killed and wounded in a Communist terrorist ambush at Betong near the Malaysian–Thai border. Among fund-raising initiatives were a sale of matchboxes in Kuala Lumpur and Petaling Jaya and a film premiere.

Straits Times Annual

An advertisement for one of Malaysia's signature products, Selangor Pewter.

1973

8 April
Pablo Picasso, 92, dies.

10 April
Israeli commandos raid Beirut to assassinate three Palestinian leaders. Lebanese PM Saib Salam resigns.

22 May
President Nixon confesses to his role in the Watergate cover-up.

20 July
Hong Kong movie star Bruce Lee dies.

2 September
The author of *The Lord of the Rings*, J.R.R. Tolkien, 81, dies.

11 September
Chilean President Allende is killed in a CIA-sponsored coup. General Augusto Pinochet's military junta takes power.

6 October
The Yom Kippur War. Egyptian and Syrian forces attack Israel.

10 October
US Vice-President Spiro Agnew resigns over a conviction for tax evasion.

Work to begin on Federal Highway

3 April Kuala Lumpur

Total reconstruction work on the Federal Highway from Kuala Lumpur to Petaling Jaya would begin in August and was expected to finish by mid-1976, said project coordinator T.A. Jegaraj. The work would begin at the Guinness factory in Sungai Way, he said.

The project would include widening of lanes, special lanes for motorcycles, five flyovers, subways and footbridges. Parts of the highway would be widened to six lanes and the section from the EPF junction to Jalan Pantai Baru would be eight lanes.

Malaysian film icon P. Ramlee dies

29 May Kuala Lumpur

Actor P. Ramlee, 44, died of a heart attack and was buried at the Muslim cemetery in Jalan Ampang. Hundreds of friends and fans flocked to pay their respects. According to his wife Saloma, Ramlee collapsed in his house in Jalan Dedap, Setapak half an hour after complaining of chest pains at 4.30am. He was taken to the General Hospital where he died an hour later.

Ramlee, who was born on 22 March 1929 in Penang, made nearly 200 films in his star-studded career. His last film, *Laksamana Do Re Mi*, was still being shown in theatres at the time of his death.

Thais agree to help replenish rice stock

23 May Songkhla

Thailand agreed to help Malaysia replenish its rice stock. The amount of rice to be supplied was not disclosed. An agreement was reached following talks between Tun Abdul Razak and Thai Prime Minister Tun Thanom Kittikachorn in Songkhla.

In Kuala Lumpur, the National Rice and Padi Board (LPN) assured the public that the price of rice would go down. LPN chairman Tan Sri Syed Nasir Ismail said it would import 45,000 tons of rice over the next three months, of which 30,000 tons would come from China. State committees would be set up to coordinate prices and there would be action against hoarders.

Malaysia tops region for life expectancy

28 May Kuala Lumpur

If average life expectancy is a yardstick of the standard of health care, then West Malaysia headed the list among developing areas in Southeast Asia with 65 years. Sri Lanka was next with 62 years, followed by South Korea with 58, Thailand with 56, the Philippines with 55, Pakistan with 51 and India with 50.

The UN Economic Commission for Asia and the Far East noted that Asia as a whole had benefited from steady, though far from spectacular, progress in health conditions in recent years.

This was due to increased public health consciousness, growing appreciation of the possibilities in preventive medicine, changes in medical practices, greater medical knowledge, improved organisation of health care and increased financial and human resources in medical fields.

MIC president to step down

27 June Kuala Lumpur

Tun V.T. Sambanthan announced his decision to step down as president of the MIC. He said the decision was made in the hope that 'turbulence would subside' in the trouble-stricken party.

He said there was obviously no harmony or brotherhood in the MIC now, which is

why he had decided to relinquish the presidency. He added that he would not be attending the party's Central Working Committee meeting on 30 June. No successor had yet been named.

The Yang di-Pertuan Agong presents the new colours of the Royal Malaysian Navy to standard bearer Lt Sheikh Othman Ahmad at the naval base at Woodlands, Singapore, on 3 July.

Tun Razak first Chancellor of UKM

23 June Kuala Lumpur

Prime Minister Tun Abdul Razak was proclaimed the first Chancellor of Universiti Kebangsaan today. Finance Minister Tun Tan Siew Sin and Deputy Speaker of Parliament Tan Sri Nik Ahmad Kamil were proclaimed the university's Pro-Chancellors. The proclamation and convocation ceremony, held in the Banquet Hall of Parliament House, was witnessed by 105 representatives of universities all over the world.

Sub to the rescue after collision in straits

26 July Kuala Lumpur

A 20,000-ton Cypriot tanker, *Anson*, and a 7,000-ton Panamanian-registered freighter, *Carnation*, collided in the Straits of Malacca, 65 miles northwest of Port Klang.

Thirty-five survivors from the *Carnation* were picked up by a British nuclear submarine, *Dreadnought*, which was on its way to Singapore when it received a signal from the vessels. The *Anson*'s crew remained aboard. There was no report of fatalities.

$85m investment to join container 'revolution'

The May edition of the magazine *Malaysian Business* provided a preview of the Port Klang Authority's containerisation project on which work was to start in August.

Containerisation, it said, was first tried by the Americans at the beginning of the century but in the 1960s began to spread rapidly and 'has swept the world.' Port Klang decided in 1969 to join this 'revolution in shipping'. It became clear, the magazine reported, that though the project would be expensive it would cost more to do nothing because shipping costs would increase so much without a container port.

Eventually $85.5 million was budgeted for the expansion of Klang's North Port. About $3 million was being spent on dredging to allow ships of 40ft draught to enter. Another $34 million was going on new 2,800ft-long wharves capable of taking 60,000-ton ships. Two 85ft-high container cranes—so high that they had to have aircraft warning lights—costing $3.75 million each and able to carry 35-ton loads were also part of the plans, as were eight bright yellow $1.5 million straddle cranes.

Sports' Hall of Fame

18 July Kuala Lumpur

Dashing hockey striker M. Mahendran and athlete Junaidah Aman were named Sportsman and Sportswoman of The Year 1972 at the Lake Club, beating 28 other candidates. It was the second year in succession that Junaidah had been awarded the title.

Mahendran said he was 'really surprised' at being voted as sportsman' after the presentation by Prime Minister Tun Abdul Razak who was also president of the OCM and the Malaysia Hockey Federation.

Hero's funeral for Tun Dr Ismail

2 August | Kuala Lumpur

Acting Prime Minister Tun Dr Ismail Abdul Rahman, 57, died of heart failure at his residence. He was survived by his wife Toh Puan Norashikin and six children. Hours before his death, he had launched the silver anniversary celebrations of the Federation of Malay Student Unions and then visited his wife, who was in hospital, before returning home. Prime Minister Tun Abdul Razak, who described Tun Dr Ismail as his 'tower of strength', rushed home from Ottawa on hearing the news.

The first Deputy Prime Minister to die in office, Tun Dr Ismail was laid to rest on 4 August at the National Mausoleum, a burial ground for national heroes. He was the first person to be buried there. Among those to pay their last respects were former Prime Minister Tunku Abdul Rahman, the King and Queen, Cabinet Ministers and other dignitaries as well as representatives of Indonesia, Thailand and Singapore.

Thousands of people watched from outside the mausoleum, some taking chartered buses to pay their last respects at the National Mosque.

The public lining up to pay their last respects.

Hussein Onn named DPM

14 August | Kuala Lumpur

Datuk Hussein Onn (below) was sworn in as the Deputy Prime Minister. The former Education Minister was also appointed Minister of Trade and Industry, a portfolio held by his predecessor, the late Tun Dr Ismail.

Others in the new Cabinet line-up were Datuk Ghazali Shafie (Minister of Information), Datuk Hamzah Abu Samah (Minister of Defence), Lee San Choon (Minister of Technology, Research and Coordination of New Villages), Datuk Ong Kee Hui (Minister of Local Government and Housing), Tengku Ahmad Rithaudeen (Minister with

Special Functions), Haji Mohamed bin Yaacob (Minister of Education), Ali Haji Ahmad (Minister of Culture, Youth and Sports) and Michael Chen (Minister with Special Functions).

Tunku to retire from Islamic Secretariat

5 August | Penang

Tunku Abdul Rahman announced that he would retire as secretary-general of the Islamic Secretariat in December. He was succeeded by Egypt's Hassan Tohamy.

'Collaborators' held

22 September | Kuching

Twenty-eight people in Sibu, including lawyers, doctors, architects, businessmen and other prominent citizens, were detained over three days for alleged collaboration with Communist terrorists.

Chief Minister Datuk Haji Abdul Rahman Yaakub said he was shocked to find his good friends among those arrested for giving material support to the guerrillas.

Later, on 1 October, Sarawak tycoon Datuk Ling Beng Siew was the 29th person to be detained under Operation Judas. He was picked up on 23 September at the Kuala Lumpur International Airport.

Malaysia joins boycott of IMF conference

26 September | Nairobi

Malaysia joined other Asian and African nations in a boycott of the International Monetary Fund conference here when South African Finance Minister Nicolaas Diederichs took the floor.

The decision to boycott was taken by African Ministers. A statement from the Organisation of African Unity said it would be abnormal if member States did not show their hatred of apartheid.

Pledge of more aid from World Bank

28 September | Nairobi

World Bank president Robert McNamara promised Finance Minister Tun Tan Siew Sin an increase in bank aid to ensure the success of the Malaysian Government's efforts to redress economic imbalances. Malaysia was among the few developing countries that had never asked for a rescheduling of loan repayments and McNamara felt there would be no problems servicing additional loans.

Malaysia's voice in the Philippines

1 October | Kuala Lumpur

Home Affairs and Information Minister Tan Sri Ghazali Shafie launched the Philippines service of Suara Malaysia (Voice of Malaysia), RTM's overseas service.

He said the broadcasts would further strengthen mutual understanding and a good relationship between the two Southeast Asian nations.

First big oil pact signed

3 October | Kuala Lumpur

The Federal Government signed a 30-year petroleum production-sharing agreement with the Sabah Shell Petroleum Co Ltd, the first agreement of its kind.

A total of 4,500 sq miles was reserved for exploitation but drilling work in each exploitation area was limited to a three-mile radius. Initial production of crude oil was expected by mid-1975.

Miss Malaysia Narimah Mohd Yusoff (right) in London for the Miss World contest, with two other contestants, Miss Mauritius (left) and Miss Brazil.

Malaysia's year of 'miraculous' growth

12 November | Kuala Lumpur

A gross national product of $15 billion or an increase of more than 20 per cent over the previous year marked 1973 as a year of what the press described as 'miraculous' growth.

As a result, the average annual rate of growth since the launch of the Second Malaysian Development plan was expected to be much higher than the planned target of 6.5 per cent per year.

Maramah Ismail, who in September became the Royal Malaysian Air Force's first female air traffic controller.

Seven-gold haul at SEAP Games

3 September | Singapore ▶ Malaysia won another seven golds at the 7th SEAP Games here, gathering two for track and field, two for shooting, two for cycling and one in women's badminton. This brought the team's tally so far to 10 golds, 19 silvers and 12 bronzes. At the top was Burma with a total of 15 golds, eight silvers and five bronzes while host Singapore was second with 14 golds, 17 silvers and 21 bronzes.

The Malaysian contingent with the contingents of the other participating countries at the opening ceremony of the SEAP Games in the Singapore National Stadium.

1973

14–15 October
Thai troops with tanks attack student demonstrators, killing 300. PM Thanom Kittikachorn and the army chief flee the country.

16 October
US Secretary of State Henry Kissinger and North Vietnam's Le Duc Tho win the Nobel Peace Prize. Tho declines, saying there is still no peace in his country.

16 October
Israeli tanks cross the Suez Canal and encircle two Egyptian armies.

17 October
An Arab oil embargo against countries supporting Israel triggers an energy crisis.

20 October
The Sydney Opera House opens.

11 November
Egypt and Israel sign a ceasefire accord.

25 November
Greek dictator George Papadopoulos is ousted days after a student revolt against his regime is crushed.

23 December
OPEC doubles the price of oil.

Bomb blast in KL injures eight

19 October Kuala Lumpur

A bomb explosion outside the Lincoln Cultural Centre injured seven city council workers and a passer-by. Police believed the bomb was planted among vegetables in a plastic pail outside the centre minutes before it exploded. Police did not establish a motive immediately but the centre was the target of student demonstrations a few days earlier against US involvement in the Arab-Israeli war.

Police keep a close watch outside the premises after the blast.

Police form a protective cordon (above) around the AIA building in Jalan Ampang, Kuala Lumpur, as thousands of protesters (right) gathered to demonstrate against the US.

Sacked MCA men join Gerakan

19 December Penang

Dr Lim Keng Yaik announced that he and a group of sacked MCA members had applied to join Gerakan. The group included Dr Tan Tiong Hong and Alex Lee, and others from Perak, Selangor, Negeri Sembilan, Malacca and Johor.

Earlier, on 30 May, Dr Lim resigned as Minister with Special Functions in Charge of New Villages, stating that 'attacks' on him by MCA Ministers would result in open clashes that would embarrass the Prime Minister and the Cabinet. On 1 June, MCA president Tun Tan Siew Sin sacked Dr Lim and Ulu Kinta chairman Yong Su Hian from the party.

Sime Darby boss sacked

1 November Singapore

Singapore police arrested Dennis W. Pinder (below) on a charge of criminal breach of trust after he had been dismissed as chairman and managing director of Sime Darby Holdings, one of the largest companies in Singapore and Malaysia. He has been released on bail, understood to be $1 million. Also dismissed from Sime Darby was Angus W. Scott, a former chairman of the group, who resigned as a director in March the previous year to become the

London adviser to the board. On 20 October 1975 Pinder was sentenced by the Singapore First District Court to 18 months' imprisonment for the offence.

Road displaces railmen

20 December Kuala Lumpur

Demolition work started on railway quarters in Jalan Bangsar to make way for a new highway. Ninety-six families had been moved to new two-room flats in Jalan Maarof earlier in the year but 30 families were still to be relocated.

Zubeidah's batik

Batik-maker Tunku Zubeidah Abu Bakar wrote a personal account in the *Straits Times Annual* of what the article called 'the tribulations of a backyard batiker'.

Tunku Zubeidah and one of her team in her backyard batik factory in Petaling Jaya.

100 dead in ferry sinking

27 December Sarikei

Nearly 100 people were feared drowned after the inter-island passenger vessel *Pulau Kidjang* sank in rough seas. It had just entered Kuala Rajang in Sarawak's Sixth Division on its way to Sarikei and Bintang. Forty-one people were rescued.

50 buried alive by mountain

18 October Ipoh

More than 50 people were buried alive when a 50ft slab of mountainside detached from Gunung Kroh and crashed on to a row of 10 houses including a shop and a laundry.

The military, police, fire brigade and volunteers mounted an all-night rescue operation for possible survivors with the help of searchlights.

By the end of the next day, rescuers pulled out six severely-injured survivors and 13 bodies. Another 30 bodies were believed to be still buried under the tons of rock and rubble in what was thought to be the worst such tragedy in Malaysia's history. A total of 15 families were living in the row.

On 23 June, seven mine workers were buried alive in a landslide in Gunung Rapat near here.

Rescuers at the foot of the huge slab of rock which crashed down from the mountainside of Gunung Kroh on to a row of houses.

1974

In what has been described as a diplomatic coup, Tun Abdul Razak made a historic visit to China, paving the way for the establishment of full diplomatic relations between Malaysia and the People's Republic of China. One of the beneficiaries of this visit may have been the Barisan Nasional when 90 of its candidates were returned unopposed in the general election, including Tun Razak and his deputy Tun Hussein Onn. In Sabah, Barisan won 15 of the 16 Parliamentary seats. The year was also marked by student demonstrations at the University of Malaya and Universiti Kebangsaan Malaysia ostensibly against issues such as inflation and corruption. Meanwhile, a language society at UM was implicated in a communist-inspired plot.

FEBRUARY
Kuala Lumpur is declared a Federal Territory.

JUNE
Inspector General of Police Tan Sri Abdul Rahman Hashim is shot dead by two gunmen in Kuala Lumpur.

SEPTEMBER
Education Minister Dr Mahathir Mohamad says the University of Malaya will be closed following riots by students, but it is later announced that classes will continue as usual.

DECEMBER
The National Savings Bank is launched by Prime Minister Tun Abdul Razak.

May: Prime Minister Tun Abdul Razak makes history as the first Malaysian leader to visit China.

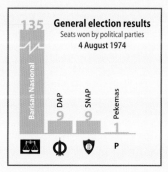

General election results
Seats won by political parties
4 August 1974

135 Barisan Nasional
9 DAP
9 SNAP
1 Pekemas

'We will not allow anyone to act outside the law, be they students or other people.'

Tun Abdul Razak, on student riots, 7 December 1974.

1974

world news

Special Branch man murdered

4 January Ipoh

A Special Branch detective was shot dead by two gunmen, believed to be Communist terrorists, in Malim Nawar. Police, who put the area under a 24-hour curfew and arrested eight people, said the shooting was part of a terror campaign to strike fear into the hearts of security forces personnel, particularly by singling out officers of Chinese origin for a 'death list'. The murder of Lew See Kaw was similar to that of Special Branch detective Chong Kok Onn in Sungei Siput on 23 October 1973 and of Chief Inspector Chin Chin Kui in Serdang on 13 July.

Lew was watching television with his wife and three children at their home when the gunmen knocked on the door. They asked if he was 'Ah Lew' and when he said he was they opened fire at point-blank range. He was buried with full honours in Penang; while in Malim Nawar, 6,000 people demonstrated to condemn the murder.

Tribute to heroes

14 January Kuala Lumpur

Former Prime Minister Tunku Abdul Rahman and Japanese Premier Kakuei Tanaka paid tribute to Malaysia's war heroes at the National Monument. Tanaka laid a wreath and signed the visitors' book before leaving for Jakarta after a three-day official visit. Tanaka also announced that Japan would provide another yen credit to Malaysia for projects under the Second Malaysia Plan.

Air force called in to wipe out terrorists

15 January Betong

RMAF Tebuan jets armed with rockets were deployed to wipe out a band of Communist terrorists trapped in the Sungai Liang area near Raub in Pahang. Defence Minister Datuk Hamzah Abu Samah said security forces were also attacking the area with mortar bombs.

Meanwhile, a number of people, believed to be members of the 'Malayan National Liberation Front', who had been supplying the terrorists with food and ammunition, were detained.

Tun Razak receives a bouquet from Kuala Lumpur Mayor Tan Sri Yaacob Latiff after unveiling a plaque marking the event.

KL proclaimed Federal Territory

1 February Kuala Lumpur

Kuala Lumpur was declared a Federal Territory in a colourful ceremony at the Balai Rong Seri of Istana Negara. The proclamation agreement was signed between the Yang di-Pertuan Agong on behalf of the Federal Government and the Sultan of Selangor for the State Government. The Sultan shed tears as he signed the papers.

After that, Prime Minister Tun Abdul Razak read the proclamation, followed by a 21-gun salute in the palace grounds. The ceremony was broadcast live over radio and television. Later, Tun Razak laid the foundation stone of a monument at the confluence of the Klang and Gombak rivers to commemorate the event. Shah Alam became Selangor's new capital.

Tun Razak reads the royal proclamation declaring Kuala Lumpur a Federal Territory.

Tycoon's son shot dead

8 February Kuala Lumpur

The son of a millionaire, racehorse owner David Sung, was shot dead as he got out of his car after parking it in a side lane off Jalan Treacher.

It was believed that three assailants had tried to kidnap Sung and shot him when he put up a struggle. The next day, police posted a $5,000 reward for information leading to the arrest of the person or persons responsible for the killing. On 10 February, police arrested two men.

Trapped boy rescued

24 February Kuala Lumpur

A schoolboy, trapped on top of a 300ft cliff at Batu Caves for more than 24 hours, was brought to safety after a rescue party spotted him looking dazed and shouting for water.

The boy, V. Ayaree, 17, said later that a stallholder had challenged him to climb the cliff and take down a flag tied to a tree there. He had previously taken part in five climbing expeditions, he said, but he vowed: 'I will never accept another challenge.'

Sarawak curfews end after mass surrenders

4 March Kuching

Chief Minister Datuk Haji Abdul Rahman Yaakub announced that for the first time in 11 years, the whole of Sarawak was curfew-free after 482 Communist terrorists had rejoined society in the past 4½ months.

The lifting of the curfew was to give remnant terrorist groups the chance to surrender. Some 200 members were still in the jungle. The leader of the so-called North Kalimantan People's Guerrilla Force was one of those who laid down arms and came out of the jungle. Datuk Rahman led a parade round Kuching to mark the event.

20 killed in caves of death

4 February Ipoh

At least 20 people were killed and 10 others injured when the bund of the Chong Poh tin mine here burst. More people were believed to be trapped in houses near the Sam Poh Tong Cave Temple. The temple was submerged in about 20ft of slime.

The next day, Menteri Besar Datuk Sri Haji Kamaruddin warned 15,000 people in Kampung Rapat to prepare for evacuation as another mine was in danger of bursting its bund. Eighty-three residents of an old people's home there were moved to safety by the State Welfare Department. Once a top tourist attraction in the state, Perak's famous Sam Poh Tong Cave Temple became a scene of death and desolation. Precious relics and idols were either swept away or buried under tons of mud and slime. Large sums of money and years of painstaking work would be required to restore the temple to its former glory.

The temple was built in one of the many limestone caves in the region by a Buddhist priest, the Revd Cheng. His successor, the Revd Chong Kam, almost died in the mudslide. The mud had reached up to his neck when rescuers pulled him out. A nearby Taoist temple Nam Thin Tong suffered a similar fate though other cave temples, including Loong Thau Ngam and Perak Thong, remained intact.

Straits Times Annual

The human face of banking is stressed in this advertisement.

Israel trade ties cut

4 March Kuala Lumpur

The Government was severing all trade ties with Israel following a decision at the Islamic Nations Summit in Lahore, said Deputy Prime Minister Datuk Hussein Onn. Malaysia's trade with Israel was described as 'very negligible'.

Watch out, streakers!

20 March Penang

Policemen on beat duty and patrol cars were ordered to arrest streakers following the sighting of two in Penang. Streakers were liable to be fined $25 or up to 14 days in jail. A strict watch was maintained, especially in the Batu Ferringhi and Teluk Bahang tourist areas.

University campus in Sabah

18 March Kota Kinabalu

Sabah Chief Minister Datu Mustapha Harun said Universiti Kebangsaan Malaysia would establish a campus in Kota Kinabalu, describing it as a historical achievement of the Sabah Foundation In Education to provide better educational facilities in the State. It would be named Universiti Kebangsaan Malaysia Limauan Kota Kinabalu and be located at Kinarut.

Big gas find off Pahang coast

2 April Kuala Lumpur

The Continental Oil Company (Conoco) struck natural gas and condensate in a well, 110 miles off the Pahang coast. Conoco's Malaysian president, Mr Charles C. Brenig Jr, said further drilling was required to determine the commercial significance but initial tests indicated a productive rate of 12.7 million cubic feet of gas and 172 barrels of condensate a day.

Perseverance pays

7 April Kuala Lumpur

After 11 years of trying, Hong Kong driver Albert Poon won the 50-lap Malaysian Grand Prix in Batu Tiga.

However, a jubilant Poon said his day was over as racing had become so sophisticated that 'if you don't have a good mechanic or sponsor, you are nowhere'.

Tan Siew Sin quits

8 April Kuala Lumpur

Tun Tan Siew Sin resigned as Finance Minister and president of the MCA. He said he was strongly advised by medical advisers to reduce his commitments in view of his recent ill health and operation for a non-malignant lung condition. His Ministry was taken over by Prime Minister Tun Abdul Razak, who said he accepted Tun Tan's resignation with 'deep regret and a sense of great personal loss'. The MCA said Tun Tan would be made honorary president and chief adviser. Meanwhile, Datuk Lee San Choon would be acting president.

American ordered out

16 April Kuala Lumpur

American-born Dr Shirle Gordon was ordered to leave the country after failing in her application to the High Court to set aside a Banishment Order signed on 25 March. Dr Gordon, 45, director and secretary of the Malaysian Sociological Research Institute, wept as she was led away by Pudu Prison warders. She was the author of several publications and editor of *Intisari* and *Benih*.

Sultan of Pahang dies

5 May Pekan

The Sultan of Pahang, Sir Abu Bakar Riayatuddin Aimu'adzam Shah ibni Al-marhum Sultan Abdullah, passed away at the Istana Peninjau here. He was 70. The late Sultan was laid to rest in the royal mausoleum at the Sultan Abdullah Mosque on 7 May. The Government proclaimed 100 days of mourning for the royal family and 44 for the public. Tengku Haji Ahmad Shah ibni Al-marhum Sultan Abu Bakar, 44, would be proclaimed the new Sultan.

Drivers warned of fake licence scam

12 April Petaling Jaya

A fake driving licence racket was uncovered in the grounds of the Registrar and Inspector of Motor Vehicles office here. At least 10 cases were reported in March.

Posing as officials, the tricksters would walk up to people who had just passed their tests or were waiting to renew their licences and offer to help.

However, they would then ask for payment for the licence and another $20 'to speed up work'. Victims would only find out the licences they received were false when they tried to renew them.

Miracle escape

5 May Penang

A family of seven on their way to a picnic survived a three-car crash in Tanjung Tokong Road. Harbour master C.S. Sawanni, 40, and his family were unhurt but two tourists from Singapore were injured when their Mini Morris somersaulted twice before landing in a ditch. The driver of the Rasa Sayang hotel van in which the tourists were travelling escaped after the vehicle turned turtle.

MIT closed after demo

22 April Kuala Lumpur

The Mara Institute of Technology was closed temporarily following demonstrations by students in the city. MIT students were told to go home but those sitting for external examinations were told these would be held as scheduled. By afternoon 131 students had been charged with unlawful assembly. Police said the demonstrations were in connection with the Government's delay in granting a request to elevate MIT to university status.

More Bahasa for schools

12 April Kuala Lumpur ▶ Changes would be made in the educational system in line with the objective of making Bahasa Malaysia the medium of instruction in national-type English schools from next year, said director-general of Education Haji Hamdan Sheikh Tahir.

The first step, he said, was that this year's assessment examination for Standard Five pupils would be in Bahasa Malaysia. From next year, the LCE examination in geography, history, art, handicrafts and music would be in the national language and all national-type English primary schools would become national primary schools. Remove classes using English as the medium of instruction would also be abolished.

1974

28 April
Last Americans
evacuated from Saigon
after its fall
to the Vietcong.

6 May
West German
Chancellor Willy
Brandt resigns over
a spy scandal.

9 May
Impeachment hearings
against President
Nixon begin.

18 May
India becomes the
sixth nation
to detonate
a nuclear bomb.

2 June
Jigme Drak Gyalpo
Jigme Singye
Wangchuck, 18,
is crowned
King of Bhutan.

17 June
An IRA bomb explodes
in Westminster Hall,
Houses of Parliament,
London.

1 July
Argentinian President
Juan Peron, 78, dies.
His wife Isabel takes
over as President.

7 July
West Germany defeats
the Netherlands 2–1
to win the
FIFA World Cup.

Sound war on crows

12 June Klang

The Sultan of Selangor had ordered that they must not be harmed, so Klang Town Council officials organised an audio blitz on the thousands of crows here.

It was a two-pronged approach. Officials using loudspeakers blasted nerve-shattering sounds at the birds, driving them to Sungai Klang. There, boats with speakers and officers firing guns in the air drove the crows further inland.

Crows were first brought to Klang from Ceylon during the Japanese Occupation to clean up Carey Island, five miles from here.

IGP shot dead on busy road

7 June Kuala Lumpur

Inspector General of Police Tan Sri Abdul Rahman Hashim was shot dead by two gunmen near the Lee Yan Lian building in busy Jalan Tun Perak.

His Mercedes was stopped at a junction on his way home from his office when the men appeared on either side of the car and opened fire.

At least 11 shots were fired, seven of them hitting the IGP. His driver was also hit but survived and chased the killers but could not catch them.

Federal police, who held several people for questioning, offered a $250,000 reward for information leading to the arrest of the assassins. It was the biggest ever offered by the Government for the purpose.

Tan Sri Abdul Rahman, who had been awarded the title only two days previously, was given a State burial on 8 June at the Jalan Ampang Muslim cemetery. Thousands of people lined the route to the cemetery to pay their last respects and Ministers were unable to control their tears. Encik Hanif Omar was appointed acting IGP (*see 24 March 1977*).

Malaysia and China establish ties

31 May Peking

An enthusiastic crowd waves the Malaysian flag to welcome Tun Razak on his visit to China. Right: Tun Razak meets Chairman Mao.

Prime Minister Tun Abdul Razak, on an historic visit to China, reached an agreement with Chinese Premier Zhou Enlai on 'matters of bilateral and international interest'. The two nations agreed to establish full diplomatic relations and to exchange ambassadors 'as soon as practicable'.

Malaysia became the 94th country, but the first Asean nation, to forge diplomatic ties with Peking. Tun Razak said differences in ideology, size and approaches to some international issues 'should not present obstacles to the development of fruitful relations and beneficial co-operation' between Malaysia and China and that it was important that 'we do what we can to contribute towards world peace'. The two Prime Ministers agreed that in recent years, the situation in Asia had undergone deep changes favourable to the people of all countries.

Tun Razak earlier met Chairman Mao Zedong, something regarded by observers as highly significant in protocol-conscious China. Tun Razak said Malaysia and its neighbours were taking the first steps towards freeing the region from the constant threat of war. He suggested that China could now play a constructive role in promoting the cause of peace and harmony in Southeast Asia.

Meanwhile, consular relations with Taiwan were terminated and all offices belonging to Taiwan in Kuala Lumpur were to be closed.

Tunku called to the Bar

4 July Penang

Former Prime Minister Tunku Abdul Rahman was called to the Bar. In moving the petition for admission, member of the Bench Datuk Eusoffe Abdoolcader described the occasion as 'unique' in the history of Malaysia. He was confident the Tunku's admission to the Bar would add lustre to the legal profession, he said.

Toast to the King

12 July London

The Yang di-Pertuan Agong and Raja Permaisuri Agong ended a four-day State visit to Britain with a farewell toast by Queen Elizabeth at a banquet in Buckingham Palace. The royal couple were staying privately in London until leaving for Madrid on 20 July. This was the first State visit by a Head of State of Malaysia to Britain.

New Cabinet

4 September Kuala Lumpur

Prime Minister Tun Abdul Razak announced his new Cabinet line-up, naming former Sabah Chief Minister Tun Datu Haji Mustapha bin Datu Harun as Defence Minister, Dr Mahathir Mohamad as Education Minister and Datuk Musa Hitam as Primary Industries Minister. There were 12 new faces among the 16 Deputy Ministers as well.

Tun Razak was also Foreign Affairs Minister, Datuk Hussein Onn, Deputy Prime Minister and Finance and Public Corporations Minister; Tan Sri V. Manickavasagam, Communications Minister; Datuk Lee San Choon, Labour and Manpower Minister; Tan Sri Ghazali Shafie, Home Affairs Minister; Encik Abdul Ghafar Baba, Agriculture and Rural Development Minister; and Datuk Hamzah Abu Samah, Trade and Industries Minister.

'Paper Tiger' to be shot in Malaysia

12 July Kuala Lumpur

Oscar winner David Niven and Toshiro Mifune were signed to star in the US$5-million film *Paper Tiger* that would be shot mainly in Malaysia. About 15–20 Malaysians would be in the cast, said producer Euan Lloyd, and local technicians would be hired. Shooting would be in Kuala Lumpur, Genting Highlands and Malacca.

Niven played an Englishman hired as tutor to the son of a Japanese Ambassador (Mifune) and who was kidnapped with the boy by terrorists.

Film star David Niven reads to a boy actor during a break in the filming of *Paper Tiger*.

Student unrest

Above: Tear gas fills the air as men from the FRU (Federal Reserve Unit) stand by near the entrance to the Universiti Kebangsaan (4 December).

Left: University of Malaya students take a solidarity pledge at the gate of the university while steel helmeted men of the Police Field Force watch silently (10 December).

University of Malaya situation tense

23 September Kuala Lumpur

Tension mounted in the University of Malaya as police stood guard outside the gates. It was feared that a clash might erupt between members of the University of Malaya Students' Union, who had earlier seized the university, and the National Supreme Council, which took back control and handed it to the authorities. Both student groups were feared to be gathering support for a showdown. Education Minister Dr Mahathir Mohamad said the university would be closed though he hoped an amicable settlement could be reached. But it was later announced that classes and lectures would go on as usual.

Student agitation 'must be stopped'

7 December Jitra

Students were warned to stop trying to organise demonstrations in villages. Such activities were similar to those of the Communist terrorists, said Education Minister Dr Mahathir Mohamad.

He told 1,000 villagers from five kampongs in the Malau mukim that some students were trying to meet and talk to villagers, inciting them to oppose the Government and to hold demonstrations supposedly to champion the cause of the poor.

The following week, Tun Abdul Razak warned that action would be taken against anyone, including students who 'use the democratic process to destroy democracy'.

No support for demos, say villagers

17 December Kuala Lumpur

Residents of Kampung Kerinchi off the Federal Highway denied supporting students in recent demonstrations. Village headman Haji Akasah Ahad said there were no deaths or injuries as a result of police action against demonstrating students on 13 December.

But the firing of tear gas led villagers to leave their homes. They did not do so to support the students. Some of the students were renting houses in the kampong. Two days earlier, Home Affairs Minister Tan Sri Ghazali Shafie advised six University of Malaya students to come forward and clear themselves of any connection with subversive documents found in a house in SEA Park in Petaling Jaya.

Singapore deports union officials

11 December Singapore

Five Malaysian student officials of the University of Singapore Students Union were arrested in a pre-dawn raid on a university hostel and deported two hours later. Thirty Immigration Department and Internal Security Department officials took part in the raid.

Police hold leaders in pre-dawn raids

7 December Kuala Lumpur

In a 2am swoop on Universiti Kebangsaan and University of Malaya campuses, police arrested almost all the student leaders responsible for staging demonstrations over the previous few days. The students were demonstrating over social issues such as inflation, corruption and allegations that farmers in Baling, Kedah, were facing starvation because of the falling price of rubber.

Tun Abdul Razak said it was clear that the students of University of Malaya and Universiti Kebangsaan had misused the freedom of the universities by using the campus as their stronghold to organise and hold demonstrations and disrupt public peace (*see 3 March 1975*).

BN has walkover in 90 parliamentary seats

8 August Kuala Lumpur

The Barisan Nasional was assured of a victory in the coming polls as 90 of its parliamentary candidates were returned unopposed. Heading the list were Tun Abdul Razak and Datuk Hussein Onn. The most stunning performance was in Sabah where the Barisan swept 15 of the 16 parliamentary seats.

On polling day, 24 August, Barisan won a landslide victory. In Penang, Opposition strongholds fell to the Barisan Nasional and Dr Lim Chong Eu won his Padang Kota State seat to remain Chief Minister. In Kuching, Sarawak's Deputy Chief Minister Datuk Stephen Yong's defeat in his Kuching Timur State constituency came as a shock to both Barisan and Opposition members.

Meanwhile, in Johor Bahru, a 120-year-old man went to the polls for the first time. Haji Tahir bin Khamid from Hujung Tambak in Gerisek, Muar, cast his vote at the Sekolah Kebangsaan in Bukit Rahmat in Tangkat.

His identity card showed that he was born in 1854.

Sardon (Call me Don) quits

31 July Kuala Lumpur

Communications Minister Tan Sri Sardon Jubir resigned from his post and announced his retirement from politics. Tan Sri Sardon, 57, was MP for Pontian Utara and his most famous line to newsmen was 'call me Don'. He had served as a Minister for 20 years.

Born, in Kampung Sungai Kluang, Rengit, Johor, he went to London to study law in 1937. On his return to Malaya in 1941, he worked in Johor Bahru as a magistrate, becoming Deputy Public Prosecutor later.

When Umno was formed in 1946, with Kesatuan Melayu as an affiliate member, he was nominated to the Umno council as the Kesatuan Melayu representative. In 1947, he was elected president of the Malay Union in Singapore and in 1951, national president of Umno Youth, a post he held for 13 years. In the 1955 Federal elections, he won the Segamat Utara parliamentary seat and was appointed Minister of Works.

Tan Sri Sardon was the first Malayan to receive the Magsaysay Award in 1958, in recognition of his contributions to youth organisations in Malaya and Asia.

Tan Sri Sardon shares a joke with a caller over the telephone in this 12 May picture.

1974

world news

15 July
A military coup overthrows President Makarios of Cyprus.

20 July
Turkish forces invade Cyprus.

23 July
Greece returns to civilian rule.

8 August
US President Nixon resigns.

15 August
South Korean President Park Chung-Hee escapes an assassination attempt that kills his wife.

8 September
US President Gerald Ford pardons Nixon.

12 September
Emperor Haile Selassie is deposed by Marxist military officers.

30 October
Muhammad Ali regains the world heavyweight title from George Foreman in Zaire.

22 November
The UN General Assembly grants the PLO observer status.

26 November
Japanese PM Kakuei Tanaka resigns over accepting a bribe from Lockheed Aircraft.

Women police prove deadly in the jungle

2 September Kuala Lumpur

Thirty women officers of the Police Field Force 'killed' five Communist terrorists in an hour-long battle in thick jungle after an ambush near Ulu Kinta. It was only a training exercise conducted for the filming of a TV Malaysia programme in conjunction with National Day.

The women's trainer, Insp Appadorai, 30, said his job was 'a little challenging' although the women were able to master whatever they were taught.

The leader of the team in the training exercise, Insp Rubiah binti Abdul Ghani, said: 'There is no reason why women cannot undertake such duties.' A team member, Corporal Fatima binti Ahmad, added: 'Now is the time for women in Malaysia to stand together with the men.'

Two policewomen walk a tight rope as part of their jungle training while (top) two other policewomen manoeuvre their way through an obstacle course.

Hunt for killer tiger

24 September Kuantan

A massive hunt began for a tiger which terrorised two kampongs, killing a woman in each one. Loggers reported seeing a tiger moving among a herd of wild elephants near one of the villages. Chek binti Lemak, a 62-year-old Orang Asli woman who was killed at Kampung Ronchang Ulu Serai, was the latest victim. Earlier in the month, an eight-months' pregnant woman was killed at Kampung Tualang Palong in the Pekan district.

Chek's neighbour Atom binti Mangis said she saw the tiger attack Chek and drag her away. She ran to alert the village headman and the villagers following the tiger's footprints later found Chek's body.

National Savings Bank launched

5 December Kuala Lumpur

The Prime Minister launched the National Savings Bank here, describing it as a vital Government instrument in its fight against inflation. He said less money in circulation would lead to a lower demand for goods and easing of pressure on supply. The money accumulated would be channelled to development. As the bank used post offices, the service was readily available to the public, even those in rural villages.

Bank chairman Datuk Syed Nahar bin Tun Syed Sheh Shahbuddin said more than 2.5 million people had deposited $537 million in the bank.

New oil law

1 October Kuala Lumpur

State Governments ceased issuing concessions to oil companies as Petronas took over all oil rights and concessions in accordance with the Petroleum Development Act.

Petronas chairman and chief executive Tengku Tan Sri Razaleigh Hamzah said the corporation would be 'fully operational' from Sunday.

Its first task was to negotiate oil concessions with State Governments and it hoped to complete this by February 1975.

Its operations were expected to involve all aspects of the industry—from exploration to distribution.

Soccer ace meets Pele

30 November Singapore

It was the moment he had dreamt of. Malaysian soccer ace Soh Chin Aun finally met his idol, the former soccer maestro Pele, in a hotel here.

Soh, voted Footballer of the Year by a Singapore magazine, *World Star Football*, received his award and several gifts from Pele.

The four-times Brazilian World Cup soccer star inquired about Soh's interest in becoming a professional in Hong Kong but Soh said he was satisfied to be an amateur.

Radio Malaysia Regional Station opens in Sibu

7 December Sibu

Sarawak Governor Tun Datuk Patinggi Tuanku Haji Bujang declared open the new Radio Malaysia Regional Station in Sibu. The station costing $3.8 million had five studios and an auditorium which could accommodate 200 people. It relayed programmes of Radio Malaysia Kuching, giving people in Sarawak's Third, Sixth and Seventh Divisions better radio reception.

Flu hits the north

19 December Kuala Lumpur

The Health Ministry confirmed an outbreak of influenza in the northern States but said it had not reached epidemic levels. The outbreak was blamed on the rainy season.

Mara blacklist

9 December Penang

Deputy Prime Minister Datuk Hussein Onn told a Mara senior officers' seminar that those 'smearing the good name' of Mara would be blacklisted. He said the 'opportunists' were using Mara for their own ends. Some even refused to repay loans given by Mara and some threatened to use violence against Mara officers trying to collect rent for shops. Only a small group was involved, he said, but he regretted that it included prominent people and community leaders.

He cited several examples of the way they were perverting attempts to assist Bumiputras in business.

Some who had Mara shops rented them out to non-Bumiputras for 'coffee money'. Some batik makers received cloth from Mara at cheap duty-free prices then sold it on to non-Bumiputras at a higher price.

Reds inflitrate Chinese language societies

19 December Kuala Lumpur

A Government White Paper implicated the University of Malaya Chinese Language Society in a Communist propaganda offensive to win public support.

The paper said the threat posed to national security by Communist elements through language bodies in institutions of higher learning must be exposed so that the people would be made fully alert to similar approaches.

1975

Communist terrorists and sympathisers attempted to foment unrest though violence. Near the Kedah–Thailand border, 60 terrorists killed seven members of the security forces in an ambush; a militant communist organisation was believed to be responsible for the bomb blast at the National Monument; the Chief Police Officer of Perak and two other police officers were shot dead by communist agents at a road junction in Ipoh; a goods train was blown up in Kelantan; and Dr Mahathir warned civil servants and university students to be wary of communist attempts to exploit their protests and impending strike. In an unrelated incident, gunmen from the Japanese Red Army stormed the US consular office in the AIA Building in Kuala Lumpur.

APRIL
Vietnamese refugees begin to arrive by boat in Peninsular Malaysia.

JUNE
'The fight of a lifetime': Muhammad Ali defeats Joe Bugner in Kuala Lumpur.

AUGUST
Japanese Red Army gunmen take 53 hostages including US Consul and Swedish Chargé d'Affaires. All hostages are later released unharmed and the gunmen flown to Libya.

AUGUST
A bomb blast severely damages the the National Monument in Kuala Lumpur.

March: Malaysia in action during the third hockey World Cup hosted by Malaysia at Merdeka Stadium. The national team reached the semi-finals, ultimately losing to India in front of a crowd of 45,000.

Malaysia Facts		
12.3 million	Population	
$23.8 billion	Gross Domestic Product	
$1,873	Gross National Income (per capita)	
30.7	Crude Birth Rate (per 1,000 persons)	
32.2	Infant Mortality (per 1,000 live births)	
33.0	Consumer Price Index (base 2010=100)	

'By this wanton act of vandalism these anti-national elements have shown how alien their cause is.'

Information and Special Functions Minister Datuk Abdul Taib Mahmud, on the Communist destruction of the National Monument, 27 August 1975.

1975

10 January
Japanese soldier Teruo Nakamura surrenders on the Indonesian island of Morata. The war is finally over for him.

15 January
Portugal grants independence to Angola.

11 February
Margaret Thatcher becomes leader of the Conservative Party in the UK.

25 March
King Faisal of Saudi Arabia is shot dead by a nephew with a history of mental illness.

5 April
Taiwan's President Chiang Kai-Shek dies at 88.

13 April
A Palestinian attack on a church in Lebanon sparks a 15-year civil war.

17 April
The Khmer Rouge captures Phnom Penh. Pol Pot becomes Prime Minister of the Democratic Republic of Kampuchea.

30 April
Saigon is taken. South Vietnam surrenders to North Vietnam.

Navy 'attacking' tanker oil spill

11 January Kuala Lumpur

Work continued to clean up oil slicks from the grounded *Showa Maru* in the Straits of Malacca.

The Royal Malaysian Navy had been 'attacking' the oil slicks and most of the patches would be clear by 14 January.

In view of the incident, Malaysia backed Indonesia's calls for joint action to fight pollution, a joint claim for compensation, a joint policy on the need to limit tonnage and draught, and other shipping safety measures in the Straits.

Indonesia made the call to Malaysia and Singapore after the *Showa Maru* ran aground in the straits on 6 January and leaked thousands of tons of crude oil.

MP guilty of sedition

14 January Kuala Lumpur

Fan Yew Teng, DAP MP for Menglembu and Selangor State Assemblyman for Petaling, was fined $6,000 or six months' jail in default for publishing a seditious speech.

The speech, by Dr Ooi Kee Saik, was published in the December 1970 issue of *The Rocket*, the official DAP publication. Fan was its editor. The conviction, if upheld, meant Fan would automatically lose his parliamentary and State Assembly seats.

Three young men dig in the area of Bukit Buluh, Pulai Chondong, Kelantan, after rumours of a diamond find.

Former Prime Minister Tunku Abdul Rahman leads his part-owned race horse Think Big, winner of the Melbourne Cup in Australia, on 4 November.

NEB men held

26 January Kuala Lumpur

Eleven National Electricity Board workers were detained as a strike by 4,000 NEB workers entered its sixth day. They were charged under the Industrial Relations Act with intimidating other employees.

The workers were protesting against alleged changes made by the Public Services Department to the Harun Report. The Harun Commission was set up in 1971 to make recommendations on salaries and conditions for employees of statutory bodies and local authorities.

Extra eggs cause a cheap sell-off

29 January Kuala Lumpur

Selangor had a glut of eggs because of poor sales. Despite the proximity to the Chinese New Year, hundred of thousands remained unsold. The Selangor Egg Dealers' Association resorted to selling leftover eggs to other States at a lower price. Penang and Perak also experienced production exceeding supply, with the Perak Poultry Farmers' Association calling on the public to eat more eggs.

Off to a head start

16 February Kuala Lumpur

The law requiring motorcyclists and their pillion riders to wear helmets was enforced in Kuala Lumpur, Petaling Jaya, Ipoh and Penang. Checkpoints were set up in all four places to book those not wearing helmets and advise others on the right types to use.

Deputy Works and Transport Minister Richard Ho described enforcement of the new rule as satisfactory. He said it might be implemented elsewhere in the country.

Plans for a garden city

1 February Kuala Lumpur

Kuala Lumpur Mayor Tan Sri Yaacob Latiff said City Hall sought to develop the capital into a clean and delightful metropolis with greenery and colour everywhere and ensure that development does not spoil the environment.

The hope was expressed in a message to mark City Day and the first anniversary of the foundation of the Federal Territory.

City Hall's other plans included increased housing facilities, promoting relations among Kuala Lumpur's multiracial population, encouraging faster development to meet the requirements of the growing population and creating more opportunities for Bumiputra participation in the city's economic life.

14,000 jobs lost

1 February Kuala Lumpur

A total of 14,063 Malaysian workers were laid off between August 1974 and January 1975, Labour and Manpower Minister Datuk Lee San Choon said. Of these, 6,563 were in Peninsular Malaysia, and the others in Sabah and Sarawak.

There were also unconfirmed reports that a further 2,470 workers lost their jobs in Sabah and Sarawak in that period.

Datuk Lee added that another 2,121 workers in Peninsular Malaysia were expected to be retrenched by the end of the month.

$400 million pledged

3 February Kuala Lumpur

Prime Minister Tun Abdul Razak returned from a 14-day trip to Saudi Arabia and the Gulf States with pledges of at least $400 million in loans. Saudi Arabia pledged $200 million, and Kuwait and Abu Dhabi $100 million each. Tun Razak also visited Qatar, Oman, Bahrain and Dubai. The trip, he said, had brought Malaysia much closer to the Arab countries.

Baby stolen from GH

27 February Kuala Lumpur

A housewife became the victim of a cruel hoax and nearly lost her baby at the maternity ward of the Kuala Lumpur General Hospital. Choo Peng Kwang was told by a woman that her husband had been seriously injured and was in the Assunta Hospital.

She rushed there, leaving her six-day-old son. When she returned to the general hospital he was missing. He was returned safe a day later.

Government must keep costs down, says PM

2 March Kuala Lumpur

Prime Minister Tun Abdul Razak warned that the Government might take drastic measures if it failed in its efforts to reduce expenditure in face of falling exports.

'We—the Government as well as individuals—cannot allow our expenditure to increase which will mean that we will be living beyond our means.' He called for public support in what he described as a difficult moment as the Government tried to reduce unnecessary expenditure.

At the Kuala Lumpur mayor's annual dinner, Tun Razak said although the Government sympathised with employees in the lower-income groups, there had to be a limit to its spending.

Volume 1, Number 1 of *Wings of Gold*, the quarterly inflight magazine of Malaysian Airline System.

Smashing start

3 March Kuala Lumpur

Angered by their refusal to stop when hailed, members of the public smashed windscreens and rear windows of at least three taxis. Kuala Lumpur cabbies were staging a rush-hour boycott in pursuit of a claim for a 10-cent increase in fares for the first mile. Only a few privately owned taxis were accepting fares.

Kidnap victim freed

5 March Ipoh

Millionaire pioneer miner Foong Seong, 78, was released by his kidnappers a week after five men broke into his house in Anderson Road, Ipoh. It was believed that a ransom of $500,000 was paid.

Foong owned several mines, foundries and property in the Kinta area and in Hong Kong and Australia.

Rubber pricing pays off

5 March Kuala Lumpur

A Government emergency programme of intervention to stabilise rubber prices yielded an additional $96.3 million in export earnings in three months. Under the programme, launched at the end of November 1974, rubber exports earned a total of $467.9 million.

70 die as boat sinks

6 March Tawau

Up to 70 people were feared drowned when a motor launch carrying 200 people from Tawau, Sabah, to Nunukan Island in Indonesia sank a few miles off Sebatik Island near Tawau. Most of the passengers were Indonesian workers in Tawau going home on holiday.

From waste to paper

7 March Kuala Lumpur

Local company Industrial Patents Sdn Bhd announced a technique for processing agricultural waste such as padi straw and lalang grass for making paper.

The process, using ammonia, was devised in Penang by engineer J. Thaillaimuthu and was developed over three years.

'Hockeymania' greets World Cup action

2 March Kuala Lumpur

The Yang di-Pertuan Agong declared open the Third World Cup hockey tournament in front of 28,000 people at Merdeka Stadium. Twelve nations took part in the tournament, which sparked 'hockeymania' in the country. After a slow start with two goalless draws against New Zealand and Spain, Malaysia defeated Poland 3–1 before going down to 1–2 to Pakistan.

The Malaysian team then sent the nation into raptures when it reached the semi-finals after defeating defending champions Holland 2–1, a result described by Tun Abdul Razak, president of the Malaysian Hockey Federation, as the best birthday gift he had received.

Malaysia went down fighting in the semi-finals, losing 2–3 to India after extra time in front of 45,000 supporters.

Americans' big stake

24 April Boston

American investment in Malaysia totalled US$500 million (M$1.1 billion), Malaysian Ambassador to the United States Mohamed Khir Johari told American businessmen at a reception in his honour in Boston. He said American businesses were generally satisfied with conditions in the country, chief of which was a stable Government.

Boat people start to arrive

25 April Tumpat

Two Cambodian navy vessels loaded with refugees arrived in Malaysian waters near Tumpat, Kelantan. The refugees were among the first of thousands of Vietnamese illegal immigrants who began to arrive on Malaysian shores following the fall of Saigon—putting Malaysia in the international spotlight and creating a controversial issue that would endure for several years (*see 18 April 1996*).

Limit your actions, Dr M warns student leaders

3 March Ipoh

Education Minister Dr Mahathir Mohamad criticised student leaders who used baseless issues to demonstrate the force of the students. He was referring to recent demonstrations on the purported issue of starvation in Baling. At the Menglembu Umno division's political and economic seminar, Dr Mahathir agreed that students should be aware of the country's political issues, but cautioned them against taking action without limitations.

Kelantan flies high

6 April Alor Star

Kelantan retained the National Kite-Flying Championship at the Pesta Wau Kebangsaan at the Sungai Petani golf course in Kedah. There were 32 entrants from Kelantan, Terengganu, Perlis and Kedah.

Border hunt for Reds

9 April Alor Star

Sixty Communist terrorists killed seven members of the security forces in an ambush in the Mong Gajah area, near the Kedah-Thailand border. Ten other soldiers were wounded. The soldiers were travelling in a convoy of four trucks from their post back to camp when they were ambushed.

Reinforcements were rushed into the area in attempt to seal the terrorists' escape route. This was the area where six Police Field Force men were killed in another ambush in 1972. In another attack, in upper Perak, 70 miles away from Mong Gajah, terrorists opened fire on a Land Rover carrying eight soldiers, injuring the driver. During the follow-up operations, another three soldiers were injured when they stepped on a booby trap.

Turtle secret revealed by fishermen's friend

13 April Malacca

An unknown species of turtle was revealed to have been laying eggs on the beach at Tanjung Kling, Malacca, for the past 70 years. Local fishermen had been keeping it a secret for all that time so they could harvest the eggs for themselves.

But the discovery was made by State Governor Tun Dr Haji Abdul Aziz bin Haji Abdul Majid, who was also patron of the Malayan Nature Society, after making friends with some of the fishermen. He said the turtle was very different from the leatherback which lays its eggs on the beaches of Terengganu and that research should be done on the species.

Local company builds bigger buses

15 April Kuala Lumpur

A Bumiputra company, TAB General Agencies Sdn Bhd, started building 77-passenger buses with seats for 53 passengers and standing room for 24.

The new buses were built with chassis imported from India. Earlier buses had seats for 44 and standing room for 14. Twelve operators signed up to use the new buses.

1975

world news

15 May
The US Navy and Marines take back the merchant ship *Mayaguez*, seized by the Khmer Rouge, but the rescue costs the Americans 38 lives.

16 May
India annexes Sikkim.

16 May
Japanese Junko Tabei is the first woman to climb Everest.

25 June
An Emergency is declared in India after PM Indira Gandhi is found guilty of electoral malpractice. She rules by decree for the next 19 months.

17 July
A US *Apollo* and a Soviet *Soyuz* spacecraft dock together in orbit.

2 August
A dam in Hunan province, China, collapses after a typhoon, drowning 200,000 people.

11 August
Governor Pires of Portuguese Timor abandons the capital Dili after a coup and an outbreak of civil war.

Million dollar fire

22 May Sibu

A fire that broke out at Sarawak House Complex at 7.45 in the morning was a surprise for most residents. The year-old King's Theatre, reported to be the most modern cinema in East Malaysia, was burnt and at least $1m worth of property damaged.

A cleaner at the theatre was trapped by the fire and was rescued by firemen. The fire station was located just a few feet away from the complex.

The complex housed the King's Theatre, Premier Hotel, Grandeur Restaurant and Nightclub and shophouses. The hotel was not affected by the fire.

Police unit revived to crack down on gangs

5 May Kuala Lumpur

The police Anti-Secret Society Branch was revived only a year after it was disbanded under a reorganisation of the CID. The re-establishment came after an upsurge of gang activity in the capital.

It was reported that the branch would work closely with the homicide and robbery squads.

At least 15 major gangs operated in the city, among them the 18 Immortals, Loong Foo Thong, the Gang of 21, the Gang of 24 and the Gang of 360.

Companies 'trying to blackmail Petronas'

1 June Kota Bharu

Petronas chairman and chief executive Tengku Razaleigh Hamzah said several companies were trying to blackmail Petronas by making comments and publicly expressing the view that the Petroleum Act would drive away investors.

The campaign began after Parliament had passed the Act, he said at a dinner given by the Kelantan branch of the Malaysian Malay Chamber of Commerce and Industry.

Tengku Razaleigh said these companies should understand that the New Economic Policy was designed to meet the needs and aspirations of the people.

Champ comes to town

11 June Kuala Lumpur

More than 25,000 people flooded Subang Airport to greet world heavyweight champion Muhammad Ali. Cheering crowds also lined the route from Subang to Kuala Lumpur.

On 1 July Ali successfully defended his title against Joe Bugner in front of a crowd of 10,000 in Merdeka Stadium. The bout was telecast live on RTM, bringing the nation to a

'I am the champion.' Ali in typical pose at the weigh-in.

standstill. Kuala Lumpur's streets were almost deserted and absenteeism was rife as all those who could stayed glued to their televisions or radios.

Two people, Malacca CID chief Deputy Supt Abdul Aziz Abdul Karim and Batu Pahat gardener Musa Tahir, collapsed and died while watching the broadcast.

Boom town

23 May Kuala Lumpur

With the country's economy growing, development was beginning to change the face of many towns. Photographs taken by cameraman Saleh Osman during a trial flight to Langkawi operated by local company Bintang Travel System showed the rapid development that has transformed the Klang Valley. The photographs were taken from 3,000 feet.

Navy to get upgrades

5 July Singapore

The Royal Malaysian Navy would get modern ships and equipment in its expansion programme under the Third Malaysia Plan, Prime Minister Tun Abdul Razak told 1,000 officers and men at a Navy Day parade at KD Malaya, the Navy base in Woodlands, Singapore. He said the expansion would allow the Navy to carry out its growing responsibilities efficiently.

At a dinner at the naval base that night, the Prime Minister paid tribute to the Navy's progress under Rear Admiral Datuk K. Thanabalasingam, saying: 'In recognition of his leadership and dedication to the Navy, I must say that your bachelor admiral, one of the most eligible in the country, has contributed no less to the country than his bachelor counterpart Tengku Tan Sri Razaleigh Hamzah, the chairman of Petronas… Our nation is indeed fortunate to have these two bachelors at this time.'

Former Speaker killed in car crash

27 June Ipoh

Former Speaker of the Dewan Rakyat Tan Sri C.M. Yusuf Sheikh Abdul Rahman and his great nephew died after the car they were in collided with an express bus near Telok Anson in Perak.

Tan Sri Yusuf, 69, was a lawyer and one of the founders of Umno in 1946. He was Perak Umno president from 1947 to 1951 and Umno Malaya vice-president from 1951 to 1954. He was appointed Dewan Rakyat Speaker in 1965 and retired in 1974.

Muhammad Ali visits Sabah

4 July Kota Kinabalu

By agreeing to defend his title in Malaysia, world heavyweight champion Muhammad Ali had put the country on the world map, said Sabah Chief Minister Tun Datu Mustapha Harun at a reception at the Community Centre in honour of the boxer. Ali was in Sabah after winning his title bout against Joe Bugner on 1 July.

Foundry boss shot dead

24 July Kuala Lumpur

Foundry owner Chak Ong was shot dead in broad daylight behind his house here. Police believed that the killing, which happened at noon as he returned home for lunch, was a case of mistaken identity. Robbery was ruled out as a motive because he was still carrying cash and his identity card.

PPP founder dies

5 July Ipoh

Dato' Seri S.P. Seenivasagam, a founder of the People's Progressive Party, died in Ipoh, where he was president of the municipal council. The 58-year-old was a lawyer and a senator.

More than 10,000 people were in the mile-long funeral procession the next day, while thousands more lined the route.

Dato' Seri S.P Seenivasagam takes the oath at a Senate meeting just months before his death.

Fuad to join Berjaya

28 July Kota Kinabalu

Tun Haji Mohamed Fuad Stephens resigned as Sabah Yang di-Pertua Negeri and joined the Berjaya party. Announcing his resignation, Tun Fuad accused Chief Minister Tun Datu Mustapha of plotting to take Sabah out of Malaysia and form a new State.

He said he had submitted his resignation to the King during an audience here on 23 July and it was accepted. A day later, Tun Fuad was named Berjaya president, and former Usno deputy president Datuk Mohamed Indan Kari was named Sabah Yang di-Pertua Negeri.

Rukun Tetangga is for all, says PM

29 July Ipoh

All able-bodied men aged 18 to 55 were required to register for Rukun Tetangga duty. Describing it as one of the best ways of combating urban guerrilla warfare and crime, Prime Minister Tun Abdul Razak said Rukun Tetangga was aimed at instilling a neighbourhood spirit among the people.

After presiding a joint Perak–Kedah Security Council meeting in Ipoh, he said everyone, including millionaires, had to do their duty. On 29 August the Prime Minister launched the first Rukun Tetangga patrol in Kampung Kasipillai in Sentul, Kuala Lumpur.

Tun Razak visits a Kuala Lumpur Rukun Tetangga post.

Reds will exploit strike, Mahathir warns

6 September Changloon

Education Minister Dr Mahathir Mohamad cautioned that if 300,000 civil servants carried out a threat to strike, Communist terrorists would exploit the ensuing chaos.

He called for better understanding of the Government's current financial difficulties and its commitment to maintaining peace and security in the country.

In a dialogue session here, Dr Mahathir said the Government's spending-spree days were over, adding that it sometimes did not have enough money to pay the salaries of civil servants.

Jobs freeze ordered

1 August Kuala Lumpur

The Government ordered a jobs freeze with respect to existing and new vacancies in Government, statutory bodies and public corporations to cut back expenditure. A statement from the Prime Minister's Department added that any job that needed to be filled required the specific approval of the Cabinet or Prime Minister. The temporary measures were taken in view of the financial problems the country was facing.

Four brothers to hang

5 July Kuala Lumpur

Four brothers, including a pair of twins, were sentenced to death by the High Court for the April 1974 murder of a pork seller in the Petaling Jaya old town market.

Tham Chee Kong, Tham Kai You, 27, and the 34-year-old twins Tham Ming Yau and Tham Ming Fook were unanimously found guilty by a seven-man jury of killing Loh Kah Han, 37. Kai You and Ming Fook were assistants to the murder victim.

Rain in wrong place so water is cut off

26 August Kuala Lumpur

Low water pressure at the reservoir in Klang Gates Dam resulted in regular interruptions to the water supply to certain areas of Kuala Lumpur and Petaling Jaya.

It had rained in Kuala Lumpur and Petaling Jaya for a month, but little of it fell in the Ulu Klang catchment area. Petaling Jaya residents said they had never experienced such a widespread water shortage.

Ministers take pay cuts

11 September Kuala Lumpur

Ministers and Deputy Ministers agreed to a pay cut of five per cent beginning in October due to the country's economic difficulties. Prime Minister Tun Abdul Razak said the Government had suspended the fourth quarterly annual bonus payment for civil servants earning $1,000 and above.

Ministers were paid $3,000 a month and Deputy Ministers $2,000. The Prime Minister got $5,000 and his deputy $4,000.

An inspector of the Police Field Force orders his men to fan out around the AIA building and keep crowds away as the hostage drama unfolds within.

A member of the Red Army holds a gun to an official as they board an airliner that was to take them to Libya.

Gunmen grab 53 hostages

5 August Kuala Lumpur

Five gunmen claiming to be members of a left-wing terrorist group, the Japanese Red Army, stormed the American consular office in the AIA Building and seized the American Consul Robert C. Stebbin, Swedish Chargé d'Affaires Frederick Bergenstrahle and 51 other people.

They shot their way into the office on the ninth floor of the building, wounding two policemen and a watchman. After taking over the ninth floor, the gunmen threw out of the window typewritten sheets making a number of demands, including the release of seven Red Army prisoners held in Japan.

'The Malaysian Government will do its best to meet the demands or to come to a compromise,' said Communications Minister Tan Sri V. Manickavasagam, who was appointed Government negotiator. The next day five of the prisoners arrived on a flight from Japan and they and the gunmen were flown to Libya along with two Japanese and two Malaysian officials.

All the hostages were released, some before the siege ended. Among these were an Australian mother and three children. The children said they were given sweets by their captors but told to behave or they would be shot dead.

Communist bomb attack on National Monument

27 August Kuala Lumpur

A bomb blast removed a 4½-ton bronze statue and the heads off three other statues at the National Monument. The 5am blast was believed to have been carried out by four members of the Malayan National Liberation Front, a militant Communist organisation. The explosion also opened a 2ft-long vertical crack in the monument's marble foundation and shattered windows of houses in the nearby Lake Gardens area (*see 11 April 1977*).

The National Monument after the attack by the Communists.

1975

world news

15 August
Bangladesh President Mujibur Rahman and most of his family are killed in a coup.

5 September
A follower of cult leader Charles Manson tries to assassinate US President Gerald Ford.

22 September
US President Gerald Ford survives a second assassination attempt in three weeks.

27 September
Death of former Ethiopian Emperor Haile Selassie, 83.

11 November
Australian Governor-General Sir John Kerr dismisses PM Gough Whitlam and replaces him with Malcolm Fraser.

20 November
Spanish dictator Franco, 83, dies.

7 December
Indonesia invades East Timor, which declared independence from Portugal on 28 November.

21 December
Terrorists attack an OPEC summit conference in Vienna They kill three hostages, extort a ransom of US$5 million and escape.

15 'subversive elements' arrested

15 September | Johor Bahru

Two women were among 15 people held in a pre-dawn swoop on their homes by Special Branch officers here. Described as 'subversive elements', among the 15 were former officials of the deregistered Shoe Industry Workers' Union. At least eight were former workers of the Nanyang Shoe Factory, which closed in 1973 after experiencing enormous losses from 1968 to 1972 because of strikes, go-slows and other forms of industrial action.

While most workers accepted the compensation offered, some refused and continued picketing the factory for two years after it closed.

Reds blow up train

16 October | Kota Bharu

Communist agents blew up a goods train in Kelantan. No one was hurt but 15 wagons were blown off the tracks. The train was on its way to Kuala Lipis when it triggered a bomb laid on the track between Kemubu and Bertam.

The explosion extensively damaged the track and wagons. Train services between Gua Musang and Kuala Kerai and between Kota Bharu and Gua Musang were suspended, while the Kelantan State Government declared a 24-hour curfew in the area.

Officers search for clues after a Communist grenade attack on the Police Field Force headquarters in Jalan Pekeliling, Kuala Lumpur on 3 September.

Perak CPO among three shot dead

14 November | Ipoh

Three police officers, among them the Chief Police Officer of Perak, were murdered in the space of 10 days. The killings were believed to have been carried out by Communist agents.

CPO Tan Sri Koo Chong Kong (below) and his driver, Constable Yeong Peng Cheong, were attacked by two gunmen at a road junction. Yeong died on the spot, while Tan Sri Koo died of his wounds two days later.

Police said the CPO was hit by four bullets fired into his official car as he was driven home for lunch. Yeong was hit twice as he jumped out of the car to return fire.

Within days leaflets were plastered up around Ipoh condemning the killings and signed 'The Voice of a Group of Ipoh Citizens'. Meanwhile, Tan Sri Koo was posthumously awarded the Panglima Setia Makhota, which carries the title Datuk.

Twelve days later, in Malacca, Special Branch detective Sgt Loh Kim Fong was killed while driving home from work.

After the murders, police launched anti-Communist operations in Perak, Malacca, Negeri Sembilan and Johor, detaining a number of suspects for questioning.

Police uncover print workshop

16 December | Kuala Lumpur

Police found a printing workshop operated by the Malayan National Liberation Front, a branch of the Communist Party of Malaya, in Cheras.

The workshop, hidden in a cellar under a hut, had two duplicating machines, a hand-operated duplicator, printing ink and paper and 4,802 copies of subversive documents. Two Communist agents sleeping in the hut were arrested.

The discovery came after the capture and interrogation of a high-ranking underground agent who had been on the wanted list for seven years.

Boy hero cheered by 10,000 children

26 October | Kuala Lumpur

Stadium Negara rang with cheers as boy hero Amran bin Ahmad, in national dress and with an escort of Boy Scouts, paraded round the running track after receiving the Pingat Hang Tuah from the Yang di-Pertuan Agong. Children ran down the steps of the stands to get a closer look at him as he waved to the 10,000 spectators.

Amran received the award for his bravery in rescuing two schoolboys from the Sungai Dong in June 1974. He was standing on the river bank after a swim when he saw them in difficulties. He jumped in and pulled them out in turn. After the award ceremony he admitted that he was 'quite scared'.

Little Amran bin Ahmad walks tall in Stadium Negara with his escort of Boy Scouts.

Selangor MB faces corruption charges

25 November | Kuala Lumpur

Selangor Menteri Besar Datuk Haji Harun Idris was charged with 16 counts of corruption, misappropriation, criminal breach of trust and failure to furnish the Government with a statement of his assets.

Other charges alleged that he bought properties and shares for himself, his wife and son and that he alienated State land to his son's benefit. Datuk Harun, who was questioned by National Bureau of Investigation officers on 23 November, pleaded not guilty to all charges. Datuk Harun was granted long leave by the Sultan of Selangor to prepare his defence. He was granted bail of $100,000 (see 26 March 1976).

Reds 'not involved' in police shooting

24 November | Kuala Lumpur

At least two gunmen shot and wounded City deputy CID chief Deputy Superintendent S. Kulasingam at the Jalan Davis–Jalan Pekeliling junction in Kuala Lumpur.

Although the gunmen fired at least 11 shots, only one hit the target. DSP Kulasingam, who was driving home at the time, was later operated on at the Kuala Lumpur General Hospital. Police believed that the shooting was carried out by criminals rather than Communist agents.

Medical first

15 December | Kuala Lumpur

Martin Rinyeb became the first person in Malaysia to have a kidney transplant. Rinyeb, a Land Dayak from Sarawak, received the kidney from his younger brother.

The five-hour operation at the Kuala Lumpur General Hospital was performed by seven doctors led by Dr Hussein Awang, head of the hospital's Institute of Urology and Nephrology.

Kamahl sings for elephants

31 December | Kuala Lumpur

Malaysian-born Australian singing star Kamahl came home to do his bit for Malaysian wildlife.

Reputedly the highest-paid entertainer in Australia, he said conservation was the main reason for his visit. He had recently recorded *The Elephant Song*, which was the No. 1 single in Holland for six weeks and won him an audience with Prince Bernhard. The song, about an imaginary conversation between two elephants, was recorded for a television show on conservation of the rainforest.

The sales of the record would help the Malaysian World Wildlife Fund to support scientists working on an elephant project in Malaysia, said its director Ken Scriven. Kamahl said he was willing to record the song in Bahasa Malaysia if someone would write the lyrics for him.

1976

Ups and Downs. Prime Minister Tun Abdul Razak died in London of leukemia, aged 53. Selangor Menteri Besar Datuk Harun Idris resigned following his expulsion from Umno. Sabah Chief Minister Tun Mohamed Fuad Stephens died in a plane crash. Police shot and wounded Botak Chin, the most wanted man in Selangor. Pilgrim ship *Malaysia Raya* caught fire in Port Klang. On the upside, new Prime Minister Datuk Hussein Onn was upbeat when he called for the creation of zones of peace in various parts of the world. At home, Finance Minister Tengku Razaleigh Hamzah reiterated the Government's plans to implement fully the aims and objectives of the Third Malaysia Plan. In football, Malaysia beat Japan to win the Merdeka Cup.

APRIL
Residents evacuate following a shootout between police and an armed gang.

JUNE
Sabah Chief Minister Tun Mohamed Fuad Stephens dies in plane crash.

AUGUST
Mokhtar Dahari lifts the Merdeka Cup after scoring two quick second-half goals to defeat Japan 2–0 and win the Merdeka Cup.

DECEMBER
Tun Tan Siew Sin appointed chairman of Sime Darby.

August: The pilgrim ship *Malaysia Raya* burns for more than 24 hours before the fire was brought under control.

'We can look forward to the rapid development of our oil and gas resources.'

Datuk Hussein Onn, on Petronas' agreements with Sarawak Shell, Sabah Shell and Exxon, 17 November 1976.

1976

world news

8 January
The death of Zhou Enlai, 78, Premier of China since 1949 and Foreign Minister 1949–1958.

12 January
Dame Agatha Christie dies at 86.

29 January
A dozen IRA bombs hit the West End of London.

30 January
George Bush becomes Director of the CIA.

4 February
An earthquake kills more than 22,000 people in Guatemala and Honduras.

24 March
Argentinian military officers overthrow President Isabel Peron.

1 April
Apple Computer Company is formed by Steve Jobs and Steve Wozniak.

5 April
In Peking, a crowd laying wreaths at Tiananmen Square for Zhou Enlai displays poems decrying the Gang of Four.

27 June
Palestinians hijack a plane in Greece and force it to fly to Entebbe, Uganda.

Stop the rot, bank governor appeals

8 January | Kuala Lumpur

Bank Negara Governor Tan Sri Ismail bin Mohamed Ali called for drastic measures to stop what he described as the decline in moral standards in business and Government 'at the highest levels'.

'People want to become millionaires quickly, regardless of the means in making themselves rich,' he said. He attributed such practices to 'booming conditions and inflation' which forced people to resort to whatever means were available to meet rising expenses.

Tan Sri Ismail said a booming economy followed by recession could have led businessmen to cutting corners and resorting to 'questionable practices' to make ends meet.

145 defiant MIT students give up

10 January | Shah Alam

The last 145 dissident students, who had 'occupied' the Mara Institute of Technology for four days, surrendered to the police. The 78 girls and 67 boys did not resist as they were taken away by members of the Federal Reserve Unit to have their photographs taken and their identities noted by police and MIT staff members.

Deputy Inspector General of Police Datuk Mahmood Yunus said 20 were detained for questioning but 16 of these were later released. MIT director Datuk Lokman Musa said each case would be assessed on individual merit and action would be taken according to MIT rules and regulations.

If it was found necessary to expel some students it would be done, he said. However, no damage was done during the occupation, he added.

Students man a checkpoint at the institute gates during the occupation.

Tun Razak dies

14 January | Kuala Lumpur

Prime Minister Tun Abdul Razak died of leukaemia in London, aged 53. His body was flown home in a specially chartered MAS Boeing 707, with people weeping openly as it landed at Subang Airport the following evening. Thousands had gathered at the airport before Tun Razak's body arrived in an oak casket draped in the national flag and thousands more lined the streets. Millions of others across the nation watched on television in their homes.

Tun Razak's eldest son Najib, 22, and his youngest son Nazir, 9, entered the plane when it landed, followed by the Sultan of Pahang, Datuk Hussein Onn, Datin Suhaila and immediate relatives.

Minutes later, Toh Puan Hajjah Rahah emerged, followed by her three other sons, Johari, Nazim and Nizam, and proceeded to the rear of the plane. Tun Razak's casket was carried to the hearse by officers of the Royal Malay Regiment. The cortege, led by outriders, circled the tarmac and left for Seri Taman. Along the way, people lining the streets fell silent as the cortege passed. At Seri Taman, the casket was taken into the living room and placed on a satin-covered dais. The next day, Tun Razak's body lay in state at the Banquet Hall in Parliament House to enable the people to pay their last respects.

It was then taken to Masjid Negara and before Friday prayers, Tun Razak was laid to rest at the National Mausoleum.

Tun Razak's cortege passes through the packed but silent streets of Kuala Lumpur.

Hussein is new PM

15 January | Kuala Lumpur

Datuk Hussein Onn was sworn in as Prime Minister at a ceremony at Istana Negara, witnessed by Cabinet Ministers and other dignitaries. A generally publicity-shy person, he was welcomed in his new position as the country' leader by all sections of society. A strong disciplinarian, Datuk Hussein was strict with regard to integrity and doing one's duty.

Petrol price up

16 February | Kuala Lumpur

From midnight, the price of premium petrol rose to $3.38 a gallon, an increase of 28 cents, and regular went up to $3, or 25 cents more. Diesel went up by 18 cents and kerosene by one cent. They were the first increases since the Organisation of Petroleum Exporting Countries raised crude oil prices by 10 per cent in October 1975. The previous price increase in Malaysia was on 9 May 1974.

$100,000 haul as armed gang holds up 40 people

2 February | Kuala Lumpur

Eight men, believed to be members of a gang led by the notorious criminal Botak Chin, held up 40 people, including 10 women and 20 children, in a shop 500 yards from the Jalan Bandar police station and escaped with $100,000 in cash, jewellery and watches. They were armed with two sub-machine guns, a shotgun, pistols and three grenades. They also seized three pistols belonging to three businessmen playing mahjong at a Chinese New Year get-together in the shop.

Hot and dry spell

12 February | Kuala Lumpur

Bush fires, burning out of control because of drought, destroyed thousands of acres of crops across the Peninsula. Areas most affected included Kedah, Perak, Malacca, Johor and Kelantan. All leave for firemen was cancelled. Villagers faced an acute shortage of drinking water in the drought, which started late in January. People were urged not to waste water and Public Works Department tankers ferried supplies to most of the affected areas.

Smugglers 'used as pathfinders' by Reds

15 February | Ipoh

Communists in South Thailand were using smugglers as pathfinders for infiltration into Malaysia, said Brig-Gen Datuk Jaafar Onn, Commander of the 2nd Malaysian Infantry Brigade. Most of the Communists' jungle trails were being closely watched by security forces, but smugglers were successful in bringing cattle across the border. This also means that guns and ammunition could be smuggled into Malaysia.

Botak Chin held after two-hour gun battle

17 February Kuala Lumpur

The most wanted man in Selangor, Botak Chin alias Wong Swee Chin, was arrested after he was shot and wounded in a two-hour gun battle with police. Two of four men with him were killed and two wounded in the head and body. They were also arrested.

Acting on a tip-off, 160 policemen had surrounded a squatter hut behind a sawmill off Jalan Ipoh. The gang opened fire on them and police sealed off the area. The police and the gang shot it out for more than two hours.

Later, three other men, believed to be members of the gang, were held in Jalan Alor. Police recovered a total of five pistols, a revolver, a shotgun, four grenades and 116 rounds of ammunition (*see 11 January 1977*).

Power-cut timetable

19 February Kuala Lumpur

The National Electricity Board drew up a timetable for staggered power cuts at factories and mines due to a temporary power shortage. Those affected were informed in advance to allow them to adjust their production.

NEB workers would visit mines and factories to switch the power off and on manually so as not to affect homes and essential services. But the public was urged to cut consumption by switching off unnecessary lights and air-conditioning.

Menteri Besar of Selangor resigns

26 March Klang

Datuk Harun Idris resigned as Selangor Menteri Besar after an overwhelming vote of no confidence by the Selangor State Legislative Assembly in which he was the only dissenting voice.

The vote followed his expulsion from Umno on 19 March. He had declined to heed the Umno supreme council's advice to resign 'from all offices in Umno and the Barisan Nasional and also as Menteri Besar'. The decision to expel Datuk Harun was taken at a special meeting of the supreme council chaired by Datuk Hussein Onn.

A magazine cover portrait of Datuk Harun.

Datuk Harun was charged on 12 March with forgery and criminal breach of trust involving $8 million in shares and stocks belonging to Bank Kerjasama Rakyat, of which he was chairman. He was jointly charged with bank general manager Ismail bin Din. Both pleaded not guilty and were allowed bail of $100,000.

On 27 March, the Sultan of Selangor appointed Datuk Hormat Rafei acting Menteri Besar (*see 18 May 1976*).

Sixth King installed

28 February Kuala Lumpur

Tuanku Yahya Petra ibni Al-marhum Sultan Ibrahim kissed the Kris of State in a gesture that symbolised his installation as the nation's sixth Yang di-Pertuan Agong.

The ceremony was held at the Dewan Tunku Abdul Rahman and was attended by Rulers, Governors, the Yang di-Pertua Negeri of Sabah, Cabinet Ministers, members of the diplomatic corps and other VIPs.

After the ceremony, the King expressed his faith in a fine future for the country, provided the Government and the people worked together towards achieving it.

Asean is for Southeast Asians, says Hussein

8 March Kuala Lumpur

Prime Minister Datuk Hussein Onn warned big powers to lay off Asean. 'We are not the tools of any extra-regional big power and we do not intend to be,' he said when addressing the second meeting of the Asean Economic Ministers.

'Asean is an association of Southeast Asians, by Southeast Asians and for Southeast Asians,' he said. He added that the association was open to all nations in the region, including Burma, Cambodia, Laos and Vietnam.

Four gangsters die in shootout with police

7 April Petaling Jaya

Four members of an armed gang which robbed a jeweller in Paramount Garden here were trapped and shot dead by police about half a mile away from the scene of the robbery. Police recovered most of the loot, worth about $300,000, in a suitcase.

Kuala Lumpur deputy CID chief DSP S. Kulasingam, who led the first police party into action, was shot in the chest. However, after the bullet was removed in hospital, he was reported to be out of danger.

Police believed six men were in the gang which had been involved in at least six gangland killings and two robberies. Nearly 100 policemen took part in the operation.

Maternity unit overworked

17 April Malacca

Doctors and nurses in the maternity unit of the General Hospital here were overworked, Dr Abdul Onny bin Yahaya told a Royal Commission of Inquiry investigating allegations of abnormal numbers of infant deaths at the hospital.

The commission was told that 15 infants—11 in the maternity unit and four in the children's ward—died between 21 November and 30 November 1975. Dr Abdul Onny, who was posted to the unit in June 1975, said he was not satisfied with the facilities. Staff shortages resulted in dislocation of normal services and incubators, wrappings and intravenous equipment were inadequate.

Helicopter downed

27 April Sungai Petani

Communist terrorists shot down an RMAF Nuri helicopter, killing all 11 security force members on board. Deputy Defence Minister Encik Mokhtar Hashim said all the bodies were recovered from the crash at Gubir in the Ulu Muda forest reserve near the Kedah–Thai border. The helicopter was dropping food supplies to soldiers in the jungle when the terrorists opened fire.

3,000 troops join border ops

22 April Alor Star

About 3,000 troops joined a search for Communist terrorists who fled when a detachment of commandos attacked their camp in the Ulu Muda forest reserve near the Thai border. Three commandos were injured by booby traps during the assault.

Malaysian jet fighters attacked areas around Wang Rai village in the Betong district and bombed suspected terrorist positions in Thailand in an apparent violation of a rule which allowed ground troops the right of 'hot pursuit' but did not permit the use of heavier weaponry.

Thai officials along the border said they were not informed before the bombing incident and Malaysian pilots said they mistook the bombing site for a target in Malaysia.

In Mentakab, schoolchildren spotted two red flags near a railway station. They alerted the police who later found four home-made bombs planted at a railway bridge about 400 yards from the station. A bomb disposal unit removed the explosives.

The authorities believed the terrorists wanted to derail a troop train on its way to Kelantan.

Towering inferno at shopping complex

9 April Kuala Lumpur

Fire destroyed the Campbell Shopping Complex, including its 20-storey office block, in what was the country's worst fire in a high-rise building. The complex in Jalan Campbell burned for nearly 24 hours. There were no casualties as the fire started late at night. The cause was an electrical short-circuit.

The burning of numerous partitions within the complex caused very dense smoke and heat, hindering the firemen's work. The firemen were also hampered by very strong winds.

The Local Government and Federal Territory Ministry said it would set up a commission of inquiry to investigate the fire and to review the Federal Territory's fire-fighting personnel and equipment.

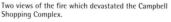

Two views of the fire which devastated the Campbell Shopping Complex.

1976

world news

Razaleigh heads ADB

23 April Kuala Lumpur

Finance Minister Tengku Razaleigh Hamzah was elected chairman of the board of Governors of the Asian Development Bank at its general meeting in Jakarta.

$3m loss in factory fire

23 April Johor Bahru

A fire in a building housing a garment factory and a row of five workshops in Jalan Datuk Abdullah Tahir here caused damage estimated at $3 million.

Tons of textiles and machinery in the Li Sheng Garments Manufacturing Sdn Bhd premises were destroyed along with stock in a battery and tyre shop, a chrome shop, a motor-repair workshop, an engineering workshop and a pump service centre.

Police pay increased and widows get help

7 May Kuala Lumpur

Under a new pay scheme, about 40,000 members of the police force were given substantial pay rises, in some cases nearly equal to their present salaries. The increases were backdated to 1 January.

Prime Minister Datuk Hussein Onn said the Government would also pay pensions to police widows whose husbands had died in the course of duty and allowances would be provided for their children's education.

Literary award surprise

29 May Kuala Lumpur

Datuk Hussein Onn sprang a $60,000 surprise on literary circles with a new Hadiah Pejuang Sastra (Literary Pioneer Award) which he conferred on six people for their contribution to the nation's literature.

The six, who received $10,000 each, were journalist Ishak Haji Muhamad (Pak Sako), *New Straits Times* managing editor Samad Ismail, Dewan Bahasa dan Pustaka editor-in-chief Kamaludin Muhammad (Keris Mas), *Dewan Sastra* editor Usman Awang (Tongkat Warrant), *Berita Harian* editor A. Samad Said and Universiti Sains lecturer Shahnon Ahmad.

Harun found guilty

18 May Kuala Lumpur

Former Selangor Menteri Besar Datuk Harun Idris was sentenced to two years' jail on three charges of corruption and ordered to pay $225,000 to Umno Selangor. He was allowed bail of $100,000 pending an appeal to the Federal Court. Mr Justice Raja Azlan Shah found him guilty of soliciting and accepting a total of $250,000 from the Hongkong and Shanghai Banking Corporation. A charge of criminal breach of trust against Datuk Harun and the former general manager of Bank Kerjasama Rakyat Ismail Din was reduced to one of abetment (*see 8 March 1978*).

Police station attacked

11 May Seremban

A policeman was killed and two others and a woman wounded in an attack on the Simpang Pertang police station by gunmen believed to members of the 'Malaysian Liberation Front'. Over the next few days police arrested 16 suspects, eight of them in a 3am raid in Kampung Titi.

Shock win by Berjaya in Sabah state election

15 April Kota Kinabalu

Tun Mohamed Fuad Stephen's Berjaya Party scored a shock victory over the ruling Sabah Alliance led by Tun Datu Mustapha, ending its nine-year rule. Tun Mustapha had resigned as Chief Minister in October 1975 following political differences with Federal leaders and had been succeeded by Tan Sri Mohammed Said Keruak.

Sabah CM killed in plane crash

6 June Kota Kinabalu

Sabah Chief Minister Tun Mohamed Fuad Stephens and 11 other people, four of them members of his Cabinet, were killed when a 14-seater Nomad aircraft they were in crashed into the sea as it approached the airport at Kota Kinabalu.

The following day Tun Fuad was laid to rest in the Warriors' Mausoleum at the State Mosque, the first State leader to be buried there. His Cabinet colleagues Datuk Haji Salleh Sulong, Datuk Peter Mojuntin, Mr Chong Thien Vun and Mr Darius Binion were also buried with full State honours.

Datuk Hussein Onn ordered aviation experts to investigate the crash.

Top award for soldier

17 July Kuala Lumpur

The Yang di-Pertuan Agong, Tuanku Yahya Petra, posthumously awarded the nation's highest gallantry award, the Seri Pahlawan Gagah Perkasa to Capt Zainal Abdul Rashid who was killed in a shootout with Communist terrorists recently. The award is only given for conspicuous bravery or eminent self-sacrifice.

$6.5m for Ali–Bugner fight 'was not repaid'

12 August Kuala Lumpur

The High Court was told that stocks and shares worth more than $6.5 million belonging to Bank Kerjasama Rakyat had been pledged to the First National City Bank. This was to obtain credit facilities enabling Tinju Dunia Sdn Bhd to stage the Muhammad Ali–Joe Bugner heavyweight championship boxing match here.

Tinju Dunia, which was incorporated in May 1975 to promote the fight, failed to repay the loan and FNCB was still holding three million Dunlop Estates Sdn Bhd ordinary shares and $1 million KL-Kepong debenture stocks which were pledged.

On trial were Datuk Harun Idris, former bank manager Ismail Din and former bank director Datuk Abu Mansor Basir. All three faced a joint charge of forging the minutes of the bank's investment committee with the intention of cheating the bank (*see 24 January 1977*).

Local people bid farewell to a Police Field Force detachment leaving Betong on 7 June after operations against terrorists.

Jungle training for police recruits

4 June Ipoh

All police recruits would be required to serve in the Police Field Force before being assigned to other duties, said Inspector General of Police Tan Sri Hanif Omar. Jungle training would ensure they were able to tackle any emergency, he said after 20 police recruits had been ambushed when they stumbled on a Communist terrorist camp in the jungles of Simpang Pulai. Four were killed on the spot and a fifth was wounded in the first burst of fire. Tan Sri Hanif praised the recruits for showing courage in facing the enemy, even after their instructor was slain. A curfew was imposed in the area.

Pilgrim ship ablaze for 24 hours

23 August Kuala Lumpur

The pilgrim ship *Malaysia Raya* caught fire at its berth in Port Klang and burned for more than 24 hours before the blaze was brought under control. The 14,000-ton vessel, belonging to Great Malaysia Lines and leased to the pilgrims' fund, Tabung Haji, had been in Port Klang for a month waiting to take pilgrims to Mecca.

Twisted metal and burnt-out lifeboats aboard the *Malaysia Raya* after the fire.

Buffer fund target

16 August Colombo

Malaysia planned to seek wide support from the non-aligned conference for the speedy implementation of the United Nations Conference on Trade and Development's integrated programme on primary commodities. The most important measure, aimed at stabilising commodity prices and ensuring fair returns, was a common buffer stock fund.

Developing nations had pressed for the multi-billion dollar fund to which consumers and producers would contribute to help stabilise price fluctuations of primary commodities.

No to delaying tactics

17 August Kuala Lumpur

Finance Minister Tengku Razaleigh Hamzah said the Government would not allow any interruption or obstacles or delaying tactics in the implementation of the Third Malaysia Plan. In winding up the debate on the Plan, he said the Government was determined to implement in full the aims and objectives of the Plan.

Super Mokh scores twice

22 August Kuala Lumpur

Two quick second-half goals from striker Mokhtar Dahari enabled Malaysia to beat Japan 2–0 and win the Merdeka Cup football tournament.

The star striker said he would remember the two goals for the rest of his life.

Hunt for police killers

27 August Johor Bahru

Det Cpl Gan Cheng Tack was shot dead while on motorcycle patrol. The following day police detained 48 secret society members and subversive elements in the hunt for the killers.

A curfew that had been imposed on Tampoi new village was later lifted.

State CID chief Asst Commissioner Gian Singh said police were interrogating those detained.

Film subtitles in Bahasa a must, says Minister

28 August Kuala Lumpur

All foreign films must have Bahasa Malaysia subtitles before they could be sent to the Censorship Board, Home Affairs Minister Tan Sri Ghazali Shafie said.

About 18,000 films previously approved by the board would be allowed to be shown without subtitles until 31 December. They would have to have subtitles if they were re-shown afterwards.

Advertising films would also be required to have subtitles and would have to have at least 80 per cent local content.

Six buried alive

27 August Ipoh

Six mineworkers, including two women, were buried alive when the wall of a mining pit they were working in caved in at the Sin Yew Sing tin mine in Pulau Atap, near Tanjung Tualang. The mine supervisor was the only one to escape when tons of slime, rocks, earth and dead wood crashed down, burying the workers 30ft deep.

Zones of peace are urgent need, says PM

18 August Colombo

The creation of zones of peace in various parts of the world has become necessary and urgent as a means of lessening tension and eliminating big-power rivalry and arms escalation, Prime Minister Datuk Hussein Onn told the Non-Aligned Summit Conference here. 'We should therefore give further impetus to the early creation of zones of peace in strategic areas such as the Indian Ocean and Southeast Asia.'

He added that the proposal was consistent with the principles of non-alignment which the movement had pledged to uphold and on which it had been established.

The next day, he told Hanoi that Malaysia gave its full support for the newly-unified Vietnam to be admitted into the United Nations.

While civil servants eagerly anticipate a pay hike on Datuk Hussein's return from an overseas trip, Lat's take is that the Prime Minister is not in any particular hurry.

Gift from Mecca for Prime Minister

24 September Mecca

Datuk Hussein Onn received a gift of cloth covering the Ka'aba in the centre of the mosque in Mecca from Mecca Governor Amir Fawaz ibni Abdul Aziz during a recent trip to Saudi Arabia. During his five-day trip, Datuk Hussein and his delegation also performed the umrah (minor haj).

Ex-editor confesses

1 September Kuala Lumpur

Former *New Straits Times* managing editor Abdul Samad Ismail, 52, confessed that he had dedicated three-quarters of his life to Communist causes.

In an interview broadcast by TV Malaysia, he said he had been a member of the Communist Party of Malaya since 1940 under the party name of 'Zainal'.

He said his directive was to penetrate Umno and get 'closer to the core of Umno leadership' through the younger generation.

He said he had gained the confidence of some Umno leaders to the extent of being consulted on such vital issues as planning for the general elections.

The confession followed the arrest on 22 June of Encik Samad and *Berita Harian* assistant editor Samani bin Mohamed Amin, 43, under the Internal Security Act.

A Home Ministry statement said the two were arrested for 'direct involvement in activities in support of the Communist struggle for political power'.

1976

6 October
A bomb planted by opponents of President Castro kills 73 people on a Cuban plane flying out of Barbados.

6 October
Right-wing militia and army troops attack students at Thammasat University, Thailand. A military coup follows, ousting PM Seni Pramoj. He is succeeded as PM by Tanin Kraivixien.

10 October
Taiwan Governor Hsieh Tung-Ming is injured by a letter bomb sent by a pro-independence militant.

12 October
Hua Guofeng is named successor to Mao Zedong as Chairman of the Communist Party of China. He ends the Cultural Revolution and ousts the Gang of Four from power.

19 October
The chimpanzee is placed on the list of endangered species.

2 November
Jimmy Carter defeats the incumbent Gerald Ford to become the first elected US President from the southern States since the Civil War.

Shell signs oil pact

30 November | Kuala Lumpur

Petronas signed production-sharing contracts with two oil companies, Sarawak Shell Bhd and Sabah Shell Petroleum Company Ltd, covering oil and gas exploration and production. The agreements, effective from 1 April 1975, were for 20 years with an extension of four years for oil and 14 years for gas.

Eight days later, Petronas and Exxon also signed three production-sharing contracts. Petronas chairman Tan Sri Abdul Kadir Shamsuddin said they would improve the investment climate and pave the way for the development and production of petroleum resources discovered in the contract areas.

A cake in the shape of the tailfin of Malaysian Airline System's latest aircraft, the DC10-30, was the highlight of a dinner on 30 September to mark its inaugural flight.

Takeover battles 'not part of national policy'

6 December | Kuala Lumpur

Deputy Prime Minister Dr Mahathir Mohamad said it was not the policy of the Government to nationalise corporations. But if the legitimate acquisition of shares and control by Malaysians resulted in the *de facto* Malaysianisation of companies, the Government was not going to prevent it.

'The boardroom strategies and manoeuvres of individuals or groups do not constitute national policies any more than raids by marauding economic buccaneers from abroad on companies in this area can be considered as deliberate economic policies of the nations which harbour these pirates,' he said, adding that the Government could not be held responsible for every boardroom decision.

Malaysian arrested for smuggling heroin

7 December | Rome

Police arrested a Malaysian and a Singaporean at Rome's airport yesterday and seized 20kg of heroin with a street value of more than US$4 million hidden in four paintings. Those arrested were identified as Koh Bak Kin, 30, of Singapore, and Syed Mohamed bin Syed Faizada, 34, of Kelantan.

Lat's view: For maximum effect, the VIP ensures he is in the thick of things, in this case getting all wet in the floods, when he speaks to the press.

22ft terror gets new home

27 December | Kuala Lumpur ▶ Residents of Jalan Aman had a scare when a 15-year-old schoolboy ran down the road screaming that a monster snake had tried to attack him. Zoo Negara was contacted and two expert snake catchers searched the undergrowth for half an hour until they found and captured a hungry 22ft python. It was taken to the zoo.

Nine buried in landslip

14 December | Kuala Lumpur

The side of a tin mine off Jalan Puchong collapsed, burying nine people. The dead were a lorry driver, five mine workers, a milk vendor and two children.

Mining authorities were trying to evacuate the residents of Kampung Bohol, on the fringe of the mine, as they were in danger of being swept down the mine.

Another 150 people cheated death in the collapse because the mine owners had managed to persuade them to move out some weeks earlier.

They had been living in huts right on top of the mine wall which collapsed. Rescue workers were trying to recover the bodies of the dead with the help of tracker dogs.

Deputy Ministers resign

2 December | Kuala Lumpur

Deputy Minister of Science, Technology and Environment Datuk Abdullah Ahmad and Deputy Minister of Labour and Manpower Encik Abdullah Majid resigned. The next day, they and four other politicians were arrested under the Internal Security Act.

The others were DAP MP for Batu Gajah Mr Chian Heng Kai, national chairman of Partai Sosialis Rakyat Malaya Encik Kassim Ahmad, DAP assistant treasurer Mr Chan Kok Kit and MCA chief executive secretary Mr Tan Kien Siew.

Police said the six were arrested for involvement with the Communist United Front (*see 22 February 1981*).

Tun Tan is Sime boss after board battle

9 December | Kuala Lumpur

Tun Tan Siew Sin became chairman of Sime Darby, ending a battle that had started in November over the composition of the board. Also elected were three new directors, Tunku Ahmad bin Tunku Yahya, Mr Sixto Kalaw Roxas and Mr Wee Cho Yaw. They were expected to take the seats on the board vacated by former chairman James Bywater and directors K.N. Eales and K.J. Morton.

Tun Tan thanked all those who had contributed to the amicable settlement of the dispute and said: 'There were obvious misunderstandings in the beginning, a phenomenon not uncommon where human relations are concerned.'

1977

Two plane crashes shattered Malaysia's good aviation record. A Japan Airlines passenger liner slammed into a hill near Subang Airport, killing 36 people. Three months later a hijacked MAS jetliner crashed in Johor, killing all 93 passengers and seven crew. In the law courts, charged and found guilty were ex-Menteri Besar Dato Harun Idris of forgery and abetting criminal breach of trust, Botak Chin of unlawful possession of firearms, May Wong of conspiracy to smuggle drugs, and a juvenile sentenced to death (later commuted) for possession of firearms. Also, Lim Woon Chong was charged with the 1974 murder of Inspector General of Police Tan Sri Abdul Rahman Hashim. In sports, Marina Chin became one of the top 10 fastest women sprinters in Asia.

JANUARY
In London, heiress-turned-drug-dealer May Wong is sentenced to 14 years' jail.

APRIL
Five die when Super Saloon driver Harvey Yap loses control of his car during the Malaysian Grand Prix at Batu Tiga.

JULY
Malaysia defeats Japan in the Asian women's hockey championship final in Kuala Lumpur.

NOVEMBER
The King declares a State of Emergency in Kelantan and a Federal Director of Government, Hashim Aman, takes control of the State Government.

May: A view of Kuala Lumpur featured in a May 1977 *National Geographic* article on Malaysia.

'[The Malays should] ... strive to make a success of the New Economic Policy.'

Datuk Hussein Onn, in his speech at Umno's 31st anniversary celebrations, 12 May 1977.

1977

world news

18 February
Maiden 'flight' of the space shuttle *Enterprise*, sitting on top of a 747.

20 March
Indian PM Indira Gandhi ends the Emergency and calls for elections. The Congress Party wins only 153 seats, a major comedown from its previous total of 350. Indira and her son Sanjay Gandhi lose their seats.

22 March:
Indira Gandhi resigns as Indian Prime Minister.

27 March
Collision between two 747s at Los Rodeos airport, Tenerife, Canary Islands kills 583.

17 May
Likud led by Menachem Begin wins the elections in Israel.

23 May
Moluccan terrorists take over a school and a train in the Netherlands.

24 May
Soviet President Podgorny is ousted for resisting Brezhnev's desire to be chairman as well as secretary-general of the party.

May Wong's crime days are over

11 January London

The trial of beautiful Malaysian heiress-turned-drug-dealer Shing Mooi Wong, better known as May Wong, drew to a close as she was sentenced to 14 years' jail for conspiring to smuggle £500,000 worth of heroin into Britain.

The former Roedean pupil originally began her life of crime in the 'Overlords'—a crime organisation based in Malaysia and Singapore—in order to seek revenge on the gang leaders who were responsible for the murder of her father, a bullion merchant in Singapore. Leaving behind her husband and children, she arrived in Britain in the spring of 1975 to help set up the organisation's sophisticated heroin network in London.

Along with her lover Li Jaafar Mah, she began taking in £9,000 ($39,600) a day from her pool of clients—between 250 and 900 users in London alone. Within seven months she had reportedly earned more than £50,000, and she lived the high life, wearing designer dresses and expensive jewellery.

She was finally caught in a police trap set for her in Heathrow Airport on 26 October 1975 on her way back from Singapore. Mah, arrested earlier, had voluntarily led the police to the north London flat that had been their 'warehouse' for heroin—where they found £700,000 worth of drugs and two automatic pistols with ammunition.

PJ expands with new municipal council

2 January Petaling Jaya

Petaling Jaya expanded to include Subang Jaya, Sungai Way–Subang, Sungai Way New Village, Damansara Utama and Damansara Village. With a population of 200,000 over an area of 17.4 sq miles, it became a municipality, administered by a 22-member municipal council, which replaced the now-defunct town board. The council was expected to have an annual budget of $15 million, and would need at least six months to complete the takeover of the new areas.

Drug bosses switch smuggling tactics

4 January Kuala Lumpur

The Central Narcotics Bureau revealed that following the arrests of local carriers in recent months, international drug syndicates had since switched tactics, using Western tourists to smuggle drugs from Malaysia to European capitals. The tourists were recruited because large numbers visited the region.

The information was relayed to the bureau by anti-narcotic agencies in other countries used by the smugglers.

Botak Chin sentenced to hang

Wong being led out of the High Court by the police to a waiting Black Maria after hearing the death sentence verdict.

11 January Kuala Lumpur

Wong Swee Chin, alias Botak Chin, was given the mandatory death sentence following his guilty plea to two charges of unlawful possession of firearms and ammunition. He had turned down an offer by Mr Justice Chang Min Tat to reconsider his plea as well as the assistance of a counsel assigned to defend him. Through the court interpreter, he said that he understood perfectly the nature and consequences of his plea, and had nothing to say in mitigation. The judge commended his bravery and honesty, though Chin interjected: 'Not bravery, My Lord—that was foolishness!' He was presumably referring to his criminal career (*see 1 April 1980*).

Thronged by supporters, Datuk Harun Idris is escorted out of the courtroom by Federal Reserve Unit men.

Former Menteri Besar found guilty

24 January Kuala Lumpur

Former Selangor Menteri Besar Datuk Harun Idris was sentenced by the High Court to six months' jail for forgery and fined $15,000 or six months' jail for abetting criminal breach of trust involving nearly $6.5 million worth of Bank Rakyat's stocks and shares.

The two other accused in the trial, former Bank Rakyat managing director Datuk Abu Mansor Mohd Basir and former general manager Ismail Din, were sentenced to two years' jail and one year's jail respectively on the same forgery charge. Datuk Mansor was also fined $25,000 for criminal breach of trust while Ismail was fined $15,000 for abetting Datuk Mansor in committing criminal breach of trust. All three have given notice of appeal.

The three were found guilty of forging minutes of a meeting of the bank's investment committee for the purpose of cheating the bank by pledging the stocks and shares it owned to the First National City Bank here as a security for obtaining letters of credit for Tinju Dunia Sdn Bhd to promote the Muhammad Ali–Joe Bugner fight in 1975, causing Bank Rakyat a loss of $7.9 million.

More than 10 months later, on 6 December, the Federal Court of Appeal upheld Datuk Harun's conviction and increased his sentence to four years' jail, describing him as 'the principal actor in this drama'. Datuk Mansor's sentence was also increased to three years' jail. Ismail, however, had his sentence reduced to a day's jail for forgery and a $10,000 fine (*see 8 March 1978*).

Floods hit Pahang

5 January Bentong

The flood season left hundreds stranded on both sides of Karak, 14 miles from here, as five-feet-high flood waters cut the main road linking the east and west coasts of the peninsula.

Bentong town itself was not been spared—with several parts of the town under at least three feet of water, three schools had to close.

The floods were due to the overflow from Sungai Bunus that had resulted from heavy rain .

'Lion of Umno' dies

14 January Johor Bahru

The 'Lion of Umno' and head of Umno Youth, Tan Sri Syed Jaafar Albar, died after a heart attack. He was 62.

He suffered the attack while addressing a Johor Umno Youth executive committee meeting at about 5pm, and was rushed immediately to the Muar hospital.

He was buried the following day at the Heroes' Mausoleum in the National Mosque, Kuala Lumpur.

He was survived by his wife Puan Sri Sharifah Fatimah and 11 children.

ISA detainees confess

4 February Kuala Lumpur

Five of six political leaders detained under the Internal Security Act last December had confessed to their involvement in activities to help the Communist United Front, Inspector General of Police Tan Sri Hanif Omar said on Radio and Television Malaysia.

The six detainees were Datuk Abdullah Ahmad (former Deputy Minister of Science, Technology and the Environment), Abdullah Majid (former Deputy Minister of Labour and Manpower), Tan Kwee Shen (MCA executive secretary-general), Chan Heng Kai (DAP MP for Batu Gajah), Chan Kok Kit (DAP national assistant treasurer) and Kassim Ahmad (chairman, Partai Sosialis Rakyat Malaysia).

Until the time of their arrests they had, either knowingly or unknowingly, acted for the benefit of the Communist Party of Malaya—by subtly inserting pro-Communist ideas in their writing and conversation.

Three of them had expressed the wish to make statements over television and over the next two days two of them did make nationally-televised confessions: Datuk Abdullah Ahmad and Encik Abdullah Majid. Another ISA detainee, former editor-in-chief of *Sin Chew Jit Poh*, Chan Kien Sin, made a televised confession on 12 February (*see 22 February 1981*).

Moonshine crackdown

29 January Petaling Jaya

A special police operation against moonshiners uncovered four massive underground distilleries in the jungle near Subang Jaya. Altogether, they had the capacity to produce enough samsu to supply the whole of Petaling Jaya and Klang. Samsu was largely sold and consumed by squatters and rubber tappers, and unhygienic conditions and shoddy production were largely the reason for cases of samsu poisoning.

Man charged with murder of IGP

24 March Kuala Lumpur

Lim Woon Chong, 21, was tentatively charged in the magistrate's court here with the 1974 murder of Inspector General of Police Tan Sri Abdul Rahman Hashim. He was alleged to have committed the offence with another still at large at the junction of Lorong Raja Chulan and Jalan Tun Perak at about 8.20 am on 7 June.

Hours earlier in the Ipoh magistrate's court, Lim was charged, with Ng Foo Nam, 22, with the similar murder in 1975 of Perak Chief Police Officer Tan Sri Koo Chong Kong and his driver Sgt Yeong Peng Cheong.

One year later, Lim and Ng were sentenced to death for the murder of Tan Sri Koo and Sgt Yeong.

New pay offer

25 January Kuala Lumpur

The Federal Government rejected the recommendations of the Ibrahim Ali Commission on public-sector pay and announced a new pay scheme drawn up by a Cabinet committee at a meeting between union representatives and the Prime Minister.

On 30 January the union umbrella group Cuepacs responded with a strike threat but affiliated unions called it off after a four-hour meeting. Instead each union would decide itself whether to accept the recommendations, though the meeting 'strongly deplored the arbitrary manner in which the Government had acted'.

Sibu to have new airport

1 April Miri

A new airport was to be built in Sibu to cater for the use of Boeing 737 aircraft, announced Sarawak's Assistant Communications and Works Minister Chong Klun Kong. Speaking at a reception at Miri airport to mark the inaugural MAS Boeing 737 flight into Miri, he said the site had already been acquired by the Government.

The flight time between Kuching and Miri was halved with the introduction of Boeing 737s to replace Fokker Friendship aircraft. Miri was the second Sarawak town to have such a service.

Dogs to detect drugs in Subang Airport

16 March Kuala Lumpur

Dogs would soon be a standard feature for Customs officers detecting drugs. The introduction of the dog unit was to intensify checks against narcotics smugglers in the country, announced Deputy Finance Minister Mr Richard Ho. 'At present, there is no machine or electronic device in the world which can detect drugs,' he said at a press conference here.

The Finance Ministry's tax division's secretary, Encik Badruddin Samad, said he hoped that Muslims would be able to understand that dogs are necessary in the fight against drugs, 'since we do not wish to see more Malaysian youths, especially Muslims, taking to drugs'.

National Geographic feature, May issue

Bronze warrior restored

11 April Kuala Lumpur

Thanks to Mr Christopher Carney, a lecturer at the Mara Institute of Technology's School of Art and Design, the National Monument was restored. It took him and his men about a year to complete the restoration work. A bomb blast, which occurred at about 5am on 26 August 1975, destroyed a 4½-ton bronze statue and the heads of three other military figures. The blast was believed to have been caused by agents of the Malayan National Liberation Front, a militant Communist organisation. Mr Carney estimates that the project will be completed by 15 May.

Youthful nation with growing pains

An overview of the country from the outsider's perspective, a feature in *National Geographic* magazine cast a spotlight on distinctive traits that make up Malaysia. It was 'a land of faunal riches', whose thick tropical jungles were also the home for still-present Communist guerrillas, 'old allies' that had turned into 'new enemies'. In summarising the history of Kuala Lumpur, the magazine also described the 13 May 1969 incident as Malays rioting in the streets, fearful of the growing political power of the Chinese, that left several hundred people dead.

Malaysia was also 'a captivating place on which the blessing of prosperity has been called down'—being the world's chief supplier of natural rubber, as well as tin (the world's largest open-cut tin mine being on the outskirts of Kuala Lumpur) and palm oil. Along with other raw materials like timber and Sarawak pepper, they gave Malaysia a sound economic footing, stable enough to withstand shocks such as terrorist attacks or 'the growing animosity between Malays and Chinese'. But that ethnic jumble, in the magazine's opinion, were unlikely to merge into a harmonious unity, and it predicted rough times ahead for the nation.

1977

world news

25 May
George Lucas' *Star Wars* premieres, soaring to astronomical box-office numbers.

5 June
Apple II, the first personal computer, goes on sale.

11 June
Dutch Marines storm a train held by Moluccan terrorists. Six terrorists and two hostages killed.

15 June
Spain's first elections after 41 years under the iron-hand rule of Franco.

25 June
American Roy Sullivan is struck by lightning ... for the seventh time.

5 July
General Mohammed Zia ul-Haq overthrows Pakistan Prime Minister Zulfiqar Ali Bhutto.

13 July
New York suffers a blackout lasting 25 hours, during which time there is widespread looting and mayhem.

22 July
Purged Chinese leader Deng Xiaoping is restored as Vice-Premier, and the Gang of Four is expelled from the party.

250-strong terrorist gang routed by troops

11 April Padang Besar

Operation Daoyai Musnah II, a joint operation between Malaysian and Thai security forces, scored another success by smashing the sanctuary of the Communist Party of Malaya's Revolutionary Faction and routing the 250-strong group of terrorists. The terrorist sanctuary was 30 miles northeast of here, in the middle of the Khao Namkhang Range in Sadao district, and had existed since 1955. In the 28-day operation 15 enemy camps were captured and a terrorist-run tin mine and its supply network destroyed. This will put the terrorists 'two years behind'.

The remains of Harvey Yap's Escort BDA after it went off the track and crashed into the fence.

Grand Prix tragedy

24 April Batu Tiga

A freak accident turned the Malaysian Grand Prix motor race into a tragedy when saloon ace Harvey Yap's Escort BDA went out of control and smashed into the crowd, killing five children. The crash, dubbed the worst in Malaysian motor racing history, also injured 23 others.

Yap was leading in the fourth lap of the 25-lap Super Saloons event when eyewitnesses saw his Escort spin, veer 15 yards off the track and hit the fence. Several children were run over as the car rolled along the fence for about 20 yards, tearing away about 15ft of chain-link fencing. It was believed that the car suffered a puncture in the right rear tyre on the 150mph back straight. Yap himself suffered a leg injury and was treated at Assunta Hospital. He broke down when he saw the dead and injured spectators as bystanders helped to pull him out of his car.

The Selangor State Government ordered the circuit closed the next day and would reconsider opening it only after it had received the report of the investigation by the International Automobile Federation (FIA) that it had asked the FIA to conduct.

Raja Muda of Johor gets six months' jail

17 April Johor Bahru

The Raja Muda of Johor, Tunku Mahmood Iskandar, was sentenced by the High Court here to six months' jail on a charge of culpable homicide not amounting to murder. He was also fined $6,000 or six months' imprisonment in default.

The Raja Muda had pleaded guilty to causing the death of Teo Ah Bah at Jalan Pasir Pelangi on 15 October last year. In mitigation, the defence for the Raja Muda argued that the accused was exercising the right of making a citizen's arrest, to stop smugglers from escaping and had no intention to cause death. He was later pardoned.

Dr M tells why English is a must

1 May Alor Star

By 1980, the medium of instruction in all Government-aided secondary schools will be Bahasa Malaysia, Education Minister Dr Mahathir Mohamad reiterated today. English, however, would be taught as a compulsory second language. English was important, according to Dr Mahathir, because the language was mostly used in science and technology the world over. Not only would it ensure Malaysia could progress in science and technology along with other countries but it could also help the country progress faster.

Fire on luxury liner

2 June Port Dickson

Nearly 1,000 people abandoned the luxury liner MS *Rasa Sayang* when it caught fire off the coast here early in the morning. Four crewmen were killed and a fifth was missing. The operators of the ship said two bodies were later recovered.

All 646 passengers were taken ashore as well as the estimated 330 crew members. Eight were admitted to the district hospital here, while a more serious case was transferred to the Seremban General Hospital. Twenty-two others were given outpatient treatment.

The 18,500-ton liner was on a pleasure cruise from Singapore to Penang with a stopover at Port Klang when the fire broke out at about 2am.

Black magic robbers

13 June Kuala Lumpur

Police detained nine men in their hunt for a burglary gang that used 'pukau' on their intended victims. 'Pukau' is a spell that is supposed to put people to sleep, and the gang used it before they struck their targets. The police had been on the trail of the gang for the past month, and the nine (including seven Indonesians) were being held on suspicion of breaking into the homes of at least 12 prominent people here and stealing about $200,000 worth of valuables. Among their victims were the secretary-general of the Treasury, Tan Sri Abdullah Ayub, the Chief Inspector of Mines, Datuk Salleh bin Abdul Majid, and former Sabah Chief Minister Tan Sri Said Keruak.

Massage parlour blaze

1 July Ipoh

Half-naked patrons scampered out into the streets when a massage parlour caught fire during lunch hour here. It was a sight that amused the large crowd that gathered to watch the blaze (above). The fire also destroyed two other shops and partially damaged two others in Jalan Yang Kalsom, in the heart of Ipoh's shopping area. Overall, property damage was estimated at $500,000.

Rafidah on cover of magazine

July Kuala Lumpur

Recently appointed Deputy Finance Minister Senator Rafidah Aziz earned the distinction of being the first woman to grace the cover of *Sarina*, a local current affairs magazine.

7777 a hot number for lottery punters

7 July Kuala Lumpur

Today was a fortuitous date for many gamblers, with the lucky number seven repeated four times. The number was sold out early in the morning at Empat Nombor Ekor offices, much to the disappointment of hopeful latecomers. The combination will only come up again in the 21st century, on 7 July 2077. In the 20th century, the next date with such a recurrent number would be 8 August 1988.

Anti-Red air strikes

9 July Betong

Malaysian Tebuan jets strafed a large Communist camp this morning, believed to be the 12th Regiment headquarters of the Communist Party of Malaya, about 15 miles north of here. The Cahaya Bena I operation is another joint cooperation with Thai armed forces.

Later, on 25 July, Operation Cahaya Bena II scored a major coup when Malaysian and Thai forces successfully seized the camp of terrorist leader Rashid Mydin.

An ecstatic Zahrah Mokhtar (left) slipping a goal past the Japanese goalkeeper Miyoko Sazaki in the 60th minute of the game.

Malaysia beat Japan in women's hockey final

23 July Kuala Lumpur ▶ Malaysia scored two goals (both by Zahrah Mokhtar) over Japan in the Asian women's hockey championship final at the Mindef Stadium. The victory erased doubts about Malaysia's performance after their below-par showing in the preliminary matches. Japan's coach Dr Kimiji Sugiyama paid tribute to the Malaysian halfline 'for building up the attacking moves and regrouping in turn to defend so well'.

Philippine claim to Sabah dropped

6 August Kuala Lumpur

Philippine President Ferdinand Marcos announced that the Philippines was dropping its claim to Sabah without any conditions. The claim has been a thorn in the two countries' diplomatic relations and a burden to the Asean community as a whole. The withdrawal of the claim, however, would have to go through procedures that had been established and certain obstacles would have to be eliminated first, but they are not insurmountable.

Marina Chin shatters 100m national mark

28 August Dusseldorf

Malaysian sprinter Marina Chin shattered the 12-second barrier in the 100 metres, clocking 11.9 seconds in a local meet at Schwetzingen, Germany. This meant she held the Malaysian women's 100-metre record. This put her in the top-10 bracket of Asia's women sprinters.

Big move to Bangi by Universiti Kebangsaan

16 September Kuala Lumpur

Universiti Kebangsaan Malaysia began its transfer from Kuala Lumpur to its new campus in Bangi, some 15km south of the capital.

The first stage of the move was to take six weeks, with the campus ready to receive the students coming in for the new academic session in November.

Only the non-science faculties were making the initial move. The Bangi campus would provide accommodation for about 60 per cent of the student population. The campus also featured an Olympic-standard sports complex.

Once the new highway was completed, it will only take 15 minutes to reach the campus from Kuala Lumpur.

14-year-old sentenced to death

25 August Penang

For the first time, a juvenile was sentenced to death by the High Court under the Internal Security Act.

The 14-year-old boy, described as 'of higher intelligence', was found guilty of possessing a pistol and ammunition. His was the first case in which a juvenile was charged under the ISA and tried under the Essential (Security Cases) Amendment Regulations 1975.

On 14 October, the Pardons Board commuted the boy's sentence to detention at the Yang di-Pertuan Agong's pleasure.

Club Med takes shape

15 September Kuantan

The first project of its kind in the country, the RM20-million Club Mediterranée tourist complex was being built based on the concept of the traditional Malay house. The complex was located at Cherating beach, 45km from Kuantan. It was expected to be completed in March 1979.

The project was a joint venture between the Tourist Development Corporation, the Pahang State Development Corporation and Club Mediterranée, a French travel organisation with one million members worldwide. The club would operate the complex and handle the marketing.

PM: Let's spread goodwill among all

14 September Kuala Lumpur

In his Hari Raya broadcast over Radio and Television Malaysia, Prime Minister Datuk Hussein Onn hoped that the year would see even more non-Muslims joining their Muslim friends in celebrating the auspicious occasion. Such a practice, according to him, would strengthen both the bonds of friendship and goodwill among the communities. 'Strengthening the feeling of goodwill is the duty of every Malaysian who truly loves this nation of ours,' he said.

Jeanette Chew graces the pages of Bahasa Malaysia magazine *Selecta Femina*. A model from Kuala Lumpur, she hopes to make a name for herself in the industry.

117-year-old man buys his lady love's freedom

5 October Alor Star

Lebai Omar bin Datuk Panglima Garang, a 117-year–old silat instructor, kept his promise to get his 40-year-old bride-to-be out of jail. He mortgaged a portion of his small farm plot in Kampung Labi, threw in his savings, and cycled all 27 miles to get to the prison in Jalan Sultanah here to free Doyah binte Dan. Both held for khalwat, she could not pay the $200 fine imposed by the kadi's office. They planned to marry as soon as possible, maybe even that night, if there was a kadi available.

Federal rule imposed in Kelantan

8 November Kuala Lumpur

Following the ongoing political crisis in Kelantan, the Yang di-Pertuan Agong proclaimed a State of Emergency in the State. A Bill to extend the executive authority of the Federal Government to the State was tabled in the Dewan Rakyat.

In response to the move to impose Federal rule on the State, five Pas members, led by its national president Datuk Haji Mohamed Asri Che Muda, quit the Federal Government.

With this ruling, Kelantan was to be administered by a Director of Government directly responsible under the Prime Minister. He was ro be given all the authority, powers, duties and functions of both the Menteri Besar and the State Executive Council.

1977

world news

12 August
The space shuttle takes its first free flight.

16 August
Elvis Presley, 42, dies of a drug overdose in Memphis, Tennessee.

10 September
The guillotine is used for the last time in France.

12 September
South African activist Steve Biko is murdered by police.

9 November
Egyptian President Anwar Sadat becomes the first Arab leader to visit Israel and to address the Knesset in Jerusalem.

14 December
Jean-Bedel Bokassa crowns himself Emperor of the Central African Empire. His coronation ceremony duplicates the coronation of Napoleon and costs US$100 million.

25 December
'The Tramp' Sir Charles Chaplin dies, at 88.

36 die and 43 survive in plane crash

Firemen hosing down the fuselage of the JAL DC-8 aircraft amid the wreckage at the Elmina Estate in Sungai Pulong.

27 September | Kuala Lumpur

In the first commercial air crash and the worst in Malaysian aviation history, a Japan Airlines DC-8 airliner crashed into a hill about 20 miles from here. Thirty-six people were feared dead but 43 others survived, though many of them were seriously injured. One of the survivors later died at the General Hospital.

Some of the survivors trapped among the debris of the crash clapped their hands to attract the rescue teams.

Initial findings released on 8 October revealed that the aircraft flew too low on its landing approach which, coupled with bad weather, resulted in it crashing into a small hill about four miles north-northwest of Subang Airport near Kuala Lumpur.

MAS jet crashes in Johor

4 December | Johor Bahru

After September's aircrash horror there was further disaster when an MAS jetliner was hijacked shortly after it took off from Penang and crashed into Tanjung Kupang, Johor at 8.35pm. No survivors were found among the 93 passengers and seven crew on board the downed Boeing 737, making the tragedy Malaysia's worst air crash in history. Among those killed was Agriculture Minister Dato' Seri Ali Haji Ahmad.

With no survivors, the true story of the hijack would not be known until the flight's 'black box' could be recovered, though allegations of the Japanese Red Army's involvement were dismissed. Later in the month the cockpit voice recorder was found.

As it was difficult to identify the remains and thus separate burials were impossible, and after discussion with religious leaders, the remains of the 100 victims were buried in a special burial site off Jalan Kebun Teh in a multi-religious ceremony (*see 8 September 1978*).

The wreckage of the MAS Boeing 737 in Tanjung Kupang, near Gelang Patah, on the southwest coast of Johor.

Miss Malaysia pulls out at the last minute

18 November | Kuala Lumpur

In protest over the participation of a Miss South Africa, Miss Christine Lim, Malaysia's Miss World finalist, decided to withdraw from the contest on Government advice. The Government said it would compensate the sponsors of the Miss Malaysia-Miss World contest for expenses incurred in sending her to London where the final was being held.

India, Indonesia, the Philippines and Singapore also pulled out. This was the second time a Malaysian representative had pulled out of the contest in protest over South Africa's participation, in line with the country's anti-apartheid policy.

More forest reserves planned in Malaysia

3 December | Kuala Lumpur

Deputy Minister of Primary Industries Mr Lew Sip Hon said today that State Governments in Peninsular Malaysia have agreed to set aside 12.8 million acres of permanent forest reserves, and to limit the opening of forests to 166,000 acres a year. This new policy would enable Government agricultural land to be worked in stages according to the development schedule, and help reduce timber wastage and thus increase forest revenue collection in all of the peninsular States.

Under the Third Malaysia Plan, the Ministry has planned 12 projects costing over $18 million.

BN votes to expel Pas

13 December | Kuala Lumpur

The Barisan Nasional Supreme Council gave Pas until 17 December to expel its MPs who voted in Parliament in November against Federal rule in Kelantan. If the party did not do so, it would be expelled from the BN. BN chairman Datuk Hussein Onn said the expulsion would be automatic once the deadline had passed and there would be no more meetings on the matter.

The next day, Pas national president Datuk Haji Mohamed Asri announced that the party considered itself expelled from the BN and would now start to play the role of an opposition party.

SEA Games get off to a bright start

19 November | Kuala Lumpur

Malaysia played host to the Ninth SEA Games beginning today. Prime Minister Datuk Hussein Onn lit the SEA Games flame at Parliament House the previous day, watched by 500 officials and spectators under cloudy skies. The cauldron stayed lit until former Thomas Cup player Abdul Rahman Mohamed lit the Games torch from it, starting the long relay of torch-carrying runners to Merdeka Stadium.

Malaysia did not do too badly—finishing fourth behind powerhouses Indonesia, Thailand and the Philippines, and closed the Games in style by winning gold in the final three events: the team and individual cycling titles as well as football. Athletics was the major contributor to Malaysia's haul with track king and queen Ishtiaq Mobarak and Marina Chin winning medals in their respective events.

Tan Sri Nik Kamil dies

20 December | Petaling Jaya

The Speaker of the Dewan Rakyat, Tan Sri Nik Ahmad Kamil, who was in Government service for more than 30 years before entering politics, died aged 68.

At his funeral the next day, Prime Minister Datuk Hussein Onn described him as 'a wise and prominent leader held in high esteem by the nation.' He was survived by six children.

1978

The end of the Vietnam War saw an exodus of refugees, many of them travelling in rickety boats and landing illegally on Malaysian shores. A number of them perished in choppy seas. In one incident, 200 drowned off Kuala Terengganu when their boat capsized. Datuk Hussein Onn romped home with a resounding victory for him and Barisan Nasional in the general election. And Malaysians' appetite for 'magic potions' was whetted but not satisfied by claims that a red-tea fungus was a panacea for 32 ailments. When the craze it Kuala Lumpur, many made a beeline for Chinese medicine shops and had to be content with promotional leaflets about the product but no tea because of a lack of suppliers.

FEBRUARY
Malaysia's largest integrated cane sugar complex opens in Kedah.

MAY
Yasmin Yusuff (centre) wins the Miss Malaysia/Universe title at the Kuala Lumpur Merlin Hotel.

AUGUST
National Museum Director Shahrum Yub receives the Ramon Magsaysay Award for outstanding Government service.

DECEMBER
Prime Minister Datuk Hussein Onn launches colour television in Malaysia.

November: Deng Xiaoping makes a historic visit to Malaysia.

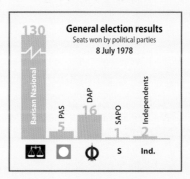

General election results
Seats won by political parties
8 July 1978

Barisan Nasional	PAS	DAP	SAPO	Independents
130	5	16	1	2
⚖	◯	✡	S	Ind.

'I would rather do the right thing and be cursed than do the popular but wrong thing and be applauded.'

Datuk Hussein Onn, on the Barisan Nasional manifesto, 2 July 1978.

1978

world news

7 January
Emilio Palma is the first baby born in the Antarctic.

18 January
The European Court of Human Rights finds Britain guilty of mistreating prisoners in Northern Ireland.

23 January
Sweden is the first country to ban aerosol sprays to spare the ozone layer.

24 January
A Soviet satellite burns up in the Earth's atmosphere, scattering debris across Canada.

11 February
China lifts a ban on the works of Aristotle, Shakespeare and Charles Dickens.

15 February
Rhodesian Prime Minister Ian Smith meets with black leaders and agrees to a transfer of power to black majority rule.

21 February
Electrical workers find the Great Pyramid of Tenochtitlan in the middle of Mexico City.

3 March
Ethiopia admits that, aided by Cuban troops, it is fighting with Somalia.

Vietnam 'will not back Reds in Malaysia'

1 January Jakarta

Vietnam would not support Communist terrorists in Malaysia and Thailand, Deputy Foreign Minister Vo Dong Ghiang said here. Vietnam considered the insurgencies as the two countries' internal affairs, he added, and 'we do not export our revolution and we hope others will not export their counter-revolution to us'.

Green Book Plan halted

18 January Kuala Lumpur

The Green Book Plan, started by the late Tun Abdul Razak to promote agriculture in 1974, appeared to have ground to a halt. Implementation of the plan was sluggish because farmers were slow to embrace it. Nature also had caused great setbacks with the drought in early 1976 and at the present time.

The attitude of the people was that since the plan was a Government campaign, it was up to the Government to provide all the necessary things, such as seeds and fertilisers.

'All the Government can do is to pave the way for them to practise modern, intensive and commercial farming, but they don't seem to realise that,' said a Government official who wished to remain anonymous.

Prime Minister Datuk Hussein Onn signs the visitors' book at the opening of a new palm-oil factory on 9 February.

Invention gets the point

3 January Kuala Lumpur

A jarum sulam (embroidery needle) designed by a Mara Institute dropout could make anyone an embroidery expert in less than 10 minutes, it was claimed. Syed Shaharuddin, who spent months of research to create the 'magic' needle from copper plates and electrical wires, said that even a child could easily be taught to use the needle. 'It takes less than 10 minutes to learn how to thread the needle and use it to sew whatever you want,' Syed Shaharuddin said. 'Just prick the cloth with the threaded needle and the designs will come out the way you want them.'

World's happiest ex-Prime Minister

6 February Kuala Lumpur

'I can still box. In fact, I can take on any youngster for at least one round'
—Tunku Abdul Rahman

The Tunku and his wife in the garden of their home.

Tunku Abdul Rahman, on the eve of his 75th birthday, showed no sign of relinquishing his claim to be the world's happiest and maybe fittest ex-Prime Minister. The speech might be a little slower and the eyesight not so strong, but the Tunku was in excellent shape and bouncy as ever.

'I can still do my physical jerks,' he said, standing, erect and straight, and down he goes, vigorously swinging his arms left to right and touching his toes. 'I can still box too,' he added in an interview with *The Star*. 'In fact, I can take on any youngster for at least one round.'

Content to be in Tunku's shadow

The newspaper feature to mark the Tunku's 75th birthday gave prominence to his wife Tun Sharifah Rodziah, describing her as a soft-spoken woman who enjoyed the simple things in life, like going to the market, tending the garden and caring for her husband. 'I don't have any qualifications that make a good leader,' she said modestly, 'but I am fortunate to be the wife of a great one.'

The article noted that she was cautious in talking about the man in her life but as she warmed up it was quite apparent that she had for him great respect and love.

'I wouldn't make it as a leader under my own steam. I was involved in politics only because I was the Prime Minister's wife.'

The house that Mubin built

8 January Petaling Jaya

It was the only one of its kind in Petaling Jaya yet it was hardly considered architecturally fashionable. Even when it was built in 1958, timber houses were looked on with disdain.

Still, Tan Sri Mubin Sheppard's timber-and-glass house was the end product of careful thought and taste backed by a deep understanding of technical skill and an intimate knowledge of the world of art and local history, said the magazine *Parade*. The interior walls were richly panelled, a tribute to the Terengganu craftsmen who carved the walls and screens. The doors and windows are also carved with simple yet beautiful designs.

Tan Sri Mubin had no problems maintaining his timber home, the magazine said, except that he had to treat and varnish the exterior every year to stop it decaying.

The majesty of the law

14 January Kuala Lumpur

About $2 million was allocated to furnish the new Federal and High Courts after the move to the Sultan Abdul Samad building.

Lord President Tun Suffian Hashim said that court buildings should be designed to symbolise the rule of law and the independence of the judiciary. 'We rejected the new court buildings in Jalan Duta because they look like a shopping complex. That's why the late Tun Abdul Razak agreed to let us have this building,' he said. 'We won't make any alteration to the exterior.'

Minibus drivers strike

20 January Kuala Lumpur

Minibus drivers staged a lightning strike, leaving thousands of commuters stranded in rush hour. Drivers and conductors said the strike was in protest against a police crackdown on them.

Claims of filming nude scenes spark row

28 January Kuala Lumpur

There was a hue and cry among Malays over the filming of alleged nude scenes by an Italian company using local extras in supporting roles. The film *Mountain of the Jungle* starred Ursula Andress. Malay newspapers, the Malaysian Actors' Association and the National Union of Film Producers criticised the production.

Largest sugar complex in Malaysia opens

16 February Alor Star

The Sultan of Kedah opened the multi-million-dollar Gula Padang Terap Berhad at Kuala Nerang, about 30 miles from Alor Star. The brainchild of the Kedah State Government, the project was an integrated cane sugar complex, the largest in Malaysia.

Hussein kidnap threat

20 February Kuala Lumpur

Datuk Hussein Onn cut short a visit to Australia and returned to Malaysia because of a kidnap threat in Melbourne. He had been advised by Australian security officials that more than one Malaysian had gone to Melbourne 'to kidnap me and to do something harmful to me', he said.

Melbourne security officials refused to comment on the kidnap threat, but the *Sydney Morning Herald* reported that the sudden change of plans followed an anonymous telephone tip-off to its newsroom, implicating a group identifying itself as the Malaysian Freedom League.

Police shot in ambush

27 February Seremban

Two patrol car constables were shot last night in Jalan Templer by two gunmen who fired 16 rounds at point-blank range. Only two shots missed. PC Hussein Ali, 46, died of nine gunshot wounds but the driver, PC Yusof Osman, 50, survived even though he had five wounds. Negeri Sembilan CPO Zaman Khan said: 'This is a Communist-inspired attack. It is believed that two men on motorcycles drew up along both sides of the car and opened fire.'

Pas battered in Kelantan

12 March Kuala Lumpur

The Barisan Nasional–Berjasa combination battered Pas in State elections to take decisive control of Kelantan. The Barisan-Berjasa combination won 34 seats against Pas's two. All 10 independent candidates lost.

Syndicate cheating EPF

18 March Kuala Lumpur

The National Bureau of Investigations uncovered a syndicate cheating the Employees' Provident Fund. NBI director-general Datuk Abdullah Ngah said a number of people including EPF head office staff had been arrested. The syndicate made fraudulent withdrawals of EPF contributions, resulting in the EPF losing more than $160,000. 'The fraud was committed with the connivance of a small number of EPF staff who possess a working knowledge of the computerised system in the EPF head office,' he said.

New $32.3m Sibu Port opens

29 April Sibu

Several hundred Rajang Port Authority workers enjoyed two days off as all operations ceased for two days to facilitate the opening of the new Sibu Port by Prime Minister Datuk Hussein Onn.

Existing facilities at the port had been improved and incorporated into the new port to facilitate operations. The objective of the expansion was to increase the capacity of the port from 175,000 tons a year to 450,000 tons.

Usually closed to the public, the port was opened to visitors from 2pm to 5pm after the opening ceremony.

Tan Sri Omar Ong (left) and Tan Sri Syed Nasir with their wives.

New Dewan Rakyat Speaker installed

21 March Kuala Lumpur

Tan Sri Syed Nasir Ismail was installed as Speaker of the Dewan Rakyat in the presence of the Yang di-Pertua Dewan Negara Tan Sri Omar Ong Yoke Lin and members of both Houses of Parliament.

Zoo Negara 'breaking the law'

16 March Kuala Lumpur

Zoo Negara had been keeping animals and birds illegally for six long years since the Protection of Wild Life Act 1972 was enforced, it was reported.

The Act says that 'no person shall take, house, confine or breed a protected animal or a protected bird unless he holds a licence, permit or special permit'. The zoo had 80 protected animals and 34 protected birds but no licence or permit, according to a reliable source.

The Act also says that 'no licence or permit shall be granted in respect of any totally protected wild animal or wild bird except by special permit from the Minister of Science, Technology and Environment'.

Unrest over Harun sentence

8 March Kuala Lumpur

The Yang di-Pertuan Agong rejected an appeal for pardon by Datuk Harun Idris on the advice of the Federal Territory Pardons Board. Datuk Harun was sentenced to six years' jail for corruption involving the Hongkong and Shanghai Banking Corporation and for forgery involving Bank Rakyat.

He was barricaded in his Taman Duta house on 23 February by his Selangor Umno Youth supporters who refused to allow him to go to jail. He was supposed to have reported himself to Pudu Prison that morning.

Umno Youth then sent a petition to the King requesting a pardon. On 28 February the Federal Court ordered his immediate arrest, saying that his crimes were 'shameful and unpardonable.'

On 1 March, Datuk Harun left his house and surrendered to police outside. He was taken to General Hospital for an operation to remove a cyst. At the hospital, he was handed over to the prison authorities (*see 1 August 1981*).

Life in chains

8 April Kuala Lumpur

Intellectually-disabled twins Kim Choong and Kim Seng, 18, were chained in their house in Cheras for 10 years by their parents who could not cope with them.

Ever since they could walk they had been extremely naughty and destructive, their father Yong Sin Wah, 61, said. They could hardly talk but they could understand their parents.

Yong, a partially-paralysed invalid, said: 'Since my wife goes out to work as a labourer and I can't control them they have to be chained up.'

Marine Police component

10 April Kota Kinabalu

The Marine Police Branch Sabah is one of the supporting units of the Royal Malaysia Police Force for the Sabah component headquartered in Kota Kinabalu. The branch was formed in the 1950s, when the headquarters was in Sandakan, to combat piracy and rampant smuggling off the Sabah coast. It now has seven ocean-going fast patrol craft, 17 sea-going craft and 28 riverine and harbour patrol craft to police the 900-mile-long coast and enforce the laws of the seas.

Red-tea fungus boom

4 April Kuala Lumpur

A craze for red-tea fungus hit Kuala Lumpur. Shops selling booklets on it quickly sold out. None of the shops, however, sold the fungus as they could not find a regular supply.

The fungus was in demand because of claims for its power to heal 32 ailments. Many people were growing it at home in glass jars and urns, having obtained it from friends.

The fungus's origin was unknown, but it was believed that the formula passed from China to Korea and Japan before arriving in Southeast Asia.

Gentleman thugs

7 April Ipoh

Two robbers walked into a firm here and announced in English to the staff of seven: 'Hello ladies and gentlemen, this is an armed robbery.' But the 'gentleman' robbers found only $80 in cash and $500 in valuables. In a fit of anger, one fired a shot into a chair. They then fled.

Popular singer Sharifah Aini is featured in the May issue of Bahasa Malaysia magazine *Selecta Femina*.

Providing power: Work in progress on the Temenggor hydro-electric project in February.

1978

world news

11 March
Palestinian guerrillas kill 34 Israelis. Three days later Israeli forces advance into Lebanon.

18 March
Zulfikar Ali Bhutto is sentenced to death for ordering the assassination of a political opponent in Pakistan.

25 June
Home team Argentina defeats the Netherlands 3–1 after extra-time to win the FIFA World Cup

25 July
Louise Brown, in the UK, is the first baby born from in-vitro fertilisation.

19 August
Fire in a cinema in Tehran kills 477. In Abadan, Iran, the following day extremists set fire to a cinema, killing nearly 400.

25 August
US soldier Walter Robinson 'walks' across the English Channel in 11½ hours using 'water-shoes' he designed himself.

Drivers in the dark over tinted glass for cars

15 April Kuala Lumpur

Motorists got a reprieve from the Works and Utilities Ministry after only 10 cars passed out of 1,000 tested in its attempt to enforce its ruling of 70 per cent light penetration for tinted car glasses.

Deputy Minister Dr Goh Cheng Teik said the light-penetration figure would be 35 per cent. Motorists whose windows did not allow 35 per cent or more light to pass through would continue to be prosecuted. Dr Goh admitted that there had been teething problems.

'Educated illiterates'

23 April Kuala Lumpur

Malaysian universities are turning out graduates who are functional illiterates, according to the acting head of the English Department of the University of Malaya, Associate Professor Ooi Boo Eng. He said a high percentage were poor writers and they had also been getting worse over the last 10 years.

Sudirman one of the best

9 April Kuala Lumpur

Sudirman Haji Arshad again won the Best TV Entertainer award 1977. Best Actor and Best Actress awards went to Sidek Hussein and Umi Kalthum respectively.

Umi Kalthum receives her award from her husband Roomai Noor.

Tunku comments on 'crocodiles'

10 April Kuala Lumpur

Tunku Abdul Rahman, in his popular column 'As I See It' in *The Star*, wrote: '*The Far Eastern Economic Review* of 31 March came out with a picture of Prime Minister Hussein Onn stepping across troubled waters over a number of ferocious crocodiles to reach the bank before the next election.

'There were Tun Mustapha, Datuk Harun, the Kelantan election and Tunku with the eyes closed.

'What it is intended to mean, I comprehend and so will many other people. These are the difficulties Datuk Hussein Onn will have to overcome before the next general elections, according to the writer.

'But for myself I have offered him no resistance but rather assistance for most of his policies except of course those which I have pointed out in the course of my writings, from time to time, on the education policy, Bumiputra business participation and the promotion of racial harmony of the various races living in this country.'

Yasmin's Miss Malaysia dream comes true

20 May Kuala Lumpur

Yasmin Yusuff's wish came true when she won the Miss Malaysia/Universe title at the Kuala Lumpur Merlin. Yasmin was a runner-up in the Miss Bradford contest when she was a student at Bradford University in England. She also won the Miss Genting Highlands crown last year and came in second in the Miss Inter-Hotel contest. Her 36-25-37 figure and a good height of 5ft 6in helped her to clinch the title.

Sticky situation

29 May Kuala Lumpur

Officials said sufficient pulut (glutinous rice) had been released for the Sarawak Gawai Festival and the Chinese Dragon Boat Festival, but wholesalers and retailers claimed there was a shortage in the city.

Although the National Padi and Rice Authority (LPN) had given each wholesaler 20 bags of 163 katis each, the wholesalers said that the supply had been sold out and they were unable to replenish their stocks.

LPN's rationale for limiting the supply was to fight hoarding. LPN director Datuk Mohamed Sopiee Sheikh Ibrahim said Thailand, the main supplier of pulut to Malaysia, was facing a shortage.

Sentry foils attack on police station

6 June Kuala Lumpur

Police foiled an attempt by a group of Communist terrorists to attack the Sungai Ruan police station in Raub. The attack was believed to have been carried out by the Communist Party of Malaya to mark the anniversary of its insurgency which began on 20 June 1948.

It came a few hours after Inspector General of Police Tan Sri Hanif Omar advised police to be prepared and to maintain maximum vigilance against Communist attacks.

A Field Force member on sentry duty at the back of the Sungai Ruan police station saw two or three figures in civilian clothes approaching. When he challenged them, they fired two or three shots without hitting him. He returned fire, forcing them to flee.

Surprise strike at Reds

28 April Bangkok

Malaysian troops and artillery crossed into Thailand in surprise strikes at some 3,000 Communist Party of Malaya guerrillas hiding in the jungle hills just north of the border in a combined Thai–Malaysian military operation. One soldier was wounded.

Bank Buruh director arrested for CBT

17 June Kuala Lumpur

Bank Buruh's director of business promotions, ex-MP Yeoh Teck Chye, 53, was arrested on charges involving more than $6 million of the bank's money. Also arrested were the bank's Kuala Lumpur manager Lim Hong Pung, 52, and housing developer Liew Chin Yam alias Chin Huat, 39.

Yeoh, a Pekemas adviser and former Pekemas MP for Bukit Bintang, was alleged to have committed criminal breach of trust of $6,073,889.75. Liew was accused of abetting Yeoh and Lim faced one charge of abetting Yeoh and two of abetting Liew.

Ungku Aziz named Royal Professor

18 June Kuala Lumpur

Vice-Chancellor of the University of Malaya Ungku Aziz was given the title of Royal Professor at the university's annual convocation ceremony. It was the first time this honour had been bestowed on a Malaysian.

Ungku Aziz was also recently awarded the Tun Razak Award for his leadership in the field of education. Datuk Musa Hitam said that as Vice-Chancellor, Ungku Aziz had made invaluable contributions to promoting higher education.

Candidates canned

22 June Klang

Election history was created when all four candidates for the State Assembly seat of Kampung Jawa were rejected because their forms were wrongly completed.

Prime Minister Datuk Hussein Onn greets his Australian counterpart Malcolm Fraser as he arrives for an official visit on 18 June.

Nation celebrates its 21st birthday

31 August Kuala Lumpur

A generation came of legal age this year and today the country turned 21. That was how *The Star* newspaper put it. There was a feeling of special significance to the 1978 National Day celebration, it said. While the various States had their own celebrations, most of the nation's eyes were focused on Kuala Lumpur.

Thousands made their way to the Selangor Club padang in the city centre, where in 1957 the cries of 'Merdeka' rent the air. The newspaper said: 'In those days the rest of the country followed the proceedings and heard the cries over the radio and imagined the scene with the help of a running commentary. Today millions of eyes will be glued to television sets watching the pageant unfold in graceful order in Kuala Lumpur'.

A unicycling clown adds to the fun and excitement at the National Day parade in Kuala Lumpur.

Cops found guilty over death of suspect

4 August Kuala Lumpur

Mr Justice Datuk Harun Hashim found four policemen guilty on a reduced charge of causing hurt to a suspected housebreaker, Nordin bin Hamzah, 16, who had died while in police custody.

Originally six policemen were accused of culpable homicide not amounting to murder. One was acquitted because he was not there and another because the judge felt he was not part of the team that carried out the 'intensive interrogation' of Nordin.

Museum head wins Magsaysay award

13 August Kuala Lumpur

National Museum director Encik Shahrum Yub was watching TV news when he saw he had won the Ramon Magsaysay Award for outstanding Government service. The award recognised his innovations in 'making the museum an enlightening experience for all ages and for fostering a national culture awakening.' It carried a US$10,000 prize and a gold medal.

Serve the people or get out, says PM

18 August Kuala Lumpur

Serve the people or get out, Prime Minister Datuk Hussein Onn told Government officers. 'These people do not have a place in our people's Government,' he declared when he opened the multi-million-dollar computerised National Operations Room at the Prime Minister's Department here.

Home nursing service runs out of money

3 September Kuala Lumpur

An ideal that had worked for eight years was said to be dying for want of public sympathy. Malaysia's only free nursing service for the housebound poor, the KL Home Nursing Service, had run out of funds, said its patron president Datuk Bandar Tan Sri Yaacob Abdul Latif.

Its two dedicated workers, Sister Margaret Chai and Nurse C.H. Ho, had gone without pay for four months. Unless more money was raised, 30 very ill people who needed constant medical care at their own homes would have to suffer. Tan Sri Ya'cob said: 'Our kitty's spent. We need money to save the poor souls.' The patients are victims of cancer, stroke and diabetes and mentally-challenged people.

Sarawak CM quits

13 September Kuching

Datuk Patinggi Tan Sri Haji Abdul Rahman Yaakub announced his resignation as Sarawak Chief Minister. He did not give reasons for his decision or say when it would take effect.

He said he would leave the choice of a successor to the Prime Minister, and the three Barisan Nasional components in Sarawak.

They are the Parti Bumiputra Bersatu (PBB), which the Datuk Patinggi himself leads, the Sarawak National Party (Snap) and the Sarawak United People's Party (SUPP).

He said that his decision to resign had been made for sometime but it needed the right timing. 'The timing was now proper,' he said.

Hijack plane pilots were shot, says report

8 September Kuala Lumpur

The pilot and first officer of the MAS Boeing that crashed last year were shot by a hijacker or hijackers minutes before it plunged into a Johor swamp killing all 100 on board, according to an official report.

Three shots were fired. Transcripts of conversations in the cockpit show that the pilot, Capt G.K. Ganjoor, pleaded 'No, please, don't' before he was shot.

It happened as the jet was descending to 4,000 feet and coming in to land at Paya Lebar Airport, Singapore. Before the shots were fired a voice was heard saying: 'You bluff us.' A foreign language was also heard, though the report did not identify the hijackers' nationality.

After the pilots were shot, and possibly dead, someone else tried to fly the plane. The flight data recorder showed abnormalities, indicating that someone was interfering with the controls. The aircraft was pitching after the shooting. It finally hit the ground at 450 knots.

Hussein confirmed as Umno president

16 September

Datuk Hussein Onn was confirmed as Umno president, trouncing challenger Haji Sulaiman Palestin by 648 votes at the 29th Umno general assembly here.

Datuk Hussein polled 898 votes against 250 for Haji Sulaiman. The three vice-presidents' posts were won by Finance Minister Tengku Razaleigh Hamzah, Barisan Nasional secretary-general Encik Ghafar Baba and Education Minister Datuk Musa Hitam.

Barisan manifesto

2 July Kuala Lumpur

Message from Datuk Hussein Onn

My Fellow Malaysians,

Once again the time for decision has come. The nation's future is in your hands.

As Prime Minister, I have tried my very best to do what is right for Malaysia and for the people of Malaysia. The office of the Prime Minister carries with it a heavy responsibility and I have tried to discharge it without fear or favour and with the fullest sense of honesty and integrity. In carrying out my duties, I put first the safety, honour and welfare of the country; my own ease, comfort and safety will always come last.

I would rather do the right thing and be cursed than do the popular but wrong thing and be applauded. I will always be guided by God's Commandments, the dictates of reason, the interests of the nation. I am ready to continue with the responsibility of office, to soldier on, to serve the country and the people.

I come to you to ask for your support in our struggle to eradicate poverty, to build upon the foundation of racial harmony and national unity a peaceful, clean, just and prosperous Malaysia and a secure future for our children.

Our record is one of achievements, not promises. Let no one demean what the people of Malaysia and the Government of Malaysia have accomplished.

Malaysia today is at peace. The economy is sound. The nation is securely on the road to social justice and a better life for all for all races, all citizens, whether they live in the countryside or in the towns.

We should thank God for all these blessings. We must take nothing for granted—not our harmony, not our prosperity, not our achievements in bringing social justice to all our citizens.

I urge you to entrust your today and your children's tomorrow to us again.

There is still so much to be done. The agenda for the nation is a long one.

Give us again your trust. Give us again your support. Without your help, we cannot succeed. With your help, and the guidance of the Almighty, we cannot fail.

God bless you.

BN triumphant at all levels

10 July Kuala Lumpur

The Barisan Nasional swept back to power, winning 94 of the 114 parliamentary seats in Peninsular Malaysia and taking firm control of all the State Assemblies, with clean sweeps in Terengganu, Pahang and Perlis. The Barisan was already within striking distance of a two-thirds majority even before votes for the 40 seats in Sabah and Sarawak had been counted. Four of the 40 were won by the Barisan unopposed.

Datuk Hussein Onn is carried by Barisan colleagues to celebrate its victory.

1978

world news

world news

8 September
Iranian troops fire on demonstrators in Tehran, killing 122 and wounding 4,000.

17 September
The Camp David Accords are signed.

28 September
Pope John Paul I dies after only 33 days of his papacy.

1 October
Vietnam attacks Kampuchea.

16 October
Pope John Paul II (Cardinal Karol Wojtyla) becomes the 264th Pope.

27 October
Anwar Sadat and Menachem Begin win the Nobel Peace Prize.

18 November
Cult leader Jim Jones leads a mass murder–suicide in Guyana that claims 918 lives, including more than 270 children.

11 December
Two million Iranians demonstrate against the Shah of Iran.

KL zoning system soon

14 November | Kuala Lumpur

Very soon Kuala Lumpur will have a zoning system with users paying charges based on the areas through which they travel. The zoning system will apply to more than 13 roads in the city centre, but only be used during certain hours. Under the system, vehicles entering the designated zones will have to have no fewer than four passengers, while taxis will have to have no fewer than three passengers.

A gantry for the zone system under construction at Jalan Belanda.

Adele Koh dies of cancer

24 October | Adelaide

Adele Koh, the Malaysian wife of South Australia Prime Minister Don Dunstan, died of cancer, aged 35. Formerly a member of Mr Dunstan's personal staff, she married him in 1976.

UTM convo put off

6 October | Kuala Lumpur

Universiti Teknologi Malaysia's convocation was postponed indefinitely due to 'unavoidable reasons'. More than 600 graduands were to have received their degrees or diplomas at the convocation on 7 October. However, there had been controversy over a dress ruling. In 1977 all students wore the national dress for the convocation but for this year's ceremony, the Ministry of Education allowed non-Bumiputra students to wear lounge suits and songkoks. The student union opposed the ruling and demonstrated on the campus in September.

Regional arbitration centre inaugurated

17 October | Kuala Lumpur

The Regional Centre for Arbitration, established under the auspices of the inter-governmental Asian-African Legal Consultative Committee, opened. The centre promotes international commercial arbitration throughout the region.

Lim Kit Siang guilty

8 November | Kuala Lumpur

DAP secretary-general Lim Kit Siang was found guilty of five charges under the Official Secrets Act and fined $15,000. The charges related to information he had received regarding the Government's purchase of four fast-strike craft for the Royal Malaysian Navy.

Deng is first Chinese leader to visit Malaysia

10 November | Kuala Lumpur

China's Senior Vice-President Deng Xiaoping became the first Chinese leader to visit Malaysia since diplomatic ties were established with Peking in 1974.

Prime Minister Datuk Hussein Onn said at a dinner in Parliament House that big-power rivalries in 'whatever form or manner or for whatever reason' would not be in the interest of Southeast Asia. Malaysia would like to be left 'free from any form of interference, subversion or incitement,' he said.

A toast at the dinner honouring Deng Xiaoping.

Monsoon studies

2 December | Kuala Lumpur

A regional experiment to study the monsoon over the South China Sea began. The monsoon experiment or Monex was aimed at gathering data from existing meteorological stations, through a combined effort by countries in the Southeast Asian region. In Malaysia it worked from the Operations Centre at the Meteorological Forecast Office which collected data to enable scientists to study monsoon phenomena.

Non-Bumiputras 'will not miss out on education'

12 December | Kuala Lumpur

Places will be given to non-Bumiputra students in all the local universities, Education Minister Datuk Musa Hitam said. The Government was considering expanding all the local universities and, in this process, more places would be given to non-Bumiputras, he said.

Airport heroin haul

15 December | Kuala Lumpur

Police seized 42lb of heroin at Subang airport and arrested 14 people. The largest haul of Grade 3 heroin, 40–60 per cent pure, in recent years, it was bound for Amsterdam.

Concorde can fly through

16 December | Kuala Lumpur

The Government lifted a ban on flights through Malaysian airspace by the Concorde supersonic airliner for a trial period of six months. it would be reimposed if it was found to be harmful to the environment.

Colour TV arrives

28 December | Kuala Lumpur

Datuk Hussein Onn pressed the button to launch colour television and the Prime Minister's dark suit suddenly turned brilliant blue on colour TV sets nationwide (*see 19 January 1979*).

43 Viets drown as police stop them landing

3 December | Pasir Puteh ▶ Forty-three Vietnamese were drowned and 99 were missing after their boat broke up in heavy seas about 100 metres off Pantai Ru, Semarak. Another 148 were rescued but a child died later in a temporary shelter.

The deaths happened after police and Rela men stopped the Vietnamese from landing. Two were prevented from swimming ashore. The boat remained at anchor about 100 metres offshore until the waves caused difficulties. This was the second such incident in 10 days. Two hundred Vietnamese drowned off Kuala Terengganu when their boat capsized on 22 November (*see 25 January 1979*).

What the foreign press said

Barring the boat people

Despite the hazards of escape, never since the massive exodus following the fall of Saigon in 1975 has the South China Sea been so strewn with refugees seeking safe harbour, *Time* magazine said. 'The flow is so great,' reported correspondent Richard Bernstein, 'that countries in the area are becoming increasingly reluctant to accept new arrivals, even temporarily. And as the tide of refugees rises, it is straining the ability—and the willingness—of more distant nations to grant them permanent asylum. Malaysia is the most striking case in point.

'Many of the refugees have heard that acceptance in Malaysia is easier than in other nearby countries. But the number of Vietnamese in Malaysian refugee camps—packed, foetid shanty towns, where food and water are scarce—has surged from a mere 5,000 last spring to more than 40,000 today, and the Government has grown progressively anxious about new arrivals.'

1979

The nation came close to a major transport crunch when four port unions threatened to take industrial action in support of a strike by Malaysia Airlines System employees. The Government acted swiftly to neutralise the influence of international trade unionists who supported the MAS employees' action and arrested 18 union members and MAS workers. Meanwhile, the number of illegal Vietnamese boat people arriving each month swelled to 14,000. A group of miscreants who desecrated several Hindu temples incurred the wrath of Deputy Prime Minister Dr Mahathir Mohamad who said their actions were in conflict with Islamic teachings and could spark racial enmity. A Government White Paper exposed serious malpractice in Bank Rakyat.

APRIL
Former beauty queen Jean Sinnappa is stabbed to death in a car.

JUNE
The Government announces it will take firm measures to prevent further entry by Vietnamese illegal immigrants or boat people.

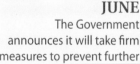

JULY
Kuala Lumpur Police Commissioner Datuk Mansor Mohamed Noor retires after 30 years of successful crime fighting.

OCTOBER
The 70-year old Station Hotel closes, leaving its workers homeless and unemployed.

February: MAS workers on strike.

'Sime Darby is well placed to share in and support Malaysia's future growth.'

Tun Tan Siew Sin, Sime Darby chairman, on the company's transfer of its domicile to Malaysia, 16 November 1979.

1979

world news

1 January
The US and the Peoples' Republic of China establish full diplomatic relations.

7 January
Vietnam announces the fall of Phnom Penh. Pol Pot and the Khmer Rouge retreat to the Thai border.

16 January
The Shah of Iran and his family flee to Egypt.

1 February
Ayatollah Khomeini returns to Iran after 15 years of exile.

10–11 February
The Iranian Army mutinies and joins the Islamic Revolution.

14 February
In Kabul, Afghanistan, the US ambassador is kidnapped. He is later killed during a rescue attempt by Afghan police.

17 February
China invades northern Vietnam to punish it for invading Kampuchea. They advance as far as 40km into Vietnam, but are completely withdrawn by 16 March.

Kungfu granny throws punch, robbers flee

5 January

A 70-year-old grandmother sent two armed robbers fleeing empty-handed when she bravely executed a backhand punch at one of them. Madam Ong Cheng Hwa was entering her house after visiting the market when a man grabbed her from behind and held a knife at her throat, while another armed with a gun held up her daughter.

The grandmother's counter-attack came when the robber was distracted by her granddaughter who ran out of the house shouting for help.

Dewan Budaya

'Khat' master

It has long been the dream of Sheikh Omar Basaree to see Malaysia having its own Islamic calligraphy (known as 'khat') art gallery, said an article in Dewan Budaya. Himself a 'khat' master, he had amassed a collection of about 60 artworks, displayed in a niche of his house in Kuala Lumpur. Islamic calligraphy comes in a variety of scripts, the more popular styles being the Nasakh, Riq'a, Kufic, Thuluth and Diwani, all of which are on display at his own mini art gallery. Sheikh Omar, described as the enfant terrible of the Malaysian khat scene by fellow artist and critic Syed Ahmad Jamal, was one of its shining stars.

A khat work in the Thuluth style done on glass.

Share-grab ploy exposed

12 January Kuala Lumpur

Malay workers were being used as tools by their superiors to buy shares allotted to Bumiputras, said Umno Youth's Economic and Finance Bureau chairman Datuk Najib bin Tun Razak.

He said this 'share-grab' tactic was uncovered recently by the parliamentary secretary to the Prime Minister's Department, Encik Shahrir Samad, in the course of his investigations. Datuk Najib voiced concern that if not curbed, this practice would hamper the implementation of the New Economic Policy.

Orang utans at risk

15 January Kuching

The number of orang utans in Sarawak had dwindled to 250 from about 900 in 1960 because of hunting and forest development, according to wildlife sources.

The animals breed every three years under natural conditions but the felling of timber using noisy machinery meant the orang utans, if they bred at all, did so only once in eight years.

House passes crisis Bill

16 January Kuala Lumpur

The Dewan Rakyat passed the Emergency (Essential Powers) Bill after a four-hour debate, with only two MPs dissenting. DAP members were absent when the Bill was put to a voice vote. Only four Opposition members, all from Pas, were present.

Law Minister Dato' Seri Hamzah Abu Samah denied that the Government was in the habit of amending the laws whenever it lost a court case. He said the Government would only amend a piece of legislation if the implications of the court judgments involved the maintenance of security and public order and if the amendments improved any weaknesses in the law for the benefit of the people.

Colour TV prices drop

19 January Kuala Lumpur

The Government announced maximum prices for colour television sets, with reductions ranging from $8 to $790 per set.

Dewan Budaya Magazine feature

The floating villages of Sabah

Along the coast of Sabah, each town has a place or locality where homes are built on water, said the January issue of *Dewan Budaya* magazine. 'In these communities, houses are linked to each other by wooden walkways extending hundreds of metres into the sea'.

The houses' appearance differs between places, it said, each community displaying the character of the livelihood of its inhabitants. Most of these houses are inhabited by fishermen, such as in 'Ice Box' Tawau, Kampung Panji Lahad Datu, Kudat and Berhala Darat Sandakan.

The inhabitants of coastal towns in Sabah prefer to build their homes over water even where land is plentiful, separated from inland society. To accommodate this strong desire, the Housing Commission of Sabah built houses equipped with piped water and electricity over the sea in Berhala Darat Sandakan. The inhabitants of these houses work on land as clerks, teachers, traders, labourers.

The floating village in Kota Kinabalu is built in an orderly manner.

'Toothless' terrors behind bars

19 January Kuala Lumpur

Eight members of the Boh Geh (toothless) robbery gang, who had been terrorising people at nightspots and eating stalls in the Bukit Bintang area, were behind bars, said deputy CID chief (Investigating) Supt S. Kulasingam. They were serving a total of 65 years' jail for armed robbery. Police also recovered about $20,000 worth of jewellery and watches.

Pakistan welcomes PM

26 January Islamabad

Prime Minister Datuk Hussein Onn's four-day official visit to Pakistan began with a 21-gun salute as he and his wife Datin Suhaila were greeted by President Zia-ul Haq and his wife Begum Zia.

Umno to discuss its constitution changes

3 February Kuala Lumpur

A proposal to amend the Umno constitution would be discussed at the 20th Umno general assembly beginning on 6 July, said Datuk Hussein Onn.

A special committee headed by Encik Ghafar Baba, an Umno vice-president, was working on the proposed amendments, which were necessary to streamline the constitution to suit the present situation, he added.

Student terrorists

3 February Muar

Seven Johor students who had become armed Communist terrorists were shot dead along the Malaysian–Thai border. Another four surrendered.

Nation mourns King

31 March Kuala Lumpur

Thousands of Malaysians from all walks of life paid their last respects to the late Yang di-Pertuan Agong Tuanku Yahya Petra ibni Al-marhum Sultan Ibrahim, who died on 30 March.

Among the first to pay their respects at Parliament House where his body lay in state were Prime Minister Datuk Hussein Onn, Finance Minister Tengku Razaleigh Hamzah and Foreign Minister Tengku Ahmad Rithaudeen.

Government offices, private firms and places of entertainment throughout the land were closed. Flags flew at half-mast. Special services were held in mosques, churches and temples.

Power cuts from today

29 March Kuala Lumpur

The National Electricity Board announced fresh power cuts expected to last for two weeks. Production in factories would be affected, it said.

An NEB statement said load-shedding in some parts of the country was necessary because of technical problems and very dry weather in hydro-power catchment areas.

Time to buckle up

2 April Kuala Lumpur

Traffic police here would begin an extensive campaign on the wearing of seat belts from 3 April, said City deputy traffic chief Deputy Supt Yunus Yacob.

Why Malaysia turns away boat people

25 January Kota Kinabalu

Malaysia was turning away Vietnamese boat people because they were being aided by a group providing them with maps, compasses and other navigation aids, said Deputy Prime Minister Dato' Seri Dr Mahathir Mohamad.

He said the group, known as 'The World Vision', also instructed the Vietnamese, whose intended final destination was not Malaysia but the United States or Europe, to sink their boats on reaching Malaysian waters so that they would be allowed into the country.

In view of this, the Government has decided not to allow any more Vietnamese illegal immigrants. All future refugee boats would be towed out to international waters. He added that the Government was doing everything possible to get the 54,000 illegal immigrants in the country out as soon as possible (see 19 June 1979).

You cannot have everything: Dr M

3 April Kuala Lumpur

National unity depended on the readiness of the majority of Malaysians to accept the fact that they cannot have all the things they want, Dato' Seri Dr Mahathir Mohamad said today.

Once there was acceptance, antagonism among the races would be reduced, if not eliminated altogether, the Deputy Prime Minister said at the launching of the unity services of the University of Malaya Students' Union here.

He said there was a tendency for every race to ask for more than society could give. For instance, he said, the Bumiputras felt that opportunities in higher education should be made their exclusive domain. Similarly, the non-Bumiputras thought that opportunities should only be open to them.

Teacher stabbed to death in car

8 April Petaling Jaya

A widowed teacher, Mrs Jean Sinnappa, 33, was stabbed to death in a car and her brother-in-law S. Karthigesu, 31, was knocked unconscious at the Federal Highway–Subang Airport Road bypass.

Mrs Sinnappa, a former beauty queen, was stabbed at least seven times. Police believed that several people could have been involved.

They ruled out robbery as a motive because expensive jewellery belonging to her was not taken (see 1 August 1980).

MAS strike

Striking workers singing the protest song *We Shall Overcome* in an effort to garner support for their action.

18 held under ISA

14 February Kuala Lumpur

Police arrested 18 people here and in Petaling Jaya in connection with the Malaysian Airline System industrial dispute. They included members of the Airline Employees' Union and MAS employees. The arrests under the Internal Security Act followed a Government directive suspending all MAS flights with immediate effect.

Transport Minister Tan Sri V. Manickavasagam said it was suspected that MAS aircraft had been tampered with. The Minister had earlier reported to Prime Minister Datuk Hussein Onn and Deputy Prime Minister Dato' Seri Dr Mahathir Mohamad the latest developments in the dispute.

Lay off, Hussein warns trade unions

16 February Kuala Lumpur

Prime Minister Datuk Hussein Onn warned trades unions that the Government would 'retaliate in full' against any action that could jeopardise the nation. He particularly told the International Transport Workers' Federation to 'cease forthwith' its interference in Malaysia's affairs. The Prime Minister appealed to the 'good sense' of union members to co-operate with the Government.

International union man is kicked out

17 February Kuala Lumpur

International Transport Workers' Federation leader Johann Hauf, whose visit pass to Malaysia was cancelled for contravening conditions of his entry, left for Bangkok 16 hours after his Asian representative Donald Uren was detained under the Internal Security Act. Mr Hauf, the assistant general-secretary of the ITWF who was in Penang for an ITWF conference, was met by five police officers who took his passport, gave him a receipt and told him to leave the country.

On 17 April, Uren was released on police advice. Home Affairs Minister Tan Sri Ghazali Shafie said Uren had made full disclosure of the manner in which he had misused his position to incite trade unionists, in particular MAS workers, to go against the law.

Cargo keeps moving

17 February Kuala Lumpur

The MAS cargo department was operating at full swing to clear the backlog of goods at the warehouse in Subang caused by the industrial action taken by MAS employees. A MAS spokesman said workers in the cargo department were cooperating and working overtime as required.

'No-nonsense' message from Mahathir

18 February Kuala Lumpur

Malaysia will tolerate no nonsense from any person or country out to destroy its economy, said Dato' Seri Dr Mahathir Mohamad. The Deputy Prime Minister said Malaysia would retaliate against any country so involved.

His warning was issued after four port unions threatened to take industrial action if the MAS dispute was not immediately resolved.

Their threat was withdrawn after a three-hour meeting with the Transport Ministry. Meanwhile, Local Defence Force members were put on standby to take over if the workers went on strike.

Dr Mahathir said the Government was aware that the port unions had met the International Transport Workers' Federation's Asian representative Donald Uren, who threatened to disrupt the nation's trade relations and to 'bring Malaysia down to its knees'.

1979

world news

18 February
It snows in the Sahara Desert for half an hour.

4 March
Photos sent back by the *Voyager 1* space probe reveal the rings of Jupiter.

1 April
Ninety-eight per cent of the votes cast in Iran referendum say yes to an Islamic republic.

2 April
A Soviet bio-warfare laboratory in Sverdlovsk, Russia, accidentally releases anthrax spores, killing 66 people and livestock.

4 April
In Pakistan, Zulfikar Ali Bhutto is executed.

11 April
Tanzanian troops capture Kampala, Uganda. Idi Amin flees.

4 May
Margaret Thatcher becomes Prime Minister of the UK.

1 June
The first black-led Government in Rhodesia takes power.

2 June
Pope John Paul II visits his native Poland, the first Pope to visit a Communist country.

Datuk Hussein Onn is greeted by the top Chinese leaders Hua Guofeng (left) and Deng Xiaoping on 3 May during the Prime Minister's visit to China.

Egypt's Mubarak briefs Hussein on peace treaty

1 May Kuala Lumpur

Egyptian Vice-President Hosni Mubarak met Datuk Hussein Onn for more than two hours here today and briefed the Prime Minister on the current situation in West Asia, particularly the peace treaty between Egypt and Israel.

The Vice-President, who arrived from Jakarta with a message from President Anwar Sadat, explained at length the various issues involved in the peace treaty.

Pro-Reds in Johor given ultimatum

1 May Johor Bahru

Communist supporters and sympathisers and others involved in anti-national and subversive activities in Johor had 14 days to surrender to the authorities, said Menteri Besar Tan Sri Haji Othman Saat.

'This is their chance to come forward and say they have made a mistake and wish to return to the right path,' he added. He noted that 89 people were arrested recently and 'most had repented.'

Diesel shortage now nationwide problem

2 May Kuala Lumpur

Random checks indicated that many petrol stations in major towns throughout the country had either run out of diesel or expected to unless supplies were received immediately from the oil companies.

A spokesman for the Petrol Dealers' Association claimed that the oil companies were deliberately holding up supplies to create a shortage and force prices up.

Kidnap gang held

4 May Ipoh

Perak police arrested six people in connection with the activities of a gang specialising in kidnapping schoolchildren. In an investigation lasting two years, police identified a farm in the Tambun area as being used as a hideout. The gang was believed to have been responsible for kidnapping 10 children, most on their way to or from school, in Ipoh since 1977.

Hottest May in 20 years

25 May Kuala Lumpur

This was the hottest May in 20 years in the city and Petaling Jaya. The average temperature recorded during the dry spell was 28.1°C (81°F) while the hottest single day was 37°C (99°F).

Stars at charity auction

27 May Kuala Lumpur

Television personalities raised thousands at a charity auction for the Malaysian Association for the Blind. Patrick MacNee's famous bowler hat from *The Avengers* fetched $900 and *Six Million Dollar Man* Lee Majors' sold a scarf for $550.

Tun Sambanthan dies, aged 59

19 May Kuala Lumpur

The executive chairman of the National Unity Board, Tun V.T. Sambanthan, died of a heart attack aged 59. Tun Sambanthan, a leader of the nation's struggle for independence, left a wife Toh Puan Uma Sambanthan and daughter Deevakunchari, 20.

Tun Sambanthan was president of the MIC for 18 years, elected in May 1955. The same year, he became a member of the Federal Assembly after the first Federal elections, and was appointed Minister of Labour. In September 1957, he became Minister of Health. In the 1959 general election, he was elected MP for Sungai Siput and was then made Minister of Works, Posts and Telecommunications, a portfolio he retained until 1971. On 1 January 1972, he became Minister of National Unity and held the post until 1974. He did not stand in the 1974 general election.

Tun Sambanthan was a member of several Malaysian delegations abroad, including that to London in 1957 led by Tunku Abdul Rahman to finalise the Constitution of an independent Malaya.

The funeral procession of Tun Sambanthan passing through Sungai Siput town.

Dr M attacks group 'seeking racial strife'

26 May Alor Star

Deputy Prime Minister Dato' Seri Dr Mahathir Mohamad hit out at a group of Muslims who had desecrated several Hindu temples in the country. Their actions were in conflict with Islamic teachings and could spark racial enmity, he said, adding that the group had made use of twisted interpretations of Islamic teachings for the benefit of several of its leaders and intended to cause racial strife in the country by propagating such false teachings.

Barisan leaders to meet over vandalism

28 May Kuala Lumpur

Prime Minister Datuk Hussein Onn today said Umno would call a meeting of Barisan leaders soon to discuss acts of vandalism against idols and temples by 'certain irresponsible people'.

He said the problem of vandalism did not involve only one religion. The actions by 'certain people who have a misconception of Islam' could have adverse consequences on community harmony.

45 feared dead in bus tragedy

8 June Kuching

A bus carrying 68 people plunged into a disused gold-mining pool at Bau, 22 miles from here. Forty-five people were feared dead. Rescue teams recovered 31 bodies, 30 of them pupils of the Bau Lake Secondary School, and one a trainee teacher. Twenty-three people, including the bus driver and conductor, survived.

Donation from Sabah benefits foundation

10 June Kuala Lumpur

The Tun Razak Foundation received the land title to its 2,500-acre cocoa estate located near Tawau.

It was handed over by Sabah Chief Minister Datuk Harris Salleh to Deputy Minister of Energy, Telecommunications and Posts Datuk Najib Tun Razak on behalf of the foundation. The donation was made by the Sabah Government last year.

Cricketer of the Year

29 June Kuala Lumpur

Dr Risya Ratnalingam was awarded Cricketer of the Year by the Yang di-Pertuan Agong after he captained the Malaysian cricket team in the ICC Trophy tournament in England. He took three wickets in Malaysia's first game though in the end Canada won by 44 runs. He was the first Malaysian to win the prestigious Rhodes scholarship in 1966, enabling him to complete his Doctor of Philosophy in Physics at Oxford University.

Formula agreed for university intake

29 June Kuala Lumpur

Umno and MCA leaders agreed a formula to redress imbalances in higher education opportunities. An MCA statement said both parties 'had a thorough discussion on the various imbalances prevailing in our multi-racial society, particularly on imbalances in higher educational opportunities.'

No more being 'nice'

19 June Kuala Lumpur

The Government would take firm measures to prevent further entry of Vietnamese illegal immigrants, said Prime Minister Datuk Hussein Onn.

Any boat carrying them that tried to enter Malaysian waters or attempted to land would be towed away and given assistance to proceed on its journey. The Prime Minister said in a message to UN Secretary-General Kurt Waldheim that Malaysia had reached the limit of its endurance and 'this is the only way open to us to contain the problem that is severely affecting the country'. Waldheim had made an official request for information on the Government's policy towards the Vietnamese.

One step taken was to divert Malaysian naval ships from the Straits of Malacca to the South China Sea. On 5 June, Deputy Prime Minister Dato' Seri Dr Mahathir Mohamad had said there were 73,000 Vietnamese boat people in the country, up from about 50,000 only months earlier, and there were 14,000 arrivals in one month alone. He said there was a necessity to be 'harsh' with the boat people because Malaysia was being burdened by this problem and on top of this was accused of being inhumane.

Bank Rakyat's inside story laid bare

22 June Kuala Lumpur

A Government White Paper exposed serious malpractice in Bank Rakyat. It said malpractice was the primary cause of the bank's $65.2-million losses.

The White Paper, based on a report by the accounting firm Price Waterhouse, listed four major factors which contributed to the bank's losses up to 31 December 1975, including lack of proper plans and studies for operations and expansion of activities; systemic weakness and poor control over lending activities; dishonesty and lack of responsibility, in particular on the part of the chairman Datuk Harun Idris and the managing director Abu Mansor Basir, and poor supervision and control.

The White Paper said that to protect the interests of members of the bank legal actions were being taken 'against those responsible' for the losses.

Invasion of tiger grasshoppers

6 July Seremban

Several estates here are under the threat of an invasion by ravaging tiger grasshoppers (*Valanga nigricornis*). The grasshoppers had damaged about 100 acres of cover crops in Chembong Estate, about 30 miles from Labu Estate, where about 500 acres of young oil palm trees were also affected.

City crime fighter to call it quits after 30 years

11 July Kuala Lumpur

The man who helped to reduce crime in the capital city, Commissioner Datuk Mansor bin Mohamed Noor, announced his retirement having worked 30 years in the police force.

When he took over as city Police Chief in 1976, Datuk Mansor launched a series of drives known by the code name Operation Sapu (Sweep) against criminals and the Communist underground movement. These constant drives paid off as crime fell.

Progress not fast enough, says Razaleigh

13 July Alor Star

Finance Minister Tengku Razaleigh Hamzah expressed concern that Bumiputra progress in commerce and industry was not as fast as expected although they had generally attained economic improvement.

He said the implementation of the New Economic Policy had helped to reduce poverty, increase employment opportunities, upgrade Bumiputras' skills and enhance their income but they were still not progressing fast enough in commerce and industry, particularly in the diversification of their enterprises.

Speaking at the opening of the Kedah National Malay Chamber of Commerce and Industry, he warned that Bumiputras should not depend entirely on Government help in their business undertakings.

Tin smugglers pose as businessmen

6 August Johor Bahru

Tin-ore smugglers were employing a new tactic, conveying the ore in new and expensive cars driven by well-dressed men posing as businessmen. This came to light after Customs officers detained four men and seized $34,807 worth of ore from expensive new cars in three separate cases.

MIC president Manickavasagam dies, aged 53

13 October Kuala Lumpur

Minister of Transport and MIC president Tan Sri V. Manickavasagam died of a heart attack. Tan Sri Manickavasagam, who celebrated his 53rd birthday eight days earlier, left five children and two grandchildren. His wife Kamala Devi died in 1968.

Seen here voting in the 1969 election, he was a founder member of the MIC and became the secretary of its Klang branch under the presidency of the late Mr Letchumanan Chettiar. He contested his first election in 1955 when he was returned unopposed to the Selangor State Council in Klang South constituency. In 1958, he was elected vice-president of the MIC and, the following year, was returned to the Federal Parliament in the Klang constituency.

Immediately after his success in the elections, he was appointed an Assistant Minister of Labour and was elevated to the full rank of Minister of Labour in 1964. He held that portfolio until 1974 when he was appointed Communications Minister. The Ministry was redesignated the Transport Ministry last year. He was made Tan Sri in 1970.

Trekking in the foothills of Everest is Ipoh-born computer analyst Zaini Sharani, 28, (Above) who reached 24,200 feet up the world's highest mountain with a Canadian friend and a Sherpa guide. They could not go any higher because they lacked the equipment.

Terengganu Ruler dies

21 September Kuala Terengganu

The Sultan of Terengganu, Tuanku Ismail Nasiruddin Shah ibni Al-marhum Sultan Zainal Abidin, passed away at Istana Badariah here. He was 72.

Sultan Ismail was the 14th Sultan of Terengganu and had ruled the State for 35 years. He also served as the fourth Yang di-Pertuan Agong. The Yang di-Pertuan Agong, the Raja Permaisuri Agong, members of the Terengganu royal family, the Menteri Besar and the State Secretary were at his bedside.

The following day the Yang di-Pertuan Muda, Tengku Mahmood ibni Al-marhum Sultan Ismail Nasiruddin Shah, 49, was proclaimed the new Sultan at the Istana Maziah throne room. The proclamation was made by the president of the State Regency Council.

Petrol and diesel prices rise again

31 August Kuala Lumpur

The retail prices of both premium and regular petrol rose, by 21 cents and 25 cents a gallon respectively. Diesel and kerosene also increased by 10 cents and 20 cents a gallon. The new prices in Kuala Lumpur were $3.69 a gallon (81.2 cents a litre) for premium and $3.35 (73.7 cents a litre) for regular petrol, and $1.30 a gallon for diesel and kerosene.

Prices elsewhere varied according to transport cost.

1979

16 July
Iraqi President Hasan al-Bakr resigns. Replaced by his deputy Saddam Hussein.

31 July
Four hundred Iranians are killed after clashes with Saudi security forces in Mecca.

27 August
Lord Mountbatten is assassinated by the IRA. On the same day, another bomb kills 18 English soldiers.

26 October
South Korean President Park Chung-Hee and five of his bodyguards are killed by the head of the Korean CIA.

4 November
Three thousand Iranians invade the US Embassy in Tehran, taking 90 hostages.

20 November
About 200 Muslim militants occupy Mecca's Grand Mosque. After bloody fighting, the toll is 250 dead, and about 600 wounded.

24 December
The Soviet Union invades Afghanistan.

Big rubber breakthrough

6 October Geneva

The International Natural Rubber Agreement on Price Stabilisation, regulating trade in the commodity, was agreed, giving Malaysia victory in a long battle to secure international guarantees for her top foreign exchange earner.

Negotiators from 55 leading producing and importing nations resolved the last remaining issues here. This was the first international agreement to regulate the natural rubber trade.

300 homeless after fire

16 October Kuala Lumpur

About 300 people were made homeless when fire razed some 30 houses, 15 shophouses and four factories in Jalan Klang Lama here today. Damage was estimated at millions as expensive machinery was destroyed. The fire was believed to have started in a candle factory.

Tax cuts for all in bold Budget

19 October Kuala Lumpur

Finance Minister Tengku Razaleigh Hamzah unveiled a bold Budget in which he slashed income tax and offered new incentives for private investment and export-oriented industries.

Personal relief for married couples was raised to $7,000, meaning that from 1980 a married couple with two children and an income of just over $700 a month need pay no tax. The tax cuts amounted to $482 million, the biggest in the nation's history.

Station Hotel closes doors after 70 years

31 October Kuala Lumpur

Sadness filled the air as about 60 workers of the 70-year-old Station Hotel here collected their last pay packet.

The Station Hotel was vacating the Malayan Railway building in Jalan Hishamuddin and to at least 20 of the workers, it meant more than losing their jobs. They also had to leave the hotel, their home as well as their workplace.

Oil to replace rubber as No.1

19 October

The petroleum and manufacturing sectors would become the country's leading export earners in 1980, replacing rubber, the Treasury's Economic Report 1979/1980 said.

The bulk of the increase in export earnings in 1980 would be generated by the petroleum and the manufacturing sectors, which were anticipated to grow in value terms by 43 per cent and 11 per cent to $5,400 million and $4,773 million respectively.

In view of this, the report said, major exports were expected to remain relatively buoyant.

Taking A Long View To Safeguard Malaysia's Oil Future

PETRONAS

Petronas advertises its faith in the future of oil.

Sime Darby to shift domicile to Malaysia

16 November Kuala Lumpur

Shareholders of Sime Darby Holdings Limited approved the transfer of its domicile to Malaysia. The new Malaysian parent company of the Sime group, Sime Darby Bhd, would take over the assets and liabilities of the old limited company incorporated in Britain. The transfer was expected to be effective on 20 December.

Tun Templer dies

26 October London

Field Marshal Tun Sir Gerald Templer, one of the chief architects of the successful anti-Communist campaign in Malaya, died at the age of 81.

A distinguished soldier in two world wars, he was British High Commissioner and Director of Operations in Malaya at the height of the Communist insurrection from 1952 to 1954. He resettled some 400,000 people in fenced 'new villages', denying the terrorists food. He also started the country's first vigilante corps, the Home Guard.

25 buried in landslip at flood relief centre

28 November Kuala Krai

At least 25 people were feared killed when the Kuala Balah clinic, used as a flood-relief centre, was buried in a landslip. Police confirmed that up to 30 people were in or around the clinic at the time.

Police said heavy rain had apparently dislodged a huge boulder and several trees from the hilltop, causing an avalanche of rocks and earth which rained on the clinic.

Boatman saves $9,000 in five-cent coins

7 December Muar

Not knowing how to spend his small change, boatman Abdul bin Montok began saving it in two small jars and several boxes over 10 years. Then he had rescuers baffled when he refused to budge from his house in the face of rising flood waters.

With police intervention, he reluctantly agreed to go, but not without taking the jars and boxes. It was found they contained 182,000 five-cent coins, a total of $9,100.

14-year-old bookie

16 December Kuala Lumpur

A girl aged 14 was among 20 people arrested in raids on an illegal bookmaking and lottery racket here.

Free schooling for all

17 December Kuala Lumpur

Education would be free for all national-type secondary school students from 1980 with the change-over of the medium of instruction to Bahasa Malaysia, according to a Cabinet committee report on the implementation of the language policy.

Previously free places were offered to not more than 10 per cent of students in such schools. Education in all primary schools and national secondary schools was free. The report also said private schools would be placed under closer Education Ministry supervision.

UK warned over rise in student fees

23 December Kuala Lumpur

Education Minister Datuk Musa Hitam said the high cost of education for foreign students in Britain would have 'far-reaching implications' on Malaysian–British relations. He expressed his concern to the British High Commissioner here, Sir Donald Hawley.

Datuk Musa said the British proposal to increase fees from September 1980 would reduce the number of Malaysian students studying there.

This, he added, would adversely affect the social, cultural and economic ties between Malaysia and Britain (*see 8 March 1981*).

Felda puts $2b into land development

30 December Kuala Lumpur

Established in 1959 as the country's major land development agency, the Federal Land Development Authority (Felda) has spearheaded agricultural development in the country, said a review of the year in the *Sunday Times*.

So far it had developed 1.2 million acres of land, about 900,000 acres in the last 10 years. More than 700,000 acres were under oil palm, 390,000 acres rubber, 21,600 acres cocoa, 13,000 acres sugar cane and 3,700 acres coffee. It had also created settlements for about 55,000 settler families with a total population of some 370,000. It had already invested some $2 billion in land development schemes and would probably have to invest another $2 billion in the next decade at the current rate of development.

1980

The national soccer team qualified for the Olympic Games by winning their qualifying match against South Korea. But Malaysia's participation in the Olympics hung in the balance following an earlier Cabinet decision to advise the Olympic Council of Malaysia to boycott the games in Moscow. The decision followed a resolution passed at the Islamic Foreign Ministers conference in Islamabad to stay away from the Games. Several religious fanatics were killed when they stormed the police station in Batu Pahat, prompting the Government to vow to stamp out deviationist Muslim teachings. Amidst what he claimed was a malicious campaign against him, DAP stalwart Lim Kit Siang resigned as secretary-general of the party.

APRIL
Malaysian football team qualifies for the Olympic Games.

MAY
Fans go beserk for the Osmonds.

JULY
Tuanku Ahmad Shah is installed as the seventh Yang di-Pertuan Agong.

NOVEMBER
A dramatic rooftop rescue by helicopter takes place when the 12-storey former Bank Bumiputra headquarters catches fire. One person dies.

June: Three people are killed, scores injured and more than $20 million of damage caused by powerful explosions at Port Klang.

Malaysia Facts		
13.9 million	Population	
$54.3 billion	Gross Domestic Product	
$3,786	Gross National Income (per capita)	
30.6	Crude Birth Rate (per 1,000 persons)	
23.8	Infant Mortality (per 1,000 live births)	
66.5 / 71.0	Life Expectancy (male / female)	
41.2	Consumer Price Index (base 2010=100)	

'Our intention was to strengthen further the provisions in the Trade Unions Ordinance ... never to suppress.'

Datuk Hussein Onn, on the new labour laws applicable to trade unions, 29 March 1980.

1980

world news

4 February
Ayatollah Khomeini names Abolhassan Bani-Sadr as President of Iran.

27 February
Guerrillas take over the Dominican Embassy in Colombia and take 60 hostages, 14 of them ambassadors.

18 March
A rocket explodes at the Plesetsk Cosmodrome in Russia while being refuelled, killing 50.

27 March
A Norwegian oil platform in the North Sea collapses, killing 123 of its crew.

1 April
A flotilla of boats carrying thousands of Cuban refugees, many of them criminals released from prison, sets out for the US.

7 April
The US severs diplomatic relations with Iran and imposes economic sanctions.

10 April
Spain and the UK agree to re-open the Gibraltar border, closed since 1969.

12 April
Samuel Doe takes over Liberia in a coup after more than 130 years of democracy.

RM12m complex for medical school

5 January | **Kuala Lumpur**

Universiti Sains Malaysia's (USM) Medical School will have a $12-million building complex to cater to its first student intake next year. The complex will be used until the school shifts to its permanent site in Kubang Kerian, Kelantan in 1983. Other schools will occupy the complex when that happened.

Two million workers to enjoy Socso coverage

8 January | **Kuala Lumpur**

In a major expansion drive, the Social Security Organisation (Socso) scheme has been extended to cover about two million workers in Peninsular Malaysia.

An additional 698,564 workers are to enjoy coverage under the expansion programme.

According to Socso director-general Nik Mohd Amin Nik Abu Bakar, another 15,988 employers were expected to register with the scheme in 1980. As at September 1979, 29,725 employers took part in the scheme involving 1.2 million workers.

Bintang RTM winners

8 January | **Kuala Lumpur**

Competition was stiff in the Bintang RTM 1979 final but the night belonged to Perak's Jamal Abdillah who won the solo section at the Angkasapuri auditorium here. Sharing the limelight was Penang's OFYZA which took the group title. First and second runners-up (solo) were Lanny Lim Mui Lan of Seremban and Flora Santos of Sabah and (group) KS5 and Sealegs.

Learn from India

23 January | **Kuala Lumpur**

Malaysia would find it worthwhile to emulate innovative ideas adopted by India in promoting its small-scale industries, said Deputy Prime Minister Dato' Seri Dr Mahathir Mohamad. 'This is because Malaysia is one of the areas in this region with a substantial amount of Indian investment and as far as possible, we would like to see more.'

Windfall for 26,000 pensioners

23 January | **Kuala Lumpur**

Some 26,000 pensioners under the Suffian Scheme can look forward to receiving higher pensions in an award by the Public Services Tribunal. They are also due arrears amounting to $80 million. With the increase in pension factor from 1/800 to 1/600 effective from 1 January 1970, the pensioners are to receive about $118 million in arrears but it was ruled that a 20 per cent supplementary allowance granted in 1977 will be deducted.

Tribunal chairman Mr Justice Abdul Hamid said it was the tribunal's view that although the amount involved was significant, what was more significant was the effect of the decision on the country's economy.

He said that the main issue was for the tribunal to determine whether the recommendation made by the Suffian Salaries Commission to reduce the pension factor for officers in public services who retired between 1 January 1970 and 31 December 1975 was 'an anomaly' and, if so, whether it needed rectification.

He said the tribunal felt that an anomalous situation had indeed arisen, adding that it was clearly established that the aggrieved persons were public officers by reason of their employment during the relevant period. Cuepacs hailed the award as a significant milestone in the history of the civil service.

Why villagers throw stones at trains

1 February | **Kuala Lumpur**

Anger over passengers throwing empty bottles, half-eaten food and other rubbish from coaches led villagers to retaliate by throwing stones at trains, said Malayan Railway passenger manager Encik Zainal Abidin bin Abdul Talib.

He appealed to passengers to put their rubbish into the bins provided instead of throwing it on the floor or, worse, out of the windows.

The metric problem for drivers: working out how much it will cost to fill their tanks.

Going metric

16 February | **Kuala Lumpur** ▶ Malaysians had no clue about how much a kilogram of rice was or what distance a kilometre was, according to an article in the *New Sunday Times*. The Government was aware of the problem, it said, but was convinced that the nation must go metric. Metric is the system for the future since 90 per cent of the world has gone or is going metric. It was simple to use, the Government argued, as everything was in 10s and divisible by 10 (*see 2 January 1982*).

Students up in arms over fees increase

2 February | **London**

Twenty thousand Malaysian students in Britain and Ireland, along with their Singaporean counterparts, launched a nationwide campaign against what they termed the British Government's 'racist fees policy' which imposed discriminatory fees on overseas students and proposed to charge 'full economic cost' fees from this year.

The planned action included a month-long campaign to collect signatures for petitions to the Prime Ministers of Malaysia, Singapore and Britain.

Book to end Bahasa Malaysia 'pollution'

5 February | **Penang**

A committee set up to study the 'pollution' of Bahasa Malaysia recommended that a Bahasa Malaysia guidebook be published. The book, said its chairman Prof Datuk Awang Had Salleh, would be invaluable.

Call to boycott Olympics

6 February | **Kuala Lumpur**

The Cabinet advised the Olympic Council of Malaysia (OCM) not to take part in the Olympic Games in Moscow in July. This followed a resolution passed at the Islamic Foreign Ministers' conference in Islamabad shortly beforehand, regarding the participation of member-States in the Games.

PM's double joy

12 February | **Kuala Lumpur**

When Prime Minister Datuk Hussein Onn celebrated his 54th birthday today, former Prime Minister Tunku Abdul Rahman, who celebrated his 77th birthday on 8 February, came to congratulate him. Datuk Hussein and his wife Datin Suhaila Tan Sri Noah were also celebrating their 32nd wedding anniversary.

Among others who called at Sri Taman were Cabinet Ministers and friends as well as officials and staff of the Prime Minister's Department. An MCA delegation, led by party president Datuk Lee San Choon, turned up with a birthday cake.

Malaysia says 'no' to Asean defence pact

19 February | Kuala Lumpur

Deputy Foreign Minister Datuk Mokhtar Hashim said Malaysia was opposed to any Asean defence pact. Such an alliance, he said, would be a setback to the realisation of a zone of peace, freedom and neutrality in Southeast Asia.

He was commenting on a report from Manila quoting Philippine President Ferdinand Marcos as saying that Asean should become more involved in mutual security arrangements to meet threats from Indochina. Datuk Mokhtar said Malaysia believed that efforts should instead be made to attain regional neutrality.

8 Communists shot dead in clash

5 March | Kuantan

Security forces shot dead eight Communist terrorists in a three-hour battle in the jungles of west Pahang. State Security Council chairman Datuk Kamarulzaman bin Abdul Rahman said it was 'the biggest single success in Pahang since the Communist bid to gain a foothold in the State in 1973'.

The crack security force unit came upon the group of heavily armed terrorists at 8.55am and a 20-minute battle ensued, resulting in the death of five of the terrorists. The rest fled, but a second clash occurred at 9.40am. Three more terrorists died but the rest managed to escape.

Razak Chair set up at Ohio University

17 March | Kuala Lumpur

The establishment of the Tun Abdul Razak Chair at Ohio University in the United States would enhance Malaysia's image in the field of education, said Education Minister Datuk Musa Hitam. The establishment of the Chair was announced jointly by the Government and Ohio University.

Datuk Musa said the Chair would play an important role in introducing social, cultural, economic and political aspects of the Malaysian way of life. It would involve a Malaysian scholar going to Ohio University every two years for teaching and research in their chosen field (*see 16 August 1983*).

Riding keeps me fit, says sporting King

29 March | Kuala Lumpur

Riding horses is one way in which Yang di-Pertuan Agong Sultan Ahmad Shah keeps fit and healthy. The King revealed that he regularly went riding in the mornings and evenings as well as played tennis and golf. He said he loved horses but that, like a father who cannot afford to have a favourite child, he did not have a favourite horse.

His Highness led his team to a stunning 12–2 victory over the visiting Dundee Polo Club of Scotland to capture the Dr Vijay Lukshumeyah trophy at the Selangor Polo and Riding Club. Referee Akhbar Khan said the King played a cool and collected game with spirited moves.

Five 'Holy Army' leaders held

2 April | Kuala Lumpur

Five leaders of the illegal Pertubuhan Angkatan Sabilullah (Holy Army) were arrested under the Internal Security Act, three in Kedah, one in Kuala Lumpur and one in Johor.

Police said investigations had established that the organisation was neither a silat group nor a secret society but 'a secret illegal organisation formed by the more extremist faction of the defunct Tentera Sabilullah to advance their extra-constitutional political objectives'.

Controls on trade unions tightened

4 April | Kuala Lumpur

The Dewan Rakyat passed two Bills to amend the Trade Unions Ordinance 1959 and the Industrial Relations Act 1967 imposing tighter controls on unions after a marathon 8½-hour sitting. The changes were introduced by Labour and Manpower Minister Datuk Richard Ho.

Dato' Seri Dr Mahathir Mohamad said the Bills were to protect the interests of workers and curb trade disputes that might wreck the country's industrialisation plan. Unions protested against the laws through the Malaysian Trades Union Congress. Secretary-general V. David said the MTUC would continue to reject the amendments.

Botak Chin tried again

1 April–16 May | Kuala Lumpur

Wong Swee Chin, alias Botak Chin, caused a stir when he was brought to trial for the second time on arms charges under the Internal Security Act, three years after he was first charged. He interrupted proceedings twice to consult counsel and also asked to see the judge in private. Two days later, the retrial was adjourned for a month for Chin to undergo observation at a mental institution. His lawyer told the court that four years in solitary confinement had taken a toll on Chin's mind.

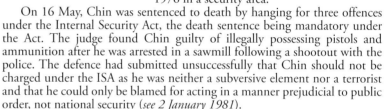

Botak Chin under heavy guard as he is led back to Pudu Prison.

Chin had pleaded guilty in 1977 to arms charges under the Internal Security Act, the only person in history to have done so. The ISA provided for a mandatory death penalty on conviction. But the Privy Council recommended in 1979 that the conviction and sentence be quashed, ruling that the Essential (Security Cases) Regulations, under which the charge was framed, were outside the powers of the Constitution. A retrial was ordered. Chin was charged with having unlawful control of three pistols and possession of ammunition on 16 February 1976 in a security area.

On 16 May, Chin was sentenced to death by hanging for three offences under the Internal Security Act, the death sentence being mandatory under the Act. The judge found Chin guilty of illegally possessing pistols and ammunition after he was arrested in a sawmill following a shootout with the police. The defence had submitted unsuccessfully that Chin should not be charged under the ISA as he was neither a subversive element nor a terrorist and that he could only be blamed for acting in a manner prejudicial to public order, not national security (*see 2 January 1981*).

Operation Hammer restrictions lifted

5 March | Kuching

The Government lifted all restrictions in the Operation Hammer Area along the Kuching–Serian Road. This meant that residents in the area were able to move about freely as in other parts of Sarawak.

The restrictions were set up in 1966 to counter the Communist insurgency in the area. Chief Minister Datuk Patinggi Tan Sri Haji Abdul Rahman Yaakub said the security situation in the State was very much under control.

THE ASIA MAGAZINE

The leaning tower of Teluk Anson

The cover of *Asia Magazine* on 11 May featured the clock tower in Teluk Intan (previously Telok Anson), Perak, which began leaning soon after construction in 1885 because of an underground stream that ran nearby.

Malaysian soccer win

6 April | Kuala Lumpur

James Wong put Malaysia in the Olympic soccer competition for the second time since the 1972 Munich Games. He struck home three minutes before the final whistle in a qualifying match against South Korea, giving Malaysia a 2–1 win after they had weathered a Korean onslaught.

James Wong (right) gets involved in the goalmouth action in an earlier tie.

1980

First drug pusher to be hanged

4 April Kuala Lumpur

Hong Hoo Chong, 32 and a confectioner by trade, became the first person to be hanged in the country for a drug offence. He was executed at 6am.

Hong had originally been jailed by the Penang High Court for life and ordered to receive 14 strokes of the rotan for trafficking in 1,550.1g of heroin in Penang on 24 March 1978.

$653,000 gems grab

9 April Kuala Lumpur

In the country's biggest jewel robbery, two men escaped with $653,000 worth of gems after a shootout with the police. They also took $3,250 from jeweller Lee Ah Swee, 28.

The gang abducted Lee, owner of Camy Goldsmith, after faking an accident in Jalan Kuching. They tied Lee's wife to a tree and forced him to go to his shop and hand over the gems. Mrs Lee escaped and called the police who sped to the scene and confronted the robbers. But they managed to escape.

The next day, three gunmen got away with $1.28 million in gold bars and jewellery from Lee Wing Goldsmith. Its manager, Tang Pack Kie, 42, was found dead in the morning, apparently suffocated in the boot of a car in which he had been left by the robbers.

On the same day in Penang, seven men, five armed with pistols, grabbed $200,000 worth of gems from the Cheong Loong Goldsmith in Penang Road.

MTUC given ultimatum

15 May Kuala Lumpur

Civil service trade unions gave the Malaysian Trades Union Congress a month to reorganise itself into a confederation of three trades union federations. Otherwise, they said, they would pull out of the congress.

Two federations should cover unions in industry and those in quasi-government bodies and local authorities. Cuepacs would be the third federation, covering the civil service.

'We will not have a police state'

17 April Kuala Lumpur

Lord President Tun Mohamed Suffian upheld the conviction and sentence of four police officers for causing hurt to a 16-year-old suspect, saying that Malaysia should not be allowed to develop into a police state. Former Chief Inspector Lai Kim Hon was convicted, together with three other policemen, of causing hurt to Nordin Hamzah for the purpose of extorting a confession and information from him at the Cheras police station in June 1977.

Nordin died two days after he was arrested and a post-mortem examination found abrasions all over his body caused by blows with a rubber hose, falls, punches and kicks.

You're not wanted, Usno tells Tun Mustapha

7 May Kuala Lumpur

Usno was not keen on former Sabah Chief Minister Tun Mustapha Harun contesting the State election under the party's ticket, according to party sources. He was planning a return to politics after the party lost miserably to Berjaya in 1976 following rumours that a snap poll might be held later in the year. 'There is no place for Mustapha who, being a former Chief Minister, cannot be just an ordinary member of the party and stand for elections,' said the sources.

Port blasts kill eight

5 June Port Klang

Three people died and at least 200 were injured when powerful explosions ripped through godowns and devastated the South Port here. Damage was estimated at between $20 million and $25 million. South Port was closed indefinitely as the Government ordered a full-scale investigation. The fire destroyed chemicals, fertilisers, canned food, rubber and palm oil stored in seven godowns. It was believed to have started in one of the godowns used to store chemicals at 2.30am.

Some 3,000 residents living around the port were evacuated as the explosions tore down squatter huts, shattered windows and blew away roofs. The dead were a Burmese seaman and two women struck by the debris of their home. At least 30 people were admitted to hospital with severe injuries, among them port officials and firemen. Victims were assured by Prime Minister Datuk Hussein Onn that they would get Government help and that houses would be found for those made homeless. The fire came barely a month after the port authority obtained a $5-million firefighting ship with modern equipment meant for fighting fires on board ships.

Hours after the blasts, Port Klang remained enveloped in a dark cloud as a downpour trapped thick smoke from the fires on the ground.

The next day, as a massive clean-up and repair work started, Port Klang secretary Mohamed bin Haji Abdul Hamid assured shippers that South Port 'will be reopened in a few months'.

Firemen damp down oil drums on the quayside at Port Klang as the battle against the fire is won.

Donny and Marie Osmond wow the Malaysian audience.

Stampede to get glimpse of Osmonds

26 May Kuala Lumpur

A handful of schoolgirls waited patiently at the lobby of Hotel Equatorial here hoping for a glimpse of their idols, the pop group the Osmonds who were in the Federal capital for a concert, but unfortunately they were waiting at the wrong exit of the restaurant where the Osmonds were having a meal.

When they heard that Marie Osmond was coming out, there was a stampede and suddenly the number of girls had swollen to 200, almost crushing the Osmonds to the wall.

And then they gave ear-piercing screams of 'I saw her! I saw her!'

Head count begins

10 June Kuala Lumpur

The count for a population census began at 7pm. The deputy secretary-general of the Information Ministry and acting chairman of the publicity committee of the Census Board, Datuk Wan Mahmood bin Pawan Teh, said census enumerators would wear identification tags, carry cards bearing the Government crest and their name and photograph, and a green box file stating Census 1980.

Enumerators would travel on trains and ships and would man roadblocks to make sure no one was left out of the count. He assured the public that all information taken was confidential and would not be used against any person under any circumstances.

Seventh King is installed

10 July **Kuala Lumpur** ▶ Tuanku Haji Ahmad Shah Al-Musta'in Billah ibni Al-marhum Sultan Abu Bakar Ri'ayatuddin Al Mu'adzam Shah was installed as the seventh Yang di-Pertuan Agong.

On the eve of the ceremony, strings of lights added a fairyland atmosphere to the city. Main streets were transformed into carnival grounds with arches, banners and bunting strung with thousands of coloured bulbs. People turned out in droves to watch the cultural show Gemala Setia at the Selangor Club padang.

The Yang di-Pertuan Agong.

Death for murder of sister-in-law

1 August **Kuala Lumpur**

Specialist Teachers' Training College lecturer S. Karthigesu, 38, was found guilty and sentenced to death for the murder of his sister-in-law, former beauty queen Mrs Jean Sinappa, 33 (pictured below). Karthigesu was calm as sentence was passed by Mr Justice Mohamed Azmi. The courtroom was so packed that many of Karthigesu's friends and family had to stand in the corridors.

The seven-man jury returned a 5–2 majority verdict after deliberating for four hours and 10 minutes. The prosecution had described the killing as 'a crime of passion triggered by intense jealousy and avariciousness' (*see 31 May 1981*).

Hunt is on for gold and diamond deposits

1 August **Ipoh**

Alluvial gold deposits were identified in Kelantan and Pahang, prompting a gold rush among local firms in both East Coast states. Six other alluvial gold areas had also been identified in Negeri Sembilan. Additionally, a contract to drill for diamonds had been awarded while drilling in a potential base metal area in Pahang would start soon.

Primary Industries Minister Datuk Paul Leong said the Geological Survey Department had accelerated its mineral exploration programme in the north-central part of the peninsula's central belt.

Petrol prices up again

15 August **Kuala Lumpur**

At midnight the price of premium petrol went up by 59 cents a litre to $4.62 in Peninsular Malaysia and increased by 52 cents in Sabah and Sarawak. This was the second time that prices of petroleum products had increased this year.

Regular petrol went up 58 cents while diesel and kerosene went up 18 cents and 20 cents respectively. There was also an 11.5 per cent increase for cooking gas.

Meanwhile, cement manufacturers asked the Government for an adjustment in the ex-factory and ceiling retail price of cement. The request was submitted in January after fuel costs went up by $77.54 per ton last October to $413.72 per ton in January. Fuel costs made up about 35 per cent of the total production cost. The manufacturers told a press conference that the fuel price increase together with higher electricity rates had raised production costs by $12.98 per ton. The retail price of cement was $6.50 per bag ex-factory. Retail prices varied from town to town; in Kuala Lumpur it was $7.60 per bag.

Dayabumi project taking off

18 September **Kuala Lumpur**

The RM200-million Dayabumi project will be the biggest re-development project undertaken by the Urban Development Authority (UDA) on what used to be the Malayan Railway Administration's north goods yard. UDA deputy chairman Ahmad Khairummuzamil Mohamad Yusof defined the area, which contained 17 blocks of old godowns before re-development, as 'a classic case of gross under-utilisation of an immensely valuable piece of real estate.'

Menglembu groundnut king dies

20 July **Kuala Lumpur**

Menglembu groundnut king Ngan Yin died of a heart attack while taking his daily morning walk at the foot of the Klendang Hills. He was 61. He left two wives, four sons and six daughters.

Ngan was the biggest manufacturer of Menglembu groundnuts and owned four groundnut factories near Kampar. His groundnuts were sold all over the peninsula as well as in Sabah, Sarawak, Hong Kong and the United States.

Two promoted in Cabinet reshuffle

15 September **Kuala Lumpur**

In his first major Cabinet reshuffle since the 1978 elections, Prime Minister Datuk Hussein Onn scrapped the Law Ministry and promoted Datuk Mokhtar Hashim and Datin Paduka Rafidah Aziz to full Ministers.

Datuk Mokhtar became Culture, Youth and Sports Minister and Datin Paduka Rafidah Public Enterprises Minister.

Datuk Hussein also relinquished the Federal Territory Ministry, a portfolio he had held himself, to Datuk Amar Haji Abdul Taib Mahmud. Datuk Hussein replaced Datuk Amar Haji Abdul Taib at the Defence Ministry.

Six 'heavy' projects worth $2.7b in 4MP

29 September **Kuala Lumpur**

Six major projects costing $2.76 billion were earmarked for implementation under the Fourth Malaysia Plan (4MP), marking the beginning of intensified involvement in heavy industries.

The projects were a $500-million iron ore venture, four cement factories—two in Perak, one in Pahang and one in Kedah—each with RM300 million capital, a $600-million aluminium plant in Bintulu, a factory to produce iron sheets with a capital of $400 million, a $60-million venture to produce metal-based products, and a factory manufacturing light machinery, the cost and location of which would be decided later (*see 27 March 1981*).

8 die in attack by 'fanatics'

16 October **Batu Pahat**

Eight men among a group of 17–20, all dressed in white, were killed when they stormed the district police station here. Inspector General of Police Tan Sri Hanif Omar described the group as 'religious fanatics'. Seven of the dead were believed to be locals and one a Kampuchean refugee. Six were killed at the police station at 9.30am and two were killed in a house in Parit Jorak Darat, six miles away, at 1.15pm.

Tan Sri Hanif said 14 policemen, six office workers at the station, an office boy, two members of the public and a boy were also injured. Eleven of them were in serious condition.

The attackers were dressed entirely in white, including white shoes, and carried swords partly wrapped in white cloth bearing the words 'Lailahaillallah Muhammadar Rasullullah'. They stormed the station shouting 'Allahu Akhbar'.

A week later, Minister Without Portfolio Datuk Haji Mohamad Nasir said a study would be carried out soon to stamp out deviationist Muslim teachings.

He warned the public not to entertain such groups in their homes and not to be misled by their teachings (*see 4 January 1981*).

Higher electricity rates to beat $1m-a-day deficit

30 October **Kuala Lumpur**

The Government has announced new electricity rates effective from 1 December. Low usage consumers will pay a little less while high usage consumers will pay more, some by up to 40 per cent.

The higher rates are aimed at wiping out a loss of $1 million a day which the National Electricity Board has been facing due to the increased cost of fuel.

The Government has been subsidising the NEB since January but will stop doing so from December.

English remains official language in Sarawak

30 October **Kuala Lumpur**

English will remain the official language in Sarawak for another three years, according to Dewan Bahasa dan Pustaka's director-general Datuk Hassan Ahmad.

This followed a request by the Sarawak Government for the continued use of English at official level for various reasons, among them, the fact that the majority of the local people had yet to fully master Bahasa Malaysia. Sarawak has a multi-ethnic community with at least five indigenous groups plus Chinese, Indians and others.

1980

world news

23 June
Sanjay Gandhi, 34, son
of Indira Gandhi, dies
in plane crash.

27 July
The deposed Shah of
Iran dies in Cairo.

2 August
A terrorist bomb at
the railway station in
Bologna, Italy, kills 85.

12 September
Kenan Evren stages
a military coup
in Turkey.

17 September
The Solidarity trade
union is formed in
Poland with Lech
Walesa as its leader.

22 September
Iraq orders its army
to 'deliver a fatal blow'
to Iran, beginning the
Iraq–Iran war.

4 November
Ronald Reagan
defeats incumbent
Jimmy Carter in the US
presidential election.

20 November
The trial of the Gang of
Four begins in Beijing.

8 December
John Lennon
is shot dead by
Mark David Chapman,
a deranged fan.

Helicopters in roof rescue

4 November Kuala Lumpur

Daring helicopter pilots have airlifted 12 people from the roof of the 12-storey former Bank Bumiputra headquarters when fire broke out. Thousands of office workers watched the drama at the Jalan Gereja–Jalan Melaka junction this afternoon.

There were some 30 people in the building when the fire started. One body was found on the sixth floor. Some managed to escape but 12 were trapped and made their way to the roof.

A helicopter from Genting Highlands flew the survivors to the Selangor Club padang and set them down before returning to pick up more people. Its pilot, Capt Baharuddin Sabilan, 39, said a delay in refuelling his craft at Segambut before a planned flight to Genting meant that he was available to help. If he had already left it would have been too late.

His helicopter and another piloted by Capt Nasir Ma Lee took turns landing on the roof of the building and taking people off to applause from crowds watching on the ground.

An aerial view of the building at the height of the blaze.

900km North–South Expressway

12 November Kuala Lumpur

The Malaysian Highway Authority was set up today to design, construct and maintain a 923km four-lane expressway which would run from Bukit Kayu Hitam in Kedah to Tampoi in Johor.

The expressway was scheduled for completion in 1986. Works and Utilities Minister Datuk S. Samy Vellu said toll charges would be imposed to recoup the construction cost (see 13 February 1982).

Collision at port

23 November Kuala Lumpur

Four barges loaded with 250 tons of sawn timber sank after they were sandwiched by three ocean-going ships when they were hit by strong currents at low tide today. Quick action by a tugboat pilot saved a fifth barge. The ships were only slightly dented.

No one was on board the barges but damage was estimated at $1 million. Thanks to a warning by sailors from one of the big ships, five men aboard the barges managed to scramble to safety.

Malaysia to lead world in rubber products

11 November Kuala Lumpur

Malaysia aspired to be one of the world leaders of manufactured natural rubber products by end of the 1980s, according to Deputy Prime Minister Dato' Seri Dr Mahathir Mohamad.

He said Malaysia had served the world well as the largest producer of natural rubber although this role did not fulfil the country's aspirations for the 1980s.

Personalised car registration plates

24 November Petaling Jaya

The Road Transport Department is considering the introduction of personalised number plates for cars, said Transport Minister Datuk Lee San Choon.

If the scheme is introduced, he said, owners of personalised plates will have to pay a fee. Under the existing system anyone wanting a specific number plate had to tender for it. Datuk Lee said there was a great demand for such numbers.

Freedom bid fails

22 November Kuala Lumpur

Former Selangor Menteri Besar Datuk Harun Haji Idris failed in his bid to be released from prison when the High Court dismissed his contention that his continued detention after 29 October was wrongful and illegal.

In May 1976, Harun was jailed for two years for corruptly accepting $250,000 from the Hong Kong and Shanghai Bank and for six months for forgery and fined $15,000 for abetting criminal breach of trust of about $6.5 million worth of Bank Rakyat shares.

He was also sentenced to six months' jail for forgery and abetting criminal breach of trust of Bank Rakyat shares in January 1977. The Federal Court, after hearing the appeal in December of that year, extended the jail term from six months to four years and varied the fine of $15,000 to three years' jail. The sentences were to run concurrently (see 1 August 1981).

DAP members give their backing to Lim Kit Siang.

DAP strongman 'quits'

29 November Petaling Jaya

The DAP MP for Petaling, Mr Lim Kit Siang, resigned as secretary-general of the party. He tendered his resignation to the party's national chairman Dr Chen Man Hin. Mr Lim gave the reason for his resignation as a 'malicious campaign' waged against him which sought to destroy his political credibility.

If his resignation was accepted, the party's deputy secretary-general, Mr Lee Lam Thye, would have taken over. However, Mr Lim immediately came under great pressure to withdraw his resignation and agreed to carry on in the post.

University Act 'meant to bring about peace'

1 December Kuala Lumpur

The Government has no intention of repealing the Universities and University Colleges Act, said Deputy Education Minister Datuk Najib Tun Razak.

The Act was drawn up, he said, to control activities that would not benefit students and to ensure an atmosphere of peace and order in the campus. Students should devote themselves to their studies first. 'After that, they can be active in politics.'

Kuwaiti nod for oil venture

15 December Kuala Lumpur

Kuwait will hold a 20 per cent stake in the Petronas oil refinery project in Malacca, which was expected to come on-stream in 1983 with a production capacity of 150,000 barrels of crude oil a day. The Kuwaiti participation would be in the form of supplying crude oil for the proposed refinery.

Finance Minister Tengku Razaleigh Hamzah, who announced the partnership, also said Malaysia had agreed to swap its lighter crude oil for the heavier Kuwaiti crude in addition to participating in joint oil exploration with the Kuwaitis.

Taxi men show unity

27 December Kuala Lumpur

About 1,000 city taxi drivers showed their solidarity at the funeral of a colleague, Lee Yun Choi, who was killed by a robber. The drivers, in about 900 taxis and other vehicles, formed a procession more than a mile long to the crematorium at Sungai Besi.

Aerobus rapid transit system may cost $9m

30 December Kuala Lumpur

The aerobus system, now under study by the Federal Territory Ministry as a possible mass rapid transport system for Kuala Lumpur, could cost $9 million for a 1½-mile route. But Federal Territory Minister Datuk Amar Haji Abdul Taib Mahmud said this figure was 'just on paper and the actual cost might be different'.

1981

Due to ill health, Datuk Hussein Onn stepped down as Prime Minister and his deputy Dato' Seri Dr Mahathir Mohamad took over the reins. Two months later, Malaysia made world headline news when, in a 'dawn raid' on the London stock market, Permodalan Nasional Berhad (PNB) bought a controlling share of plantation giant Guthrie Corporation Ltd, previously wholly British owned. Britain reacted by tightening some of its regulations to discourage similar takeovers in future. Later in the year the Malaysian Government adopted a 'Look East' policy under which Japanese and South Korean development models were considered more relevant to Malaysia which had previously focused on Western countries for training and education.

FEBRUARY
Prominent journalist and former *New Straits Times* managing editor Samad Ismail is released from detention.

MAY
Floods hit Kuala Lumpur leading to 6,000 people being evacuated.

JULY
Dr Mahathir takes over as Malaysia's Prime Minister from Datuk Hussein Onn.

NOVEMBER
Civil court proceedings begin to be conducted in Bahasa Malaysia. Language classes are later introduced for court officials.

December: A MAS Fokker Friendship crash-lands while taking off in Penang. No one is killed.

'Power is given to us not to lord it over others, not to improve our standing nor to enrich ourselves.'

Tun Hussein Onn, 1981.

1981

13 January
Donna Griffiths, a British schoolgirl, has a sneezing fit which lasts 978 days.

19 January
The US and Iran agree on release of 52 US hostages held in Iran for 14 months.

23 January
Under international pressure, South Korea commutes the death sentence of opposition leader Kim Dae Jung to life imprisonment.

25 January
Jiang Qing, widow of Chairman Mao, is sentenced to death.

23 February
Spanish Civil Guards invade Parliament. The right-wing coup collapses after 18 hours.

30 March
US President Reagan is shot and wounded by John Hinckley Jr.

11 April
Riots in Brixton, South London.

13 May
Pope John Paul II is shot in St Peter's Square.

21 May
François Mitterrand is elected President of France.

Dacing banned

1 January Kuala Lumpur

The Ministry of Trade And Industry announced that the use of the *dacing* (balance scale) was banned except in Chinese medicine shops. Only weighing scales such as spring scales, platform scales, banging scales and other machines approved by the Inspector of Weights And Measures could be used.

Botak Chin attempts to escape death row cell

2 January Kuala Lumpur

Wong Swee Chin, better known as Botak Chin, made a daring attempt to break out of his death row cell at Pudu Prison. He stabbed three wardens in the attempt but was overpowered. Botak Chin sustained serious head injuries and was taken to Kuala Lumpur General Hospital.

He began his life of crime with a robbery in 1969 in Jinjang, Selangor. By the time of his capture in 1976, he had committed more than 30, including those at the Overseas Union Bank in Jalan Imbi, Kuala Lumpur, and at the Selangor Turf Club in which his gang got away with $218,000. He was sentenced to death by the High Court in 1980 under the Internal Security Act.

On 12 June Botak Chin was hanged at Pudu Prison. He was 30. In a final meeting with his family, he asked to be cremated and his ashes thrown into a river or drain as he did not deserve a proper burial.

Fanatic gang gets 10 years' jail

4 January Muar

Six members of a fanatic group—Mohamed Nasir, 24, Muhamed Arpin Jailani, 43, Sulaiman Ismail, 21, Yusof Haji Abdul Karim, 41, Dasman Kiman, 24, and Kormain Abdul Rashid, 59—who attacked the Batu Pahat police station in October 1980 were jailed for 10 years each.

With the exception of Kormain, all were also sentenced to the rotan. The six were members of a religious sect headed by a Cambodian, Mohamed Nasir Ismail, who claimed he was the Imam Mahadi.

4 years later, Samad Ismail is freed

3 February Kuala Lumpur

Former managing editor of the *New Straits Times* Samad Ismail was released after 4½ years' detention for Communist activities. He was detained in 1976, and was released after making a live broadcast statement of his confession on television.

During his confession,

Samad is greeted by family members after his release from detention.

Samad denounced the Communist movement and warned the people, particularly the young, against being enslaved and exploited by the Communists.

Asked about his future after he got home to be reunited with his family, Samad said he planned to go to Mecca with his wife to perform the Haj.

CPM chief surrenders

6 January Kuala Lumpur

The chairman of the outlawed Communist Party of Malaysia, Musa Ahmad, and his wife Zainab Mahmud had surrendered, it was announced.

They gave themselves up in November 1980 after they were smuggled out of China where they had been living for the previous 24 years.

Samsu deaths

26 January Kulim

Twenty-nine people in Lunas, Kulim, died after consuming illicit samsu. Most of the victims were rubber and oil palm plantation workers.

The worst hit was the Wellesley Lunas Rubber Estate, where at least three-quarters of the 50-odd families lost relatives. One family lost six members.

In Kuala Lumpur, Inspector General of Police Tan Sri Hanif Omar urged those who possessed information on distillers of illicit samsu to come forward to help the police.

Shares at all-time high

25 February Kuala Lumpur

The NST Industrial Index surged 18.12 points to close at 1,004.99, the first time it had ever gone past the 1,000 mark. The market surge was part of a continuous boom that had lasted 15 months.

Take it to the ring

29 January Kuala Lumpur

In a light-hearted reference to a feud between the MIC and MCA, Barisan Nasional secretary-general Abdul Ghafar Baba offered to organise a boxing match between acting MIC president Datuk S. Samy Vellu and Selangor MCA chairman Datuk Lee Kim Sai.

PM to go for heart surgery

29 January Kuala Lumpur

Prime Minister Datuk Hussein Onn would undergo a coronary bypass operation in London, it was announced. During his absence for about a month, Dato' Seri Dr Mahathir Mohamad would be acting Prime Minister. A statement from the Prime Minister's Office said tests conducted in London showed a narrowing of the blood vessels and a bypass was recommended.

Control on foreign labour

18 February Labuan

Malaysia planned to regulate the inflow of Indonesian workers, said acting Prime Minister Dato' Seri Dr Mahathir Mohamad, adding that the entry of Indonesian workers to Malaysia should be conducted in a proper manner. Dr Mahathir described the Indonesians as good workers who had helped Malaysia's development.

Ex-Deputy Minister released

22 February Kuala Lumpur

Internal Security Act detainee Abdullah Majid was released after the Government decided he was no longer a security threat. The former Deputy Labour and Manpower Minister was arrested in 1976 on the grounds that he had been involved in Communist activities since the early 1950s. He was arrested around the same time as former Deputy Minister in the Prime Minister's Department Datuk Abdullah Ahmad. Both were expelled from Umno in 1977.

Fire sweeps Fitzpatrick building

19 February Kuala Lumpur

Fire destroyed offices on the 15th floor and damaged the 16th floor of the old Fitzpatrick building in Jalan Raja Chulan this evening. Damage was estimated at more than $1 million. No casualties were reported, although four firemen received treatment after being overcome by fumes.

The old Fitzpatrick building at the height of the fire.

Federal Highway gets RM100m upgrading

25 March Kuala Lumpur

An estimated $100 million would be spent over two years to upgrade the Federal Highway into a three-lane dual carriageway. All traffic lights along the highway (excluding slip roads) would be removed to allow for free traffic flow from Kuala Lumpur to Klang. Additionally, a motorcycle lane would be built to segregate motorcyclists from other vehicles.

The tiny twins after the successful operation.

Siamese twins separated at UH

6 March Petaling Jaya

University Hospital made medical history by successfully separating Siamese twins joined at the pelvis. The twins, seven-month-old girls from Ipoh, were under intensive care and their condition was stable. The 10-hour operation, the first in Southeast Asia, was carried out by six surgeons, eight anaesthesiologists and a 12-member nursing team.

No more students for UK as fees are increased

8 March Kuala Kubu Baru

The Government has decided to stop sending students to the United Kingdom following the British Government's decision to increase university fees for overseas students by 20–25 per cent.

Education Minister Datuk Musa Hitam said he had given up hope that the British Government would accede to the wishes of the foreign student committee there.

After opening the Selayang Umno Youth work camp here, Datuk Musa said his Ministry would find alternative places for Malaysian students in the United States, Australia and New Zealand.

Woman's 18 dogs saved

13 March Kuala Lumpur

An Ipoh woman with 18 dogs, which the local council wanted put down because her house was overcrowded, was told they had been offered a home on a farm in Tambun.

111 DAP members quit

1 March Bukit Mertajam

One hundred and eleven DAP members resigned en masse following the expulsion of three State leaders, secretary Goh Lim Eam, publicity chief Chin Nyok Soo and Bukit Mertajam branch chairman Seow Hun Khim, who was also MP and State Assemblyman for Bukit Mertajam.

The three, along with the DAP State Assemblyman for Kampung Kolam, Ooi Ean Kwong, who had recently resigned from the party, witnessed the mass resignation. All 111 were from the party's Bukit Mertajam branch, leaving the branch with only 43 members. They also removed the DAP signboard in front of the branch office.

Eight days later, DAP secretary-general Lim Kit Siang described the previous four months as the most agonising period of his 15-year political career.

31 buried by tin mine landslip

26 March Kuala Lumpur

Thirty-one people, including children, were believed to have been buried alive when a landslip in Kampung Kandan in Puchong swept away their homes at the edge of a tin mine. Initial reports said at least 24 people from six families are missing. The other seven were workers of Capitol Mining Sdn Bhd, where the landslip happened. Police also ordered the evacuation of 200 other residents.

4MP: No room for complacency

27 March Kuala Lumpur

The Fourth Malaysia Plan (4MP) was unveiled by Prime Minister Datuk Hussein Onn, who warned that 'greed and extremism on the part of any group would undermine and destroy the peace and prosperity we now enjoy'. Of the $102.6 billion to be invested, $28.5 billion would come from the public sector. The main objective was to provide greater incentive for the implementation of the New Economic Policy (see 18 April 1981).

Parliament agrees to emergency powers

11 April Kuala Lumpur

The Dewan Rakyat passed the Constitution (Amendment) Bill by an overwhelming 118 votes to 12. It took two years to formulate the amendments.

Bomohs to quit Pemadam

11 April Kuala Lumpur

Thirty-six bomohs and dukuns (traditional healers) planned to quit the anti-drug organisation Pemadam as they were unhappy with its policies. Their president, Haji Radin Supatan Haji Radin Sanusi, said that Pemadam had not given enough importance to the role of bomohs and dukuns in the fight against drugs. He said there was no reason why they could not help drug addicts.

Taib Mahmud is 4th Sarawak Chief Minister

26 March Kuching

Datuk Amar Haji Taib Mahmud was sworn in as Sarawak's 4th Chief Minister today. He pledged to continue with the efforts of his predecessor, Datuk Patinggi Tan Sri Haji Abdul Rahman Yaakub, to make Sarawak a model State in the country.

Societies Act amended

9 April Kuala Lumpur

The Dewan Rakyat passed by a voice vote the controversial Societies (Amendment) Bill 1981 after a 6½-hour debate. In presenting the Bill for debate, Home Affairs Minister Tan Sri Ghazali Shafie said those who opposed the amendments had no real understanding of what the Government was trying to do.

He said that the amendments were merely aimed at streamlining the Act to regulate the activities of public organisations. 'The amendments are merely to determine the type and nature of societies so that they function according to the objectives stipulated by the societies themselves. It is nothing but calling a spade a spade,' he said. There was a need, he said, for societies to openly state if they were political or non-political and to function accordingly.

Petrol prices go up

18 April Kuala Lumpur

The prices of premium and regular petrol went up by six cents and five cents per litre, respectively. The new prices in Peninsular Malaysia were $1.08 for premium and $1.02 for regular. A statement by the Ministry of Trade and Industry also announced a 6.6-cent increase per litre for diesel and kerosene. Prices of cooking gas also went up, by between $2.35 and $3.10 per cylinder depending on capacity.

The last price rise was in August 1980, with increases of between 11 and 15 per cent. Since then, however, the OPEC countries had raised crude prices by 13 per cent, the Ministry said.

The woman who tried to seduce hotel room boy

S.H. Tan

HOTEL staff in Peking have been asked to report foreign guests who try to seduce them in their rooms.

They have also been asked not to look at pornographic books and magazines and nude photographs left by overseas visitors.

A room boy in the Peking Hotel, the biggest and most expensive in the city, was praised when he reported to his superiors that a foreign woman had tried to seduce him.

Far be it for me to ridicule any man who would complain let alone report, if he had tried any hanky-panky with him. But isn't it possible that there had been a misunderstanding?

After all, when two people do not speak the same language, even the most inno-

cent gesture could be misinterpreted.

Take the Caucasian singer on a three-month contract with a first class hotel in K.L.

She was friendly and unassuming. She treated the hotel's junior staff as her equal. And in no time at all she decided to master a few words of Bahasa Malaysia.

Unluckily, the man she picked as her 'ce'gu (teacher) was a waiter well-known for his pranks.

When she asked him what 'good morning' was in Bahasa Malaysia, he said: "Saya cinta ku". (I love you).

"Saya cinta ku," she repeated after him. H'm...that was a push-over.

The next question was: what is "thank you" in Bahasa Malaysia?

"Easy," beamed the waiter. "Cium," (kiss).

"Cium," she repeated.

Two common words mastered, the singer said that she would pick up a few more as she went along.

The next morning, when a room boy knocked on her door and entered the room with her morning tea, she cooed: "Saya cinta ku".

The room boy, who had not been kept in the picture, could

not believe his ears. So he maintained a straight face and left the tea tray on the coffee table.

"Cium," the singer said.

Room boys are used to seeing Caucasian women in scanty clothes or without bras. But a come hither? And so early in the morning?

He fled and reported to the front desk manager the attempt to outrage his modesty.

The front desk manager went to the singer's room to investigate. And when he too was greeted with a "saya cinta ku" he realised that a joke had been misfired.

The singer's education in Bahasa Malaysia was given a quick revision.

Luckily for all concerned, she said that she truly loved all Malaysians — for their sense of humour.

Newspaper editor S.H. Tan's column in the *Malay Mail* on 4 June 1981. The daily column ran for 11 years.

1981

world news

30 May
Bangladesh President Ziaur Rahman is assassinated in Chittagong.

5 June
Five homosexual men in Los Angeles are the first recognised AIDS cases.

6 June
A bridge collapse in Bihar, India, sends a train plunging into a river, killing 800.

7 June
Israeli planes destroy Iraq's Osirak nuclear reactor.

22 June
Iranian President Bani-Sadr is dismissed by Ayatollah Khomeini.

29 June
Hu Yaobang, protégé of Deng Xiaoping, is elected chairman of the Chinese Communist Party.

30 June
The Chinese Communist Party criticises the late Chairman Mao's policies.

17 July
Israeli bombers destroy PLO headquarters in Beirut.

Malaysia must work harder, says Razaleigh

18 April Kuala Lumpur

The country needed to intensify economic diversification efforts, increase productivity and make optimum use of manpower to face the bleak world economy of the 1980s, said Finance Minister Tengku Razaleigh Hamzah.

Industrialised countries facing slow economic growth would cut imports from developing nations, he warned. Tariff barriers would also be tightened, resulting in reduced international trade. Tabling the Fourth Malaysia Plan in the Dewan Negara he said Malaysia would have to depend more on its own diversified economy to achieve annual growth of eight per cent (*see 19 August 1982*).

The launch of the share sale by the Prime Minister.

ASN shares go on sale to help small investors

21 April Kuala Lumpur

Prime Minister Datuk Hussein Onn launched the sale of Amanah Saham Nasional shares with a call to Bumiputras to show their determination to meet the objectives of the New Economic Policy.

Datuk Hussein launched the sale at Dewan Tunku Abdul Rahman with a personal investment of $10.

Datuk Hussein said the Government had taken great pains to work out the scheme to help ensure that a 30 per cent of share equity in the corporate sector was owned by Bumiputras by 1990. Deputy Prime Minister Dato' Seri Dr Mahathir Mohamad said the ASN scheme allowed Bumiputras to invest on a small scale. This, he said, ensured that the benefits of the New Economic Policy would be enjoyed by all.

By the end of the first week, a total of $30 million ASN shares had been sold throughout the country.

Keris Mas honoured

22 April Kuala Lumpur

Writer Haji Kamaludin Muhammad, better known as Keris Mas, was awarded the National Literary Award 1981. The award includes a scroll of honour and a cash prize of $30,000. Education Minister Datuk Musa Hitam, as chairman of the panel, said Keris Mas's works had brought a new image to short stories.

Compensation to Selangor for FT takeover

24 May Morib

The Federal Government agreed to pay $3.5 billion in compensation to Selangor for its takeover of the 94-square mile Federal Territory. Advances totalling $625 million had already been made while the rest would be paid over a period of 10 years beginning 1982, Finance Minister Tengku Razaleigh said after opening the Selangor Umno convention here. Under the agreement, Selangor would continue to receive $18.3 million a year in return for revenue losses.

Karthigesu thanks his jailers after his release.

Karthigesu freed

31 May Kuala Lumpur

Lecturer S. Karthigesu, who was sentenced to death last year for the murder of his sister-in-law and former beauty queen Jean Sinappa, was freed by the Federal Court after a key prosecution witness at his trial, Bandhulananda Jayatilake, admitted that he had lied when giving evidence.

Waist-deep water poses problems for residents in Kuala Lumpur's 'worst floods since 1971'.

6,000 evacuated as floods hit KL

25 May Kuala Lumpur

Six thousand people were evacuated in Kuala Lumpur as floods hit the capital and outlying areas. Described as the worst since 1971, the floods followed four hours of torrential rain. Rail services were disrupted after the railway tracks in Serdang were washed away, leaving 850 commuters stranded. The city also experienced massive traffic jams as several main thoroughfares were flooded or blocked by fallen trees and branches. Hundreds of motorists were held up for at least five hours.

Sarawak leader dies

9 July Kuching

Former Minister for Sarawak Affairs Datuk Patinggi Tan Sri Temenggong Jugah anak Barieng died at the Kuching General Hospital after a long illness. He was 81.

Temenggong Jugah was founder of Parti Pesaka Anak Sarawak and later became founder of the Sarawak Alliance, dedicated to the fight for Sarawak's independence through Malaysia.

After the formation of Malaysia in 1963, he joined the Federal Cabinet as Minister for Sarawak Affairs. He retained the post after winning in the 1970 general election and retired from active politics in 1974.

Temenggong Jugah's outstanding qualities as a community leader and as a politician in a career that spanned more than 50 years earned him national and international recognition.

Woman to hang for ISA offence

25 July Kuala Lumpur

Thye Siew Heong (pictured right under police escort) became the first woman to be sentenced to death for an offence under the Internal Security Act. The 39-year-old seamstress and her husband Lim Re Song, alias Lim See Kiew, 38, were found guilty by the High Court of possessing nine primed hand grenades in 1977. The grenades, along with three unprimed ones and jungle-green uniforms, were found during a Special Branch raid on a room occupied by the couple in Hot Spring New Village in Setapak, Kuala Lumpur.

Hussein steps down

16 July | **Kuala Lumpur**

Datuk Hussein Onn stepped down as Prime Minister today. He had announced at the Umno general assembly in May that he would not seek re-election as Umno president and would step down as Prime Minister. The news was greeted with tears from some delegates.

He had held the post since January 1976, following the death of Tun Abdul Razak. He made his decision to resign for health reasons after undergoing a coronary bypass operation in January. He told the 32nd Umno general assembly that he was staying on until 16 July at the request of the new party president Dato' Seri Dr Mahathir Mohamad.

Dr M takes over

17 July | **Kuala Lumpur**

Dato' Seri Dr Mahathir Mohamad was sworn in as Prime Minister in a 10-minute ceremony at the Istana Negara.

He received his letter of appointment from the Yang di-Pertuan Agong before taking his oath before His Majesty and signing the instrument of office witnessed by acting Lord President Raja Tan Sri Azlan Shah and Chief Secretary to the Government Tan Sri Hashim Aman.

Dr Mahathir receives his letter of appointment as Prime Minister from the King.

The ceremony was witnessed by Datuk Hussein Onn, Cabinet Ministers and other dignitaries. The King then conferred on Datuk Hussein the Seri Maharaja Mangku Negara, which carries the title Tun.

Arrested: political secretary with KGB links

14 July | **Kuala Lumpur**

The former political secretary to the Deputy Prime Minister, Siddiq Mohamed Ghouse, was arrested under the Internal Security Act for activities prejudicial to the security of the country, said by Home Affairs Minister Tan Sri Ghazali Shafie in a statement.

The arrest came after more than two years of surveillance by the Special Branch. Equipment, including cameras and a portable radio set which transmitted signals for rendezvous, were also recovered from Siddiq's house. Three Soviet diplomats had been identified as KGB agents—V.P. Romanov, Z.I. Khamidouline and G.I. Stepanov. They were declared persona non grata and given 24 hours to leave the country.

Harun Idris freed

1 August | **Kuala Lumpur**

Former Selangor Menteri Besar Datuk Haji Harun Idris was freed after serving 3½ years in prison on a corruption charge. He was granted remission from his six-year sentence.

He walked out a free man from the General Hospital in Kuala Lumpur where he had been for two months with arthritis and other ailments.

A day earlier, 21 ISA detainees, including former Deputy Minister in the Prime Minister's Department Datuk Abdullah Ahmad and Partai Sosialis Rakyat Malaya chairman Kassim Ahmad, were released unconditionally from the Kamunting detention camp. Also freed were DAP MPs Chan Kok Kit and Chian Heng Kai. All four were arrested on 3 November 1976 for their involvement in the Communist United Front. Ten taxis were called to ferry the 21 men back to their families.

Roads closed for flyover

5 August | **Kuala Lumpur**

The Federal Highway–Jalan Barat–Jalan Utara junction in Petaling Jaya closed for two years for the construction of a flyover from Jalan Barat to Jalan Utara.

Malaysian Business Magazine

Primer on condominiums

Although there was a growing interest in condominiums, few house buyers were fully familiar with the concept and its legal implications, according to the June issue of *Malaysian Business*.

It noted that initial occupation of condominiums in Kuala Lumpur was mainly by expatriates renting units from investors.

The article also explored the problems that come with joint ownership of property, including restrictions on use and the sharing of costs of maintenance and improvements.

Clocking in but tea-breaks are out

10 August | **Kuala Lumpur**

Ministers and senior Government officials were told they might have to clock-in with junior staff as part of the new administration's effort to improve efficiency.

This followed a trial of the clock-in system which had succeeded in making Government servants more time-conscious.

Twelve days later it was announced that tea-breaks might be a thing of the past for Government servants.

Manpower Administration Modernisation and Planning Unit director-general Dr Mohamad Nor Abdul Ghani said that civil servants could have their tea or coffee brought to them by tea boys or girls.

Homes found for fire victims just 14 hours after blaze

12 August | **Kuala Lumpur**

Fourteen hours after losing their homes in fire, 28 families from Kampung Riverside in Kuala Lumpur were offered new places to stay. Kuala Lumpur City Hall offered flats in Jalan San Peng to the 158 people. Moreover, the flats were to be rent-free for the first month.

An aerial view of the fierce blaze at Kampung Riverside.

1981

world news

29 July
Lady Diana Spencer marries Charles, Prince of Wales.

12 August
US President Ronald Reagan orders US jets to attack targets in Libya.

6 October
Egyptian President Anwar Sadat is assassinated at a military parade. Vice-President Hosni Mubarak succeeds him.

23 November
US President Reagan signs a secret directive authorising the CIA to recruit and support Contra rebels in Nicaragua.

11 December
Peruvian Javier Perez de Cuellar becomes UN Secretary-General.

13 December
Polish leader Jaruzelski declares martial law. Solidarity leader Lech Walesa is arrested.

14 December
Israel annexes the Golan Heights which it seized from Syria in 1967.

15 December
A car bomb destroys the Iraqi Embassy in Beirut, killing 61. Syrian military intelligence is blamed.

Asia Magazine
'Bukit Kepong': the movie

Film director Jins Samsuddin on the set of his latest film, *Bukit Kepong*, a $1-million movie recreating the killing spree at Bukit Kepong, Johor. There, on 23 February 1950, 18 policemen, outnumbered 10 to one by Communists, fought a 5-hour battle which left 14 policemen, two of their wives and a great number of the terrorists dead.

Revamp of cattle agency ordered

11 September **Kuala Lumpur**

Majuternak, the Government agency responsible for cattle-rearing and beef supply, will have its general management, role and projects revamped, said Agriculture Minister Datuk Abdul Manan Othman. This was necessary, he said, because 'there is something wrong somewhere' that caused two cheques issued by Majuternak to bounce in August.

He had earlier ordered an inquiry into allegations of corruption and malpractice at the agency and expressed dissatisfaction over its award of tenders, accounts and purchases of imported cattle. He also ordered the shutdown of the agency's milk production programme, involving 2,500 cows, which had run up a deficit of $3 million.

Government acts on British goods

3 October **Kuala Lumpur**

Government departments and agencies will need to get the endorsement of the Prime Minister's Department before they can award any tender to a British company, said Prime Minister Dato' Seri Dr Mahathir Mohamad. The decision was made at a Cabinet meeting two days earlier, he said, adding that all submissions would need to include an alternative non-British choice (*see 2 April 1983*).

Guthrie in Malaysian hands

8 September **Kuala Lumpur**

In a well-timed four-hour 'dawn raid' on the London stock market, Permodalan Nasional Berhad bought a controlling share of plantation giant Guthrie Corporation Ltd. Guthrie, which held nearly 200,000 acres of land in Malaysia, was previously almost wholly British-owned. Permodalan bought 7,995,500 shares for $131 million to take its total holding to 15,790,500 shares, or 50.4 per cent. PNB chairman Tun Ismail Mohamed Ali said an offer to buy up the remaining shares would follow soon. PNB said its takeover was essential to protect its substantial investment in the company. Tun Ismail expressed satisfaction at the outcome but Guthrie managing director Ian Coates said the move was 'nationalisation by the front door'.

What the foreign press said

In a special article headed 'Why the Malaysians grabbed Guthrie' (8 September), *The Times* said the takeover 'fits in with the avowed policy of the Kuala Lumpur administration to control all its own primary resources.' It went on: 'It also touches on the differences between the indigenous Malays who hold much of the political power and the Chinese and Indians who control a great deal of the economy.' The Malaysians were 'highly sensitive to what they regard as foreign manipulation,' the article said.

Court proceedings in Bahasa Malaysia

2 December **Johor Bahru** ▶ The Johor Bahru High Court became the first court in the country to conduct the proceedings of a civil suit in Bahasa Malaysia. However, both parties were Malays. The proceedings relating to a land issue were before Mr Justice Mohamed Yusof Rashid. A switch to English was made only when both counsels made their submission.

Bahasa Malaysia classes for officials were introduced later, as Lat pointed out.

New standard time for Malaysia

4 December **Kota Kinabalu**

Peninsular Malaysia would adopt Sabah/Sarawak time as the standard Malaysian time effective 1 January 1982. Deputy Prime Minister Datuk Musa Hitam described the move as yet another effort by the Federal Government to forge greater integration of Sabah and Sarawak with the rest of Malaysia. In Singapore, Prime Minister Lee Kuan Yew said the island republic, too, would move half-an-hour ahead in line with Peninsular Malaysia's time switch (*see 1 January 1982*).

'Japan and South Korea more relevant to us'

16 December **Kuala Lumpur**

Prime Minister Dato' Seri Dr Mahathir Mohamad said the Government was 'looking East' because development in countries like Japan and South Korea is much more relevant to the nation's growing economy than the West.

He explained that Malaysia's decision to look East would give it a more balanced view of the world as it had previously concentrated on countries in the West for training and education.

A crane lifts the crashed plane off the runway.

Plane crashes while taking off

31 December **Penang**

A MAS Fokker Friendship crash-landed at Penang Airport while taking off. The plane landed on its belly and slid more than 300 metres down the runway before coming to a halt. No one was killed in the incident.

The aircraft was en route to Ipoh and Kuala Lumpur with 30 passengers and a crew of five.

1982

Moving with the times is essential, but moving ahead of time is optional. But this is an option that Malaysia decided to take when it moved local time 30 minutes forward in Peninsular Malaysia to standardise it with Sabah and Sarawak. At 29 years of age Datuk Najib Tun Razak became the youngest Menteri Besar when he assumed the post in Pahang. Time was not yet up for Foreign Minister Tan Sri Ghazali Shafie who was presumed dead after the plane he was in crashed into the jungles in Pahang. He was found slightly bruised but very much alive the next day. Making up for lost time, the Sidek brothers—Razif and Jalani—made badminton history when they won the All England doubles championship which had eluded Malaysia for 11 years.

JANUARY
Foreign Minister Tan Sri Ghazali Shafie survives a plane crash.

SEPTEMBER
Petronas strikes oil for the first time since its inception.

NOVEMBER
Local sprinter Rabuan Pit becomes the fastest man in Asia.

NOVEMBER
Raja Azlan Shah is sworn in as Lord President before the Yang di-Pertuan Agong.

March: The Sidek Brothers win the elusive All England doubles title.

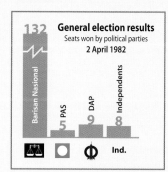

General election results
Seats won by political parties
2 April 1982

Barisan Nasional	PAS	DAP	Independents
132	5	9	8

Ind.

'People who rely on the talents and skills of others are not free'

Dato' Seri Dr Mahathir Mohamad, speaking at the LUTH foundation stone-laying ceremony, 16 January 1982.

1982

11 January
Mark Thatcher, son of British PM Margaret Thatcher, is lost in the Sahara Desert during the Paris–Dakar Rally. Found 14 January.

3 February
Syrian President Hafez al-Assad orders the army to purge the city of Harran of the Muslim Brotherhood.

25 February
The European Court of Human Rights rules that teachers who cane children against their parents' wishes are in violation of the Human Rights Convention.

2 April
Argentina invades the Falkland Islands.

25 April
Israel completes withdrawal from the Sinai. Protesting settlers have to be forcibly removed.

2 May
A British submarine sinks the Argentinian cruiser *General Belgrano*, killing 323 sailors.

4 May
HMS *Sheffield* is hit by an Exocet missile, killing 20.

The men responsible for making the monumental time change happen at work in the Sultan Abdul Samad clock tower.

Malaysia changes time

1 January | **Kuala Lumpur**

Upon ushering in the New Year, Peninsular Malaysia moved its local time 30 minutes forward to standardise time with Sabah and Sarawak. It was the third time in the nation's history that a time change had been enforced.

At 10.30pm on New Year's Eve, a five-men team led by Ching Hin Sian, acting superintendent of the Survey Department instruments workshop, went up to the clock tower at the Selangor State Secretariat building to prepare for the countdown. At 11.25pm, the pendulum had to be slowed down before bringing it to a stop. The escapement arm, which controls the speed of the swing, was held back to allow the minute arm to move fast.

A plank was placed between the hammer and the bell and another piece inside the bell to muffle the 11.30pm chime. After releasing the plank, the clock stopped just three seconds before midnight. The team brought with them a radio to wait for the time signal from Radio Malaysia. The escapement arm was released to give time for the pendulum to return to its normal pace. As Radio Malaysia announced the hour, the clock tower chimed.

Lim Kok Wing's take on the effect of the time change.

Switch to metric system

2 January | **Kuala Lumpur**

The year began with a new system of measurement with the change from the Imperial system to the metric system.

Mokh and Maradona

14 January | **Kuala Lumpur**

Malaysian soccer ace Mokhtar Dahari had a golden opportunity to meet the soccer great Diego Maradona face-to-face at the Merdeka Stadium for a match between Selangor Invitation and Boca Juniors. They exchanged mementoes before the kick-off. Boca won 2–1.

Mokhtar Dahari wrote enthusiastically in his regular column 'On Target' in the *New Straits Times* about Maradona's unrivalled playing skills.

Change attitudes, Muslims told

16 January | **Kuala Lumpur**

Prime Minister Dato' Seri Dr Mahathir Mohamad called on Muslims to change their 'indifferent and passive' attitudes if they did not want to be manipulated and be dependent on others.

At the foundation stone laying for the Pilgrim Management and Fund Board here, he said such attitudes were unhealthy and should change. 'People who rely on the talents and skills of others are not free, are looked down upon, and can be manipulated,' he added.

Fire at rubber factory

27 January | **Bukit Mertajam**

Fire caused massive destruction at the Alma Rubber Estate in Bukit Mertajam. About 3,000 tons of rubber went up in flames. It took 45 firemen and seven engines from five nearby towns more than three hours to put out the fire.

Three tanks of diesel were situated near the building but firemen contained the fire which had spread rapidly.

Foreign Minister in plane crash drama

11 January | **Kuala Lumpur** ▶ Foreign Minister Tan Sri Ghazali Shafie, 59, had a miraculous escape from a plane crash while on his way to Kuala Lipis to attend an Umno division committee meeting. He was accompanied by his aide-de-camp, ASP Charon Dann, and chief flying inspector of the Royal Selangor Flying Club Varghese Chacko when the six-seater Cessna 206 crashed into a hill at Janda Baik, Pahang. A distress call was picked up at 9.17am by an aircraft from the club flying near the area and the pilot spotted possible wreckage.

A ground search began the same afternoon but hilly terrain and failing light hampered the hunt which continued the next morning. At noon, search teams found the bodies of ASP Charon and Mr Chacko still strapped to their seats. At 2.15pm, Tan Sri Ghazali was found 65 metres from the crash site with only slight injuries.

Left: The ill-fated Cessna. Right: Tan Sri Ghazali is greeted by astonished search teams assigned to find him.

Bungling burglars turn on each other

10 February | Slim River

In Slim River, two burglars landed in hospital after they accidentally slashed each other with weapons in the house of their intended victim.

In total darkness, they mistook each other for the house owner and swung their parangs. In the confusion, the house owner overpowered them and called the police who called the ambulance.

Oriental fashion is in

2 January | Kuala Lumpur

TV smash hits *Shogun* and *Dynasty* brought about a revival of Oriental fashion for women. The sexy female warrior look was in: high-waisted obi sashes for belts, kung-fu style pants and kimono jackets with European proportions and embroidered Chinese ideograms on materials which looked silky, chic and seductive.

In fashion: Samurai-styled attire for the trendy.

North–South Highway ready by 1986

13 February | Kuala Lumpur

Works and Utilities Minister Datuk S. Samy Vellu announced that the $2.7-billion North–South Highway would be completed by 1986. Parts of the 475-kilometre highway were already completed while work on six interchanges and all other facilities on the KL–Seremban highway would be complete by 1985. This would form the future inter-urban toll highway system.

An open toll system would be adopted meaning that anyone passing through one toll plaza would pay when passing through the next. The northern toll plaza near Sungai Besi was to have 11 lanes while the southern plaza north of Seremban would have nine lanes. The number of lanes was based on a rate of 350 vehicles per hour or 10 per second.

Tin difficulties

4 March–25 August | Kuala Lumpur

Thirty gravel mines would close 'very soon' due to the continuous drop in tin prices, warned Primary Industries Minister Datuk Paul Leong. More would close as miners and mining companies 'go into the red,' he said. 'Unwarranted and ill-timed' disposal of tin by the US General Services Administration was the cause, he added. The disposal of 8,000 tonnes of tin, with another 22,000 to be sold, came at a very bad time for the tin industry worldwide. A rules change by the London Metal Exchange favouring short sellers had worsened the situation, he added. All this led to 'great difficulties' for the industry.

Datuk Leong commented that no one could blame tin producers if they contemplated an alternative arrangement should the International Tin Agreement fail to get off the ground in July when the extended term of the present one expired. In fact, Malaysia was already consulting Indonesia and Thailand, which together with Malaysia were responsible for two-thirds of the world's tin production. Malaysia was suggesting a tin producers' association, a joint marketing arrangement and consultation on output.

Indeed foreign press reports suggested that Malaysia was buying up tin in an attempt to corner the market. *Time* magazine quoted an industry insider as saying: 'The general feeling is that Malaysia, Indonesia and Thailand got together and decided that if they couldn't get a higher price they would buy all the tin available and move the price up.' But the fall continued. On 26 April the Penang tin price fell below its floor level. The following day the US dumped another 100 tons on the market. Penang prices could only be maintained by heavy buffer-stock buying. By July more than 170 gravel-pump mines had closed with the loss of more than 4,000 jobs.

On 25 August, *The Times* of London reported that Malayan Tin Dredging and the Malaysian Mining Corp, the world's biggest tin miner, were to merge and that 'the long standing foreign domination of the local tin industry will be virtually at an end'.

Four years later, the Reuters news agency reported that Malaysia had lost $209 million in the effort to prop up 'an export industry that later collapsed'.

Sportsman and Sportswoman of the Year

21 February | Kuala Lumpur

Walker V. Subramaniam was named Sportsman of the Year and sprinter Mumtaz Jaafar Sportswoman of the Year. Both were included in the Malaysian squad for the Commonwealth Games in October.

Far left: V. Subramaniam (right) in a winning moment. With him is team-mate B. Kumarasamy.

Left: Mumtaz Jaafar rewarded for her outstanding achievements.

Thousands rush to apply for 300 houses

21 February | Petaling Jaya

Two thousand people camped overnight at the Taman Bukit Kuchai site office. At sunrise, the crowd had swelled to 10,000. They queued up for application forms for only 300 low-cost flats up for sale; only 3,000 forms were available. When the crowd became unruly, two hundred police and FRU personnel were called in to restore order. All the forms were distributed by 2.20pm. The flats were going for RM20,000 to RM35,000 each. They were being built under Phases Two and Three of the housing scheme along the 8th mile Jalan Puchong in a joint venture between the Selangor State Government and a private developer.

Thousands rush in an attempt to secure low-cost houses.

The Sidek Brothers...

Win championship

29 March | London

Razif and Jalani Sidek made badminton history when they beat champions Billy Gilliland and Dan Travers 8–15, 15–9, 15–10 to win the All England doubles title, which had eluded Malaysia for 11 years.

The triumphant brothers with their trophies.

...but lose the Sidek Service advantage

London ▶ The International Badminton Federation banned the famous Sidek Service, which involved holding the shuttlecock upside down and hitting it feathers first with a backhand motion so that it rotates in flight, making it difficult for the receiver to return the service.

This was the second time the IBF had banned the service. In 1980 it imposed its first ban, and then sanctioned it a year later. The reason cited for the latest ban was that the shuttlecock was developed to be hit at the base and not the feathers.

1982

world news

25 May
Another British ship is lost to an Exocet missile.

6 June
Defence Minister Ariel Sharon leads Israeli forces into Lebanon.

9 June
Israeli jets wipe out all Syrian SAM sites in the Bekaa Valley, Lebanon.

13 June
In Alberta, Canada, 15 members of a karate club demolish a house with their bare hands and feet…with the consent of the owner.

14 June
Argentina surrenders in the Falklands. On 18 June, Argentinian military dictator Galtieri resigns over the defeat.

2 July
A Los Angeles truck driver soars 16,000 feet into the air with 42 balloons hitched to a lawn chair. Must have been fed up with the jams.

8 July
Iraqis in Dujail, angered by the execution of a Shi'ite leader, fire on Saddam Hussein's convoy, killing several but missing him. In retaliation, hundreds are imprisoned and about 380 killed.

First open-heart surgery

18 April Kuala Lumpur

Kuala Lumpur General Hospital's cardiothoracic unit performed its first open-heart surgery on 6 April. The team leader, Dr Rozali Wathooth, said the patient, M. Maheswaran, 19, was doing fine.

Dr Rozali's team of surgeons had spent eight months in Sydney in 1981 for training in cardiothoracic surgery.

International Islamic University in Malaysia

7 March Kuala Lumpur

Malaysia would set up an international Islamic university open to students of all races and religions with teaching staff comprising Muslims and non-Muslims in a year's time.

Prime Minister Dato' Seri Dr Mahathir Mohamad said the idea received all-round support from various groups he had spoken to during his 10-day visit to the Gulf States and Jeddah.

Dr Mahathir likened the proposed university to the United Nations-sponsored Asian Institute for Broadcasting and Development at Angkasapuri and the Southeast Asian Centre for Mathematics Studies in Glugor, Penang.

As such, the university should not be subject to Malaysia's education policy, Dr Mahathir noted, in reference to the use of English and Arabic as the university's mediums of instruction.

Pas–DAP pact?

3 April Kuala Lumpur

The DAP denied that it had entered into an electoral pact with Pas for the up-coming general elections after Deputy Prime Minister Datuk Musa Hitam said there was an 'unholy alliance' between them.

Pas president Datuk Asri Che Muda also denied the party had reached an agreement with DAP, saying Pas did not need any help from other parties to secure victory.

Lat's depiction of the claimed alliance, playing on its unlikelihood because of the vast differences in political agenda and voters' preferences.

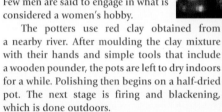

Bamboo-and-paper 'Jaws' of Pas

21 April Kota Bharu

The public was fascinated with this display in town. It took Pas supporters three days, and a lot of bamboo and posters, to build this 'Pas Shark' in Kota Bharu for the upcoming polls. It was three times as long as an average car.

Wings Of Gold magazine

The women potters of Sayong

Kampung Kepala Bendang, a small village just outside Kuala Kangsar in Perak's Sayong district, has acquired a reputation for producing fine black clay pots, according to an article in *Wings Of Gold* magazine (Volume 8, No. 3). The potters are usually housewives who each make a pot or two a week in between cooking, cleaning and minding their children. Few men are said to engage in what is considered a women's hobby.

The potters use red clay obtained from a nearby river. After moulding the clay mixture with their hands and simple tools that include a wooden pounder, the pots are left to dry indoors for a while. Polishing then begins on a half-dried pot. The next stage is firing and blackening, which is done outdoors.

Sadly, according to one potter, Siti Fatimah, not all her children are interested in the craft. A few of them have left to work in nearby Ipoh and Kuala Kangsar. 'That's life,' she philosophised.

Top: A variety of black pots made by the villagers. Above: The pots are blackened in a pit filled with rice husks.

A Malay movie with a difference

22 April Kuala Lumpur

The Malay film industry, known for its melodramatic plots, saw a significant departure with the release of a new film, *Pemburu*, by Fleet Communications. The film, starring Ahmad Yatim, was produced by Datuk Junus Sudin and directed by Rahim Razali. The story revolves around a man who leaves his native kampong for the city, in search of those responsible for the rape and murder of his daughter.

Bidin Mohd Hashim with one of the three cobras that appear in Pemburu.

No entry into BN

29 April Kuala Lumpur

Barisan Nasional (BN) would not admit as members five independent candidates backed by the Berjaya party who had won in Sabah's parliamentary election.

The candidates, who had contested against BN candidates from Usno as a result of animosity between Usno and Berjaya, would 'sit on the Opposition side', according to Prime Minister Dato' Seri Dr Mahathir Mohamad.

The candidates were Affendy Stephens (Merudu), Yahaya Lampong (Kota Belud), Hassan Alban Sandukong (Lubuk Sugut), Abdullah Hamid (Silam) and Yusuf Yakob (Hilir Padas).

Youngest Pahang MB

3 May Kuantan

Datuk Najib Tun Razak became the youngest Menteri Besar to assume office when he was sworn in as Pahang Menteri Besar at the age of 29. His appointment was announced in late April by outgoing Pahang MB Datuk Abdul Rashid, who forwarded Datuk Najib's nomination on behalf of Dato' Seri Dr Mahathir Mohamad to the Regent of Pahang.

KLSE trading put off for one week

11 May **Kuala Lumpur**

The KLSE was closed for trading for a week after fire partly damaged its premises during the weekend. Brokers, however, continued trading using the prices of the Singapore Stock Exchange (SSE) as indicators while dealing by the rules of the KLSE.

Biggest loan in Asia

19 August **Kuala Lumpur**

Malaysia signed a US$1.1-billion loan, the biggest so far in Asia, with Malayan Banking and nine other financial institutions. It was divided into three: a Eurodollar tranche of US$510 million, a UK tax-sparing tranche of US$150 million and US domestic prime rate tranche of US$440 million. The lenders were 70 financial institutions located in 13 countries. The loan was intended to help finance development programmes such as the Fourth Malaysia Plan.

Television star in KL

27 May **Kuala Lumpur**

Stephanie Powers, star of hit TV series *Hart to Hart*, arrived in Malaysia on a personal visit.

TV favourite Stephanie Powers graces Kuala Lumpur.

Ban on smoking in all Government offices

22 August **Kuala Lumpur**

The Chief Secretary to the Government, Tan Sri Hashim Aman, issued a directive banning smoking in the premises of all State and Federal departments and statutory bodies. The first step to help ensure the success of the campaign involved leaders, officers and other Government employees. Notices were put up in meeting rooms, in waiting rooms, over counters and in offices. State Governments would be asked to prohibit any cigarette advertisements on billboards along roadsides.

New Straits Times Annual

25,000 at 25th Merdeka parade

The 25th Merdeka parade near the Sultan Abdul Samad building, Kuala Lumpur.

31 August **Kuala Lumpur**

This year's special anniversary Merdeka parade saw 25,000 Malaysians taking part in a show of colours and performance in front of the Sultan Abdul Samad building. The celebration was different because there was no show of creatively-designed floats, synchronised martial arts performance or queues of armoured vehicles and weaponry. The release of 268 prisoners, including 47 ISA detainees, was another special cause to celebrate. According to the Pardons Board, the detainees had demonstrated their willingness to reform and return to society and no longer posed any threat to the security of the nation. This year's anniversary motto was 'Discipline, Diligence, Progress'.

Highway security boost

4 July **Grik**

Reports from Battalions 303 and 304 of the 10th Brigade in Perak and Battalions 301 and 302 of the 8th Brigade in Kelantan confirmed that security threats along the 115km East–West Highway were almost nil. Calling themselves 'the Highway Guys', the security forces had managed to deter Communist elements from sabotaging the construction of the highway. Vigilant patrols on land and water were conducted to ensure that the contractors, their workers and highway users were constantly safe.

Most of the areas in upper Perak including near the Temenggor Dam were considered security sensitive. The Government had approved 56 projects in these areas costing an estimated $56 million. Development along the highway at the heavily-forested fringes near the town of Grik would cost $14.2 million for housing and plantations.

Leaders take pay cuts

4 June **Segamat**

The Prime Minister and Deputy Prime Minister each took a $1,000 pay cut to support the Government's belt-tightening efforts in view of the global recession. They encouraged other Cabinet members to take cuts of $500–$1,000.

French woman jailed

26 August **Kuala Lumpur**

The Federal Court reduced the sentence for drug trafficking of French secretary Beatrice Saubin, 22, from death to life imprisonment. She was found guilty of trafficking in 534 grams of heroin worth $1.2 million on 17 June.

Saubin committed the offence at Bayan Lepas Airport in Penang on 27 January 1980. Legal circles said that life imprisonment meant Saubin would have to serve a 20-year jail term, but with good behaviour could serve less.

Beatrice Saubin, a French national, was sentenced to life imprisonment after the Federal Court reduced her previous death sentence.

Bogus doctors trapped

23 June **Kuala Lumpur**

The discovery of a bogus doctor at the Kuala Lumpur General Hospital prompted a nationwide alert as authorities began to increase their surveillance of all medical staff. On 25 May, Zainal Mohamed Salleh was arrested by police for posing as a doctor at the hospital. He pleaded guilty to the charge and was sentenced to one year's jail and fined $1,000 or six months' imprisonment by the magistrate's court.

Another imposter was discovered when a prison warder, who happened to come to the hospital, recognised the man as a former inmate of Pudu Prison.

A hospital assistant was also suspicious of the 'doctor' who had taken a patient to the outpatient department for a prescription and managed to convince a medical officer that he was on a course at the hospital. The imposter was caught when he took the patient back to the casualty department.

Prime Minister Dato' Seri Dr Mahathir Mohamad walks past his slogan which means 'Clean, Efficient, Trustworthy'.

Cartoonist Lat's depiction of the 'illegal' telecast of the 1982 World Cup with reference to the news reports.

'Illegal' World Cup telecast

26 June **Malacca** ▶ An earth satellite station in Lendu, 25 miles from Malacca, became the venue for an unauthorised reception and viewing of the 'live' World Cup match between France and Czechoslovakia.

A tip-off sent 13 Anti-Corruption Agency officers to the scene at 12.10am, where they caught 30 men watching the match on a large-screen colour monitor. The show was 'hosted' by off-duty Telecoms officers charging outsiders between $5 and $10 fee each.

The irony was that the *Malay Mail* was striving to raise funds to enable the public to watch one game. It was understood that many had been converging on the station every night since the World Cup started. No arrests were made.

1982

11 July
Italy beats West Germany 3–1 to win the World Cup in Spain.

20 August
A multinational force lands to supervise PLO withdrawal from Lebanon.

14 September
Lebanese President Bashir Gemayel is assassinated in Beirut.

14 September
Princess Grace (Kelly) Rainier, 53, dies in a car accident.

15 September
Israeli forces move into Beirut.

1 October
Sony launches the first compact disc player.

8 October
Poland bans the trade union Solidarity.

3 November
A petrol tanker explodes in the Salang Tunnel, Afghanistan, killing 2,000 people.

2 December
Barney Clark, 61, becomes the first man to have a permanent artificial heart. The operation is performed at the University of Utah. Clark lives for 112 days with the device.

Malaysia criticises US arms supply to Israel

1 October New York

In his address to the 37th UN General Assembly, Dr Mahathir Mohamad criticised the United States for its role in supplying arms to Israel.

Calling the superpower a 'bully', he urged the US to reconsider its position in supplying arms to the Jewish State.

Asri quits Pas post

24 October Kuala Lumpur

Datuk Asri Che Muda resigned as Pas president amidst mounting pressure from party members seeking his removal.

Yusof Rawa assumed the post, with Fadzil Noor as deputy president.

Pas leaders described the resignation as a timely means of saving Datuk Asri's face in view of dissatisfaction over his leadership since the last election. Two other party stalwarts also resigned.

Massive killer croc hunt in Sarawak

6 November Kuching ▶ In Sarawak, an increasing number of crocodile attacks in recent years prompted concerted efforts in Kuching, Bandar Sri Aman and Sarikei to get rid of the reptiles. Special operations such as Operasi Buaya Ganas were launched after a recent death in Batang Belawi. Authorities successfully shot dead two 15-footers. One crocodile was stuffed and put on display in Bandar Sri Aman and later moved to the Sarawak Museum in Kuching.

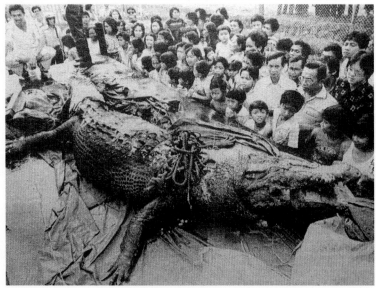

Locals view one of the crocodiles shot dead in Operasi Buaya Ganas.

Petronas strikes black gold

8 September Kuala Lumpur

For the first time since its incorporation in 1978, Petronas Carigali, a wholly-owned subsidiary of Petronas, struck oil. A well, located about 125km east of Kuala Terengganu, was drilled, tested and completed on board the drillship *Cora*.

Production tests revealed a total of 5,565 barrels of oil per day and 10 million standard cubic feet of non-associated gas per day.

The depth of the well was 74 metres and the reservoir zones were at a depth of about 1,200 metres.

Petronas was now producing about 125,000 barrels a day from the South China Sea.

Malaysia's potential oil reserves are believed to be about 2.5 billion barrels. Natural gas reserves off Terengganu have been estimated at more than 15 trillion cubic feet, enough to be exploited for up to 60 years.

Construction of Malaysia's largest port under way

2 September Kemaman

The construction of Malaysia's largest port, with a capacity to handle ships up to 130,000 deadweight tons (dwt), started at Tanjung Berhala in Terengganu and was due for completion in August 1984.

The port was to be Malaysia's first specialised port, catering for the petroleum and petroleum-related industries and the Heavy Industries Corporation (Hicom) project, according to Deputy Prime Minister Datuk Musa Hitam.

There was a possibility of increasing the handling capacity of the port to 220,000dwt vessels, making it one of the largest in Southeast Asia, according to the State Economic and Development Corporation.

Local film giant dies

3 October Kuala Lumpur

Pioneer filmmaker Ho Ah Loke died aged 82. Ho was the Malaysian movie giant who successfully developed the local industry during the 1950s and 1960s.

He was the only Malaysian able to challenge the Shaw Brothers monopoly of Malaysian filmmaking by producing hit movies such as former Prime Minister Tunku Abdul Rahman's *Mahsuri* and the infamous *Pontianak* series.

In 1948 Ho and Datuk Loke Wan Tho, owner of the International Theatre chain, started the Cathay Organisation, one of the biggest movie companies in the region.

He went later to Singapore to open Cathay Keris Studios and Keris Film Productions where he scouted the talents of S. Roomai Noor, M. Amin, Mat Sentul and the late Noordin Ahmad.

He and Loke were also the founders of the Asian Film Festival, started in 1954 in Manila, then called the Annual Film Festival of Southeast Asia.

Ho was also the president of the Malaysian Producers' Association which sought Government help to improve the local film industry by creating a financial pool to help sustain local moviemaking and production.

His foresight and insight into the film industry were highly respected by industry people.

Raja Azlan Shah is new Lord President

13 November Kuala Lumpur

Mr Justice Raja Tan Sri Azlan Shah was sworn in as Lord President before the Timbalan Yang di-Pertuan Agong at Istana Negara. He took over from Mr Justice Tun Mohamed Suffian who retired after 21 years on the Bench.

Mr Justice Raja Azlan Shah had been Chief Justice of the High Court in Malaya since March 1979. He was appointed High Court judge in 1965; at 37 he was the youngest judge in the Commonwealth (*see 11 August 1983*).

Rabuan Pit becomes fastest man in Asia

Rabuan Pit made Malaysia proud as he was named the fastest man in Asia.

29 November New Delhi

Despite a foot injury, Rabuan Pit won the 100m sprint event at the Asian Games in New Delhi, earning him the title of the fastest man in Asia.

Braille money: Bank Negara goofs

1 December Kuala Lumpur

Despite good intentions, Bank Negara's diamond-shaped Braille codes on the $20 and $500 currency notes introduced on 1 September were of no help for the blind because the dots were hardly discernible; they were printed on, and not embossed.

Sources said the bank had failed to consult the Malaysian Association for the Blind before introducing the notes.

1983

Malaysia moved to preserve its heritage and honour its past: several buildings were gazetted under the Antiquities Act, the armed forces celebrated the golden jubilee of the Royal Malay Regiment which was formed as an experimental Malay army unit, and the Sultan Idris Training College (SITC)—touted as the cradle of Malaysian nationalism—celebrated its diamond jubilee. At the same time, Malaysia moved ahead with the introduction of new policies—Malaysia Incorporated and privatisation—that, according to Prime Minister Dr Mahathir, were keystones to national development. Special attention was also given to primary schoolchildren of whom some 150,000 were found to be underweight.

JANUARY
Fire breaks out on the upper floors of the Komtar Tower, Penang's tallest building, during its construction. Firemen are unable to tackle the blaze as they lacked equipment for fires at that height.

APRIL
Barisan Nasional component party youth wing members demonstrate against threatened Soviet support for Communist insurgents in Asean.

AUGUST
Lord President Raja Azlan Shah is appointed Raja Muda of Perak.

DECEMBER
An MAS Airbus flying from Kota Kinabalu crashes near Subang Airport. All 247 passengers survive.

August: Malaysia shocks India at hockey tournament.

'Our future depends on how well many different kinds of people can live and work together.'

Tunku Abdul Rahman, on his 80th birthday, 8 February 1983.

1983

Prison escape

3 January Kuala Lumpur

With the help of iron spikes and bedsheets, four convicts broke out of Pudu Jail. Azhar bin Ibrahim, 28, Ghazali bin Awang, 29, Raja Yusuff bin Raja Mohamed and Razali bin Ismail, both 22, tunnelled under their cell with the spikes and slipped down the three-metre-high perimeter wall with the help of the knotted bedsheets.

Dressed in their prison garb of white shirts and khaki shorts, they then sprinted across Jalan Hang Tuah towards Jalan Davidson and disappeared into the night. Police believed that the convicts took the spikes from the prison workshop and had been digging under the cell wall for the past two days. A fifth convict in the cell stayed behind.

Police, aided by 100 prison warders, staged a massive manhunt that included the use of tracker dogs. They also set up roadblocks and a house-to-house search in the Jalan Davidson area, while search teams went over various parts of the city without success.

The last breakout was in November 1972 when two convicts scaled the prison wall. One, named Chan Tit Kong, was recaptured in 1974 and the other, Low Wah Chai, was caught two years later.

Two of the escapees under guard after their recapture.

106 dead after boat capsizes

11 January Kota Kinabalu ▶ A barter trade boat, the *Al-Malyn*, sailed into heavy storms about 3km east of Tambisan, an island off the tip of the Dent peninsula on Sabah's east coast. The boat flipped over and broke into pieces.

It had departed from the fishing village of Bongao Island in the southern Philippines, en route for Sandakan. The 226 Philippine Muslims packed into the boat were tossed into the Sulu Sea.

Within 10 hours, 95 men, 13 women and 12 children had been rescued. Fourteen bodies were recovered and 92 other passengers were reported missing.

Boat captain Sahak Mohd Said was washed ashore along with 45 others on Tambisan. He could not explain why the boat's manifest named only 135 passengers although there were 81 more than that on board, excluding the crew. A police launch transferred them to Sandakan where they were met by their friends and relatives.

Malay nationalist Boestamam dies

19 January Kuala Lumpur

Former chairman of political party Pekemas, Datuk Abdullah Sani bin Raja Kechil, better known as Datuk Ahmad Boestamam, died at the General Hospital this morning.

The ardent Malay nationalist famed for his left-wing politics was 62 and had been battling lung cancer for the past six months. Boestamam was the general secretary of the Malayan Nationalist Party, which was formed to fight British colonialism after the Japanese Occupation.

He founded the party's youth wing, Api, which had the motto *Merdeka dengan darah* (Bloody struggle for independence). Two years later the party was banned and he was interned for 7½ years for sedition. Upon his release he founded Party Rakyat (Socialist Party). The party joined forces with the Labour Party to form the Malaysian Peoples' Socialist Front, with Boestamam as chairman. In 1958, he won a seat in Parliament. In 1961, he resigned as chairman of the Socialist Front to concentrate on leading Party Rakyat. When Malaysia was formed, Boestamam was detained yet again, this time for four years. In this period he wrote four novels, sat for the Higher School Certificate and learnt Mandarin. He resigned from Party Rakyat after his release due to differences with the newer, younger, leadership and formed the Partai Marhaen Malaysia which later merged with Pekemas, a party formed by Dr Tan Chee Koon.

When Dr Tan resigned due to ill health in 1977, Boestamam became the party president. In August 1978, he resigned and rejoined Party Rakyat as an ordinary member.

Peace Corps march away after 21 years

13 February Kuala Lumpur

The Peace Corps made its first visit to Malaysia in 1962 and left with over 3,500 volunteers having served in the country over the years. It was initially made up of young adults who gave up two years of their lives to serve in underdeveloped nations, to promote understanding, help the host country and expand their own horizons. Over the years the focus changed gradually with emphasis on older, more experienced specialists.

The scene at Batu Caves after the stand collapsed.

VIP stand collapses at Thaipusam festival

29 January Kuala Lumpur

A packed three-metre-high VIP platform at the Thaipusam celebration at Batu Caves came crashing down just after the arrival of the guest-of-honour, Selangor Menteri Besar Datuk Ahmad Razali Ali.

As he was about to take his seat for the opening ceremony, having been garlanded by MIC president (also Works and Utilities Minister) Datuk S. Samy Vellu, the stand caved in, injuring 54 people.

No one was seriously hurt. Some casualties received attention at the medical centre in the temple grounds and others at the General Hospital. Volunteers quickly restored order.

Towering inferno

23 January Penang

Firemen watched helplessly as fire raged on the 43rd floor of Kompleks Tun Abdul Razak (Komtar) because their skylifts could not carry their water hoses to that height. The fire continued unabated and spread to four floors above for about eight hours before it died down. There were also several explosions thought to have been caused by oxygen cylinders, left behind by building workers, overheating in the blaze.

Flames rise from Komtar's upper floors during the blaze.

Bapa Malaysia celebrates 80th

8 February Kuala Lumpur

Bapa Malaysia Tunku Abdul Rahman turned 80 and was in the pink of health as the Barisan Nasional threw a dinner to celebrate the occasion.

Prime Minister Dato' Seri Dr Mahathir Mohamad (pictured below looking on as the Tunku cuts his cake) said the peace and prosperity Malaysians enjoyed were the result of the leadership of the Tunku.

The Kedah prince played a key role in assisting Malaya to Independence in 1957, uniting Umno, the MCA and MIC into one party, the Alliance, to formalise the country's multiracial concept of nation building. He left office in 1970 but his achievements in laying down the foundations for a peaceful and prosperous country would never be forgotten, Dr Mahathir told the gathering.

Dr M hails Malaysia Inc

25 February | **Kuala Lumpur**

The Malaysia Incorporated policy and the concept of privatisation are keystones to speeding up national development, according to Prime Minister Dato' Seri Dr Mahathir Mohamad.

He was speaking at the launch of forums organised by the National Institute of Public Administration (Intan). The Malaysia Inc system envisioned the public and private sectors working closely together, he said. The Government should play the role of a service agency to assist the private sector in producing goods and services. There were numerous problems faced by the private sector that Government officers did not understand, he said, while the private sector on occasions had not assisted the public sector in its work. Instead of working at a tangent, both sectors should work towards common goals. He pointed out that this formula proved very successful in Japan.

With regard to privatisation, he said it was a process by which public-owned utilities and corporations would be either fully or partly transferred to the private sector to be better run, more efficient and more profitable. It was not necessarily good for the country to have Government-owned and managed businesses. Public-owned enterprises were often not profitable or efficient. Indeed, profitable privately owned enterprises had ceased making money after being nationalised.

Lat's view: Dr Mahathir gets some advice on growth.

Minister to hang

5 March | **Kuala Lumpur**

Culture, Youth and Sports Minister Datuk Mokhtar Hashim was found guilty of the murder of Datuk Mohamed Taha Talib, 10 months after the former State Assemblyman was found shot dead outside his house. A village headman, Rahmat Satiman, 54, who was charged jointly with the Minister, was also found guilty. Both were sentenced to death.

Trial judge Mr Justice Hashim Yeop Sani said that as the scientific evidence was unchallenged, it meant the two bullets found in the victim came from Datuk Mokhtar's pistol which was in his control and custody at all times.

Datuk Mokhtar and Rahmat gave notice of appeal and were granted a stay of execution. Rahmat appealed his conviction and was released later in the year (*see 2 March 1984*).

King scores two goals

18 February | **Kuala Lumpur**

The Yang di-Pertuan Agong's XI, an occasional team, defeated the Malaysian Diplomatic and Administration Service (PTD) 8–2 in a friendly hockey match at the Tun Razak Stadium yesterday.

PTD took an early 2–0 lead, but the King struck two goals to bring the teams on level terms before his side, which featured notable veteran hockey stars including Freddie Vias, Raj Kumar and Ismail Bakri, hit another six for an easy win.

Party Islam launched

24 March | **Kota Bharu**

The Hizbulmuslimin Malaysia (Hamim) or Party Islam has been formed. It aims to set up a system of administration, laws and justice based on Islamic values.

'Buy British last' policy called off

2 April | **Kuala Lumpur**

The Prime Minister's Department will no longer vet contracts and tenders involving British firms for Government agencies and departments, Dato' Seri Dr Mahathir Mohamad said today.

In 1981, just before he became Prime Minister that July, Dr Mahathir lashed out at the British attitude to Malaysia. The relationship between the two countries had become strained due to various factors, such as Britain's decision to impose higher fees on overseas students and to reduce technical assistance.

In October that year, the Government ordered the vetting of proposals to award contracts and tenders for Government projects to British firms. This was dubbed the 'Buy British last' policy. The relationship thawed after Dr Mahathir met Britain's Prime Minister Margaret Thatcher in March this year.

Malaysia's first Lord President dies

9 April | **Kuala Lumpur**

Sir James Thomson, the first Lord President of Malaysia, died in Scotland aged 81. He was instrumental in implementing the Malayanisation of the judiciary. He was made Chief Justice in 1956, the highest judicial appointment in the country.

He was integral in maintaining the independence of the judiciary and getting funds to send promising young officers to qualify in law in England.

Sir James was Lord President from 1963 to 1967, by which time all the courts in Malaysia were manned entirely by local people.

Sir James (right) in his days in Malaysia.

Amateur athlete in trouble over ad

29 April | **Kuala Lumpur**

Track queen Marina Chin may have infringed her amateur status by appearing in an advertisement for a motorcycle without permission from the Malaysian Amateur Athletic Union. As a result she has withdrawn from the national athletic trials to select the team for the upcoming SEA Games in Singapore.

Under International Amateur Athletic Federation rules, an athlete must have permission to appear in an advertisement.

Singing idol of French teenagers comes home

7 May | **Kuala Lumpur**

Malaysian singer Shake, who became an idol of teenagers in France, gave his first concert in his home country at the Dewan Tunku Canselor, Universiti Malaya. The star, whose real name is Datuk Sheikh Abdullah bin Ahmad, sang in French and spoke Malay haltingly, not surprisingly as he had been away from Malaysia for about 10 years.

Born in Johor Bahru, he sang in local clubs before leaving for London and Paris. In 1975 his first single, *You Know I Love You*, sold a million copies.

Force 136 featured in BBC documentary

21 May | **Grik**

Former Perak Menteri Besar Dato' Seri Haji Wan Mohamed Haji Wan relived his time in Force 136, the World War II anti-Japanese resistance movement, for a BBC documentary. A team from the BBC was shooting a nine-part documentary on Force 136. Produced and directed by Vivienne King, the documentary was to be screened in Britain and Australia.

Heritage buildings in KL

Several buildings in Kuala Lumpur were gazetted in 1983 under the Antiquities Act 1976. They included courthouses, a mosque, offices, theatres and schools. Below are four of them.

Town hall and municipal offices, built 1903–1904, gazetted 13 October.

Chartered Bank of India, Australia and China/Standard Chartered Bank, Jalan Raja, built 1908–1909, gazetted 22 March.

Institute of Medical Research, Jalan Pahang, gazetted 22 March.

Masjid Jamek, Jalan Tun Perak, built 1908–1909, gazetted 13 October.

1983

17 May
Lebanon, Israel and the US sign an agreement on Israeli withdrawal from Lebanon.

9 June
British PM Thatcher wins a landslide election victory.

13 June
US space probe *Pioneer 10*, launched in 1972, becomes the first spacecraft to leave the solar system.

1 July
Death of visionary American architect, inventor of the geodesic dome, Buckminster Fuller, 88.

22 July
Diana Ross gives a free concert in Central Park, New York City to 800,000 people.

25 July
Anti-Tamil riots in Sri Lanka leave 3,000 dead.

21 August
Despite tight security, Benigno Aquino Jr, the Philippine opposition leader, is assassinated at Manila Airport on his return from exile.

1 September
Korean commercial flight 007 strays into Soviet airspace and is shot down, killing all 269 on board.

Biggest bank robbery

15 June Penang

Three masked gunmen robbed Citibank in Jalan Aman Shah of $700,000 in the biggest hold-up in the country's history.

The pistol-packing thugs entered the bank through a side door, floored the single guard with a punch, and proceeded to the main office. They then emptied the drawers of cash before making their escape in a car driven by an accomplice. About $500,000 of the haul was from the payroll of the Royal Australian Air Force base at Butterworth.

The gang was believed to have been responsible for all six bank robberies in the State since April the previous year in which a total of $1.3 million had been stolen. It was believed the gang was based in Thailand.

A curious crowd gathers outside the Citibank branch where masked gunmen, believed to be based in Thailand, got away with $700,000 in what is believed to be Malaysia's biggest ever hold-up.

5,000 in anti-Soviet demo

15 April Kuala Lumpur

Youth wing members of Barisan Nasional component parties gathered at the Chinese Assembly Hall here to condemn the Soviet Union's threat to support Communist insurgent movements in Asean countries.

The rally, which was organised by Umno Youth and drew a crowd of 5,000, was in response to a statement by Soviet Deputy Foreign Minister Mikail Kapitan, who the previous week in Singapore had warned Asean nations that the whole infrastructure of Southeast Asian countries would erode if Asean did not end its confrontation with Vietnam and its allies in Laos and Kampuchea.

The protesters pledged to uphold the nation's honour and to support any move by Prime Minister Dato' Seri Dr Mahathir Mohamad to defend Malaysia against the Communist threat.

Super Zaiton

2 June Singapore

Zaiton Othman grabbed the only gold medal of the day for Malaysia, winning the heptathlon with 5,322 points to beat Nene Gamo of the Philippines at the SEA Games in Singapore.

Zaiton Othman leaps to success in the heptathlon at the SEA Games in Singapore.

Cradle of Malaysian nationalism celebrates

1 August Tanjung Malim

The Sultan Idris Training College (SITC), cradle of Malaysian nationalism, launched its diamond jubilee celebrations.

Founded in 1922, and located in Tanjung Malim, 80km from Kuala Lumpur, it is the oldest existing teachers' training college in the country.

Many politicians, educationists and literary figures studied at the SITC, including Harun Aminurashid, Masuri B.N., Abdullah Sidek, Zainal Abidin bin Ahmad (Za'ba), Aminuddin Baki, Awang Had Salleh and Ghafar Baba.

Deputy Prime Minister Datuk Musa Hitam paid tribute to the college.

Azlan Shah named Perak Raja Muda

11 August Ipoh

Lord President Raja Tun Azlan Shah ibni Al-marhum Sultan Yusuff Izzuddin Shah was appointed Raja Muda of Perak, making him the first in line to succeed to the Perak throne. The appointment had been widely expected.

Raja Tun Azlan Shah had been the Raja Kecil Besar, traditionally third in line to the throne, since 1 August 1978. He studied at Nottingham University in the English East Midlands and was called to the English Bar in 1954. On his return to Malaysia he served as assistant state secretary in Perak and subsequently held a number of legal posts. He was appointed Lord President in 1982.

First woman for Tun Razak Chair

16 August Kuala Lumpur

Professor of Curriculum Development at the University of Malaya, Puan Sri Fatimah Hamid Don, was appointed by the Government as distinguished professor for the Tun Abdul Razak Chair of Southeast Asian Studies at Ohio University in Athens, Ohio, in the US.

The appointment was for the 1982–1984 academic years, which ran from September to June the following year.

Malaysia stuns India in hockey

25 August Kuala Lumpur

In their first win in seven years over the Olympic champions, Malaysia shocked India with a 3–2 victory in the International Pentangular hockey tournament at the Tun Razak Stadium here. Malaysia had beaten India only twice before, in 1964 and 1976.

The Malaysians played beyond themselves and showed more determination and spirit than the visitors. Colin Sta Maria converted a penalty stroke in the seventh minute followed by M. Surenthiran's fine finish in the 19th minute. Sta Maria scored again in the 53rd minute.

Action gets hectic at the Tun Razak Stadium where Malaysia beat India 3–2.

Nine-year-old scales Gunung Tahan

31 August Klang

Standard Four student Kenneth Chin Hseng Kuang climbed the 7,174ft-high Gunung Tahan in 5½ days.

The La Salle primary school student was a member of a team that included his father and six others. He said he felt a little tired when climbing the steeper slopes but did not have much difficulty otherwise and had learned a lot.

'The only time I was scared was when strong winds blew away our tents but my daddy was there all the time beside me,' he said.

His father Chin Yik Poh, 38, who had already climbed Gunung Tahan seven times, said 11 people started the climb but only eight, including two women, reached the top.

He calculated that all in all they had walked 120 miles and climbed 37 hills.

Performers herald the launch of the school milk scheme.

150,000 children underweight

12 September | Kuala Lumpur

About 150,000 schoolchildren are underweight, the Health Ministry said. This figure constituted five per cent of all primary school pupils in schools throughout the country. Deputy Education Minister Datuk Tan Tiong Hong disclosed the figures at the launching of a $5-million scheme to provide free and subsidised milk to primary school pupils. With the subsidy, a packet of milk was to be sold for only 30 cents. About 200,000 students would benefit. Another 20,000 would benefit under the free milk scheme.

Prime Minister
urges clean living

2 October | Kuala Lumpur

Prime Minister Dato' Seri Dr Mahathir Mohamad launched a nationwide cleanliness campaign.

He reminded the public that keeping the cities, towns and their whole environment clean was part of their responsibility.

Launching the month-long campaign at the Jalan Munshi Abdullah car park in Kuala Lumpur, he said the people should practise cleanliness for the good of all.

Mr Clean: Dr Mahathir chats to workers at the launch of the cleanliness campaign.

Misbun shows his winning style.

Badminton ace
Misbun turns pro

7 October | Kuala Lumpur

Misbun Sidek turned professional when he signed up with International Management Group (IMG), managers of superstars such as Paolo Rossi, Arnold Palmer, Bjorn Borg and Sebastian Coe.

The 23-year-old Malaysian, who signed a three-year contract, was the first sportsman in the region to be recruited by the management group.

New port opened

4 September | Bintulu

The $558-million Bintulu Port in Tanjung Kidurong was declared open by Sarawak Yang di-Pertua Negeri Tun Datuk Patinggi Haji Abdul Rahman Yaakub.

The deepwater port, which took three years to complete, was equipped with the latest radar surveillance systems.

Chief Minister Datuk Patinggi Haji Abdul Taib Mahmud said the port would serve the rich hinterland of northern Sarawak, handling exports of timber, timber products, ammonia, urea, coal, LNG, crude oil and general cargo.

Soviet visit cancelled

7 September | Kuala Lumpur

Following the downing of a Korean Airlines jumbo jet with 269 people on board by a Soviet fighter aircraft, Malaysia asked Moscow to cancel the planned visit here by a Soviet Foreign Ministry delegation.

Malaysian public opinion would not allow the visit, Deputy Foreign Minister Abdul Kadir Sheikh Fadzir said. One victim of the disaster was 23-year-old Malaysian Siow Woon Kwong. The Soviet Ambassador was summoned to the Foreign Ministry where a verbal protest was delivered over the incident. Soviet radio messages intercepted by Japan clearly showed that the aircraft was shot down despite its commercial aircraft status.

Two other countries scheduled to be visited, Thailand and Singapore, also called for an indefinite postponement of the trip.

Ancient river traditions
part of royal wedding

10 September | Kuala Kangsar

Five boats sped off to seven tributaries of the Perak River to collect water for the wedding celebrations of the Tunku Mahkota of Johor, Tunku Ibrahim Ismail, and Perak princess Raja Zarith Sofiah binti Sultan Idris.

The ceremony was preceded by a procession of seven Land Rovers carrying the Pawang Raja and his assistant, court officials, heralds, 16 bearers of silver spears and court musicians.

The river water was to be sprinkled over the bridal couple as is the tradition.

VIP visitors

Turkish leader in trade talks

6 September | Kuala Lumpur

Turkish Prime Minister Bulend Ulusu conferred with Prime Minister Dato' Seri Dr Mahathir Mohamad after his arrival for a five-day official visit, the first by a Turkish Prime Minister.

The discussions at the Prime Minister's Department centred on bilateral cooperation. Turkey

The two leaders' wives at the airport.

hoped to buy more Malaysian rubber and palm oil through direct trade instead of going through third parties, said Mr Ulusu. A maritime transport agreement between Malaysia and Turkey was in the works.

King Hussein voices concern

24 September | Kuala Lumpur

King Hussein of Jordan, on his visit to Malaysia, had discussions with acting Prime Minister Datuk Musa Hitam regarding the Palestinian crisis.

They agreed to consult each other on moves to implement the Geneva Plan of action to solve the crisis.

The two leaders also discussed the situation in Afghanistan and Kampuchea and agreed that both were basically victims of invasions and political solutions were needed to restore the two countries' independence and sovereignty. The Iran–Iraq war was also cause for concern despite efforts to bring it to an end.

Somare heads delegation
from Papua New Guinea

20 November | Kuala Lumpur

The Papua New Guinea Prime Minister, Michael Somare, and his wife Veronica arrived here to begin a four-day official visit.

The Prime Minister was accompanied by a 16-strong delegation. They were greeted on arrival by the Prime Minister Dato' Seri Dr Mahathir Mohamad and Foreign Minister Tan Sri Ghazali Shafie.

Mr Somare inspects a guard-of-honour with Dr Mahathir.

1983

world news

5 October
Lech Walesa wins the Nobel Peace Prize.

9 October
A bomb in Rangoon, blamed on North Korea, misses South Korean President Chun Doo Hwan but kills several of his Cabinet Ministers.

12 October
Former Japanese Prime Minister Tanaka is found guilty of corruption and jailed for four years.

27 October
Pope John Paul II visits his would-be assassin Mehmet Ali Agca in prison to offer him forgiveness.

26 November
In London, 6,800 gold bars worth £26 million are stolen from a vault in Heathrow Airport.

17 December
An IRA car bomb kills six Christmas shoppers outside Harrods, London.

31 December
Brunei gains independence from the UK.

Constitution is amended

15 December | Kuala Lumpur

Lat's gardener returns with advice on roots.

The Constitution (Amendment) Bill was signed by the Timbalan Yang di-Pertuan Agong. It established the Government as the supreme ruling body ahead of the Rulers, who were not required to play any role in political matters.

The signing of the Bill, introduced in August, was delayed, which led to unrest in the country. There was strong support for the Bill and after meetings between the Government and Rulers, the Timbalan Yang di-Pertuan Agong signed the Bill in place of the King who was on holiday. However, a special session of Parliament was called to introduce a new Bill incorporating a Government compromise offered to the Rulers as a way out of the four-month impasse over the issue.

Royal Malay Regiment marks golden jubilee

15 September | Kuala Lumpur

In 1933 the British picked 25 young Malay men for an experimental unit to see if the Malays made good soldiers. They were so impressed that by the second year, the unit was expanded to 150 and Askar Melayu, the Malay Regiment, was born.

In the years that followed, the regiment saw service in the defence of Malaya against the Japanese invasion, the Emergency, the Congo civil war and the Confrontation with Indonesia. The Di-Raja (royal) title was bestowed on the regiment in 1958.

Soldiers on parade to mark the golden jubilee of the Royal Malay Regiment.

Smallest baby to have heart surgery

9 December | Petaling Jaya

A surgeon at the Universiti Hospital scored a first when he performed open-heart surgery on a seven-month-old baby weighing only 4kg.

The patient, Rohaidah bte Mohamad Rashid, was the smallest infant in the country to have undergone such surgery to patch up a hole in the heart. She was said to be progressing well.

The surgeon, Dr Razalli Hashim, 37, said he undertook the operation because there was no other means of saving the baby.

It was a high-risk procedure that was rarely used, he said.

PM goes ghostbusting

12 December | Kuala Lumpur

Following a rash of press reports of near-daily sightings of spirits and vampires, such as the 'Kum Kum' said to have been spotted in Kuala Lumpur, and outbreaks of mass hysteria, Prime Minister Dato' Seri Dr Mahathir Mohamad decided to lay ghosts in the minds of Malaysians to rest.

He started with the media. 'Reading too many tales of the supernatural and horror stories could turn you into a nervous, hysterical person, afraid of your own shadow,' he said at the Press Awards presentation dinner here tonight.

The wreckage of the MAS airliner, with the top of its fuselage blown off, lies in a swamp near the airport.

247 survive in MAS Airbus crash

18 December | Petaling Jaya

All 247 people survived, with only 27 injured, when a Malaysia Airlines Airbus, apparently stuck by lightning, crash-landed in a swamp 1.5km from Subang Airport. Moments after everyone had safely left the plane, three explosions rocked the aircraft, blowing off the top of the fuselage. On board the flight from Kota Kinabalu were 233 passengers and 14 crew members.

The Central Market building could be a thriving centre for local arts and crafts, said campaigners.

Fight to save Central Market

24 November | Kuala Lumpur

Kuala Lumpur's Central Market should be given a new lease of life, campaigners said. It was planned to move the market and pull down the 50-year-old building, the largest enclosed space in the city, to make way for a high-rise block.

But critics said it could be turned into a lively cultural and crafts centre that would be a Malaysian version of London's famous Covent Garden.

NEP extended as targets are not achieved

14 December | Kuala Lumpur

The New Economic Policy (NEP) would be extended beyond 1990 because it failed to meet its targets, Datuk Musa Hitam said.

He told members of the Malay Chamber of Commerce and Industry at their annual dinner that the country's economic position had upset earlier forecasts.

A recent review had sunk hopes of achieving the anticipated results and a thorough re-think was needed.

He said he was confident an amended policy draft would be ratified by the Cabinet and tabled in Parliament next March.

A meeting of the National Planning Council he attended yesterday put the final touches on the revamp.

Landslide victory for Barisan in Sarawak

30 December | Kuching

The Barisan Nasional-plus Government of Chief Minister Datuk Patinggi Amar Haji Abdul Taib Mahmud won handsomely in the Sarawak State election, securing 44 of the 48 seats.

1984

Protests, more protests and yet more protests: Telephonists, Kuala Lumpur residents, tow-truck operators, squatters, and Chinese guilds held separate protests over a host of issues. Other contentious issues included MCA phantom members and the attempted disruption of government administration by deviationist groups. Yet another controversy brewed over the question of a new dance craze to grip youngsters—breakdancing. The Government threatened to ban the dance sensation because of its 'public nuisance' value. There were no protests however when seven members of a jury were fined $100 each by the High Court for contempt after talking with prosecution witnesses. Judge Ajaib Singh ordered a retrial for the accused.

JANUARY
The Hotel Majestic in Kuala Lumpur closes after 50 years.

JUNE
The Government decides to go ahead with the construction of a radioactive waste dump in Papan despite vocal protests against it.

JULY
Yasser Arafat, Chairman of the Palestine Liberation Organisation (PLO), speaks at a mass rally at Stadium Negara.

OCTOBER
Squatters clash with police at Kampung Bercham, Ipoh, when a Land Office enforcement unit arrived to demolish illegal homes.

February: More than 4,000 runners take part in the KL International Marathon.

'No thought or consideration was given to provide convenience for kampong people.'

Tunku Abdul Rahman, commenting on the colonial administration in his newspaper column 'As I See It' in *The Star*, 15 October 1984.

1984

world news

New Year increase in bus and taxi fares

1 January | **Kuala Lumpur**

The withdrawal of a Government diesel subsidy of 10.66 cents a litre meant that Malaysians would pay more for bus and most taxi fares.

With diesel costing 58.6 cents in Peninsular Malaysia, bus fares and those of chartered, outstation and air-conditioned taxis would be allowed to rise, Transport Minister Tan Sri Chong Hon Nyan said. The price of kerosene also rose, to 63 cents a litre in Peninsular Malaysia.

The bad news for Sabah and Sarawak motorists was that part of the exemption from excise or import duties on petroleum products was withdrawn, pushing up petrol prices by two cents a litre.

Rulers' immunity challenged

9 January | **Kuala Lumpur**

Immunity of Rulers from court proceedings did not mean they could commit criminal acts, Dato' Seri Dr Mahathir Mohamad told the Dewan Rakyat. The Prime Minister, who tabled the Constitution (Amendment) Bill 1984, explained that even though no Ruler could be brought to court in his personal capacity, this did not mean a Ruler was free to commit crimes, abuse anyone, seize property or refuse to pay debts. The purpose of Article 181(2) was only that no Ruler could be tried in a court.

After a six-hour debate, the Dewan passed the Bill by a 141–10 vote. The Bill stipulated that under Article 66, financial measures passed by Parliament must be assented to by the Yang di-Pertuan Agong within 30 days of their being presented to him.

For other Bills, the King could return them to the House within 30 days, stating the reasons for his objection. But any Bill reconsidered by Parliament would be presented again to the King for the royal assent. If the King failed to give his assent within 30 days, it would become law as if he had assented. A Bill would automatically become law after 30 days if the King did not give his assent and raise any objection within the specified time.

The giant waterslide at the recreational resort of Mimaland, which opened this year. The pool was said to be the largest in Southeast Asia. The resort, in the hills of Gombak, also featured boating, fishing and jungle trekking.

Above: The elderly head waiter on his last day at work.

Right: The Majestic, symbol of a slower age.

Hotel Majestic closes after 50 years

1 January | **Kuala Lumpur**

After 50 years, the Hotel Majestic, one of the Federal capital's landmarks, closed. It served its final meal on New Year's Eve, and said 'Hello' to 1984, and then the doors closed.

The hotel, from a gentler, slower era, was to be turned into a national art gallery, though that later moved to new premises, leaving the hotel building empty.

A regular guest at the hotel said he wished hotels such as this did not have to close down. He likened the Majestic, which was built in 1932, to Raffles Hotel in Singapore and to the Taj Mahal in Bombay.

Carrian boss sued

2 January | **Kuala Lumpur**

Bumiputra Malaysia Finance sued George Tan, 49, chairman of the collapsed Hong Kong property group Carrian, for US$138 million. The suit stated that Tan stood guarantee for loans and credit facilities which BMF gave to seven companies in October 1981.

BMF was the first Carrian Group creditor to sue Tan as guarantor and the move surprised the banking industry in view of the close links between BMF and Carrian before the latter's collapse in 1982.

In November 1983, BMF obtained a winding-up order against Carrian with a petition for outstanding loans of HK$145 million and US$84 million (see 17 May 1984).

4,000 telephonists on work-to-rule

4 January | **Kuala Lumpur**

About 4,000 Telecoms telephonists in Peninsular Malaysia decided to stop metering international and trunk calls in protest against 'non-recognition of services and inadequate salaries'.

Telephonists were supposed to note the time, duration and cost of every trunk call and send details to the accounts section for billing of subscribers.

But they felt that since their maximum salaries were the same as PABX operators, who only connect calls from switchboards to extensions, they would do only what was required of them. Metering, they said, should be handled by the administrative staff of Telecoms.

Fiery start to tow-truck operators' strike

16 January | **Kuala Lumpur**

A three-day strike by tow-truck operators got off to a fiery start when one of their vehicles in Gombak caught fire. The owner claimed someone started the blaze. The strike, called by the Federal Territory and Selangor Automobile Repairers' Association, was in protest against the classification of workshops by the General Insurance Association of Malaysia.

Two die in tanker blaze

20 January | **Teluk Intan**

Two engineers were killed when fire broke out on board the oil tanker *Sitiawan* loaded with more than 800 tonnes of high-grade petroleum and moored at the Perak River here. Their charred bodies were found in their cabins and it was believed they were trapped by the fire. Twelve other crew members escaped unhurt despite a series of explosions.

Head of new varsity

26 January | **Alor Star**

The Vice-Chancellor of Universiti Kebangsaan Malaysia, Tan Sri Prof Dr Awang Had Salleh, was appointed the first Vice-Chancellor of Universiti Utara Malaysia. His place in UKM was taken by Prof Datuk Dr Abdul Hamid Abdul Rahman, dean of UKM's Medical Faculty.

Demerit system starts

31 January | **Kuala Lumpur**

The demerit points system for drivers would begin on 1 February but traffic offenders would not be penalised until after 3 March, Road Transport Department director-general Mohamed Hassan Mohamed Hashim said. The first two months would be used to familiarise the public and for the authorities to solve teething problems. Offenders would only be issued warning notices.

100,000 phantom members on MCA rolls?

18 February | **Kuala Lumpur**

MCA branches with 'phantom members' might be suspended and barred from taking part in party elections, said acting party president Datuk Dr Neo Yee Pan. The phantom members would also be struck off the membership list.

A dispute over the presence of phantom members caused senior MCA leaders Datuk Dr Ling Liong Sik and Datuk Lee Kim Sai to walk out of a steering committee meeting when they were denied access to the master list of members.

Both had wanted the list for a check of phantom members as there were allegations of at least 100,000 such members on the rolls. Datuk Dr Neo said the central committee decided the master list would be distributed to branches by the end of the month (*see 6 May 1984*).

Malaysian of the Year

31 January | **Kuala Lumpur**

The country's first Prime Minister Tunku Abdul Rahman Putra Al-Haj was named Malaysian of the Year 1983 by *The Star* newspaper. It was a year of drastic change and unexpected soul-searching, the newspaper said, 'in politics, in our perceptions of many of the institutions that we had for so long taken for granted or regarded as immutable.'

But in a year of turbulence and tests of unity, the newspaper said that one person stood out for his moderating influence, his commonsense views, for his unflagging moral courage and for sheer durability as an elder statesman, speaking up 'forcefully and bravely', counselling and setting an example 'for the muddled and the uncertain'.

Law officers 'overworked'

28 February | **Kuantan**

Kuantan High Court judge Mr Justice Shaik Daud Haji Ismail said many judicial and legal service officers were resigning because of the overwhelming workload.

Describing the resignation rate as alarming, he said the authorities should not let them be overloaded.

He said this when he admitted to the Bar Raub Sessions Court president Daphne Sebastian and Pahang assistant legal aid director Thong Siew Keng.

He used Daphne as an example of an overworked judicial officer.

Besides being Raub Sessions Court president, she was Raub High Court assistant registrar and a magistrate for Bentong, Kuala Lipis and Raub.

Death sentence commuted

2 March | **Kuala Lumpur**

Datuk Mokhtar Hashim's death sentence was commuted to life imprisonment after a meeting of the Pardons Board. A statement from the Prime Minister's Department said the Yang di-Pertuan Agong decided to commute the sentence after a meeting of the board at Istana Negara.

Datuk Mokhtar, a former Culture, Youth and Sports Minister, was found guilty of murdering former Negeri Sembilan Legislative Assembly Speaker Datuk Mohamed Taha Talib in Gemencheh on 14 April 1982 (*see 16 April 1991*).

What a marathon

12 February | **Kuala Lumpur**

The KL International Marathon, held in conjunction with the city's 10th anniversary, was not only a carnival for city people but helped put the capital on the world map. More than 4,000 runners entered in various sections of the race, ranging from the 42km marathon to a section for veterans and a 20km mini-marathon.

As the runners came into the Merdeka Stadium, the 5,000-strong crowd who had gathered, including the King, applauded. In the main event, Sweden's Tommy Persson was home first with a time of 2:23:06. The women's champion was Lone Dybdal of Denmark who finished in 2:48:03. Malaysia's P. Rajakumari came in third in 3:27:03.

Patrick John shows his moves in the fancy dress category of the KL International Marathon.

Salleh Abbas is new Lord President

2 March | **Kuala Lumpur**

The Yang di-Pertuan Agong presented the letter of appointment as Lord President to Tan Sri Haji Mohd Salleh Abbas. Mr Justice Tan Sri Abdul Hamid Omar was appointed Chief Justice to take Tan Sri Salleh's place.

Asiaweek magazine featured the rising stars of Umno on the cover of its 27 April issue, among them Abdullah Ahmad Badawi, Rais Yatim, Anwar Ibrahim and Najib Razak.

Gaya Street carnival

1 April | **Kota Kinabalu**

Thousands of people witnessed the inaugural Sunday Gaya Street Fair which featured a wide range of cultural and commercial activities. Acting Sabah Chief Minister Tan Sri Suffian Koroh launched the event. The highlight was German Ernst F.C White who exhibited the hang glider with which he made a historic flight from the top of Mt Kinabalu on 23 March.

$5m start to fund

1 May | **Kuala Lumpur**

Prime Minister Dato' Seri Dr Mahathir Mohamad donated $500,000 on behalf of the Federal Government when he launched a foundation dedicated to wiping out poverty. A total of $5.2 million in donations and pledges was received for Yayasan Gerakbakti Pemuda. Umno Youth, which started the foundation, donated $100,000.

Go for five children, urges Mahathir

6 April | **Kuala Lumpur** ▶ Maternity leave and benefits would be extended to five children instead of the current three to encourage population growth, said Prime Minister Dato' Seri Dr Mahathir Mohamad. 'We need manpower to develop the country,' he added. If the current growth rate was maintained, the population would only reach 35 million in about 115 years.

He made comparisons between the population of Malaysia, with 14.8 million, and that of the Philippines, with 40 million people, and Indonesia, with more than 150 million.

1984

world news

17 April
A policewoman is killed by rifle shots from the Libyan Embassy in London.

22 April
French researchers discover the human immunodeficiency virus, HIV, responsible for AIDS.

8 May
The Soviet Union announces a boycott of the Olympic Games in Los Angeles.

5 June
Indian troops storm the Golden Temple in Amritsar, the Sikhs' holiest shrine, to flush out Sikh separatists. Up to 1,000 Sikhs and 200 Indian soldiers die.

18 July
In San Ysidro, California, a man kills 21 in a McDonald's restaurant.

25 July
Cosmonaut Svetlana Savitskaya is the first woman to walk in space.

11 August
US athlete Carl Lewis collects four Olympic golds, for the 100m, 200m, long jump and 4x100m relay.

Jury fined and sacked

8 May | Ipoh

Legal history was created when all seven members of a murder retrial jury were fined $100 each by the High Court for contempt after talking with prosecution witnesses. Mr Justice Ajaib Singh also fined a prosecution witness $500 for contempt of court for passing certain 'highly prejudicial' remarks to the jurors.

He ordered a second re-trial for driver I. Arumugam, 32, who was charged with the murder of two constables in Sungai Buloh New Village, Sungai Siput, in 1981.

'Sunken treasure is ours'

9 May | Kuala Lumpur

Sunken treasure found off the Mersing coast near Babi Tengah Island belonged to Malaysia as it was found in Malaysian waters, said Dato' Seri Dr Mahathir Mohamad. The Government would get in touch with the Singapore authorities to salvage the treasure, said to comprise silver and tin ingots, ivory, gold and other jewellery.

He was commenting on a report that the Dutch Government had claimed that the treasure was on board a Dutch merchant ship that sank in 1727 and was interested in salvaging it.

Disruptive elements

25 May | Kuala Lumpur

Dato' Seri Dr Mahathir Mohamad warned that certain groups were disrupting the administration by giving extremist interpretations to the efforts to introduce Islamic values in Government. He said these groups made out Islam to be so intolerant that Muslim employees were not allowed to befriend non-Muslims or to visit them during festivals.

Singing mayor outshines stars at charity show

13 May | Kuala Lumpur

An auction of items belonging to Hollywood stars at a Celebrity Tennis Gala dinner here raised $450,000. But the true star was Kuala Lumpur Datuk Bandar Datuk Elyas Omar.

Celebrities and VIPs paid $100,000 to hear him sing *Always On My Mind*. The money was for five charities.

Battle in MCA

6 May | Kuala Lumpur

The MCA was divided into two camps over the question of how to resolve the issue of phantom members in the party, with each side putting on shows of strength and claiming majority support. Acting president Datuk Dr Neo Yee Pan and his arch-rival Tan Koon Swan were to meet Prime Minister and Barisan Nasional chairman Dato' Seri Dr Mahathir Mohamad separately to brief him on the outcome of their meetings. Datuk Dr Neo and other leaders were at Wisma MCA for an emotional 35th anniversary party attended by 3,000 newly-elected general assembly delegates and rank-and-file members.

At the same time, at the KL Hilton, 1,616 delegates of the last general assembly held an EGM not sanctioned by the party leadership. Resolutions passed by secret ballot called for 14 party members, including Mr Tan, Datuk Dr Ling Liong Sik and Datuk Lee Kim Sai, expelled in March, to be reinstated and an ad-hoc committee to be set up to investigate the phantom members issue. Datuk Dr Neo said the EGM was illegal and the party would not implement the resolutions (*see 25 November 1985*).

Acting Air Force chief Datuk Mohamed Ngah Said takes the salute at a passing-out parade of members of the women's wing of the RMAF. In all, 2,000 men and women, including 14 officers, paraded on 1 May after finishing their training.

Sentenced to death

17 May | Hong Kong

Mak Foon Than, 33, was sentenced to death for the murder of BMF assistant general manager Jalil Ibrahim here on 18 July 1983. Mak strangled Jalil in the Regent Hotel, Kowloon.

Musa stays in post

25 May | Kuala Lumpur

Umno voted for continuity by retaining Datuk Musa Hitam as deputy president, and for a combination of experience and youth by choosing Dato' Seri Wan Mokhtar Ahmad, Datuk Abdullah Ahmad Badawi and Encik Ghafar Baba as vice-presidents. Party president Dato' Seri Dr Mahathir Mohamad said the result was a clear-cut decision with no ambiguity but declined to answer questions on Tengku Razaleigh Hamzah's Cabinet position and his post as treasurer of the party.

Datuk Musa won 744 votes to Tengku Razaleigh's 501. Datuk Harun Idris came third with only 34. Tengku Razaleigh said he accepted the decision of the delegates and would continue to serve the party.

Files destroyed in courtroom blaze

6 June | Seremban

Thousands of files were destroyed in a fire that swept through the courtroom, registry and library of the High Court here. It did not affect the judges' chambers, a strongroom containing exhibits and other parts of the building. Two empty petrol cans were found in the registry.

Senior assistant registrar Toh Ching Chong said it would be an immense task to reconstruct the destroyed files, some of which were for pending or partly heard cases. Police said 'investigations on all possible angles' were under way.

Proton Saga is the name

7 June | Kuala Lumpur

The made-in-Malaysia car would be called the Proton Saga, said Tan Sri Jamil bin Mohamed Jan. The chairman of Perusahaan Otomobil Nasional Sdn Bhd (Proton) said the winning entry came from Staff Sergeant Ismail Jaafar of Penang who would receive a Proton Saga 1300.

The contest for the name attracted about 103,000 entries.

The name was picked because 'it was easy to pronounce and had a good meaning'. The saga seed, *Adenanthera pavonina*, or coral tree, was used in the old days by goldsmiths as a measure and signified power, strength and durability.

In fact, saga is derived from the Arabic word for goldsmith. In English, saga means a tale of heroic deeds, while in Japanese it means social custom.

A total of 5,500 Sagas were expected to be made in 1985 (*see 10 July 1985*).

Clan associations urged to venture into business

15 June | Kuching

Deputy Chief Minister of Sarawak Tan Sri Datuk Sim Kheng Hong urged Chinese clan associations to venture into commerce and industry. He was speaking at the opening of the $10m five-storey Wisma Hopoh in Jawa Road. He said these associations should pool resources and modernise business practices for their own benefits and as a contribution to the modernisation of the national economy.

Nuclear waste protest

5 June Bangi

The Government would go ahead with the construction of a controversial radioactive waste dumping ground in Papan, said Prime Minister Dato' Seri Dr Mahathir Mohamad. Every precaution necessary had been taken and experts thought it was not dangerous provided all the rules and restrictions were observed, he said at the Tun Ismail Atomic Research Centre here.

However, he added, the Government could not guarantee the safety of the people if they went into the area, dug the soil, bathed in it or threw it over their heads. He said radioactive waste could not be dumped into the sea because 'it would be harmful and if nobody wants the dump to be situated anywhere, it would put an end to the nuclear industry in the country'.

Banner-waving protestors at the proposed waste site.

Visas for India

19 June Kuala Lumpur

All Malaysian visitors to India must have a visa, a statement from the Indian High Commission here said.

No reason was given, but the requirement was believed to be a security measure to prevent overseas Sikhs going to support extremists in Punjab.

New face in Finance Ministry

14 July Kuala Lumpur

In a surprise move, Prime Minister Dato' Seri Dr Mahathir Mohamad appointed millionaire businessman Daim Zainuddin, 45, to his new Cabinet as Finance Minister and Umno treasurer.

Former Finance Minister Tengku Razaleigh Hamzah was moved to the Trade and Industry Minstry, lost the party treasurer post and was replaced as Kelantan Umno chief.

Tengku Razaleigh no longer held any national or State party post.

Dr Mahathir dismissed allegations that Tengku Razaleigh was being punished for having challenged Deputy Prime Minister Datuk Musa Hitam for the Umno deputy presidency.

He said Cabinet Ministers were being moved around to gather experience in different fields.

6,000 get stolen exam papers

21 June Kuala Lumpur

A security breach led to the theft of eight of the 78 examination papers for the Sijil Tinggi Persekolahan Malaysia (STPM) in 1983. This resulted in about 6,000 candidates obtaining questions and model answers.

Malaysian Examinations Council chairman Royal Prof Ungku Aziz said the council 'will try to do its best to prevent any more penetration of security'. An official report on the affair said cartridge tapes from electric typewriters were stolen from the council storeroom and the questions were read off the tape.

PLO chairman says thanks

24 July Kuala Lumpur

Palestine Liberation Organisation chairman Yasser Arafat told a mass rally at Stadium Negara that Palestinians would win their struggle against Zionist aggression with the support of their 'Muslim brothers'. He also thanked Malaysians for their support. Arafat was on a three-day official visit.

Prime Minister Dato' Seri Dr Mahathir Mohamad offered Palestinian students places for training in Malaysian medical faculties and said Malaysia would also consider giving Palestinian students scholarships and places in its universities.

'Power struggle' at City Hall office

24 June Kuala Lumpur

Several City Hall officers locked themselves in their office in Jalan San Peng when a group of residents arrived to protest at the removal of extension wires in their homes.

The residents gathered outside the office after a City Hall worker removed illegal extensions in some flats. They claimed they needed the extensions as each flat was only allotted two power points. City Hall enforcement director Roslin Haji Hassan said the extensions were removed because they often caused electrical overloading.

'No' to Bukit China plan

7 August Malacca

Ninety Chinese guilds, clubs and associations disagreed with the State Government's proposal to develop Bukit China for commerce and housing, the trustees of the hill said today.

Earlier, acting MCA president Datuk Dr Neo Yee Pan said the spirit of the 1949 Ordinance incorporating the Cheng Hoon Teng temple which owned Bukit China should be maintained.

He said the land was given as a gift to the temple and the trustees should not give it up for the sake of commerce.

33 massacred in boat attack by pirates

15 August Kota Kinabalu

Three pirates murdered 33 people, including seven women and three children, when they attacked a boat on its way from Semporna in Sabah to Sintangkal in the southern Philippines.

They also kidnapped three teenaged girls before fleeing in a boat, leaving another 15 women and children adrift in the vessel. All 23 men, including the boat's skipper, were shot.

Sabah State Commissioner of Police Haji Yahaya Yeop Ishak said the survivors of the cold-blooded murder were spotted drifting in the rough seas off Tungku in Tawau and rescued by Police Field Force personnel. Two days later, Sabah police said the three pirates, all of them aged between 20 and 25, were from the 10-strong Bahang Abijisu group.

World's largest cave to open to public

The awesome Sarawak Chamber in the Gunung Mulu National Park, Sarawak.

14 June Kuala Lumpur

The world's largest cave, at Sarawak's Gunung Mulu National Park, was likely to be opened to visitors once accommodation and travel facilities to the park were developed. The cave chamber is believed to have a volume of between 10 and 13 million cubic metres, big enough for 40 jumbo jets with room to spare. The National Park covers 52,865 hectares of primary rainforest.

Licences needed to operate printing presses

23 August Kuala Lumpur

The Printing Presses and Publications Act, 1984, passed in March to make licensing of certain printing presses mandatory, would be enforced from 1 September, said Deputy Home Minister Radzi Sheikh Ahmad.

He urged all owners of printing presses which could print 1,000 or more copies in an hour to apply for licences immediately.

A licence would cost $500 a year, the Deputy Minister said.

Tin dredge capsizes

8 August Puchong

At least seven people were feared drowned after a tin dredge capsized in a mining pool at 21km Jalan Klang this evening. Of the 21 other workers who managed to swim to safety, three were in hospital and others were treated for bruises. Rescue workers and navy divers remained at the scene, but search efforts were likely to be called off due to poor night visibility.

Employees of Sungai Klang Dredging Sdn Bhd said a leaking pontoon, one of 12 supporting the dredge, was believed to be the cause of the tragedy. The Mines Department and the Factories and Machinery Department would jointly investigate, said Primary Industries Minister Datuk Paul Leong, who added that the findings could help prevent similar accidents.

1984

15 September
A research team at the University of Leicester finds that DNA sequencing is specific to individuals.

20 September
A Hezbollah car bomb kills 22 at the US Embassy in Beirut.

12 October
An IRA bomb kills five at a hotel during the Conservative Party conference.

16 October
Desmond Tutu, Anglican Archbishop of Cape Town, is awarded the Nobel Peace Prize.

31 October
Indian PM Indira Gandhi is assassinated by Sikh bodyguards. Anti-Sikh riots leave 1,000 dead.

6 November
Ronald Reagan is re-elected US President.

3 December
A toxic gas leak at a Union Carbide pesticide plant in Bhopal, India, kills more than 2,000 villagers, many in their sleep. Another 5,000 die later.

19 December
Britain agrees to return Hong Kong to China in 1997.

Petronas to the rescue

15 September   **Kuala Lumpur**

Finance Minister Daim Zainuddin eased concerns following the Bumiputra Malaysia Finance loans scandal over how the problem of bad debts would affect Permodalan Nasional Bhd which owned more than 80 per cent of the shares of Bank Bumiputra.

The Minister announced a rescue package that freed PNB of the burden at little cost to it. Petronas would buy out the PNB stake for $933 million. The package ensured that 1.5 million unit-trust holders in the PNB's Amanah Saham Malaysia were protected and that confidence in the trust was maintained. Bank Bumiputra executive chairman Dr Nawawi Mat Awin said this had ended doubts about the bank's strength and stability (*see 18 January 1985*).

> *'The Malays realise that without the support of the non-Malays, we could never have overcome the barriers of divide-and-rule and won independence. For this reason, they have accepted each other as fellow citizens and are living at peace with one another.'*
>
> Tunku Abdul Rahman
> *The Star*, 15 October 1984.

Government pledges to break up the dancing

7 September   **Kuala Lumpur**

The Government and the police were out to cool the breakdance fever that had hit the country. Culture, Youth and Sports Minister Datuk Dr Sulaiman Daud said he would consider a proposal that the dance sensation should be banned while police warned they would act

against breakdance groups creating a public nuisance. The statement prompted about 30 dancers to stage a noisy protest-cum-breakdance session at the Esplanade skating rink in Penang. A spokesman for the Ipoh YMCA said breakdancing was no more dangerous than gymnastics. 'If youngsters can indulge in those sports I don't see why they shouldn't do breakdancing. There is nothing immoral about the dance,' he said.

In Alor Star, two youths, one a student, were fined $70 each for disorderly behaviour, the first breakdancers to be charged in the country. Two more students and another youth were fined for various offences committed during a breakdance session in the town on the night of 6 September.

8th King installed

15 November   **Kuala Lumpur**

The Sultan of Johor, Sultan Iskandar ibni Al-marhum Sultan Ismail, took the oath as the eighth Yang di-Pertuan Agong at Istana Negara. After the King had read the royal oath, there were shouts of 'Daulat Tuanku' (Long live the King).

Pioneer palm oil refinery faces bankruptcy

17 August   **Kuala Lumpur**

Socoil Corporation Sdn Bhd, one of the country's largest and most established palm oil refineries, was placed under receivership, a victim of the slump in crude palm oil prices following a recent crisis in the Kuala Lumpur Commodities Exchange. According to industry sources, Socoil bought 40,000 to 50,000 tonnes of crude palm oil at a fairly high price with the expectation of it going up even higher. CPO prices fell instead to around the current $950 level. It was believed that Socoil owed its creditors $28 million.

Clash at squatter village

10 October   **Ipoh**

About 500 squatters and their supporters clashed with the police in an exchange of rocks, bottles and tear gas as a Land Office enforcement unit arrived to demolish illegal homes in Kampung Bercham here. Earlier, the Land Office had told the inhabitants of 64 squatter homes to move out by 8 October as the squatter houses were to be demolished to make way for the construction of 9,000 low-cost flats.

Ten people, including a policeman and DAP publicity secretary Kok Weng Kok, were injured and 12 people arrested, including two children and SDP secretary-general Fan Yew Teng.

Nine squatters were charged in the magistrate's court with obstructing the police and the Ipoh assistant district officer in the performance of their duties.

On 1 October, the Land Office had bulldozed four houses before they were stopped by a human barricade of 100 people led by Kepayang State Assemblyman Lau Dak Kee. Some of the squatters, mainly labourers, had lived there for 20 years.

A protestor is marched off by police.

Close fight for Gerakan posts

29 September   **Kuala Lumpur**

The keenly contested election for top Gerakan posts was a heart-stopper but two incumbents—party president Datuk Dr Lim Keng Yaik and his deputy Datuk Paul Leong—managed to retain their posts. Datuk Leong only managed to secure his seat after three counts. The close margin drew gasps from the crowd attending the 13th national delegates' conference.

Bank Negara to prop up ringgit

5 October   **Kuala Lumpur**

The central bank came to the rescue of the ringgit today to prevent possible chaos in the local financial market. It stepped in after rumours circulated in the market that the ringgit would be devalued, leading to a strong demand for the US dollar. However, Bank Negara's heavy selling of the greenback restored the ringgit's stability. 'It is our policy to maintain orderly conditions in the market,' a Bank Negara official said.

Four workers killed in Penang Bridge tragedy

22 October   **Butterworth**

A huge crossbeam of the Penang Bridge collapsed, killing four workers. Four more were injured and one was still missing. Three of the four dead were from South Korea, as was the missing worker.

They plunged into the sea along with 320 tonnes of concrete and steel in the worst mishap since work began in 1979. At least 10 others died in other accidents.

King calls off debate

8 November   **Kuala Lumpur**

A scheduled Umno–Pas debate was cancelled by the King with the concurrence of the Rulers, said the Keeper of the Rulers' Seal, Datuk Ahmad Zainal Abidin Yusof.

He said that under the Constitution the Rulers, as religious heads of States, had been vested with all powers on Islamic matters, so no one other than they had the right to make a decision on the kafir–mengkafir issue, in which some Pas officials had branded as kafir, or infidel, Muslims who did not support the party.

1985

Highs and Lows. The Highs: Malaysia entered the ranks of car-manufacturing nations with the debut of the Proton Saga; the 65-storey Komtar building in Penang was 'capped'; Parliament celebrated its 25th anniversary; crowds walked over the yet-to-be-opened Penang Bridge; University Hospital created medical history when surgeons conducted open-heart surgery on a month-old baby; athlete B. Rajkumar won gold medal in the Asian Games; and Sidek brothers Razif and Jalani won the only SEA Games badminton gold. The Lows: an uprising in Baling left four policemen and 14 criminals dead in one of the darkest chapters in Malaysian history; and a 33-year-old intravenous drug user was confirmed as the first known AIDS carrier in the country.

JANUARY
The Supreme Court is inaugurated to replace the Federal Court.

MARCH
Malaysia celebrates 25 years of the Parliament's establishment in 1959.

MAY
Political drama and violence in Sabah follows the victory of Joseph Pairin Kitingan's Parti Bersatu Sabah (PBS) in the State election.

NOVEMBER
Writer A. Samad Said receives the National Literary Award (Anugerah Sastera Negara).

September: Prime Minister Dr Mahathir and his wife Dr Siti Hasmah pose with the Proton Saga on the Penang Bridge.

Malaysia Facts		
15.9 million	Population	
$79.9 billion	Gross Domestic Product	
$4,652	Gross National Income (per capita)	
31.5	Crude Birth Rate (per 1,000 persons)	
16.4	Infant Mortality (per 1,000 live births)	
67.8 / 72.5	Life Expectancy (male / female)	
51.6	Consumer Price Index (base 2010=100)	

'The Saga will add one more dimension to our own saga of development like the little red seed that grows into a great tree.'

The New Straits Times, 'No compromise on quality', 9 July 1985.

1985

15 April
South Africa ends a ban on interracial marriages.

13 May
To end a stand-off with the radical group MOVE in Philadelphia, police drop from a helicopter a bomb that kills 11, including five children, and burns out 61 homes.

29 May
Fans riot during the European Cup final between Liverpool and Juventus at Heysel Stadium, Belgium. Thirty-eight are killed when a wall collapses.

31 May
Eighty-eight die as 41 tornadoes hit the US and Canada in eight hours.

10 June
Israel pulls out of Lebanon after 1,099 days of occupation.

10 June
Xintan on the Yangtze is obliterated as a landslide sends a 128ft surge down the river.

23 June
All 329 on board an Air India 747 die when a bomb brings the plane down over the Atlantic. Sikh militants are responsible. A bomb meant for another Air India flight goes off in Narita Airport, Japan.

Lim Kok Wing's *Guli Guli* imagines the public's reaction to the emergence of the country's first batch of firewomen.

4 January ▶ Ten firewomen graduated from the Fire Services Department training programme, creating the first batch of firewomen.

'Capping' of Komtar

1 January Penang

The Kompleks Tun Abdul Razak (Komtar) got the final touches from Yang di-Pertua Negeri Tun Datuk Dr Awang Hassan in the official 'capping' ceremony. This marked the completion of the structural work for the 65-storey building. Construction began in 1974. Komtar proudly stands at 232m, the largest urban renewal project undertaken by the Penang State Government.

Komtar towers over other buildings in the heart of George Town, Penang.

Cops and robbers: one killed

8 January Kuala Lumpur

Crime did not pay for three robbers when a witness raised the alarm as he saw them enter a shop in Jalan Sungai Besi. Within minutes, police arrived and a shootout ensued in which one gunman was killed and the other two escaped. The gunman and his accomplices had entered the shop and had extorted $50,000 from the shopowner when the police surprised them. In the gun battle, PC Nordin bin Ujud had a close brush with death when two shots went through his helmet. However, he escaped injury. Police recovered a .38 Smith and Wesson revolver from the dead robber Lee Nam Fan.

First Lumut naval chart published

11 January Kuala Lumpur

Malaysia has produced its own navigational chart. The Hydrographic Directorate of the Royal Malaysian Navy released the Lumut Naval Chart, which was recognised by the International Hydrographic Organisation (IHO), of which Malaysia had been a member since 1975. The chart was described as very detailed and useful.

Supreme Court reigns supreme

8 January Kuala Lumpur

The Supreme Court was inaugurated today, ending the jurisdiction of Britain's Privy Council which was previously the final court of appeal. All 10 Supreme Court judges, the Chief Justice of Malaya Tan Sri Abdul Hamid Omar and the Chief Justice of Borneo Tan Sri Lee Hun Hoe attended the simple ceremony.

The Supreme Court replaced the former Federal Court. The Lord President Tan Sri Mohd Salleh Abas said the setting up of the Supreme Court as the final court of appeal meant 'our responsibilities become more grave'.

Lorrain Osman sued for $27 million

18 January Kuala Lumpur

The High Court granted Bank Bumiputra and Bumiputra Malaysia Finance (BMF) injunctions to freeze the assets of former BMF chairman Lorrain Esme Osman.

The bank and BMF also filed a writ for the return of $27 million, alleged to be secret profits made by Lorrain while he was managing them. Lorrain, chairman from 1978 to 1983, allegedly approved loans of US$770 million to the Carrian Group of companies in 'questionable circumstances' between January and December 1983.

Super shopping

20 February Kuala Lumpur

Supermarkets were making rapid progress in Malaysia because they provided 'convenience for everybody, especially the working group', said Cold Storage retail division general manager John Pinnick.

Dora leads the way as tribe's first doctor

4 February Kuala Lumpur

As a child growing up in a remote longhouse, Dora Ubang Taja hardly ever saw a doctor but she admired the nurses she saw coming to the help of tribespeople. 'For a long time I wanted to be a nurse', she said.

But she went one better, to become the first of the Sarawak Kenyah tribe to qualify as a doctor. Dr Dora, the third of 11 children in a planter-hunter family, graduated from the University of Malaya and went to work at the obstetrics and gynaecology department of Kuching General Hospital.

The first thing she did as a medical student in Kuala Lumpur, she recalled, was to have her traditional long ear-lobes, lengthened by wearing heavy earrings as a child, cut off. The old custom, she said, was 'a way of telling the world that we are still Kenyah. But today this seems superfluous. You are who you are and outward appearances are just that, appearances, nothing more.'

Daim Zainuddin is tops in business

1 January Kuala Lumpur

Daim Zainuddin has worn many hats. In 1985 he was a lawyer-turned-business tycoon and Malaysia's Finance Minister—and was named Man of the Year by top business magazine *Malaysian Business*.

When asked what philosophical approach he adopted in juggling many responsibilities, Daim replied: 'In business, keep things pure and simple, attend tasks urgently, bear no waste. I think that is equally applicable to the task of Government and administration.'

Skyhawk squadron

23 February Kuantan

Prime Minister and Defence Minister Dato' Seri Dr Mahathir Mohamad officially received 10 A-4 Skyhawk fighter jets from the Grumman Aircraft Corporation on behalf of the Royal Malaysian Air Force.

In the same ceremony, he launched the Sixth A-4 squadron. The ceremony marked the start of the Skyhawk squadron, replacing the RMAF 10th Squadron, a helicopter unit which completed its service here in 1984. The helicopter unit was to be redeployed to Kuala Lumpur.

The deal was concluded under the auspices of the Government's $320-million expenditure plan to buy 40 aircraft, all of which were to be completely refurbished and overhauled by Grumman Corporation.

'Ninja' robs bank

4 May Kuala Lumpur

Armed with a sickle, a robber dressed as a 'ninja' slipped into the Chase Manhattan Bank and managed to grab $110,000 seven minutes before the bank opened for business. Reports said that the 'ninja' was believed to have been hiding in the ceiling above the banking hall.

Dr Mahathir on BBC

13 May Kuala Lumpur

Dato' Seri Dr Mahathir Mohamad was a guest on a 45-minute BBC phone-in programme, *It's Your World*. He answered questions from listeners from around the world on topics ranging from the New Economic Policy to developments in Asia, Malaysian–British ties and the Government's stand on Internal Security Act detainees.

Parliament celebrates 25th anniversary

30 March Kuala Lumpur

Prime Minister Dato' Seri Dr Mahathir Mohamad launched a celebration marking the 25th anniversary of the setting up of Parliament in 1959. Newspapers recalled the times when MPs paved the way towards creating efficient legislation for the country. Special reports documented Parliament's achievements. Parliament started with the

Prime Minister Dato' Seri Dr Mahathir Mohamad giving a speech commemorating Parliament's 25th anniversary.

setting up of the Federal Council in 1909 with a membership that gradually expanded over the years. The council was dissolved in June 1959 when the general election was held. Parliament's official opening was at Dewan Tunku Abdul Rahman but the first session was conducted at a Ministry building in Jalan Maxwell (now Jalan Tun Ismail). In 1960, an area in Lake Gardens was set aside for a permanent building which was completed in 1963.

Bank Negara flushes millions into economy

30 March Kuala Lumpur

Bank Negara reduced the statutory reserve requirements for commercial banks to four per cent, starting from April, flushing $440 million into the economy to increase its growth. In its annual report for 1984, Bank Negara revised reserve requirements for merchant banks up to 2.5 per cent. The report also revealed that in 1984, Malaysia had the largest merchandise surplus since 1979. Therefore, and due also to reduced Government expenditure, the country could borrow less in 1984. Exports for 1985 were not expected to be good because the largest industrial economies seemed to be slowing down. Petroleum was the leading single export item ($8.1 billion), comprising 23 per cent of gross exports ($38.1 billion) while palm oil came in second ($4.5 billion), forming 11.9 per cent of gross exports. Manufactures accounted for 31.3 per cent of exports ($11.9 billion). Malaysia's main export markets were Japan (22.6 per cent of exports), Singapore (20.8 per cent), the United States (13.7 per cent) and South Korea (5.1 per cent).

Pairin's PBS defeats Berjaya

21 April Kota Kinabalu

Parti Bersatu Sabah (PBS), led by Datuk Joseph Pairin Kitingan, swept into power, ousting Parti Berjaya which had ruled Sabah for the previous nine years. Pairin formed the party in March after he resigned from Berjaya. PBS defeated all members of the Berjaya Cabinet, including Chief Minister Datuk Harris Salleh who was beaten in the Tenom constituency by a political unknown, Encik Kadoh Agundong of PBS.

A tale of two Chief Ministers

22 April Kota Kinabalu

Datuk Joseph Pairin Kitingan, 44, was sworn in at 8.20pm as the new Chief Minister of Sabah by Yang Dipertua Negeri Tun Haji Mohd Adnan Robert.

Earlier in the day, a state of confusion arose when Harris and Usno's Tun Datu Mustapha met Tun Haji Adnan at 5am to ask the latter to swear in Mustapha as the new CM. The appointment was withdrawn 15 hours later.

On 27 May, Mustapha filed a writ to nullify Pairin's appointment, claiming that the PBS government was unconstitutional. In his widely publicised statement of defence submitted to the court in June, Head of State Tun Haji Mohd Adnan Robert said he had 'faked' Tun Mustapha's swearing-in ceremony as Chief Minister in order to make a group of Usno and Berjaya leaders leave the Istana. He explained that the leaders had made him fear for his safety and that of his family (see *16 April 1986*).

Datuk Joseph Pairin Kitingan.

Tun Datu Mustapha Datu Harun.

Bomb blast in KK

25 May Kota Kinabalu

A bomb blast rocked the Segama shopping complex injuring Puan Chiam Keng Mee, the wife of the proprietor of one of the shops in the area. There could have been more injuries or even deaths had it not been raining heavily which caused few people to be in the vicinity.

The bomb, which was planted at the back of the Mow Tang Goldsmith Shop, went off at about 2.30pm. It shattered the windscreen of a nearby car, badly damaged a motorcycle and blew a hole in the lower corner of the gate of the goldsmith's shop. The following day, a bomb hoax at the Kojasa supermarket caused panic.

This was the second time that the State capital was rocked by a bomb blast soon after an election. The first time was in 1976 when two bombs exploded at two petrol stations on the same day (see *12–22 March 1986*).

1985

world news

10 July
A Greenpeace boat, *Rainbow Warrior*, protesting at French nuclear tests in the Pacific, is sunk in Auckland Harbour by French agents. A Dutch photographer is killed.

13 July
Live Aid concerts in London, Philadelphia, Sydney and Moscow raise nearly US$100 million for famine relief in Ethiopia.

1 August
The French Government begins testing all donated blood for AIDS after some 1,300 haemophiliacs, mostly children, are infected.

12 August
A JAL 747 on a domestic flight crashes into a mountain, killing 520 dead, the world's worst single-plane accident.

17 August
Iraqi jets armed with Exocet missiles attack Iran's Kharg Island oil terminal.

19 September
An 8.1-magnitude earthquake hits Mexico City. More than 9,000 are killed.

1 October
Israeli jets target PLO headquarters near Tunis, killing 68.

PM goes on jumbo ride

2 May Kuala Lumpur

Prime Minister Dato' Seri Dr Mahathir Mohamad went on a jumbo ride at the Selangor Club padang and caused a scare when the giant hot air balloon disappeared out of sight. The 'flying jumbo' was commissioned by *Forbes* magazine to commemorate its motorcycle friendship tour of Malaysia, Singapore, Thailand and Brunei. Piloted by the magazine founder, Malcolm Forbes, the balloon finally landed in the vicinity of the Lake Gardens, 20 minutes later. Traffic came to a halt as security officers rushed to the scene. In-flight commentary was provided by Dr Mahathir who pointed out to Forbes the major landmarks in Kuala Lumpur such as the Parliament building.

The giant Forbes elephant balloon carries Dr Mahathir away.

Nationwide alert on cattle disease

10 June Kuala Lumpur

Since the discovery of foot-and-mouth disease in cattle in Kelantan over the past six months, the Government stepped up efforts to contain the disease before Hari Raya Puasa on 20 June. This was the fifth outbreak of the disease since 1973.

The Veterinary Services Department sought the help of police, immigration, Customs and anti-smuggling units in border areas to curb cattle smuggling throughout the country.

All movements of cattle and the transportation of beef from Kelantan were prohibited. Additionally, permits for the entry of cattle from Thailand were temporarily frozen.

PWTC ready for business and events

22 June Kuala Lumpur

It was announced that the first function to be held at the new Putra World Trade Centre would be the Umno general assembly in September.

Peninsular power fails

30 June Kuala Lumpur

An accidental tripping of electricity transmission lines caused power failures throughout Peninsular Malaysia. The failure also reduced water supply to a trickle in many parts of the country as there was no power to work the pumps. The National Electricity Board restored supply to most parts by nightfall.

Malaysians cope with life in the dark.

Nanas Johor makes debut

5 July Pontian

Nanas Johor, a hybrid pineapple suitable for canning, has made its debut. It started as a Mardi cultivation project more than 10 years before. The project owed its success partly to the three-year participation on a trial basis of pineapple smallholders who did not mind investing time at the institute's research station in Pontian Kecil.

Hitting the right note

In Lahat, Ipoh, a piano manufacturing-cum-assembly factory has made an impression on the music industry overseas. The owner of the Musical Products Sdn Bhd factory, T.W. Hoe, said the secret of his success originated from his grandfather who ran a piano factory in China. Hoe developed the expertise after visiting piano manufacturers in Taiwan, West Germany and Britain.

Air show horror

15 July Kuantan

Three thousand spectators watched in horror as two Royal Malaysian Air Force pilots plunged to their deaths in their twin-seater jet plane during an air show in conjunction with the 27th anniversary of the RMAF. The plane, an advanced trainer, crashed into a rubber-holding only a kilometre from the RMAF base.

Proton Saga makes its debut

10 July Shah Alam

Malaysia joined the ranks of the world's car manufacturers when its own car, the Proton Saga, rolled off the assembly line in Shah Alam. The automobile project was a joint venture between Proton and Mitsubishi Motor Corporation of Japan. Proton was a subsidiary of Heavy Industries Corporation of Malaysia (Hicom). Some 20,000 components were required in the manufacture of the car; the local content was 36 per cent. The first model was named Proton Saga after a national car-naming contest. Two versions, with different engine sizes, cost $17,575 and $19,005, respectively.

Malaysia's first car—the Proton Saga—is a symbol of historic achievement.

UH's youngest open-heart surgery patient

22 July Kuala Lumpur

University Hospital successfully operated on a month-old baby, creating medical history. A team headed by Dr Razalli Hashim operated on Tan Kwee Tjong, who had two holes in the heart and was suffering from ventricular septal and atrial septal defects.

In the three-hour operation, the team used the 'profound hypothermia and circulatory arrest' technique, which involves bringing down body temperature to 18 degrees Celsius and cutting off blood supply to the heart.

TV dinners
Malaysian style

The Malaysian Agricultural Research and Development Institute (Mardi), has developed the potential for local foods to be processed as TV dinners or freeze-dried products.

According to Mardi's food technology division, the process of lowering temperature and pressure has enabled Mardi to develop 27 food items such as nasi lemak, mee rebus, laksa assam, kuah pecal, kuah satay and fried kuay teow.

MAS and BA sign accord

1 August Kuala Lumpur

Malaysia and Britain agreed to a weekly passenger quota of 1,550 seats on the five MAS flights from Kuala Lumpur to London starting in July 1986. British Airways would introduce a fifth flight on the route from the same date. The agreement, which was said to be of benefit to both countries, was reached after two days of negotiation.

Islamic insurance

2 August Kuala Lumpur

Prime Minister Dato' Seri Dr Mahathir Mohamad launched the country's first Islamic insurance company, Syarikat Takaful Malaysia Sdn Bhd, as part of Government efforts to encourage Islamic businesses. The firm was one of only 10 in the world based on Islamic concepts.

Amphibious planes for the RMAF

17 August Kuala Lumpur

The Royal Malaysian Air Force has bought two SU-16B Albatross amphibious transports from the US Grumman Corporation costing US$4 million. The introduction of the amphibious aircraft was said to add more dimension to the operational capability of the RMAF. Such aircraft would be used for long-range communication and search-and-rescue operations.

Crowds on Penang Bridge before its opening

9 September Penang

Malaysians took their only chance to take a walk on the new Penang Bridge before it was officially opened. The non-motorists' day on the bridge was special because once it opened, people would never again be able to cross on foot. The hot sun did not deter the crowds appreciating the 13.5km bridge's monumental impact.

Two events in one historic occasion

2 August Penang

Dato' Seri Dr Mahathir Mohamad drove a Proton Saga across the new bridge from Penang to the mainland. It was the first trip for the national car on a highway in public view and the first ceremonial use of the bridge.

Asean news centre in KL

2 September Kuala Lumpur

The Asean News Exchange (Anex) centre was transferred from Philippines Communications Incorporated (Philcom) in Manila to the Malaysian National News Agency (Bernama) headquarters in Kuala Lumpur. The transfer of news items for the exchange would be routed by direct satellite circuits from Manila, Jakarta and Seoul and by submarine cable from Tokyo to Bernama's computer.

The system, costing $2.5 million, was one of the most sophisticated news agency systems in the region, able to handle three million words of news items and information from 40 destinations worldwide in a day. The switchover would provide a more efficient system for regional news exchange.

Cheaper electricity

1 September Kuala Lumpur

Electricity rates were cut for the commercial and industrial sectors. The cuts ranged from four to 15 per cent for most businesses, and from 16 to 20 per cent for hotels, depending on their monthly consumption. The new rates would cost the National Electricity Board $163 million in lost revenue but it hoped to recoup this through lower operating costs and higher electricity consumption during off-peak periods.

City Hall sued by Scorpions' organisers

13 September Kuala Lumpur

Organisers of a concert by the rock group the Scorpions filed a $1.1-million suit against City Hall for 'suffering humiliation and loss of reputation' over the cancellation of the show that was to have been held at Merdeka Stadium on 24 June.

The organisers claimed that City Hall had given its approval on 2 May and that they were told to proceed with the sale of tickets and to pay the required entertainment tax.

But in June, City Hall said the Ministry of Culture, Youth and Sports had objected to the performance and therefore withdrew the approval. After their appeal to the Ministry was rejected, the organisers filed court action against the Minister and the Government.

In late August, the High Court ruled that under the Theatres and Places of Public Amusement (Federal Territory) Act 1977, power to approve lay with the Federal Territory Minister, not the Minister of Culture, Youth and Sports. The organisers had sued the wrong Ministry.

1985

7 October
Palestinian gunmen hijack an Italian cruise ship, *Achille Lauro*, in the Mediterranean. They kill a disabled American and throw him and his wheelchair overboard.

10 October
US jets force an Egyptian plane carrying hijackers of the *Achille Lauro* to land in Italy.

13 November
A volcano buries the 23,000 inhabitants of Armero, Colombia, under 30ft of mud.

17 November
Lon Nol, 72, dies in California. He was the architect of the US-supported coup in Cambodia that deposed Prince Sihanouk in 1970. He fled the Khmer Rouge takeover in 1975.

24 November
Egyptian commandos storm an Egyptian plane hijacked to Malta, killing 58.

27 December
Palestinian gunmen open fire in the airports of Rome and Vienna, killing 15 before they are shot dead.

Pirate menace in Sabah

24 September | Kota Kinabalu

Clad in jungle-green fatigues and armed with M-16 rifles, 20 marauders opened fire as they raided a bank and the Malaysia Airlines office in Lahad Datu. Police arrived on the scene to intercept the men at the wharf as they tried to escape and engaged in a series of shootouts. One policeman and two pirates were killed. The next day, in a joint operation by Sabah police, the Police Field Force, marine police and the Royal Malaysian Navy, heavy gunfire was exchanged at sea near Pulau Mataking. Five pirates were shot dead.

Gold for track ace

27 September | Jakarta

Malaysian middle-distance track ace B. Rajkumar won the gold in the Asian Track and Field Championships in Jakarta and also broke the national 800m record of 1:47:59 with a time of 1:47:37.

B. Rajkumar at track practice.

Novelist wins literary award

20 November | Kuala Lumpur

A. Samad Said has been awarded the National Literary Award (Anugerah Sastera Negara), making him the fourth winner, the first being in 1981.

Kampung Memali clash

21 November | Baling

A five-hour police operation ended one of the darkest chapters in local history when an uprising here left four policemen and 14 criminals dead. Supporters of Ibrahim Mahmud, also known as Ibrahim Libya for his short educational stint in that country, armed with parangs, Molotov cocktails, bamboo spikes and poison-tipped arrows, had a head-on clash with three police teams that closed in on them at their jungle hideout. Ibrahim was among the 14 killed.

The Government banned 1,686 political meetings in six States a day after the incident, but lifted the ban in December. A ban was also imposed on all books about the Baling clash, and the Cabinet announced that a White Paper on the incident would be published.

An array of weapons, ranging from arrows to guns, seized during the incident.

Bakun Project on

30 November | Kuching

The Government had decided to implement the Bakun hydroelectric project, announced Deputy Prime Minister Datuk Musa Hitam. Speaking at the opening of Wisma SESCo at Petrajaya, he said that the administration was convinced the project was technically feasible and that electricity generated from the project would accelerate industrial development in Sarawak and nationwide. Part of the energy generated would be channelled to Sabah and to the peninsula. The long-term benefit of the project would justify the cost, he added (*see 29 June 1996*).

New MCA president

25 November | Kuala Lumpur

Businessman Tan Koon Swan, who was sacked from the MCA in March 1984 and reinstated in January 1985, won the MCA presidency at the party's general assembly with a stunning majority of 1,906 votes over rival Datuk Dr Neo Yee Pan, who obtained 809 votes. The deputy president's post went to Datuk Dr Ling Liong Sik, who beat two contenders.

At the XIII SEA Games in Bangkok

10 December

Swimming ace Nurul Huda Abdullah wins two golds in the 400m medley and 800m freestyle events.

13 December

Malaysia strikes five golds in track and field events. The *Negaraku* serenaded victories by V. Subramaniam (below, centre) in the 10km walk, S. Muthiah in the 1,500m, Nordin Jadi's 400m, Ramjit Nairu in the high jump and Hanapiah Nasir's 110m hurdles.

16 December

The Sidek brothers, Razif and Jalani, score over Indonesia's Liem Swie King and Kartono Hariatmanto to win the only SEA Games badminton gold.

First known AIDS carrier

28 December | Kuala Lumpur

A 33-year-old-man from Johor Bahru, who admitted he was an intravenous drug user, was confirmed as the first known AIDS carrier in the country. He was admitted to the Sultanah Aminah General Hospital in Johor Bahru for pulmonary tuberculosis and shingles infection.

1986

The lengthy legal battle between Tun Datu Mustapha of Usno and Datuk Joseph Pairin Kittingan of Parti Bersatu Sabah over who was the rightful Chief Minister of Sabah ended when the High Court in Kota Kinabalu ruled in favour of the latter. In Kuala Lumpur police commandos stormed the Pudu Prison and freed two medical personnel held hostage by six prisoners, ending a six-day standoff. In politics, Barisan Nasional retained its two-thirds majority in Parliament in the August general election. Earlier Musa Hitam resigned as Deputy Prime Minister and was succeeded by Ghafar Baba. Showman extraordinaire Sudirman drew a capacity crowd at an open air concert in Kuala Lumpur's Chow Kit Road.

FEBRUARY
Datuk Musa Hitam resigns as Deputy Prime Minister and UMNO deputy president.

JUNE
Tun Mohamed Suffian becomes the first Asian International Labour Organisation judge.

JULY
Australian drug traffickers Brian Chambers (right) and Kevin Barlow (centre, on crutches) hanged at Pudu Prison.

OCTOBER
The Pudu prison hostage drama ends without a single shot fired.

March: Political upheaval in Sabah.

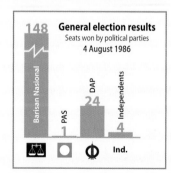

General election results
Seats won by political parties
4 August 1986

- Barisan Nasional: 148
- PAS: 1
- DAP: 24
- Independents: 4

'We should accept the judgment in the spirit of democracy and fair play.'

Datuk Joseph Pairin Kitingan, on the judgment by the High Court that he is Sabah's legitimate Chief Minister, 16 April 1986.

1986

---

world news

28 January
The space shuttle *Challenger* disintegrates 73 seconds after launch, killing all aboard.

28 February
Philippine President Ferdinand Marcos goes into exile in Hawaii after two decades of rule. His wife leaves behind 5,400 pairs of shoes. Corazon Aquino becomes the first woman President of the country.

28 February
Swedish PM Olaf Palme is shot dead as he is walking home from the cinema.

15 April
US planes bomb Tripoli, the Libyan capital, and Benghazi.

17 April
In retaliation for the US bombing of Libya, a British journalist is kidnapped in Beirut (released August 1991) and three other British hostages are killed.

24 April
Wallis Simpson, Duchess of Windsor, for whom King Edward VIII gave up a kingdom, dies at 89.

Nation emerges from 'problematic year'

1 January | Kuala Lumpur

Auditor General Tan Sri Ahmad Noordin Zakaria described 1985 as a 'problematic year for Malaysia during which the country's financial and economic strength came under increasing pressure.'

Apart from the Bumiputra Malaysia Finance scandal, the recession posed 'considerable problems in relation to our budgetary position, adversely affecting the country's balance of payments.'

Police move in on the 'hell riders'.

A rowdy New Year

1 January | Kuala Lumpur

More than 80 policemen detained nearly 130 motorcyclists at the Selangor Club padang overnight as more than 5,000 revellers gathered to usher in the New Year. The unruly crowd threatened to pull down a canvas partition to get into the club but police prevented them. When police moved in, the crowd moved on. More gathered at the Dayabumi Complex, a popular place for so-called hell-rider motorcycle racers.

Musa quits Cabinet

27 February | Kuala Lumpur

Datuk Musa Hitam resigned from his Cabinet posts and as Umno deputy president effective from mid-April. He was the first Deputy Prime Minister to resign. He would, however, continue as MP for Panti and Segamat Umno division head. Accusations that he was involved in efforts to discredit Dr Mahathir and to topple him formed the basis of his decision to resign, sources said.

Datuk Musa Hitam with Prime Minister Dato' Seri Dr Mahathir Mohamad.

He believed that statements from several party leaders about 'certain people' attempting to topple the Government and tarnish the good name of the Prime Minister referred to him, which greatly upset him; he felt that his commitment had been eroded as he was no longer trusted and so could not serve with all his heart. Under such circumstances, the motives for his actions would be called into question and he might be accused of acting out of his own political interest.

Datuk Musa, 52, entered politics in 1965 as political secretary to then Transport Minister Tun Sardon Jubir. He was expelled from Umno in 1969 and left to take a master's degree in Britain. He returned in September 1970 and three months later was elected deputy president of Umno Youth. The following year he was elected to the Supreme Council.

Tunku named 'Father of Malaysian Sports'

14 January | Kuala Lumpur

Tunku Abdul Rahman was not just Bapa Malaysia, but also Bapa Sukan, Father of Sport. During his tenure as PM, the Tunku left an indelible mark on Malaysian sports. The SAM-Benson and Hedges Gold Award for Leadership presented to the Tunku acknowledged this. Soccer, golf and horse racing were among the sports that benefited from his leadership.

Eight RMAF officers die in plane crash

5 February | Kuala Lumpur ▶ Eight Royal Malaysian Air Force officers were killed when their aircraft crashed near the Sabah–Sarawak border. The aircraft, a twin-engined Cessna 402B of a type that the RMAF had been using for 10 years, was returning to the Labuan base after checking on flood relief operations in Sandakan.

The crash was the worst in RMAF history and the fourth since July 1985. The crew had reported they were experiencing bad weather but had not sent out any distress signals. A board of inquiry was appointed to examine the possible causes of the crash.

The shattered wreckage of the Cessna.

BMF-Carrian final report delivered to MPs

9 March | Kuala Lumpur

The final report and confidential briefs on deals between Bumiputra Malaysia Finance and the Hong Kong property group Carrian which led to the BMF being saddled with $2.5 billion in unrecoverable loans were delivered to MPs. Included in the 6,600-page package were six confidential briefs that the Ahmad Noordin Committee of Inquiry originally did not recommend be made public. Three of the briefs had previously been made public by the Government; the other three dealt with various loans.

In tracing the story of BMF and Carrian, the committee was understood to have traced the source of the loans affair to a concerted plan to make money at the start of a property boom in Hong Kong, the first proposal being to buy a building and sell it off for a quick profit to the Malaysian Government in 1980. It was believed that the proposal fell through but huge sums continued to be loaned to Carrian and other companies. Sources said the committee apparently discovered that what started out to be a simple loan of $5 million in 1979 went up to about HK$4 billion ($2.5 billion) (*see 7 November 1986*).

P. Ramlee library opens

22 March | Kuala Lumpur

The former home of the late singer, film star and film director P. Ramlee in Setapak opened as the P. Ramlee Memorial Library and Museum after four months of renovation work costing about $200,000, on what would have been his 57th birthday.

More than $750,000 was raised from donations over two years to set up the library. On display were more than 3,000 items owned by the late star, including albums, cassettes, videotapes, films, photographs, newspaper clippings, books, musical instruments, awards, trophies, documents, down to his identity card and birth and death certificates, and some of his clothes. Even his old car, a Datsun 1200, was parked permanently outside.

The museum was mooted soon after P. Ramlee's death in 1973, but preparations began only after the death of his widow Saloma in 1984.

P. Ramlee's director's chair, among the exhibits at the museum in his old home.

RMN's new minehunters

28 March | Port Klang

The Royal Malaysian Navy's four new mine counter-measure vessels, KD *Mahamiru*, KD *Kinabalu*, KD *Jerai* and KD *Ledung*, berthed here after a three-year delay in delivery from the Italian shipbuilder.

The four new vessels off Port Klang.

Riot police move in as smoke from one of the many fires darkens the sky over Kota Kinabalu.

Bomb blasts rock Sabah

12–22 March Kota Kinabalu

Seven plastic explosives were set off in the town centre on 12 March, injuring four people. The explosions occurred as some 3,000 people were demonstrating against the Head of State and the State Government near the court premises. The explosions, all within a radius of about 100 metres, were heard throughout the town centre. Four people were slightly injured.

On 19 March, a 6pm-to-6am curfew was imposed following a demonstration that turned into a riot, leaving two dead, at least seven injured and damage worth more than $6 million. Sabah Police Commissioner Haji Ahmad Maulana Babjee said police had to open fire when rioters ignored orders to turn back and instead set fire to cars, vans, shophouses and godowns. A policeman was slashed on the shoulder with a parang.

In Tawau, a bomb-disposal squad detonated a bomb found outside a Parti Bersatu Sabah office. Eighteen fires were put out in Sandakan, Tawau and Kota Kinabalu but 30 three-storey shophouses were destroyed. Rioters also burnt 29 vehicles and damaged 30.

Pairin is Sabah CM, High Court rules

16 April Kota Kinabalu

The High Court here ruled that Parti Bersatu Sabah president Datuk Joseph Pairin Kitingan was the legitimate Chief Minister of Sabah.

It dismissed with costs Usno president Tun Datu Mustapha Harun's writ challenging the legitimacy of Datuk Pairin's appointment. The court also dismissed Tun Mustapha's appointment as Chief Minister on the night of 22 April 1985. It had been illegal as the Head of State had been under duress.

However, it allowed an application by Queen's Counsel Raymond Kidwell, representing Tun Mustapha, for leave to file an appeal in the Supreme Court against the decision.

PBS in power again with big majority

7 May Kota Kinabalu

Parti Bersatu Sabah swept into power again, winning with a two-thirds majority in the Sabah elections. It won 34 of the 48 seats, nine more than in the previous election in 1985.

Berjaya, which had ruled Sabah for nine years, was almost wiped out, with its sole seat won by its president Datuk Mohamad Noor Mansor. Berjaya had put up a total of 37 candidates. Usno, the other main opposition party, lost ground too, winning 12 seats compared to 16 previously.

The newly-formed Parti Cina Sabah and the Parti Murut Sabah were trounced, with several of their candidates losing their deposits.

Rehabilitated Reds released

27 April Kuala Lumpur

Forty-three former Communist terrorists who surrendered between 1981 and 1983 were released after a rehabilitation programme to help them return to society. They were all formerly members of a Communist Party of Malaya unit in central Perak.

The group, said to be the largest released in Peninsular Malaysia, comprised 23 men and 20 women.

There were still 206 armed terrorists in the jungles of Perak, Pahang and Kelantan. The total armed strength in Peninsular Malaysia and southern Thailand stood at 2,000, of whom 1,300 belonged to the Communist Party of Malaya under Chin Peng and 700 to the Communist Party of Malaysia, a breakaway faction. Of the 43 freed, two were Thais and one a Singaporean. The Thais were given permanent residence and arrangements were being made to repatriate the Singaporean.

Ghafar greeted by supporters at a Barisan election rally.

Ghafar Baba is the DPM

8 May Kuala Lumpur

Umno vice-president and Barisan Nasional secretary-general Ghafar Baba would be appointed Deputy Prime Minister and National and Rural Development Minister, Cabinet spokesman Datuk Rais Yatim said.

Prime Minister Dato' Seri Dr Mahathir Mohamad also announced a minor reshuffle involving the Education, Home and Defence Ministries.

Dr Mahathir assumed the Home Ministry portfolio. His post as Defence Minister went to Datuk Abdullah Ahmad Badawi. Encik Anwar Ibrahim became Education Minister and Datuk Seri Sanusi Junid became Agriculture Minister.

New Straits Times Annual

How Kuala Lumpur has changed.

Above: Jalan Sultan Ismail, 1972.

Left: The same area of the Golden Triangle in 1986, with more and higher highrises.

Sudirman's concert at Chow Kit

14 April Kuala Lumpur

A sea of people converged at the Chow Kit area for an open-air concert by the singer Sudirman. The crowd jammed the stretch of Jalan Tuanku Abdul Rahman from Jalan Raja Muda to Jalan Raja Alang. The 2½-hour concert was held in conjunction with the Pacific Area Travel Association conference. Sudirman made a grand entrance on a skylift. And as expected, he sang his hit song *Chow Kit Road*.

Sudirman makes his entrance, lowered to the stage on a skylift at the open-air concert.

1986

world news

26 April
One of the reactors at a nuclear power station in Chernobyl, Ukraine, explodes and burns for 10 days. Thirty-one people are killed immediately, but thousands are to die of cancer in years to come, and vast territories of Ukraine and Belarus are uninhabitable.

3 May
Tamil Tigers bomb a plane at Colombo Airport, killing 16.

25 May
At least five million people form a human chain across the US from New York City to Long Beach, California to raise funds for the fight against hunger and homelessness.

29 June
Argentina beats West Germany 3–2 in Mexico City to win the FIFA World Cup.

31 August
A cargo ship leaves Philadelphia carrying 14,000 tons of toxic waste. It is destined to sail the seas for 16 months trying to find a place to off-load its cargo.

Sweeping general election victory for Barisan

4 August | **Kuala Lumpur**

The Barisan Nasional secured more than a two-thirds majority in the seventh general election, with 148 seats in the 177-seat Dewan Rakyat. The DAP was the big winner among the opposition parties. The Pas challenge fizzled out with the party winning only one seat, its stronghold of Pengkalan Chepa in Kelantan.

Barisan supporters on the campaign trail before the party's general election victory which resulted in a majority of more than two-thirds.

The biggest majority went to Barisan's Datin Paduka Zaleha Ismail who won by 31,472 votes in Selayang against her Pas opponent Haji Talib Bakti. Three other candidates won by more than 30,000 votes, the Barisan's Lim Ann Koon in Ampang Jaya (30,721), Umno deputy president Datuk Musa Hitam (30,633) and the DAP's Lee Lam Thye (30,145).

100 angry investors ransack firm's office

15 May | **Klang**

About 100 angry investors ransacked a company operating a get-rich scheme here after they failed to meet with a director. A company worker said the crowd demanded to meet the director and rushed into the office when he did not show up. They ransacked it and carted away furniture and office equipment.

Police arrived minutes later and prevented the crowd from causing further damage. Four people were detained for questioning and the office was sealed.

This was the second incident involving investors in get-rich schemes. On 29 April, when about 100 people found they had been cheated by an investment company in Banting, they ransacked a house where one of the company's partners was believed to be living.

15 schools in Johor infiltrated by Reds

20 May | **Johor Bahru**

The outlawed Communist Party of Malaya had infiltrated 15 secondary schools in Johor and persuaded more than 100 students to join secret societies, State Secretary Datuk Rahim Ramli said.

Six of the schools were in the Johor Bahru district, three in Segamat, two each in Muar and Pontian and one each in Kota Tinggi and Batu Pahat.

Malaysia joins Games boycott

17 July | **Kuala Lumpur**

The Cabinet has decided that Malaysia would boycott the Commonwealth Games to be held in Edinburgh in protest against Britain's reluctance to impose sanctions on South Africa's apartheid regime.

Malaysia was the first Commonwealth member outside the African continent to join a boycott already announced by Tanzania, Kenya, Ghana, Nigeria and Uganda. India was said to have postponed the departure of its contingent to Edinburgh to await a decision by the Government.

Six killed and two lost in collision at sea

10 July | **Port Klang**

Six seamen were killed and two others reported missing when an oil tanker and a supertanker collided in the Straits of Malacca. Fourteen others, all from the Singapore-registered *Pantas*, were rescued by another tanker, *Soon Hill*. The collision between the *Pantas* and the supertanker *Bright Duke* occurred about 15 nautical miles off the coast near Batu Pahat.

A tugboat tackles the fire aboard the *Pantas*.

Opposition front peters out

15 July | **Kuala Lumpur**

A much-talked-about Opposition United Front to fight the Barisan Nasional in the general election became just an electoral pact among four parties: Pas, SDP, PSRM and Nasma. They would not be known as Harakah Keadilan Rakyat (People's Justice Movement) as had been agreed earlier, but would use their own party symbols in the election. The leaders of the four parties signed a joint declaration on the pact after a seven-hour meeting.

Suffian first Asian to be made ILO judge

19 June | **Kuala Lumpur**

The Former Lord President, Tun Mohd Suffian, became the first Asian to be appointed a judge of the International Labour Organisation's administrative tribunal. His appointment for a three-year term was announced by the Labour Ministry, which said the former judge was elected by the ILO conference meeting in Geneva. Tun Suffian said he would accept.

The tribunal, the final place of appeal for all disputes involving international civil servants in Europe, is made up of three judges and four deputy judges.

Australian drug traffickers hanged

7 July | **Kuala Lumpur**

Australian drug traffickers Brian Chambers and Kevin Barlow were executed at the Pudu Prison at 6am. Their bodies were taken to the General Hospital mortuary.

Barlow's body was claimed by his brother Christopher and an Australian High Commission official. Chambers, a 29-year-old building contractor from Sydney, and Barlow, 28, a welder from Perth, were sentenced to death by the Penang High Court on 1 August 1985 for trafficking 179g of heroin at the Bayan Lepas Airport, Penang, on 9 November 1983.

Chambers (in tie) and Barlow (far right) leaving the Supreme Court which turned down their death sentence appeal on 18 December 1985.

Ang to pay $2.8 million

30 August | **Kuala Lumpur**

Mohammed Abdullah Ang, the former managing director of Malaysian Overseas Investment Corporation, was ordered by the High Court to pay Perlis Plantations $2.8 million. The money was the balance of an advance the company had made to him to buy a piece of land in 1983. He was also ordered to pay costs (*see 14 August 1989*).

Rock concerts banned

9 September Kuala Lumpur

Police were instructed not to issue permits for rock concerts throughout the country as more State Governments considered banning them.

The Information Ministry was also pondering whether to ban the transmission of rock concerts over RTM and TV3. Perak and Terengganu banned rock concerts following violence during a 'Battle of the Bands' in Penang on 7 September. Selangor, Kelantan, Kedah and Johor were also considering bans.

The Musicians' Union appealed to authorities to reconsider such decisions as bans affected the livelihood of musicians.

Murder among escapees

11 September Kuala Lumpur

Three Internal Security Act detainees who had escaped killed a fourth when he wanted to surrender, and buried him in the jungle in Serendah, about 40km from here. Police exhumed the body of Tan Swee Hoo hours after they caught two of the other escapees. The third escapee gave them the slip.

Breakout by five

25 September Kajang

Five criminals escaped from Kajang Prison after sawing off the bars on the windows of their cells. One wrote a note in chalk on the floor of his cell, saying: 'Very sorry. I have suffered enough and I have to escape. I have other big cases pending in the courts. Thank you.' It was signed Free Man.

I was like you once, Dr M tells the young

16 September Kuala Lumpur

Prime Minister Dato' Seri Dr Mahathir Mohamad said the younger generation 'wanted everything overnight' and in the process some of them hurt the feelings of their fellow Malaysians.

'I understand what the younger generation is going through now because I was also like them during my younger days. But now I would advise them to exercise restraint,' he told a Malaysia Day rally at the Putra World Trade Centre.

New MAS regional building

26 October Kuching

Sarawak Chief Minister Datuk Patinggi Abdul Taib Mahmud opened the new $5.8m MAS office. MAS chairman Raja Tan Sri Mohar Raja Badiozaman said the airline would launch a large-scale campaign in Australia the following month to draw more tourists to Sarawak.

Hockey team scores first win over Pakistan

26 September Seoul ▶ For the first time Malaysia beat Pakistan, the three-times and current world hockey champions. Malaysia's 2–1 victory in a preliminary round at the Asian Games in Seoul came through goals by forward M. Surenthiran and halfback Sarjit Singh. And the result sealed Malaysia's position at the top of the table.

Celebrations follow Malaysia's win at the Asian Games.

BMF boss pleads guilty to fraud and corruption

7 November London

Datuk Hashim Shamsuddin, former director of Bumiputra Malaysia Finance, created a stir in the Bow Street magistrates' court here when he pleaded guilty to four charges of fraud and corruption involving US$139 million ($356.2 million). He agreed to go back to Hong Kong to face sentencing. He admitted to charges relating to loans made by BMF to the Carrian Group and George Tan companies between 1981 and 1982.

The charges were conspiracy to defraud Bank Bumiputra of US$97 million, conspiracy to defraud the bank of US$90 million, corruptly receiving HK$30,726,680 and corruptly receiving HK$2 million. Datuk Hashim told the court that he received only HK$8 million out of the HK$30,726,680.

Each of the charges Datuk Hashim admitted carried a maximum sentence of seven years' jail in Hong Kong. His counsel George Carman asked the court not to commit him on the remaining 39 charges he faced and the court accepted his plea (*see 27 March 1987*).

One road accident every six minutes

3 October Kuala Lumpur

There was one road accident every six minutes and 40 seconds in 1985, according to the Road Safety Council annual report. The total number was 82,059. Statistics in the report showed that most happened on Saturdays or Mondays and were at noon or in the evening rush hour.

The statistics also showed that most of those involved in serious accidents were aged between 16 and 25. Speeding and reckless driving were the main causes.

Hostage drama at Pudu Jail

23 October Kuala Lumpur

One of the hostage takers in the hands of the police.

Twelve police commandos stormed the Pudu Prison clinic and freed two medical volunteers held hostage by six prisoners, ending a six-day standoff. The 15-minute operation was accomplished without a shot being fired. The scuffle inside the clinic lasted only one minute. Director of Internal Security and Public Order Datuk Zaman Khan Rahim Khan told reporters: 'It's all over...we've got a 100 per cent success. The hostages are safe and the prisoners captured.'

Specialist Dr Radzi Jaafar and lab technologist Abdul Aziz Majid, both from Universiti Kebangsaan Malaysia, suffered minor cuts in the rescue operation. All six prisoners also received minor injuries. Prisons director-general Datuk Ibrahim Mohamed said a phone call from a prisoner asking for food set the rescue into motion. Datuk Ibrahim told him: 'If you are hungry, you should help me by giving yourself up.' The line was then cut. A short while later, the phone rang again, and the same prisoner told Datuk Ibrahim: 'This is the time to act.'

Datuk Ibrahim did in fact go into action with the commando team. He entered the clinic area with several of them, armed with rattan canes and batons, and took up positions outside the clinic entrance and waited for 10 minutes. They then rushed the clinic, bringing down a barricade of beds stacked against the door by the prisoners.

'We were lucky because we had the element of surprise. They tried to fight back but were not successful because they were caught by surprise and were weak,' Datuk Ibrahim said.

Police on watch outside the main entrance of the prison during the siege.

Malaysia makes things easier for investors

1 October New York

Malaysia relaxed its investment rules, allowing foreigners 100 per cent ownership in manufacturing concerns under certain conditions. Foreign companies would also find it easier to employ expatriates under new rules announced by Prime Minister Dato' Seri Dr Mahathir Mohamad. Companies with a foreign paid-up capital of US$2 million would be automatically allowed five expatriate posts during the first 10 years. Changes of personnel would not require fresh work permits and additional expatriate posts might be allowed.

The Prime Minister told about 200 American industrialists, businessmen, bankers and consultants after a seminar on investment opportunities that the conditions would apply to new foreign investments in industries whose products would not compete for the domestic market. Foreign investors would be allowed 100 per cent equity if their companies exported 50 per cent for cent or more of their products, sold 50 per cent or more in free trade zones or licensed manufacturing warehouses, employed 350 or more full-time Malaysian workers and adopted an employment policy reflecting the racial composition of the country.

Israeli visit: Causeway blocked in protest

29 November Johor Bahru

Three thousand people blocked the road to Singapore in a protest against the recent visit to the republic by Israeli President Chaim Herzog.

Singing and jeering at Singapore vehicles, they marched on to the Causeway after a rally, stopping about 100 metres from the border and preventing vehicles from going into the island state. The protest lasted about 10 minutes.

1986

world news

6 September
In Istanbul, two Abu Nidal terrorists kill 22 people in a synagogue during Sabbath services.

6 October
A Soviet nuclear submarine sinks east of Bermuda. A sailor sacrifices himself to shut down an overheating reactor manually.

2 November
Mike Tyson, 20, becomes the youngest heavyweight boxing champ, pounding Trevor Berbick in Las Vegas.

21 December
The number of students demonstrating for democracy in Shanghai grows to 500,000.

23 December
The Rutan Voyager, an experimental aircraft, completes the first non-stop circumnavigation of the world without refuelling after nine days and three minutes.

29 December
Former British PM Harold Macmillan, dies at 92.

Usno joins Umno

30 November Kota Kinabalu

Usno delegates voted overwhelmingly to dissolve the party and merge with Umno, with 45 of the party's 48 divisions supporting the resolution at an extraordinary general meeting here. But they demanded that stiff conditions be met first, including party president Tun Mustapha Datu Harun being made a Cabinet Minister and Umno vice-president.

Only one division, Moyog, voted against dissolution and merger. Representatives from two other divisions, Nabawan and Matonggong, were absent.

The Usno Youth and Wanita wings also agreed to the proposal.

Beauty tells why she posed for 'Playboy'

22 November Petaling Jaya

Jacinta Lee with a copy of the magazine in which she appeared topless.

Former Miss Malaysia runner-up Jacinta Lee said she posed braless for the latest Hong Kong edition of *Playboy* 'for the sake of art and personal promotion.'

'If models can pose nude for paintings what's wrong with posing the same way for the camera?' she asked on her return at Subang Airport. Jacinta, 26, said she had received several Hong Kong film offers since the publication of the photographs.

'I've accepted one and shooting is scheduled to begin on 15 December,' she said. 'However I wouldn't pose in the nude for a movie. That would require action and, moreover, I wouldn't be given control of the final product.' Five pictures of her appeared in *Playboy*, including the centrefold. She was paid $26,000 for each.

Official Secrets Bill passed

6 December Kuala Lumpur

The Government withdrew the controversial Official Secrets (Amendment) Bill 1986 and tabled a new version with several changes, including specifying who could classify and declassify a secret document. The much discussed schedule which specified the types of documents deemed to be official secrets was narrowed.

The Dewan Rakyat passed the Bill by 131–21 after a stormy debate which saw the DAP's Mr Karpal Singh and Mr Hu Sepang ordered out of the House.

Daim sells

10 December Kuala Lumpur

Finance Minister Daim Zainuddin said his family companies were selling their stakes in 17 corporations, of which 13 are listed on the KLSE, in line with the Cabinet directive for all Ministers to dispose of direct and indirect holdings in quoted companies.

Paddling his own canoe: An upturned table becomes an improvised boat in floods on the East Coast on 2 December. At least eight people died in the flooding in Terengganu and Kelantan and thousands were moved to relief centres.

Langkawi set to be tourist attraction

6 December Kuala Lumpur

Langkawi would be made a free port in 1987 to place it among the country's major tourist centres, Finance Minister Daim Zainuddin said. Most import, export and excise duties would be abolished and sales and service taxes would not be imposed.

Sideks end Grand Prix on winning note

21 December Kuala Lumpur

Razif and Jalani Sidek completed the Grand Prix badminton circuit in grand fashion when they won the Grand Prix Finals title by beating Hadibowo Susanto and Eddy Hartono of Indonesia.

Co-op chief gets 12 years' jail

23 December Kuala Lumpur

Former Koperasi Belia Bersatu (Kosatu) chairman Tee An Chuan was jailed for 12 years and fined $50,000 by the High Court today after pleading guilty to criminal breach of trust of more than $603,000. Counsel Ronald Khoo said later that he would appeal to the Supreme Court. In passing sentence, Mr Justice N.H. Chan said: 'The punishment is meant to be punitive. It is meant to reflect this court's abhorrence of this type of mean criminal conduct' (*see 6 January 1987*).

Cooperative depositors reject rescue plan

9 December Kuala Lumpur

Depositors with funds in 24 suspended cooperatives said they believed they could still get a full refund of their money and rejected a Government rescue plan to pay back half of it over two years and convert the rest into shares in the cooperatives. The chairman of the National Action Committee to Safeguard Deposit-taking Cooperatives, Mr Ng Kek Kiong, said the Government had never officially offered the rescue plan to the depositors but they learnt of it and rejected it during general meetings held in all the States in September.

Mr Ng was replying to a statement from Deputy Prime Minister Abdul Ghafar Baba that depositors had to decide whether they wanted to accept or reject the rescue plan. According to an article in *Malaysian Business*, nearly half a million Malaysians, mostly Chinese, had lost $1.5 billion of their savings in the failing cooperatives which offered high interest rates and were backed by powerful politicians. But, said the article, there were indications as far back as early 1985 that all was not well. In July 1986 reports that Koperasi Belia Bersatu Bhd (Kosatu) was in financial trouble led to heavy withdrawals. The same month saw Bank Negara given extra powers which enabled it to freeze the assets of Kosatu and investigate its affairs. This was not enough. A run began on other DTCs, with $150 million withdrawn before the Government froze the assets of 23 others in early August.

The 24 DTCs in trouble had taken $1.5 billion in deposits, but most of this was tied up in property and shares whose values had plunged in the recession. Only 9.1 per cent of their total gross assets was in cash and most of this was pledged against bank loans, needed to meet heavy withdrawals. The end result was that liquidation of two DTCs was recommended, one to be unfrozen and 21 to be taken over and restructured by banks and finance companies.

DTC depositors gather outside the Bank Negara headquarters in Kuala Lumpur.

1987

Winners and Losers. Swimming sensation Nurul Huda Abdullah won seven gold medals at the SEA Games in Jakarta; the Barisan Nasional coalition was returned to power in the fifth Sarawak State election; Malaysia's first test-tube baby was born; and Malaysian clothing designer Joe Pui made a name for himself in England. Police launched Operation Lalang and arrested 53 people under the Internal Security Act in an attempt, the Government said, to defuse racial tension. They included politicians, social activitists, educationists, and religious teachers. The saga of the BMF scandal continued in court. Two flowers on the Malaysian entertainment scene—Rose Chan and Rose Yatimah—and popular violinist Hamzah Dolmat passed away.

MARCH
Malaysia's first test tube baby is born. The picture shows three more test tube babies born in June.

JULY
Renowned violinist Hamzah Dolmat passes away.

SEPTEMBER
Malaysia's golden girl Nurul Huda wins seven gold medals in swimming in the 14th SEA Games.

OCTOBER
Child of the Year 1987 winners, Putri Roslina Abdul Latiff (left) and Mohamad Anuwa Abdul Rahman.

January: The keys to Carcosa are handed to the Malaysian Government.

> 'I have often said that nobody is going to get 100 percent of what they ask for ... we have to share and we have to make sacrifices.'
>
> Prime Minister Dr Mahathir Mohamad, in an interview published in *Asiaweek*, 20 November 1987.

1987

world news

16 January
President Cordero of Ecuador is kidnapped and exchanged for the release from prison of a general.

22 February
American pop artist, Andy Warhol, 58, dies. He turned Campbell's Soup into art.

1 April
Steve Newman completes his walk round the world, the first man to achieve this feat.

13 April
Portugal signs an agreement to return Macau to China in 1999.

6 May
On the orders of South Africa, a building in London housing the offices of the Congress of South African Unions is bombed.

14 May
Lt-Col Rabuka stages a bloodless coup in Fiji.

17 May
The USS *Stark* in the Persian Gulf is struck by two Exocet missiles from an Iraqi fighter. Thirty-seven men die.

Stores shut after co-ops crisis

6 January Kuala Lumpur

Amid demonstrations and sit-ins outside Bank Negara and offices of deposit-taking cooperatives (DTCs), it was announced that at least 10 of 23 DTCs, whose assets were frozen, would refund depositors their full principal sums in stages. Bank Negara Governor Datuk Jaafar Hussein announced that nine of the cooperatives had concluded agreements with their appointed financial institutions on arrangements to repay their depositors at least 20 per cent immediately. Meanwhile, 18 DTCs were placed under receivership in the wake of applications in the High Court by Bank Negara. Applications involving five more DTCs were postponed.

Bank Negara action was initiated after allegations that several cooperatives had violated the Finance Companies Act. It was later estimated that nearly 500,000 people had lost money in the DTCs. Jitters in the business community worsened with the closure of three superstores in the first quarter of the year. Lower purchasing power was blamed for the closures due to the DTC losses and unemployment reaching a high of 12 per cent.

January: Perwira Habib Bank staff picket in protest against the management's non-compliance with the bonus clause in their collective agreement and 'intimidation'. The dispute was later resolved by their union and the management.

Hostage magistrate rescued in shootout

10 January Kuantan

A woman magistrate, held hostage for 24 hours by three Indonesian prisoners at the Kuantan Prison, was rescued when a Special Action Squad (SAS) team stormed the building where she was held captive.

Two of the prisoners were shot dead and the third was wounded. Magistrate Mariana Yahya, 27, who was unharmed, had been at the detention centre of the prison to fix the hearing dates for cases involving 120 detainees when the three men, facing charges of murder and possession of firearms, rushed in from an adjoining waiting room and grabbed her. They later demanded a getaway car, but the prison was stormed shortly before their noon deadline. The wounded prisoner was later tried and sentenced to death for kidnapping.

Cash incentives for champion sportsmen

17 January Kuala Lumpur

The Government said it would award $80,000 to gold medal winners at the Olympics or world-level events. Runners-up will receive $40,000 and bronze medallists $20,000. Culture, Youth and Sports Minister Dato' Seri Najib Tun Razak said the financial rewards heralded 'the entry into a new era where excellence will be pursued and quality will be recognised'.

Escaping detainees strangle constable

30 January Malacca

Seven detainees broke out of the Melaka Tengah police station after strangling a constable and injuring another. After a nationwide manhunt, four of the escapees, who were aboard a Seremban–Tampin bus, were captured at a roadblock within 20 hours. Two others were caught three days later sleeping near a reservoir in Negeri Sembilan. The last suspect was caught five days later walking along Jalan Munshi Abdullah in Malacca.

Two of the escaped prisoners are led back to jail in handcuffs.

1,000 made homeless in kampong blaze

2 February Kuala Lumpur

Fire destroyed 150 wooden houses in Kampung Datuk Keramat, leaving about 1,000 people homeless. Deputy Prime Minister Ghafar Baba said they would be offered new homes at a low price.

$1.5m bank cash lost in highway robbery

6 February Alor Gajah

Four robbers, wearing ski masks and armed with guns, pulled off one of the country's biggest robberies in recent years after shooting at an armoured car and forcing it to stop along the Malacca–Alor Gajah Highway.

The gang, who had trailed the armoured car from Malacca, escaped with $1.5 million, a haul only exceeded by the Bank of Tokyo robbery in 1985. The money was the weekend collection of the Chung Khiaw Bank in Malacca and was being delivered to Bank Negara in Kuala Lumpur by a security agency. One of the three security guards was armed but the robbers stole his gun.

Good TV shows hurt video rental trade

11 February Kuala Lumpur

Radio Television Malaysia's showing of popular Chinese serials, the World Cup and good films sponsored by cigarette companies have brought a halt to the video craze. Rentals of video cassettes began dropping in the middle of 1986, said video shop operators. One operator claimed RTM's improved programming was causing a 20 per cent drop in profits.

Party paper gets OK

1 March Kuala Lumpur

The Home Ministry approved the publication of the Pas weekly newspaper *Al-Harakah*. The publication made its debut in early April before the opening of the party's general assembly.

'Resign' ultimatum to Sarawak Chief Minister

10 March Kuching

Sarawak was plunged into a political crisis when 28 State Assemblymen in the 48-member Legislative Assembly gave Chief Minister Datuk Patinggi Abdul Taib Mahmud an ultimatum to resign or face a vote of no confidence.

Among dissenting Assemblymen were four State Ministers and three Assistant Ministers who were said to have resigned from the State Cabinet. One said they wanted the Chief Minister to step down because 'he can no longer administer the Government properly and has failed to look after the interests of the Bumiputras.'

Datuk Patinggi Abdul Taib said he would request dissolution of the State Legislative Assembly if it was determined that he had indeed lost the support of the majority of the Assemblymen. Two days later, he announced the dissolution of the State Assembly, paving the way for fresh elections in the State (*see 16 April 1987*).

Carcosa residence returns to Malaysia

31 January Kuala Lumpur

Carcosa, the official residence of the British High Commissioner for almost a century, was handed back to the Malaysian Government.

It was built as the official residence of Sir Frank Swettenham, appointed in 1896 as the first Resident-General. In 1957, it was presented to the British Government by Prime Minister Tunku Abdul Rahman to serve as the official residence of the British High Commissioner.

The imposing facade of Carcosa, now a hotel.

Green turtle eggs pride of Sandakan

19 March Sandakan

The eggs might not have come from the giant leatherback but those sold in the market here came from the green turtle (*Chelonia mydas*) and were harvested from three Philppines islands—Lihiman, Bakkungan Besar and Taganak—as Sabah's own 'turtle farms' at the islands of Selingaan, Bakkungan Kecil and Gulisan, which are about 50km away, had been converted into turtle sanctuaries in 1971.

Najib unhurt in helicopter crash

9 March Bentong

A Royal Malaysian Air Force helicopter with Culture, Youth and Sports Minister Dato' Sri Najib Tun Abdul Razak and four others on board crash-landed near here. No one was hurt. It was a 'very close shave indeed,' he said.

He was returning to Kuala Lumpur from his constituency, Pekan, when there was an explosion and the helicopter began losing altitude. The pilot spotted a patch of cleared land next to the highway and managed to land there. The undercarriage was damaged.

Malaysia's first test-tube baby

12 March Petaling Jaya

A 2.7kg girl, Malaysia's first test-tube baby, was born. The infant was the product of the in-vitro fertilisation process whereby fertilisation takes place outside the woman's body, and the resulting embryo is transferred to the uterus.

Three more test-tube babies born later in the year.

Pivet Laboratory (Malaysia) Sdn Bhd together with six Malaysian doctors and nursing staff members collaborated in the project which resulted in the delivery, through natural childbirth, of a single child, although twins had been originally expected. The parents did not want to be identified.

Tycoon's son strangled with telephone wire

25 February Penang

The managing director of Kah Motors, Loh Kah Kheng, 39, the adopted son of tycoon Datuk Loh Boon Siew, was found dead in his bedroom at his seaside villa in Tanjung Bungah.

His body was found by his brother-in-law who broke into the locked room after Loh failed to show up for work in the morning. Kah Kheng's hands were tied with a telephone wire that was also looped around his neck.

Police detained a suspect in his thirties in connection with the murder.

The deceased was said to have been groomed to take over his father's business empire. He was also the managing director of NGK Sparkplugs and a director of Yuasa Battery (Malaysia) and Oriental Holdings (*see 18 June 1990*).

Documents on three projects declassified

13 April Kuala Lumpur

The Government declassified minutes of meetings in which decisions were taken to embark on the Dayabumi Complex, the Penang Bridge and the national car project. Prime Minister Dato' Seri Dr Mahathir Mohamad said anyone could apply for the documents, adding that they had been declassified to make known the truth about the projects. The three projects had been questioned by a faction aligned to candidate for the Umno presidency Tongku Razaleigh Hamzah, and deputy president Datuk Musa Hitam.

Mahathir beats off Umno leadership challenge

24 April Kuala Lumpur

Umno party leader Dato' Seri Dr Mahathir Mohamad staved off a major challenge to his leadership and was elected as party president for a third term. Encik Ghafar Baba was elected his deputy. In the closest elections in Umno history, Dr Mahathir defeated challenger Tengku Razaleigh Hamzah by 43 votes while Ghafar defeated incumbent Datuk Musa Hitam by 40 votes. For the first time, two leaders from the same State—Penang—were elected vice-presidents. Datuk Abdullah Ahmad Badawi retained his post and Anwar Ibrahim (who resigned his post as Umno Youth leader the previous day) was voted in. Abdullah polled 879 votes and Anwar received 850 (*see 28 April 1987*).

BMF $120m to be repaid

27 March Kuala Lumpur

Former Bumiputra Malaysia Finance (BMF) director Datuk Hashim Shamsuddin, in jail in Hong Kong for fraud and bribery, has agreed to pay more than $120 million to Bank Bumiputra and BMF in connection with two suits filed against him and others two years ago.

One of the suits filed by Bank Bumiputra and BMF was for the recovery of US$47.5 million (about $119 million). By consent, Hashim, 49, was ordered to pay the amount to the banks plus costs of the action.

Former BMF chairman Lorrain Esme Osman, former senior general manager and alternate director of BMF Dr Rais Saniman and former BMF general manager Ibrahim Jaafar were the other defendants named. Bank Bumiputra and BMF claimed that the defendants 'by their own neglect, want of skill or misconduct in management' caused the loss of US$40 million loaned to Carrian Nominee Ltd and US$7.5 million loaned to Fitarget Investments Ltd. They were alleged to have misled the bank's supervisory committee to believe that the sum was for moneymarket loans to banks instead of companies belonging to Carrian boss George Tan.

Hashim was sentenced to 4½ years' jail in Hong Kong in January for fraud and bribery. He had admitted to two counts of conspiring with Tan and others to defraud Bank Bumiputra, its Hong Kong subsidiary BMF, Permodalan Nasional Berhad and the Malaysian Government of US$137 million by getting the bank to lend the money to the Carrian property group. He also pleaded guilty to two counts of accepting a bribe from Tan of more than HK$15.7 million between September 1981 and May 1982. However, on application by the Attorney-General his sentence was increased to 10 years by the Appeal Court (*see 17 August 1993*).

Jail break!

30 March Miri

Fifteen prisoners escaped from Miri Central Prison but three were shot dead by police and two recaptured. Another 10 remained at large.

Deputy Divisional Police Chief ASP Ambrose Chung said a Police Field Force party spotted a group of the escapees in the jungle and ordered them to surrender. When the escapees ignored the order and tried to flee, the police opened fire and shot three of them. Two were recaptured. They had suffered cuts on their bodies believed to have been inflicted while scaling the barbed wire fence of the prison.

Chung warned that the remaining 10 were dangerous as they were armed with parangs stolen from nearby farms.

Two quit Cabinet, seven are dropped

28 April Kuala Lumpur

After their defeat at the Umno elections, Trade and Industry Minister Tengku Razaleigh Hamzah and Foreign Minister Datuk Rais Yatim resigned from the Cabinet. Prime Minister Dato' Seri Dr Mahathir Mohamad dropped seven other Cabinet members who had opposed his leadership. Three of them were full Ministers and four Deputy Ministers.

1987

1 June
Lebanese PM Karami is killed off the coast of Lebanon by a remote-controlled bomb planted in his helicopter.

4 July
Martina Navratilova wins her eighth Wimbledon title, beating Steffi Graf.

15 July
Taiwan ends 37 years of martial law.

30 July
Fifty thousand Indian troops arrive in Jaffna to disarm the Tamil Tigers and to enforce a peace pact.

31 July
Four hundred Iranian pilgrims are killed in clashes with Saudi security forces in Mecca.

1 August
Responding to events in Mecca the day before, Iranians attack the Saudi Arabian and Kuwaiti embassies in Tehran.

19 October
Black Monday. The Dow Jones drops 22.6 per cent, the biggest-ever one-day plummet. The rest of the world follow suit like dominos.

Barisan holds Sarawak

16 April Kuching

The Barisan Nasional coalition was returned to power in the fifth Sarawak State election with 28 seats. BN party members Parti Pesaka Bumiputera Bersatu (PBB), Sarawak United People's Party (SUPP) and Sarawak National Party (Snap) won 14, 11 and three seats respectively.

Although a BN component, the Parti Bansa Dayak Sarawak (PBDS) which won 15 seats—the largest number of any one party—contested under its own banner. PBDS president Datuk Leo Moggie said the party had doubled its representation in the State Assembly due to Dayak dissatisfaction with the administration of Chief Minister Datuk Patinggi Abdul Taib Mahmud.

'PBDS will not work with Datuk Taib at State level, but will remain with Barisan Nasional at Federal level,' he said.

The Chief Minister comfortably beat Datuk Wan Yusof Tuanku Bujang in Sebandi, with a majority of 2,194 votes. Voter turnout—approximately 75 per cent—was described as 'very good' by the Election Commission. In the 1983 election, turnout was 65 per cent.

Asia Magazine

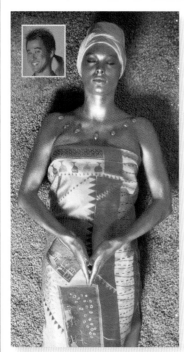

Asia Magazine featured a Malaysian designer, Joe Pui, making a name for himself in Bradford, England, with his favourite technique of printing on a pre-dyed background in a range of fabrics from silk to wool.

Ex-striptease queen Rose Chan dies

26 May Penang

Striptease queen of the 1960s Rose Chan died at her home in Butterworth after a seven-year battle with cancer. She was 62.

Hysterical schoolgirls scream for blood

18 May Alor Star

Fourteen girls from the Raudzatul Ulum religious school, armed with knives, sharp instruments and shards from broken window panes, ran amok in the school compound. Three held a fellow student hostage, wanting to exchange her for a woman teacher. After two hours, they calmed down and no one was hurt.

On 24 May, seven girls became hysterical again, screaming for blood and abusing other students. The other seven girls were on leave from school. One student suffered a leg injury. The students calmed down after being consoled and prayers were said. The school had hysteria outbreaks in the 1960s and 1970s, all affecting girls.

Apology to Mahathir from magazine

27 May Kuala Lumpur

The *Far Eastern Economic Review* apologised to Prime Minister Dato' Seri Dr Mahathir Mohamad for any embarrassment caused by a report in its 21 May issue on the purported sale of Limbang in northeast Sarawak to Brunei. It also retracted all allegations made against the Prime Minister in its report which had claimed that Dr Mahathir had raised the possible sale of Limbang to Brunei for US$6 billion in private talks with the Sultan while on a two-day official visit to Brunei.

Bronze Age skeletons found in Perak cave

1 July Lenggong

At least five Bronze Age human skeletons were discovered in the Gua Harimau limestone cave by a 25-member excavation team led by Associate Professor Dr Zuraina Abdul Majid of Universiti Sains Malaysia's Anthropology Department and assisted by officers of the National Museum.

The find was made after 10 days of painstaking excavation. The Neolithic skeletons were believed to be at least 2,000 years old.

Nine soldiers die in grenade explosion

9 July Gurun

Nine soldiers were killed and five others injured at Camp Hobart, one of the two main army training centres in the country, during a training exercise. The soldiers, all from the 24th Battalion Royal Malay Regiment, were being shown how to detonate grenades that they had earlier hurled but did not go off. The unexploded grenades had been collected by the sergeant training them and placed on the ground. When the men gathered around him to watch him demonstrate how to detonate them, there was an explosion, killing the sergeant and eight others.

Sarawak's Penans urged to resist logging

28 August Kuching

Swiss environmentalist Bruno Manser, in cassette recordings addressed to native Penans in the Baram and Ulu Limbang areas, urged them to 'stand firm' in their blockades against logging concessionaires that were affecting their homes in the jungles. The taped advice, in the Penan language, however, stated that they 'must not shed blood' when they defended their land against the authorities. Manser had been living illegally among the Penan since his permit to stay in the country expired almost three years earlier.

23 Malaysians killed in Thai airliner tragedy

30 August Phuket

All 83 passengers and crew members, including 23 Malaysians, on board a Thai Airways Boeing 737 died when the aircraft plunged into the sea near here. It was the worst air crash involving Malaysians abroad and also believed to be the worst in Thai aviation history.

A Kuala Lumpur travel agency said 15 of the Malaysians, plus a Japanese couple, had booked a five-day tour of Haadyai and Phuket. A spokeswoman said the group was flying from Haadyai to Phuket.

Celebrated violinist Hamzah Dolmat dies

12 July Kuala Lumpur

Malaysia's most celebrated violinist Hamzah Dolmat, 64, died at the General Hospital after an asthma attack. Hamzah was born in Kallang Batin, Singapore, in 1923, into a family of musicians. His father was a violinist, composer and singer and his mother a mak yong prima donna.

In the 1940s, he played for Radio Malaya in Singapore and later in Kuala Lumpur, where he had a 15-minute traditional music slot twice a week for six years. Responsible for the soundtracks of a number of Shaw Brothers Malay films, Hamzah was invited in 1957 by Tunku Abdul Rahman to record *Lanchang Kuning*—the Prime Minister's composition for his film *Mahsuri*. In 1964, he was awarded the Ahli Mangku Negara for his efforts to popularise Malay traditional songs, and in 1978, received an honorary degree from the University of Malaya.

KLSE's new complex officially opened

14 August Kuala Lumpur

Ringing an antique bell on the dot of 10am, Prime Minister Dato' Seri Dr Mahathir Mohamad signalled the start of the day's trading at the Kuala Lumpur Stock Exchange's new trading floor and symbolically opened the new KLSE premises at the Bukit Naga Complex. The antique Indian temple bell had been used to signal the start of trading at the KLSE since the 1960s. The Prime Minister was later taken on a tour of the new offices.

NZ housewife sentenced to death over drugs

1 September Penang

New Zealander Lorraine Phyllis Cohen, 44, (above under police escort) was sentenced to death by the High Court for trafficking 140.76g of heroin at the Bayan Lepas International Airport on 9 February 1985.

Her son Aaron Shelton, 20, who was jointly charged, was sentenced to life imprisonment and six strokes of the rotan (cane) on an amended charge of possessing 34.16g of heroin. The judge said he had accepted Aaron's defence that the drug found on him was for his own consumption and that he was not a trafficker.

80kg of 5-sen coins compensation for worker

12 September Klang

The winner of an industrial dispute, production officer Mohamad Tarmizi Ismail found out the hard—and heavy—way the meaning of being short-changed.

He was given a bag of five-sen coins weighing 80kg by his previous employers as part-payment for the $6,500 compensation the Industrial Court had awarded him on 6 August for wrongful dismissal.

The company, saying it was short of funds, gave him the coins—loose change accumulated over 10 years—claiming there were 64,000 pieces amounting to $3,200.

A bank came to Tarmizi's rescue when the press highlighted the monumental task he had been facing in trying to count the money.

With the aid of a coin-counting machine, it took two hours to find out that the coins amounted to $2,800.

Tycoon Kuok rescued, kidnappers shot dead

11 September Johor Bahru

After 74 days as a hostage, philanthropist tycoon Datuk Kuok Ho Yan, 72, was rescued by police in pre-dawn raids which saw six kidnappers shot dead.

The simultaneous 4am raids here and in Labis were conducted after a tip-off and 'discreet investigations' by police who had learnt that Datuk Kuok was being held in a house in one of the two places.

Five kidnappers, one of them a woman, were killed in the 15-minute exchange of fire in a house in Jalan Petrie, Johor Bahru, from which Datuk Kuok was rescued unhurt. The other gang member was shot dead in a house in Labis.

On the night Datuk Kuok went missing after a meeting, his Mercedes, with lights on and doors ajar, was found a short distance from his house.

This was the second time Datuk Kuok had been abducted. On the first occasion, he was held for 66 days and released after a ransom, believed to have been between $3 million and $4 million, was paid. The first kidnapping was also believed to have been by the same gang.

Highway toll system implemented

1 October Kuala Lumpur

The closed-toll system came into force along the Kuala Lumpur–Ayer Keroh and Ipoh–Changkat Jering expressways amid protest demonstrations by the DAP at toll plazas in various States. A DAP youth leader was detained for allegedly preventing a traffic police officer from carrying out his duties at an anti-toll protest gathering and was later released on bail of $300. The pay-as-you-drive system differed from the previous one under which motorists were charged a flat rate of 2.5 sen per kilometre. The new system meant motorists did not need to stop at every booth to pay but only when entering or leaving the expressway, at a rate specified by the Government.

Placard-carrying demonstrators stand in the road to protest the introduction of highway tolls.

Two held for spreading apostasy misinformation

30 September Kuala Lumpur

Two men claiming to be former Christian missionaries were arrested under the Internal Security Act for spreading false information that could cause public disorder. Haji Kamaluddin Haji Tahir @ Haji Kamaruddin, 48, and Salleh Omar @ Mat Omar, 47, had been conducting lectures on the activities of Christian missionaries.

Their activities had been monitored by the police for two months. Inspector General of Police Tan Sri Hanif Omar said police took a serious view of any activity that could cause unrest, disunity and anxiety among Muslims and followers of other religions, especially in connection with claims of apostasy.

Dazzling 'air-crobatics'

10 October Kuala Lumpur

The US Air Force aerial demonstration squadron, the Thunderbirds, whooshed across the sky at Subang in a soaring display of 0skill and precision. They were here as part of the squadron's Far East tour, its first in the region since 1959.

Name change and new logo for airline

15 October Kuala Lumpur

Malaysian Airline System launched its new corporate logo, a Kelantan

kite that had been given an aerodynamic look, and announced that it would be renamed Malaysia Airlines. Performing the launch, Transport Minister Datuk Dr Ling Liong Sik watched the most recent addition to the MAS Boeing 737 fleet—fitted with the new livery—land at the international airport in Subang. The new design, produced by a local design house, cost the airline about $1 million.

Swimmer Nurul Huda starts the gold roll

10 September Jakarta

Swimming sensation Nurul Huda Abdullah, 15, gave Malaysia a splashing start by winning her first two events, one of them in record time, at the much-anticipated 14th SEA Games.

By the end of the 12-day games, she had won seven gold medals to equal her last haul in the Bangkok SEA Games. Swimmer Jeffrey Ong also proved to be a winner with two record-breaking golds. The final medal tally for Malaysia was 36 gold medals, 41 silver and 67 bronze.

1987

19 October
US warships destroy three Iranian oil platforms in the Persian Gulf in retaliation for an Iranian missile that had hit a Kuwaiti tanker.

22 October
The US navy says it has deployed five dolphins in the Persian Gulf to hunt for Iranian mines.

29 November
A South Korean commercial flight blows up over the Andaman Sea, killing 115. Fingers are pointed at North Korea.

1 December
Digging begins on the Chunnel linking the UK and the continent.

8 December
The Palestinian Intifada protests against Israel begin in the Gaza Strip and the West Bank.

16 December
First presidential elections in South Korea in 16 years. The Government's candidate Roh Tae-woo wins. The opposition alleges fraud.

Soldier on shooting spree kills man, injures two

18 October   **Kuala Lumpur**

A soldier, armed with an M-16 rifle, went on a shooting spree at 11.30pm in the Chow Kit area, killing a man and injuring two others. He also shot at passing cars and attempted to set fire to a petrol station. In the absence of his senior officers on the scene, Inspector General of Police Tan Sri Hanif Omar led the police operation to disarm the soldier.

Private Adam Jaafar, 23, from Camp Syed Putra in Tambun, Ipoh, surrendered at 3.45pm the next day after holding police at bay for three hours while holed up in a flat. On 2 November, Adam was charged with the murder of smallholder Che Soh Che Mahmud, 53, and with illegal possession of a firearm and ammunition.

Inspector General of Police Tan Sri Hanif Omar leaps into action as a soldier goes on a shooting spree in the Chow Kit area of Kuala Lumpur.

Sultan strips Minister of 'Datuk' title

23 October   **Kuala Lumpur**

The Sultan of Selangor withdrew two awards given to Labour Minister Datuk Lee Kim Sai, the Datuk Paduka Makhota Selangor award that carries the title 'Datuk', and the Setia Mahkota Selangor award.

Lee had received the Datuk Paduka Mahkota Selangor award in 1979. The Sultan said the withdrawal of the awards was to serve as a warning to others not to raise racial issues in public and to belittle the sovereignty of Rulers. The withdrawal of awards was the fifth in the State's history.

Smuggling puts a halt to cross-border train service

1 November   **Kangar**

Rampant smuggling of rice from Thailand into Malaysia by commuters on the Arau–Padang Besar train service has forced Malayan Railway to terminate this service.

The service was earlier suspended for a month from August to break the back of the smugglers but when the service resumed in September, the smuggling also resumed. Deputy Transport Minister Datin Paduka Zaleha Ismail said the authorities were forced to close the service, though the railway would lose about $50,000 a month.

KLCE launches tin futures contract

1 October   **Kuala Lumpur**

The Kuala Lumpur Commodities Exchange began a tin futures contract, establishing the world's first international market for trading tin on a forward month basis. It traded in Malaysian, Thai and Indonesian tin, which together made up about 50 per cent of the world's production.

The KL exchange projected a rapid growth in contracts from an estimated 30 a day in the first quarter of trading to 500 a day in the first half of the fourth year. The contracts were of one tonne priced in US cents per kilogram.

The official opening of the futures contract.

63 detained as threat to national security

27 October   **Kuala Lumpur**

Twenty-nine politicians, nine social activists, three educationalists, two religious teachers and 20 other people were detained by the Special Branch under the Internal Security Act at the start of Operation Lalang. The following day, more arrests were made. Prime Minister Dr Mahathir said the police action was necessary to defuse racial tension that had reached 'dangerous proportions'. He said the country—facing an economic recession and high unemployment—could not afford racial riots. He also announced a nationwide ban on any gathering or rally, including any previously approved.

Inspector General of Police Tan Sri Hanif Omar explained that the police operations were for the sake of national security and had nothing to do with politics. 'Sometimes, the political situation may have a bearing on the security situation, but for us, we view these things from the security angle… If we don't take action now, it may be too late,' he said.

The Ministry of Home Affairs also withdrew the publishing permits of four newspapers: *The Star* and its companion *The Sunday Star*; the Chinese-language daily *Sin Chew Jit Poh*; and the bi-weekly Malay-language tabloid *Watan*. By 7 November, a total of 106 people had been detained. On 20 November, 11 of them were released unconditionally after investigations showed they were not a threat to national security (*see 23 March 1988*).

Manila House drops Sabah claim

11 December   **Manila**

A Bill dropping the 25-year-old Philippine claim to Sabah was overwhelmingly approved by the Philippine House of Representatives and was tabled in the Senate. Sponsored by 14 Senators, the Senate version of the Bill included a provision that it would take effect only upon settlement of the proprietary rights of the Sultan of Sulu and the signing of two treaties with Malaysia, one on friendship and cooperation, and the other on border patrols and crossings.

On 15 December, the six Asean leaders signed the Manila Declaration pledging commitment to the early achievement of a zone of peace, freedom and neutrality (Zopfan) and a nuclear weapons-free zone in Southeast Asia. The signing ended the two-day Third Asean Summit.

'Darling' of Malay film fans Rose Yatimah dies

14 December   **Petaling Jaya**

Popular Malay actress Rose Yatimah, 44, died of cancer at her home in Subang Jaya. At 15, Rose Yatimah gained fame as the 'darling' of Malay filmgoers in Southeast Asia with her first movie *Pendekar Bujang Lapok* starring P. Ramlee.

Brunei royal wedding for Malaysian singer

10 December   **Bandar Seri Begawan**

In a private ceremony at the Istana Darul Hana, popular songstress Mazuin Hamzah was married to Brunei prince Pengiran Muda Haji Sufri. The royal family was represented by the bridegroom's

younger brother Pengiran Muda Jefri Bolkiah, who is also Brunei's Finance Minister. The bride was given away by her elder brother Mazlan.

Man crushed in rockfall

29 December   **Ipoh**

A watchman was killed and three other people injured when the face of the Gunung Tunggal limestone hill collapsed onto an orchard, off the Ipoh–Kampar road some 26km from Ipoh.

The watchman was in his office-cum-quarters when the incident occurred at dawn. His 70-year-old mother and a relative, 14, who were partially buried in the rockfall, were rescued by firemen and villagers. A lorry driver, on his way to work at a quarry at the foot of the hill, was injured by falling rocks.

1988

Two events this year had long-lasting repercussions on the nation's psyche and future. One was the High Court declaration that UMNO was an unlawful society. (A few days later, the Registrar of Societies rejected an application to form UMNO Malaysia. A week later, a new party, UMNO Baru was registered with Dato' Seri Dr Mahathir Mohamad as president). In the other unprecedented move, Tun Mohamad Salleh Abbas was removed as Lord President. Two Malaysians had set their sights on going to US in pursuit of academic excellence and movie stardom respectively—boy genius Chiang Ti Ming, 12, wanted to study nuclear physics, and bodybuilder Malek Noor headed to Hollywood to star in a movie.

FEBRUARY
Former MCA President Tan Koon Swan is sentenced to jail for criminal breach of trust.

JUNE
Illusionist David Copperfield visits Malaysia and is mobbed by fans everywhere he goes.

AUGUST
Twelve-year-old genius Chiang Ti Ming heads to university in the United States.

DECEMBER
Gold fever in Marang leads to a rush for gold prospecting licences.

October: The first Umno Baru general assembly.

'The challenges before us are numerous and we still have a long way to go in achieving health for all and child survival.'

Datin Seri Dr Siti Hasmah, upon her receipt of the Kazue Kimura McLaren Leadership Achievement Award, 22 January 1988.

1988

3 January
Margaret Thatcher becomes the longest-serving British PM of the 20th century.

1 March
In the first such long-range rocket attack in the war, Iraq fires 16 missiles into Tehran.

16 March
Iraqi forces use poison gas on the village of Halabia. An estimated 5,000–7,000 villagers die. This is the latest attack in a campaign that started in February, since when poison gas has been used to kill 50,000–100,000 Kurds judged friendly with Iran, and 4,000 villages have been bulldozed to rubble.

14 April
The Soviet Union signs an accord in Geneva, agreeing to the withdrawal of its troops from Afghanistan. Afghan rebel forces reject the pact, saying the fighting will continue until the Kabul regime falls.

16 April
PLO commander Abu Jihad is killed by Israeli commandos on a raid in Tunisia.

Introducing the Vescar

1 January Sabak Bernam

It looks like a half-finished pick-up truck and sounds like a scooter but it can move at 25km per hour and carry a load of 1,000 coconuts while negotiating difficult terrain and climbing hill slopes.

Named Vescar by its designer Khidir Marjiki, 21, the contraption is the buzz in Kampung Sungai Apong, near Klang. There are seven such vehicles using scooter engines and the chassis of cars including a Toyota, Mazda, Morris and Volkswagen.

Youth leader guilty of CBT

29 January Kuala Lumpur

Former MCA Youth leader Datuk Kee Yong Wee was jailed for two years after pleading guilty to two counts of criminal breach of trust involving $3.3 million belonging to Koperasi Pembangunan Pemuda Malaysia (Komuda). The Sessions Court also fined him $2.5 million or 15 months' jail in default.

Presiding Judge Wan Adnan Wan Mohammed said if Kee had been honest, he would not have allowed Komuda to invest in Malaysian Resources Corporation Berhad which was then 'in the red'. Kee had a vested interest in the companies and had diversified his interests at the expense of Komuda depositors.

Datuk Kee with his wife outside the Sessions Court.

$62.5m soccer deal

2 February Kuala Lumpur

The Football Association of Malaysia signed a 10-year contract worth $62.5 million with the Dunhill cigarette company.

Bapa Malaysia is 85

8 February Penang

Old friends and well-wishers turned up at Tunku Abdul Rahman's residence, Takhdir, with cakes, flowers and presents to wish Bapa Malaysia a happy 85th birthday. With his wife Sharifah Rodziah Barakbah at his side, the Tunku was his usual jovial self as he received visitors including acting Penang Chief Minister Datuk Khoo Kay Por, State Executive Councillors, former Cabinet Ministers and his former colleagues. Also there were former Umno members headed by Tengku Razaleigh Hamzah.

Yesterday, at the opening of the headquarters of the Muslim Converts' Association of Penang, the Tunku urged Malays to interact with Muslim converts as Islam was meant for all races. He said Malays should not isolate themselves but should welcome their Muslim brothers into their homes.

Call to immunise children

12 February Kuala Lumpur

The Health Ministry warned that diphtheria was a killer and urged all parents to complete the immunisation programme for their children.

Commenting on an incident in Klang this month when a young boy died of diphtheria, Health Services director Dr Jones Varughese said only a small percentage of the population was not immunised and most cases were reported in Sabah and Sarawak where medical services were not fully developed.

Ching Dynasty wedding

15 February Ipoh

A $400,000 Ching Dynasty-style wedding put the quiet village of Lawan Kuda on the map and brought the police out to control the crowd.

Dressed in full traditional costume, contractor Woi Sook Kooi, 40, rode a horse to the house of hairdresser Wong Foong Mee, 21, and brought her back in a sedan chair. Woi, who left the village 20 years ago to seek his fortune, returned a wealthy man, building a $1-million house and driving a BMW car.

The Hash House Harriers were founded, probably by colonial civil servants, in Kuala Lumpur in 1938, and since then have grown into an international network of thousands of runners' (and drinkers') clubs. There are even two branches in Antarctica.

HASH HOUSE HARRIERS CELEBRATING THEIR 50TH YEAR OF RUNNING... BUT I HAVE A FEELING THIS BUNCH IS WAY—WAY— OFF COURSE...

'Cavalry' at Batu Caves

2 February Kuala Lumpur

Mounted police of the Federal Reserve Unit were called in to help control the 700,000-strong crowd at Batu Caves near Kuala Lumpur during the Thaipusam festival. But the riders and their horses became attractions as much as the kavadi bearers and pilgrims.

A mounted policeman on duty at Batu Caves.

PM's wife wins award for health care work

21 January Kuala Lumpur

The wife of the Prime Minister, Datin Seri Dr Siti Hasmah, became the first Malaysian to receive the Kazue Kimura McLaren Leadership Achievement Award. US Ambassador to Malaysia John Monjo presented the award to her for her contributions to primary health care.

Jailed for CBT

4 February Kuala Lumpur

The Sessions Court here sentenced former MCA president Tan Koon Swan to 30 months' jail for criminal breach of trust involving $23.3 million belonging to Multi-Purpose Holdings in 1985. He was also fined $1 million or nine months' jail in default. On 11 September his jail term was reduced to 18 months and the fine was quashed.

Kidnapped Thai baby reunited with mother

24 February Kuantan

One of five kidnapped Thai babies rescued by police was reunited with his mother after 11 months. Prasong Netana Tevasana, 16 months, cried when Nol Thippawan hugged him in a tearful reunion at the Tengku Ampuan Fatimah Children's Home. He obviously did not recognise her.

Kidnapped in March last year and smuggled across the border, Prasong was sold to a rubber tapper for $8,500. Police rescued him and detained a woman.

Action on drug islands

28 February Ipoh

The marine police disclosed that 12 islands clustered in two isolated groups off the Perak coast are being used by drug traffickers to store and process their products. The first group of islands is 17km from Pulau Pangkor and the other near Pulau Jerak.

Marine police (northern division) chief Supt A.G. Lopez said a major operation was being planned with the Perak anti-narcotics division, using dogs trained to detect dadah. He said constant harassment by the police had driven the traffickers to the islands.

Leap-year Dragon babies

29 February Kuala Lumpur

It was a triple special day for babies born today—a double digit year, a leap year and the Year of the Dragon. Leap-year babies numbered 31 in Malacca, 29 in Kuantan, 28 in Kuala Lumpur and Petaling Jaya, 31 in Penang and 31 in Ipoh.

Commando gets bravery dagger

1 March Kuantan

Commando Kapten Ali Amir received the army's Combat Dagger for bravery in leading 20 men in a successful operation against Communist terrorists in west Pahang on 27 July 1987 despite being outnumbered by the enemy.

Kapt Ali, 27, of the Special Services Regiment in Sungai Udang, Malacca, was the seventh recipient of the award.

Make mosque a centre of learning, says Sultan

12 March Shah Alam

The Sultan of Selangor wanted the $162-million Masjid Sultan Salahuddin Abdul Aziz Shah to be an institution for Islamic scholars. At the official opening, the Sultan said the State mosque should revive the functions of mosques in Islam's early days.

Sports awards

13 March Kuala Lumpur

National swimmer Nurul Huda Abdullah became the first person to win the Sportswoman of the Year award for the third consecutive year while cyclist M. Kumaresan won Sportsman of the Year in a ceremony at the Stadium Negara.

'I dedicate the award to my mother,' said Nurul Huda.

Dr Mahathir launches the campaign at Lubuk Jong, where the legend of Awang Buntar was born.

Mahathir urges new spirit of cooperation

6 March Lubuk Jong

Prime Minister Dato' Seri Dr Mahathir Mohamad launched the Semarak movement, aimed at generating a new spirit of industry and cooperation and encouraging leaders to identify themselves with the people.

Lubuk Jong was a significant venue because of the legend of Awang Buntar, a humble villager who became a rich merchant. He grew ashamed of his roots and of his mother. One day, his junk sank, near Lubok Jong, and all aboard drowned except for his third wife who had earlier stopped him beating his mother.

'Let's not just point to the failures of our respective races in getting certain things without accepting and showing the achievements of the community.'

Dato' Seri Dr Mahathir Mohamad

Qur'an in Braille

13 March Kuala Lumpur

Blind Muslims in Malaysia were able read the Qur'an with the printing of the holy book in Braille, thanks to a joint effort by the Islamic Centre, the Muslim Women's Welfare Board and the Malaysian Association for the Blind. The idea was mooted by the MAB in 1980. The project took Encik Mohamad Nor Awang Ngah, a blind teacher at the Islamic Centre, six years to complete. Since Braille characters are larger than normal ones, each of the 30 chapters was printed in a separate volume.

Japan top investor

13 March Kuala Lumpur

Foreign equity in industrial projects approved in 1987 was $1.599 billion, with Japan accounting for 23.2 per cent, Parliament was told.

Upheaval in politics

Umno declared unlawful

4 February Kuala Lumpur

The High Court dismissed a suit against Umno and in its decision declared that Umno was an unlawful society when its 38th general assembly and election took place last 24 April. Mr Justice Harun Hashim said he did not have to declare the assembly and election null and void because 'it was a nullity all the way'.

The Umno general assembly. The 1987 gathering and the party election were unlawful, the High Court ruled.

He said that as branches were established without the approval of the Registrar of Societies, Umno as the parent society was an unlawful society. Therefore, the remedies sought by the 11 could not be granted.

The plaintiffs wanted the divisional delegates' meeting for the election of delegates to the general assembly declared unconstitutional and ultra vires with regard to the party constitution. They also asked for an order compelling Umno and its secretary-general Dato' Seri Sanusi Junid to make arrangements for a fresh general assembly and election.

The next day, Prime Minister Dato' Seri Dr Mahathir Mohamad said the Government was not affected by the ruling as it was elected into power by the people in 1986 and was still in power. 'We still have a Government and decisions of the Government are not affected.'

Umno Malaysia application rejected

15 February Kuala Lumpur

The Registrar of Societies has turned down an application to set up Umno Malaysia on 8 February, said Former Trade and Industry Minister Tengku Razaleigh Hamzah. He said the initiative to form the party was to 'provide a lifeline to Malays who had been deprived of a political platform' and not to advance any particular group's interest or to form another Umno.

Umno Baru formed

16 February Kuala Lumpur

A new party, Pertubuhan Kebangsaan Melayu Bersatu (Baru) or Umno Baru (New Umno), has been registered, announced Prime Minister Dato' Seri Dr Mahathir Mohamad. The party had been accepted as a member of the Barisan Nasional by the latter's supreme council.

Members of its pro-tem committee were Dr Mahathir (president), Deputy Prime Minister Ghafar Baba (deputy president), Information Minister Datuk Mohamed Rahmat (secretary) and Finance Minister Datuk Paduka Daim Zainuddin (treasurer). The party replaced the old Umno, which was deregistered following a High Court decision on 4 February declaring it an unlawful society (*see 28 October 1998*).

1988

15 May
After eight years of bloody stalemate, Soviet troops begin withdrawing from Afghanistan.

15 June
Hong Kong, swamped by an endless tide of boat people, announces that new arrivals unable to prove religious or political persecution will be returned to Vietnam.

3 July
An Iranian commercial flight is shot down by American missiles in the Persian Gulf.

20 July
Ayatollah Khomeini accepts truce with Iraq, though he likens it to drinking poison.

30 July
Jordan's King Hussein renounces sovereignty over the West Bank, ceding it to the PLO.

8 August
8888 Uprising. Thousands of Burmese are killed during anti-Government demonstrations.

Constitutional changes

18 March Kuala Lumpur

The Dewan Rakyat passed the Constitution (Amendment) Bill which sought changes, among others, to matters relating to the judiciary and Federal jurisdiction over land matters, with 142 MPs from Barisan Nasional and Independents supporting it while 17 DAP MPs and the sole Pas representative voted against. Prime Minister Dato' Seri Dr Mahathir Mohamad said the amendments were not aimed at curbing judicial powers but were necessary because some judges had ignored laws made by Parliament.

Swimmer cracks 16-minute barrier

23 March Kuala Lumpur

Jeffrey Ong became the first Malaysian to crack the 16-minute barrier in the 1,500m freestyle when he finished in 15:59:36 in the British inter-club championship, second to current British champion Tony Day.

National Sports Council's acting director-general Mazlan Ahmad said it received details of Ong's smashing performance two days ago.

Virus in Malaysia stumps scientists

9 April Kuala Lumpur

A virus that killed dozens of people in Malaysia was the first of its kind, an American health official said, and virologists were stumped about how it spreads. Scientists from the US and other experts from Australia, Taiwan and Japan arrived in Malaysia several weeks earlier to help the Southeast Asian country determine the nature of the virus believed to be spreading from pigs to humans.

At first, officials thought all of the deaths were caused by Japanese encephalitis, which they believed was being transmitted from pigs to humans by mosquitoes. Malaysia had slaughtered hundreds of thousands of pigs in an attempt to stop the epidemic. About 230 people in the country were believed to have been infected in the previous six months.

Tan Siew Sin dies

18 March Kuala Lumpur

Tun Tan Siew Sin: MCA leader for 13 years.

Former Finance Minister Tun Tan Siew Sin died after a heart attack, just four days short of his 72nd birthday. Members of his family were at his bedside at the Pantai Medical Centre. He was buried on 22 March in the family burial ground in Malacca, near the grave of his father Tun Sir Tan Cheng Lock.

National and party leaders from all over the country, including Deputy Prime Minister Ghafar Baba, attended the funeral.

Tun Tan served as Finance Minister for 15 years and was MCA leader for 13 years. He was also the only Malaysian to be listed in the *International Who's Who of Intellectuals*.

'ISA arrests necessary'

23 March Kuala Lumpur

The activities of some politicians, Communists and religious and other pressure groups had created a dangerous situation, according to a Government White Paper detailing the days preceding arrests under the ISA in October 1987. It said sensitive issues had been exploited and communal sentiments fanned to a point where bloodshed was imminent, making the arrest of 106 people necessary to restore stability.

The 24-page paper, entitled 'Towards Preserving National Security', was released by the Home Affairs Ministry and tabled as an 'information document' in Parliament, meaning it was not for debate. It listed issues exploited as those relating to the Education Act, the development of Bukit China, losses incurred by deposit-taking cooperatives, the school pledge, the University of Malaya ruling on elective subjects, the language used on signboards and the posting in Chinese schools of senior assistants and afternoon supervisors.

Tackling samsu issue

13 April Kuala Lumpur

The Cabinet directed Attorney-General Tan Sri Abu Talib Othman to draft a law providing the most severe punishment for illicit samsu distillers.

Works Minister Datuk S. Samy Vellu, who was also MIC president, had earlier advocated the death penalty for the distillers and proposed that their properties be seized.

Ex-Deputy Minister jailed

9 May Kuala Lumpur

The Sessions Court has sentenced former Deputy Youth and Sports Minister Wang Choon Wing to nine months' imprisonment on two counts of criminal breach of trust involving $211,000.

Wang, 46, pleaded guilty to committing both offences at the premises of Ruban Enterprises Sdn Bhd in Wisma Stephens, Jalan Raja Chulan, Kuala Lumpur.

He was a director of the company at that time of the offences.

'Crying' over platinum

4 April Kuala Lumpur

He had a talent for singing...and crying. Andrian Andy, whose LP *Sayangi Daku* scored a platinum, was in tears when he sang *Ayah* at the launch today of his second album *Pedekar Silat*. But Andrian wiped them away and switched his mood and rhythm for the next rock number, Perpaduan. The 8-year-old who received his platinum album from Datin Seri Rosmah Mansor, wife of Youth and Sports Minister Dato' Seri Najib Tun Razak, left for Istanbul the next day to perform at a cultural show sponsored by City Hall.

Recovering from his tears, Adrian Andy smiles shyly for the camera.

Eerie 'twilight' of the solar eclipse

18 March Kuala Lumpur

It was 8.34am. The sun disappeared and temperatures dipped as morning took on a twilight feel at the peak of a partial eclipse of the sun that cast a veil of grey over the city. Life came to a momentary halt as workers, students, housewives and children paused to observe the sun being 'eaten' up.

Founder and president of the Astronomical Society of Malaysia Lim Ju Boo said the morning's solar eclipse attracted shiploads of people from the United States and Britain to Pulau Bangka, off Sumatra, where a total eclipse took place.

A curious crowd gathers at the scene of the robbery.

Cops and robbers: three killed

29 April Kuala Lumpur

Three armed Indonesians who held up the Sabah Finance Berhad branch in Jalan Tuanku Abdul Rahman today were shot dead by police waiting in ambush outside the building, while a fourth man escaped with $18,401. The assistant manager of the company, shot in the back earlier by the robbers, was recovering at the General Hospital. While the robbery was in progress, an alert passer-by telephoned the police and a patrol squad nearby rushed to the scene. Police seized a .32 Smith and Wesson revolver and three eight-inch daggers. They recovered part of the loot amounting to $28,529 along with valuables that the gangsters had taken from the company employees during the raid.

Wisma Tani on fire

3 May Kuala Lumpur

Fire broke out on the top floor of Wisma Tani, the nine-storey Agriculture Ministry building in Jalan Mahameru, destroying files, records and data. Also destroyed were computers, fish samples and equipment belonging to the Fisheries Department. There were no reports of casualties although there were nine people working late in the building at that time. The fire, which spread quickly, shattered glass windows and spread to part of the eighth floor. Firemen took three hours to bring it under control.

A firefighting platform is used to tackle the blaze.

End of RAAF Mirage era

3 May Butterworth

The last batch of 10 Royal Australian Air Force (RAAF) Mirage fighter jets took off at 11.30am, marking the end of their 20-year presence here. The Mirages were first deployed at the Butterworth, Penang, air base in 1967.

Witnessing the event were over 200 RAAF and RMAF personnel, including RAAF Chief of Air Staff Air Marshal R.G. Funnel and RMAF Air Region II commander Brigadier-Jen C.S. Huang. Air Marshal Funnel said Australia's link with Butterworth would enter a new era with the start of regular deployments of FA-18 Hornet aircraft and F-111s for extended joint exercises to contribute to the Integrated Air Defence System.

Air Marshal Funnel said Australia would continue to base a detachment of Orion P3 maritime reconnaissance aircraft at Butterworth.

Stevie Wonder in KL

10 May Kuala Lumpur

Blind American singer Stevie Wonder talked of love as he arrived at Subang Airport tonight for a concert at Stadium Negara on the following evening. 'Songs can help move people all the way forward as one united family,' he said.

He was one of the US pop artistes behind the 'USA for Africa' benefit song for the Ethiopian famine victims. 'When we did *We Are The World,* it wasn't political. If you are hungry, you want to eat,' he said.

New UN representative

14 May Kuala Lumpur

Datuk Razali Ismail, deputy secretary-general (I) of the Foreign Affairs Ministry, has been appointed Malaysia's Permanent Representative to the United Nations in New York. He succeeded Datuk Mohamed Yusof Hitam, who has been appointed Foreign Ministry secretary-general.

Singer back in rehab

27 May Seremban

Singer Jamal Abdillah was back in the Serenti drug rehabilitation centre in Tampin for after-care treatment and to protect him from drug pushers, a senior Home Ministry official said.

Released in April, Jamal, 29, was taken back in after a field officer was convinced that the singer might be tempted to return to drugs.

China bounces Malaysia out of Thomas Cup

4 June Kuala Lumpur

The Chinese trounced Malaysia soundly in the Thomas Cup final at the Stadium Negara, winning 4–1. It was all over in two hours and one minute, with Misbun Sidek surrendering to the indestructible Yang Yang, Foo Kok Keong unable to stand up to Xiong Guobao and Rashid Sidek falling to Zhao Jianhua.

Handy way to fish

16 June Kuala Besut

No lines, no hooks. Trishaw rider Husin Dollah, 42, just uses his bare hands when fishing. He said he found he had this skill when he visited a fishing complex here and saw a lot of ikan kelang and ikan duri in the water under the jetty. Both species have rough skin under the head that makes them easy to hold with bare hands.

He tried his luck the next day, waving the bait in his last three fingers and catching the fish between his thumb and index finger. Now, to supplement his income, the father of nine went fishing every afternoon, catching a basketful in half an hour. He makes $5 a day selling the fish.

David says sorry

16 June Kuala Lumpur

Secretary-general of the Malaysian Trades Union Congress Dr V. David admitted that he had attempted to get an American labour organisation to petition the US Government to withdraw trade privileges accorded to Malaysia under the Generalised System of Preferences (GSP). He had earlier denied doing so.

Labour Minister Lee Kim Sai said David had expressed willingness to rectify the matter after he realised the adverse effects of his action on hundreds of companies and thousands of workers here.

Tun H.S. Lee dies

20 June Kuala Lumpur

The country's first Finance Minister, Tun Sir Henry H.S. Lee, died after a long illness. He was 87. He left a widow, Toh Puan Lady Lee Kwan Choi Lin, four sons, a daughter, five sons- and daughters-in-law, 17 grandchildren and two great-grandchildren. Tun Lee, one of the eight signatories to Malaya's independence, was a founder member of the MCA and

played a key role in the formation of the Alliance (the coalition of Umno, MCA and MIC). He was Malaya's Finance Minister from 1957 until he resigned on health grounds in 1959.

Dataran Merdeka

20 May Kuala Lumpur

It was up stumps at the Royal Selangor Club padang as the famous cricket ground was to make way for a multi-million-dollar underground car park and shopping arcade. The city

Work goes on at the underground car park in Merdeka Square.

fathers had promised to build a concrete Merdeka Square at the site where the nation proudly proclaimed its independence from British colonial rule on 31 August 1957. However, after the car park was completed, part of the area was later returfed and cricket resumed.

No illusion here

20 June Kuala Lumpur

Master of illusion David Copperfield did not do any disappearing acts despite the thousands of fans who mobbed him everywhere he went in the city. Instead, he turned on the charm everywhere he went, endearing himself to the unending sea of admirers. The magician, whose tricks have included walking through the Great Wall of China and levitating himself across the Grand Canyon, was here to perform in a series of shows.

Singapore agrees to offshore gas price

28 June Kuala Lumpur

Singapore signed a memorandum of understanding with Malaysia agreeing to pay a premium of not less than S$20 million in its first-year purchase of Terengganu offshore natural gas. The agreement, signed by Prime Minister Lee Kuan Yew and Prime Minister Dato' Seri Dr Mahathir Mohamad, also made provision for Singapore to draw more water from Malaysia.

1988

12 August
Sein Lwin resigns as President of Burma, and is replaced by a civilian, Maung Maung, who lasts for a month before it's business as usual with the military.

17 August
Pakistan President Muhammad Zia-ul-Haq and the US ambassador are killed in a plane crash near Bhawalpur.

20 August
The Iran–Iraq War ends. The death toll for both countries adds up to a million, give or take…

11 September
Three hundred thousand Estonians demonstrate for independence from the Soviet Union.

17 September–2 October
South Korea plays host to the Summer Olympics. Canadian sprinter Ben Johnson has the 100 metres gold medal stripped from him after testing positive for anabolic steroids.

Datin Seri Dr Siti Hasmah, wife of the Prime Minister, signs autographs for the women's paratroop squad.

Superwoman

16 July Kuala Lumpur

Superwoman mother-of-four Cpl Jamilah Dahlan, 34, a member of the Royal Malaysian Police's first woman paratroop squad, made her first parachute jump in February. Since then she has chalked up 71 jumps, mostly from 3,000 metres.

The six-member squad made its first public jump in a dress rehearsal at the Bandar Tun Razak Lake in Cheras.

Karpal back in detention

19 July Kuala Lumpur

The Supreme Court ruled that MP for Jelutong Karpal Singh should not have been released from detention under the Internal Security Act. Karpal was to have been detained under the ISA for two years from 19 December 1987 but was released by the High Court on 9 March. He was re-arrested about nine hours later.

Five held for arson

19 July Kuching

Since 23 June, five people, including a senior Customs officer and the managing director of a newspaper, had been arrested under the Internal Security Act in connection with 18 fires in and around Kuching between 28 April and 7 June, it was announced. Premises affected included Government offices and business premises. Police said the aim of setting the fires was to 'create alarm and despondency, undermining peace and stability in the State'.

31 killed in jetty tragedy

31 July Butterworth

The passenger platform at the Sultan Abdul Halim ferry terminal here collapsed at 4.40pm, killing at least 31 people and injuring more than 800. Of the injured, 390 were admitted to hospital and 54 were given outpatient treatment. It was believed that the structure collapsed under the sheer weight of the unusually large crowd in the waiting area; thousands were returning home from the St Anne Festival in Bukit Mertajam and others were on their way to the island for the Kuan Yin Festival procession.

Passengers were rushing to board a ferry when the platform crashed down on motorcycles and three cars waiting on the lower deck. Using forklifts to lift beams and planks, Penang Port Commission firemen and State Fire Services Department staff took three hours to recover all the bodies.

On 3 August, Prime Minister Dato' Seri Dr Mahathir Mohamad said a Royal Commission would be set up to inquire into the tragedy.

Soccer fans reach the heights by climbing the floodlights at the Seremban stadium.

Soccer mania rides high

17 July Seremban

Selangor soccer fans would go to any height to watch their team win. When nearly 20,000 fans jammed the Seremban Municipal Stadium that was built to hold only 10,000 comfortably, these fans resorted to climbing right up to catch a bird's eye view of the action when Negeri Sembilan played Selangor.

MIC sacks 1,760

21 July Kuala Lumpur

The MIC dismissed 1,760 elected committee members of 80 branches for 'gross inefficiency and negligence' which resulted in their branches being declared defunct. These included 68 which failed to submit their membership dues and 12 which were deemed to have been formed unconstitutionally. MIC president Datuk S. Samy Vellu said the branches would be revived under a restructuring exercise. Four days later, vice-president M.G. Pandithan and 13 of his supporters were expelled and another vice-president, S.S. Subramaniam, was suspended for a year.

Longest lemang record

24 July Kuala Lumpur

To the beat of the kompang, six young men ceremoniously carried a 10-metre-long lemang to the front of Restoran Rasa Utara, organiser of an effort to make the world's longest lemang. Still encased in bamboo, it was cut into 400 pieces and sold in aid of the Cheras Rehabilitation Centre for the Physically Handicapped. Made from 30kg of glutinous rice and milk from 34 coconuts, the lemang took five hours to cook and cost $270.

Boy genius for US varsity

15 August Kuala Lumpur

Zero is very quiet
It does not like to mix with 1,2,3…
For zero to mix anything to the right
It'll lose its neutrality
If zero mixes with anything to the left
It'll go astray…
Zero! It has conquered mankind!
But why… ha!… ha!…
Has mankind ever wasted time…
On nothing!
On zero!

This is part of a poem written for Teacher's Day by 12-year-old Chiang Ti Ming, who was heading for the United States to major in computer science or nuclear physics. His parents decided he should skip Form Six and go straight to university.

Ti Ming planned to appeal to the Education Ministry to allow him to sit for the STPM examination without going through SRP and SPM. Meanwhile, a university lecturer, John Huddleson, was personally tutoring him in computer science.

Ti Ming said he wanted to be a nuclear physicist or a scientist (*see 1 August 1989*).

Karen Lian gives the victory sign after her win at the International Open Bowling Championships.

Girl's perfect game

21 August Singapore

Karen Lian from Ipoh shot a perfect game during the Master's final in the Singapore International Open Bowling Championship, just 11 days after her 20th birthday.

She was the first woman bowler in Asia to achieve the feat in an Asian FIQ-sanctioned tournament. She won S$50,000 and a BMW318i worth S$94,000. It was a fruitful trip, as two days later she also won the Singapore International title.

Upheaval in judiciary

Lord President to be removed

8 August **Kuala Lumpur**

The Yang di-Pertuan Agong directed that Tun Mohamed Salleh Abbas be removed as Lord President. A statement from the Prime Minister's office said that the King had concurred with the recommendations of a tribunal investigating charges against Tun Salleh (*see 17 April 2008*).

Tun Salleh on 2 June announcing that he had appointed Raja Aziz Addruze (left) to represent him.

In March, Tun Salleh, claiming to represent all the country's judges, wrote to the King on developments in the relationship between the executive and the judiciary.

Then, on 28 May, he wrote to Prime Minister Dato' Seri Dr Mahathir Mohamad to say he had decided on early retirement. But the next day he called a press conference to announce that he had been suspended from office.

On 31 May, the Prime Minister's Department issued a statement saying that Tun Salleh had been suspended and would face a tribunal to hear charges against him including 'prejudice and bias against the Government'.

Tan Sri Abdul Hamid Omar was appointed acting Lord President on 1 July, and his appointment was confirmed on 10 November (*see 27 January 1989*).

Protests over suspensions

16 August **Kuala Lumpur**

The Prime Minister's office announced that a six-man tribunal would hear charges of 'gross misbehaviour' against five Supreme Court judges suspended on 6 July, in relation to the removal of Lord President Tun Mohamed Salleh Abbas.

Several members of the Bar protested against the suspensions at the High Court building in Kuala Lumpur.

Later, on 8 October, two judges, Tan Sri Wan Suleiman Pawan Teh and Datuk George Seah Kim Seng, were found guilty and ordered to be removed. The suspension of Tan Sri Haji Mohamed Azmi Datuk Haji Kamaruddin, Tan Sri Eusoffe Abdoolcader and Tan Sri Wan Hamzah bin Haji Mohamed Salleh was lifted.

Lawyers stage a protest at the High Court in Kuala Lumpur over the removal of judges.

Strongman Malek for Hollywood

23 August

Kuala Lumpur

Bodybuilder Malek Noor, who won the Asian heavyweight title for the fourth consecutive year, landed a role in a Hollywood film, *Key To Freedom*. The star would be Roger Moore, said Malek.

Strongman Malek is set to make his mark with former 007 star Roger Moore.

Largest national flag, at Angkasapuri

29 August **Kuala Lumpur**

The biggest-ever Malaysian national flag was hoisted by 500 employees of the Information Ministry and unfurled to cover the façade of Angkasapuri in the run-up to the 31st National Day celebrations. The exercise was led by Information Minister Datuk Mohamed Rahmat and Dato' Seri Dr Mahathir Mohamad who dropped in to lend a hand. The flag, which measured 83.5m by 24.3m, would stay up for a week.

The huge flag covers the entire facade of Angkasapuri.

New union for 80,000

2 October **Petaling Jaya**

Ten days after the Government announced that it had dropped its non-unionisation policy for the sector, the National Union of Electronics Industry Workers was set up. It represented a workforce of 80,000.

First Olympic medal

19 September **Johor Bahru**

At only 5ft 2in, Vasugi Maruthamuthu, 20, might be petite in size but she scored big for the country. Despite a foot injury, she won a bronze medal for taekwondo. Unfortunately, taekwondo was only a demonstration sport and the medal did not count in the official medal tally.

Sports Aid

18 September **Kuala Lumpur**

The major charity event of the year was Sports Aid 1988. A charity run and the first live telethon was part of the activities to raise funds for needy children of the world. Though millions were pledged, the organisers found it a little difficult collecting but Malaysians came through in the end and a sizeable sum was donated to children's charities around the globe.

Probe launched into Skyhawk crashes

4 October **Kuala Lumpur**

Prime Minister Dato' Seri Dr Mahathir Mohamad directed the Defence Ministry to appoint an independent board of inquiry to look into recent Skyhawk crashes. The remaining 33 Skyhawks would be grounded until the RMAF proved their air-worthiness.

In the latest incident, a Skyhawk on the way to Labuan from Kuantan crashed into the South China Sea, about 120 nautical miles from Miri. Its pilot was picked up by a navy ship 15 hours after he ejected to safety. There had been five crashes involving Skyhawks since 1985.

1988

world news

18 September
General Saw Maung, chairman of SLORC (State Law & Order Restoration Council), puts Aung San Suu Kyi under house arrest.

11 October
Women are allowed to study at Magdelene College, Cambridge for the first time.

30 October
Brazilian Ayrton Senna wins his first Formula One championship by winning the Japan Grand Prix. He wins it starting 16th on the grid.

16 November
In Pakistan, Benazir Bhutto wins the first free elections in 11 years and becomes Prime Minister, a position held by her father in the 1970s.

12 December
PLO leader Yasser Arafat accepts the right of Israel to exist.

21 December
A Libyan bomb planted on Pan Am Flight 103 blows up over Lockerbie, Scotland, with the loss of 270 lives.

First Umno Baru general assembly

28 October | **Kuala Lumpur**

Prime Minister Dato' Seri Dr Mahathir Mohamad received a standing ovation at the first Umno Baru general assembly today.

Recognition for Palestinian State

15 November | **Kuala Lumpur**

The Foreign Ministry said Malaysia recognised the new State of Palestine and the political declaration made by Palestine Liberation Organisation chairman Yasser Arafat. 'This is a historic development and Malaysia has full confidence that the establishment of a separate and independent Palestine State will enable the Palestinian people to regain their sovereignty', it said.

Tokoh Wartawan award given to 'people's voice'

19 November | **Kuala Lumpur**

Veteran journalist Haji Abdul Samad Ismail was awarded the Tokoh Wartawan Negara for his outstanding contribution to journalism in the country. Haji Samad, 64, had been the 'people's voice' for almost half a century.

Haji Samad (right) receives the coveted award from Dato' Seri Dr Mahathir Mohamad.

Fans take the plunge

20 October | **Kuching**

Led by Sarawak soccer coach Awang Mahyan Awang Mohamed, about 100 fans jumped into the Sarawak River from the Jalan Satok bridge here. Among those who jumped were the State players. Awang, 37, had said that if Sarawak won the Malaysia Cup, he would jump from the new bridge.

Inquiry launched into 'death by noodles'

23 October | **Ipoh**

Three licensed wet noodle and loh shee fun makers in Kampar were asked to suspend operations for a week for investigations into the deaths of 11 children.

Most of the victims were from areas around Kampar and Teluk Intan. It started when eight pupils of a primary school were taken ill and two of them died of acute salicylate poisoning.

It was found later that most of the victims had eaten loh shee fun from the Kampar manufacturers.

However, not everyone who ate the noodles was affected while some were only affected mildly.

A veteran force: men of the Royal Malaysian Navy form a guard of honour.

Older than they think

2 December | **Kuala Lumpur**

The Royal Malaysian Navy was established long before the official date of 1 July 1952. A naval committee spokesman said the RMN grew out of the Straits Settlements Royal Naval Volunteer Reserve founded in 1934, with 50 British officers and 200 Malays based in Singapore.

It was renamed the Malayan Royal Navy Reserve in 1939. The Malay Navy or Malay Section was formed out of that, with a force of 1,400 in 1942.

Rush for gold permits

3 December | **Marang**

Struck by gold fever, more than 3,000 people crowded the Marang district office for prospecting licences. As the hours passed, some of those waiting lost their patience and threw eggs at the clerks on duty. As a result, riot policemen had to be called in to restore order.

In past weeks, large crowds had been panning for gold in a stream running through a rubber estate in Lubuk Mandi (*see 26 February 1989*).

Gold fever: crowds of prospectors panning for the precious metal in the stream.

'Spiderman' dies in crash

18 December | **Petaling Jaya**

R. Arumugam, the former national goalkeeper was killed when his car crashed into an embankment off the Federal Highway as he was on his way home to Port Klang after dinner with friends. Popularly known to fans as 'Spiderman', he was 35.

30 KTM wagons derailed

21 December | **Butterworth**

Thirty goods wagons left the railway track at Permatang Saga today with damage estimated to run into millions of ringgit. Only nine wagons of the whole train were spared. A KTM source described it as one of the worst derailments in the country.

Third-time lucky for composer Ahmad Nawab

24 December | **Kuala Lumpur**

It was third-time lucky for veteran composer Ahmad Nawab who walked away with the top songwriting award of $10,000 and a trophy at TV3's Juara Lagu '88. His song, *Kau Kunci Cinta Ku Di Hati Mu*, was sung by Ramlah Ram, who won the best performer award.

1989

Women to the fore. National Archives director-general Zakiah Hanum won the Ramon Magsaysay Award for Government service in recognition of her work that made the National Archives 'the most professional and technically advanced in all of Southeast Asia'; Lt Emelia Kamaruddin became the nation's first woman fighter pilot; singer Sheila Majid was a shining star in Japan with her hit song 'Sinaran' topping the charts there; and women activists lambasted some male MPs for their insensitive remarks during the debate on amendments to the Penal Code on cases of rape. Ibu Zain, who fought for the emancipation of Malay women in education and politics, and who was one of the early women MPs, passed away.

MARCH
Singing lawyer Sudirman wins the first Asian Popular Music Award.

APRIL
Tan Sri Hajah Zainun Sulaiman, the early woman MP better known as Ibu Zain, passes away at the age of 86.

JULY
The five Shanmugan brothers at a joint wedding ceremony in Penang.

NOVEMBER
Muzium Negara director Datuk Shahrum Yub is awarded the British Museum medal.

March: Malaysian peacekeepers do the nation proud. Fifteen Malaysian army officers who returned from a six-month stint under the United Nations Iran–Iraq Military Observer Group are seen here being welcomed home by Defence Minister Tengku Ahmad Rithauddeen.

'The frivolous reaction towards rape is indicative of moral decadence by those who cannot see the seriousness of the issue.'

Professor Syed Hussein Alatas, on the reaction of some MPs to the issue of rape, 26 March 1989.

1989

7 January
Emperor Hirohito of Japan, 87, dies. Crown Prince Akihito succeeds to the throne.

10 January
Cuban troops withdraw from Angola, ending a 13-year involvement in the civil war.

14 January
Union Carbide agrees to pay US$470 million compensation for the 1984 Bhopal industrial accident tragedy in India.

23 March
An asteroid misses the Earth by 500,000km, a hair's breadth in astronomical terms.

26 March
First free elections in the Soviet Union. Boris Yeltsin is elected, while the Communists barely take a quarter of the seats.

15 April
In Sheffield, England, 96 Liverpool football supporters are crushed to death at the Hillsborough Stadium.

2 May
Hungary dismantles 150 miles of barbed wire fencing, opening its border to Western Europe.

Cruise ship grounded

1 January | Kuala Lumpur

The 346 New Year revellers on board Feri Malaysia's *Cruise Muhibbah* had a rude shock when the ship ran aground at 5.20am near Pulau Jangkat, off Tanjung Piai in Johor. There were no casualties.

Initial investigations showed that the ship had sailed into shallow waters and hit a reef. By 8.20pm, all passengers had been taken off the ship to Singapore though Capt Abdullah bin Haji Jamil and most of the crew remained on board.

Fish bombs : a warning

2 January | Kuala Lumpur

Fishermen using plastic explosives and detonators in waters off Sabah were causing damage to oil and gas pipelines as well as endangering the lives of divers and oil platform workers, according to oil exploration companies.

Since April last year, 19 such cases had been reported, said the companies. Police said the devices were brought in from the Philippines by fishermen operating from Mantanani Island near Kota Belud and in Kudat and Kota Kinabalu.

Winning start for badminton brothers

8 January | Hong Kong

It was a great start to the New Year for Razif and Jalani Sidek who beat Indonesians Eddy Hartono and Gunawan to win the Fuji International Grand Prix doubles title at the Queen Elizabeth Hall here.

A jubilant Jalani said he hoped the victory was a sign of success to come. This was their second GP success. In 1986, they defeated Eddy Hartono and Hadibowo Susanto of Indonesia for the title.

Bear attacks family

8 January | Seremban

Two bears attacked and injured an Orang Asli couple searching for bamboo in a forest reserve at Jelebu, 90km from here. Tan Rantip, 31, had a deep gash below his left eye while his wife, Dayang, 18, suffered a fractured arm. Their seven-month-old daughter, Rano, who was being carried across Dayang's chest, was unhurt.

111 pupils in hospital with food poisoning

23 January | Kota Bharu

A breakfast of fried rice, boiled eggs and tea with milk landed 111 students of the Falahiah Secondary School in hospital with suspected food poisoning.

Nine were admitted and the others were given outpatient treatment. This was the third such incident in the school in Pasir Pekan near here. The last one happened two years previously.

Tan Sri Hashim (at head of table) briefs new magistrates on their duties.

New Chief Justice appointed

27 January | Kuala Lumpur

Tan Sri Hashim Yeop Abdullah Sani was appointed Chief Justice of Malaya. He received his letter of appointment from the Yang di-Pertuan Agong at Istana Johor.

He succeeded Tan Sri Abdul Hamid Omar, who was appointed Lord President on 20 November 1988. Tan Sri Hashim created ripples in law circles while serving at the Ipoh High Court when he set aside judicial tradition by wearing a songkok instead of a wig on the Bench.

Musa Hitam rejoins Umno

31 January | Kuala Lumpur

MP for Kota Tinggi Datuk Musa Hitam and four of his Johor supporters have decided to rejoin Umno. The four were Tawfik Tun Ismail (Sungai Benut MP), Kadri Sabran (Endau State Assemblyman), Adam Hamid (Bandar Tenggara State Assemblyman) and Hamdan Yahya, an Independent candidate. Datuk Musa said their decision was influenced by the party's willingness to compromise to preserve Malay unity.

Wrong man cremated

25 January | Sungai Petani

The children of pensioner K. Nadaraja cried hard at his funeral. But, even before the flames of the pyre had died out, they were told that their father was alive and in a temple nearby. His son Subramaniam then rushed to the temple, saw his elderly father there and took him home. They were left wondering who it was they had cremated. The man had died in a road accident.

'The dead man looked like my father. He had the same facial features and was of the same height,' said Subramaniam, still not recovered from the shock. Nadaraja was in the habit of leaving the house for a day or two and often relatives would find him in other towns.

Glimpse of a blimp

15 January | Kuala Lumpur

While motorists in the capital wondered if it was a UFO they were seeing, anxious technical staff of Malaysia Airlines hotly pursued a $250,000 thermal airship which was blown off course towards Jalan Kuching. The blimp was a gimmick to announce the airline's first Golden Boutique outlet in the city.

ISA detainees freed

26 January | Taiping

DAP national deputy chairman Karpal Singh (right) and deputy secretary-general P. Patto were among five Internal Security Act detainees released from the Kamunting detention centre. The others were Insan chairman Dr Nasir Hashim, and Pas officials Yusof Hussin and Che Kamaruzaman Che Ismail. Only two of the 106 people detained in October 1987 under Operation Lallang were still under detention. They were DAP secretary-general Lim Kit Siang and his son Lim Guan Eng, MP for Kota Melaka.

Flying Tigers plane crashes in Puchong

19 February | Kuala Lumpur

A cargo plane belonging to Flying Tigers Line crashed into a hillside and burst into flames in Puchong. Its four American crew members were believed killed though only one charred body was recovered.

The crash occurred in fog at 6.36am just before the Boeing 747-200 was due to land at the Kuala Lumpur International Airport in Subang with a cargo of textiles. The explosion rocked about 50 houses nearby.

Police and workers sift through the wreckage of the cargo plane which crashed into a hillside.

Part of $22m stolen from bank recovered

2 February Kuala Lumpur

After the arrest of nine people, police recovered $718,900 of $22.2 million missing from Bank Negara. Forged documents were said to have been used to transfer the money from Bank Negara to a law firm's account in Bank Bumiputra. A week later, $11 million more was recovered. On 5 May, a former Bank Negara clerk, Harun Osman (pictured right under police escort) admitted stealing $22.2 million from the bank and was sentenced to five years' jail and fined $50,000 or 18 months' jail.

A curious crowd gathers at the scene of the hotel shooting in Kuala Lumpur.

Bank raid foiled as robbers are shot dead

21 February Kuala Lumpur

Police burst into a hotel room in Jalan Hicks and shot dead six bank robbers, including a woman, who were planning a bank raid in Taman Tun Dr Ismail. They also arrested a couple, believed to be members of the gang, in another room on the sixth floor of the Imperial Hotel.

The gang members, who were described as 'ruthless and trigger-happy', were said to have been responsible for the killing of four security guards and a policeman and injuring eight others in 16 armed hold-ups in two years.

Police seized four revolvers, one of them silver-plated, and ammunition including deadly 'dum-dum' bullets. They believed that one of the dead was the gang leader.

PM has heart bypass

5 February Kuala Lumpur

Prime Minister Dato' Seri Dr Mahathir Mohamad was discharged from the Kuala Lumpur General Hospital after a successful coronary bypass operation.

Dr Mahathir was admitted to hospital on 18 January after complaining of chest pains. He was operated on by a team comprising cardiac surgeons Yahya Awang and Rozali Wathooth and chief anaesthetist S. Radhakrishna.

2,000 in protest against author Salman Rushdie

24 February Kuala Terengganu

More than 2,000 Muslims gathered at Padang Hiliran near here to protest against Salman Rushdie's book *The Satanic Verses*. The book was banned in Malaysia.

The crowd gathered after Friday prayers, carrying Pas flags and placards condemning Rushdie who was under a fatwa of death from Iranian leader Ayatollah Khomeini. Among those who addressed the crowd was Terengganu Pas commissioner Haji Hadi Awang.

Former MCA chief freed after 12 months' jail

25 February Kajang

Former MCA president Tan Koon Swan walked out of Kajang prison a free man after serving 12 months in jail. He was convicted of committing criminal breach of trust involving $23.2 million belonging to Multi-Purpose Holdings Bhd in 1985.

He was greeted outside the prison by more than 30 relatives and friends.

Curbs on gambling

7 March Kuala Lumpur

In a move to tighten control over gambling, the Government pledged not to issue new gambling licences and to withdraw those of 70 per cent of slot machines. Finance Minister Datuk Paduka Daim Zainuddin said several sections of the community, including political parties and the media, had expressed concern over what they termed widespread gambling activities in the country.

Daily flights to London

12 March Kuala Lumpur

Britain has agreed to allow Malaysia Airlines two more weekly flights to London, bringing the total to seven, said Transport Minister Datuk Dr Ling Liong Sik. 'We have always wanted a daily flight to London and now we can look forward to it,' Transport Ministry secretary-general Datuk Ramon Navaratnam, leader of the Malaysian delegation, told Bernama after the talks in London that led to the agreement. Datuk Ling said Prime Minister Dr Mahathir had been informed of the success of the air talks.

Peacekeepers return

1 March Kuala Lumpur

Fifteen Malaysian army officers told how they fought intense heat, lack of water and a change in diet, and used diplomacy rather than bullets, to win the confidence of warring Iraq and Iran.

Back home after six months under the United Nations Iran–Iraq Military Observer Group, Lt-Kol Zahidi Haji Zainuddin, who led the team of peacekeepers, told of his problems in communicating with as many as 55 observers from 12 nations. But the biggest challenge, he said, was to win the confidence of the warring troops. Malaysia was one of 24 countries with representatives in an observer group monitoring the ceasefire there.

Sudirman wins music award in London

20 March London

The singing lawyer, Sudirman, won the first Asian Popular Music Award competition held at the Royal Albert Hall here last night. Sudirman was selected best performing artist, beating eight others including Anita Sarawak, Japan's Epo and Hong Kong's mega-star Leslie Cheung. The lawyer-turned-singer won the award with the song 'A Thousand Smiles', written by his manager, Dharanee Dharan Kanan.

Gold diggers killed as tunnel caves in

26 February Kuala Terengganu

Three gold diggers were killed and two others injured when a tunnel they were digging at a depth of 10 metres caved in.

Other prospectors at Rusila, 3km from the Bukit Lubuk Mandi main road, took more than an hour to pull the five out of the tunnel. One was dead and two others died on the way to hospital. Bukit Lubuk Mandi had been besieged by thousands of prospectors since traces of gold were discovered there late last year.

Two months later, on 29 April, Menteri Besar Tan Sri Haji Wan Mokhtar Ahmad ordered digging to be stopped immediately after another cave-in tragedy.

An enforcement officer warns prospectors to stay away from the area where the cave-in occurred.

1989

world news

8 May
Slobodan Milosevic is elected President of Serbia. A troubled future lies ahead for Slovenia, Croatia and Bosnia-Herzegovina.

13 May
Two thousand Chinese students begin a hunger strike in Tiananmen Square, Beijing.

20 May
Martial law is declared in Beijing.

3 June
Iranian spiritual leader Ayatollah Khomeini, 89, dies.

4 June
A leaking natural gas pipeline near Ufa, Russia, fuels an explosion that incinerates about 600 passengers in two trains.

9 July
Tennis: Germany conquers England. Steffi Graf and Boris Becker win Wimbledon titles.

23 August
Two million Estonians, Latvians and Lithuanians form an unbroken 600km human chain to demand independence from the Soviet Union.

Palm oil smear campaign in US

22 March Boston

President George Bush assured Prime Minister Dato' Seri Dr Mahathir Mohamad that he would act on allegations that the US Federal Trade Commission was unfair to Malaysia in the latter's efforts to counter the smear campaign against palm oil.

The commission had questioned posters put up by Malaysia describing palm oil as nutritious and not a health hazard. On the other hand, it did not question posters put up by the American Soybean Association and the American Heart Savers Association which alleged that palm oil was poisonous and a health hazard (*see 11 September 1990*).

Woman pioneer dies

2 April Johor Baru

Tan Sri Hajah Zainun Sulaiman, affectionately known as Ibu Zain, died in her home after two heart attacks. She had asked to be discharged from hospital the previous month to spend her last days at home with her relatives and three children—journalist Adibah Amin, Sulaiman Shaikh and Fadzilah. Among those who paid their last respects was Johor Menteri Besar Tan Sri Haji Muhyiddin Yassin.

The gutsy Ibu Zain, who fought for the emancipation of Malay women in education and politics, was one of the early women MPs.

Women rap MPs over rape debate

25 March Kuala Lumpur

The behaviour of a few MPs during a recent debate on the Penal Code (Amendment) Bill on rape roused the ire of women's groups. They were aghast that the serious subject was debated with 'levity and much male hilarity' in Parliament.

Newspapers had reported that the issue was discussed casually amid laughter and frivolous interpolations. The women's groups said that although they welcomed the mandatory minimum five-year jail sentence for convicted rapists, they regretted that unwelcome remarks were made during the debate.

'We are disgusted by their behaviour,' said All Women's Action Society (AWAM) president Irene Fernandez. It caused 'great concern,' she added.

Production boosted as UK snaps up Proton

3 April Shah Alam

Just two weeks after its launch there on 16 March, all 1,000 Proton Saga cars sent to Britain were snapped up, making it the fastest selling newly-launched imported vehicle there.

'Orders are coming in fast,' said Proton UK chairman David Brown. To meet the demand, the Proton plant in Shah Alam will increase production to between 60,000 and 80,000 units a year.

Time-bomb theory as blast rocks Dayabumi

10 April Kuala Lumpur

Four people were injured in a bomb blast that caused extensive damage to the Dayabumi Complex at 8.30 this morning.

While police were investigating, an anonymous telephone call at 10.15am warned of a second bomb in the building but this turned out to be a hoax. Police said explosives used for rock blasting were probably used in the bomb and there were indications that a timer was used.

Six killed as police plane crashes on car

17 May Kuala Lumpur

Five police officers and a six-year-old boy were killed and several other people injured when a light aircraft of the Royal Malaysian Police air wing crashed into a car. The plane was trying to make an emergency landing on the highway leading to Subang Airport when it nose-dived into the car.

Malaysian millionaire dies in Tamil Nadu

27 April Kuala Lumpur

N.T.S. Arumugam Pillai, the Bukit Mertajam millionaire, died of a heart attack in his hometown Prippur in Tamil Nadu, India. He was 74. Arumugam, who owned the Tamil daily *Thinamani*, used to own rubber plantations, oil palm estates and textile shops in Malaysia and Singapore. He arrived in Malaysia in 1939 and rose from rags to riches through land deals in Bukit Mertajam.

Soccer star suffers muscular disorder

22 May Kuala Lumpur

Malaysia's soccer superstar Mokhtar Dahari was suffering from a disorder that causes muscular weakness and wasting, according to a statement by Sir John Walton of Radcliffe Infirmary in Oxford, England.

Mokhtar is helped through the airport on his arrival.

Football Association of Selangor deputy president Mazlan Harun said the FAS council would set up a committee to manage a trust fund for the former soccer star. The FAS said Mokhtar did not want the exact diagnosis to be made public.

To boost the trust fund, it suggested that a percentage of the gate from coming football matches should be donated to it.

There were tributes to 'Supermokh' after the news broke. One sportswriter, Fauzi Omar, wrote that his symptoms showed while he was still active as a player and assistant coach with the Selangor Malaysia Cup team. Describing Mokhtar as 'one of the nicest people I have met', his column concluded: 'You will never walk alone.'

Tearful farewell for Assunta headmistress

31 May Petaling Jaya

Her Irish eyes filled with tears as Sister Enda, head of Assunta Secondary School, said goodbye after 35 years of service.

Sister Enda, who left Ireland at 19 to be a nun with the Franciscan Missionaries of Mary, said she could not imagine life without the girls of the school, who were her family. She was succeeded by Miss L.K. Tan, who will be the second headmistress of the school.

Sister Enda with Assunta School students.

Children poisoned by toxin in noodles

8 June Ipoh

Two coroners ruled today that 11 children who died of food poisoning were killed by aflatoxin in the loh shee fun noodles they ate. Aflatoxin is a fungus that grows on damp food. The coroners said it could not be determined who was responsible for the tragedy, nor could they find any criminal element in the cases.

Film star flies in for PWTC premiere

22 June Kuala Lumpur

Film star Jane Seymour flew in from London to attend the premiere of the first joint Malaysian-American film, *Keys To Freedom*, on 27 June at the Putra World Trade Centre.

Seymour, who plays a doctor in the film, said she 'missed Malaysian food and the friendly faces' and was glad to be back. She would visit the east coast, Kuching and several other destinations.

Scuffles at Maika AGM

30 June **Kuala Lumpur**

Shareholders got downright physical at the Maika Holdings Berhad annual general meeting at the Putra World Trade Centre today. Two groups exchanged blows, kicks and punches and Federal Reserve Unit personnel were called in to control the 3,000 shareholders.

MIC president Dato' Seri S. Samy Vellu said he would lodge police reports against those who instigated the scuffles.

A helmeted police officer wades into the brawling crowd.

One big wedding for five brothers

5 July **Penang**

The five Shanmugam brothers, aged between 29 and 35, made history when they each took a bride in a colourful ceremony at the Pesta Pulau Pinang site. The ceremony was witnessed by some 4,000 relatives and friends.

Malaysian Hindu Priests' Association chief priest M. Salvasamy said: 'This is the first time in my 20 years as a priest that I am marrying so many brothers at the same time.' The five newly wed couples decided against honeymooning together, preferring to go their own ways to various destinations in the country.

Five brides for five brothers making wedding history.

A first at International Islamic University

29 July **Kuala Lumpur**

When Sukhdev Singh finally realised his aspiration to be a lawyer, he also became the first student of the International Islamic University to be awarded a first-class honours bachelor's degree in law.

Sukhdev, son of a bus driver, had to work as a jaga and a waiter after he left school to finance his further education.

'Treated like slaves'

1 August **Kuala Lumpur**

Seven people who claimed that they were 'treated like slaves' while working for Saudi aristocracy, flew home this evening. Several broke down when greeted by friends and family at Subang Airport.

The seven travelled on emergency passports issued by the Malaysian High Commission in London as their passports were kept by the employers.

Child prodigy enters US university at 13

1 August **Kuala Lumpur**

Child prodigy Chiang Ti Ming, 13, was admitted to the second-year physics programme at the prestigious California Institute of Technology. He was the youngest student to be admitted into Caltech. But his parents said their biggest problem would be financing his three-year course because the university insisted that his father live with him in the US. Later the MCA pledged $120,000 to help the boy.

Ti Ming and his father (left) with MCA president Dato' Seri Dr Ling Liong Sik.

Magsaysay Award for National Archives D-G

6 August **Kuala Lumpur**

National Archives director-general Datin Zakiah Hanum Abdul Majid was named winner of the Ramon Magsaysay Award for Government service.

The Manila-based foundation said she had been selected for her expert running of the Malaysian archives. They were 'the most professional and technically advanced in all of Southeast Asia', it said.

Datin Zakiah with her award.

Probe into VIP prisoners perks

14 August **Kuala Lumpur**

Deputy Home Affairs Minister Datuk Megat Junid Megat Ayob ordered investigations into allegations that prisoners with political connections and wealth were enjoying special privileges like colour television in their cells and could leave the prison during the day.

After a *Malay Mail* report on how Abdullah Ang, the recently-released former managing director of the Malaysian Overseas Investment Corporation, could visit family business premises while still an inmate at the prison, the VIP prisoners are now back to sharing cells and eating prison meals like other inmates.

'Before the Abdullah Ang story, some of the warders acted as errand boys for these prisoners,' a source said, adding that a former convict even had a waterbed in his cell. Datuk Megat Junid said the Home Ministry took indiscipline by prison officers very seriously. Later, on 16 November, a report by the Home Ministry committee investigating the case, recommended that two senior prison officers be dismissed.

Protest against Sheila Majid concert

11 September **Kuala Lumpur**

Police arrested 22 people after breaking up a demonstration by 1,000 people during a concert by singer Sheila Majid at Dewan Tunku Canselor in University of Malaya. The two-hour concert went on uninterrupted. Deputy Vice-Chancellor Prof Madya Abdul Rashid Ahmad said the university was unaware that there would be a demonstration though the Islamic Students' Union had submitted a memorandum four days earlier to protest against allowing the concert. The demonstrators said the concert was un-Islamic and should not be part of cultural activities at the university.

Tokyo chart topper

12 September **Kuala Lumpur**

Singer Sheila Majid was shining in the Land of The Rising Sun with her hit song *Sinaran*, the No. 1 song on Sapporo radio in Tokyo. The song, released as a single in the Japanese market two months earlier, was No. 38 in the Top 40 chart, according to the Osaka cable radio station.

1989

world news

28 September
Former Philippine president Ferdinand Marcos, 72, dies in exile in Hawaii.

5 October
The Dalai Lama wins the Nobel Peace Prize.

8 November
East Germany opens its checkpoints in the Berlin Wall, allowing its citizens to travel freely to the West.

9 November
A massive crowd in a party mood starts tearing down the Berlin Wall.

29 November
Indian PM Rajiv Gandhi resigns.

22 December
After a week of bloody fighting, Ion Illiescu becomes President of Romania, while former dictator Nicolae Ceaucescu and his wife flee in a helicopter. They were captured on Christmas Day and executed.

29 December
Riots break out in refugee camps, after Hong Kong announces it will repatriate Vietnamese boat people, by force if necessary.

8 prisoners in pre-dawn jailbreak

4 September | Johor Bahru

Eight remand prisoners facing drug trafficking charges used bedsheets to escape from the prison in Jalan Air Molek.

They broke through two iron gates, wire fencing and a 7.62-metre wall topped with barbed wire. Police set up roadblocks throughout the State and launched house-to-house checks.

Protest against Central Market reshuffle'

18 September | Kuala Lumpur

The Central Market, usually quiet at night, was a scene of activity as stall operators gathered to stage a protest and refused to budge until they had talked to the management.

The operators had been evicted in a 'reshuffle and upgrading exercise'. Central Market management said some of the affected operators had been found to have sub-let their stalls while others sold items similar to those of other operators.

9th King installed

18 September | Kuala Lumpur

The Sultan of Perak, Sultan Azlan Muhibuddin Shah ibni Al-marhum Sultan Yussuf Izzuddin Ghafarullahu-lahu Shah, was installed as the 9th Yang di-Pertuan Agong. He succeeded the Sultan of Johor, Sultan Iskandar Al Haj ibni Al-marhum Sultan Ismail, whose term expired in April.

British award for museum director

1 November | Kuala Lumpur

It was a day of double joy for Muzium Negara director Datuk Shahrum Yub. First, the Treasures from the Grave exhibition opened—the result of much hard work by Datuk Shahrum who had arranged for the loan and shipment of exhibits from 40 countries, and second, he was awarded the British Museum Medal.

Spectacular end to 15th SEA Games

31 August | Kuala Lumpur ▶ Pomp and pageantry marked the end of the 15th SEA Games at the Merdeka Stadium. Thousands braved the heavy rain in a climactic finish to 11 days of sporting competition between the nine participating nations. Malaysia finished an unprecedented second to champions Indonesia with 67 golds, the last coming from football, a best-ever National Day gift for the country. Swimmers Eric Buhain of the Philippines and eight-gold winner Nurul Huda Abdullah of Malaysia were chosen as the best Sportsman and Sportswoman of the 15th Games.

The closing ceremony of the SEA Games.

Tussle for MIC leadership

1 October | Kuala Lumpur

The opening of nominations for the MIC party presidential election today was marred by scuffles between supporters of Datuk Seri S. Samy Vellu and his deputy Datuk S. Subramaniam.

Police had to step in and baton-charge the crowd when the supporters, who exchanged punches, kicks and abuse as Datuk Subramaniam arrived to file his nomination papers in the morning, refused to disperse. Fifteen people filed nomination papers for the top party post. In a nationwide poll of MIC members on 15 October, Samy Vellu was confirmed as party president.

Balmy welcome for Queen Elizabeth

14 October | Port Klang

Queen Elizabeth II arrived aboard the royal yacht *Britannia* for the start of a State visit.

She and Prince Philip were welcomed by dignitaries led by the Raja Muda of Selangor and his wife and Prime Minister Dato' Seri Dr Mahathir Mohamad and his wife. They were then whisked off to Parliament House for the official welcoming ceremony.

Queen Elizabeth also visited Lumut, Perak, where she was met by the Regent of Perak and received a traditional Malaysian welcome (pictured above).

Farmer walks down ASN road to win honour

11 November | Kuala Lumpur

Megat Sulaiman Megat Omar, 73, never earned much as a farmer. But in eight years he made 667 deposits of $3 each in his Amanah Saham Nasional account, filling up seven savings books. And each time, he had to walk 3.2km from his house to catch the bus to the post office.

He was one of four exemplary investors honoured by Permodalan Nasional Berhad at the launch of the Amanah Saham Bumiputra scheme at the Putra World Trade Centre here. They received their awards from Prime Minister Dato' Seri Dr Mahathir.

First woman fighter pilot

17 November | Kuala Lumpur

Lt Emilia Kamarudin, 27, was close to making history by becoming the country's first woman fighter pilot. She obtained her 'wings' in April 1988, making her the only woman in Malaysia qualified to undergo an advanced flight tactical course. Then she underwent a tactical fighter conversion course for the A-4 Skyhawk. She went on to become the first full-fledged woman pilot of a fighter-bomber.

Communists to dismantle booby traps

5 December | Kuala Lumpur

The army would withdraw in stages troops stationed in operational areas following the move by the Communist Party of Malaya to lay down arms, it was announced. Counter-insurgency operations would cease immediately. Army Chief Jen Tan Sri Yaacob Mohamed Zain said the withdrawal would be conducted in stages to 'give them time and space to move out and dismantle the booby traps which they had planted'.

Helicopters grounded

19 December | Kuala Lumpur

The Royal Malaysian Air Force has grounded all its Nuri helicopters after two of them crashed in Sarawak yesterday, killing all 16 on board, including two army generals.

Mej-Jen Datuk Mustaffa Awang and Brig-Jen Datuk Hasbullah Yusuf were in the helicopters which crashed into the sea near Kampung Pandang, 54km northwest of Kuching, Sarawak.

The Nuris were part of a fleet of 40 purchased in 1968. Eight of them have crashed, two this year.

1990

Beauty and the Beasts briefly grabbed Malaysians' attention this year. Malaysians rejoiced as Kavita Kaur became the first Malaysian to bag an international beauty contest title when she was crowned Miss Charm International in Leningrad; and the beasts came in the form of two drunken parents who forced their two children to beg, and caregivers in a welfare home in Klang who were exposed for their inhuman treatment of inmates. The first Visit Malaysia Year was launched in January with ambitious plans for the nation to move into 'aggressive, big league tourism'. Six months later Malaysia played host to Heads of Government at the Group of Fifteen summit meeting. Malaysia also highlighted the ugly side of the US anti-palm oil lobby.

FEBRUARY
Multi-vehicle pile-up on the Kuala Lumpur–Karak Highway leaves 16 dead.

JUNE
Renowned lawyer Datuk Param Cumaraswamy is elected to the International Commission of Jurists.

NOVEMBER
Nelson Mandela visits Malaysia.

DECEMBER
'Bapa Malaysia' Tunku Abdul Rahman passes away and is given a royal funeral.

June: The first G15 summit to be held in Kuala Lumpur.

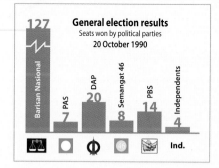

General election results
Seats won by political parties
20 October 1990

Party	Seats
Barisan Nasional	127
PAS	7
DAP	20
Semangat 46	8
PBS	14
Independents (Ind.)	4

Malaysia Facts

18.1 million	Population
$119.1 billion	Gross Domestic Product
$6,298	Gross National Income (per capita)
27.9	Crude Birth Rate (per 1,000 persons)
13.1	Infant Mortality (per 1,000 live births)
69.2 / 73.7	Life Expectancy (male / female)
56.7	Consumer Price Index (base 2010=100)

'The memory of him, his hope for us and his faith in us will keep our feet on the path of tolerance, peace and harmony.'

'Father, Patriot and Friend', obituary for Tunku Abdul Rahman in *The Star*, 7 December 1990.

1990

world news

20 January
Soviet troops attack Baku, Azerbaijan to crush separatist sentiments, killing 62 demonstrators.

2 February
South African President de Klerk lifts the ban on the African National Congress.

11 February
Nelson Mandela is released after 26 years behind bars.

20 March
After 25 years of a guerrilla war to end 75 years of South African domination, Namibia gains independence.

28 March
British Customs announce the seizure of 40 American-made devices for triggering nuclear missiles being shipped to Iraq.

18 April
The Soviet Union shuts off the crude oil pipeline that supplies Lithuania, which declared independence from the Soviet Union.

27 May
The first free elections in three decades are held in Myanmar. The military ignores the electoral results when the National League led by Aung San Suu Kyi wins 392 of the 485 seats.

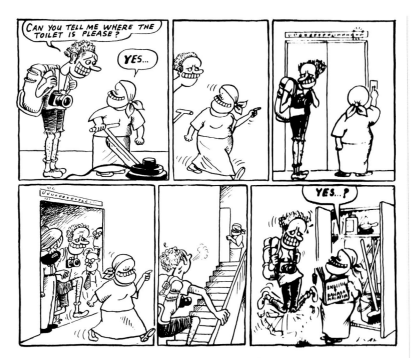

First Visit Malaysia Year launched

1 January Kuala Lumpur

The first Visit Malaysia Year was launched at a glittering party at Merdeka Square with cultural performances and a concert by local artistes. 'We're new at this game. Visit Malaysia Year is just the beginning of our move into aggressive, big-league tourism,' said Culture and Tourism Minister Sabbaruddin Chik (*see 3 January 1991*).

Missing trekkers found

5 January Kluang

Five trekkers missing for 11 days at Gunung Belumut found their way to a logging camp in Kejora near Kota Tinggi. More than 100 people had combed the dense jungle in search of the trekkers after they failed to return from their hiking trip. Singaporean Tan Aik Kee, 28, one of the trekkers, blamed a faulty compass.

Graft exists in RMAF

4 February Kuala Lumpur

There was evidence of corruption in the Supplies and Air Material Command of the Royal Malaysian Air Force, the Defence Ministry said. But it added that it was sure this had not led to inferior or imitation parts being used in any of its aircraft. All spare parts and equipment acquired by the RMAF were first scrutinised by the Aeronautical Inspection Service, said Mindef spokesman Lt-Kol Sheikh Taufik Sheikh Shukor.

500 reconditioned cars under probe

15 March Kuala Lumpur

Registration documents of about 500 reconditioned cars suspected of having been imported with false approval permits (APs) have been submitted to the police by the Road Transport Department (RTD).

According to RTD public relations officer Mohamed Hatta Said, the Federal Territory RTD registered the cars as it perceived the import documents to be in order. But the RTD was later informed by the Customs Department that the APs might have been forged.

Gone in minutes

15 March Petaling Jaya

Clutching whatever belongings they could lay their hands on, some 350 female Universiti Malaya students ran helter-skelter as fire razed their hostel in Section 16 here.

Vijandran to step down

22 February Kangar

Dewan Rakyat Deputy Speaker D.P. Vijandran, who was at the centre of a pornographic videotape scandal, would resign from his post, according to MIC president Dato' Seri S. Samy Vellu.

'He wants to reduce politicking that could affect the MIC and the Barisan Nasional ...he does not want to inconvenience the Government and the MIC,' said Dato' Seri Samy Vellu.

The controversy was sparked by certain allegations made by DAP deputy chairman Karpal Singh in the Dewan Rakyat two months earlier. He had accused Vijandran of having abused his position as MIC-owned Maika Holdings chairman. Mr Vijandran, a lawyer, will continue as Kapar MP.

Regional stock markets plunge

26 February Kuala Lumpur

Stock markets across Asia tumbled in what was reminiscent of the Black October crash of 1987. Most markets recorded the most severe one-day drop in their indices since the mini-crash of 16 October 1989. The key 225-share Nikkei Index closed 1,569.10 points lower at 33,321.87.

The Kuala Lumpur Stock Exchange's benchmark Composite Index lost 19.75 points or 3.3 per cent to close at 581.50, its biggest one-day drop in 1990.

Parents have a say in child's religion

2 March Kuala Lumpur

The Supreme Court overturned a High Court decision on the conversion of a girl to Islam by ruling that parents had the right to choose the religion of children below the age of 18. The judgment was passed on the appeal of labourer Teoh Eng Huat against a Kota Bharu High Court decision that he had no right to decide on the religion of his then 17-year-old daughter Susie. Teoh had sought a declaration that he had the right to decide Susie's religion, education and upbringing, and that her conversion from Buddhism to Islam was null and void.

49,000 scrips still missing

14 March Kuala Lumpur

Some 49,000 share scrips that were reported to have 'gone missing' were still unaccounted for although the Kuala Lumpur Stock Exchange (KLSE) had been able to verify most of them.

KLSE executive chairman Nik Mohamed Din Nik Yusof expressed strong belief that the missing scrips were still in the system. 'I must emphasise that there is no question of RM200 million worth of scrips missing as reported in the media,' he said, noting that KLSE was confident of resolving the entire problem and 'every single verified short claim will be made good.'

16 dead in 13-vehicle pile-up

28 February Karak

Sixteen people, 11 of them Federal Reserve Unit (FRU) personnel, were killed and scores of others were injured, some seriously, in an accident involving 13 vehicles at the 25km Kuala Lumpur–Karak Highway. The collision, described as the worst since the highway was built in 1978, involved an FRU truck, a bus, a trailer, an oil tanker, a lorry, two taxis and six cars.

Insurance companies were expected to pay out at least RM3 million in compensation but it might take up to three years. Officials were investigating whether a gang might be causing accidents for profit after traces of oil were found at sharp bends.

Karpov and Timman face each other in the World Chess Candidates final.

Chess grandmasters square off

8 March   Kuala Lumpur

Chess grandmasters Anatoly Karpov and Jan Timman squared off at the opening match of the World Chess Candidates final.

More than 200 chess enthusiasts packed the Kuala Lumpur City Hall auditorium to witness the battle of wits and nerves between Karpov, the Soviet grandmaster who was world champion from 1975 to 1985, and Timman, the seven-times Dutch grandmaster. Karpov beat Timman in the first game that lasted four hours and 36 moves. Karpov went on to take the title, with two wins and two drawn games.

Inhumane treatment at welfare homes

26 March   Klang

Inhumane treatment of inmates at welfare homes was exposed after a nine-year old bedridden girl suffering from severe malnutrition was rescued from a private welfare home, Rumah Kebajikan Kanak-Kanak Mufakat, in Klang.

Wong Fung Yen was described by doctors at the Tengku Ampuan Rahimah General Hospital as 'anaemic, grossly underweight and has scabies with secondary infection'.

Welfare Services Minister Datuk Mustaffa Mohamad ordered a full investigation as hospital medical superintendent Dr G. Vevegananthan confirmed 'a long history of serious neglect cases' at the private welfare home where Fung Yen was housed.

In Kedah, the Bedong Rumah Seri Kenangan was described as a 'home of horror' for 330 old people living there. The inmates were cruelly treated and lived in squalor, according to Penang Hindu Sangam social and welfare committee chairman P. Murugiah.

Malaysia–Thailand pact

26 March   Pattaya

Malaysian and Thai officials agreed to put their differences aside, paving the way for the signing of an accord to jointly exploit natural resources in overlapping offshore border areas in the South China Sea.

Consensus was reached over civil jurisdiction and sovereignty in six-hour talks which ended at 2.30am. It would lead to the formation of a joint authority for the exploration covering 7,300 sq km in the Gulf of Thailand and waters off Kelantan.

'We are cooperating and sensitive to each other's needs…we have made each other aware of what the other is doing,' said Prime Minister Dato' Seri Dr Mahathir Mohamad who earlier had talks with his Thai counterpart General Chatichai Choonhavan.

Malaysian beauty tops the world

8 May   Kuala Lumpur

Kavita Kaur, 21, became the first Malaysian woman to bag an international beauty contest title when she beat 32 other beauties to be crowned Miss Charm International 1990 in Leningrad.

Kavita Kaur, 21, the first Malaysian to win an international beauty title.

KL celebrates 100th anniversary

14 May   Kuala Lumpur

The celebration of Kuala Lumpur's 100th anniversary as a local authority was launched in front of the Sultan Abdul Samad building, with Yang di-Pertuan Agong Sultan Azlan Shah handing over the new Kuala Lumpur flag to Datuk Bandar (Mayor) Elyas Omar.

Penang hosts fleet review

18 May   Penang

Fifty-nine warships of various nations docked in Penang harbour for a four-day International Royal Fleet Review.

Some 12,000 navy personnel from 22 countries took part. One of the highlights was a march by 2,000 of them accompanied by nine bands. Deputy Culture and Tourism Minister Datuk Ng Cheng Kuai expected Penang to earn about RM50 million from the sailors.

As an acknowledgement of the RMN's long link with Penang, going back to 1934 when the Straits Settlements Naval Volunteer Reserve was founded, the State conferred on the RMN the Freedom of the City of George Town. The RMN was the first institution to receive the key.

Malaysia hosts G15 summit

1 June   Kuala Lumpur

The first Group of Fifteen (G15) summit meeting began in Kuala Lumpur attended by heads of Government and special representatives from Algeria, Argentina, Brazil, Egypt, Indonesia, India, Jamaica, Mexico, Nigeria, Peru, Senegal, Venezuela, Yugoslavia, Zimbabwe and Malaysia.

The three-day meeting would form part of a regular consultation session to coordinate and enhance cooperation among members in the context of an increasingly interdependent world. The G15 was established in September 1989, following the conclusion of the Ninth Non-Aligned Summit meeting in Belgrade.

World Cup fever

9 June   Kuala Lumpur

Hundreds of soccer fans converged at the Merdeka Square to watch a live telecast of the opening of the World Cup football tournament on a giant video screen.

Tun Hussein's casket is carried ceremoniously to the hall of the Islamic Centre in Kuala Lumpur for his lying-in-state.

Tun Hussein dies at 68

29 May   Kuala Lumpur

Former Prime Minister Tun Hussein Onn died of a heart attack in San Francisco at the age of 68 after undergoing two heart operations within six weeks. Tun Hussein, who served as Malaysia's third PM from 1976 to 1981, was laid to rest beside Tun Abdul Razak in the Heroes' Mausoleum at the National Mosque.

Johor-born Tun Hussein received his early education in Singapore and at the English College in Johor Bahru.

After leaving school, he joined the Johor Military Forces as a cadet in 1940 and a year later was sent to the Indian Military Academy in Dehradun, India.

Tun Hussein entered politics in 1945 at the age of 23. He came from a family with deep nationalistic spirit and political roots. His father was Datuk Onn Jaafar, the founder of Umno. In 1949, Tun Hussein became the first youth chief of the party.

Opposition leader Lim Kit Siang said Tun Hussein's deeds, especially in combating corruption, would always be remembered. The country's first Prime Minister, Tunku Abdul Rahman, was impressed with Tun Hussein's quiet dignity. He noted: 'He was a very good man; he hated to quarrel and he hated to be rough with his enemies.'

1990

world news

28 May
Iraqi President Saddam Hussein opens an Arab League summit in Baghdad by saying that Iraq will respond with 'weapons of mass destruction' should Israel deploy nuclear or chemical weapons.

29 May
Boris Yeltsin is elected President by the Russian Parliament.

1 June
US President Bush and Soviet leader Gorbachev sign a treaty ending chemical weapon production and destroying existing stocks.

4 June
Janet Atkins, 54, of Portland, Oregon, suffering from Alzheimer's Disease, uses a suicide machine designed by Dr Kevorkian.

21 June
A 7.3–7.7-magnitude earthquake kills an estimated 50,000 Iranians. Salman Rushdie contributes US$8,600 to the relief of victims.

2 August
Iraq invades Kuwait, claiming it as a 19th province.

Tycoon's son was murdered, says coroner

18 June Penang

A coroner's court concluded that Kah Motors managing director Loh Kah Kheng, who was found dead three years earlier at the Boon Siew Villa in Batu Ferringhi, was murdered.

The murder was planned and committed by someone 'familiar with the ins and outs' of Loh's house, according to coroner Rosilah Yop. Loh, the second son of magnate Tan Sri Loh Boon Siew, was found dead in his bedroom with a telephone wire coiled around his neck and hands on 25 February 1987.

A total of 35 witnesses including Tan Sri Loh, Kah Kheng's widow Shirley Yap and her brother, architect Jeffrey, testified at the inquest which began on 12 September 1988.

The hearing lasted more than 50 days spread over nearly two years.

Malaysian elected ICJ member

23 June Kuala Lumpur

Prominent lawyer Datuk Param Cumaraswamy was elected to the Geneva-based International Commission of Jurists (ICJ). A highly regarded advocate and solicitor, Param had been actively championing human rights and was a member of the standing advisory board on human rights of the International Bar Association. The ICJ comprises not more than 40 distinguished lawyers from all over the world and its main objective is to defend the rule of law and to work towards observance of human rights.

Rashid makes his mark

15 July Kuala Lumpur

Rashid Sidek lived up to expectations as a potential world-beater when he defeated national champion Foo Kok Keong to lift the US$165,000 Rothmans Malaysian Open singles badminton title, the first six-star tournament in the world, at Stadium Negara. Rashid bagged a US$12,500 top prize with his first Grand Prix title.

122 Haj pilgrims die in stampede

6 July Kuala Lumpur

At least 122 Malaysian pilgrims were among more than 1,400 dead in the stampede in a pedestrian tunnel (Al-Ma'aisim) between Mecca and Mina, in Saudi Arabia, Tabung Haji announced. Previously it was thought only six Malaysians were killed.

The 2 July stampede occurred when a power cut halted air supplies and sent temperatures in the tunnel soaring above 43°C, triggering panic among thousands of pilgrims heading for Mecca from Mina. Mina is located near Mount Arafat where Prophet Muhammad preached his last sermon 14 centuries ago. Many of the dead were said to have suffocated. Others were trampled to death in the 500-metre tunnel.

Tabung Haji chairman Datuk Hanafiah Ahmad said he expected the Malaysian pilgrims' mission in Mecca to have difficulty identifying the dead. The Saudi Government had buried all the dead without confirming their identities, he said.

CAF officials with the family in their rented flat, which was completely without furniture.

Drunkard parents force children to beg

2 July Petaling Jaya

A six-year-old boy and his eight-year-old sister were forced to beg for money and food for their alcoholic parents for one year before they were rescued by volunteers from the Child Abuse Fighters (CAF) group at their PKNS flat in Sungai Way.

Proceeds from the begging would be used by their 40-year-old jobless father to buy illicit liquor for him and his 32-year-old wife. When the children refused to go begging, they would be beaten.

When they were found there were marks on their bodies and they were malnourished. There was no furniture in the family home and they owed more than $2,000 in rent.

Thanks to the CAF, the father, who suffered from liver disease, was given a job as a watchman and a place to stay in Port Klang. The mother was admitted to the University Hospital for treatment for a liver ailment. The children were housed at a welfare home.

Plot to take Sabah out of Malaysia

9 July Kuala Lumpur

Police uncovered a plot to take Sabah out of Malaysia by force and detained four people, including a senior police officer, for their alleged involvement.

They were on the lookout for a Caucasian mercenary who was believed to be the group's middleman in recruiting more mercenaries.

Documents seized by the police revealed that the plot was still at the planning stage when they stepped in, according to Deputy Inspector General of Police Tan Sri Abdul Rahim Noor.

The documents revealed a plan for a 'Sabah People's Liberation Organisation' and a secret army to seize power in the State. They also seized an account book with a bank in Hong Kong showing a balance of more than US$300,000.

Investigation into the plot started in 1987 when a member of the group voluntarily exposed it to the police, Tan Sri Abdul Rahim added.

Ban on Cuba visits lifted

29 July Ipoh

Malaysia has lifted the ban on visiting North Korea, Cuba and Albania. The decision was in line with the view that these nations were no longer a threat to Malaysia due to global political changes. However, the ban on visits to Israel and South Africa remained, according to Deputy Home Minister Datuk Megat Junid Ayob.

Seeking capable Bumi managers

22 August Kuala Lumpur

Malaysia's post-1990 economy would not encounter any radical change as a result of the New Economic Policy (NEP) but would in essence be a well-thought plan geared towards achieving economic growth and equality, according to Prime Minister Dato' Seri Mahathir Mohamad.

The Prime Minister contended that the idea behind the NEP was not to channel 30 per cent of the nation's wealth to Bumiputras but instead for 30 per cent of Malaysian managers and entrepreneurs to be highly-skilled and ethical Bumiputras. The sooner the target could be met, the sooner the need for special treatment would end, he added.

Dr Ling and Lee retain top posts

28 July Kuala Lumpur

MCA president Dato' Seri Dr Ling Liong Sik successfully thwarted an attempt by his deputy Datuk Lee Kim Sai to mount a challenge against him at the eleventh hour.

Both leaders easily retained their posts and expressed satisfaction that party delegates were concerned with striking a balance.

Datuk Lim Ah Lek and Woon See Chin were retained as vice-presidents at the party's general assembly while Chua Jui Meng and former party Youth chief Datuk Yap Pian Hon were elected as the two other vice-presidents.

Haze blankets Klang Valley

29 August Kuala Lumpur

Klang Valley was blanketed by haze after a long dry spell that allowed dust from indiscriminate open burning, smoke-belching vehicles and industrial emissions to accumulate and hang in the air.

The Klang Valley suffered in particular because of an underground fire in the peat swamp forests in Ulu Klang. Such fires were extremely difficult to extinguish. At Port Klang, the Kuching-registered MV *Soon Dua* ran aground in the haze and the arrival or departure of 31 other vessels was delayed.

Lending rate up 0.5%

7 September Kuala Lumpur

Banks raised their base lending rate by 0.5 per cent in a move to control inflation by encouraging savings and lessening spending. The change was a drop of between 0.25 and 0.5 per cent to 6.75 per cent for Malayan Banking and Bank Bumiputra and to seven per cent for other commercial banks. Despite the increase, the rate was at a 20-year low and was one of the lowest in the region. At its peak in 1985, it was as high as 12.25 per cent.

Stranded Malaysians leave Kuwait

16 August Kuala Lumpur

Following the invasion by Iraq, Malaysians still in Kuwait have begun their journey to the Iraqi capital Baghdad on the way home. First to leave were 69 workers and non-essential Malaysian Embassy staff and their families. The Government had advised Malaysians in the Middle East to leave in the event war broke out in the region following the invasion of Kuwait by Iraqi troops on 2 August.

On 24 August, 55 Malaysians, most of whom were passengers of the stranded British Airways Flight 149 in Kuwait, touched down at Subang Airport at 9.15pm. Accompanied by two BA officials, the Malaysians and four foreigners were flown from Amman to Dubai in a chartered Royal Jordanian plane. The last batch of 90 Malaysians who were stranded in Kuwait and Iraq arrived home on 30 August (*see 7 January 1991*).

Lam Thye calls it a day

2 October Kuala Lumpur

DAP MP for Bukit Bintang Lee Lam Thye (above with his wife) quit as deputy secretary-general of the party less than a week after announcing that he was leaving politics but would nevertheless stay on with the party.

Lee, MP for Kuala Lumpur Bandar/ Bukit Bintang since 1974, said in a letter to party chairman Dr Chen Man Hin that he had decided to retire from politics.

Dr Chen said Lee had chosen to resign despite an appeal to reconsider.

RM100,000-a-day payout

18 September Kuala Lumpur

The suspension of toll collection at Jalan Cheras following protests from the public cost the Government RM100,000 daily in payments to the toll concessionaire, Teratai K.G. Sdn Bhd.

Prime Minister Dato' Seri Dr Mahathir Mohamad said the Government was prepared to shoulder the burden to prevent any untoward incidents following large-scale demonstrations at the highway interchange when the toll was imposed.

Anti-palm oil campaign: Malaysia hits back

11 September Kuala Lumpur

Palm oil had proved itself as a healthy choice of edible oil based on numerous scientific discoveries, chief executive officer of the Malaysian Palm Oil Promotion Council Datuk Murad Hashim said. Test results would clear various misconceptions about palm oil, he added.

'The latest result shows the importance of palm oil in a person's diet as it raises the 'good' high-density lipoprotein cholesterol,' he said, laying to rest the claims of the anti-palm-oil campaign spearheaded by American soya-bean producers.

The anti-palm-oil campaign had been acknowledged as a commercial ploy by the manufacturers of oils competing against it so that they could take advantage of changes in the marketplace.

Datuk Murad said that in fact changing from palm oil to other oils could have negative effects on consumers 'because palm oil does not need hydrogenation' (*see 1 October 1992*).

Commodity firms under fire

28 September Kuala Lumpur

Several commodity firms came under investigation for allegedly soliciting funds to trade on the overseas market. The main case involved the collection of RM7 million from 2,000 investors around the country.

Two dealers' representatives of the firm involved allegedly traded for eight operators who between them lost RM6 million in two months. The firm could be charged with syndicated trading, according to Commodities Trading Commission commissioner Ismail Ahmad.

First gold in Beijing Games

28 September Beijing

Malaysia bagged its first gold at the 11th Asian Games after its sepak takraw team battled for six hours to beat Thailand in the final match of the team tournament at the Fengtai Gymnasium.

Low turnout in general election

20–21 October Kuala Lumpur

The Barisan Nasional captured 127 of the 180 seats in Parliament with 53.38 per cent of the total vote in the general election. Turnout was 72.7 per cent, lower than in previous polls. Semangat '46 lost four of its 12 seats. Pas won seven seats and the DAP 20. In Sabah PBS won 14 seats and independents four. For the first time Commonwealth monitors observed the election process.

Dr Lim congratulating Dr Koh (left).

Designer Wong Fee Hoong and his business partner Mohammed Ali demonstrate the Forerunner 101 to an admirer.

Malaysia-made 4WD

21 October Kuala Lumpur

That he did not have a formal education in engineering did not deter a used car dealer from building another made-in-Malaysia car after the Proton Saga. Backed by 30 years of experience in the car business, Wong Fee Hoong, 47, assembled a four-wheel drive aptly named the Forerunner 101.

The car, which took two years to complete and earned the approval of the Road Transport Department, was exhibited at the Kuala Lumpur International Motor Show.

Six new Ministers in Cabinet line-up

27 October Kuala Lumpur

Six new Ministers and 11 Deputy Ministers were among appointees in Prime Minister Dato' Seri Dr Mahathir Mohamad's Cabinet. The six were Datuk Abang Abu Bakar Mustapha, Law Hieng Ding, Dr Ting Chew Peh, Tan Sri Sakaran Dandai, Annuar Musa and Syed Hamid Albar. There were 25 Cabinet posts, one more than before, with the splitting of the Trade and Industry Ministry to cater for international trade.

Youngest Penang CM

25 October Penang

Dr Koh Tsu Koon became Penang's Chief Minister, succeeding Dr Lim Chong Eu, who was the longest-serving CM having assumed office on 12 May 1969. Dr Koh, 41, who was the State Assemblyman for Tanjung Bungah, was the State's third CM and the youngest to assume the post. The deputy CM post went to Seberang Jaya Assemblyman Dr Ibrahim Saad.

1990

world news

7 August
Twice this day at 12:34:56am and pm, the notation reads 12:34:56 7/8/90.

3 October
East and West Germany become one.

13 October
Syrian forces oust the Lebanese government of General Michael Aoun.

15 October
Mikhail Gorbachev wins the Nobel Peace Prize.

28 November
Losing on a first ballot for party leader, Margaret Thatcher resigns, making way for John Major to become PM.

1 December
Workers from the UK and France breakthrough to meet 40 metres under the English Channel, establishing the first connection between the British Isles and the continent since the Ice Age.

6 December
Saddam Hussein releases Western hostages held in Kuwait.

CT terrorists' chapter closes

3 November Sibu

Fifty communist terrorists, remnants of the North Kalimantan Communist Party, left their jungle hideouts, ending the three-decade insurgency problem. The NKCP signed an agreement with the Government on 17 October to lay down arms in Kuching, 11 months after the Communist Party of Malaya signed a similar accord.

Sarawak Cultural Village opens

14 November Santubong

Prime Minister Dato' Seri Mahathir Mohamad set free white doves to declare open the Sarawak Cultural Village at Damai Beach. Set against the backdrop of the legendary Mount Santubong, the village is 35km from Kuching.

Bumi stake allocation a complex matter

30 October Kuala Lumpur

Prime Minister Dato' Seri Dr Mahathir Mohamad acknowledged that allocating a stake for Bumiputras in the corporate sector had turned out to be an arduous task that was more complex than the New Economic Policy (NEP). This was because the issue could not be resolved simply by enlarging the economic pie and granting 30 per cent ownership to Bumiputras. Dr Mahathir emphasised that the Government could not solve all problems hindering the progress of Bumiputra entrepreneurs.

Mandela on four-day visit to Malaysia

1 November Kuala Lumpur

Nelson Mandela, South Africa's anti-apartheid leader, was welcomed by the Prime Minister when he made a four-day visit to Malaysia on a 20-day tour of five Asia-Pacific countries. The 72-year-old deputy president of the African National Congress was originally scheduled to visit Malaysia on 19 October but his trip was postponed in view of the country's general election.

Malaysians sweep Asean awards

7 November Singapore

Four Malaysians were given the 1990 Asean awards for their achievements in the form of culture, communication and literary works. They were journalist A. Samad Ismail, National Literary laureate Prof Datuk Shanon Ahmad, Malaysian Junior Symphony Orchestra founder and conductor Abdul Fatah Karim and architect Hijjas Kasturi (for visual arts). Introduced in 1987, the awards were conferred only once in three years in each category.

Malaysia purchases 28 Hawk bombers

18 November Kuala Lumpur

Malaysia agreed to buy 28 Hawk fighter bombers from British Aerospace for an estimated RM2 billion. The deal comprised 10 two-seater Hawk 100s and 18 single-seater Hawk 200s. This was part of a RM4.5-billion arms deal between Malaysia and Britain agreed in September 1988. The first Hawk was expected to be delivered in 1993.

RM2.5b savings bonus

27 December Kuala Lumpur

Amanah Saham Nasional (ASN) declared a special bonus amounting to RM2.5 billion to 2.45 million unit-holders. The bonus was computed so that long-term unit-holders would reap bigger rewards from their investments, said Permodalan Nasional Bhd chief executive Datuk Khalid Ibrahim.

The casket of Tunku Abdul Rahman is carried in procession under royal umbrellas and with a military escort.

The passing of Bapa Malaysia

6 December Kuala Lumpur

Tunku Abdul Rahman died aged 87 at the Kuala Lumpur General Hospital. The country's first Prime Minister was buried at the Langgar Royal Mausoleum in Alor Star as a Sultan.

In her condolence message to the Tunku's widow Tun Sharifah Rodziah, Queen Elizabeth said she learnt of the Tunku's death with 'great sorrow', adding: 'He enjoyed a unique position in Malaysia, and was held in the highest regard in Britain, the Commonwealth and the world at large. He will be greatly missed.'

Lee Kuan Yew, who had recently stepped down as Singapore's Prime Minister, described the Tunku as a great leader loved by the Malays, trusted by the Chinese and Indians, and highly regarded by the British. 'He was a good man, shrewd in his judgment of people. He always concentrated on the essentials in a problem and often got it right,' Lee said in his condolence message to Tun Sharifah Rodziah.

With his family at the Tunku's bedside when he died were the Sultan of Terengganu, Dato' Seri Dr Mahathir Mohamad, Tengku Razaleigh Hamzah and Consumer Affairs Minister Datuk Dr Sulaiman Daud. There was a spontaneous outpouring of grief throughout the nation with Rulers, political figures and ordinary people in the streets paying fulsome tribute. His long-serving personal staff said it was like the death of a family member.

Tycoon's kidnappers shot dead by police

22 December Kuala Lumpur

Police shot dead three kidnappers an hour after they released their millionaire victim on receiving a ransom of more than RM1 million. Police said the family of the 72-year-old had refused to cooperate since his abduction 16 days earlier. CID director Datuk Zaman Khan said a mystery man notified the police of the kidnapping.

Coins to commemorate KL's centenary

8 December Kuala Lumpur

Bank Negara issued two coins in the denomination of RM25 sterling silver and RM5 cupro-nickel to mark Kuala Lumpur's centenary as a local authority. City Hall buildings of the past and present were depicted on both coins.

1991

Health and safety issues took centre stage. A nationwide dengue epidemic was alarming, said the Health Ministry which also warned that unless the public took preventive measures, it was impossible to contain the outbreak; the AIDS Task Force identified more than 1,000 HIV carriers with drug addicts topping the list; a haze that enveloped Kuala Lumpur raised concerns of respiratory ailments while snakes were reported to be a threat in the more affluent urban neighbourhoods. Among the safety issues was the question of whether there were precautionary measures at the Sungai Buloh fireworks factory which was destroyed by fire claiming 26 lives. The Selangor Government planned to set up a permanent fund for the victims.

FEBRUARY
Selangor residents take steps to store and conserve water as the State faces a serious water crisis.

APRIL
Former Culture, Youth and Sports Minister Datuk Mokhtar Hashim (right) is released from jail having obtained a royal pardon.

JULY
Artist Ibrahim Hussein is part of the team involved in producing the book *Malaysia: Heart of Southeast Asia*.

OCTOBER
Haze envelops Kuala Lumpur for the second time in a year, the first time being in March.

May: The aftermath of the Sungai Buloh fireworks factory inferno.

'Establishing a united Malaysian nation with a sense of common and shared destiny ... made up of one Bangsa Malaysia.'

Dato' Seri Dr Mahathir Mohamad on one of the challenges of Vision 2020, 1991.

1991

world news

17 January
Iraq fires eight Scud missiles at Israel.

25 January
Iraq dumps an estimated 460 million gallons of crude oil into the Gulf. Iraqi missiles strike Tel Aviv and Haifa, killing one Israeli.

28 January
Sixty Iraqi fighter-bombers take refuge in Iran and are impounded.

23 February
Citing corruption, a Thai military coup removes the Government of Chatichai Choonhavan.

26 February
Saddam Hussein announces a withdrawal from Kuwait. Retreating Iraqi forces set fire to the oilfields.

2 March
Shi'ite Muslims in the south and Kurds in the north rise against the regime of Saddam Hussein. The uprisings are crushed. About 50,000 are killed and more than a million refugees are forced into Turkey and Iran.

Ban on steel bars lifted

1 January **Kuala Lumpur**

The Government decided to temporarily lift an eight-year ban on the import of steel bars. Housing developers and builders gave local steelmillers a month to adjust production to cope with demand before resorting to imports.

The decision to lift the ban was made to overcome delays in the completion of development projects caused by a 'critical' shortage of steel bars in the country. High demand and claims of hoarding in anticipation of a price increase were blamed for the shortage.

56% increase in tourist arrivals

3 January **Kuala Lumpur**

Visit Malaysia Year in 1990 was successful in that the number of tourists increased by 56.6 per cent in the first 11 months of the year, Culture, Arts and Tourism Minister Datuk Sabbaruddin Chik said. Records showed 6,892,739 arrivals compared with 4,400,112 during the same period in 1989.

Buildings should add beauty, says architect

13 January **Kuala Lumpur**

Architect Hijjas Kasturi's LUTH building, built in 1985, had drawn both admiration and criticism for its design, said the 11–13 January issue of *Asia Magazine*. The article looked at the architect's career and said he strove to 'build something that brings enjoyment and delight to people...It should not harm the environment but add beauty'. It quoted him as saying that form should also be functional.

The LUTH building designed by architect Hijjas Kasturi, which attracted both criticism and admiration.

Malaysians urged to leave Gulf

7 January **Kuala Lumpur**

Malaysians in the Gulf States have been advised to move out as soon as possible in view of the possible outbreak of war in the region. Foreign Minister Datuk Abu Hassan Omar (right) said there were about 1,700 Malaysians (mainly workers, students and housewives) in Saudi Arabia, the United Arab Emirates, Bahrain, Qatar, Jordan and Syria.

'We are monitoring the situation closely to see whether there is a need to hire airplanes to take these people back home,' he said. 'If need be, the Government is also willing to shoulder the expenses of those who cannot afford their flight home.'

Two days later, Dato' Seri Dr Mahathir Mohamad agreed to postpone the meeting of the High-Level Appraisal Group on the Commonwealth in the 1990s and Beyond because of uncertainties arising from the Gulf crisis.

New, safe routes to Europe

3 January **Kuala Lumpur**

Malaysia Airlines has taken steps to ensure the safety of its passengers by using new routes to Europe and Jeddah. Dubai, formerly a technical stop for 23 flights by the national carrier, has been replaced by New Delhi on 10 January. At the same time all flights to Istanbul stopped. Flights to Jeddah have been reduced from twice a week to once a week. MAS senior director of operations Datuk Kamaruddin Ahmad told reporters: 'The load factor is low now and this doesn't justify the frequent flights to Jeddah.' The new schedule of flights to Jeddah would be effective on 13 January, he said.

Few cancel trips to the Gulf

25 January **Kuala Lumpur**

The prospect of war in the Middle East has not deterred people from travelling. Although there were fears of terrorism at airports, many people still went ahead with their trips. Only a few cancelled their plans. Malaysia Airlines public relations manager Siew Yong Gnanalingam said there was a slight drop in passenger numbers for flights to Europe. But she said it was difficult to know whether the drop was due to the Gulf crisis or the tourism off-peak season which began at the end of the third week of January.

First Malay thesaurus

18 January **Kuala Lumpur**

The first Malay language thesaurus, a joint effort by Dewan Bahasa dan Pustaka and Universiti Sains Malaysia, is expected to be on sale from early February. The first batch of the pilot edition of *Tesaurus Umum Bahasa Melayu* is due to hit the streets in a couple of weeks. It is already being consigned to distributors for retailing.

An improved and enlarged second edition is planned for mid-1993 followed by the third edition later. The second edition would contain 2,000 words and 15,000 derivatives. It would contain words like *wawasan* (vision), *menangani* (endorsement) and *canggih* (sophisticated).

Blacklisted for issuing bad cheques

6 January **Kuala Lumpur**

A total of 53,746 current account holders were blacklisted as of November 1990 for issuing bad cheques, Bank Negara said. Of this total, 30,225 had served their six-month suspension. Accounts of the remaining 23,521 remained suspended.

The central bank said accounts were reported to the Cheque Information Bureau if three bad cheques were issued from the same account within a year. Bank Negara noted, however, that there had been a drop in cases of dishonoured cheques due to insufficient funds.

KL hotels raise rates

14 January **Kuala Lumpur**

Hotel operators in Kuala Lumpur ushered in 1991 with increases in room rates. However, resort hotels did not generally raise their prices as they had already gone up late in 1990. Room rates at five-star hotels in the city were up by between 7.7 and 18.2 per cent.

Pay rise for civil service

23 January **Kuala Lumpur**

An interim five per cent pay rise for Government employees at the end of the month would cost an additional $409 million in the current year, Prime Minister Dato' Seri Dr Mahathir Mohamad said.

A full salary adjustment would be made by the end of the year by which time the Government expected to have completed a wage study to determine the final full salary increase.

New oil/gas discovery

5 February **Kuala Lumpur**

Esso Production Malaysia Inc made a new oil and gas discovery at North Lukut, 280km off the coast of Terengganu. It said the North Lukut 1 wildcat well started drilling on 30 December 1990 and was completed last month. Its exploration manager, Mr Dennis E. Francis, said: 'The well identified oil in five zones and gas in three others. On a production of one interval, the test flowed at rates in excess of 6,650 barrels of oil per day from a depth of 1,730 metres.'

Special grilles

10 January **Kuala Lumpur**

The Government would consider making it statutory for house and flat owners to install specially-designed grilles that enable occupants to escape in the event of a fire.

Deputy Housing and Local Government Minister Haji Daud Taha said the move would be adopted if home owners refused to accept the Fire Services Department's suggestion to install the special grilles. It had designed five types of window and door grilles. For security reasons, most urban home owners install iron grilles. In the event of fire, these immovable grilles can turn the house into a death trap.

Water tariffs up

10 January Kuala Lumpur

Water tariffs in Selangor and Kuala Lumpur were increased by between 10 and 23 per cent with effect from on 1 January.

Selangor Infrastructure Committee chairman Datuk Saidin Tamby said the increase was necessary to meet the rising cost of production.

Kelantan: no to gambling

23 January Kota Bharu

The Kelantan Government rejected an appeal by agents of Sports Toto and Empat Nombor Ekor to extend by six months their licences to operate gambling premises in the State, State Executive Councillor Datuk Halim Mohamad said. The State Government banned all forms of gambling in the State from 1 January.

Dengue alert

7 March Kuala Lumpur

A nationwide dengue epidemic was described as 'alarming'. Health Ministry public relations officer Sabtuyah Senson said 1,178 cases of the mosquito-borne disease had been reported as of 5 March. Of these, 1,046 were of dengue fever (DF) and 132 of dengue haemorrhagic fever (DHF). Five people had died. Sarawak alone had 314 DF and 41 DHF cases.

Unless the public took preventive measures, it would be next to impossible to contain the outbreak, he said.

Drugs found in fruit

7 April Kangar

Customs would intensify checks on fruit brought in from Thailand following the seizure of 7.56kg of ganja hidden inside fruit in two incidents since February, said Perlis Customs preventive chief Ahmad Akbar Zahari. Large quantities would now be inspected thoroughly.

The ploy was first uncovered when 2.86kg of ganja was found inside five pumpkins, four papayas and a watermelon on the Bangkok Express train in Padang Besar on 24 February. Subsequently, another 4.7kg of the drug was found in four durians and in the shoes of a 43-year-old suspect detained on 28 March.

Selangor water crisis

6 February Petaling Jaya

Water levels at three major dams in Selangor were steadily dropping to such an extent that water rationing had become a possibility. The level dropped between 0.1 metre and 0.5 metre from the previous day.

Selangor Waterworks Department director Liew Wai Kiat had earlier warned of rationing if water in the three dams dropped to critical levels. He said the rainy season in April was too short to refill the dams, normally filled from October to December but did not in 1990.

People collect water from a tanker during the shortage while (right) the water is hauled home in an oil drum.

Man killed boy for 4D numbers

11 March Johor Bahru

A labourer, who chopped off the head of a 16-year-old schoolboy seven years ago in a ritual that he thought would reveal four-digit numbers, was sentenced to death by the High Court. A seven-man jury unanimously found V. Krishnan, 32, guilty after deliberating for more than five hours. Krishnan remained calm when the foreman delivered the verdict. Krishnan was charged with murdering S. Rajendran in Kulai, 32km north of here.

A witness, Sinnathamby Pachiappan, 28, had told the court earlier how Krishnan had slashed Rajendran's neck twice with a parang before the victim's head was severed from the body.

Results of 400 SPM candidates withheld

12 March Kuala Lumpur

The Examination Syndicate withheld the results of 400 students throughout the country who sat for the Sijil Pelajaran Malaysia examination for various reasons including cheating. Deputy Education Minister Dr Fong Chan Onn said another reason was the students did not provide sufficient details in application forms or their answer sheets.

Plane hijacked on way to Singapore

26 March Subang

A Singapore Airlines Airbus flying from Subang Airport with 118 passengers and 11 crew on board was hijacked on its way to Singapore. Four men claiming to be members of the Pakistan People's Party demanded the release of Benazir Bhutto's jailed husband Asif Ali Zardari and other PPP members.

At Changi Airport, Singapore, they pushed two stewards out of the aircraft and demanded refuelling for a flight to Australia. When their deadline was not met they threatened to kill one passenger every 10 minutes. A special counter-terrorism unit stormed the plane and killed all four hijackers, leaving the hostages unhurt.

Craving for crabs lands woman in prison

29 April Petaling Jaya

A. Chellama was jailed for 43 days by the magistrates' court here today for stealing six crabs. The unemployed woman of Kampung Lindungan, Sungai Way, pleaded guilty to stealing the crabs from Encik Mahmood Maidin in front of a shop at Simpang Tiga, Kampung Medan. She was jailed another month for failing to produce her identity card.

Members of religious group arrested

6 March Kuala Lumpur

Police picked up 21 members of a religious group for behaving in a disorderly manner and ignoring orders to disperse at the Jalan Bandar police station here. This brought the total number of arrested members of the New Testament Church to 30.

It was learnt that police had yet to make any headway in their investigations of the group because its members were uncooperative and reluctant to speak to police about its activities.

First Malaysian boat show

7 March Port Klang ▶ The first Malaysian boat show opened in Port Klang with a line-up of about 40 sailing boats and motor-cruisers. Vessels ranging from junior sail boats to large cruising boats were on show at the event organised by the Royal Selangor Yacht Club.

It assembled the latest, most advanced and biggest sailing boats and motor-cruisers from the United States, Singapore, Hong Kong, the United Kingdom, Taiwan, Australia and Japan. Boating accessories were also exhibited and offered for sale.

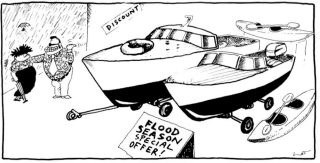

1991

world news

29 March
Argentinian footballer Diego Maradona is suspended by the Italian League after testing positive for cocaine.

14 May
Madame Mao, Jiang Qing, 77, commits suicide in prison.

21 May
In Madras, a Tamil suicide bomber kills former PM Rajiv Gandhi, 47.

25 June
Croatia and Slovenia declare independence from Yugoslavia.

22 July
Boxer Mike Tyson is charged with raping a beauty contestant in Indianapolis, Indiana.

19 August
While on holiday in the Crimea, Soviet leader Mikhail Gorbachev is put under house arrest. The coup is led by Vice-President Gennady Yanayev and seven other hardliners.

25 August
Michael Schumacher makes his debut at the Belgian Grand Prix.

Four held over theft from 26 mail sacks

29 April Kota Kinabalu

Police detained three Malaysia Airlines employees and a postal worker over three days in connection with mail pilferage at the international airport here.

State CID chief Supt Hassan Abdul Mutalip said the three were attached to the airport's cargo section. A fourth suspect was a postal worker at the General Post Office.

The arrests followed the discovery by postal officials of pilfered postal bags under thick undergrowth near a restricted area of the airport.

After a search, they recovered 26 sacks of letters, including parcels and registered mail.

Officials found some letters dated back to September 1990 while the most recent was 14 April 1991.

Jailed ex-Minister free after royal pardon

16 April Kuala Lumpur

Former Culture, Youth and Sports Minister Datuk Mokhtar Hashim, who was serving a life sentence at Kuala Lumpur's Pudu Prison, walked out a free man after obtaining a royal pardon. He was greeted by his son and daughter.

Datuk Mokhtar was arrested in Petaling Jaya on 10 July 1982. He was found guilty and sentenced to death in March 1983 for the murder of former Negeri Sembilan Legislative Assembly Speaker Datuk Mohamed Taha Talib at Kampung Seri Asahan in Gemencheh on 14 April 1982.

The sentence was subsequently commuted to life imprisonment in 1984.

Datuk Mokhtar reunited with his wife after his release.

'Safety first' says the sign but safety did not seem to be a priority. Right: A victim of the fire.

Fireworks factory inferno

7 May Kuala Lumpur

At least 26 people were killed and hundreds were injured in a fireworks factory fire in Sungai Buloh here. A series of explosions and raging fires, which completely destroyed the premises of Bright Sparklers Sdn Bhd, also gutted a nearby sawmill, three furniture factories, an animal feed producer and a chemical plant. The nation's worst industrial accident also saw at least 10 houses within a 1km radius flattened by the blasts. Many other houses were damaged, leaving about 300 people homeless.

The next day, search-and-rescue operations for survivors continued and the Police Field Force cordoned off the site to facilitate investigations. Army and police bomb squads were trying to unearth explosives stored underground.

Residents of two nearby villages complained that the authorities failed to listen to earlier appeals to close the factory. They had complained that it was a fire hazard. Selangor Menteri Besar Tan Sri Muhammad Haji Muhammad Taib confirmed that the fireworks factory was illegal. He said initial investigations revealed that the factory operator had not applied for any permit to operate in the area. A Royal Commission of Inquiry was to be set up to undertake a full investigation.

On 20 May, Selangor deputy police chief Asst Commissioner Tuffile Nawab Din said police would remove toxic chemicals from the devastated factory and store them in drums which would be kept temporarily at the factory site pending a final decision on how to dispose of them.

Empty fireworks casings litter the ground and the area around the Bright Sparklers fireworks factory looks like a battle zone after the fire and explosions. Altogether 41 people died and hundreds were injured.

Permanent fund planned for blast victims

24 June Kuala Lumpur

The Selangor Government planned to set up a permanent fund for victims of the Sungai Buloh disaster, State Secretary Datuk Abdul Halim Haji Abdul Rauf said. Apart from the $460,000 already distributed to victims, a further $200,000 from the fund would be given to 171 applicants who were late in submitting their requests for aid. The fund, which totalled $875,000 on 19 June, rose to $925,000 today following a $50,000 donation from MAS.

Radical cardiac surgery demonstrated in KL

28 May Kuala Lumpur

Treatment of cardiovascular diseases, the country's leading cause of death, saw a first when a new technique, cardiac rotablation, was performed.

The radical new procedure for clearing blocked heart arteries entailed the insertion of a tiny electric drill-like object into the heart to shave off cholesterol deposits which clog a coronary artery.

KL General Hospital director Datuk Dr Megat Burhainuddin Megat Abdul Rahman said the two-hour procedure was demonstrated by visiting American cardiologist Dr Simon Stertzer on 15 May.

The patient, a 56-year-old retired senior Government officer, was discharged from the hospital two days after undergoing the procedure. Dr Stertzer, 56, one of the world's three leading practitioners of angioplasty, a method of relieving arterial obstructon, was in Malaysia for three days, during which he also attended to several VIPs and royals.

Local TV shows to get prime-time showing

19 May Kuala Lumpur

RTM and TV3 were directed to restructure their screening schedules from 1 June to ensure that programmes of local content were given prominence during prime time. Announcing this, Information Minister Datuk Mohamed Rahmat said this was the first step towards realising the Government's policy of having 80 per cent local content and 20 per cent foreign programmes by the year 2000.

Thais drop action over border tree felling

13 June Kota Bharu

The Thai authorities decided not to go ahead with court action against nine Kelantan Forestry Department officers, including its director, Johari Baharuddin, for allegedly entering the country illegally and felling trees 1km inside the border.

Governor of Narathiwat Mr Phan Chantrapan said he would inform the Kelantan Government of the decision.

1,100 HIV carriers

27 June Kuala Lumpur

The AIDS Task Force in the Health Ministry identified 1,169 HIV carriers, with drug addicts topping the list at 974. The next biggest groups were those still under investigation (103), heterosexuals (52), homosexuals (15), users of contaminated blood products (10), prostitutes (eight) and bisexuals (seven).

AIDS Task Force head Dr Jones Varughese advised addicts not to share syringes as this was one of the most common causes of AIDS. So far this year four people had been identified as having the full-blown AIDS infection, bringing the number of such cases to 28 to date.

The release of the statistics followed news that three people had died of AIDS in three weeks at the General Hospital in Kuala Lumpur.

This brought to 19 the total number of people who had died of AIDS in the country. Dr Varughese said that drug addicts formed the biggest group of AIDS patients and HIV carriers.

What the foreign press said

By global standards, Malaysia was still not greatly affected by the scourge of AIDS, *The Times* of London reported in its 30 September 1991 issue. It went on to comment that 'Only 27 of [Malaysia's] 18 million people have died of the disease since 1986, and fewer than 1,400 are known to be infected with the virus. But according to Health Minister Lee Kim Sai, the number of AIDS cases has more than doubled since last December and Kuala Lumpur is now weighing strong measures to block the further spread of the disease'.

The paper went on to note that 'Infected individuals, for instance, would be obliged to carry special identification cards. The press would be permitted to publish the names of patients. People convicted of bringing AIDS-afflicted prostitutes into the country would be given beatings and long prison terms. Harshest of all, the Government proposes building a detention camp similar to a leper colony for those with AIDS. If that should happen, health officials believe, Malaysia would become one of the few nations in the world to try fighting the disease by detaining its victims.'

160 M'sians in Taiwan jails

5 June Kuala Lumpur

At least 160 Malaysians, including a large number of illegal workers, were languishing in Taiwanese jails for various offences, it was claimed.

So far, Taiwanese authorities had confirmed that 67 were being held but the MCA public complaints section believed the figure is higher.

Mr Michael Chong, the public complaints section head, said he would ask Interpol to trace the others.

$5.5m flood damage

17 June Penang

Damage to public and Government property during State-wide floods after five hours of continuous heavy rain in Penang on 2 June was estimated at between $2.5 million and $3 million.

Malaysians charged with surgeon's murder

15 July Kuala Lumpur

Two Malaysians, Chiew Seng Liew, 48, and Jimmy Tan, 39, were charged in Sydney with the murder of leading Australian heart surgeon Dr Victor Chang. Another was being ques-

The wanted man is led away after the court here allowed his extradition to Australia.

tioned by Australian police and a fourth, believed to be in hiding in Malaysia, was being sought by the New South Wales police task force. 'We believe the fourth man left Melbourne late last week for Kuala Lumpur,' a task force spokesman said. On 24 July, police in Malaysia received a warrant of arrest from their Australian counterparts for the wanted man.

Protest against Muslims in beauty contest

11 July Kota Kinabalu

A beauty pageant organised here drew protest from the religious bureau of the Umno Gaya pro-tem committee for allowing Muslim participants. Its chairman, Haji Abdul Ghani Nawawi, said Muslims were barred from participating in such contests by the State Government.

He urged the Sabah Islamic Council to investigate the matter and said necessary action should be taken against those involved. In the contest, air stewardess Rosidah Jane Hamid, 21, was crowned Ms Sabah/Malaysia Charm to represent Sabah at the final of Ms Malaysia Charm in Kuala Lumpur on 19 July.

Teachers asked to stage boycott

8 July Kuala Lumpur

More than 4,500 teachers in the Federal Territory were asked to boycott a five-minute anti-drug programme. The Federal Territory branch of the National Union of the Teaching Profession (NUTP) sent circulars to all its members in primary and secondary schools directing them not to participate if a section asking students to assess teachers taking part was not dropped.

NUTP Federal Territory branch honorary secretary K. Ravindran Nair said the union had always supported moves to promote anti-drug awareness among students but opposed the evaluation of teachers by students. 'It is an insult to the teaching profession and tantamount to questioning the integrity and honour of teachers,' he said.

Rare marmosets born

20 July Taiping

Three newly born cotton-eared marmosets were the pride of the Taiping zoo as the species faced extinction in its Amazon rainforest habitat. The animal was also an endangered species under the Convention on International Trade in Endangered Species. Related to macaques and leaf monkeys, and one of the smallest monkeys in the world, the three marmoset babies were born at the zoo today.

Book by top photographers launched

26 July Kuala Lumpur

Prime Minister Dato' Seri Dr Mahathir Mohamad (pictured centre in bush jacket with his wife Datin Seri Dr Siti Hasmah and the book's international photographers) launched *Malaysia: Heart of Southeast Asia* at the Artiquarium here. Forty-six top lensmen from 17 countries covered the nation to capture its charm and put it on the tourist map. Their focus was on the environment and the Malaysian way of life and on culture. British travel writer Gavin Young and US environmentalist Paul Wachtel provided the accompanying text.

Taxis under scrutiny with KL under haze

16 March: The Kuala Lumpur skyline disappeared due to very low visibility. The Department of Environment believes that it may be due to the after-effects of rain and not entirely because of excessive pollutants in the air. The source said the haze could be the result of water particles from rain coagulating with existing dust particles.

October: A Department of Environment officer checking on the level of emission from a taxi. Dry weather, factory smoke and car exhaust fumes were among the causes blamed for a haze hanging over Kuala Lumpur in March.

1991

world news

14 October
Burmese leader
Aung San Suu Kyi,
under house arrest,
is awarded the Nobel
Peace Prize.

23 October
A peace treaty is
signed in Paris
between Cambodia's
warring factions.
Khmer Rouge
president Khieu
Samphan and military
commander Son Sen
return to Phnom
Penh but beat a hasty
retreat when a mob
tries to lynch them.

2 November
Chechnya declares
independence from the
Soviet Union.

14 November
Prince Norodom
Sihanouk returns to
Cambodia after
13 years of exile.

12 November
Indonesian troops
kill over 270 people
attending the funeral
of a young man in
disturbances killed
two weeks earlier in
Dili, East Timor.

25 December
Mikhail Gorbachev
resigns as President of
the Soviet Union.

An Umno delegate (right) welcomes Dato' Seri Abdullah Ahmad Badawi on his return to the Government after an absence of four years.

CM lays foundation stone of Kuching City South

28 August | Kuching

Chief Minister Tan Sri Haji Abdul Taib Mahmud laid the foundation stone of the proposed City Hall of Kuching City South today and said the jurisdiction of the City South Council has been extended to include the airport and Tabuan Jaya.

The mayor of Kuching South, Mr Song Swee Guan, said the City Hall would go a long way to providing a more effective administration as all its divisions' offices would be under one roof.

Twins reunited after 27 years

27 October | Penang

Penang bride Tan Lay Kee could hardly contain her joy at seeing her twin sister Mashita Ahmad for the first time in almost 25 years. The twins, the fourth and fifth daughters in the family, were

The twin sisters at Lay Kee's wedding.

separated when they were just a month old. Their parents, Mr Tan Soon Huat and Madam Lim Saw Guat, had to give up Mashita due to pressure from the grandparents as Madam Lim, 51, could not produce a son after giving birth to five daughters. Lay Kee kissed her long-lost sister on the cheek and both women hugged and cried.

Mashita, from Alor Star, said she decided to visit her natural family after reading newspaper advertisements recently.

Bears on rampage at KL bourse

8 August | Kuala Lumpur

Bears went on the rampage at the Kuala Lumpur stock market, sending prices lower for the ninth consecutive session.

Investor confidence was at an extremely low ebb, with buyers staying aloof and sellers dominating trading. And with dabblers bent on selling, even firm leads from overseas bourses on certain days were ignored.

Rise in Malaysia's ageing population

30 September | Kuala Lumpur

The number of elderly in Malaysia (55 and above) was increasing rapidly, from 7.9 per cent in 1970 to an estimated 10.3 per cent in 2000. Life expectancy at birth for Malaysians was currently 68 years for males and 72 for females. Males aged 60 could expect to live 16 more years while females aged 60 could expect to live 18.2 years longer.

Pink Triangle prepares for exhibition

1 December | Kuala Lumpur

Pink Triangle members were preparing for an exhibition on AIDS-themed Sharing The Challenge, at the Central Market in conjunction with World AIDS Day. The exhibition was being jointly organised by Pink Triangle, a voluntary body established to fight AIDS, the National Council of Women's Organisations and Natural Therapy Centre.

Pink Triangle presented a short comedy sketch—but with a serious message about the dreaded and deadly disease.

Proton to raise output

23 December | Shah Alam

Perusahaan Otomobil Nasional Bhd (Proton) planned to increase the annual production of the national car from 100,000 to 120,000. To achieve this, Proton planned a series of projects including a plant expansion programme. The production increase and the continued acceleration of the incorporation of local content in the national car would also expedite the growth of the local automotive component manufacturing industry.

Up to October 1990, 67,369 Proton Sagas had been sold, capturing 63 per cent of the domestic market. The car was also exported to 13 countries with a total of 14,011 sold up to November 1990. Meanwhile, Proton announced that it had received approval from the Capital Issues Committee for public listing on the Kuala Lumpur Stock Exchange.

The winners of the national Tunas Jaya award for boys and girls, Hin Tze Yang of Penang and Sri Farhanim Mohamad of Malacca, hold their trophies at Stadium Negara on Children's Day, 19 October. The award is given for all-round achievement.

Snakes in the grass of richer neighbourhoods

24 December | Kuala Lumpur

Residents from affluent neighbourhoods called the City Hall Emergency Unit to get rid of snakes from their houses more often than those in squatter areas. City Hall's Urban Services Department was receiving an average of 27 calls a month.

Most calls were from areas such as Damansara, Bangsar, Kenny Hills and Ampang. This was probably due to the rapid development of these areas.

Penang Free School turns 175

21 October | Penang ▶ The Penang Free School turned 175. Among the honoured guests at the school's Speech Day were the Yang di-Pertua Negeri Tun Dr Haji Hamdan Sheikh Tahir and Chief Minister Dr Koh Tsu Koon. Tun Haji Hamdan was received on arrival by school principal Goh Hooi Beng.

The Yang di-Pertua Negeri inspected a guard-of-honour comprising school cadets, Scouts and Red Crescent Society units.

1992

We green the world: That was the message Malaysia passed to the Earth Summit in Rio de Janeiro where world leaders had gathered to consider ways to preserve the environment. Malaysia was committed to maintaining 60 per cent of its land area under tree cover. Dr Mahathir announced plans to ensure Malaysia became a mature nation by the year 2020. His plan, known as Vision 2020, was to see that Malaysia progressed in all respects to achieve developed nation status. Malaysians' spirit was further uplifted when the Thomas Cup returned to Malaysia after 22 years; the final match lasting more than five hours. The 96-year-old Selangor Turf Club held its last race, making way for the Kuala Lumpur City Centre project.

FEBRUARY
Entertainer Sudirman passes away.

SEPTEMBER
Most of Peninsular Malaysia experiences a massive power outage.

OCTOBER
Fire guts Subang Airport's flight control centre.

DECEMBER
Bosnian children arrive in Malaysia under an adoption programme.

May: The Thomas Cup returns to Malaysia after 22 years.

'Malaysians must ensure that their country enjoys unhampered growth.'

Dato' Seri Dr Mahathir Mohamad, 9 July 1992.

1992

1 January
Egyptian Boutros Boutros-Ghali replaces Peruvian Javier Perez de Cuellar as the UN Secretary-General.

3 January
Singapore bans the import and sale of chewing gum because 'chewing gum pollution has disrupted train transportation and is generally irritating and unsightly'.

4 January
US President Bush, visiting Singapore, announces plans to shift the navy logistics command, evicted from the Philippines, to the republic.

7 February
The Maastricht Treaty is signed. The European Union becomes a reality.

17 March
A suicide truck bomb at the Israeli Embassy in Buenos Aires kills 29.

17 March
White South Africans vote to give legal equality to blacks.

6 April
Bosnia-Herzegovina proclaims independence from Yugoslavia. Serbian forces besiege Sarajevo.

Links to Tamil Tigers

1 January Kuala Lumpur

Several Malaysians were providing financial and moral support to the Liberation Tigers of Tamil Eelam (LTTE), said Inspector General of Police Tan Sri Mohamed Hanif Omar.

This was confirmed by the Indian police during their investigations into the 21 May 1991 assassination of former Indian Prime Minister Rajiv Gandhi. The police were still gathering evidence on a group of Malaysians who allegedly had been smuggling weapons, fake currency and forged passports in support of LTTE. They were investigating how such aid was being channelled and how assistance was being provided to the LTTE.

The head of Interpol in Malaysia was reported to have alleged that three Malaysians met members of the LTTE in London shortly before Rajiv Gandhi's assassination.

Effluent discharge: Factory ordered to close

8 January Kuala Lumpur

The Cabinet ordered the immediate closure of Mardec's latex-processing factory in Durian Tunggal, Malacca, following an incident the previous week when effluent spilled into the Malacca River, disrupting water supply in some parts of the State. Mardec claimed that it was not at fault as the river had burst its banks after heavy rain and overflowed into the oxidation ponds meant to treat the effluent, causing ammonia-carrying effluent to run off into the river. Mardec had spent $3 million on anti-pollution measures, it said.

Floral entry wins US award

2 January Pasadena ▶ At the 103rd annual Tournament of Roses Parade in Pasadena, California, Malaysia's float, jointly sponsored by the Tourist Development Corporation of Malaysia and Malaysia Airlines, entitled 'Discover the Fascination', won the Best Foreign Entry. This made it Malaysia's fourth winning entry since first entering a float in the parade in 1988.

Pos Malaysia's new look

1 January Kuala Lumpur

It was reported that mail might soon be delivered by a postwoman instead of a postman as a result of the corporatisation of Malaysia's 165-year-old postal service. Other changes, such as a new logo: a stylised white pigeon gliding across red letters spelling POS on a background of blue, befitted its newly corporate status.

Singer Sahara attacked

16 January Rawang

Police were looking for two men who attacked rock and blues singer Sahara Yaacob in Jalan Gombak Lama. They were believed to be her acquaintances. The motive for the attack was not immediately established. Sahara suffered slash wounds on the head and a fractured right arm and was recuperating in hospital.

Winner of 'best compère' title

20 January Kuala Lumpur

Former stewardess Normala Shamsudin beat 11 other contestants to win the title of best compère for TV3's women's magazine programme *Nona*.

Earning top marks for appearance, character, photogenic quality, voice and intonation, Normala impressed the judges with her warmth, friendliness and rapport with the crew. She took over the job of hosting *Nona* for a month, replacing regular host Ezzah Aziz Fauzy.

Dr Mahathir's 2020 Vision

31 January Kuala Lumpur

Prime Minister Dr Mahathir Mohamad announced plans to ensure Malaysia would be a mature nation by the year 2020. Known later as Vision 2020, the plan was to see that Malaysia progressed in all respects to achieve developed nation status. At a dinner organised by the Harvard Club of Malaysia, he said that by the year 2020, Malaysians would have shared nationhood for six decades.

'We would have had 60 years of shared historical experience, of fashioning shared destinies, of cultivating common values and perceptions, of bonding the people with a common language, and of evolving without duress a uniquely Malaysian culture, identity and ethos which is organic to the Malaysian environment.

'If we are still not a mature nation by then, we would at least be well on the path to healthy nationhood,' he said. However, the nation-building process must be managed well.

He expressed his hope that by 2020 Malaysia would have overcome the socio-economic imbalances among the various ethnic groups and regions (*see 12 April 1995*).

Restoring Mahathir's kampong home

6 February Alor Star

The kampong house where Dr Mahathir Mohamad was born and spent the first few years of his life was to be restored and preserved as a national historical site. The humble-looking house is located at No. 18 Lorong Kilang Ais, right next to an ice factory. It is an example of typical kampong architecture, with large windows, but was at the time in a state of disrepair due to the weather and improper care.

High drama as Jackie Chan sparks jams

13 February Kuala Lumpur

High drama in the middle of Kuala Lumpur caused massive traffic jams in several areas, especially Jalan Raja. The drama was the shooting of a scene of a 'daring rescue' for the forthcoming Hong Kong movie *Police Story 3*, starring Jackie Chan and Malaysia's Michelle Yeoh. But while the drama was a fake, the traffic jams were real.

Several roads had to be closed for the shoot, causing chaos around Jalan Raja, Jalan Tun Perak, Jalan Tuanku Abdul Rahman and Jalan Sultan Hishamuddin.

Snake charmer in town

6 February Kota Bharu

Giving a king cobra a kiss on the head was not a big deal for Sultan Khan Rasul Khan. The 23-year-old snake charmer was in town with 150 snakes and two family members to take part in a month-long show at a resort near Pantai Cinta Berahi.

Malaysian forces aid UN

29 March Battambang

Malaysian troops took up positions along the Thai–Cambodian border to help in the United Nations repatriation of 380,000 Cambodian refugees from Thailand. According to the head of the Malaysian military contingent, the troops would be responsible for the security of the refugees from the border until they were handed over to civilian agencies supervising them in their resettlement areas.

Fans mourn death of singer Sudirman

22 February Kuala Lumpur

Superstar Sudirman Haji Arshad died at his sister's home in Bangsar. He was 37. He had been bedridden since a stroke six months before, and his death ended months of speculation that he had already died overseas. He was buried at the Kampung Chengal Muslim cemetery, next to his mother's grave. This had been one of his last wishes.

In his 16 years in entertainment, Sudirman chalked up many achievements, including performing at the Royal Albert Hall in London, holding the massive Chow Kit concert, and marketing his own brand of soft drinks.

Kelantan Sultan won't surrender sports car

26 March Kota Bharu

The Sultan of Kelantan would not pay the required \$2.1 million in Customs duties due on his Lamborghini Diablo nor would he surrender the car to Federal authorities, said a palace official.

The Sultan, who had driven the car out of the Customs' warehouse without paying the duties, believed that the car was legitimately his and did not consider that the rejection of his appeal for a waiver of duties changed anything.

Finance Minister Datuk Anwar Ibrahim said that the matter would be resolved using normal channels and within the existing regulatory framework.

National laureate Keris Mas dies

9 March Kuala Lumpur

Prominent literary figure and national laureate Kamaludin Muhammad (Keris Mas) died at the Kuala Lumpur General Hospital of a heart attack. He was 69.

Born in Bentong, Pahang on 10 June 1922, he was regarded as one of the pillars of Malay literature and was one of the founders of the literary organisation Angkatan Sasterawan 50 (Asas 50).

He was the first recipient of the Sasterawan Negara (National Laureate) award in 1981.

Smashing victory

17 May Kuala Lumpur ▶ The Thomas Cup for badminton returned to Malaysia after 22 years. The clinching match was won by doubles pair Soo Beng Kiang and Cheah Soon Kit after a gruelling game in Stadium Negara which lasted five hours and 37 minutes and which left the players exhausted but jubilant (below) and the spectators tired but ecstatic.

For every match that Malaysia won (Rashid Sidek vs Ardy Wiranata; Foo Kok Keong vs Alan Budi Kesuma), Indonesia gained ground (Razif Sidek–Jalani Sidek vs Eddy Hartono–Gunawan; Kwan Yoke Meng vs Joko Suprianto), until Cheah and Soo beat Rexy Mainaki and Ricky Subagia.

Later the players received two hectares of land each from the Selangor State Government and a RM2.5-million pledge from well-wishers.

City Hall building razed

16 March Kuala Lumpur

The former City Hall building in Jalan Raja was destroyed by fire. The fire was brought under control after raging for 1½ hours, leaving only the walls of the 95-year-old building standing. The fire also damaged the Panggung Bandaraya, a popular venue for the city's theatre groups. The building was to undergo a \$17-million facelift to house 13 courtrooms now situated in Jalan Duta.

The fire spread fast because of the plywood and softboard ceilings and the lack of modern fire-fighting equipment in the building. Due to the low water pressure, firemen were forced to use water from the nearby river to put out the fire. Jalan Raja had to be closed for several hours.

1992

world news

7 April
Palestinian leader
Yasser Arafat survives
a plane crash in the
Libyan desert.

9 April
John Major and the
Conservative Party
win the UK general
election.

15–16 April
Mujahideen forces
overthrow President
Najibullah in Kabul.

23 April
Filmmaker Satyajit
Ray, internationally
renowned for his
portraits of Indian
society, dies at 71.

24 May
Pro-democracy
protests in Thailand
climax with the
resignation of
PM Suchinda.

30 June
Fidel Ramos is
elected President of
the Philippines. The
electoral contest for
Vice-President
is won by
Joseph Estrada,
with twice as many
votes as Ramos.

22 September
The UN General
Assembly votes to
expel Yugoslavia.

Major gas field found in Bintulu

20 May Shah Alam

A new gas field with the potential to produce up to four trillion cubic feet has been discovered in Bintulu, Sarawak. Petronas president Tan Sri Azizan Zainul Abidin said this could warrant the setting up of another liquefied natural gas plant but added that this might take two to three years to develop. The existing LNG plant in Bintulu, which had targeted a doubling of its capacity to 16 million tonnes a year by 1995, would become the world's largest LNG plant in terms of capacity.

Cheque fraud solved

4 June Kuala Lumpur

Police arrested 12 suspects behind a syndicate responsible for a major financial fraud involving refund cheques with a total face value of over $16 million issued by MIDF Consultancy and Corporate Services Sdn Bhd (MIDFCCS).

13 die in tanker blast and 24-hour blaze at port

20 June Klang

Thirteen people were killed in an explosion and fire at the Shell depot in the South Port of Port Klang. The complex was set ablaze early in the morning after an explosion aboard the tanker *Chong Hong III* during an inspection of its cargo. The captain and first officer of the ship survived by jumping into the sea.

320,000 illegals beat the deadline

30 June Kuala Lumpur

At the end of its six-month campaign today, the Immigration Department registered 320,000 illegal immigrants. The scene at Immigration headquarters was chaotic as last-minute applicants rushed to register. The counters closed at 4.15pm, turning away thousands more.

The following day 2,000 policemen began a crackdown on the estimated 100,000 foreign workers who had failed to register in the exercise.

Walk the walk, Abdullah tells developed nations

11 June Rio de Janeiro

Developed nations must walk the walk, not just talk the talk in their commitment to environment and development programmes, Foreign Minister Datuk Abdullah Ahmad Badawi told the Earth Summit, attended by more than 100 countries. The North must change its wasteful pattern of production and consumption, he said. The poorer nations were already too overburdened economically and socially for them to bear the brunt if the North did not help to accelerate its development.

Woman killed, 10 injured as train jumps tracks

20 June Kuala Lumpur

Passenger Fatimah Salleh, 58, died and 10 others were injured when eight of the 11 carriages of the Sinaran Pagi express train from Butterworth went off the tracks near Kuang, about seven kilometres from Rawang. The carriages were brand new.

There have been at least eight derailments this year, although this was the first time that there had been casualties. Almost all were suspected to have been caused by vandalism.

Raja Kamarul brings children back to Malaysia

26 July Kuala Lumpur

Raja Kamarul Bahrin Shah Raja Ahmad Shah returned from Australia with his two children, Raja Muhammad Baharuddin Ismail Shah, 9, and Raja Shahirah Aishah, 7.

The nephew of the Sultan of Terengganu said he was prepared to face the consequences of his actions—he had spirited them away from his divorced wife Jacqueline Gillespie. She had filed for divorce in Australia in 1991 and was granted custody of the children. According to Raja Kamarul, he had been given custody by the Syariah Court in Kuala Terengganu in 1986.

He had acted to bring them back after receiving news that their religious status had been changed in Australia.

In 2006 the children were reunited with their mother when they individually visited her in Melbourne.

Proclamation signed

4 July Kuala Lumpur

With a few exceptions, Malay Rulers signed the Proclamation of Constitutional Principles at Istana Negara, agreeing to uphold the Constitution and not be involved in party politics or business. They also pledged to adhere to constitutional provisions pertaining to the appointment of Menteris Besar, State Executive Councillors and senior Government officers.

Keeper of the Rulers' Seal Engku Datuk Ibrahim Engku Ngah signing the proclamation.

The Sultans of Terengganu and Selangor were indisposed, but had consented and the Sultans of Johor and Kedah sought clarification on certain clauses. The Sultan of Kelantan did not sign. The proclamation was to clarify the rights and powers of the Rulers and to clear confusion up among the people.

Kuala Lumpur severs relations with Belgrade

12 August Kuala Lumpur

With immediate effect, Kuala Lumpur severed diplomatic relations with the Serbian Government in Belgrade in response to continued atrocities by the Serbs in Bosnia-Herzegovina. Malaysia was believed to be the first country to take such action. The Malaysian mission in Belgrade closed, and trading relations were suspended. The Serbian envoy was told to close his mission in Kuala Lumpur and leave the country with his officials 'as soon as possible.'

Living Skills for pupils

16 August Kuala Lumpur

With the new school year beginning on 30 November, a new subject, Living Skills, is to be introduced in 6,860 primary schools. It would be a compulsory subject for Standard Four pupils, and would be part of the curriculum for Standard Five and Six pupils. It would replace the Manipulative Skills subject currently taught on a pilot basis in certain schools. It aimed to teach pupils some basics of practical living.

M'sian contingent at the Olympics opening

26 July Barcelona

With Razif Sidek as the flag bearer, the Malaysian contingent stepped out smartly in their green baju Melayu and baju kurung for at the opening ceremony of the 25th Olympic Games here (left). The Yang di-Pertuan Agong Sultan Azlan Shah was among those present, as vice-president of the International Hockey Federation.

The badminton team scored Malaysia's first-ever Olympic medal when Razif and Jalani Sidek won the bronze in the men's doubles semi-finals against South Korea. Malaysia's second bronze came through Hu King Hong in the women's taekwondo bantamweight category.

Last race for the turf club

23 August Kuala Lumpur

The 96-year-old Selangor Turf Club held its last race after being a landmark of the city in Jalan Ampang for almost a century. The club, which opened in March 1896 under the chairmanship of Sir Frank Swettenham, was giving way to the planned Kuala Lumpur City Centre project.

'The Old Lady', as many fondly called the racecourse, would be relocated to its new grounds in Sungai Besi, off the Kuala Lumpur–Seremban highway. There would be a break in racing until the $220-million complex, currently under construction, opened. The new track would include a grandstand with a capacity of 20,000, the latest betting facilities, closed-circuit television coverage of races and modern stables for the racehorses.

It would also hold an international race offering stakes of $1 million.

This Kuala Lumpur landmark in Jalan Ampang was destined to make way for the Kuala Lumpur City Centre project.

Peninsula hit by power breakdown

29 September Kuala Lumpur

Most of Peninsular Malaysia was thrown into chaos when a massive blackout occurred, disrupting water supply, as pumps failed, the traffic system, as traffic lights went out, and business and industry too.

The massive power failure, the most serious in the country's history, was caused by a thunderstorm and lightning damaging the entire connecting system at Tenaga Nasional's Teluk Kalong sub-station in Kemaman, tripping the national grid.

All States except Kelantan, Perlis and Terengganu were affected by the blackout. Many factories in affected States reported major losses, and many companies had no choice but to send their workers home. Shopping complexes also closed early. Power supply was fully restored nationwide two days later.

Palm oil smear goes on

1 October Kuala Lumpur

Canisters of the US-produced Contadina brand of seasoned breadcrumbs, boldly labelled 'No Palm Oil', were found on the shelves of a local supermarket here.

The general manager of Golden Kerry Holdings Sdn Bhd admitted that importing the product was a blunder. All Contadina products were removed by the management, and seized by the Domestic Trade and Consumer Affairs Ministry.

Several countries in the West had recently embarked on a campaign to boycott palm oil in an effort to protect their local vegetable oil industries.

Firemen sifting through the debris in the late afternoon.

Six-storey block collapses

10 September Kuala Lumpur

A six-storey apartment block under construction in Taman Bukit Permai in Cheras collapsed during heavy rain, trapping at least four workers under concrete and steel rubble. It was one of five apartment blocks being built on a slope in Jalan Kuari, near Kampung Cheras Baru. Other workers escaped death or injury because they had left the building to take shelter from the rain.

Riding into wedded bliss

10 October Kuala Lumpur

Cycling champ M. Kumaresan and Stephanie Ramachandran (above) married at a Hindu temple in Kuala Lumpur. They met three years earlier...at a bicycle shop.

Ships collide in straits

Tanker and container vessel

20 September Kuala Lumpur

A Japanese oil tanker, *Nagasaki Spirit*, burst into flames after colliding with a container ship, the Ocean Blessing, off Belawan, Indonesia, early in the morning. It was confirmed that 21 crewmen had died and about 2,000 tonnes of crude oil were leaking into the sea.

Three days later, the *Nagasaki Spirit* was still burning, and two huge oil slicks were spotted just 30 nautical miles southwest of Penang, with a radius of between 10 and 30 nautical miles. The Department of Environment activated oil spill response measures following the sightings of the oil slicks.

The collision further heightened Malaysia's fear over the proposed passage through the Straits of Malacca of the Japanese ship *Akatsuki Maru* carrying a cargo of a tonne of plutonium.

Cruise liner and trawler

23 August Port Dickson

A Greek cruise liner, *Royal Pacific*, collided with a Taiwanese trawler at night, 12 nautical miles from here. A Singapore architect, Lau Chan Ghit, 37, and an unidentified woman died and several were listed as missing.

The liner sank quickly and submerged completely less than an hour after the collision. Two foreign vessels rescued 504 survivors. Sixty-four injured survivors were taken to Singapore, while other injured went to the district hospital here.

A crew member said most of those aboard were asleep when it happened. 'Everybody panicked and jumped into the dark sea,' he said. The accident brought into focus once again the danger of the Straits of Malacca which is known to be one of the world's busiest and most crowded shipping lanes.

1992

3 October
Bill Gates, college dropout founder of Microsoft, heads *Forbes* magazine's list of richest Americans, with US$6.3 billion.

6 October
The UN Security Council is unanimous in establishing a war crimes commission for incidents in the Balkan civil war.

8 October
West Indian poet Derek Walcott wins the Nobel Prize for Literature.

3 November
Bill Clinton wins the US presidential elections.

6 December
Hindu extremists destroy the 16th-century Babri Mosque in Ayodhya, India. This sparks off two months of violence. Thousands die.

31 December
Czechoslovakia breaks up. The next day the people wake up to two separate nations, Slovakia and the Czech Republic.

Fire again at Subang Airport

15 October | **Kuala Lumpur**

The Kuala Lumpur airport was on fire again, six months after a major blaze destroyed the South Wing of Terminal One in April. The flight control centre was gutted early in the morning, putting the airport out of operation for six hours, disrupting flights and leaving thousands stranded here and in other airports in the country.

Operations returned to normal in late afternoon, when flight movements were coordinated by the Singapore air traffic control centre in Changi, the Royal Malaysian Air Force Subang base control tower and a manual radar operated from the airport's fire department tower.

The fire resulted in a $20-million loss of revenue for MAS, mainly due to flight cancellations and the disruption to cargo service.

Firemen atop a Simon Snorkel spraying fire at the smoking flight control tower at Subang Airport.

Proton Catalyst bags three prestigious awards

22 October | **London**

The Proton Catalyst, known as the Proton Iswara at home, bagged three awards at the British International Motor Show in Birmingham, just two weeks after its debut in the UK market.

It won two gold awards in the £7,500–£9,500 saloon car and the below-£7,500 hatchback categories, as well as the Award of Excellence from the Institute of Transport Managers. The Proton Iswara Aeroback was launched in Malaysia on 15 August.

Chilean President Patricio Aylwin Azocar, with his wife Leanor Oyarzun De Aylwin, is greeted by Prime Minister Dato' Seri Dr Mahathir Mohamad.

Chilean President on three-day visit

10 November | **Kuala Lumpur**

Chilean President Patricio Aylwin Azocar arrived here on a three-day official visit. With a 120-member entourage, he was the first Latin American Head of State to pay an official visit to Malaysia.

High Court burns

2 December | **Kuala Lumpur**

A fire broke out at dawn, causing extensive damage to the High Court building here in Jalan Raja.

Cases at the High Court criminal division were heard at the adjacent Sultan Abdul Samad building, while the Sessions Court criminal division was transferred to the Jalan Duta Sessions Court. Court documents were damaged, not by the fire but by the water used to put out the blaze.

Sultan beat me, says hockey coach

6 December | **Kuala Lumpur**

Maktab Sultan Abu Bakar hockey coach Douglas Gomez has named the Sultan of Johor as the person who allegedly assaulted him at the Istana Bukit Serene in Johor Bahru a week ago.

In the police report he lodged, Gomez said that the angry Sultan had hit him in the face and verbally assaulted him.

The incident followed the forced withdrawal of the MSAB team from the semi-finals of the Malaysian Hockey Federation–Milo Champion Schools tournament. This prompted Gomez to criticise the leadership of the Johor Hockey Association for 'destroying' hockey in the State.

Prime Minister Dato' Seri Dr Mahathir Mohamad said later that the Government was studying the extent of the Rulers' legal immunity, as the privileges accorded to royalty did not extend to 'killing or beating people' (*see 9 January 1993*).

No. 1 tourist destination

3 September | **Kuala Lumpur**

Despite being a new entrant to the international tourism industry, Malaysia became the leading Asean tourist destination in 1991, overtaking Singapore and Thailand. Malaysia's share was 28.32 per cent of the tourism pie.

Bosnian children arrive in Malaysia

27 October | **Kuala Lumpur**

The first batch of Bosnian children under the Angkatan Belia Islam Malaysia adoption programme arrived in Malaysia after a 29-hour journey from Zagreb. The 41 children were accompanied by 21 Bosnian mothers.

1993

News highlights: a constitutional crisis was averted and an Umno leadership tussle was amicably settled. Tension over the question of royal immunity was eased when Yang di-Pertuan Agong Sultan Azlan Shah agreed to proposed constitutional changes. Ghafar Baba withdrew from the race for the post of Umno Deputy President to make way for Dato' Seri Anwar Ibrahim. After the neutralisation of these potential flashpoints the nation was gripped with shock when the Highland Towers, a block of luxury apartments in Kuala Lumpur, keeled over crushing to death 48 residents. Many of the victims were diplomats and other expatriates. Rescue operations were called off 12 days later.

FEBRUARY
Launch of the Proton Wira, successor to the Proton Saga.

JUNE
Cheah Soon Kit (left) and Soo Beng Kiang (right) deliver Malaysia's 43rd and final gold medal in the badminton doubles final at the SEA Games in Singapore.

JULY
Former rubber tappers seek apology and compensation from Britain for the 1948 Batang Kali incident in which British soldiers killed 24 Malayans.

DECEMBER
Australian Prime Minister Paul Keating calls Dato' Seri Dr Mahathir Mohamad 'recalcitrant' leading to a diplomatic row between Malaysia and Australia.

December: Tragedy—the Highland Towers collapse.

'All the 43 gold medals were not gifts. It was blood and sweat from the athletes.'

Datuk Khalid Yunos, chef-de-mission of the 17th SEA Games Malaysian team, 21 June 1993.

1993

19 January
Israel reverses its position and accepts that the PLO is not a criminal organisation.

12 March
Thirteen bombs explode in Bombay, killing about 300. The outrage is believed to have been organised by a crime syndicate in retaliation for the destruction of the Babri Mosque.

19 April
A 51-day standoff between the FBI and Branch Davidian cultists near Waco, Texas, ends in an explosive fire that kills 76 people including the cult leader, David Koresh.

27 April
The Zambian national football team, en route to play in a World Cup qualifying match, dies in a plane crash off Libreville, Gabon.

1 May
A Tamil Tiger suicide bomber kills Sri Lankan President Ranasinghe Premadasa.

24 May
After a 30-year civil war, Eritrea gains independence from Ethiopia.

Tension over royal immunity

9 January | Kuala Lumpur

The Sultan of Johor after the meeting at Istana Negara.

Government representatives met Rulers and expressed the hope that they would agree to draft amendments to the Constitution on royal immunity. The meeting at Istana Negara followed a proposal by the Sultan of Pahang on 27 December 1992 to meet informally before the Conference of Rulers convened 16 January to discuss proposed constitutional amendments.

Essentially the Government was seeking to remove the Rulers' privilege of immunity from legal action as well as to minimise their role in the political and governmental process. The draft was approved without changes by the Cabinet on 7 January.

Tensions over the proposed changes were raised about a week previously when the Sultan of Johor said he wanted to hold a mass audience on 8 January at the Istana Besar. It was feared that such a gathering could lead to a split among Malays as the opposition party Semangat 46, which opposed the changes, would be involved. However, the Sultan retracted the plan.

King agrees to constitutional changes

22 March | Kuala Lumpur

The Yang di-Pertuan Agong Sultan Azlan Shah consented to the Constitution (Amendment) Bill 1993, averting a rift between the Government and Malay royalty. The Dewan Rakyat had passed the Bill, with more than the required two-thirds majority, at a special meeting on 9 March. The next day the Senate voted unanimously in favour.

VIP visits

'Mr Nice Guy'

6 January | Kuala Lumpur

Thailand's Prime Minister Chuan Leekpai arrived on a three-day official visit, accompanied by an 88-member delegation.

Chuan, 55, described as the 'Mr Nice Guy' of Thai politics, became Prime Minister after his party, the Democrats, won the general election in September 1992.

Japanese PM

13 January | Kuala Lumpur

Japanese Prime Minister Kiichi Miyazawa arrived on a three-day visit on the second leg of a tour of four Asean countries. Miyazawa led a 62-member delegation which included senior officials and MPs.

First woman at top of public-listed company

3 February | Kuala Lumpur

Island & Peninsular Bhd (I&P) announced the appointment of Puan Shahrizat Abdul Jalil as its chairman, making her the first woman to head a Malaysian publicly-listed group of companies.

Shahrizat, a former magistrate and assistant Treasury solicitor, resigned from the legal and judicial service to enter private practice in 1980. In the past seven years, she had been a director of I&P and Austral Enterprise and other leading companies. She was chairman of the Women's City Core Legal Bureau of the Prime Minister's Department and a member of the National Economic Consultative Committee.

Assault charge against Johor prince dropped

26 January | Johor Bahru

Perak hockey goalkeeper Mohamed Jaafar Selvaraja Vello accepted RM1,000 compensation from the Tengku Bendahara of Johor, Tengku Abdul Majid Idris, and agreed to drop an assault complaint against him.

Tengku Abdul Majid, 22, was accused of causing hurt to Jaafar on 10 July last year after the Malaysia Games hockey final at the Johor Bahru AstroTurf stadium in which Tengku Majid had played for Johor.

Perak had beaten the home State for the title through penalty flicks.

Savings bond a hit

19 February | Kuala Lumpur

The RM1-billion Malaysian Savings Bond issued by Bank Negara was snapped up within eight days after it went on offer. Individuals and charitable organisations booked RM300 million in advance and the rest went on sale for a month. The price for each bond was RM67.55, redeemable at RM100 on maturity on 16 February 1998.

Great Malaysian Novel completed

16 March | Kuala Lumpur

The Great Malaysian Novel was finished and on display at the National Library. Organised by *The Star* newspaper the project began in early November 1991. The event took place in stages with Malaysians throughout the country completing various sections of the book after being given a basic outline.

Islamic banking now widely available

4 March | Kuala Lumpur

The Islamic alternative to conventional banking is now available at three leading banks. The syariah-compatible banking system was offered by Malayan Banking Berhad, Bank Bumiputra and United Malayan Banking Corporation.

Previously, the only bank adopting an interest-free system was Bank Islam Malaysia. The facilities, available to Muslims and non-Muslims, comprised services which do not involve interest, including savings and general investment deposits and housing and car loans.

500 mourn matriarch

6 March | Kuala Lumpur

A 1km funeral procession here comprised most of the 500 descendants of See Loy Leong, who died at the age of 102. Four generations—children, grandchildren, great-grandchildren and great-great-grandchildren—were represented, each dressed in different colours.

Funeral held for jet stowaway boy

21 March | Alor Star

Stowaway Shamsul Ramli, 16, who was found dead from exposure in the wheel-bay of the MAS 747-200 last Monday after it landed at Johannesburg, South Africa, has been buried at the Kubang Palas Mosque burial ground at Padang Senai.

The mystery of how or why he stole into the wheel-bay of the jumbo jet at the Kuala Lumpur International Airport remained unsolved.

Death of Wira, the orang utan mascot

20 April | Kuala Lumpur

Wira the orang utan with his keeper.

Wira, the orang utan which was used as the mascot of Visit Malaysia Year 1990, was found drowned in the moat of his enclosure. Wira was 11.

The trained orang utan gained fame when he graced the advertisements and billboards of the tourist promotion drive.

Melanau festival draws the crowds

23 April Mukah

Deputy Education Minister Mr Leo Michael Toyad, himself a Melanau, said the State Government had agreed in principle to include in the tourist calendar the Melanau Kaul beach festival celebrating the coming of the fishing season.

The festival features funfairs, stage shows, water sports, boat competitions and traditional games.

The fest in Mukah, where Melanau predominate, this year drew some 7,000 people, many more than in previous years.

Snail mail

20 May Penang

A letter that a grandmother wrote to her grandson in 1977 arrived at its destination in Penang recently. The grandmother Goh Ai Keow, 78, was visiting when the letter arrived at her daughter's home. The post office said it could have been wedged at the bottom of a mail bag. The letter urged Hock Lim, her grandson, then in Form One, to study hard and get his mother to cook him nutritious food.

Proton Wira launched

21 May Kuala Lumpur ▶ Dato' Seri Dr Mahathir Mohamad launched the Proton Wira at the Putra World Trade Centre. The car was a successor to the Saga and Iswara models, of which more than 400,000 had been sold. It had sleek, rounded lines, was more spacious than previous models and came in 1.5- and 1.6-litre versions, both manual and automatic.

The Wira, the result of three years of development by local engineers at a cost of RM300 million, was priced at RM39,500–RM55,000.

The Prime Minister inspects the car.

Dr M meets mentor at school reunion

30 April Kuala Lumpur

Former teacher Mohd Zain Abdul Rashid shares a joke with Dato' Seri Dr Mahathir Mohamad at a Hari Raya gathering at Sri Perdana.

The 80-year-old former teacher of the Sultan Abdul Hamid College in Alor Star was given a surprise birthday party at the gathering which the Prime Minister hosted for the old boys' association of the college.

Triad boss brought back from Bangkok

31 May Bangkok

Malaysia's most wanted Chinese triad gang leader was arrested in Bangkok and brought back to the country under heavy police guard.

Jacky Chan, 28, a leader of the Siew Sam Ong (Three Little Emperors) triad, was being interrogated at the Penang police headquarters .

Free trade appeal

14 June Washington DC

The world should be a single marketplace and trading bloc, Prime Minister Dato' Seri Dr Mahathir Mohamad told the International General Meeting of the Pacific Basin Economic Council.

Free trade was not perfect, he said, but it was the best way to ensure economic good for the greatest number. 'In the context of trade, open globalism must be the first and the best choice,' he told more than 700 top executives and officials.

It was to champion a multilateral, open global trading system that Malaysia advocated forming an East Asia Economic Caucus. Unlike in Europe and elsewhere, East Asian integration was completely market- and business-driven, said Dr Mahathir.

'We must fight for open regionalism,' Dr Mahathir urged conference participants in his speech.

Crocodile loses deadly tug-of-war in river

18 June Malacca

A market trader was recovering in hospital after fighting for his life with a three-metre-long crocodile which grabbed him by the arm in a river near here.

After a tug-of-war lasting five minutes the croc eventually let him go. It happened, said Ramli Jantan, 33, when he, his brother-in-law and a friend were netting prawns in a tributary of the Malacca River. 'I fought for dear life,' he said.

Middling marathoner walks to gold medal

14 June Singapore

Walker M. Ravindran went down on his knees to thank his mentor V. Subramaniam immediately after winning the men's 20km walk in the SEA Games at the Singapore National Stadium. The 23-year-old from Seremban said he was more interested in the marathon but Subramaniam felt he would make a better walker.

'He spent many hours motivating and encouraging me. He also got me a job with Telekom Malaysia. This gold is for him as well,' Ravindran said.

Honours for Hanif

22 June Singapore

Inspector General of Police Tun Hanif Omar was awarded Singapore's Distinguished Service Order. This is the highest service award presented to any foreigner for distinguished conduct.

Tun Hanif, 54, the first foreign police chief to be so honoured, was recognised for his contribution to closer cooperation between the police forces of the two countries. On 5 June, he was awarded the Seri Setia Mahkota by the Yang di-Pertuan Agong.

Tun Hanif was the youngest IGP, appointed in 1974 at 35 to succeed Tan Sri Abdul Rahman Hashim who was shot dead by Communist terrorists. He was the longest-serving IGP in the world and the longest-serving head of a Malaysian Government department.

Bentong Kali killed

30 June Kuala Lumpur

P. Kalimuthu, better known as Bentong Kali, a criminal involved in 17 murders as well as assault cases, armed robberies and car thefts, was killed in a shootout with police in a house in Medan Damansara. It happened just 40 minutes after he killed his last victim, a tea-stall owner.

Police carry away Bentong Kali's body.

Bentong Kali's two henchmen, identified as S. Gunalan alias Billiard and T. Gunasegaran, 30, were also killed. Kali was the country's most wanted man, with a RM100,000 price on his head.

1993

10 June
Scientists announce they have extracted genetic material from preserved remains of an insect that lived when dinosaurs roamed the Earth.

11 June
Steven Spielberg's film *Jurassic Park* premieres.

24 June
Andrew Wiles presents a solution to Fermat's Last Theorem, a mathematical conundrum that has defied solution for more than three centuries.

27 June
The US launches cruise missiles at Iraqi military targets in Baghdad, in response to the attempted assassination of former President George Bush when he visited Kuwait in April.

12 July
A 7.8-magnitude earthquake off Hokkaido launches a tsunami that kills 202.

13 August
A six-storey hotel in Nakhon Ratchasima, Thailand, collapses, killing more than 100.

Traffic police go on 'strike'

9 July Kuala Lumpur

City traffic was in chaos when an experiment to ensure smooth flow with the aid of computerised lights went awry as police withdrew their participation.

As City Hall wrestled with the massive jams, angry motorists pointed an accusing finger at the police for being conspicuously absent when they were most needed.

In an article in the *New Straits Times*, a City Hall official said the authorities could not stop the police from taking over control at the traffic junctions involved despite an undertaking to allow the Kuala Lumpur area traffic control (KLATC) to operate on its own

Under the system, the lights respond to the congestion level with the help of detector loops in the ground to detect traffic volume.

To monitor its effectiveness, traffic policemen were instructed not to direct traffic at the 81 intersections. This resulted in massive traffic jams.

Illegals drown trying to swim ashore

20 July Banting

At least 28 illegal Indonesian immigrants drowned and 40 others were missing, when they and about 50 others were forced to swim ashore off Morib beach, Selangor, early this morning.

The men and women had to abandon their Indonesian-registered boat after it ran aground 300m from shore. The 100-tonne boat, *Bara Damai*, left Dumai in Sumatra at 11am on Monday with about 120 passengers aboard.

Survivors said they were ordered to swim ashore after the boat hit a sandbar and ran aground. They were ordered off the boat as it was taking in water as a result of heavy seas.

Forty-nine passengers, aged 12 to 45, made it to shore and were detained by police while search-and-rescue teams recovered 28 bodies up to 7pm. A 2-year-old boy and a 12-year-old girl were among those who died.

Deputy Home Minister Datuk Megat Junid Megat Ayob told reporters at Parliament House that the survivors would be deported.

British 'massacre' petition

8 July Petaling Jaya

Three former rubber tappers spoke out for the first time against what they described as the massacre of 24 Malaysians by British soldiers in Batang Kali 45 years ago. The sole survivor was Mr Chong Foong, 67. Madam Foo Moi, 74, and Madam Tham Yong, 62, said their husbands and relatives were killed. And they were especially bitter that so far Britain had refused

Michael Chong reviews the petition with the villagers.

to apologise and compensate them for their loss and suffering. MCA public service and complaints section head Michael Chong accompanied the three to hand over a petition to British High Commissioner Duncan Slater.

In their petition, they appealed to Queen Elizabeth to re-open the files for the third time and prosecute those involved. Mr Chong Foong claimed that although two inquiries had been conducted in England, none of the witnesses was questioned by the British investigators.

According to the British High Commission, investigations into the Batang Kali incident had not revealed sufficient evidence to prosecute those involved. But the former village headman and constable Low Chin Sen said he had not slept peacefully since, he claimed, men of the Scots Guards killed the 24, apparently believing they were Communist terrorist supporters, and set village houses ablaze.

SEA Games

Athletes and bowlers shine for Malaysia

12–20 June Singapore

With 43 golds won out of 317 at stake and fifth place overall, Malaysia had its best outing in the SEA Games outside Kuala Lumpur.

Bowling: The men struck gold in the singles, where Ng Yiew Peng had eight consecutive strikes in the last game, doubles and all-events, and the women in trios, fives and Masters. Shalin Zulkifli, 16, was the youngest Malaysian bowler to win a Games gold medal.

Karate: Amid allegations of biased judging, Malaysia won three golds, five silvers and nine bronzes.

Swimming: Jeffrey Ong delivered gold medals in the 400m freestyle and 1,500m freestyle events. He also bagged a bronze in the 400m individual medley.

Billiards and snooker: Malaysia did well in billiards and snooker, winning two golds, one silver and three bronzes. Sam Chong won the individual billiards title and helped the three-man team to victory.

Athletics: The quartet of Josephine Mary, Rabia Abdul Salam, G. Shanti and R. Shanti set a national record of 3:35.83, in the 4x400m, ending the Thais' 12-year domination. The victory made Malaysia regional track and field kings, with 14 golds, pipping Indonesia by a gold in the overall standings in athletics.

Zaki Sadri leapt into the record books with a 16.27m effort to become the first athlete to win the triple-jump gold for the fourth consecutive Games. Lou Chee Peng soared 2.21m to rewrite his own SEA Games high-jump record.

Winks on the blink

7 August Kuala Lumpur

The manager of a goldsmith's shop tried to signal two policemen with winks during a robbery—but his attempt failed and the robbers escaped with jewellery valued at RM200,000.

It happened when two robbers forced their way into the Mei Poh goldsmith's shop in Kepong Baru at 9.40am.

They forced manager Lau Teck Seng and a female employee into the back office and told him to open the safe containing the jewellery.

At that time, the two policemen entered the shop on a routine check. The robbers ordered Lau to go out and greet them in a normal manner.

He said he 'winked and winked' at the policemen to indicate that something was wrong. But they did not get it and left after signing the shop logbook.

The robbers fled the scene after taking the jewellery.

New township, road

7 August Tebedu

Sarawak Chief Minister Tan Sri Abdul Taib Mahmud laid the foundation stone for the new Mutiara Town and said it would be linked to Serian by a tar-sealed road costing RM54.2m.

The 38km road was to be funded by the Federal Government. Mutiara Town is located 5km from the Tebedu Immigration Checkpoint near the Sarawak–Indonesian border.

Tan Sri Taib Mahmud unveiling the plaque of the clock tower at the centre of Mutiara Town.

Lorrain Osman freed

17 August | **Hong Kong**

The former chairman of Bumiputra Malaysia Finance Ltd, Lorrain Osman, was freed after eight months in Stanley Prison here. Lorrain, 62, was jailed for a year by the High Court after he pleaded guilty to fraud and conspiracy in connection with the 1983 collapse of the Carrian group. He was released after serving eight months for good behaviour.

Lorrain had earlier spent seven years in detention in Britain, fighting extradition to Hong Kong. He was Britain's longest-serving remand prisoner.

Lorrain had pleaded guilty to conspiring with George Tan, chairman of the Carrian shipping and property group, to have his company lend inadequately secured loans of US$292 million to a shelf company run by Tan.

The Carrian group, including publicly-listed Carrian Investment Ltd, left debts in excess of US$1 billion, the biggest bankruptcy in the Hong Kong's history.

Once-in-a-lifetime meteor shower

13 August | **Kuala Lumpur**

An awesome shower of shooting stars lit up the sky at Fraser's Hill early in the morning. The phenomenon was caused by space debris left by the comet Swift-Tuttle.

The sky was filled with about 50 falls of the perseids (meteorised comet dust) between 2.15am and 3.30am. Malaysian Nature Society Astronomy Group Coordinator Looi Keng Kok and some 30 people were stationed at Fraser's Hill to watch them.

The previous morning only 10 dartings had been seen in the half hour during which skywatchers gazed at the heavens from Janda Baik, Genting Highlands.

Perseids pose no danger to people on Earth. Although they strike the atmosphere at more than 200,000 kilometres per hour, they are extremely fragile, usually smaller than a grain of sand and vaporise about 100 km above the Earth's surface.

The minibus, once a familiar sight on the capital's streets.

Minibus strike

22 August | **Kuala Lumpur**

Thousands of commuters were stranded as minibus drivers went on strike. The strike was said to have been in protest against a crackdown by the authorities. The Federal Territory and Selangor Minibus Operators' Association complained that its members who went on their usual rounds had been threatened and harassed at bus terminals.

Malaysian judge for war crimes tribunal

18 September | **Kuala Lumpur**

High Court judge Datuk Wira Lal Chand Vohrah took his election to the International War Crimes Tribunal in his stride. 'One trial is like any other,' he said when asked about the differences between the cases he had been trying in Malaysia and those he would be trying at The Hague. Mr Justice Vohrah, 59, the country's senior High Court judge, was one of seven elected by the United Nations General Assembly.

The 11-member tribunal was set up by the UN Security Council to try those accused of rape, murder, torture and other atrocities in the former Yugoslavia since 1991.

Mr Justice Vohrah, who had more than 15 years' experience hearing trials for capital offences and criminal appeals from subordinate courts, was appointed for a four-year term.

The Green Man

21 October | **Kuala Lumpur**

Gurmit Singh has won the Langkawi Award—Malaysia's highest award for environmental protection. Gurmit set up the Environmental Protection Society of Malaysia (EPSM) 20 years ago to promote environmental awareness.

Sacrificing a more lucrative career as an engineer, Gurmit had dedicated his life to educating the public. Furthermore, he and his wife live an environmentally-friendly lifestyle. They kept a 'green' home, without air-conditioning, their furniture was recycled and they did not have a car. Instead, Gurmit used public transport or bicycles to his destination.

In 1978, he raced the Minister of Environment's car to Taman Titiwangsa and won, proving that traffic jams in KL were so bad that even a cyclist could beat a car. He also wore a facemask to see how much dust collected in the filter.

Landslide win for Wawasan

5 November | **Kuala Lumpur**

While Umno president Dato' Seri Dr Mahathir Mohamad and deputy president Dato' Seri Anwar Ibrahim were unopposed in the Umno election, the rest of the posts were contested by leaders aligned either to Dr Mahathir or to those who opposed him, namely Datuk Musa Hitam and Tengku Razaleigh Hamzah.

Despite Dr Mahathir's reported aversion to team politics, the group that supported him (and which became known as the Wawasan team) grabbed the three vice-president posts—Tan Sri Muhyiddin Yassin got the most votes with 1,413 followed by Dato' Seri Najib Tun Razak with 1,202 and Tan Sri Muhammad Muhammad Haji Taib with 1,189.

The victorious Wawasan team.

Change at top in Umno

Ghafar makes way for Anwar

15 October | **Kuala Lumpur**

Ghafar congratulates Anwar (left).

Encik Ghafar Baba resigned as Deputy Prime Minister, confirming widely circulating rumours that he would quit the post. A week later he withdrew from the race for the post of Umno deputy president to make way for Dato' Seri Anwar Ibrahim who therefore won unopposed.

Umno leaders praised Ghafar for his decision, describing him as a true statesman who put the party above personal interest. They said his decision should be respected and dismissed speculation that Ghafar would join Semangat 46.

Born in 1925 to a poor family in Negri Sembilan, Ghafar became a teacher and later joined Umno. He was appointed Deputy Prime Minister in 1986.

It took Anwar, a former student activist, only 11 years to rise through the ranks of Umno to its second-highest post. Soon after his entry to Umno in 1982 he was named Deputy Minister in the Prime Minister's Department. He was appointed Finance Minister in 1991.

Two sons born on Deepavali day

14 November | **Kuala Lumpur**

Housewife Low Kwan Ho did it again, giving birth to a second son on Deepavali day. Low, 31, was overjoyed when her son was delivered eight minutes after midnight at the Assunta Hospital.

Her first was born on Deepavali at the same hospital two years earlier. 'It is unbelievable that my first two children would be born on Deepavali, both two weeks premature and both sons,' she said.

Way clear for caucus

24 November | **Kuala Lumpur**

East Asian countries no longer had any excuse not to join the East Asia Economic Caucus following US President Bill Clinton's statement that he was not against it, said Prime Minister Dato' Seri Dr Mahathir. Japan and South Korea were reluctant to join due to US opposition. But Clinton said he was not opposed to the Caucus if it expanded economic opportunities.

1993

world news

13 September
Israeli PM Yitzhak Rabin and PLO leader Yasser Arafat sign an accord at the US White House granting limited autonomy to Palestinians in most of the Gaza Strip and about a third of the West Bank.

30 September
Prince Norodom Sihanouk is re-installed as the King of Cambodia.

30 September
An earthquake of 6.0–6.4-magnitude strikes southern India, killing 10,000-30,000 people.

2 October
In Son La, Vietnam, 53 Thai members of a doomsday cult commit mass suicide.

3 October
A battle between US forces and Muslim militia in Mogadishu leaves 19 US soldiers and about 500 Somalians dead.

11 November
Tamil Tigers overrun a Sri Lankan army camp, killing or capturing 600 soldiers.

Row with Australia over 'Recalcitrant' comment

Australian Paul Makucha tries to resolve the rift between Dr Mahathir and Keating by putting up this billboard in Sydney.

7 December | **Kuala Lumpur**

Foreign Minister Datuk Abdullah Ahmad Badawi described Malaysia's current displeasure with the Australian Government as 'very serious.'

He said Australian Prime Minister Paul Keating had made no sincere effort to apologise to Dato' Seri Dr Mahathir Mohamad after calling him 'recalcitrant' for boycotting the first summit of the Asia Pacific Economic Cooperation (APEC) forum in Seattle the previous month. Datuk Abdullah said Keating's recent letter of explanation to Dr Mahathir was in no way conciliatory. Asked how ties could be repaired, he replied: 'It is entirely up to Keating to undo the damage already done to the relationship by offering a sincere apology to Dr Mahathir.'

In Canberra, the Australian Government insisted that there was nothing more it could do to settle the row with Malaysia, which had raised threats of trade sanctions, saying it was now up to Kuala Lumpur to improve relations (*see 16 January 1996*).

Milk and farm profits go down the drain

30 December | **Dengkil**

Dairy farmers in Selangor were being forced to pour their daily income down the drain. 'We are losing about RM130 a day as the milk collection centre in Sepang has not been coming for our milk,' said one of the farmers, Vivellannathan Kanninadar, 28.

He said collections stopped four days earlier without prior warning from the Selangor Veterinary Services Department in Sepang which was in charge of the collection. The farmers were told the department's vehicle had broken down and it could not afford to repair it until January. The farmers were told they had to transport the milk to Sepang, 38km away, themselves.

Sky-high praise for Lima '93

11 December | **Langkawi**

The Langkawi International Maritime and Aerospace exhibition (Lima '93) drew to a close after six days of high-flying activity on the island.

Participants said there was a marked improvement in the show's marketing, infrastructure, management and logistics compared to the inaugural show, which was held in 1991.

Lima '93 would also be remembered for the big deals clinched and number of memoranda of understanding signed.

It was agreed that Germany's Dornier Seastar aircraft, the world's only all-composite amphibious aircraft, would be manufactured in Penang from 1994 on a joint-venture basis.

Satirical shocks to the system

An article in *Asia Magazine* focused on a Malaysian theatre group with the satirical name The Instant Café Theatre which featured, you guessed it, satire. The 15-strong company was performing at a Kuala Lumpur hotel, and produced pastiches of Malaysian life which came as a refreshing surprise, the article said. The children of Prime Minister Dato' Seri Dr Mahathir Mohamad were avid fans of Instant Café, and he had dropped in incognito to see the show.

48 die in condo collapse

11–24 December | **Kuala Lumpur**

Block One of Highland Towers, a 12-storey block of luxury apartments in Ulu Klang, collapsed at 1.30 pm on Saturday, 11 December following 10 days of continuous rainfall. Three survivors were found on the first day. Eighteen-month-old Nurhamidah Najib was the first to be rescued from the rubble, followed by her mother Umirah Rashida, 21, who escaped with minor injuries, and Japanese national Shizue Nakajima, 50, who later died in hospital.

The apartment block scattered like a collapsed house of cards.

Nurhamidah even managed to catch some sleep while she was trapped in the rubble. Umirah said Nurhamidah cried at first but fell asleep after she was breast-fed. Umirah said the rescue workers initially did not hear her cries for help but she stuck out a stick and managed to get their attention.

When rescue operations ceased 12 days later, 48 bodies had been recovered. Residents from the two other blocks in Highland Towers and seven nearby houses were evacuated soon after the tragedy. Highland Towers was among the first condominiums built in the Klang Valley. Block One was opened for occupation in 1979. Blocks Two and Three were completed in 1982 and 1985.

Many of the victims were diplomats and other expatriates including Koreans, Japanese, Americans, Europeans and Arabs. Also among them were former Deputy Prime Minister Datuk Musa Hitam's son Carlos Rashid, daughter-in-law Rozeetha and their part-time Indonesian maid. They were trapped in their fourth-floor apartment.

However the family's Philippine maid saved Datuk Musa's eight-month-old granddaughter Marisa, when she grabbed the child and jumped clear from the crumbling building's car park to the ground floor. The next day, a tearful Datuk Musa visited the ruins and found a book, a few photographs and some clothing that belonged to Carlos. The book was a 1990 birthday present he gave to his son.

But not all the rescue efforts were successful. In one incident 55 hours after Block One toppled, a note was pushed through the rubble reading, 'I am still alive', but rescuers could not reach the survivor. Meanwhile, looters were reportedly seen scavenging in abandoned units in the two remaining blocks.

However, the tragedy also brought out the noblest instincts in people with police, firemen, army personnel and civilian volunteers working round the clock. International aid was also not slow in coming. There was a 24-member International Disaster Relief Team of Japan which had, since 1987, assisted in disasters around the world. The team had brought technical equipment including sonic ground detectors and special cutting machines to cut through concrete and iron.

Friends and relatives clasp hands for support as work to rescue survivors continued.

1994

Two discoveries brought hope of harvesting riches from the past: one was the discovery of the British vessel *Diana* which sank near Malacca in 1817. Its cargo of Ching Dynasty porcelain was estimated to be worth RM54 million. The other was the recovery by construction workers of a chest that renewed speculation of a sunken Khmer city at the bottom of Tasik Chini. The past was also showcased in two events—a parade themed 'Best of Malaysian Heritage' at the Malaysia Fest '94; and a *panglima* (warrior) riding a howdah atop an elephant to deliver copies of old Malay letters to the National Library. On the religious front, the Institut Kefahaman Islam Malaysia (IKIM) was launched to promote understanding of Islam.

FEBRUARY
Datuk Joseph Pairin Kitingan is sworn in as Sabah Chief Minister after a 36-hour wait.

MARCH
Institut Kefahaman Islam Malaysia (Ikim) opens with Tan Sri Ahmad Sarji Abdul Hamid as chairman.

SEPTEMBER
Former colonial administrator and cultural activist Tan Sri Mubin Sheppard passes away.

DECEMBER
Prime Minister Dr Mahathir opens the Tunku Abdul Rahman Putra Memorial.

September: Cultural extravaganza—Malaysia Fest.

'Interfaith understanding is the duty of all.'
Tan Sri Ahmad Sarji Abdul Hamid, at the opening of Institut Kefahaman Islam Malaysia (Ikim), 26 March 1994.

1994

world news

23 February
The Russian Parliament thumbs its nose at Boris Yeltsin by granting amnesty to the coup leaders of 1991 and 1993.

25 February
A Jewish extremist kills 29 Muslim worshippers in the Cave of Patriarchs, Hebron, West Bank. He is beaten to death.

30 March
Serbia and Croatia sign a ceasefire agreement to end the war in Croatia. The fighting continues in Bosnia-Herzegovina.

6 April
The Presidents of Rwanda and Burundi go down with their plane; some reports suggest it was brought down by a missile. It is the pretext for the beginning of the genocide of Tutsis and moderate Hutus. Estimates range from half a million to a million dead in this first phase of communal bloodletting.

22 April
Former US President, Richard Nixon, 81, is felled by a stroke.

Malaysian to lead UN force in Somalia

6 January Kuala Lumpur

Army Field Command Headquarters chief Lt-Jen Datuk Aboo Samah Aboo Bakar was appointed Force Commander of the United Nations Operations in Somalia (Unosom II).

The post was offered to Malaysia and the Cabinet felt that the career officer, who held a master's degree in strategic studies, was the best man for the job.

Lt-Jen Aboo Samah, 54, was to replace Lt-Gen Cervik Bir of Turkey from 20 January to take charge of the 20,000-strong UN force in Somalia which had the mandate to maintain peace so that humanitarian aid could be distributed to the Somalis.

Rahim is new IGP

10 January Kuala Lumpur

Deputy Inspector General of Police Tan Sri Abdul Rahim Mohamad Noor (below) was appointed Inspector General of Police, with Director of Management Datuk Samsuri Arshad as his deputy.

Tan Sri Rahim, 50, succeeded Tun Mohamed Hanif Omar who retired after having served as IGP for almost 20 years.

Prior to his appointment as Deputy IGP in June 1989, Rahim was the Special Branch Director.

Sabah CM guilty of corruption

17 January Kota Kinabalu

Sabah Chief Minister Datuk Joseph Pairin Kitingan was convicted by the Miri High Court of corruption and fined RM1,800. The amount did not disqualify him from holding public office and contesting February's State elections. A fine of RM2,000 or more would have disqualified him for five years.

After being in the dock for 96 days in a trial that began in January 1991, Pairin was found guilty of using his position as Chief Minister to corruptly approve a RM1.4-million contract for shophouses to a company of which his brothers-in-law were directors and shareholders.

The Japanese Sogo department store in Kuala Lumpur, advertised as the largest in Asia.

Tanker suspected of sludge dumping

26 January Kuala Lumpur

Navy divers found plastic bags of sludge scattered on the seabed around the tanker *Arabian Sea*, which was suspected of having dumped hazardous waste into the sea. .

The Liberian-registered tanker had been detained off Tanjung Piai, Johor, since 17 January. Workers for the tanker's cleaning contractor admitted that they had been instructed to throw bags of sludge overboard.

There were still 300,000 bags containing some 900 tonnes of sludge aboard and it was believed that some 600 to 800 tonnes had been dumped while the tanker was en route to Singapore.

36-hour palace vigil for new Chief Minister

21 February Kota Kinabalu

Datuk Joseph Pairin Kitingan was sworn in as the seventh Chief Minister of Sabah after a 36-hour wait. His Parti Bersatu Sabah (PBS) had won 25 seats to edge out Barisan Nasional, which took 23. Datuk Pairin then went to the palace of the Yang di-Pertua Negeri Tun Mohammad Said Keruak to be sworn in, but was refused entry. Datuk Pairin, who was serving his fourth term in office, then waited in a car outside the palace gates for a day and a half with about

Datuk Pairin signs the letter of office witnessed by High Court judge Mr Justice Charles Ho.

50 supporters. After being sworn in, Datuk Pairin named his Cabinet line-up as well as six appointed Assemblymen provided for under the Sabah Constitution.

Couture hero still rooted in Malaysia

28 January Kuala Lumpur

Couture hero Zang Toi, back in Malaysia from the US, showed he had not forgotten his roots at the Asean Fashion Trade Expo held in Kuala Lumpur recently.

He treated audiences to delightful ensembles that had imaginative east-meets-west touches such as Kelantanese wayang kulit figurines emblazoned on skirts and micro tops, as well as elaborate handsewn costumes with influences taken from traditional Chinese opera. The 33-year-old grew up in Kuala Krai, where his parents owned a grocery store. In 1979 he completed his high school education in Canada, after which he moved to New York to study fashion design.

Zang Toi with models at the Asean Fashion Trade Expo.

After a stint as a freelance designer he started the Zang Toi New York label five years ago with great success.

By the 1990s his collection was sold in major department stores and boutiques all over the US and other countries including Hong Kong, Singapore and Saudi Arabia. His clients included celebrities such as Ivana Trump and Princess Yasmin Aga Khan.

'Buy British last'

25 February Kuala Lumpur

The Cabinet decided to bar British firms from new Government contracts. British educational institutions and consulting firms would be among those hit. The decision was in retaliation against a British newspaper dragging up nine-year-old allegations that a British building firm was ready to offer Prime Minister Dato' Seri Dr Mahathir Mohamad a US$50,000 bribe to win a contract.

Malaysia's move would affect projects valued at between RM14 billion and RM16 billion. In addition, all private colleges and institutions were advised to look for non-British partners for future academic cooperation.

However, it was said that 15,000 Malaysian students studying in Britain would not be recalled. International Trade and Industry Minister Dato' Seri Rafidah Aziz said Malaysia had not imposed trade sanctions against Britain and the private sector could still continue their dealings in the open market.

Soldiers missing on Mt Kinabalu found

26 March Kota Kinabalu

Five British and Hong Kong soldiers missing for about three weeks on Mount Kinabalu were found alive and airlifted out.

They were spotted by helicopter pilot Kapt Mohamad Izhar Haruan between two steep waterfalls some 1,830 metres above sea level. The five were part of a 10-man team from the Royal Logistics Corps based in Hong Kong on a training expedition on the mountain. The search involved nearly 350 Malaysian soldiers, police, Sabah Park rangers and 36 British rescuers.

Ikim to promote progressive Islam

24 March Kuala Lumpur

Prime Minister Dato' Seri Dr Mahathir Mohamad opened the office of the Institut Kefahaman Islam Malaysia (Ikim), which is dedicated to promoting a peaceful, progressive and profound understanding of Islam.

Chairman Tan Sri Ahmad Sarji Abdul Hamid said Ikim would strive to show that Islam was a just and tolerant religion with a value system that could be universally accepted by all. But, most importantly, the function of IKIM was to explain certain concepts and principles in Islam which were prone to misinterpretation and misrepresentation.

The architecture of Ikim's building blended Islamic and colonial traditions. All the components of the RM10-million structure, down to the stained glass with traditional non-figurative Islamic designs, were made in Malaysia by local artisans.

Day of shootouts and car chases in Penang

8 April Penang

A day of all-action drama ended with the police arresting six suspected snatch thieves and four suspected drug traffickers. The 15-hour operation involving 300 policemen began at 6.30pm on 7 April when two policemen in a patrol car saw six men in a car speeding off after one of them had snatched a woman's handbag in Teluk Bahang. They gave chase and a gunbattle erupted which ended in Balik Pulau, more than 15km away.

The thieves abandoned their car and fled but were tracked and captured the next day. But the action did not stop there. Police had set up roadblocks to catch the snatch thieves and a car with four men inside crashed through a barrier at Tanjung Bungah, resulting in another car chase.

The suspected drug traffickers ran into another roadblock in busy George Town, more than 10km away, where police opened fire. Three suspects were arrested at the roadblock. The fourth suspect, who was wounded, fled on foot but was also later arrested.

Wreck highlights hope of buried treasure

11 April Malacca

The discovery of the British vessel *Diana*, which sank in 1817 off the coast of Malacca, prompted the setting up of a task force to highlight the riches that lie in shipwrecks off Malaysian shores as a tourist attraction. The *Diana*'s cargo of 20 tonnes of Ching Dynasty porcelain was estimated to be worth RM54 million.

At least 12 wrecks had been identified in the State's territorial waters. Many were believed to contain antique china, gold, silver, and tin. Some vessels that sank during World War II were said to be richly laden with precious metals.

However, illegal salvage work was going on. A company allegedly involved was said to have already sold some artefacts. According to a former director of the company, these included a 200-year-old gold cannon believed to have belonged to Bugis pirate Raja Hadji.

Local 'Bonnie and Clyde' killed in police raid

17 September Kuala Lumpur

A local 'Bonnie and Clyde' couple were among the most successful robbers in Malaysian history. Loo Ywhy Hoong, 28, his Thai wife Maung Mak Rampai, 25, and their henchman Soo Kim Teck, 27, were responsible for more than 10 goldsmith shop robberies and had made off with valuables worth RM4 million since last year.

The gang's last heist was on three goldsmith shops in Jalan Tuanku Abdul Rahman here the previous Tuesday.

Acting on a tip-off, police staked out a house in Kepong and ordered the occupants to surrender. They were greeted with a hail of bullets and a gunbattle erupted, ending in the deaths of Loo, Maung and Soo.

Threat thwarted

23 July Petaling Jaya

Twenty Chinese illegal immigrants threatened to turn themselves into human fireballs in a bid to thwart deportation at Subang Airport but surrendered unconditionally after 26 hours of negotiations with the police and Chinese Embassy officials.

Gang caught with trousers down

19 April Petaling Jaya

Police arrested the 'Underwear Gang', six Indonesians believed to have committed at least 21 cases of housebreaking and robbery in the Klang Valley. Two gold dealers suspected of fencing were also held. The gang gained notoriety for breaking into homes wearing only their underwear. Police recovered RM30,000 worth of cameras, watches, necklaces and rings.

Another Malaysian peacekeeper dies

13 May Sarajevo

Malaysian peacekeeper Mejar Ariffin Zakaria died from injuries sustained in mortar fire in Bosnia-Herzegovina. He was the second Malaysian soldier killed in former Yugoslavia. Mej Ramli Shaari was killed in April by a landmine in Sibenik, Croatia.

Mej Ariffin was on patrol with an Egyptian UN observer and a Bosnian soldier in Cermenica, near Visoko, when their vehicle stalled in mud and they had to stop for the night. They were trying to get the vehicle moving again the next day when Serb forces hit them with mortar fire.

Mej Ariffin was hit in the left thigh and back. The Egyptian, Lt-Col Mohamed Kamal El Din, suffered shrapnel wounds to his legs. A Bosnian army soldier was also wounded when he and a colleague on board a tractor came under fire as they were trying to tow away the UN vehicle.

Mej Ariffin was among 21 Malaysian soldiers serving with the UN Military Observer Group. He was survived by his wife and four young children.

No to hudud laws

16 May Kuala Lumpur

The Federal Government did not recognise the hudud laws approved by the Pas Government in Kelantan because they did not reflect justice according to Islamic laws, Dato' Seri Dr Mahathir Mohamad said.

Therefore, he said, the question of amending the Federal Constitution to provide for their implementation 'does not arise at all.' He was commenting on a newspaper report that the Kelantan Sultan had given his assent to the laws.

Inventor wins award

22 April Kuala Lumpur

Dr Choo Yuen May, of the Palm Oil Research Institute (Porim), won the Best Woman Inventor award at the 22nd International Exhibition of Inventions (New Technologies and Products) in Geneva. The Malaysian scientist impressed the judges with her new process for the production of red palm oil enriched with carotene. She also won the same award at Mindex '93, the Malaysian exhibition of inventions. In all, 10 awards went to Malaysia at the Geneva event, three gold, four silver and three bronze, with Dr Choo winning two of the golds.

Dr Choo with her trophy for being Malaysia's Best Woman Inventor which she received from Prime Minister Dato' Seri Dr Mahathir Mohamad at the Malaysian Inventions and Design Society (MINDS) banquet in August 1993. Congratulating her are Science, Technology and Environment Minister Datuk Law Hieng Ding (right) and MINDS president Tan Sri Augustine S.H. Ong (second from right).

Claim for RM22.40 is settled after 21 years

29 July Kuala Lumpur

A rubber tapper's claim for RM22.40 in wages was finally settled last month, 21 years after the claim was filed. Retired Supreme Court judge Tan Sri Harun Hashim, sitting as a High Court judge, also awarded K. Govinda Pillai costs.

During the long wait for the judgment to be delivered, Govinda, his counsel D.P. Xaxier and Kinrara Estate owner Gan Teik Yeow, against whom the claim was made, all died.

Tan Sri Harun had reserved judgment in 1975 when Kinrara Estate had appealed against a Selangor Labour Court decision awarding Govinda the RM22.40.

National Art Gallery

On 15 September the well-known painting 'Gadis Melayu' was stolen from its place in the National Art Gallery, Kuala Lumpur.

1994

world news

9 May
Nelson Mandela is inaugurated as the first black President of South Africa.

23 May
About 270 pilgrims, many of them Indonesians, are killed in a crush in Mecca.

26 May
Michael Jackson and Lisa Marie Presley are married in the Dominican Republic.

8 June
Soviet Cosmonaut Valeri Polyakov takes off for what will become the longest stay in space—437 days.

21 June
The nerve gas sarin kills seven people in Matsumoto, Japan. A messianic doomsday cult, Aum Shin Rikyo, is responsible.

8 July
North Korean President Kim Il-Sung, 82, dies. His son Kim Jong-Il takes over.

31 August
In Ireland, the Provisional IRA announces a 'complete cessation of military operations'.

Malaysia to train South Africans

4 August **Cape Town**

Foreign Minister Datuk Abdullah Ahmad Badawi paid a courtesy call on South African President Nelson Mandela during his eight-day visit to the country.

Mr Mandela thanked Malaysia for its unwavering support for the South African Government and expressed his appreciation for Malaysia's willingness to provide training in various fields to South African Government employees.

The continuing bilateral operations will be coordinated through the new Malaysian High Commission in Pretoria, led by Ambassador Choo Eng Guan.

25,000 shining lights on Buddha's life

29 August **Kuala Lumpur**

A pandal standing 65ft high and decorated with 25,000 bulbs (below) was built around 17 paintings of the Buddha, depicting his life and death.

It went on display at the Sri Lanka Buddhist Temple, Jalan Tujuh in Sentul Pasar, in conjunction with a seven-day blessing for peace and prosperity for the country ahead of National Day on 31 August. A 20-minute recorded narration explained each of the paintings. Three experts from Sri Lanka took a week to build the pandal. The lights, which formed 27 patterns, were manually controlled.

Acid rain as bad as in West

17 May **Kuala Lumpur**

Acid rain levels in Malaysia's industrialised areas were comparable with those in Europe and North America. Science, Technology and Environment Minister Datuk Law Hieng Ding said the three most affected areas were the Klang Valley, Prai and the Johor Bahru Senai industrial area.

'Between 1985 and 1988, acidity levels increased threefold before stabilising after 1988,' he said at a workshop on acid rain.

Although acid rain levels were well-documented, Datuk Law said there were no studies of its impact on soil and vegetation. 'At this stage it is not possible to assess the adverse effects of acid rain due to lack of data,' he said.

Dancers at the parade which launched Malaysia Fest '94.

Heritage goes on parade at Malaysia Fest '94

10 September **Kuala Lumpur**

The theme was the Best of Malaysian Heritage, and fittingly the parade which opened Malaysia Fest '94 was a potpourri of dances and songs from all 13 States, representing the many facets of local cultures. Leading the procession was a Malay ceremonial entourage complete with elephants, horses, musicians and court heralds.

'Bad girl' to good grandma

11 September ▶ She was called 'the most beautiful woman of Malaya' by *Life* magazine photographer Philippe Halsmann and was renowned for her 'bad girl' roles in films. Indeed Umi Kalthum, now 60, was a trailblazer, a 19-year-old rebel who defied her conservative parents and left Seremban for stardom in Singapore.

Her first movie was *Dahlia*, released in 1953, and her beauty and talent ensured her success. In her countless films since for Singapore's Cathay Keris Productions, she played a good girl only once, in *Yatim Mustapha*. 'Bad girl roles are more challenging,' she said with a smile.

Umi Kalthum, the 'bad girl' film star, enjoys her retirement.

When she returned to Malaysia in 1969, she was inundated with film roles and also acted in RTM dramas, winning the Seri Angkasa award for Best Actress in 1978.

Married to actor Datuk Haji S. Roomai Noor, she was now in retirement, looking after her grandchildren, working out in the gym and gardening.

Old warrior dies

11 September **Kuala Lumpur**

Soldier and cultural activist Tan Sri Mubin Sheppard, a former administrator in the colonial service, died at the Subang Medical Centre.

Tan Sri Mubin established the National Art Gallery and the Malayan Historical Society, and founded the National Museum and the National Archives. He embraced Islam in 1957 and helped develop the Muslim Welfare Organisation of Malaysia (Perkim).

Born in Ireland in 1905, he arrived in Kuala Lumpur in 1928 as a cadet in the administrative corps. In World War II he served with the FMS Voluntary Forces and was a prisoner of war from 1942 to 1945. After the war, he was district officer in Klang and subsequently British Advisor in Terengganu and Negeri Sembilan.

Retiring from Government service in 1964, he devoted himself to documenting and resurrecting interest in Malay culture and history.

Letters give glimpse of Malay sultanates

11 September **Kuala Lumpur**

Riding in a howdah strapped to the back of an elephant, a panglima (warrior), accompanied by palace guards and musicians delivered photocopies of 100 ancient Malay letters to the National Library. The scene recreated the courier service that operated during the era of the ancient Malay sultanates.

The ceremony marked the acquisition of the correspondence, some written nearly 500 years ago, between Rulers, officials and traders. They conveyed friendship, complaints and pledges of loyalty.

British Library curator Annabel Teh Gallop spent more than a year researching and compiling the letters.

Hawking visits

13 September **Kuala Lumpur**

The quadriplegic physicist Professor Stephen Hawking, who speaks through a voice simulator, arrived to give two lectures in the city.

Cheaper chocolate through palm oil

13 September Kuala Lumpur

A Universiti Kebangsaan Malaysia researcher made a breakthrough that promised to cut the cost of making chocolates. Associate Professor Dr Mohamed Ali Abdul Rahim, who found his 'cocoa butter equivalent' by using palm mid-fraction (PMF) oil from the outer part of the oil palm fruit, claimed that it does not alter the taste or quality of the chocolates.

While cocoa butter costs about £2,500 a ton, PMF oil costs 60 per cent less, he said. 'In addition, the finished product will have a nice glossy finish. And it doesn't melt easily,' said the professor.

Athletics coach on molesting charges

4 October Kuala Lumpur

Suspended national athletics coach C. Ramanathan, 58, claimed trial in the Sessions Court to charges of molesting two teenage athletes in 1992.

He was alleged to have outraged the modesty of two girls, aged 17 and 18, in a room at Maba House in Jalan Hang Jebat here. He was convicted on 8 November 1996 and sentenced to eight years' jail. However, in 2005 he successfully appealed against his conviction.

Ninja in our midst

30 September Kuala Lumpur

James Lee Peek Kuan, 29, described his life as a ninja, a practitioner of the ancient Japanese martial art of ninjutsu, in a feature article in *The Star*.

'In the past, the ninjas started off as spies and hired out their services to the highest bidder. In peacetime, practitioners master the skills to develop physical, mental and spiritual well-being,' he said.

'Not many people know we exist.' But he denied that ninjas could fly through the air, crawl up walls, stick to ceilings upside down and disappear at will. 'Comic books, TV shows and movies have given rise to all kinds of misconceptions,' he said.

Practitioners learn to use various weapons including nunchaku (fighting sticks) and na-gi-nata (sword fixed to a pole). There are also other skills like 'silent walking', survival skills and trapping. Lee said the art was brought to Malaysia by two Japanese masters in the early 1980s. 'It was only practised by small groups and close friends and even today, practitioners do not publicise their skills.'

10th King installed

22 September Kuala Lumpur

The Yang di-Pertuan Besar of Negeri Sembilan Tuanku Ja'afar ibni Al-marhum Tuanku Abdul Rahman was installed as the 10th Yang di-Pertuan Agong in a glittering ceremony steeped in the tradition of the golden era of the Malacca Sultanate.

A symbolic kiss of the Keris Kerajaan (Kris of State) followed by the Royal Oath of Office and a pledge by Tuanku Ja'afar to discharge his duties fairly and justly officially signalled the start of the reign of the new Agong. Immediately, the nobat (royal band) began playing the *Raja Bertabal (His Majesty is Installed)*.

The Datuk Paduka Maharaja Lela (Grand Chamberlain) then shouted 'Daulat Tuanku' (Long Live the King) thrice, accompanied by those present at the Balairong Seri (Throne Room) of Istana Negara.

This was followed by a 21-gun salute and the national anthem, and then by fireworks at the Lake Gardens in the evening. Special postage stamps and first-day covers were issued in conjunction with the King's installation.

MAS stops flights to India due to plague

29 September Kuala Lumpur

Malaysia Airlines suspended all flights to India following a plague outbreak on the subcontinent. More than 2,000 passengers fly MAS to India each week and the suspension left about 500 passengers stranded here and in Madras and New Delhi.

The Government also announced other measures to keep out the pneumonic plague, including a ban on all incoming passengers from or via India. Ships from India would be inspected off Port Klang to ensure there was no infestation by rats and that crew members were not infected. An average of five vessels from India a week called at Port Klang.

The authorities were in close touch with their counterparts in Singapore and Thailand, said acting director-general of health Datuk Dr Wan Mahmud Othman.

Banned Islamic group reaches end of road

21 October Kuala Lumpur

The leader of the outlawed Al Arqam Islamic movement, Ashaari Muhammad, and seven high-ranking members confessed at a dialogue at Masjid Negara organised by the police and Pusat Islam that they had deviated from the true teachings of Islam and repented their actions.

Ashaari said he realised his claims to have Arab blood and to have had conversations with the Prophet Muhammad were nonsensical and that he was no miracle worker.

'We realise we have been misleading our followers and we realise that we have been mistaken,' he said.

The movement was branded deviant and outlawed by the National Fatwa Council on 5 August. The next month, Ashaari and several of his followers were detained under the Internal Security Act.

The movement was started in 1971 in Kuala Lumpur by Ashaari and some friends. Over the years its missionaries went preaching and set up Islamic schools and villages throughout Malaysia. It sent missionaries throughout Southeast Asia and later throughout the world and was unwelcome not just in Malaysia but also in Singapore, Brunei, Indonesia and Thailand.

Asian Games high roller

9 October Hiroshima

Sixteen-year-old bowler Shalin Zulkifli was the Malaysian darling at the Asian Games. She scorched the lanes again at the Hiroden Bowl to take the women's all-events gold medal.

It was the second gold medal for Malaysia. Earlier Shalin played a sterling role with Lydia Kwah and Shirley Chow to lift the trios gold medal. Lydia took the bronze in the all-events.

Shalin won the all-events in a Games record score of 5,016 pinfalls. She beat South Korea's Kim Sook-young, the winner of the singles and doubles gold medal, by 48 pins.

Colour TV 'most important purchase'

5 September Kuala Lumpur ▶ The 1993 Malaysian Lifestyle Study by Survey Research Malaysia (SRM), in which 2,000 Malaysian adults were interviewed, showed that for them the possession of a colour television set, with 92 per cent owning one, was far more important than life insurance policies (16 per cent) and computers (3 per cent). Other findings:

Destination of adult air travellers		Ownership of household durables	
Singapore	17%	Colour television set	92%
Thailand	15%	Refrigerator	78%
China	10%	Washing machine	50%
Indonesia	8%	Video cassettes	
Saudi Arabia	7%	recorders/player	45%
Brunei	7%	Mobile phone	3%
North America	6%		
Hong Kong	5%	**Main purpose for overseas**	
Australia	5%	**visits in past 18 months**	
India	3%	Leisure	61%
Europe	3%	Business	19%
Others	11%	Visiting families	4%
		Pilgrimage	6%
Make of car owned		Business and leisure	9%
Proton	28%	Studies	1%
Toyota	14%		
Ford	11%		
Honda	9%		
Others	20%		

SPORTS ACTIVITIES

% of Malaysians as:	Participants	Spectators
Badminton	14%	70%
Football	10%	67%
Swimming	7%	34%
Aerobics	3%	17%
Tennis	2%	32%
Squash	2%	12%
Golf	1%	19%
Wrestling	–	45%

1994

31 August
A computer beats world chess champion Gary Kasparov.

13 October
Japanese novelist Kenchaburo Oe wins the Nobel Prize for Literature.

14 October
The Nobel Peace Prize is awarded to PLO leader Yasser Arafat, Israeli PM Yitzhak Rabin and Israeli Foreign Minister Shimon Peres.

29 November
The capital city of South Korea, Seoul, celebrates its 600th year as a settlement.

4 December
Serbs release 53 of some 400 UN peacekeepers being held as human shields against NATO air-strikes.

11 December
Russian forces move into Chechnya to quell the separatist movement there.

Legend of sunken
Khmer city resurfaces

19 October Kuantan

Construction workers recovered artefacts including a chest and ancient Chinese porcelain that renewed speculation of a sunken Khmer city at the bottom of Tasik Chini. Personnel working at the mouth of Chini River to construct a RM7-million dam made the discoveries. Among the finds was an ancient plate dating back to the Chinese imperial era.

Chinese President's visit
marks 20 years of ties

10 November Kuala Lumpur

Chinese President Jiang Zemin started a four-day visit to Malaysia, his first to the country. He was accorded a ceremonial welcome at Parliament Square and was met on arrival by Yang di-Pertuan Agong Tuanku Ja'afar and Prime Minister Dato' Seri Dr Mahathir Mohamad. His visit coincided with the 20th anniversary of diplomatic relations between Malaysia and China.

Dr M opens Tunku memorial

10 November Kuala Lumpur

Prime Minister Dato' Seri Dr Mahathir Mohamad opened the Tunku Abdul Rahman Putra Memorial, commemorating the first Prime Minister's contribution to the nation.

He said the Tunku was the country's most prominent statesman. 'The country could not have achieved its present development if not for Tunku's struggles to free the people from the chains of colonialism and unite the various races,' he said. By forming the Alliance Party, he said, the Tunku had brought about tolerance, compromise and mutual respect among the races.

He added that he hoped the RM32-million memorial would serve as a centre for research on Tunku for both local and foreign scholars.

The memorial, formerly known as the Residency, is an old colonial building that Tunku occupied as Federation of Malaya Chief Minister in 1956 and as Prime Minister until he retired in 1970.

Dato' Seri Dr Mahathir (right) and Tan Sri Ahmad Sarji (second from right) admiring a memorial panel.

Raising the bar
for new lawyers

11 November Kuala Lumpur

Law graduates from foreign universities with third class degrees and below are likely to be barred from practice because they will not be allowed to sit for the Certificate of Legal Practice (CLP) examinations. CLP director Khalid Yusuff said the Bar Council had proposed the minimum standard of entry qualification be raised. At present, all law graduates are able to sit for the examination regardless of class of degree.

En Khalid said the qualifying board, which decides on the qualifications required to apply to be admitted to the Malaysian Bar, is likely to accept the proposal as it will check the declining quality of new lawyers.

Based on last year's registration for the examination, about 35 per cent of graduates from foreign universities will not quality for CLP after 1997 if the proposal was accepted, he said.

'Free trade by 2020'

15 November Bogor

Asia-Pacific leaders, meeting in Bogor near Jakarta, set two non-binding deadlines for the removal of trade barriers in the region. The advanced economies would comply by 2010 and the developing economies by 2020. The proposal gave no launch date, implementation pace, details of target tariff rates or sectors listed for tariff cuts.

Improved rural air service

1 December Kuching

The Government would build more airfields to facilitate air services to remote areas in the State, said Sarawak Chief Minister Tan Sri Abdul Taib Mahmud. In addition to the Bakun airfield, there were plans to build another at Tanjung Manis, Sarikei.

Taib said he was confident that the newly launched SAEAGA Airlines would serve the people by providing additional links to remote destinations in Sarawak and Sabah. SAEGA Airlines, a joint venture between the State Governments of Sabah and Sarawak and Ekran Bhd, had been officially launched by Prime Minister Dato' Seri Dr Mahathir Mohamad in Kota Kinabalu the previous day.

'Comfort woman'
recounts her ordeal

14 November Kuala Lumpur

A Malaysian who was among 200,000 women throughout Asia forced into prostitution as 'comfort women' for Japanese soldiers during World War II came forward to accuse her former tormentors.

In 1993, nine Malaysian 'comfort women' came forward to seek compensation from Japan but Rosalind Saw was the first to recount her ordeal publicly.

A feature in *The Star* newspaper recounted how, at the age of 25, with two children, she was dragged away from her home in Jelutong, Penang, and taken to a hotel where she was kept with 50 other girls. 'We were not allowed to leave. The Japanese soldiers would visit us at any hour of the day or night. They were filthy and drunk most of the time. Often we would be savagely beaten', she said.

Her nightmare ended when she became pregnant and was sent to hospital where she gave birth to a baby girl and then made her escape.

Chief Minister sworn
in before his father

27 December Kota Kinabalu

Datuk Mohamed Salleh (below, left) was sworn in before his father, Yang di-Pertua Negeri Tun Mohd Said Keruak, to become Sabah's ninth and youngest Chief Minister. He replaced Tan Sri Sakaran Dandai.

Salleh, 37, a political science graduate, was expected to serve the 14 months remaining for a Muslim Bumiputra Chief Minister under the formula to rotate the CM's post among Sabah's three main communities.

1995

Capital ideas! The Government announced measures to make Malaysia a premier regional capital market, including moves to encourage a greater flow of funds, reduce transaction costs and stamp duties, to facilitate speedier approval for new share issues and relax the stringent requirements for listing on stock exchange; the RM20 billion project to build Malaysia's new administrative capital Putrajaya was launched. The year's most sensational event however was the verdict of a *bomoh* and her two accomplices who were involved in the ritualistic killing of State Assemblyman Datuk Mazlan Idris and dismembering his body. The trio were sentenced to death. On football, 58 players confessed that they were involved in match-fixing.

JANUARY
The Grand Old Man of Sabah politics, Tun Datu Mustapha Datu Harun, passes on.

JUNE
Vietnamese boat people stage a sit-down protest.

AUGUST
Dutch bronze cannon retrieved during Malaysia's first marine archaeological excavation project.

NOVEMBER
A Fokker 50 aircraft crashes into a squatter village in Tawau killing 34.

December: Malaysia's first ever light rail transit, the STAR LRT.

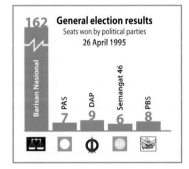

General election results
Seats won by political parties
26 April 1995

Barisan Nasional	PAS	DAP	Semangat 46	PBS
162	7	9	6	8

Malaysia Facts		
20.1 million	Population	
RM222.5 billion	Gross Domestic Product	
RM9,649	Gross National Income (per capita)	
26.8	Crude Birth Rate (per 1,000 persons)	
10.3	Infant Mortality (per 1,000 live births)	
69.4 / 74.2	Life Expectancy (male / female)	
68.9	Consumer Price Index (base 2010=100)	

> 'It's a moderate manifesto.
> We do not promise the impossible.'
>
> Dato' Seri Dr Mahathir Mohamad, on Barisan Nasional's Vision 2020 manifesto, 13 April 1995.

1995

Tun Mustapha dies

3 January   Kota Kinabalu

Tun Datu Haji Mustapha Datu Harun, one of the founding fathers of Malaysia, died aged 76. The Grand Old Man of Sabah politics was accorded a State funeral and was laid to rest at the Putatan Muslim cemetery next to his wife Toh Puan Rahmah Zulkarnian, who died in 1992.

Tun Mustapha shaped the politics of Sabah in Malaysia. He founded Usno and his election as party president in 1961 marked the start of his involvement in politics at the highest level over some three decades. As the motivating force behind Sabah's entry into Malaysia and as Usno president, he forged Sabah Alliance with the help of Tunku Abdul Rahman. Tun Mustapha sat on the Cobbold Commission in 1962 to establish whether the peoples of Sabah and Sarawak wished to join Malaysia.

Shalin is named world's best bowler

4 January   Kuala Lumpur

Teenage sensation Shalin Zulkifli was named 1994 World Bowler of the Year. The 16-year-old was the first Malaysian to win the award from the World Bowlers Writers' Association.

Shalin, voted Olympian of the Year by the Olympic Council of Malaysia, was the first Malaysian to strike gold in the FIQ Asian Championships, winning the singles gold and silver in the all-events and Masters in the competition in Guam in July. In the FIQ World Youth Championships at Monterrey in Mexico, she won bronze in the singles event and at the Asian Games in Hiroshima in October, she struck two golds.

Blind bookie tells all

8 January   Kajang

A blind man who had never watched a football game was the mastermind of a nationwide network of syndicates involved in football bribery and match-fixing.

The 50-year-old was among six bookies placed under restricted residence following police investigations into match-rigging which saw dozens of players questioned. Deputy Home Minister Datuk Megat Junid Megat Ayob said most arrests in connection with match-fixing followed information from the blind suspect.

Death sentence for bomohs

10 January   Temerloh

Bomoh Mohd Affandi Abdul Rahman, his wife Maznah Ismail alias Mona Fandey and their assistant Juraimi Husin were sentenced to death by the High Court for the murder of Batu Talam State Assemblyman Datuk Mazlan Idris. The seven-member jury unanimously returned a guilty verdict at the end of their trial, the second-longest criminal trial in the country's history.

Affandi, 37, Mona, 38, and Juraimi, 24, maintained their normal cool composure when Mr Justice Datuk Mokhtar Sidin passed the death sentence. They even joked with each other after the court adjourned, but Juraimi told the press he asked for forgiveness from Datuk Mazlan's widow Datin Faridah.

Elements of black magic in the murder caught the imagination of the public, but greed was the main motivation. Affandi met Datuk Mazlan in 1992; the politician was said to have sought his services as a bomoh to oust political enemies. On 2 July 1993, Datuk Mazlan withdrew nearly RM300,000 from his bank. The money was probably part of a ritual to increase his wealth.

That night, Datuk Mazlan was beheaded by Juraimi and his body chopped up and buried under a storeroom. Affandi, Mona and their daughter Mazdia then drove to Kuala Lumpur in Datuk Mazlan's car and spent more than RM190,000 on, among other things, a Mercedes, jewellery and plastic surgery for Mona (*see 25 October 1997*).

Still smiling: Mona after being sentenced to death.

Ramayana gallery ready

15 January   Kuala Lumpur

After 26 months of patient sculpting and painting, work on the RM800,000 Ramayana Art Gallery in the Maha Mariamman Temple at Batu Caves was completed.

Highlights of the gallery in a limestone cave were a 14.7m statue of Hanuman the Monkey God with his chest open revealing Rama and Seeta, and a breathtaking 13m reclining statue of the giant Kumbakarnan. Milestones in Rama's life are portrayed with recorded narration. Seven sculptors were brought from India to work with four Malaysians on the gallery, said temple president R. Nadarajah.

Sailing to Somalia

30 January   Lumut

Two navy multipurpose supply ships, the KD *Mahawangsa* and the KD *Seri Indera Sakti*, left to help in the evacuation of 3,000 peacekeeping troops from Somalia.

The 380 crew were accompanied by more than 50 commandos, rangers and medical personnel. Both ships were under the command of National Task Force commander Laksamana Pertama Datuk Ahmad Haron. They joined a UN fleet from the United States, Italy, France and Pakistan in a mission due to last until the middle of March. The ships were expected to reach Mogadishu in two weeks.

Jugra

Ancestral odyssey

4 February   Klang

Following the path of his ancestors, the Orang Laut or Bugis, the Raja Muda of Selangor Tengku Idris Shah set sail from Port Klang on a journey around the world that was expected to take over two years. He set out on his 70ft yacht *Jugra* with a crew of three on the first leg of the journey. Maldives was the first port of call (*see 9 November 1996*).

Local sports car is ready to roll

26 January   Kuala Lumpur

The locally-produced Bufori sports car would be manufactured by STI Bufori Sdn Bhd from March 1995, it was announced.

Chairman of the company Tunku Tan Sri Imran Tuanku Ja'afar is seen below giving a helping hand to Gerry Khouri, the car's Lebanese-Australian designer and maker, standing on the windscreen to demonstrate its strength. Vinod Sekhar, chief executive of the company, is on the left.

Two who accused police over porn found guilty

27 February Kuala Lumpur

After Malaysia's longest criminal trial, lasting 112 days, Kanaperan alias Mohamad Amin Abdullah, 43, a former detective, and Mary Anne Arokiadas, 34, were found guilty of defaming six policemen of the Selama police station in Perak and a civilian by claiming that they had forced her to act in pornographic videos in April 1991. They were also found guilty of making false reports at the Jalan Bandar police station.

During the trial a Japanese forensic pathologist reviewed pornographic tapes to determine if Mary Anne was the actress. A total of 114 witnesses were called by the prosecution and defence.

The magistrate's court sentenced her to eight years' jail plus a fine of RM69,900 or 54 months' jail, after finding her guilty of the seven charges. Kanaperan, her husband, received a similar sentence. The High Court allowed a stay of execution pending appeal. But Mary Anne was remanded to prison as she failed to post the RM18,000 bail.

Mourners pay tribute to Tan Sri Loh Boon Siew.

'Mr Honda' dies

16 February Penang

Tan Sri Loh Boon Siew, one of Malaysia's richest men, died of a heart attack at his Jalan Sultan Ahmad Shah mansion here. He was 83.

He was completely illiterate but had a powerful memory. From humble beginnings as a motor mechanic at the age of 12, he successfully built up a wide-ranging business empire. Widely referred to as 'Mr Honda', he was the man who brought the Japanese motorcycles to Malaysia.

One of the biggest foreign hotel investors in Australia and New Zealand, he was also a philanthropist, making contributions to hospitals and schools.

Dr Mahathir displays copies of the manifesto at the launch.

Closer look at Vision 2020

12 April Kuala Lumpur

Details of Vision 2020, a nine-point Barisan Nasional manifesto aimed at turning Malaysia into a fully-developed country by that year, were announced by the Prime Minister, Dato' Seri Dr Mahathir Mohamad.

The manifesto outlined a Government based on the principles of vision, justice and efficiency, continuity of development, respect for religious freedom, a confident future generation, dynamic foreign policies, environmental preservation and enhancement, high technology industrialisation, prudent financial management, and efficient and effective administration. Dr Mahathir said the Barisan aimed to double the per capita income every 10 years to reach RM40,000. The manifesto promised to continue the privatisation concept.

Bank robbers tunnel their way to millions

6 March Kuala Lumpur

Burglars tunnelled into the vault of the Mayban Finance branch in Taman Cheras and escaped with valuables believed to be worth millions of ringgit. The break-in was discovered by a member of its staff reporting for work after the long Hari Raya holidays. The burglars had crawled along a drain at the front of the finance company and tunnelled into the strongroom.

It was believed to be the first break-in of its kind in the country. Police said the burglars must have taken days, if not weeks, to burrow into the strongroom. They left behind hammers, screwdrivers and a trolley as well as mineral water bottles and leftovers of food items.

On 10 March, three forensic scientists looking for clues in the tunnel had to cut short their search when they were surprised by a two-metre-long python.

Fish killed by illegal dumping of poison

25 March Pangkor Island

When thousands of fish in three fish farms on this island started dying mysteriously, the farm owners remembered seeing someone unloading drums from a boat on to the beach the week before.

Investigating officials found 41 drums containing about 2,000kg of highly-toxic potassium cyanide at a rubbish dump on the northeast coast of the island, close to the fish farms.

The chemical is one of the most lethal of poisons known to man, and the amount had the potential to kill seven million people. Some of the rusty and dented drums were leaking.

Logging on to Malaysia

17 April Penang

Dell Computer Corp announced that it was to set up a manufacturing plant for PCs in the Bayan Lepas Free Trade Industrial Zone here. Production was expected to start in October. It would be Dell's third manufacturing plant after Austin, Texas, and Limerick, Ireland, and Dell would be the first international computer company to make PCs in Malaysia.

1995

29 April
Tamil Tigers use surface-to-air missiles for the first time, shooting down two Sri Lankan air force transports.

19 May
Mount Sinai Medical School in the US certifies the world's youngest doctor, age 17—India–born Balamurali Ambati.

25 May
NATO planes strike at the Bosnian Serbs' headquarters. In retaliation, Serbs storm UN weapons depots, attack safe areas and take UN peacekeepers as hostages.

14 June
Chechen rebels raid a Russian hospital, taking 1,500 people hostage. After a four-day stand-off, the rebels escape, with 100 hostages as human shields, in convoy of buses.

29 June
A department store in Seoul collapses, killing 501 people. A 19-year-old sales clerk is rescued from the rubble after 16 days.

Footballers admit taking RM1.32m in bribes

16 April Petaling Jaya

Fifty-eight players confessed to the Football Association of Malaysia (FAM) that they were involved in match-fixing last season and received RM1,324,000 from the bookies.

The FAM announced suspensions of between one and four years for the players who confessed. The longest were for those involved in match-fixing since the inaugural Semi-Pro League in 1989.

The FAM deputy president Tengku Abdullah Sultan Ahmad Shah said 90 per cent of the matches fixed involved Singapore. The money paid out by the bookies involved 40 matches, meaning they paid out an average of RM33,000 a match.

The biggest payout for a single player was RM96,000 for eight matches. The lowest bribe was RM500.

'Almost every match involving Singapore had one player or another agreeing to fix it,' said Tengku Abdullah.

Landslide win for Barisan Nasional

26 April Kuala Lumpur

Malaysians voted the Barisan Nasional back to power with a two-thirds majority, capturing 162 of the 192 seats in the enlarged Parliament, up from 180. It took 63.3 per cent of the total vote.

The DAP suffered one of its worst defeats, down from 20 seats to nine. The Parti Bersatu Sabah took eight seats, down from its previous 14. Semangat 46, which had eight seats previously, was down to six. Pas representation remained the same, with seven seats. When nominations closed on April 15, the coalition had captured 11 parliamentary and nine State seats unchallenged.

Dr Mahathir is borne aloft in triumph after the win.

Ban on alcohol ads

28 May Kuala Lumpur

Deputy Information Minister Dr Suleiman Mohamed announced a Government ban on all advertisements of alcohol, including beer. The ban would also apply to foreign films shown in cinemas and on television. The censors would 'crop off' any part which showed an actor drinking alcohol.

Cancer on the rise, Malaysians warned

28 May Kuala Lumpur

One in 1,000 Malaysians had cancer, according to the Malaysian Oncology Society. Its president, Professor Dr Md Tahir Azhar, said of the more than 20,000 cases in Government hospitals, a third were cancers of the colon, rectum or stomach and more than 20 per cent lung cancer.

Dr Tahir added that cancer cases were increasing along with the number of smokers. 'In fact, the number of cases will be reduced by 40 per cent if all Malaysians were to stop smoking,' he said at a public forum of the 7th Asian and Oceania Congress of Radiology organised by the Malaysian Radiological Society.

10 per cent increase in deaths on the roads

5 June Langkawi

A total of 5,159 people died in road accidents in 1994, a 10 per cent increase over the previous year, said Transport Minister Datuk Seri Dr Ling Liong Sik. He expressed concern over the sharp rise.

Boat people stage sit-down protest

5 June Petaling Jaya

Malaysia sympathised with the Vietnamese boat people but could not keep them, said Prime Minister Dato' Seri Dr Mahathir Mohamad, adding that Malaysia was a 'transit country' which accepted them only after third countries promised to take them in. But the third countries had broken their promise.

Earlier in the day, illegal immigrants tore down the fence of their detention camp and staged a sit-down protest along both sides of the Kuala Lumpur–Seremban Highway. About 300 took turns to hold knives to their bodies, threatening suicide. They returned peacefully to camp after meeting US Embassy representative Louis Mazel and two UNHCR officials. But 2,000 others supporting the 300 refused to move until the police fired tear gas.

Boat people during the protest.

Boost for capital market

22 June Kuala Lumpur

Deputy Prime Minister Dato' Seri Anwar Ibrahim announced several measures to make Malaysia a premier regional capital market centre, including moves to encourage greater flow of funds. Among them were reduced transaction costs and stamp duties, speedier approval for new share issues and corporate restructuring exercises and less stringent requirements for listing on the Kuala Lumpur Stock Exchange.

He said that with the new measures, large organisations such as the Employees' Provident Fund, Permodalan Nasional Berhad, banks and major trust agencies could play more active roles in the stock market. The liberalisation move also involved the opening up of the local stock market for greater participation by foreign fund management companies, investment bodies and more publicly-listed companies and brokerage houses.

Malaysia's stock market was the largest in Asean, the fifth largest in the Asia-Pacific region and the 15th largest in the world in terms of market capitalisation. There were also plans to make Malaysia the premier international Islamic capital market centre.

The cartoon caption reads: "WE MAY BE ABLE TO FORM A VERY GOOD PRISON'S FOOTBALL TEAM SOON..."

Dancers of the Troupa de Malacca at the festival.

In honour of St Peter

29 June Malacca

The Portuguese Settlement in Ujong Pasir was the setting for displays of Portuguese-influenced food, song and fun as the 1,000-strong community celebrated the feast of St Peter, the patron saint of fishermen.

Members of the minority community who are dispersed in other States and elsewhere in the world made it a point to come back for the Festa San Pedro, which has been held annually since the early 1930s, while tourists, both domestic and foreign, made up the rest of the crowd.

The highlight of the three-day festival was a Mass held in honour of St Peter and the blessing of the gaily-decorated boats. Although fishing was no longer the community's main occupation, with only about 60 fishermen left, the festival still survived.

Twice is too much

28 July Kuala Lumpur

A tightening of the demerit points system meant motorists caught beating the traffic lights only twice would have their licences suspended for three months. Those caught hogging the road or overtaking on the left side three times would face the same penalty. Under the new system, all the above offences would mean 15 demerit points, enough to have licences suspended for three months. Previously, only those with 20 demerit points could have their licences suspended.

Man with 10 wives jailed for 25 months

13 July Johor Bahru

A Singaporean self-proclaimed religious teacher with 10 wives was jailed for a total of 25 months and fined RM14,000 by a lower syariah court yesterday for violation of State religious laws. The court found Abdul Talib Haron @ Ahmad Habibullah As Salafi Haron, 35, guilty of 17 offences.

He was convicted of having more than four wives, collecting money and tithes from other Muslims without written permission and cohabiting and having illicit sex with six contractual wives. His four lawful wives were jailed for a month and fined RM500 each. His six contractual wives were jailed for a month and fined RM1,500.

The partially submerged wreckage of the Caribou.

Caribou down

13 July Labuan

Quick-thinking boatman Binjamul Akan saved three RMAF officers when their Caribou transport plane crashed into the sea near Labuan. Binjamul saw the plane plunging into the sea after experiencing engine problems and rushed to the scene in his boat to help. However, three other officers died in the crash.

'UN suffering from paralysis '

3 August Kuala Lumpur

Rather than celebrate, it would be more fitting to declare the United Nations' 50th anniversary a day of mourning because the world body did not live up to its role as guardian of peace and protector of the weak, said Prime Minister Dato' Seri Dr Mahathir Mohamad. 'The United Nations, the powerful and self-proclaimed defenders of justice, human rights and peace, seems paralysed when faced with genocide,' he said.

Electric train switched on

3 August Kuala Lumpur

The KTM Bhd Komuter electric train service between Rawang and Kuala Lumpur began at 6.15am today. Free tickets would be given for one week. After that the 38-minute one-way trip between Kuala Lumpur and Rawang would cost RM2.90.

The first phase from Sentul to Shah Alam had started running on 1 July. The route was to eventually cover more than 150km, from Rawang to Seremban and Sentul to Port Klang, with 22 stations and 18 halts.

Bahasa Malaysia's status affirmed

6 August Kuala Lumpur

The Education Act 1995, to be tabled in October, would reaffirm the status of Bahasa Malaysia as the national language. Umno president Dato' Seri Dr Mahathir Mohamad gave this assurance after chairing the Umno supreme council meeting. He said there would be no compromise on the status of Bahasa Malaysia as the national language, though exemptions had to be accorded in certain areas. One such exemption was diplomatic communications where English was more effective.

Dr Mahathir said national-type schools would also be exempted from using Bahasa Malaysia as the medium of instruction. 'Exemptions can also be given to certain subjects like science and technology.'

Sex-for-hire syndicates

7 August Kuala Lumpur

Police have uncovered more sex-for-hire syndicates here which cater to exclusive clients. In July police crippled a syndicate involving several TV drama actresses and models, who are said to have charged fees of RM5,000 for sex with rich and famous clients in Kuala Lumpur, and they are confident of crippling the others soon.

Kuala Lumpur CPO Datuk Ismail Che Ros said three of the artistes involved were underaged.

He also expressed concern over the rise in cases of gang rape involving youths in the city. He said most of the cases involved young girls who readily accepted lifts from men on superbikes, better known as Mat Motor, whom they met for the first time at shopping centres.

A car caught in the Genting Highlands landslide is hauled out by a crane.

Landslide kills 20

29 June Kuala Lumpur

Twenty people were killed when more than 15 vehicles were buried by a wall of mud, uprooted trees, boulders and water that swept down a hillside on the slip road to Genting Highlands. It was believed the landslide was caused by heavy rain washing tons of earth down the slope.

Witnesses said floodwaters half a metre high gushed down the road, sweeping cars travelling to the highlands back down, crashing into one another. Bus driver Lee Than Pow said scores of uprooted trees and boulders fell from the hillside and part of the hill came crashing down. Seconds later part of the road collapsed down a 70m-deep ravine, dragging with it at least four vehicles and several motorists who had abandoned their vehicles.

First Semai called to Bar

12 August Ipoh

Lisah Che Mat, 25, from Tapah created legal history by becoming the first Orang Asli from the Semai tribe to be called to the Bar at the High Court.

Lisah, from Kampung Batu 2, Sg Isoi, Tapah, is the fourth child in a family of nine. She graduated with an LLB (Honours) degree from Universiti Malaya last year.

To reach her school in Tapah, Lisah had to cycle 6km from her village at the jungle fringe along a steep laterite road in an oil palm estate, just to reach the main road. There were occasions when she had to skip lessons because of floods.

She used to study under a kerosene lamp in a corner of their one-room thatched bamboo hut at night because there was no electricity in the village.

Beauty and beefcake, 9 August. The winners of the Malaysia Manhunt 1995 Alwin Low Dai Wei (left) and Malaysia Best Model 1995 Joey Tan Eng Li.

1995

11 July
Bosnian Serbs occupy
Srebenica, as Dutch
UN peacekeepers
leave, and massacre
8,000 Muslim men.

1 September
Muammar Gaddafi of
Libya announces the
expulsion of all 30,000
Palestinians in Libya.

30 October
Quebec separatists
lose a referendum by a
margin of 50,000 votes
in a total of about five
million for a mandate
to split from Canada.

4 November
Israeli PM Yitzhak
Rabin is assassinated
by a Jewish settler
opposed to the
Palestine peace
process.

10 November
Rescue workers
save 549 hikers and
climbers after a
massive landslide in
the foothills of the
Himalayas buries 24
tourists and
32 Nepalese.

14 December
A peace treaty for
Bosnia is signed
in Paris, dividing
the country into
two autonomous
territories.

Bronze cannon from shipwreck found

19 August | **Port Dickson**

The country's first marine archaeological works started with the retrieval of a bronze cannon from the Dutch vessel *Nassau* which sank 389 years ago. The three-ton cannon was the first of 13 artefacts to be recovered by Transea Sdn Bhd.

The company had been awarded a RM3-million contract by the Government to commence an underwater archaeological excavation of the vessel, one of four which sank at Bambek Shoal.

The others were the Dutch ship *Middleburg* and two Portuguese men-of-war, *Sao Salvador* and *Don Duarte*.

The cannon from the Dutch ship sunk in 1606.

Former Minister Bahaman dies

7 September | **Kuala Lumpur**

Former Justice Minister Tan Sri Bahaman Shamsuddin (below, left) died at his home in Jalai Puteri, Kampung Baru. He was 89. He had been treated for a heart ailment at the Kuala Lumpur Hospital. He left a wife, seven children and 35 grandchildren.

Darkness at noon

25 October | **Kuala Lumpur**

Malaysians, along with millions of people from Iran to Indonesia, stopped to watch as a total solar eclipse cast a rare shadow across South and Southeast Asia.

Between 10.30am and 2.30pm the sun was slowly covered by the moon's shadow. They watched through various devices, from sophisticated telescopes to just simple exposed negatives.

At least 20,000 tourists and locals gathered in Kudat, Sabah, said to be the best place in the world to view the occurrence.

Malaysia's megacity taking shape

29 August | **Kuala Lumpur**

Putrajaya, the Federal Government's new administrative centre, would, with Kuala Lumpur and the Kuala Lumpur International Airport in Sepang, become a megacity, Dato' Seri Dr Mahathir Mohamad said at the launch of the RM20-billion project about 25km from Kuala Lumpur.

The merger of the three areas, similar to that of Kuala Lumpur, Petaling Jaya and Shah Alam, would bring immense benefits, the Prime Minister said.

Ramos says Asean is way to bright future

2 October | **Kuala Lumpur**

Philippine President Fidel Ramos (below) called on Southeast Asian countries to strive for unity to enable them to shape the future themselves. He was addressing an international conference on Jose Rizal and the Asian Renaissance at the Putra World Trade Centre.  For the first time in 500 years, Ramos said, Southeast Asia's destiny was in its own hands. He said the region's leaders should make new relationships and design new institutions to ensure enduring peace and prosperity for all.

Floods cause havoc

24 December | **Kuala Lumpur**

Floods wreaked havoc in the Klang Valley with 9,000 evacuated and several thousands trapped in low-lying areas. Hundreds of cars were stranded in flood waters as high as two metres as traffic came to a standstill in most parts of Petaling Jaya and Shah Alam.

The worst-hit residential area was Taman Sri Muda in Shah Alam, where the water level was reported to have passed the two-metre mark. About 10,000 houses and thousands of vehicles were damaged by flood water. In Sungai Buloh, 275 people were stuck in metre-deep water after a river broke its banks. The other affected areas were Kuala Kubu Baru, Batang Kali, Klang and Kuala Selangor. A spokesman for Kuala Lumpur City Hall said several areas including Jalan Klang Lama, Jalan Ipoh, Jalan Sungai Besi and Jalan Cheras were under about half a metre of water.

Other States affected included Johor, where 536 villagers in Mersing and Segamat had to be evacuated. Three hundred thousand people in the Batu Pahat district were told to prepare for evacuation as water levels of three major rivers had risen sharply. In Pahang, 386 people in three areas in the Rompin district were moved to relief centres. In Negeri Sembilan, floods hit the Tampin, Seremban and Rembau districts, forcing the evacuation of 451 people to eight relief centres. Kelantan was also in distress with the water level at Tangga Krai reported to be nearing the danger level.

Actress awarded RM400,000 in damages

1 November | **Kuala Lumpur**

Actress Sofia Jane Hisham was awarded RM400,000 in general damages over two defamatory articles in the weekly tabloid *Buletin Utama* published in July and August 1994 which alleged that she was a 'husband snatcher'. The actress had been seeking RM1.5 million in damages. She said she would donate the money to the needy.

LRT up and running

12 December | **Kuala Lumpur**

The Kuala Lumpur STAR Light Rail Transit 1 system took on its first passengers 16 years after the idea of a downtown people mover was mooted to overcome traffic congestion. The run, with about 200 guests, newsmen and STAR officials, was a five-minute journey from the Ampang LRT depot to the Maluri LRT station, part of Phase One of the project to link Ampang to Jalan Sultan Ismail with a 29km line offering a 23-minute journey time.

34 dead in Fokker crash

15 September | **Tawau**

A Malaysia Airlines Fokker 50 aircraft ploughed into a squatter village after overshooting the runway at Tawau Airport. Thirty-two passengers and two crew members were killed while 19 others on board, including two crew members, survived. Flight MH2133 from Kota Kinabalu came to a halt only after demolishing some 20 houses in the squatter colony of Kampung Seri Menanti. It then exploded. Several survivors fled to safety while others were helped out of the burning wreck. The  survivors included a baby. Many of those who died were charred beyond recognition.

Initial reports said that no squatters were killed, but nine were taken to the Tawau Hospital. Witnesses said the plane, with 49 passengers and a crew of four on board, burst into a ball of fire after the crash. The aircraft broke up into several pieces. It came down at about the same place as a PosLaju aircraft which had crashed six months earlier.

1996

From darkness to light: the nation was plunged into darkness when the national power grid collapsed, plunging homes and offices into darkness and causing massive traffic jams; the Appeals Court gave the nod for the RM13.6 billion Bakun hydroelectric project; a woman emerged alive after spending 12 dark nights wandering in the Taman Negara jungle. It was not exactly a grand sendoff, but prisoners at the century-old Pudu Prison were moved out to the newly built Sungai Buloh prison. In another 'prison', Vietnamese illegal immigrants housed in a Sungai Besi camp went on a rampage to protest against being forcibly repatriated. Malaysians celebrated Kongsi Raya when Hari Raya Aidilfitri and Chinese New Year fell in the same week.

JANUARY
Twenty-four injured in rioting at the Sungai Besi camp for Vietnamese illegal immigrants.

JUNE
The Court of Appeal clears the way for the Bakun Dam project.

AUGUST
An avalanche wipes out an entire Orang Asli settlement in Kampar, Perak.

NOVEMBER
The final batch of prisoners is relocated before Pudu Prison closes its doors.

January: The launch of Measat-1.

'Measat-1 made 19 million Malaysians proud and euphoric.'

Binariang chairman Tun Mohd Hanif Omar, at the launch of Measat-1, 14 January 1996.

1996

world news

8 January
A Zairean cargo plane crashes into a market in the country's capital, Kinshasa, killing 350.

14 February
A failed satellite launch causes a rocket to hit a village near the Xichang Space Centre, Sichuan Province, China, killing six.

23 February
Two sons-in-law of Iraqi President Saddam Hussein who defected to Jordan are lured back to Baghdad and killed.

19 March
A fire in a Quezon City nightclub kills 149 young Filipinos celebrating the end of the school year.

20 March
The British Government says that a rare brain disease that killed 10 people is probably linked to the so-called 'mad cow disease'.

17 April
Militants attack a group of Greek tourists near the Pyramids in Egypt. Eighteen people are killed.

Malaysia and Australia to foster closer ties

16 January Kuala Lumpur

A three-day visit by Australian Prime Minister Paul Keating was an important milestone, Prime Minister Dato' Seri Dr Mahathir Mohamad said. The two countries had expressed a desire to cooperate more closely and work to remove any misconceptions that could affect their strengthening ties. These have dipped in the past, especially when Keating called Dr Mahathir 'recalcitrant' for not attending the inaugural meeting of the Asia Pacific Economic Cooperation in Seattle in 1983.

Former Supreme Court judge found dead

11 January Penang

A former judge of the Supreme Court, Tan Sri Eusoffe Abdoolcader, was found dead in his home at Taman Jesselton with a gunshot wound to his head.

Tan Sri Eusoffe, 72, was found in his bedroom by his two maids, who heard gunshots at about 4pm. A .38 Smith and Wesson revolver was found beside the body. Police believed there was no foul play.

Malaysia satellite

13 January Kuala Lumpur

Malaysia took a giant leap forward in the field of regional and global telecommunications with the launch of the RM600-million Malaysia East Asia Satellite (Measat).

A scene of devastation in the Sungai Besi camp after the rioting.

Vietnamese riot in camp

17 January Kuala Lumpur

Twenty-four people, seven of them policemen, were injured in rioting at the Sungai Besi camp for Vietnamese illegal immigrants. Armed with home-made weapons and petrol bombs, the rioters set living quarters on fire and attacked police. Several were shot and wounded when they tried to wrest an automatic rifle from a sentry. The camp had been due to close in 1995 (*see 18 April 1996*).

Breast cancer rising

18 January Kota Bharu

Breast cancer, one of the major disorders affecting women in the country, was on the rise, said Deputy Health Minister Datuk Dr Siti Zaharah Sulaiman.

She said statistics showed that 36 out of every 100,000 Malaysian women had breast cancer. There were 2,321 reported cases of the disease in 1993 and 3,153 in 1994.

Salary deal

31 January Kuala Lumpur

Negotiations between the Public Services Department and the trade union Cuepacs over a RM2-billion salary revision package ended successfully after 16 months of proposals and counter-proposals.

In September 1994, Cuepacs submitted a memorandum on the 1995 salary revision seeking a 3.3 per cent pay rise for civil servants. The Government rejected it.

A marriage of two cultures in fashion

24 January Kuala Lumpur

Local fashion designer Eric Tho produced a special collection to mark the double celebration of Chinese New Year and Hari Raya this year.

Tho's designs, which played with prints on batik, crepe and jacquard silk, married Malay and Chinese cultures to bring out the best of both festivals, something all Malaysians could relate to.

MSC to cover the nation, says PM

31 January Kuala Lumpur

Malaysia's Multimedia Super Corridor (MSC) linking Kuala Lumpur, Putrajaya and the KL International Airport would be expanded to cover the nation, Prime Minister Dato' Seri Dr Mahathir Mohamad said. The proposed super corridor was to gauge how useful such technology was to Malaysia's development before expanding throughout the country, he added.

Dr Mahathir said the National Information Technology Council was looking into possible legislation to monitor the expansion of IT and usage of multimedia. On 8 February Dr Mahathir confirmed that Japan's Nippon Telegraph and Telephone Corporation had agreed to set up a task force to help the MSC. He also announced that James Clark, co-founder and chairman of Netscape Communications Corp, a world leader in Internet software, had agreed to join the National IT Council advisory panel.

Landslide on North–South Expressway

6 January Ipoh

Tons of earth and concrete at Gua Tempurung, along the most expensive stretch of the North–South Expressway, came crashing down in a massive landslide, killing a container truck co-driver. A concrete slope reinforced with rock anchors collapsed, sweeping the vehicle off the road.

Some 300 rescue workers from the army, police, Fire Services Department and Civil Defence Corps plus eight excavators, 14 lorries and 14 backhoe tractors were used to remove the fallen earth. The landslide caused a massive traffic jam through Kampar and Gopeng as motorists were diverted to the old trunk road.

Anti-colonialism hero reinterred

2 March Sibu

Rosli Dhobi, who assassinated Sir Duncan George Stewart, the second governor of Sarawak, on 3 December 1949, together with Awang Ramli Amit Mohd Deli, Morshidi Sidek and Bujang Suntong, was reburied today in Sibu, with full State honours.

All four were hanged on 2 March 1950. Rosli had requested such a funeral in his will sent to his parents that day.

Foreigners have no right to sue Rulers

7 February Kuala Lumpur

The Special Court ruled that foreigners had no right to sue the Malay Rulers and dismissed with costs a libel suit brought by Singaporean business-woman Faridah Begum Abdullah against the Sultan of Pahang in his personal capacity.

Chief Justice Tan Sri Eusoff Chin in his judgment said the Singapore Constitution stated that the President of the republic was not liable to any proceedings in any court. A Malaysian citizen could not sue the President in any Singaporean court; therefore the Ruler of a Malay State could not be sued by a Singaporean.

Heavy rainfall caused Genting landslide

8 February Kuala Lumpur

A landslide at the Genting Highlands slip road which claimed 21 lives and injured 23 people on 30 June 1995 was due to natural causes, a Government panel found.

Two hours of heavy rain that evening triggered three major landslides, resulting in a stream of debris, said the report by a technical investigation committee.

The report was released by Works Minister Dato' Seri S. Samy Vellu who said the landslides were not caused by jungle clearing or development. The Hills Action Network, a coalition of conservation groups, urged the Government to draw up a policy on the sustainable development of hills and highlands to ensure integrated land use which preserved the ecology of these areas.

Ministers are managers

9 February Kuala Lumpur

The Cabinet made Ministers fully respon-sible for the management of Government agencies and statutory bodies which they oversee. This move was to ensure there would be no mismanagement or abuse of power by the staff of these organisations, said Deputy Prime Minister Dato' Seri Anwar Ibrahim.

Drive against illegal settlements

23 March Kuala Lumpur

Eighty squatter houses in Kampung Pandan Dalam were demolished in a first step to rid Selangor of illegal settlements occupied by foreigners. In February, Deputy Home Minister Datuk Megat Junid Megat Ayob ticked off local governments for turning a blind eye to mushrooming Indonesian illegal settlements. Checks

found at least five in Hulu Langat district alone, including one township complete with a recreation centre, clinic, kindergarten, electricity, piped water and telephone lines. The foreigners were believed to have paid nearly RM1 million to a syndicate for several hectares of land in the Hulu Langat district on which they planned to build three illegal settlements.

Semangat and Pas 'not birds of a feather'

9 February Pasir Puteh

Prime Minister Dato' Seri Dr Mahathir Mohamad said that he was not surprised that ties between Semangat and Pas had soured because they were not 'birds of a feather'.

The Prime Minister said that Parti Melayu Semangat 46 would cease to exist once it gave up fighting Umno because Semangat originated from Umno and championed the same cause. Semangat could not sidestep the causes of Umno because it would then become like Pas.

New Zealander wins Langkawi cycle race

2 March Penang

New Zealander Glen Mitchell won the third stage of the Le Tour de Langkawi from Kangar to George Town. Mitchell and former-world-champion Christian Anderson of Denmark were neck-and-neck coming to the finish but Mitchell won by a length.

Third place went to Josef Christian of Switzerland. M. Kumaresan, who was reinstated in the Malaysian A team at the 11th hour due to his vast experience, was the best local rider with 12th place.

Economy grows for eighth year

28 March Kuala Lumpur

The Malaysian economy achieved another year of robust growth marked by a substantial increase in investments, mainly for capacity expansiona and infrastructure projects, said Bank Negara Governor Datuk Ahmad Mohamed Don.

Presenting the bank's 1995 report, Datuk Ahmad said the economy grew at 9.5 per cent compared to 8.7 per cent in 1994. It was the eighth consecutive year of growth.

PNG premier visits

1 April Kuala Lumpur

Papua New Guinea Prime Minister Sir Julius Chan arrived for a six-day official visit accompanied by his wife Lady Stella and a 60-member delegation.

Rainforests on film

3 April Kuala Lumpur

Six film documentaries on Malaysian forests would be launched in 1997, Renong Bhd announced. An Australian-based company would produce the documentaries, which were designed to showcase the country's commitment to forest conservation.

Police personnel in gun racket probe

16 April Kota Kinabalu

Eight people, including four police personnel, were arrested as a special team of investigators from police headquarters in Bukit Aman focused on a major syndicate involved in illegal gun sales in Sabah.

Those arrested were a corporal and three civilian employees from the Kota Kinabalu and Tuaran district police headquarters. The others were relatives of jailed firearms dealer Vincent Teo.

Police vetting urged for proposed State awards

16 April Kuala Lumpur

The Home Ministry has urged State palace officials to seek the help of the police in vetting the names of those proposed for awards and titles.

The request was to prevent a recurrence of cases where people of questionable character had been given State honours.

This was necessary to stop investiture ceremonies from becoming the subject of ridicule, said Deputy Home Minister Datuk Megat Junid Megat Ayob.

He said only names of those nominated by the office of the Sultans and Governors should be referred as candidates to the authorities.

Kongsi Raya. The rare occasion when Chinese New Year and Hari Raya Aidilfitri, the feast marking the end of Ramadan, fall in the same week, occurred this year, with decorations representing both Malay and Chinese cultures.

1996

world news

23 May
Swede Goran Kropp reaches the summit of Mount Everest—alone and without the aid of oxygen…and after cycling to Nepal all the way from Sweden.

5 July
Dolly, a sheep in Scotland, is the result of the first successful mammal cloning.

5 July
Tokyo and Osaka, the world's two most expensive cities, are joined by three new Asian entries—the third, fourth and fifth positions are now occupied by Beijing, Shanghai and Hong Kong.

14 August
Afghan PM Hekmatyar closes cinemas and bans music from television and radio. The move fails to appease advancing Taliban forces.

8 August
Ieng Sary, the Foreign Minister of the Khmer Rouge, defects with about 10,000 supporters to the Cambodian Government.

Simple majority needed to curb CM's powers

19 April Kota Kinabalu

Only a simple majority would be required in the State Assembly next week to amend State laws that curb the powers of the Chief Minister, said Sabah State Attorney-General Datuk Stephen Foo.

He said the simple-majority rule would apply because the amendments touched on ordinary laws and not the State Constitution. He added that only if the State Constitution were to be amended would a two-thirds majority be required.

Court affairs under PM's Department'

9 May Kuala Lumpur

Deputy Minister in the Prime Minister's Department Datuk Mohamed Nazri Abdul Aziz clarified in the Dewan Rakyat that court administration affairs came under the Prime Minister's Department. He said this meant it was appropriate for Prime Minister Dato' Seri Dr Mahathir Mohamad as head of the Government to deliver a keynote address and open the Judges' Conference in Kuching. However, Datuk Nazri said in reply to a question from Pas MP Mohamed Sabu that this did not mean that the judiciary was not independent.

First batch of boat people sent home

18 April Kuala Lumpur

The first batch of 317 Vietnamese illegal immigrants who had refused to sign up for voluntary repatriation were sent home by ship (left) under the Orderly Repatriation Programme (ORP).

A total of 272 adults and 45 children boarded 11 buses for the journey from the Sungei Besi camp to Tanjung Gelang, Kuantan, where they boarded the KD *Inderapura* bound for Vung Tao port in Vietnam.

The Sungai Besi transit camp, home to thousands of Vietnamese illegal immigrants since 1979, was officially closed. A symbolic lowering of the flags of the United Nations High Commissioner for Refugees and the Malaysian Red Crescent Society (below, left) signalled the departure of the last batch of 22 Vietnamese to Hanoi by air.

Since 1975, more than 255,000 Vietnamese boat people had passed through Malaysia with 249,099 resettled in a third country. A total of 8,815 had returned under the Voluntary Repatriation Programme and 721 under the Orderly Repatriation Programme.

Warning to drivers

10 May Kuala Lumpur

From August, motorists would be banned from holding cellular phones while driving, Transport Minister Dato' Seri Dr Ling Liong Sik said. Errant motorists would be charged with driving without due care.

MP calls for information on national security

10 May Kuala Lumpur

An opposition MP called on the Government to table a White Paper on defence, saying the Seventh Malaysia Plan failed to provide satisfactory information on all aspects of the armed forces. Dr Tan Seng Giaw (DAP-Kepong) said the public must be told more about national security, adding that the White Paper should address army bureaucracy, operation methods, manpower and recruitment guidelines.

Razaleigh back in Umno

10 May Kuala Lumpur

Parti Melayu Semangat 46 president Tengku Razaleigh Hamzah has decided to rejoin Umno. He met Prime Minister Dato' Seri Dr Mahathir Mohamad on 7 May and expressed his intention to return. Tengku Razaleigh left Umno in 1987.

Delegates at the Umno general assembly on 11 May celebrate the party's 50th anniversary.

RM2.98b loss at steel company

21 May Kuala Lumpur

Perwaja Steel was insolvent with accumulated losses of RM2.98 billion; the Cabinet had ordered an investigation following an audit report which exposed massive irregularities in the company's dealings, Deputy Prime Minister Dato' Seri Anwar Ibrahim told the Dewan Rakyat.

A Price Waterhouse report revealed many questionable practices and payments by the Perwaja management, he said, but the status of Perwaja was critical and a rescue plan must be launched.

Price Waterhouse had submitted four proposals for restructuring, he said. One called for maintaining the equity structure and implementing recovery through the current management with a view to privatising or listing the company on the KLSE in the future.

Dato' Seri Anwar added that four private companies had indicated an interest in restructuring the Perwaja Group. They were Lion Group, Renong Bhd, Syarikat Maju Holding Bhd and Wing Tiek Holding Bhd.

Penang tops list of cholera victims

19 May Kuala Lumpur

A total of 128 new cholera cases were confirmed, bringing to 936 the total number of people infected. Penang, where the epidemic originated, topped the list with 744, followed by Kedah (122), Perak (34), Terengganu (10) and Kelantan (nine).

There was no change in the figures for other States. Selangor had six cases, Perlis four, Kuala Lumpur three, Negeri Sembilan two, and Johor and Pahang one each.

Malacca, Sabah and Sarawak were the only States reported to be cholera-free since the outbreak of the epidemic nine days ago.

Daily dash with danger

19 April Klang

Hundreds of schoolchildren from five schools here were risking their lives to cross the busy Klang–Port Klang highway after part of an overhead pedestrian bridge collapsed on 17 April. A trailer had crashed into it.

Karpal ordered out

10 May Kuala Lumpur

Opposition MP Karpal Singh was given marching orders by the Dewan Rakyat Speaker Tan Sri Zahir Ismail and suspended for two days for disorderly conduct during the debate on the 7th Malaysia Plan. Karpal had persisted in using unparliamentary words directed at Barisan Nasional MPs.

Botanist found after 12-day jungle ordeal

7 June Kuala Tahan

Botanist Lina Santiago, lost for 12 days in the Taman Negara jungle during a camping trip with friends, was found alive. Two Wildlife Department rangers found her suffering from exposure, cuts, insect bites and blisters at Ulu Sungai Teku, near a waterfall about five hours' walk from Camp Teku.

Holiday excursion ends in tragedy

16 July Genting Highlands

Seventeen people, factory workers and members of their families on a holiday excursion, were killed when their bus plunged into a 120m-deep ravine near the Genting Highlands Resort.

Six of the dead were children. Three members of one family lost their lives. Fifteen people survived the plunge, which ripped off the roof of the bus and broke it in two.

The bus was going downhill in a downpour when its driver lost control.

Flying Dayak is fastest man in Malaysia

7 June Pahang

Sarawakian Watson Nyambek proved beyond doubt he was the fastest man in Malaysia at the Darulmakmur Stadium. The 'Flying Dayak' zoomed home in 10.33 seconds in the 100m final to beat rival Azmi Ibrahim of Pahang convincingly.

He topped the national record of 10.38 which he had jointly held with Azmi. His victory also earned him a place in the Olympic Games under Category A, which had a qualifying mark of 10.34.

Watson beats Azmi (right) to the finish.

Syariah courts change

23 July Kuala Lumpur

The Cabinet had approved a proposal to restructure all syariah courts and so improve their administration, Prime Minister Dato' Seri Dr Mahathir Mohamad announced. It had also agreed to place Islamic affairs officers in joint State–Federal service.

The Prime Minister said this did not mean the Federal Government was taking over the syariah courts. They would still be under State Governments.

Court gives OK to Bakun dam

29 June Kuala Lumpur

Ekran Bhd obtained an order from the Court of Appeal suspending a High Court declaration that could have stopped work on the RM13.6-billion Bakun hydroelectric project.

High Court judge Datuk James Foong had granted a declaration that Ekran Bhd must comply with the Environment Quality Act 1974 before work could commence.

He also declared invalid an order made by the Science, Technology and Environment Minister transferring environmental approval for projects in

The site of the Bakun dam project.

Sarawak from Federal to State administration. But on 23 June Deputy Prime Minister Dato' Seri Anwar Ibrahim said work could go on.

A report by Attorney-General Tan Sri Mohtar Abdullah did not give any definitive recommendations, Dato' Seri Anwar said, but pointed out that the court did not order work to be stopped (*see 2 July 2000*).

Smartcards on the way

1 August Kuala Lumpur

Prime Minister Dato' Seri Dr Mahathir Mohamad unveiled a plan for Malaysia to take a leap into the future with the RM5-billion Multimedia Super Corridor project. Among other things, it would produce the world's first national multi-purpose smartcards within four years and also include a networked paperless administration and a telemedicine centre.

Nation plunged into darkness

3 August Kuala Lumpur

The national power grid collapsed, causing a total blackout in Peninsular Malaysia. The massive failure was traced to the Paka power station transmission line in Terengganu. The cascading effect of the line's tripping set off a progressive shutdown of supply from all power stations.

Besides plunging homes and offices into darkness, the failure caused traffic chaos and official functions and sports were cancelled. Most factories were forced to shut down or operate at minimal capacity. There was a scramble for candles, torches and emergency food but power was restored to most areas by 11pm.

PM reaffirms Anwar as his successor

6 August Kuala Lumpur

Dato' Seri Dr Mahathir Mohamad reaffirmed Dato' Seri Anwar Ibrahim as his successor and said he was confident of Anwar's ability. The Prime Minister said his deputy was capable of taking over though they were different in style.

When asked in an hour-long interview on RTM whether he had ever doubted Anwar's loyalty and honesty, he replied: 'At times when you are inundated with all kinds of reports, you get the feeling that it may be true. I think whether I believe it or not, one day I have to withdraw from the post.'

8 September, Dato' Seri Dr Mahathir Mohamad and his wife Datin Seri Dr Siti Hasmah take a ride through Kuala Lumpur on the new STAR LRT system to mark its opening.

Unity trust fund for young Malaysians

28 August Kuala Lumpur

A trust fund aimed at bringing younger people from all races together was launched by Prime Minister Dato' Seri Dr Mahathir Mohamad.

The Prime Minister said the main objective of Amanah Saham Wawasan 2020 was to strengthen ties between the races by 2020. The unit trust scheme would help to achieve national stability and prosperity, he added.

Avalanche hits Orang Asli settlement

29 August Kampar ▶ An avalanche of logs, earth and debris swept down a hill, leaving at least 36 people dead or missing and wiping out the Pos Dipang Orang Asli settlement near here after an hour of heavy rain. The swollen Sungai Dipang swept away about 30 houses at the settlement, about 5km south of Gunung Tempurung. The tragedy was described as the worst in Perak since the great floods of 1926. The Semai tribe settlement, more than 30 years old, was one of the most developed Orang Asli settlements. It had a school and a community hall. The residents were farmers, rubber tappers and fruit collectors.

Two plead guilty to dumping cyanide

13 August Sitiawan

Company director Choo Aun Liew, 42, was fined RM5,000 or three months' jail and his brother-in-law Lee Thian Aun, 28, was fined RM10,000 or six months' jail after pleading guilty in a magistrate's court here to dumping 92 drums of potassium cyanide in Pangkor Island in 1995. The poison seeped into the water, killing fish raised in fish-farm cages nearby.

26 August
Former South Korean President Chun Doo Hwan is sentenced to death. His successor, Roh Tae-Woo, is sentenced to 22 years in prison for corruption.

15 September
All Singaporean Internet subscribers will have to go through proxy servers to screen them from sites containing nudity and sexual material.

18 September
A North Korean spy submarine runs aground in South Korea. Eleven bodies are found. The next day, seven North Koreans are tracked down and killed.

27 September
In Afghanistan, Taliban forces capture Kabul, driving out President Rabbani. The former leader Mohammad Najibullah is executed.

19 December
Benazir Bhutto's husband is released from prison and then charged with the murder of his brother-in-law Murtaza.

Tribute to Mr Opposition

14 October **Kuala Lumpur**

Tan Sri Dr Tan Chee Koon, known as the Mr Opposition of Malaysian politics, died aged 77. The unofficial title was accorded to him not because he was the leader of an opposition party with the most seats but because of his selfless devotion to his duties as an MP for Batu from 1959. This was the seat he held when he was in the Labour Party, Socialist Front, Gerakan and Pekemas.

As an MP, he worked tirelessly, championing the cause of the poor and the underprivileged, regardless of their ethnic background. Describing him as a truly outstanding Malaysian and a great human being, admirers and former colleagues said his death was a great loss to the nation.

A close friend, Associate Prof Syed Hussein Alatas, said there was mutual respect between Dr Tan and the then Prime Ministers, Tunku Abdul Rahman and Tun Abdul Razak.

He said it was an achievement to build such respect between the Government and the Opposition.

Pudu Prison closes

2 November **Kuala Lumpur**

The last of 1,580 prisoners were moved out of the century-old Pudu Prison, completing a two-day operation. They were moved to the newly built Sungai Buloh prison complex, about 32km away. The new 48ha prison, completed late the previous year, could accommodate 2,000 prisoners. There were plans to retain Pudu Prison, maybe temporarily, as a tourist attraction (*see 21 June 2010*).

KL Tower the most beautiful, says PM

2 October **Kuala Lumpur**

The KL Tower was officially opened the night before by Prime Minister Dato' Seri Dr Mahathir Mohamad amidst a dazzling display of laser lights.

The event was telecast by RTM and, for the first time in the country, a digital transmission of the spectacular launch was available on the Internet.

In his speech, Dr Mahathir described the tower as 'the most beautiful.' He said it symbolised the success of the Government's privatisation policies as it was the direct result of telecommunications privatisation.

End of S46

6 October **Kuala Lumpur**

Parti Melayu Semangat 46, which was set up on 5 May 1989, officially ceased to exist when 468 delegates led by party president Tengku Razaleigh Hamzah unanimously agreed to its dissolution at an extraordinary general assembly, paving the way for its members to rejoin Umno.

King of Pop makes history in Malaysia

26 October **Kuala Lumpur**

Some 40,000 fans thronged Stadium Merdeka for the biggest concert in Malaysia, featuring pop megastar Michael Jackson.

The King of Pop had arrived at the Sultan Abdul Aziz Shah Airport for two concerts on a world tour. Hundreds of his fans thronged the airport (below) to catch a glimpse of the star.

Tropical Storm Greg hits Sabah

26 December **Kota Kinabalu**

The worst storm to hit Sabah in a decade lashed the State's west coast with winds up to 70km per hour leaving a trail of destruction and 163 dead. Keningau, about 130km southeast of Kota Kinabalu, was badly hit and 500 houses in nine villages along the Bayouyo, Liawan and Sinagang rivers were washed away, leaving about 3,000 people homeless.

Prestigious birthday gift for Dr M

20 December **New Delhi**

Prime Minister Dato' Seri Dr Mahathir Mohamad, on a four-day official visit to India, received the prestigious Jawaharlal Nehru Award for International Understanding.

The award, named in memory of the nation's first Prime Minister, was presented by Indian President Dr Shankar Dayal Sharma, coincidentally on Dr Mahathir's 71st birthday (*see 31 March 1997*).

Selangor Raja Muda back from odyssey

9 November **Port Klang**

The Raja Muda of Selangor Tengku Idris Shah returned from a 21-month odyssey circumnavigating the globe.

The journey, which began on 4 February 1995 at Port Klang, took the Raja Muda and his crew of four through three oceans, 14 seas, three canals and 159 ports.

The inspiration for the Raja Muda's travels came from the childhood books he used to read about great adventurers such as Magellan and Columbus.

The crew and yacht which circumnavigated the globe.

Return of Mr Clean

10 October **Kuala Lumpur**

Datuk Abdullah Ahmad Badawi defied the odds to make a historic comeback as Umno vice-president, a position he lost in the party elections in 1993.

The Foreign Minister, often called 'Mr Clean', polled the second-highest number of votes at the expense of the incumbent Youth and Sports Minister Tan Sri Muhyiddin Yasin, who failed in his bid to retain the post for a second term.

Malaysia roars on

21 November **Kuala Lumpur**

Malaysia became the first nation to sponsor a Grand Prix motor racing team. Prime Minister Dato' Seri Dr Mahathir Mohamad said the decision to sponsor the Stewart-Ford Grand Prix team would promote Malaysia as a top tourist destination.

Malaysian envoy held hostage released

29 December **Kuala Lumpur**

Malaysian ambassador to Peru Ahmad Mokhtar Selat was released with 19 other hostages by Tupac Amaru Revolutionary Movements rebels after being held captive at the Japanese ambassador's residence in Lima for 12 days.

Ahmad Mokhtar said his captors treated him and the other hostages well and had told them they would not be harmed as their purpose was to secure the release of some 400 jailed comrades.

He was one of more than 400 guests taken hostage at a party on 17 December to celebrate the birthday of the Japanese Emperor. Many were released at intervals but 72 remained there for four months until Peruvian troops stormed the building.

1997

We shall overcome: Prime Minister Dr Mahathir Mohamad urged Malaysians not to despair over economic problems caused by currency trading and expressed confidence that Malaysia could resist attacks on the ringgit. The Government set up the National Economic Action Council to steer Malaysia out of economic doldrums caused by a weakened ringgit and a depressed Kuala Lumpur Stock Exchange. But the IMF called on Asian countries affected by the financial crisis to 'take painful measures' to stop the economic contagion. Malaysians' sense of confidence was boosted also by the conquest of Mount Everest by M. Magendran and N. Mohanadas, and the nation's best-ever SEA Games haul as the athletics team contributed 16 goals.

MARCH
Corporate figure Tan Sri Yahaya Ahmad dies in a helicopter crash in Pahang.

MAY
Teacher M. Magendran (left) and administrative assistant N. Mohanadas (right) become the first Malaysians to reach the summit of Mount Everest.

SEPTEMBER
Haze caused by forest fires reaches hazardous levels.

DECEMBER
Prime Minister Dato' Seri Dr Mahathir Mohamad slams speculator George Soros over the Asian Financial Crisis.

March: The Malaysian hockey team qualifies for the 1998 World Cup.

'We must be fully disciplined and must not panic.'
Dato' Seri Dr Mahathir Mohamad, to Malaysians on the nation's economic problems, 4 October 1997.

1997

Cars buried in mud in the aftermath of 'Greg'.

RM130m damage as 'Greg' roars through

1 January Kota Kinabalu

Tropical storm Greg and subsequent floods killed at least 173 people and caused damage totalling RM130 million to Government property and homes in Sabah, where efforts continued to determine the number of dead and missing people.

Chief Minister Datuk Yong Teck Lee said Special Task Force officials would meet 72 major employers to assess the number of people missing in Keningau district. He said there were 4,077 registered foreign workers in Keningau district and this figure would be used as a basis to determine the number of those unaccounted for.

Datuk Yong said the damage was to roads, bridges, water supply facilities, Kota Kinabalu port, Government property and kampong houses.

Siphoning petrol

22 January Penang

Police caught three men near Bukit Mertajam siphoning petrol from a lorry tanker of a major oil firm into empty drums for adulteration with kerosene.

Boys saved after 16 days at sea

23 January Miri

Miri teenagers Kassim Drahman and Muliadi Baderi were found alive huddled inside a drifting fibreglass icebox after being missing in the South China Sea for 16 days. Sarawak Shell Bhd workers found the two in the icebox which had floated to an oil rig 125 nautical miles from here.

Kassim, 16, and Muliadi, 19, were weak but could talk. They had survived on rainwater, along with biscuits and rice they had with them when they left port with two others on New Year's Day.

They told their rescuers they were to have returned on 7 January, but their engine broke down on that day and their boat drifted for four days before it sank.

The other two, Alix anak Arpat, 25, and Rajaiee Hanapi, 26, remained missing, but their families hoped to find them alive because they, too, had packed themselves into an icebox.

Motorcycle ambulances planned to beat jams

5 February Petaling Jaya

Motorcycle ambulances would be introduced to beat traffic jams by the end of the year, Health Minister Datuk Chua Jui Meng said.

Ten to 20 of the three-wheeled motorcycle ambulances would be in operation in the Klang Valley by the end of the year, he said. Each unit would cost RM200,000–RM300,000. He said the Kuala Lumpur Hospital already had three bicycle ambulances for emergencies.

TMnet hacked twice

21 February Kuala Lumpur

A hacker broke into the TMnet system for the second time, altering the corporate homepage by adding the message 'This Site Has Been Hacked Again!' in large blinking letters. Two days earlier, a hacker had broken into the system and changed TMnet's homepage by adding the words 'This Site Has Been Hacked!!!'

In an anonymous letter to the press someone claiming to be the intruder said his attacks were not malicious but intended simply to 'wake TMnet up' to security holes in its systems.

Plane nosedives, killing 3

3 March Langkawi

Two Filem Negara cameramen and a pilot were killed when the aircraft they were aboard crashed into a swampy area in Kelibang, about 5km from Kuah town.

The dead were identified as Abdul Razak Mohd Nor, 43, Ishak Latif, 32, and pilot Capt Nik Alfian Abdul Ghani, 26. Ishak and Capt Nik Alfian died on the spot. Abdul Razak died while being flown by a police helicopter to Langkawi Hospital.

The aircraft, a Cessna 172, belonged to Mofaz Air Sdn Bhd and the pilot was an employee of the company.

Ishak with his wife in happier times.

Cut trees must be replaced

4 March Kuala Lumpur

All trees cut for development projects, including the proposed highway to link the peninsula's three highland resorts, must be replaced, Prime Minister Dato' Seri Dr Mahathir Mohamad said.

The Government was also keen for landscaping to be made a requirement for all development projects.

'We realise that some trees will have to be cut for the highway to the highland resorts. But we expect the developers to replace them by planting trees along the route. The effort will not only ensure that the greenery is maintained but also benefit the developers in the long run as the trees will hold the earth along the highway together and prevent erosion,' Dr Mahathir said after launching the National Tree Planting Campaign in Gombak.

Royal yacht on fire

13 March Johor Bahru

The 20-metre yacht *Bonita*, belonging to the Sultan of Johor, was gutted in a fire after it was struck by lightning during a storm in Johor Bahru yesterday. The interior of the yacht, docked at the Sultan's personal harbour in Stutang, was destroyed. Nobody was injured.

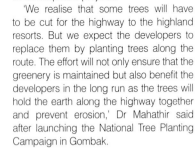

Malaysia makes it to hockey World Cup

14 March Kuala Lumpur

Players wept and danced while fans invaded the pitch and hung around long after the lights had been switched off.

Malaysia's hockey team and its fans had realised their dream of finishing in the top six at the pre-World Cup tournament in Kuala Lumpur and qualifying for the 1998 World Cup in Utrecht, Holland. The dream had taken 16 years to come true. That was how long Malaysia had been out of the World Cup.

The Malaysians started out with a 4–5 defeat to Poland, then beat Canada 4–1, South Africa 4–3 and drew with Switzerland 2–2, lost to Spain 2–5 and, in a key match, defeated Belgium 3–0 to qualify for the 5th-6th placing match against Canada. Malaysia lost 1–3 but it was enough to seal their ticket to the World Cup proper.

Unknown species found in Sarawak caves

4 March Miri

An American expedition discovered several hitherto unknown species of amphibians and fish in the Gunung Buda caves near Limbang, northern Sarawak.

The team of 20 scientists, cave explorers and adventurers stumbled upon a rare species of crab that is white and blind, and lives its entire life in complete darkness. Another discovery was a frog that does not live in water but clings to the roots of a plant. It lays its eggs in water. Expedition leader George Prest said the team had never seen these species before although they had explored caves and mountains in almost every continent. 'We also discovered unusual species of spiders and insects inside the caves, and a very unusual fish with an eel-like body,' he said.

RMAF helicopters crash

18 March Kota Kinabalu

Two RMAF Nuri helicopters, on a routine supply mission with 11 men on board, crashed within minutes of each other in a remote, jungle-clad hilly area near Sipitang, 200km south of here.

The Nuris were returning to their base on Labuan island after delivering supplies to army and police units in the remote district of Long Pasia when they crashed. All aboard were killed.

The wreckage of one helicopter was found in a 150m-deep ravine amid thick jungle at Ilukit Moningoton near Gunung Lumaku. The other was 4.8km away.

Sabah CID chief Senior Asst Comm II Mazlan Tyan said there were two captains, two lieutenants, three sergeants, two corporals and two privates on board the helicopters. The bodies of all 11 RMAF crewmen were recovered within 48 hours.

Dr Mahathir with the South African President.

Mandela has high praise for Malaysia

7 March Kuala Lumpur

South African President Nelson Mandela praised Malaysia for being among the leading countries in the global struggle against apartheid, 'keeping strong links of friendship and solidarity with the democratic forces of our country.'

He said the support became more evident in the build-up to the historic 1994 general election in the republic. 'Today, South Africa is free. And our nations share common objectives in political, economic and social matters,' he said at a State banquet hosted by the Yang di-Pertuan Agong Tuanku Ja'afar.

On economic co-operation, Mr Mandela said bilateral trade had more than doubled within three years, and Malaysia was now the fourth largest investor in the republic.

Yahaya Ahmad dies

2 March Kuala Lumpur

Leading corporate figure Tan Sri Yahaya Ahmad and his wife Puan Sri Rohana Othman were killed in a helicopter crash near Kuala Lipis while on their way to visit his ailing mother in Terengganu.

After a mid-air explosion, the six-seater Agusta-109P plunged 2,900m into rubber trees just metres away from houses in Kampung Along, Jerangsang, about 25 miles southwest of Kuala Lipis.

The pilot, Mej (R) Azlizan Abdul Manas, 32, from Batu Pahat, was also killed. The bodies were found by police and villagers about two hours after the crash. The position of the bodies suggested that Yahaya, 50, and Rohana, 48, were embracing.

What was left of the helicopter after it crashed.

The helicopter, belonging to Gadek Aviation Helicopter Sdn Bhd, one of Yahaya's companies, was believed to have had engine trouble about 30 minutes after it took off from the Segambut helipad in Kuala Lumpur.

Yahaya, who was said to control more than RM5 billion worth of assets through 12 companies, had left a reunion dinner at Dato' Seri Anwar Ibrahim's residence heading for Marang to see his mother Mandak Omar, 77, who was in the coronary care unit of the Kuala Terengganu Hospital.

KL hit by floods again

23 March Kuala Lumpur

Parts of the city came to a standstill in the evening when a three-hour downpour caused massive floods. Rising waters cut at least 10 major roads, resulting in traffic chaos. Flood waters rose as high as 1.5m on some roads, forcing motorists to abandon their vehicles. Water flowed into basement car parks of shopping complexes.

At Kampung Chendana and Kampung Periuk, two areas in Kampung Baru, police and Civil Defence Department and City Hall workers rescued more than 150 people trapped in their houses.

Boats had to be used as water levels rose to two metres. A number of low-lying squatter areas were reported to be in more than a metre of water.

Lee says sorry

22 March Kuala Lumpur

It all started when Singapore's Senior Minister Lee Kuan Yew filed a sworn affidavit in a Singapore court in his defamation suit against opposition candidate Tang Liang Hong. One

passage read: 'I was baffled. He [Tang] claimed that his life was under threat. But, of all places, he went to Johor. That place is notorious for shootings, muggings and car-jackings. It did not make any sense for a person who claims to be fearful for his life to go to a place like Johor.'

His comments led Malaysia to issue a protest to Singapore. Lee apologised and asked to have his statement deleted from court records. Malaysia decided at a weekly Cabinet meeting to freeze all fresh bilateral ties with Singapore. The decision was made at the weekly Cabinet meeting chaired by Deputy Prime Minister Dato' Seri Anwar Ibrahim.

1997

world news

13 April
Tiger Woods, 21, becomes the youngest winner of the US Masters, with a record 18-under par 270.

2 May
Tony Blair, 44, becomes the youngest British PM in 185 years.

28 June
Boxer Mike Tyson is disqualified during a title fight with Evander Holyfield for biting his opponent's ear.

30 June
The first title in J.K. Rowling's *Harry Potter* series is published.

1 July
Hong Kong reverts to Chinese control again after 156 years of British governance.

1 July
Thailand lets its baht float and it devalues by 20 per cent, heralding the start of an Asia-wide financial crisis.

4–5 July
Cambodia's Second Prime Minister Hun Sen overthrows First Prime Minister Norodom Ranariddh.

15 August
India celebrates 50 years of independence.

'Spiderman' warms up with 14-storey climb

28 March | **Kuala Lumpur**

The French free climber, 'Spiderman' Alain Robert, took only eight minutes to climb the 14-storey Melia Hotel in Kuala Lumpur as a warm-up for his proposed climb of the 88-storey Petronas Twin Towers. Robert climbed the hotel by clinging to the window frames without any safety harness.

New road link to Singapore approved

24 March | **Pasir Gudang**

A proposal to build a bridge across the Tebrau Straits to replace the Johor–Singapore Causeway was approved. Work was expected to begin in 1998. Works Minister Dato' Seri S. Samy Vellu said the Cabinet gave the nod at a recent meeting and picked a consortium for the project. The idea to replace the Causeway with a bridge was mooted by the PM.

Two awards for Dr M

31 March | **Kuala Lumpur**

Two awards won by Dato' Seri Dr Mahathir Mohamad were 'for the people. I only went there to accept them on their behalf,' he said at a dinner to honour him for the Jawaharlal Nehru Award for International Understanding and the King Faisal International Award, given by India and Saudi Arabia respectively.

Curbs on share market and property

28 March | **Kuala Lumpur**

Bank Negara Malaysia announced two 'pre-emptive strikes' against excessive lending to share market and property operators. Presenting Bank Negara's 1996 annual report, governor Datuk Ahmad Mohd Don said there was too much money in the banking system and it was being increasingly channelled to 'less productive sectors'.

The first measure put a ceiling on the amount of loans banks could provide for buying shares and non-Government unit trusts, including loans to holding and investment companies.

Loans for investment in Amanah Saham Nasional, Amanah Saham Bumiputra, Amanah Saham Wawasan 2020 and unit trust funds established by State Governments were exempted.

Under the second measure, financial institutions could extend a maximum of 20 per cent of their loans to the property sector. This restriction excluded loans for lower-cost housing, infrastructure projects, industrial buildings and factories. The lending curbs came into effect the following week.

New shark species found off Sabah

12 April | **Kota Kinabalu**

At least three species of shark completely new to science are believed to be in the coastal waters off Sabah.

Their discovery came as part of a study that resulted in the recent finding of a rare freshwater shark, *Glyphis* species B, thought to be extinct for more than 100 years. Scientists stumbled on it during their regular forays to fish markets in Sabah.

Commonly known as the Borneo river shark, it was caught in the Kinabatangan River by a fisherman and handed over to scientists involved in the Elasmobranch (sharks and rays) Biodiversity, Conservation and Management project. The 80cm shark was taken to the Likas research centre of the State Fisheries Department, which was carrying out the study with the World Conservation Union shark specialist group.

Opening of river channel

22 April | **Kuching**

The river channel through the Sungai Sarawak Regulation Scheme barrage was timely and necessary to develop a ring road for Kuching and to serve as a gateway to other major towns and districts, said Sarawak Chief Minister Tan Sri Abdul Taib Mahmud.

The RM150-million project included the cost of a four-lane road linking Pending with Sejingkat and the second causeway.

Dr Mahathir: Malays can succeed

12 May | **Kuala Lumpur**

Dato' Seri Dr Mahathir Mohamad said he no longer believed in the view that Malays lacked the ability to succeed as he suggested in his book *The Malay Dilemma*.

The Prime Minister said he was now of the view that the Malays had the necessary ability and confidence.

'I admit that at the time I felt very disappointed. I spoke to many people my age then who did not have the confidence. I too was not confident that Malays could achieve success. Now I reverse my stand. I no longer believe what I had written,' he said to applause during his address at a forum organised by Umno Youth in conjunction with the party's 51st anniversary.

The book, published in 1970, dealt with problems besetting the Malays. It was banned shortly after it was released. The ban was only lifted when Dr Mahathir became Prime Minister in 1981.

The Umno president said what was more important now was that the Malays must have the confidence and willingness to acquire knowledge and expertise until they had mastered them.

PM chats online

16 April | **Kuala Lumpur**

In the biggest online chat of its kind in Malaysia, Dato' Seri Dr Mahathir Mohamad spoke to ordinary Malaysians about the Multimedia Super Corridor project and how it would change their lives.

Dr M appeals for all-Asean cyber laws

18 May | **Sepang**

Malaysia would try to persuade other Asean countries to adopt its cyber laws so that an international court could be set up to enforce them, said Prime Minister Dato' Seri Dr Mahathir Mohamad.

Setting up the court would be a matter for Asean but it would be discussed at ministerial level before being presented to the leaders, he said.

'Eventually the world will have to come to terms with this new technology which has no respect for borders,' Dr Mahathir told reporters at the ground-breaking ceremony of the 7,000-ha Cyberjaya city near here. Dr Mahathir first proposed the need for an international cyber court in a lecture at Stanford University earlier in the year.

Selangor MB quits

12 April | **Kuala Lumpur**

Tan Sri Muhammad Muhammad Taib quit as Selangor Menteri Besar amid controversy relating to a court case he was involved in and properties worth millions in Australia. Dato' Seri Dr Mahathir Mohamad announced the resignation after an Umno supreme council meeting. It took effect on 14 April.

Muhammad, 51, also resigned as Selangor and Federal Territory Umno liaison chief and State Barisan Nasional chairman but remained as party vice-president. Asked whether the resignation was an admission of guilt, Dr Mahathir replied: 'I don't know if this is admission of guilt. But it is his own decision. Any investigation is not against Umno but on him.'

Muhammad faced two charges of attempting to transfer A$1.2 million out of Australia and making a false declaration. He was also being investigated by the Anti-Corruption

Agency (ACA) in connection with his ownership of several properties in Australia reported to be worth millions of ringgit (*see 28 May 1998*).

Magendran (right) proudly displays the national flag on the summit of Everest. Sitting next to him is Mohanadas.

Malaysia on top of the world

24 May Kuala Lumpur

A teacher and an administrative assistant became national heroes when they successfully set foot on the summit of Mount Everest. Crawling the last few metres, his progress hindered by 80km/h winds, teacher M. Magendran, 33, planted the Malaysian flag on the 8,848m-high peak at noon. He was followed soon after by administrative assistant N. Mohanadas, 36.

Their success was relayed by walkie-talkie to expedition team members at base camp while the nation was kept informed by expedition member Aminuddin Abu Samah through radio and television. The achievement brought congratulations from Prime Minister Dato' Seri Dr Mahathir Mohamad and his deputy Dato' Seri Anwar Ibrahim.

Gary Choong and Mohamed Fauzan Hassan, the two others in the team attempting the final assault on Everest, were forced to return to Camp 4.

On their return, the victorious team was welcomed by more than 5,000 people on arrival at the airport in Subang.

MAS flying high

30 May Kuala Lumpur

Malaysian Airline System Bhd recorded a group pre-tax profit of RM349.4 million, the highest in its corporate history, for the financial year to 31 March.

Profit was up 39.1 per cent over last year's RM251.1 million. The airline achieved the record profit despite stiff competition, challenging market conditions and higher fuel costs.

Group after-tax profit rose 43.3 per cent to RM333.97 million against RM233.036 million in 1996. Group turnover rose 13.5 per cent to RM6.484 billion from RM5.713 billion.

Earnings per share increased to 43.8 sen from 33.3, while net tangible assets per share stood at RM6.76 against RM6.23 in the previous period.

Helicopter plunge

14 June Kuala Lumpur

A Bell 206L-4 helicopter broke up and crashed at the Sri Damansara light industrial area here. The helicopter had been attempting to hoist a tripod metal structure for a telecommunications tower when the pilot lost control.

Three on board the aircraft and two on the ground died in the tragedy.

The wreckage of the helicopter.

Islamic Civilisation to be compulsory subject

24 June Kuala Lumpur

Islamic Civilisation will soon be a compulsory and standard subject in all public and private institutions of higher learning in a move to foster religious tolerance.

Minister in the Prime Minister's Department Datuk Dr Abdul Hamid Othman said the subject would ensure better religious understanding among Muslims and non-Muslims which would help strengthen unity.

Ten die in plane crash

6 September Miri

Ten people, including six Malaysians, were killed when a chartered Dornier-228 aircraft crashed into hilly terrain at the Lambir Hills National Park near here. The others who died were two Japanese, a Singaporean and a Sri Lankan. The pilot and the co-pilot of the 19-seater aircraft belonging to Merpati Intan Sdn Bhd were among the Malaysians killed.

Flight B1839 from Bandar Seri Begawan in Brunei bound for Miri broke into three when it crashed at Lambir Hill, about 14km south of the Miri airport.

Razali criticises US for not paying UN dues

17 September New York

The United States was criticised by Tan Sri Razali Ismail, the president of the 51st United Nations General Assembly, for not paying up its old dues of US$1.5 billion. This, he said, had considerably slowed efforts to reform the UN.

Razali, who was ending his one-year term as president, said: 'The issue of non-payment is the most disappointing part of the 51st General Assembly. The huge arrears add to the tension and as a result the momentum of reform is affected'. He said the US had officially offered a partial payment of US$500 million to the UN, far short of the amount needed. 'There's no reason why a special arrangement should be made for the most powerful country in the world', he said.

Firefighters to battle Sumatra blaze

22 September Klang

Malaysian firefighters gathered at Port Klang before leaving for Sumatra to help put out the forest fires that had caused Malaysia to be engulfed in thick haze for two weeks. The 1,210 men left on two navy vessels, KD *Mahawangsa* and KD *Sri Banggi*, for Dumai and from there would travel by road to the fires in the south.

Haze causes havoc on land and sea

27 September Petaling Jaya

Haze which had been particularly dense for a week continued to play havoc, causing two ships to collide just off the coast of Port Dickson and sending the Air Pollutant Index (API) in Penang to soar above the hazardous 301 level.

The haze had already been blamed for the air crash in Sumatra earlier in the week which killed more than 234 people, including at least one Malaysian.

Twenty-nine people on board the Madras-registered cargo vessel *ICL Vikraman* were feared drowned when their ship sank after colliding with another cargo ship, the *Mount 1*.

Four survivors, including a woman, were rescued by the Thai-registered vessel *Teen Glory* and a fifth was picked up by the RMN frigate KD *Lekir*.

The API in Penang hit a new high when it reached 371, the highest in the peninsula since the haze alert began in August.

Games countdown

10 September Kuala Lumpur

The countdown to the 16th Commonwealth Games in Kuala Lumpur in 1998 was launched by Youth and Sports Minister Tan Sri Muhyiddin Yassin. It was displayed on a RM300,000 three-dimensional billboard in Dataran Merdeka.

1997

world news

Best-ever SEA Games haul for Malaysia

20 October Jakarta

There was no overseas training stint for the athletics team. They also only had three foreign competitions. But in this SEA Games, the Malaysian athletes reigned supreme. The 38-member athletics team contributed 16 golds. They also won seven silvers and five bronzes. The 16-gold haul was Malaysia's best ever in the SEA Games. The previous best was 14, achieved in Singapore in 1993.

However Malaysian Amateur Athletic Union coaching chairman J.V. Jayan was not too happy. 'We won 16 golds and this is something to be proud of after having returned with only eight from Chiang Mai two years ago,' said Jayan.

'But look at our athletes' winning marks. I don't think they are impressive at all. Except for one or two athletes, they did not meet the target set for them.'

Controversial gold

13 October Jakarta

Malaysia were almost robbed of the women's artistic gymnastics gold medal in a competition where the winners were not decided until two hours after it was complete. And the Malaysian gymnasts had Indonesia to thank for the win at the 19th SEA Games. Malaysia (who had originally been silver medallists) and the Philippines were eventually adjudged joint champions at the Radin Gymnastics Hall as a result of the controversy stirred up by Indonesia.

Bomohs fail in appeal against death sentence

25 October Kuala Lumpur

Bomoh couple Mohd Affandi Abdul Rahman and Mona Fandey and their assistant Juraimi Husin failed to get their conviction for the murder of Bukit Talam State Assemblyman Datuk Mazlan Idris overturned. They also failed in their appeal against the death sentence. The Court of Appeal panel found unanimously there had been no substantial miscarriage of justice in their trial. Counsel were seen assuring their clients they could still appeal to the Federal Court. However, their appeals were dismissed in 1999 and they were hanged on 2 November 2001.

Financial crisis

'No need' for despair over economy

4 October Montevideo

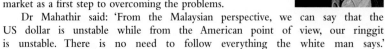

Dato' Seri Dr Mahathir Mohamad urged Malaysians not to despair over economic problems. The Prime Minister expressed confidence that Malaysia would surmount the pressures resulting from attacks on the ringgit. 'We must be fully disciplined and must not panic,' he said at the end of a two-day visit here. Dr Mahathir said the Government was compiling information on the effects of the depreciation of the ringgit and the slide in the share market as a first step to overcoming the problems.

Dr Mahathir said: 'From the Malaysian perspective, we can say that the US dollar is unstable while from the American point of view, our ringgit is unstable. There is no need to follow everything the white man says.'

Malaysia had gone through several tough patches, he said. In 1973 inflation hit 17 per cent when oil prices shot up and in 1985 many people went bankrupt when the property market crashed. 'We managed to overcome all that.'

Prime Minister slams speculator Soros

2 November Kuala Lumpur

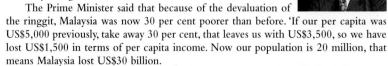

George Soros should stop speculating in the world's financial markets if he had a conscience, according to Dato' Seri Dr Mahathir Mohamad. 'I do hope he realises that he is profiting from the misery of other people,' the Prime Minister said. The international financier should realise that speculation in the financial markets had disrupted the economy and growth of other countries.

The Prime Minister said that because of the devaluation of the ringgit, Malaysia was now 30 per cent poorer than before. 'If our per capita was US$5,000 previously, take away 30 per cent, that leaves us with US$3,500, so we have lost US$1,500 in terms of per capita income. Now our population is 20 million, that means Malaysia lost US$30 billion.

'There is Indonesia, the Philippines, Thailand and Taiwan. So they [speculators] have a lot of money. All this trouble they have caused to the whole world, disruption of the economy, growth, is in order to give profit to a very few people who are already rich. This is what makes me very unhappy,' he said.

'Globalisation has its perils'

4 November Kuala Lumpur

Dato' Seri Dr Mahathir Mohamad, in a reminder to developing countries over the lack of a clear definition of globalisation, has called on the Group of 15 to ensure they are not taken advantage of. He said if countries were to accept globalisation, there must be a fair system of trading in goods and services, shares or currency.

'I would like to refer to currency trading in which we had no say and now we find it impossible almost to correct the system even when it is clearly to our disadvantage,' he said when opening the seventh G15 summit here yesterday.

Leaders attending the three-day summit included Indonesia's President Suharto, Egyptian President Hosni Mubarak, Peruvian President Alberto Fujimori, Algerian President Liamine Zerouel and Zimbabwean President Robert Mugabe. Describing the present currency trading arrangements as 'unethical and unfair' to countries whose currencies were under attack, Dr Mahathir called for a fair system of currency trading.

Powerful panel set up to revitalise economy

20 November Kuala Lumpur

The Government decided to set up a National Economic Action Council to overcome effects of the weakened ringgit and the depressed Kuala Lumpur Stock Exchange. The panel, chaired by Prime Minister Dato' Seri Dr Mahathir Mohamad, would have powers similar to those used in an emergency situation.

The decision to set up the council was made at a three-hour Umno supreme council meeting.

IMF chief calls for 'painful measures'

2 December Kuala Lumpur

Asian countries could rebuild confidence and ambitions rocked by economic turmoil by taking painful measures via structural and policy changes, IMF managing director Michel Camdessus said. He said Governments should draw on current developments to decide what they should change to manage their economies.

'Governments must realise that they are more vulnerable to crisis in other markets than their own economic fundamentals would suggest,' he told the Asean Business Forum here. Asian Governments must also promote a more orderly working of financial markets, he added.

Dr M calls for salaries of execs to be cut

13 December Subang Jaya

Dato' Seri Dr Mahathir Mohamad called on the private sector to reduce 'unreasonable' salaries paid to top and middle-level executives as part of its contribution to the austerity drive.

Citing executives' high salaries as one of the reasons for the increasing cost of contracts, he said salaries should be commensurate with profits or management costs incurred by companies.

1998

This was a tumultuous year. The Government moved quickly to address the deepening economic crisis by introducing currency controls amid predictions of dire consequences for the nation. Anwar Ibrahim was sacked as Deputy Prime Minister and subsequently arrested for 'offences including illegal assembly, rioting, vandalism, using criminal force and causing public disorder'. In September Anwar pleaded not guilty in the Sessions Court to five charges of corruption and four of sodomy. But it was not all doom and gloom: the new Kuala Lumpur International Airport opened in Sepang and Malaysia pulled off a coup by successfully hosting the biggest sporting extravaganza ever staged in Malaysia, the 16th Commonwealth Games.

MARCH
Microsoft chairman Bill Gates fully backs the Multimedia Super Corridor.

JUNE
Kuala Lumpur International Airport (KLIA) opens.

SEPTEMBER
Dato' Seri Anwar Ibrahim is sacked as Deputy Prime Minister and arrested.

NOVEMBER
Lina Teoh comes in third in the Miss World finals.

September: The colourful opening of the Commonwealth Games in Kuala Lumpur.

'If the international community cannot change, then Malaysia must undertake its own reform.'

Dato' Seri Dr Mahathir Mohamad, about Malaysia's recession, 16 January 1998.

1998

world news

10 April
The anti-impotence drug Viagra is introduced.

15 April
In Cambodia, Khmer Rouge leader Pol Pot dies at 73.

21 May
Suharto resigns after 32 years as Indonesian President.

16 June
In Afghanistan the Taliban order the closure of more than 100 girls' schools.

22 June
South Korea captures a small North Korean submarine entangled in a fishing net. The nine crewmen commit suicide.

8 July
The Taliban ban television, VCRs, videos and satellite dishes.

12 July
France beats Brazil 3–0 to win the FIFA World Cup in France.

17 July
A 23ft tsunami hits Papua New Guinea after an earthquake in the Solomon Islands, killing 2,500-3,000.

Malaysia first in region to set up foreign campus

16 January Kuala Lumpur

Australia's Monash University would be the first foreign tertiary education institution to set up a campus in Malaysia, said Education Minister Dato' Seri Najib Tun Razak.

He said it would be an 'offshore branch campus' in which a foreign university teams up with a local institution.

'If I am not mistaken, we [Malaysia] will be the first country in the region to have such a prestigious educational arrangement,' he said.

The proposed campus would offer degree courses in the fields of information technology, engineering and business management. 'The degrees to be given out will be like the ones given out by Monash in Melbourne,' he said.

Second link opens

3 January Johor Bahru

The Malaysia–Singapore Second Link opened to traffic. The bridge from Kampung Ladang, Tanjung Kupang, in Johor connects to Jalan Ahmad Ibrahim at Tuas, Singapore. The total length of the bridge is 2km and it was built at a cost of RM1.3 billion.

On 19 April the link was officially opened by Prime Minister Dato' Seri Dr Mahathir Mohamad and his Singapore counterpart Goh Chok Tong. The official opening meant tolls had to be paid, though at half the previously published rate due to earlier public protests.

Noble act brings new life

10 February Kuala Lumpur

The noble act of a 22-year-old brain tumour victim put 51-year-old technician R. Sathrugnan in the record book as the first man in Malaysia to have a heart transplant. Sathrugnan underwent surgery at the National Heart Institute on 18 December 1997 after being on the waiting list for seven months.

R. Sathrugnan (holding baby) with his family after he had recovered from surgery.

Financial crisis

Out of the gloom, an economic 'miracle'

16 January Kuala Lumpur

Signs that the economic crisis in Malaysia was deepening came slowly. Indeed the year started on a note of hope when International Monetary Fund managing director Michel Camdessus said Malaysia did not need an IMF bailout. The statement followed a two-day consultation with Malaysian leaders and authorities.

The country's financial sector was strong, its economic policy was sound and tough pre-emptive measures had been taken to tackle economic problems, said Camdessus. 'Malaysia is not facing a similar crisis to that faced by the neighbours,' he said. 'IMF will, however, offer policy advice and technical assistance.'

On 3 March 1998, Bank Negara said Sime Bank, Bank Bumiputra, Abrar Finance and Cempaka Finance Bhd were in need of recapitalisation. Sime Bank were in need of RM1.2 billion and Bank Bumiputra of RM750 million; merger negotiations between them were at an advanced stage. Share trading in Sime Darby, which owned 60.3 per cent of Sime Bank, was suspended. However Bank Negara Governor Tan Sri Ahmad Mohd Don assured depositors that their savings were protected.

The next warning sign came the following day, from overseas, in a report in *The Australian* newspaper. The number of visas issued to students from Malaysia, Australia's biggest overseas student market, in the crucial enrolment month of January was down 45 per cent from the previous year, it said.

Enrolment from other Southeast Asian countries was also down, it said, sparking fears of an Asian currency fallout.

  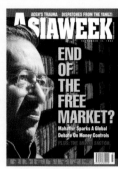

The following month, on 18 April, Prime Minister Dato' Seri Dr Mahathir Mohamad said companies that had 'proven themselves' were likely to be given aid to ensure they survived the economic slowdown. 'Their problems are not the result

Singaporean cartoonist Heng's view

of bad management but due to the depreciation of the ringgit and the value of shares,' he said.

By this stage, the ringgit had fallen from a rate of about 2.55 to the US$ in early 1997 to about 3.75. The currency continued to fall, reaching a level of RM4.2 in August, largely due to speculation on the foreign exchange market.

On 1 September Tan Sri Ahmad resigned as Bank Negara Governor, along with his deputy Datuk Fong Weng Phak. The resignations took effect immediately. Assistant Governor Datuk Zeti Akhtar Aziz took over in an acting role.

The same day the Government took what it called a series of 'shocking measures' to protect the economy, chief of which was pegging the ringgit to the US dollar at RM3.80, to take effect the following day, and declaring the ringgit no longer legal tender in foreign countries after 1 October. International Trade and Industry Minister Dato' Seri Rafidah Aziz said the drastic measures would not harm long-term investors who were able to maintain foreign-currency accounts. The decision was lauded by local economists.

In an interview with *Time* magazine in September, Dr Mahathir strongly defended his actions. 'Malaysia cannot wait,' it quoted him as saying. 'Malaysia has chosen to become a heretic, a pariah if you like.

'Our appeal to the world community to regulate and bring order to the market has gone unheeded. If the international community cannot change then Malaysia must undertake its own reform.'

'We may fail, of course, but we are going to do our damndest to succeed even if all the forces of the rich and powerful are aligned against us. God willing, we will succeed.'

What the foreign press said

Malaysia 'falls into recession'

28 August Brisbane

The *Courier Mail* in Brisbane said Malaysia had entered a full-blown recession. It said this was admitted by Dr Mahathir and reported by Bernama. It quoted him as saying the second-quarter GDP had contracted a further 7 per cent, from 1.8 per cent in the first quarter. The economy, which had expanded 7.8 per cent in 1997, had fallen into its worst recession in 13 years, according to the newspaper.

Open letter to Mahathir

4 September Sydney

An open letter to Dr Mahathir from Paul Krugman of the Massachusetts Institute of Technology in the United States was published in the *Australian Financial Review.* An edited version follows:

Dear Dr Mahathir,
I was as surprised as anyone when you announced sweeping new currency controls yesterday, and am still unclear about some of the details. However since my recent Fortune article did suggest that temporary currency controls are part of the solution for Asia, I cannot deny some responsibility for your policy turn. Let me therefore say that, like yourself and, of course, the people of Malaysia, I fervently hope that this dramatic policy move pays off.
Paul Krugman
Department of Economics, MIT

Dr M 'turns lessons of Suharto on their head'

5–6 September Sydney

The *Australian Financial Review* commented that 'just as some faint glimmers of hope began to glint in Asia, Dr Mahathir Mohamad has retreated into an ugly and dangerous experiment in economic and political reaction. Mahathir's course is ugly because it defies principle. And it is dangerous because it could not only jeopardise Malaysia's future, but also encourage imitators across the region. It seems that Mahathir has looked at the experience of his neighbour, Indonesia's Suharto, and drawn precisely the wrong lessons.'

UN lends support to currency controls

21 September Geneva

Malaysia was justified in imposing foreign exchange controls in the current 'extreme' conditions, said United Nations Conference on Trade and Development secretary-general Rubens Ricupero. He told *The Australian* in Geneva that other Asian countries should perhaps look at what Malaysia was doing to solve its problems.

Soros hurting poor: Mahathir

12 December Melbourne

The Melbourne newspaper *The Age* said Dr Mahathir had stepped up his attack on the American financier George Soros. 'In an extraordinary new outburst,' it said, Dr Mahathir, when asked whether he regarded Mr Soros as a criminal, answered: 'Well, as much as people who produce and distribute drugs are criminals because they destroy nations, the people who undermine the economies of poor nations [are too].'

Dr M in Brunei talks

18 February Bandar Seri Begawan

Prime Minister Dato' Seri Dr Mahathir Mohamad visited Brunei for a private meeting with Sultan Hassanal Bolkiah at the Royal Brunei Golf and Country Club.

Gates committed to MSC

18 March Kuala Lumpur

Microsoft chairman and chief executive officer Bill Gates pledged his total support for Malaysia's Multimedia Super Corridor (MSC) project and said he would offer maximum investment in the project.

Gates, who was visiting Singapore, the Philippines and Australia as well as Malaysia, was a member of the MSC's International Advisory Panel. Prime Minister Dato' Seri Dr Mahathir Mohamad said the Microsoft boss was also keen to participate in the country's education programme, especially in smart schools, universities and information technology training.

Bill Gates speaks, overshadowed by himself on a giant TV screen.

Chair for Dayak Studies

16 March Kuching

Dayak leaders and Universiti Malaysia Sarawak (Unimas) set up a Chair for Dayak Studies. Unimas pro-chancellor Chief Minister Tan Sri Abdul Taib Mahmud said this would help the Dayak community to go through socioeconomic transformation as they enter the 21st century.

Malaysia receives Games baton

9 March London

Datuk Punch Gunalan, the former badminton gold medallist, received the Commonwealth Games relay baton from Queen Elizabeth II at Buckingham Palace.

The specially designed silver baton, modelled on a gombek, an instrument used to pound sireh leaf, was carried for the first time in relay through other Commonwealth countries before arriving in Kuala Lumpur for the opening of the Games in September.

The handover of the baton was accompanied by a colourful display, with kompang drummers, and a 'Malay warrior' and 'Malay princess' in attendance.

What the foreign press said

Is Kuala Lumpur able to host Games?

19 March Brisbane

The Asian financial crisis aside, Malaysia was hoping to make the Commonwealth Games in Kuala Lumpur a showpiece for its technological advancement, the *Courier Mail* in Brisbane reported.

But it claimed Kuala Lumpur's ability to host the Games was not looking good. In 1997 city haze had forced locals and tourists to walk the streets of Malaysia's capital with gas masks and the city's major hotels were empty, it wrote. Added to that, the Asian financial crisis had crippled the local economy and Kuala Lumpur was, at one stage, staring down the barrel of an international sporting disaster. The country's ability to put on a sporting extravaganza was at risk (*see 11–22 September 1998*).

Intelligent passports

23 March Kuala Lumpur

Malaysia became the first nation to incorporate computer chips into passports. The biometric data included was a digital photograph of the bearer's face and images of his or her two thumbprints. The technology was developed by a Malaysian company.

1998

world news

7 August
Bombs at the US embassies in Dar es Salaam, Tanzania, and Nairobi, Kenya, kill 224.

19 August
US President Bill Clinton admits a relationship with Monica Lewinsky.

20 August
US cruise missile attacks in retaliation for the US Embassy bombings in East Africa hit the main camp of Osama bin Laden in Afghanistan.

1 September
After half a century of unbridled deforestation, the Chinese Government bans all logging upstream of the Yangtze.

22 September
Iranian President Mohammad Khatami says the fatwa on the head of Salman Rushdie is over.

25 September
Frenchman Benoit Lecombe completes a 72-day swim across the Atlantic, landing on the Brittany coast.

8 October
Japan apologises to the people of South Korea for 35 years of brutal colonial rule.

Water rationing in dry Klang Valley

27 March | **Petaling Jaya**

Water rationing began in 350 areas in the Klang Valley, affecting about 600,000 residents. On 10 April the rationing was extended to Seremban and on 20 April to more than 700 Klang Valley localities, affecting more than 1.8 million people.

People were warned that the rationing, involving rolling water cuts, could last for six months due to the prolonged dry spell that had taken a toll on water levels at the Semenyih and Kuala Langat dams.

Some residents complained that they had not been told about the rationing by the authorities and that the only information they had was from newspapers. In fact the drought ended in September.

Elephant resettlement a jumbo operation

18 April | **Kuala Gandah**

The Elephant Management Centre in Kuala Gandah, Pahang had a jumbo task translocating wild elephants whose habitat had been encroached on by human beings in the name of development.

Through the unit's efforts, the wild elephant population had risen to 1,200 but the number needed to rise to 2,000 to ensure a stable and healthy population, said Mohd M. Khan, a former Department of Wildlife and National Parks director-general. Fears were growing that the task would be near impossible given the rate of decline due to logging, highway construction and land conversion for agricultural use.

Lawyers investigated

19 April | **Kuala Lumpur**

The Advocates' and Solicitors' Disciplinary Board said it was probing alleged professional misconduct by more than 300 lawyers nationwide. The board's director Ramdhari @ Jai Ram JBS noted that there had been a three-fold increase in complaints against lawyers since mid-1996. There was at least a complaint a day, with the bulk from the Klang Valley, Johor and Penang. Most were about excessive fees, lawyers acting as stakeholders and not returning the money, holding up cases and disregarding clients' interests.

Goodbye Subang, welcome Sepang

27 June | **Sepang**

The Yang di-Pertuan Agong Tuanku Ja'afar opened the RM9-billion KL International Airport here. It was completed in a record time of 36 months. Following the opening, a Malaysia Airlines 777, dubbed Super Ranger, landed at the KLIA with 150 villagers from Sepang and invited Press members on board.

The 10,000ha of land where the KLIA is sited was previously an oil palm and rubber estate and a swamp forest. It was transformed with futuristic-looking buildings and carefully designed landscape.

Two days later, the Sultan Abdul Aziz Shah International Airport at Subang sent off its last international flight, about seven hours before the first commercial flight from the KLIA took to the skies.

A symbol of the future: Fireworks (top) celebrate the opening of the ultra-modern Kuala Lumpur International Airport.

First Bank Negara Governor dies

6 July | **Kuala Lumpur**

Former Bank Negara Governor and Permodalan Nasional Bhd chairman Tun Ismail Mohamed Ali died at the Ampang Puteri Specialist Hospital. He was 79.

The longest-serving central bank governor (he had served from 1962 to 1980) left two sons, Iskandar, a merchant banker, and Ahmad Kamal, an architect. His wife Toh Puan Maimunah Abdul Latiff died in 1996. He was buried at the Ampang Muslim cemetery. Tan Sri

Ramon Navaratnam, the former Finance Ministry deputy secretary-general, said Tun Ismail's death was a loss to the nation as he had been a great patriot and an outstanding civil servant.

Dr M moves to quash claims of cronyism

20 June | **Kuala Lumpur**

Prime Minister Dato' Seri Dr Mahathir Mohamad released at the Umno general assembly two lists of privatised projects and the companies which won them. The lists also contained names of principal shareholders of the companies.

He said the lists were released in response to allegations that the Government had practised cronyism and nepotism in awarding contracts. Umno leaders supported the party leadership's move to make the details public, saying it showed the Government had nothing to hide. Umno vice-president Dato' Seri Najib Tun Razak said the call for greater transparency prompted the Government to release the lists of recipients.

Later, on 26 June, Dr Mahathir said foreigners, especially the Western media, had come up with terms like nepotism, crony capitalism and corruption and used them in such a way as to persuade Malaysians to topple the Government.

He said the West wanted Malaysia to dismantle all the systems and policies that had maintained political and economic stability. 'As they had failed to erode our strong stand they are now trying to change the country's leadership.'

Ex-MB cleared in Brisbane

28 May | **Brisbane**

Former Selangor Menteri Besar Tan Sri Muhammad Muhammad Taib was acquitted of two charges of falsely declaring money he carried into Australia in December 1996 and failing to declare more than A$1.2 million (RM2.9 million) when he left Australia.

...then charged in Malaysia

10 June | **Kuala Lumpur**

Tan Sri Muhammad Muhammad Taib pleaded not guilty in the Sessions Court in Kuala Lumpur to a charge of failing to declare all his and his family's assets last year. His case was then transferred to the High Court in Kuala Lumpur after the Sessions Court allowed the prosecution's request. The High Court fixed trial for 7 to 18 December later in the year.

Tan Sri Muhammad, 53, was charged with committing the offence, under the Prevention of Corruption Act 1961, on 26 May last year. He was charged with knowingly ignoring conditions in a statutory declaration dated 23 May 1997 by declaring assets worth, at the time of acquisition, only RM10.82 million and A$3.46 million. On 29 December Tan Sri Muhammad was found not guilty.

Tan Sri Muhammad with his wife.

National Sports Complex opens

11 July Bukit Jalil

Prime Minister Dato' Seri Dr Mahathir Mohamad opened the National Sports Complex in Bukit Jalil, the venue for the 16th Commonwealth Games, in a glittering ceremony before a large crowd. Spectators included Ministers, the diplomatic corps and Commonwealth Games Federation president Michael Fennell.

To mark the opening of the stadium, Dr Mahathir lit the cauldron using a torch he received from bowler Shalin Zulkifli. Earlier, he launched the Sistem Transit Aliran Ringan (STAR) LRT, which links the city and the sports complex. He then took the 24-minute ride from the Jalan Sultan Ismail station in the city to the RM23-million Bukit Jalil station, a distance of 12km.

Dwarfed by an MAS airliner, the new plane.

Malaysia's aircraft

3 August Kuala Lumpur

Transport Minister Dato' Seri Dr Ling Liong Sik launched Langkawi 1, Malaysia's first two-seater aircraft. The light aircraft, given a flying permit by the Department of Civil Aviation, was a collaboration between Eurodynamic Sdn Bhd (ESB) and Association of Malaysia Airlines Licensed Aircraft Engineers (Amalae). At the ceremony, the light plane flew for 10 minutes at the Sultan Abdul Aziz Shah Airport in Subang.

Anwar shock

Injunction granted against book

31 July Kuala Lumpur

Dato' Seri Anwar Ibrahim obtained a court injunction to stop the distribution of *50 Dalil Mengapa Anwar Tidak Boleh Jadi PM (50 Reasons Why Anwar Cannot Become Prime Minister)*. High Court judge Datuk Wira Mohamed Noor Ahmad held that there were other public interests in the case which overrode journalistic freedom. He also dismissed with costs the application of the author, Abdul Khalid alias Khalid Jafri Bakar Shah, and the publisher, Media Pulau Legenda, to set aside the interim injunction which Anwar had obtained against them on 17 June.

Deputy PM sacked

2 September Kuala Lumpur

Dato' Seri Anwar Ibrahim was removed as Deputy Prime Minister and Finance Minister, and stripped of all posts he was holding in those capacities, the Prime Minister's Department said. The Yang di-Pertuan Agong has been informed and a letter to this effect was delivered to Anwar at his residence by a top government official. The same night, Anwar's was dismissed as Umno deputy president by a meeting of the party's supreme council. The meeting was originally scheduled for 8 September.

Duo jailed for sodomy

19 September Kuala Lumpur

Sukma Darmawan Sasmitaat Madja, 37, an adopted brother of former Deputy Prime Minister Dato' Seri Anwar Ibrahim, and his Pakistani friend Dr Munawar Ahmad Anees, 50, were jailed for six months each having been convicted of allowing Anwar to sodomise them.

11 arrested after rally sparks riots

20 September Kuala Lumpur

Police arrested Dato' Seri Anwar Ibrahim at his house in Bukit Damansara after a rally which he addressed sparked several incidents of unrest, including a crowd throwing stones at the Prime Minister's residence and calling for his resignation. Negeri Sembilan Umno Youth chief Ruslan Kassim and 10 others were also arrested (*see 14 April 1999*).

Supporters surround Dato' Seri Anwar as he is arrested at his home in Bukit Damansara.

Police said Anwar was held for offences including illegal assembly, rioting, vandalism, using criminal force and causing public disorder. The next day police used tear gas and water cannons to disperse a crowd of more than 3,000 who gathered in front of the magistrate's court in Kuala Lumpur expecting Anwar to be charged there. On 27 September 29 people were arrested when more than 3,000 people gathered at Dataran Merdeka shouting the Anwar supporters' slogan 'Reformasi'.

On 29 September Anwar pleaded not guilty in the Sessions Court in Kuala Lumpur to five charges of corruption and four of sodomy (*see 14 April 1999*).

Street demos go on

17 October Kuala Lumpur

Police dispersed supporters of Dato' Seri Anwar Ibrahim who gathered in Jalan Tuanku Abdul Rahman, Dataran Merdeka and the surrounding area. Shouting anti-Government slogans, the crowd broke into several groups at about 3.50pm, two hours before the wife of former Deputy Prime Minister Dato' Seri Anwar Ibrahim, Datin Seri Dr Wan Azizah Wan Ismail, arrived at the scene in an open-top multi-purpose vehicle. Some people were seen distributing T-shirts bearing the word 'Reformasi'.

Al Gore praises 'Reformasi'

16 November Kuala Lumpur

At an APEC Business Summit dinner, US Vice-President Al Gore saluted the 'brave people of Malaysia who supported the Reformasi', the rallying cry of supporters of former Deputy Prime Minister Dato' Seri Anwar Ibrahim. 'Democracy confers a stamp of legitimacy that reforms must have in order to be effective,' said Gore.

The next day, Barisan Nasional and Opposition MPs condemned him for criticising Malaysia's democratic practices.

What the foreign press said

Malaysia's reputation 'on the line'

17 November Adelaide

Australia has warned Dato' Seri Dr Mahathir Mohamad that he should guarantee Anwar Ibrahim a fair trial or risk inflicting damage to his country's international reputation, according to the Adelaide newspaper *The Advertiser*. It said Australian Prime Minister John Howard had also revealed that the Foreign Minister Alexander Downer had held a secret meeting with Anwar's wife Dr Wan Azizah Wan Ismail in Kuala Lumpur.

1998

14 October
Amartya Sen, 64, wins the Nobel Prize for Economics for his work on the causes of poverty and famine.

29 October
John Glenn, the first American to orbit the Earth in 1962, becomes the oldest man in space at 77, blasting off in the space shuttle *Discovery*.

13 November
The warring factions in Cambodia settle differences. Hun Sen heads a coalition Government and Prince Ranariddh becomes president of the National Assembly.

14 November
Extensive rioting and looting in Jakarta are directed against shopping malls, banks, car dealerships and Chinese-owned businesses and shops.

25 November
President Jiang Zemin arrives in Tokyo for the first visit by a Chinese Head of State since World War II.

26 November
Former President Suharto hands over seven family-controlled foundations with assets of over US$530 million.

Concert hall opens

17 August Kuala Lumpur

The Dewan Filharmonik Petronas, or Petronas Philharmonic Hall, was opened by the patron of the Malaysian Philharmonic Orchestra, Datin Seri Dr Siti Hasmah Mohamed Ali, accompanied by her husband Prime Minister Dato' Seri Dr Mahathir Mohamad.

Dr Siti Hasmah said the opening of the hall and the orchestra's gala performance which launched it were yet another Malaysian dream come true. 'We have indeed arrived at another major milestone in our progress towards achieving the cultural agenda set out in Vision 2020.' The design of the hall, with a seating capacity of 885, was inspired by the traditional shoe-box shape of 19th-century European concert halls.

Beating the drum: Dr Mahathir and Dr Siti Hasmah at the opening of the Dewan Filharmonik.

Malaysia Boleh

26 November Kuala Lumpur

Miss Malaysia/World 1998 Lina Teoh Pick Lim was placed third in the Miss World finals in Mahe, Seychelles. The 22-year-old model and actress was second runner-up behind France's Veronique Caloc, 23, a language student, and Miss Israel, model Linor Abargil, 19, who won the crown. Malaysia's previous best showing in the pageant was when Miss Malaysia/World 1997 Arianna Teoh made it to the last 10.

Devoted husband gives up kidney for his wife

2 December Kuala Lumpur

On daily dialysis since suffering kidney failure in 1997, Suriyawati Senin, 30, was given a kidney by her husband in the first spousal transplant operation in the country, it was announced. The operation took place on 9 May at University Hospital. Husband Tajularus Bahari said he gave his kidney because he could no longer bear to see his wife suffering.

The nephrologist who led the transplant team, Associate Professor Dr S.Y. Tan, said the Kuala Lumpur Hospital had conducted about 500 transplants between living relatives in 23 years and University Hospital 50 since 1990. But the number was shrinking as families got smaller.

'Modern medicine has made spousal transfer safe as long as the blood group matches,' he said.

Developers launch home ownership campaign

12 December Kuala Lumpur

Property developers united to hold a month-long Home Ownership Campaign, offering houses at discounted prices. Some 22,036 units of property worth RM5.2 billion were registered for sale, most in Selangor and Kuala Lumpur. Incentives included up to 80 per cent financing for cheaper homes and up to 70 per cent for the more expensive. Stamp duty would be waived. Other incentives included Government loans for civil servants after one year of service, down from five years.

Asia's Newsmaker of 1998

22 December Kuala Lumpur

Prime Minister Dato' Seri Dr Mahathir Mohamad was named *Time* magazine's Asia's Newsmaker of 1998. 'No one drove the news with such ferocity this year as Dr M and that makes him Asia's Newsmaker of 1998,' it said. *Time* described Dr Mahathir, who turned 73 on 20 December, as brisk, modern, quick to diagnose and even readier to prescribe. It said the events of 1998 had put a sharp focus on the Dr Mahathir era and his outspokenness has put Malaysia, indeed the developing world, on the map.

The Malaysian team enters the National Stadium for the opening of the Commonwealth Games, the biggest sporting event ever held in Malaysia.

16th Commonwealth Games

11–22 September Kuala Lumpur

After six years of hard work, the 16th Commonwealth Games, the biggest sporting extravaganza ever staged in Malaysia, opened in spectacular fashion. The Yang di-Pertuan Agong Tuanku Ja'afar officiated at the lively and colourful event which lasted four hours.

The Games were also the biggest since their inception in 1930. Apart from the 100,000 people in the National Stadium, a record 800 million television viewers watched worldwide. There were 5,000 performers in the cultural show after the opening ceremony.

Bowling, the newest sport in the Commonwealth Games, gave Malaysia its first gold through Kenny Ang and Ben Heng. Despite a broken arm, Nurul Huda Baharin won Malaysia's first-ever Commonwealth Games gold in shooting. The country's grand total of golds was 10.

Giant dragons featured in the cultural presentation at the Games' opening ceremony.

The Games closed on the night of 22 September with another spectacular ceremony which featured the 20,000 volunteers who had worked for the event's success.

Nurul Huda's keen eye won Malaysia its first-ever Commonwealth Games gold in shooting.

Ben Heng and Kenny Ang (right) celebrate their victory in bowling.

1999

Afterwards and aftermath: the recession was 'comfortably over' said Bank Negara Malaysia; IGP Tan Sri Abdul Rahim Noor quit after taking responsibility for Anwar Ibrahim's black eye; Anwar Ibrahim was sent to jail after being found guilty on four counts of corrupt practice; the bulls were back at KLSE; and the IMF admitted that Malaysia's capital controls were the right prescriptions for its economic malady. Onward and forward: the Prime Minister's Office moved to Putrajaya; the inaugural Petronas Malaysia F1 Grand Prix was a resounding success; brothers Gerald and Justin Read walked to the North Pole; and *Kampung Boy*, the animated series, won a top prize at the Annecy Awards, one of the oldest and largest animation festivals in France.

FEBRUARY
Penang's heritage area is transformed into 19th-century Bangkok for the Hollywood film *Anna and the King.*

APRIL
Brothers Gerald and Justin Read are the first Malaysians to walk to the North Pole.

AUGUST
Datuk Azhar Mansor becomes the first person to sail solo around the world on a new west–east route.

SEPTEMBER
Sultan Salahuddin Abdul Aziz Shah of Selangor is installed as the 11th Yang di-Pertuan Agong.

June: The new Prime Minister's Office, Putrajaya.

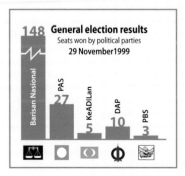

General election results
Seats won by political parties
29 November 1999

Party	Seats
Barisan Nasional	148
PAS	27
KeADILan	5
DAP	10
PBS	3

'Confidence has returned. The industries themselves have increased production.'

Bank Negara Governor Tan Sri Ali Abul Hassan Sulaiman, on the end of the recession, 26 August 1999.

1999

world news

8 January
Two officials of Salt Lake City in the US resign in a bribery scandal connected with the award of the 2002 Winter Olympics to the city.

5 February
Bill and Melinda Gates donate US$3.3 billion to their charitable foundations.

14 February
Megawati Sukarnoputri launches the PDI Struggle Party in Indonesia.

16 February:
Turkish commandos capture Kurd leader Abdullah Ocalan in Kenya. Kurds seize Greek missions round Europe and take hostages.

15 March
The Indonesian Government closes 38 banks, takes over seven and bails out nine to revitalise the financial system.

19 March
Bertrand Piccard and Brian Jones complete the first non-stop circumnavigation of the world in a balloon.

IGP quits

7 January Kuala Lumpur

Taking responsibility: Tan Sri Rahim.

Inspector General of Police Tan Sri Abdul Rahim Noor has announced his resignation after taking full responsibility for injuries suffered by former Deputy Prime Minister Dato' Seri Anwar Ibrahim while in police custody.

He said his decision followed a statement from Attorney-General Tan Sri Mohtar Abdullah which held the police fully responsible for Anwar's injuries. Datuk Seri Anwar was arrested on 20 September last year. He appeared in the Sessions Court on 29 September with a black left eye and told the court that he was beaten unconscious on the first night of his arrest.

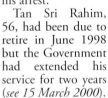

'Beaten unconscious': Dato' Seri Anwar.

Tan Sri Rahim, 56, had been due to retire in June 1998 but the Government had extended his service for two years (*see 15 March 2000*).

Pulling out the stops

29 January Kuala Lumpur

The 44-stop Klais pipe organ in the Dewan Filharmonik Petronas at the KL City Centre was inaugurated with three days of recitals by one of the world's leading organists, Simon Preston. The 2,977 pipes range in length from just 2.5cm to 10m.

The huge organ dominates the rear of the orchestra platform in the Dewan Filharmonik.

Abdullah is Deputy PM

8 January Kuala Lumpur

Dato' Seri Abdullah Ahmad Badawi (below) became Deputy Prime Minister and Home Minister. Announcing this after an Umno supreme council meeting, Prime Minister Dato' Seri Dr Mahathir Mohamad also named Tun Daim Zainuddin as Finance Minister. Dato' Seri Abdullah's appointment was welcomed by Barisan Nasional leaders, who said they felt it would strengthen the nation's political stability.

Buried alive in landslip

7 February Sandakan

Seventeen people were buried alive in Kampung Gelam near Sandakan, when mud and boulders rolled over four squatter homes. The dead were three mothers and 14 children. Two other girls were injured.

Guilty plea to firearms possession charge

2 February Kuala Lumpur

Former Magnum Corporation Bhd public affairs director Datuk S. Nallakaruppan, 52, was sentenced to 42 months' jail by the High Court after he pleaded guilty to keeping 125 bullets without a permit.

He was originally charged under the Internal Security Act which provides for the death sentence but this was amended by the prosecution. Judge Datuk Arifin Jaka said Nallakaruppan 'should thank his lucky stars' for that. He ordered that Nallakaruppan's jail term begin from the date of his arrest, 31 July 1998.

Graveyards found

20 February Kota Tinggi

The Johor Heritage Foundation uncovered two burial sites at Ulu Sungai Che Omar and Bukit Telepok, with about 40 graves. Its director Zalil Baron said the tombstones had Quranic inscriptions, indicating that the graves belonged to Malay Rulers, court officials and warriors, but added that it had yet to identify who was buried there.

MCA's proven record

17 February Sitiawan

The MCA had always worked closely with Chinese associations in the interests of community and nation-building, its president Dato' Seri Dr Ling Liong Sik said at the party's 50th anniversary celebrations organised by Lumut MCA.

Shall we dance? Filming goes on in the streets of Penang.

Hollywood comes to Penang

28 February Penang

Location shooting of *Anna and the King* in Penang's heritage enclave area brought traffic there almost to a standstill as thousands of people hoped to catch a glimpse of stars Jodie Foster and Chow Yun Fat. They played Englishwoman Anna Leonowen and King Mongkut respectively. The presence of 10 elephants, several oxen and goats also made for a curious sight.

Traffic police had to close off some of the roads in the vicinity of Armenian Street which was transformed, depicting a thriving market place in 19th-century Bangkok.

A Johor Heritage Foundation curator makes notes at the graves found at Bukit Telepok.

All about Malaysia

3 March Kuala Lumpur

The launch of the first five volumes of *The Encyclopedia of Malaysia*, published by Editions Didier Millet, marked a significant milestone in the country's publishing history. The entire encyclopedia was to consist of 15 volumes (later extended to 16 volumes) containing 1,100 double-page articles and almost 10,000 illustrations. More than 450 contributors were involved, most of them leading Malaysian academics.

Fisherman mourns as freed dugong dies

10 March Pasir Gudang

Barely 48 hours after it was released into the open sea by Johor Fisheries Department officials, Si Tenang the baby dugong was found dead by a fisherman near the spot where it was released.

Well-wishers gather round as the dugong is cared for.

Just 30 metres away, Atan Husin, the fisherman who cared for the badly-bruised dugong when he found it in his net on 25 January, was keeping vigil, hoping for Si Tenang to return. When Si Tenang's carcass was brought to his kelong, Atan, 50, broke down and cradled it in his arms. The carcass was taken away for examination.

The World Wide Fund for Nature (WWF) Malaysia said lessons could be learned from the death of the dugong which, it said, could have survived had it been released immediately. 'Every day that a wild animal is in captivity reduces the chances of its surviving in the wild,' said WWF marine biologist Chitramala Nadarajah.

BN wins in Sabah

13 March Kota Kinabalu

Barisan Nasional emerged the clear winner in Sabah's State elections with an unexpected 31 seats out of the 48 contested. But three of BN's component party leaders fell. They were Chief Minister and Parti Demokratik Sabah leader Tan Sri Bernard Dompok, Deputy Chief Minister and Parti Bersatu Rakyat Sabah president Datuk Joseph Kurup and State MCA chief Chau Tet On.

New IGP appointed

16 April Kuala Lumpur

Deputy Inspector General of Police Tan Sri Norian Mai, 52, was appointed Inspector-General of Police. A history graduate, he joined the police in 1969.

The appointment, effective 8 January when his predecessor resigned, was announced by Deputy Prime Minister Dato' Seri Abdullah Ahmad Badawi who was also Home Minister.

Graft: Anwar found guilty

14 April Kuala Lumpur

Former Deputy Prime Minister Dato' Seri Anwar Ibrahim was found guilty and jailed for six years by the High Court on four counts of corrupt practice. He was accused of interfering in police investigations into allegations of sexual misconduct against him.

He was sentenced to six years' jail on each of the four charges, the sentences to run concurrently. Judge Datuk S. Augustine Paul ordered the sentence to take effect from today and disallowed bail pending appeal.

Anwar was sacked as Deputy Prime Minister and Finance Minister on 2 September 1998 amid allegations of sexual misconduct leading to the trial that began on 2 November.

After learning of the verdict, groups of Reformasi demonstrators protested and some clashed with police near the High Court building, throwing stones and empty bottles at riot police who replied with water cannon and tear gas. Calm returned by late evening (*see 8 August 2000*).

Demonstrators on the day the court handed down its verdict.

New 'Nipah' virus discovered as 92 die

26 March Kuala Lumpur ▶ The Health Ministry spelt out precautionary measures for pig farmers, farm workers, lorry drivers, attendants and abattoir workers to counter an outbreak of what was believed to be Japanese encephalitis (JE). Abattoir workers were advised to wear protective clothing.

Health Minister Datuk Chua Jui Meng advised them to seek medical treatment if they had drowsiness, giddiness, headache or fever. He said 14 of 52 reported deaths and 29 of 159 reported cases had been confirmed as JE while the other casualties were believed to have been caused by a new type of virus which spreads from pigs to humans. More than 420,000 pigs were surrendered for culling.

Later it was discovered that the new virus was responsible for many of the deaths. The number killed by JE and the new virus was 92, including 15 at a pig-farming community in Ipoh.

The new virus, which crippled the pig-rearing industry, was named Nipah after the village Kampung Baru Sungai Nipah in Negeri Sembilan where it was first detected by Universiti Malaya experts on 18 March. Datuk Chua said the Nipah virus, the first known example of its kind in the world, was discovered by Dr Chua Kaw Ping from the Medical Microbiology Department of Universiti Malaya.

Parti Keadilan launched

4 April Kuala Lumpur

Datin Seri Dr Wan Azizah Wan Ismail, wife of the former Deputy Prime Minister Dato' Seri Anwar Ibrahim, launched Parti Keadilan, claiming that it marked a new dawn in Malaysian politics. Party deputy president Dr Chandra Muzaffar said its first task, if elected to power, would be to seek a royal pardon for Dato' Seri Anwar. 'If this is granted then the Prime Minister will be Anwar Ibrahim,' he said.

RM3.9m auction

4 April Kuala Lumpur

Dana Khas Negara, a fund which enables Malaysians to donate gifts to the Government in times of economic difficulty, said it expected to raise more than RM3.9 million from an auction of items including foreign banknotes worth RM30,000 given by the Prime Minister, jewellery and a RM300,000 bungalow.

Brothers Gerald (right) and Justin Read show their determination before setting out on their walk.

Malaysian brothers reach North Pole

19 April Kuala Lumpur

Gerald and Justin Read became the first Malaysians to walk to the North Pole. Gerald, 25, and Justin, 19, were elated at their conquest. Justin was especially thrilled as he might have set a new world record as the youngest person to have made the journey. The brothers began their walk on 12 April accompanied by a guide and two film crew members.

Bulls back at KLSE

5 May Kuala Lumpur

The KLSE composite index breached the psychological 700-point mark in a 13-month high. The heavy trading seemed to confirm that confidence was back in the market. The market opened stronger and rapidly went up on high volumes with heavy buying on blue-chip stocks.

Traders pointed out that it was obvious from the quality of stocks moving upwards that it could not be syndicates or punters moving the market.

Viagra for Malaysians

12 May Petaling Jaya

The first consignment of the much-awaited 'wonder drug' Viagra to treat erectile dysfunction in men arrived for distribution to hospitals, clinics and pharmacies, but would only be dispensed with a doctor's prescription. Orders worth more than RM1 million had been received before the product arrived. Erectile dysfunction was said to affect an estimated 1.6 million Malaysian men. In July, a year's supply of Viagra was a prize in a charity golf tournament in Petaling Jaya.

Hulu Kelang landslides

15 May Kuala Lumpur

More than 1,000 people from the Athenaeum and Wangsa Permai condominiums and a row of 20 double-storey houses facing the condominiums in Bukit Antarabangsa, Ampang-Hulu Kelang were told to evacuate their homes after several landslides hit the area.

Ampang Jaya Municipal Council president Mohamad Nik said the residents were told to leave for their own safety.

Drug offender sought after rape-murder case

21 May Kuala Lumpur

Police set up a team to track down a man whom they believe may be able to help them solve a rape-cum-murder case.

They had a photograph of the man taken when he was arrested earlier by police for drug offences.

The body of Audrey Melissa Patinathan, a Form Five pupil of the Methodist Girls' Secondary School, was found in the undergrowth not far from her school off Jalan Kinabalu.

1999

17 April
The BJP coalition loses a vote of confidence in the Indian Parliament by one vote. PM Vajpayee resigns. The Congress Party will form the new Government.

20 April
In the Columbine High School, Jefferson County, Colorado, in the US, two teenagers gun down 12 students then kill themselves.

7 May
Three Chinese Embassy staff in Belgrade are killed when NATO planes mistakenly attack the building.

12 July
Taiwan President Lee Teng-Hui abandons the 'one-China' policy in favour of a State-to-State relationship with the mainland.

15 July
Indonesian election results give Megawati's party 34% of 122 million votes and the ruling Golkar Party 22%.

17 August
A 7.4-magnitude earthquake strikes Izmit, Turkey, killing more than 17,000.

'Kampung Boy' wins top award

14 June **Kuala Lumpur**

An episode of *Kampung Boy*, the animated series, won a top international prize at one of the world's oldest and largest animation festivals, the Annecy Awards, in France. The episode, *Oh, Tok!*, defeated contenders from Iran, Canada, Britain and Spain, and even the American cartoon series *Dennis the Menace*.

The cartoonist Datuk Mohamed Nor Khalid, better known as Lat, created the series based on his cartoon book *Kampung Boy*.

Kampung boy: Datuk Lat with his creation.

Giant mattress sets a record

29 May **Kuala Lumpur**

Visitors to the Tax-Free Sales Carnival at the Bukit Jalil Sports Complex managed to grab a snooze too. Mattress manufacturer Far East Foam Industries entered the *Malaysian Book of Records* with a giant mattress measuring 11.7m by 24.6m, placed outside the carnival enclosure. The public was given a chance to lie down on the mattress and 250 people of all ages and sizes did so.

Cyberjaya 'is proof of commitment'

9 July **Cyberjaya**

The quick completion of Cyberjaya despite recent economic difficulties was proof of Malaysia's commitment to all investors in the Multimedia Super Corridor (MSC), said Prime Minister Dato' Seri Dr Mahathir Mohamad at the official opening of Cyberjaya and the 3rd MSC International Advisory Panel meeting at Cyber View Lodge.

Even during the downturn, the MSC was given priority in terms of both budget allocation and policy support. Thirty-two world-class web-shapers had obtained MSC status, though the target was only 50 by 2003. Out of 85 companies applying for MSC status 25 had obtained it, with 21 companies, including eight with MSC status, already located in Cyberjaya.

New CLOB deal

30 June **Kuala Lumpur**

A new effort was made to resolve the impasse over the Central Limit Order Book International (CLOB) when Telekom Malaysia Bhd and United Engineers (M) Bhd made a joint bid to acquire all Malaysian shares previously traded on CLOB.

Trading of Malaysian shares on CLOB stopped after capital controls were imposed by the Government in 1998. The system was now defunct and the RM3.7 billion in shares, mainly held by Singaporeans, left in limbo.

The Telekom–UEM bid was based on the day's closing prices on the Kuala Lumpur Stock Exchange. Trading of Telekom and UEM shares on the KLSE was suspended following their announcements.

Economy bouncing back into growth

23 June **Kuala Lumpur**

The Malaysian economy was back in positive mood, posting growth of 1.4 per cent for February and March compared to the same period a year earlier.

However, for the first three months of the year, gross domestic product was still 1.3 per cent lower than previously.

Overall, the first quarter performance was a sharp improvement from the 10.3 per cent contraction experienced in the fourth quarter of 1998, prompting Bank Negara Governor Tan Sri Ali Abul Hassan Sulaiman to say that the official one per cent growth forecast for 1999 would likely be exceeded.

Fire hits cruise ship on the high seas

20 May **Penang**

All 1,090 passengers and crew members of the Bahamas-registered luxury cruise vessel *Sun Vista* were rescued from its burning deck by 14 ships, including two navy vessels from Lumut and one each from the Marine Department and the Marine police, and two ferries sent by the ill-fated ship's agent.

Good weather aided the rescue operation. There were no fatalities. The ship sank at 1.22am, about 60 nautical miles south of Penang and 45 nautical miles off Kuala Sepetang.

The 437 passengers of some 20 nationalities, including Americans, British, Canadians and Japanese, left for Singapore the next day.

Former RTM newscaster jailed

23 July **Kuala Lumpur**

The magistrate's court sentenced former RTM newsreader Sharma Kumari Shukla to 12 weeks' jail after she was found guilty of giving false information to a policeman.

She had falsely claimed that four men had attempted to kidnap her son from his school in Bangsar.

Magistrate Mohamed Ilhami Idris rejected an application for a stay of execution pending her appeal. Four days later, however, she was granted a stay (*see 24 January 2000*).

P. Ramlee's eldest son Nasir shows off the range of stamps.

Special P. Ramlee stamps

24 July **Kuala Lumpur**

Special commemorative stamps and a first-day cover of the late Tan Sri P. Ramlee went on sale at post offices. Pos Malaysia Bhd said the special issue came about due to demands from stamp collectors and fans of the late actor-director-singer.

The first-day cover would have four stamps in the denominations of 20, 30, 50 sen respectively and RM1. The most special feature was the P. Ramlee special-edition stamp album which cost RM25.

Open university starts classes with 238 students

7 August **Kuala Lumpur**

The country's own distance-learning university, Universiti Terbuka Malaysia (Unitem), started operations with 238 students at the Universiti Teknologi Malaysia campus.

The first session was for the bachelor's degree course in electrical engineering. The university would use self-study modules, video conferencing, face-to-face tutorials and Internet help.

PM moves into new office in Putrajaya

21 June **Putrajaya**

Prime Minister Dato' Seri Dr Mahathir Mohamad began his first day in his new office in the nation's new administrative capital Putrajaya with a tour of the massive complex and breakfast in the cafeteria.

After a short *doa selamat* prayer ceremony with the staff, he inspected the new office block. He also announced that he had no intention of staying on as Senior Minister when he retired, an implicit reference to former Singapore premier Lee Kuan Yew who is currently Senior Minister.

Dr Mahathir arriving for work at the new office.

Dispute over Spratlys 'deal'

21 July Kuala Lumpur

Malaysia has denied that it has scuppered a plan put forward by some of its neighbours to draw China into discussions over the disputed Spratly Islands. It has also denied having 'cut a separate deal' with Beijing.

The South China Sea has been one of the main topics raised during Asean-China Senior Officials' Consultations in the past six years. The Spratlys, said to be rich in hydrocarbon resources, are currently claimed, wholly or partly, by China, Malaysia, the Philippines, Brunei, Vietnam and Taiwan. All except Brunei have placed troops on the islands.

The Philippines has submitted a draft of a Regional Code of Conduct for the South China Sea that included addressing the overlapping claims over the Spratlys. The draft was commissioned by Asean Foreign Ministers in 1996. It was initially to be a joint effort by the Philippines and Vietnam, but the latter subsequently withdrew, saying it was in no position to make any contribution.

Datuk Azhar waves to those welcoming him as he arrives.

Azhar sails home

11 August Langkawi

Datuk Azhar Mansor, 40, made history as the first person to sail solo round the world on a new west–east route. Escorted by two Royal Malaysian Navy vessels and a marine police vessel, his yacht, *Jalur Gemilang*, crossed the finishing line at 11.37pm.

As he stepped out after spending 190 days at sea, he was greeted by a large crowd which included his wife Sara Maria Abdullah and their three children, his family, friends, Prime Minister Dato' Seri Dr Mahathir Mohamad and Datin Seri Dr Siti Hasmah. Datuk Azhar had sailed some 25,333 nautical miles.

KLSE back on US indices

13 August Kuala Lumpur

American financial services company Morgan Stanley said it would reinstate Malaysia on its stock market indices. The move is expected to attract billions of ringgit in foreign funds into the KL Stock Exchange. News of the impending decision led to frantic buying on the KLSE, pushing the composite index up to 728.

SEA Games gold haul

15 August Bandar Seri Begawan

As the 20th SEA Games drew to a close, Malaysia basked in its best performance yet with a total gold haul of 57, finishing second behind Thailand. As early as the third day of the Games Malaysia swept 14 gold medals in athletics, bowling, karate, swimming, taekwondo and diving in a single day. The Malaysian contingent also won 45 silver and 42 bronze medals.

Going for gold: the medal-winning karate team.

ITM becomes UiTM

26 August Shah Alam

After 43 years and several name changes, Institut Teknologi Mara (ITM) became a university in recognition of dynamic progress and achievement in its educational programmes, said Dato' Seri Dr Mahathir Mohamad.

However, the Prime Minister added that ITM's existing function, to provide privileges for Bumiputras pursuing higher education, remained.

A spectacular part of the 1999 Merdeka Day celebrations, a fireworks display in the KLCC Park produced this image of a starburst between the Petronas Twin Towers.

Recession 'comfortably' over, says Bank Negara

24 August Kuala Lumpur

Malaysia was 'comfortably out of a recession', said Bank Negara Malaysia Governor Tan Sri Ali Abul Hassan Sulaiman when he announced that gross domestic product grew by 4.1 per cent in the second quarter. In the preceding quarter, the GDP contracted by 1.3 per cent.

'Confidence has come back and is a reflection of improvements in the banking and finance sectors. The capital controls have also enabled the Government to focus on restructuring the economy,' he said at a briefing on the second quarter economic performance at Bank Negara. Private sector activity had been driven by improved exports.

Super Titus

22 August Kuala Lumpur

At only 13 years old Titus James earned a place in the *Malaysian Book of Records* by juggling a football 5,680 times at the National Stadium in Bukit Jalil. The La Salle Brickfields student took one hour 14 minutes to achieve the feat in front of 20,000 spectators.

1999

world news

12 October
Pakistani PM Nawaz Sharif attempts to dismiss army chief Gen Musharraf. He orders Karachi Airport not to allow a plane carrying the general to land. The army takes over the airport and the plane lands with just a few minutes of fuel left.

12 October
According to the UN, on this day the world's population passes six billion.

19 October
After months of violence by pro-Indonesian militia following a referendum vote for independence and the intervention of the UN, Indonesia relinquishes its claim to East Timor.

20 December
The administration of Macau reverts to China from Portugal.

31 December
Millennium celebrations begin around the world.

11th King installed

23 September **Kuala Lumpur**

Selangor's Sultan Salahuddin Abdul Aziz Shah Alhaj Ibni Al-marhum Sultan Hisamuddin Alam Shah Alhaj was installed as Malaysia's 11th Yang di-Pertuan Agong. The Raja Permaisuri Agong Tuanku Siti Aishah was also present at the ceremony at Istana Negara.

Drivers let-off

16 September **Shah Alam**

Police revoked all notices of traffic offences issued this year because of what they described as difficulty in identifying the drivers.

Malaysian to head UN outer space affairs

15 September **Kuala Lumpur**

Professor Datuk Dr Mazlan Othman, director-general of the National Space Science Division, was appointed to head the United Nations Office for Outer Space

Affairs, based in Vienna, for two years. The appointment underlined the UN's recognition of Malaysia's contribution to the call for the peaceful use of outer space and space technologies.

Military team will join UN force in Timor

16 September **Kuala Lumpur**

Malaysia agreed to send a team of military officers to join a United Nations force going to East Timor to restore order and would deploy a larger peacekeeping force there, Foreign Minister Dato' Seri Syed Hamid Albar said. The decision followed a review of developments in East Timor.

IMF admits capital controls were right

9 September **Kuala Lumpur**

The International Monetary Fund, which criticised Malaysia for imposing selective capital controls, admitted that the measures produced 'more positive results than many observers had initially expected'.

A document summarising the IMF's review of the Malaysian economy said the controls have been applied in a 'pragmatic and flexible way'.

When it introduced selective capital controls, including fixing the ringgit's exchange rate at 3.80 to the US dollar, on 1 September 1998, the Government made it clear that the measures were aimed at insulating domestic interest rates from continuing pressures and volatility in the foreign exchange market.

Going strong at 102

30 December **Malacca**

At 102, Tampi Kasan Muniat was one of the rare few who lived through the whole of the 20th century. Tampi was born in Java, Indonesia, in 1897.

To celebrate, she would spend New Year's Day with her only son, 79-year-old Ahmad Nor, 12 grandchildren, 40 great-grandchildren and 21 great-great-grandchildren.

Mahathir takes UN to task

30 September **New York**

Dr Mahathir addressing the United Nations.

Prime Minister Dato' Seri Dr Mahathir Mohamad said no change could be expected of the United Nations as long as it was controlled by its five permanent members, the United States, Russia, China, the United Kingdom and France.

'The structure of the United Nations will continue to reflect the glorious victory of these nations 50 years ago,' he said in a scathing address to the 54th session of the UN General Assembly. Small member States, said the Prime Minister, would have to be content with making annual speeches at the General Assembly and the various UN anniversaries. Occasionally, they would be elected to the Security Council.

He took to task the world body for practising what he called 'rather unusual principles', and went on to cite the selection of UN human rights commissioners. He was clearly referring to the appointment of the UN Commission of Human Rights' Special Rapporteur on the Independence of Judges and Lawyers, Datuk Param Cumaraswamy, who had clashed with the Government.

First Malaysian GP a roaring success

15 October **Sepang**

The best in the world: F1 cars in action at the Grand Prix.

The fine weather helped make the inaugural Petronas Malaysia F1 Grand Prix a big success with few hitches and plenty of excitement. Led by Dato' Seri Dr Mahathir Mohamad, Malaysians were in a frenzy at the Sepang circuit which took on a carnival-like atmosphere.

Veteran TV commentator Murray Walker of the United Kingdom-based ITV, who had covered Formula One at every circuit for 51 years, declared: 'This circuit is absolutely fantastic. It not only met my best expectation but exceeded it. This is without a doubt the finest Formula One venue in the world.'

Alex Lee dies

31 October **Kuala Lumpur**

Former National Unity and Social Development Deputy Minister Datuk Alexander Lee Yu Lung succumbed to his injuries while scuba diving in Papua New Guinea today. He was 60. His wife Datin Irene Jucker was with him when he was flown to a hospital in Darwin, Australia, where he was pronounced dead.

Tribute to Iban leaders

17 November **Kuching**

At the launching of the book, *A Life Story Of Temenggong Koh*, Sarawak Chief Minister Tan Sri Haji Abdul Taib Mahmud paid tribute to two Iban leaders — the late Temenggong Koh and Tun Jugah—saying that they had transformed the community. He described Temenggong Koh as a visionary and warrior.

Wedding couples aboard LRT

11 September **Kuala Lumpur**

Some 20 couples took the LRT to their wedding ceremony at the National Stadium in Bukit Jalil. They boarded specially-decorated STAR-LRT coaches from Masjid Jamek station in Kuala Lumpur. The event was held in conjunction with the launch of the Domestic Tourism Campaign and Malaysia Fest '99.

2000

A massive fireworks display at the Petronas Twin Towers ushered in the millennium year before new challenges faced the nation. In April, pirates took 20 hostages on Sipadan Island, off Sabah. Six months later, Abu Sayyaf gunmen abducted three Malaysians from Pulau Pandanan, also off Sabah. Anwar Ibrahim was sentenced to nine years' jail for sodomy. Women again made headlines: squash wonder Nicol David was named Sportswoman of the Year, Datuk Dr Zeti Akhtar Aziz was appointed the seventh Governor of Bank Negara, and Datuk Ainun Mohamed Saaid became the first woman Attorney-General. Other news: Malaysians were amused to read that a global sex survey had found them to be among the world's most inactive people in bed.

JANUARY
The Kuala Lumpur skyline in the new millennium.

APRIL
Datuk Dr Zeti Akhtar Aziz becomes the first woman to head Bank Negara Malaysia.

OCTOBER
Johor declares an outbreak of hand, foot and mouth disease in the State.

NOVEMBER
The Government Multi-Purpose Smart Card replaces the Malaysian identity card.

April: The Sipadan hostage-takers pose for a photograph.

Malaysia Facts		
23.3 million	Population	
RM343.2 billion	Gross Domestic Product	
RM13,378	Gross National Income (per capita)	
24.5	Crude Birth Rate (per 1,000 persons)	
5.7	Infant Mortality (per 1,000 live births)	
70.2 / 75.0	Life Expectancy (male / female)	
80.4	Consumer Price Index (base 2010=100)	

'It is important to ensure that national unity and social harmony remain the overriding objective of national development.'

Statement by Malaysia to the 28th Session of the International Fund for Agricultural Development Governing Council, 2000.

world news

29 February
Independence war veterans invade and occupy 36 white-owned farms in Zimbabwe.

16 March
A Pakistani judge sentences a murderer of 100 children to the same fate as that suffered by his victims: strangulation, dismemberment and dissolving in acid. The man hangs himself before sentence is executed.

18 March
Chen Shui-bian is elected President of Taiwan, ending 51 years of Nationalist Party rule.

26 March
Vladimir Putin is elected President of Russia.

13 June
Kim Jong-Il of North Korea and Kim Dae Jung of South Korea meet face-to-face in talks on reconciliation, the first time leaders of the two countries have doe so.

29 June
A ferry carrying 492 refugees fleeing from sectarian violence in the Moluccas sinks. Only 10 survive.

Millennium party: No glitches

1 January Kuala Lumpur

As the clock struck 12, Malaysians joined people in the same time zone to usher in the Year 2000 with fireworks and partying in the streets and without the much-publicised Millennium Bug glitches. One of the most spectacular celebrations in Kuala Lumpur was a massive fireworks display at the Petronas Twin Towers.

Ex-newsreader jailed

24 January Kajang

Former RTM newsreader Sharma Shukla was sent to the Kajang Prison after losing her appeal in the High Court against her conviction and 12-week jail sentence for giving the police false information.

On 24 July 1999, magistrate Mohamed Ilhami Idris found her guilty of giving false information when she said four men were attempting to kidnap her son from his school and had alleged that Judge Abdullah Sani Mohd Hashim was the brother of one of the four men.

In a separate case, Mr Justice Dr R.K. Nathan also dismissed with costs her appeal against a decision not to set aside a bankruptcy notice filed by Abdullah Sani and a plea from her to disqualify him as judge in the cases.

Sharma is led away to jail.

Trade surplus soars

4 February Kuala Lumpur

Malaysia recorded its largest trade surplus to date: RM72.3 billion in 1999, almost 24 per cent higher than the previous year's total. The increase was led by exports of electrical and electronic products, according to the Statistics Department.

Exports were up 12.1 per cent, at RM321.2 billion, continuing to outpace imports, which rose 9.1 per cent to RM248.9 billion, a 'remarkable' performance, said the department.

Wave of bank mergers

14 February Kuala Lumpur

Bank Negara Malaysia had granted approval for the formation of 10 banking groups through a series of mergers, Governor Tan Sri Ali Abul Hassan Sulaiman announced. Each would have an asset base of at least RM25 billion, he said.

Killer croc found dead

7 February Gedong

A 5.2m crocodile was found dead at the place where it attacked and killed 10-year-old girl Ros Umba anak Wat from Kampung Sg Benat Ulu in Sarawak's Simunjan District recently. The crocodile, named Bujang Gedong, was believed to have taken baits set by bomohs.

Landmark turtle statue removed

1 March Kuala Terengganu

Terengganu, the land of the turtle, no longer had a monument to represent this after a turtle statue at a roundabout near Ladang in Kuala Terengganu was removed by Public Works Department workers. The statue was put up in the 1970s under the then Barisan Nasional State Government. No reason was given for its removal.

Dr Mahathir wins unopposed

26 March Kuala Lumpur

Prime Minister Dato' Seri Dr Mahathir Mohamad was returned unopposed as Umno party president. He received nominations from 35 divisions, giving him the required 133 nominations to win the seat uncontested. DPM Dato' Seri Abdullah Ahmad Badawi won the Umno deputy presidency the following day after receiving 133 nominations.

Cap on mobile phone access fee removed

31 March Kuala Lumpur

The RM60 cap on mobile phone access fees was removed so that rates could be determined by market forces, said Minister of Energy, Communications and Multimedia Datuk Leo Moggie.

Ex-IGP jailed over Anwar beating

15 March Kuala Lumpur

Former Inspector General of Police Tan Sri Abdul Rahim Noor was sentenced to two months' jail and fined RM2,000 by a Sessions Court for punching Dato' Seri Anwar Ibrahim, who was blindfolded and handcuffed at the time, at the Bukit Aman lock-up about 10.45pm on 20 September 1998. Judge Akhtar Tahir allowed an application for a stay of execution pending appeal to the High Court and released Tan Sri Abdul Rahim on bail of RM5,000.

On 15 December, the High Court upheld the sentence. Judge Datuk Zulkefli Ahmad Makinudin, however, set aside the RM2,000 fine imposed.

Tunku's widow dies at 80

12 March Penang

Tun Sharifah Rodziah Syed Alwi Barakbah, widow of the first Prime Minister and Bapa Malaysia Tunku Abdul Rahman, died at the Penang Hospital, aged 80.

Prime Minister Dato' Seri Dr Mahathir Mohamad, his wife Datin Seri Dr Siti Hasmah and deputy Dato' Seri Abdullah Ahmad Badawi were among the dignitaries who paid their last respects at her funeral the following day. Dr Mahathir paid tribute to the way she had supported her husband.

Sporting awards

3 April Subang Jaya

Cyclist Shahrulneeza Razali (top) and squash wonder Nicol David were named the National Sportsman and Sportswoman of the Year 1999. Each won RM10,000 and a trophy.

Shahrulneeza won the honour for winning two gold medals at the Brunei SEA Games and Nicol won it for bagging the World Junior title in Antwerp, Belgium as well as team and individual gold medals at the SEA Games.

More score 10 A1s

4 April Kuala Lumpur

The number of students who scored 10 A1s in the Sijil Pelajaran Malaysia examination increased from 65 in 1999 to 189 in 2000. Perak had the highest number of top scorers (38) followed by Malacca (24), Kuala Lumpur (22) and Kedah and Negeri Sembilan (18 each).

Cloned ATM cards

5 April Penang

Ban Hin Lee Bank handed to the police more than 40 cloned automated teller machine cards after they investigated withdrawals from several branches in Penang. Another 183 cases amounting to more than RM300,000 were reported to the police later. Fraudulent withdrawals were also detected in Selangor, Kuala Lumpur, Kedah, Perak and Johor.

Dato' Seri Abdullah Ahmad Badawi told banks to investigate immediately and prevent such cloning. 'Unless something is done to check the problem, the public will lose confidence in the institution and start a run on the country's banks,' he said.

'No' to unisex salons

10 April Kuala Terengganu

The Kuala Terengganu Municipal Council has banned unisex hairdressing salons in line with the State's policy to introduce an Islamic administration.

Medium 'raped hawker'

3 May Batu Pahat

A 36-year-old hawker who went to a medium to help improve business was told 'evil spirits' were in her. The medium told her to strip so that he could find them, then raped her twice, said Michael Chong, head of the MCA Public Services and Complaints Department.

Addicts hit by lightning

3 May Rawang

Five drug addicts undergoing rehabilitation at the Pusat Serenti here were killed when they and 17 others were struck by lightning while having a tea break in the garden. Fourteen were badly injured.

Hostages taken in island raid

23 April Sipadan Island

A Filipino doctor, watched by gunmen, treats two of the Sipadan Island hostages.

Six heavily-armed gunmen took nine Malaysians and 11 foreigners hostage on Sipadan Island, off the Sabah coast. Police said the gunmen were armed with AK-47 assault rifles and a bazooka. Inspector General of Police Tan Sri Norian Mai said the kidnappers fled with the hostages in two boats towards Philippine waters. Three days later, Philippine Defence Secretary Orlando Mercado said the captives were being held in Talipao town on Jolo Island by a unit of the Abu Sayyaf, confirming for the first time the group's claim that it was behind the kidnapping (*see 10 September 2000*).

Apology as patient gets HIV-tainted blood

17 May Kuala Lumpur

The Cabinet issued an apology over the incident where a 47-year-old woman was given blood contaminated with HIV at the Jitra Hospital in Kedah in April. Acting Health Minister Datuk Dr Fong Chan Onn said it had also directed the Health Ministry to review blood-screening procedures to prevent a recurrence. 'We are very sorry and will provide her with medical treatment and the necessary support to make her life comfortable and help her family to continue leading normal lives,' he said.

Exports push GDP up

24 May Kuala Lumpur

It was reported that Malaysia's Gross Domestic Product grew by 11.7 per cent during the first quarter of 2000.

This was underpinned by strong demand for exports and rising private sector expenditure.

70% failed UPSR, says Ministry

20 May Kuala Lumpur

More than 70 per cent of pupils failed the UPSR school examination in 1999, according to an Education Ministry survey of 1,786 primary schools nationwide.

MCA president Datuk Dr Ling Liong Sik said the 'under-performing schools' comprised 433 Chinese schools, 402 Tamil schools and 951 national schools.

Return of a legend

31 May Kuala Lumpur

Descendants of Mahsuri, the beautiful maiden of the island of Langkawi who was falsely accused of adultery and executed but became the island's heroine, were invited to return from Phuket, Thailand.

Culture, Tourism and Arts Minister Datuk Abdul Kadir Sheikh Fadzir said homes, education and suitable jobs would be provided.

James Puthucheary dies

4 April Kuala Lumpur

James Puthucheary, anti-colonial fighter, politician, lawyer, trade unionist, economist, intellectual, poet, political activist, and chairman of the Central Provident Fund and Industrial Promotion Board of Singapore, died of a stroke today at the age of 77.

Born in India, Puthucheary moved to Malaya at a young age and was educated in Johor and Singapore before graduating with a Bachelor of Arts honours degree from the University of Malaya in Singapore in 1954.

Always the activist (he was jailed from 1956 to 1959), nevertheless upon his final release from detention in November 1963, Puthucheary declared that he would go into private law practice, which he did until 1993, fulfilling his ambition of a 'quiet life of law'.

Woman head for Bank Negara

22 April Kuala Lumpur

Datuk Dr Zeti Akhtar Aziz was appointed the seventh governor of Bank Negara. The first woman to lead the central bank, Datuk Dr Zeti, 52, took over from Tan Sri Ali Abul Hassan Sulaiman. Her appointment became effective on 1 May.

Datuk Dr Zeti's appointment proved that Malaysian women could reach the top position in their field of expertise, said Deputy Prime Minister Dato' Seri Abdullah Ahmad Badawi. 'It is a show of respect for her abilities, capabilities and expertise and not because she is a woman.'

Datuk Dr Zeti, the daughter of former Universiti Malaya Vice-Chancellor Royal Professor Ungku Aziz, joined the economics board of Bank Negara in 1985 and was appointed secretary to its board in 1987. Prof. Ungku Aziz and his wife Puan Azah Aziz expressed joy at the appointment of their only child.

Datuk Dr Zeti: Appointment was show of respect for her abilities.

2000

Take a walk on the skybridge

30 May **Kuala Lumpur**

The Petronas Twin Towers was open to the public today. Hundreds of Malaysians and foreign tourists waited for their turn to get inside and up to the skybridge connecting the 88-storey towers at the 41st and 42nd floors.

The 41st floor is 170 metres above street level and there are 29 double-deck high-speed lifts and 10 escalators in each tower. At least 400 visitors were expected to visit the skybridge each day.

The Twin Towers building was officially opened by Prime Minister Dato' Seri Dr Mahathir Mohamad on 31 August 1999.

Admission to the skybridge was and remains free but there were only 1,300 timed tickets for a 10-minute stay a day, given out on a first-come-first-served basis, which meant long queues formed.

Two young visitors admire the view from the Petronas Twin Towers skybridge.

Back to driving school

5 June **Kuala Lumpur**

Motorists with the maximum 15 demerit points for traffic offences could soon take a three-day advanced driving skills course instead of having their licences suspended, said Road Transport Department director-general Datuk Shahar Sidek. The option would be available once the curriculum for the course was finalised.

Brothers in crime

14 June **Kuala Lumpur**

Police said they had arrested two unemployed brothers aged 26 and 30 believed to have been involved in 79 snatch thefts.

Brickfields OCPD ACP Koh Hong Sun said police had recovered ID cards, handbags, ATM and credit cards, several BonusLink cards and a motorcycle.

Sanctuary for orang utan

10 June **Taiping** ▶ A two-hectare sanctuary was being developed for the conservation and breeding of animals at the orang utan island in Bukit Merah Laketown Resort, near Taiping. It would provide an opportunity for researchers and students to study and observe orang utan in a natural habitat.

Taste of Malaysia

19 June **Birmingham**

From roti canai makers to suppliers of bubur pulut hitam, a three-day European Ethnic Food Exhibition in Birmingham, UK, became a platform enabling Malaysian manufacturers of convenience meals and condiments to tap the RM30-billion British ethnic food industry.

No charges against 49 people in night spots

28 June **Petaling Jaya**

No charges would be brought against 49 people detained by officers of the Religious Department (Jais) at three nightspots here on 11 June as there was not enough evidence, said Menteri Besar Dato' Seri Abu Hassan Omar.

They included singer Azlina Abbas, who was held for 'being in premises where alcohol is served'. Dato' Seri Abu Hassan said Jais enforcement officers were not empowered to detain Muslims who entered or were in a place where liquor was sold. It was not an offence for Muslims to be in such a place.

Petronas records its best-ever results

29 June **Kuala Lumpur**

Petroliam Nasional Bhd (Petronas) recorded an 83 per cent increase in pre-tax profit of RM21.6 billion for the year ended 31 March, its best-ever result.

'The last financial year has been very exciting and rewarding,' said Petronas chairman Tan Sri Azizan Zainul Abidin. The strong performance was a result of the decision to globalise, integrate and add value to Petronas's business.

Stolen shoes sold at pasar malam

29 June **Kuala Lumpur**

Bangsar residents whose shoes and slippers were stolen from their doorsteps found them on sale at the area's pasar malam, said Bukit Bandaraya Residents Association spokesman K. Kanagandram. He described it as 'a nightmare come true.'

Teenage genius runs away from home

3 July **London**

Sufiah Farooq Yusof, a teenage prodigy who in 1997 secured a place at Oxford University to read mathematics at the age of 12, vanished from her flat in Oxford for 17 days before Thames Valley police found her safe and well.

Before she was found, her father Farooq Yusof, a Pakistani Briton, and her Malaysian mother Halimahton Yusof said she could have been kidnapped or influenced by certain quarters in order 'to break the family'. But she was adamant that she would not return home (*see 5 April 2008*).

Go ahead for Bakun

2 July **Kuching**

The Bakun Hydroelectric Dam project would go ahead, with the backing of the Federal Government. Sarawak Deputy Chief Minister Tan Sri Dr George Chan said work on the dam's diversion tunnels was expected to be completed very soon. The project was estimated to cost between RM12 billion and RM14 billion.

Ecstasy crisis

1 August **Kuala Lumpur**

The MCA declared war on the Ecstasy pill menace with a procession around the city distributing anti-Ecstasy posters. The campaign was aimed at creating awareness of the dangers of the pills among youth in the country, their parents and enforcement authorities.

The Government had warned that offenders would be charged in court for possession and use of the drug.

Anwar found guilty

8 August Kuala Lumpur

Dato' Seri Anwar Ibrahim was sentenced to nine years' imprisonment by the High Court in Kuala Lumpur for sodomy. Judge Datuk Arifin Jaka ordered Anwar to serve the sentence after the completion of his current six-year jail term for corruption.

Anwar's adopted brother Sukma Darmawan Sasmitaat Madja, who was jointly tried with him, was sentenced to six years' jail with four strokes of the rotan. Anwar was spared the cane which is limited to those aged 49 years and below. He turned 53 on 10 August (*see 2 September 2004*).

KL Olympic host bid fails

28 August Lausanne

Kuala Lumpur failed in its bid to host the 2008 Olympics after the International Olympic Committee here slashed in half the 10 cities battling for the plum job.

But KL was on the starting block in Tashkent, where it bid for the 2006 Asian Games at the Olympic Council of Asia executive board meeting. The other three cities bidding for the Games were Doha, New Delhi and Hong Kong.

Woman killed in man's shooting spree

22 August Kuala Lumpur

Accountant Lee Good Yew was shot dead when a 50-year-old businessman went on a shooting spree at Jalan Bukit Petaling, near Wisma Putra, after driving on the wrong side of the road. Police recovered seven used cartridges at the scene and seized a Walther P5 from Kenneth Fook Mun Lee @ Omar Iskandar Abdullah, who was detained for questioning. The victim and attacker were not related. Kenneth was the grandson of the late Tun Sir H.S. Lee, Malaysia's first Finance Minister. His father Datuk Douglas Lee was a well-known banker and his mother was Datuk Paduka Ruby Lee the former Malaysian Red Crescent secretary-general.

The High Court sentenced Kenneth to eight years' jail on 30 June 2003 for manslaughter. However, the Court of Appeal on 26 March 2005 set aside the High Court's findings, convicted him of murder and sentenced him to death. On 10 June 2006 the Federal Court affirmed the death sentence.

Deputy Prime Minister Dato' Seri Abdullah Badawi and Transport Minister Dato' Seri Dr Ling Liong Sik examine the Proton Waja. Sales bookings opened on 30 August.

Waja unveiled in Penang

19 August Penang

The new Proton Waja made its debut in Penang at the Jalan Hatin Umno branch's golden jubilee carnival.

It was expected to go on sale in September. It was the first Proton model to be designed and engineered largely in-house with 95 per cent local content.

Petrol sees first price rise since early 1980s

30 September Kuala Lumpur

The Cabinet announced today that petrol would cost 10 sen more—up from RM1.10 to RM1.20 a litre—from 1 October.

The price of diesel was increased by five sen to 70.1 sen while liquefied petroleum gas would cost 10 sen more at RM1.28 per kg. The last increase was in the early 1980s.

Ban on arcade games

4 October Kuala Lumpur

The Cabinet imposed a total ban on video-game arcades. The Government would not issue new licences for such arcades, said Deputy Prime Minister Dato' Seri Abdullah Ahmad Badawi, and existing licences would be revoked within two months.

Dato' Seri Abdullah said the ban was 'overall' and would even include Genting Highlands. Inspector-General of Police Tan Sri Norian Mai said the police fully supported a ban on arcades and sterner action against their operators.

Amok kills four

6 October Kota Bharu

Four people were killed and five injured when a mentally-unstable man ran amok with a parang at Kampung Kubang Kawah, Pasir Mas. Among those who died from slash wounds was the man's mother.

More island hostages snatched

10 September Sabah

Just six months after gunmen took 21 Malaysians and foreigners at nearby Sipadan, it has happened again. Armed Filipino gunmen abducted three hotel staff from Pulau Pandanan, off the east coast of Sabah. It was later confirmed that Abu Sayyaf terrorists were responsible for the abduction.

Police officers said an air-and-sea search began within hours of the three men's being reported missing. The incident began when a group of unidentified gunmen arrived by speedboat on the tiny island of Pulau Pandanan, brandishing military-style M16 rifles and firing shots into the air.

There were no guests staying at the diving resort and most of the local staff fled into the surrounding jungle. The gunmen stole television sets and other booty before escaping, apparently towards international waters. All the hostages were later freed.

The hostages in captivity photographed by a freelance journalist.

Schumi wins Malaysian Grand Prix

21 October Sepang

The crowds went wild and the circuit wasa sea of Ferrari red when newly-crowned world champion Michael Schumacher, in winning the Malaysian Grand Prix, ensured that Ferrari retained the constructors' title with 170 points to McLaren's 152.

Schumacher had won his third world title in Japan two weeks ago, becoming the first Ferrari driver since South African

Michael Schumacher celebrates in traditional champagne-spraying style.

Jody Scheckter in 1979 to take the championship. It was Schumacher's ninth victory of a triumphant season, equalling the all-time record, his fourth win in succession and the 44th of his career on a day when Ferrari extended their team record to 10 wins in one year.

Outbreak of HFM disease

11 October Johor

With three deaths, Johor formally declared an outbreak of hand, foot and mouth (HFM) disease.

The Johor Government also closed all kindergartens and childcare centres in Johor Bahru district and advised people to be extra vigilant and to take their children to the doctor if they showed symptoms of the disease.

The previous day, Singapore officials had warned that the republic's worst outbreak of hand, foot and mouth disease, linked to the deaths of four children in September, was not over yet despite a decline in the number of cases.

Global sex survey

17 October Kuala Lumpur

Malaysians, it seems, were too busy for sex. The Durex Global Sex Survey 2000 found Malaysians to be among the world's most inactive people in bed. They polled second last, only higher than the Japanese, when asked how often they had sex.

Malaysians, according to the survey, had sex on average 62 times a year, while the Japanese managed only 37 times. Americans scored 132 times a year, Russians 122, French 121, Greeks 115 and Brazilians 113. At the bottom with Japan and Malaysia were China, Thailand and Taiwan.

2000

11 November
Indonesian police crack down on tens of thousands demonstrating for Acehnese independence, killing 27.

13 November
The Philippines House of Representatives approves an impeachment trial for President Joseph Estrada on corruption charges.

10 December
Jack Kilby is awarded the Nobel Prize for Physics for his invention of the microchip.

12 December
Dozens of nightclubs in Jakarta are attacked and damaged by Muslim militants.

24 December
Two dozen churches in Jakarta and other Indonesian cities and towns are bombed. Nineteen die.

Malaysia is polio-free

28 October | Kuala Lumpur

The World Health Organisation declared 37 countries, including Malaysia, Singapore, the Philippines, Brunei, Vietnam and Cambodia, and areas in the western Pacific region polio-free. Shigeru Omi, regional director of WHO in the western Pacific, said it was a victory for 1.6 billion people against the once-dreaded disease.

Bitter-sweet victory

17 November | Bangkok

After being easily defeated 2–0 by Thailand, Malaysia beat favourites Vietnam to win the bronze medal in the Tiger Cup soccer competition at the Rajamangala Stadium here. Two-goal hero Rusdi Suparman led the Malaysians to this unexpected victory with Rosdi Talib putting them ahead in the first half, followed by two goals from Rusdi in the second. An elated Malaysian coach Abdul Rahman Ibrahim said this was one of Malaysia's better matches and that the reserve players he fielded gave a good account of themselves.

Errors in SPM paper

27 November | Kuala Lumpur

The Education Ministry apologised for problems encountered in the Sijil Pelajaran Malaysia examination. The parliamentary secretary to the Education Ministry, Datuk Mahadzir Khir, was responding to complaints about insufficient question papers, missing pages and errors in some questions. Several parents had complained to the media and the Ministry that there were mistakes in the Physics and Additional Mathematics questions.

Historic win

9 December | Kuala Lumpur

At the Jalan Duta courts here, Asian squash champion Ong Beng Hee won the OSK Malaysian Open squash championships. The first Malaysian to win this title, he beat Australian John Williams 16–17, 15–6, 15–8, 15–10 in 88 minutes to win his third Professional Squash Association (PSA) title of the year.

Assemblyman shot dead

4 November | Bukit Mertajam

Lunas Assemblyman Dr Joe Fernandez was gunned down by two men on a motor-cycle in busy Jalan Maju here while driving alone to his nearby Taman Bukit home. The Kedah deputy MIC chairman, 54, was shot twice in the head and once in the abdomen. He left a wife and daughter.

Former Bank Negara executive fined

5 November | Kuala Lumpur

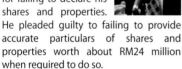

Former Bank Negara assistant governor Datuk Abdul Murad Khalid, 47, was fined RM500,000 or six months' jail in default by the Sessions Court in Kuala Lumpur for failing to declare his shares and properties. He pleaded guilty to failing to provide accurate particulars of shares and properties worth about RM24 million when required to do so.

Airport limo drivers end strike

A long line of empty limos outside the airport at the height of the strike.

10 December | Sepang

It was business as usual for drivers of Airport Limo (M) Bhd, following an agreement to end a strike and begin negotiations for better working conditions. Many of the 600 drivers were picking up passengers from the arrival hall of the Kuala Lumpur International Airport. But one stressed that if negotiations failed they might contemplate resuming their strike.

Submarines arrive

19 December | Lumut

Two former Dutch Navy Swordfish-class submarines arrived at the PSC-Naval Dockyard Sdn Bhd at Lumut for refurbishment and modernisation. The submarines were then to be offered for sale with the Government a potential buyer.

Smart Card to replace ID card

25 November | Kuala Lumpur

In efforts to speed up the country's transformation into a paperless society, the Government Multi-Purpose Smart Card (GMPC) would replace Malaysian identity cards, it was announced. The world's first multi-application smart card would be introduced to the Multimedia Super Corridor and KL in April 2001.

The GMPC would have a microchip with six applications: consolidating personal particulars, driver's licence, passport and health data. It could also be used as a debit/cash card and for public key infrastructure applications.

Kinabalu Park made World Heritage Site

30 November | Cairns

Sabah's Kinabalu Park, dominated by Mount Kinabalu, was declared a World Heritage Site by UNESCO at the 24th Annual Session of the World Heritage Committee here in Cairns, Australia. The park was inscribed for its natural values which include a wide range of habitats exceptionally rich in species.

Year-end joy

13 December | Kuala Lumpur

It was a joyous end to the year when the Government announced that some 800,000 civil servants would be getting bonuses amounting to half a month's salary or a minimum of RM500. The bonus payment would involve an additional operating expenditure of RM500 million. Payment would be made before the end of the year.

Tajudin sells back MAS shares

20 December | Kuala Lumpur

Tan Sri Tajudin Ramli signed an agreement to sell back to the Minister of Finance the 29.09 per cent equity he held in Malaysian Airline System Bhd, through Naluri Bhd, for RM1.792 billion cash or RM8 a share.

First female Attorney-General

19 December | Kuala Lumpur

Datuk Ainum Mohamed Saaid was appointed Attorney-General for a two-year term from 1 January 2001, the first woman to serve in this capacity.

Chief Justice retires

20 December | Kuala Lumpur

Chief Justice of the Federal Court Tun Eusoff Chin retired after six years in the post. Born in Batu Gajah, Perak, he began his judicial career as a magistrate in 1959. He was succeeded as Chief Justice by Tan Sri Dzaiddin Abdullah.

2001

Malaysia can learn from the rest of the world and the rest of the world can also take lessons from Malaysia. This message was underlined by Prime Minister Dato' Seri Dr Mahathir Mohamad at two separate functions in July. He told guests at the exhibition to mark 'Six Centuries of Islamic Art' in China that Malays should learn more about Islam in China where it was widely practised before it arrived in Malaysia. At another function, he said Malaysia held great potential for the world's genome-based industry as its forests were among the oldest in the world. Dr Mahathir expressed sadness over the 11 September New York Twin Towers horror. Women again became the focus of attention when a Women's Affairs Ministry was created.

JANUARY
Datuk Shahrizat Abdul Jalil heads the new Women's Affairs Ministry.

FEBRUARY
Putrajaya is declared a Federal Territory.

SEPTEMBER
Banners for the 21st SEA Games are put up throughout Kuala Lumpur.

NOVEMBER
The 11th Yang di-Pertuan Agong, Sultan Salahuddin Abdul Aziz Shah, dies. A seven-day period of national mourning is declared.

June: Universiti Malaya's Dewan Tunku Canselor destroyed in a fire.

'Women have proven over time that they are committed to and serious about any struggle they undertake.'

Dato' Seri Dr Mahathir Mohamad, at the launch of Puteri Umno, 4 August 2001.

12 January
Gloria Macapagal-Arroyo is sworn in as President of the Philippines after the armed forces and several Cabinet Ministers withdraw support from President Estrada.

23 January
Five members of Falun Gong, a banned spiritual organisation, immolate themselves in Tiananmen Square, Beijing.

26 January
A powerful earthquake hits Gujarat, India, killing more than 20,000.

26 February
Taliban leader Mullah Mohammed Omar orders the destruction of all pre-Islamic statues and sanctuaries in Afghanistan.

10 April
In Singapore, doctors complete a four-day operation to separate 11-month-old twins from Nepal joined at the head.

6 May
US millionaire Dennis Tito, 61, is the first 'space tourist', paying US$20 million.

Sensitive issue settled

5 January   **Kuala Lumpur**

Suqiu, the Chinese Election Appeals Committee, in a joint announcement with Umno Youth, 'put aside' seven 'contentious points' which touched on Malay rights. Both also 'expressed regret over the unintended reaction within the Malay and Chinese communities which have arisen'.

Umno Youth chief Datuk Hishammuddin Hussein and Suqiu's Quek Suan Hiang made this announcement after an hour's meeting. Hishammuddin said both parties had agreed not to question the seven points as the special privileges enjoyed by the Bumiputra community were enshrined in the Constitution. Both parties, however, agreed to continue discussions on the remaining 76 election appeals which they described as 'acceptable'.

Suqiu had, before the 1999 general election, submitted to the Government a 17-point memorandum containing 83 appeals. The appeals drew severe criticism and protests from various groups led by Umno Youth, the 4B Youth movement and later the Federation of Peninsular Malay Students.

The Suqiu committee comprised 11 Chinese associations. Among them were United Chinese School Committees Association of Malaysia (Dong Zong), United Chinese School Teachers Association of Malaysia (Jiao Zong) and Nanyang University Alumni Association of Malaysia.

The moon goes into shadow during the total lunar eclipse on 10 January, pictured above the Putra Mosque in Putrajaya. It took more than five hours for the sun to overshadow the moon. The total eclipse lasted 62 minutes.

Welcome to the Third Millennium

1 January   **Kuala Lumpur**

Technically speaking, the Third Millennium started at midnight but celebrations were noticeably more subdued than those of 2000. In Kuala Lumpur, the festive mood began early as people thronged the KLCC Park to watch fireworks and a team of international skydivers leap off the 452m Twin Towers as the countdown began.

Large seizure of drugs and weapons

11 January   **Penang**

Police seized 427kg of ganja worth almost RM600,000 in what was described as the State's biggest seizure after a 12-hour standoff at the suspected traffickers' double-storey rented house in Taman Idaman, Simpang Ampat.

Police also discovered 20 hand grenades, four pistols including a fake, a submachine, a shotgun and 483 rounds of ammunition—believed to be the biggest seizure of weapons since that from Al-Ma'unah in July 2000. Two suspected drug traffickers, aged 27 and 31, one of whom believed to be a former army commando, were arrested. Some 150 police were involved in the operation.

Population rises by 4.6m in 10 years

3 January   **Kota Kinabalu**

The Malaysian population increased by 4.6 million in a decade and stood at 22.2 million, according to the population and housing census. Males numbered 11,212,525 and there were 10,990,089 females, a ratio of 102 men to every 100 women.

The gender imbalance was most marked in Johor, Selangor and Negeri Sembilan, indicating a tendency for men to move to such places seeking jobs.

New Ministry for women's affairs

17 January   **Kuala Lumpur**

A new Ministry was created to handle women's affairs. Datuk Shahrizat Abdul Jalil was promoted to full Minister to head the Women's Affairs Ministry.

Shahrizat, 47, MP for Lembah Pantai, was seen by many as a hands-on person who freely spoke her mind. Women's leaders and organisations welcomed the formation of the Ministry, saying it reflected the Government's seriousness with regard to problems faced by women.

Prime Minister Dato' Seri Dr Mahathir Mohamad said: 'We value the contributions of women and their role and that is why we created the new Ministry.'

Putrajaya becomes a Federal Territory

1 February   **Putrajaya**

Prime Minister Dato' Seri Dr Mahathir Mohamad declared Putrajaya a Federal Territory at the Dataran Perdana here.

Dr Mahathir handed over the Putrajaya flag to the president of Putrajaya Corp, Tan Sri Azizan Zainul Abidin. The corporation is entrusted with developing, managing and administering Putrajaya on behalf of the Federal Government.

Putrajaya was the country's third Federal Territory after Kuala Lumpur and Labuan. It is 25km south of Kuala Lumpur and 20km north of the KL International Airport in Sepang.

Dr Mahathir said Kuala Lumpur would remain the commercial centre but it was the pre-independence capital and the nation needed a symbol identified with the country.

The Putrajaya flag is raised at the ceremony.

70 held as three die in kampong clashes

10 March   **Petaling Jaya**

Police detained 70 people following clashes in which three people died in Kampung Lindungan and surrounding areas off Jalan Klang Lama. They seized parangs, knives, steel rods and samurai swords. Those detained included five soldiers attached to the Sungai Besi army camp and a Rela member.

The clashes followed a quarrel between a car owner and several teenagers. Then another group, not involved in the initial argument, spread rumours that a gang clash had broken out.

100,000 Ecstasy pills seized at KLIA

31 March   **Petaling Jaya**

A major consignment of Ecstasy pills heading into the country from Germany was foiled by the Customs Department, which acted on a tip-off, at the Kuala Lumpur International Airport.

The 100,000 pills, worth an estimated RM10 million, were well wrapped in paper packets and placed in two computer casings. Customs deputy director-general (Prevention) Datuk Zaleha Hamzah said investigation revealed that the seized packages were addressed to a condominium in Kuala Lumpur.

Malaysia not ready to re-peg currency

9 April Kuala Lumpur

Malaysia would not be pressured to devalue the ringgit, which remained close to fair value and consistent with the fundamentals of the economy, said Bank Negara Governor Tan Sri Zeti Akhtar Aziz.

Malaysia could not afford to set its exchange rate on the basis of short-term developments in the international markets, she said. In view of weak external demand, depreciation would lead to higher costs.

Four arrested under ISA

12 April Kuala Lumpur

Police detained four opposition politicians and activists under the Internal Security Act in connection with a 'Black 14' gathering. 'Black 14' was a phrase coined by activists to mark the conviction of former Deputy Prime Minister Dato' Seri Anwar Ibrahim on 14 April 1999.

Those detained were Parti Keadilan Nasional Youth chief Mohamad Ezam Mohd Nor, its vice-president Chong Tian Chua (Tian Chua), former student leader Hishamuddin Rais and Jemaah Islam Malaysia president Saari Sungib, a 'Black 14' organising committee member.

Police claimed the four were planning protests to topple the Government.

Affordable hope for infertile mothers

18 April Kuala Lumpur

There was hope for infertile women in Malaysia to conceive, thanks to the affordable in-vitro fertilisation (IVF) service rendered by the Universiti Kebangsaan Malaysia Hospital (HUKM) in Cheras. It made a breakthrough when a girl, Alia, was born to a mother in her 30s who had gynaecological problems that prevented normal fertilisation.

Consultant Associate Prof Dr Zainul Rashid Mohamad Razi said the hospital charged RM8,000 to RM10,000 for its IVF service while private hospitals were likely to charge double that price range.

10-year plan for growth

3 April Kuala Lumpur

Prime Minister Dato' Seri Dr Mahathir Mohamad unveiled a 10-year socio-economic plan aimed at achieving higher growth, eradicating poverty and raising the Bumiputra stake in the economy. 'Economic growth will be promoted alongside efforts aimed at poverty eradication and restructuring of society, as well as reducing social, economic and regional imbalances,' he said when tabling the Third Outline Perspective Plan in the Dewan Rakyat.

The thrust of the National Vision Policy (NVP), which formed the basis of strategies and programmes under the OPP3, was to establish a progressive, prosperous and harmonious Bangsa Malaysia. The NVP succeeded the National Development Policy, and was an economic and social development blueprint that spelled out key strategies to enable Malaysia to become a developed country by 2020. It also provided the broad policy parameters for the formulation of the Eighth Malaysia Plan which will be tabled in Parliament later this month.

It's Datuk Michelle Yeoh

20 April Ipoh

The Ipoh-born film sensation Michelle Yeoh, star of the martial-arts epic *Crouching Tiger, Hidden Dragon* and the James Bond film *Tomorrow Never Dies*, was created a datuk. She was among the 987 award recipients on the occasion of the Sultan of Perak Sultan Azlan Shah's 73rd birthday.

PM's son quits business

26 April Kuala Lumpur

Datuk Mokhzani Mahathir, chief executive officer of Pantai Holdings Bhd and Tongkah Holdings Bhd, announced his withdrawal from the corporate world. The Prime Minister's son said his decision was prompted by personal disappointment at allegations by irresponsible groups who tarnished his family name.

48 years' service

1 May Kuala Lumpur

The country's longest-serving civil servant, Benedict Nettar, retired after working for 48 years and six months. The 76-year-old private secretary to Works Minister Datuk Seri S. Samy Vellu planned to go to India to visit his siblings and to do church work.

Stock Market boost after levy abolished

3 May Kuala Lumpur

The Government abolished the 10 per cent profit levy, that had been imposed in 1998 during the financial crisis, to encourage the return of foreign funds to the local stock market. The move had a powerful effect on the KLSE with the Composite Index surging 27 points to 611 points, a rise of 4.6 per cent.

Move to boost health tourism

6 May Kuala Lumpur

Private hospitals and clinics were given the green light to advertise their services in an effort to woo health tourists. Health Minister Datuk Chua Jui Meng said amendments would be made to existing laws governing medical professionalism and ethics.

In 1999, private hospitals in Malaysia generated RM15.8 million in revenue from foreign patients as opposed to RM10 million the year before. The number of foreign patients in private hospitals had also risen.

It won't bite: A father and daughter show different reactions to a Tyrannosaurus Rex replica on show at the Dinosaur Alive exhibition in Petaling Jaya in May.

'Firebird' found

18 April Penang

An amateur botanist has discovered a new species of ginger at the new Perlis State Park. Named *Zingiber mythianum* and nicknamed Firebird (right), it was found by Datuk Lim Chong Keat, the younger brother of former Penang Chief Minister Tun Dr Lim Chong Eu. The striking plant, also found in southern Thailand, was thought to be *Z. rubens* until Datuk Lim introduced it as a new species.

Dr M gets Green Beret

5 May Malacca

Armed Forces Chief Jen Datuk Seri Hashim Hussein and Special Forces commander Brig-Jen Ahmad Rodi Zakaria give Prime Minister Dato' Seri Dr Mahathir Mohamad a helping hand to adjust his beret at the Sungai Udang camp in Malacca. Dr Mahathir was conferred the honorary Green Beret for his determination and spirit.

2001

world news

1 June
Crown Prince Dipendra kills his parents, the King and Queen of Nepal, and other members of the royal family, then shoots himself.

1 June
A Hamas suicide bomber kills 21 teenagers in a disco in Tel Aviv, Israel.

6 June
Thaksin Shinawata's Thai Rak Thai party wins 248 of 500 seats in the Thai elections.

23 July
Indonesian President Abdurrahman Wahid declares a state of emergency. The military refuses to carry out his orders and Parliament votes unanimously to remove him. Megawati Sukarnoputri is the new President.

24 July
Thirteen Tamil Tigers suicide bombers destroy three airliners and eight military aircraft at Bandaranaike International Airport, Colombo.

3 August
The Constitutional Court of Thailand acquits PM Thaksin of corruption charges.

Performers on stage during a show to mark the official opening of KL Sentral.

KL Sentral to spur growth

13 June Kuala Lumpur

Deputy Prime Minister Dato' Seri Abdullah Ahmad Badawi officially opened KL Sentral Station tonight, saying the RM5-billion project would become a catalyst to propel Malaysia into a new growth area.

'KL Sentral will become the nucleus of the new transport network and at the same time, it will offer links to the ports, industrial areas, cities and even neighbouring destinations in Singapore and Thailand,' he added.

ISA duo freed

30 May Shah Alam

High Court judge Datuk Mohd Hishamudin Mohd Yunus today ordered the police to free Abdul Ghani Haroon and N. Gobalakrishnan who had been arrested under the Internal Security Act and detained since April, saying their detention was unlawful.

Gawai Dayak celebration

1 June Kuching

Sarawak Chief Minister Tan Sri Abdul Taib Mahmud, who attended the Gawai Dayak Celebration in the State capital, promised that the economic cake would be shared with all communities in the State.

He added that there would be opportunities for all and no one would be discriminated against.

Pathmanaban dies

9 June Kuala Lumpur

Former Deputy Health Minister Datuk K. Pathmanaban died aged 63. He left three sons and two grandchildren.

Daim resigns

2 June Kuala Lumpur

Finance Minister Tun Daim Zainuddin had resigned, said Prime Minister Dato' Seri Dr Mahathir Mohamad. Dr Mahathir said he had accepted the resignation. The announcement ended speculation that had been rife since Tun Daim went on two months' leave which ended on 31 May. Dr Mahathir said Tun Daim wanted to resign two months earlier but he had told him to go on leave first and reconsider. This was Tun Daim's second resignation as Finance Minister. The first was in 1991.

'Holy war' gang

7 June Kuala Lumpur

A local militant group linked to international terrorists was involved in the assassination of Lunas Assemblyman Dr Joe Fernandez in November 2000, said Inspector General of Police Tan Sri Norian Mai.

It also planned to wage jihad, he said. Its members were responsible for bombing a church and a Hindu temple and attacking the Guar Chempedak police station. The group, heavily armed with sophisticated weapons, also planned to attack American citizens.

MCA gets varsity

8 July Ipoh

The Education Ministry approved the MCA's application to set up the Tunku Abdul Rahman Universiti.

MCA president Dato' Seri Dr Ling Liong Sik said details of courses, funding, location and opening date would be discussed and a proposal submitted to the Education Ministry. The university, he said, would be open to all races.

Dinner for 25,000

15 July Kuala Lumpur

A dinner to celebrate Dato' Seri Dr Mahathir Mohamad's 20th anniversary as Prime Minister, attended by an estimated 25,000 people in Malacca, made it into the *Malaysian Book of Records*, breaking the previous record attendance of 20,200 at a dinner in Negeri Sembilan.

Temple of 15,000 bottles

25 June Alor Star

A Buddhist temple in Sik decorated with 15,000 bottles was ready to open. The first of its kind in the country, the 'bottle' wat is adorned with recycled drink bottles of various shapes and sizes from the foundations to the rooftop. The temple belongs to the 200-year-old Wat Caruk Padang and is located in Pekan Batu Lima.

Wat tiler: A workman on the temple roof.

Malaysia needs to be more innovative

24 July Petaling Jaya ▶ Malaysia was ranked 30th among 72 countries in the United Nations Human Development Report 2001's Technology Achievement Index, introduced with the Human Development Report 2001 by the United Nations Development Programme.

The index was intended to measure how well a country was 'creating and diffusing technology and building a human skill base.' Although the country had the potential to be a technology leader by virtue of its being among the top 10 exporters of high-technology products, its achievement was dampened by its low Internet penetration, a mere 2.4 users per 1,000 people in 2000, by far the lowest among the 37 countries categorised as technology leaders and potential leaders.

Arson probe after fire at Universiti Malaya

29 June Kuala Lumpur

Universiti Malaya's Dewan Tunku Canselor was razed in an early morning fire. Police are probing all angles, including the possibility of arson. A special team would be set up to investigate the cause of the fire. The fire, which started at 3.40am, engulfed the 38-year-old building in minutes, destroying the wooden structures, the stage, the roof, furniture and audio-visual equipment. Firemen arrived at 4am and managed to control the fire after an hour, but 90 per cent of the building had been destroyed.

Damage was estimated at RM12.4 million but the real loss was a sentimental one. The hall was opened by first Prime Minister Tunku Abdul Rahman in 1966, and some 50,000 graduates had since walked through to receive their scrolls. For the first time in the university's history, this year's convocation, scheduled for 1–4 August, would not be held here.

The fire-damaged entrance to the university hall.

Forests are for us, says Dr M

2 July Kuala Lumpur

Dato' Seri Dr Mahathir Mohamad told rich nations to stop dictating how Malaysia should use its forests when they have destroyed theirs. 'Malaysians and local non-governmental organisations should not get so carried away with the so-called environmental consciousness of the foreigners that we are forced to sacrifice our forest's economic importance for their comfort,' he said.

'While we need to preserve our forests, we should be able to derive income from it, particularly logging, to develop the country. We also need forest areas to generate electricity and for agriculture purposes.' He said Malaysia's forests were among the oldest in the world and had great potential for the genome-based industry, so instead cooperation should be extended to foreign researchers to gather and keep samples and data of plant and animal genomes.

He added that this is why the Government has agreed to develop a bio-technology valley within the Multimedia Super Corridor.

Red Devils in town

21 July Kuala Lumpur

David Beckham signed autographs as the Manchester United football team flew into KLIA to be greeted by more than 100 fans who had waited since dawn.

The next night, United took on the national team in a friendly match at the National Stadium watched by 85,000 fans.

As far as the fans were concerned, it was a United show. The English champions gave the young local side a 6–0 mauling in which Ruud van Nistelrooy and Juan Sebastian Veron enjoyed a winning debut.

Religious militants held under ISA

4 August Kuala Lumpur

The son of Kelantan Menteri Besar Datuk Nik Abdul Aziz Nik Mat and a Pas supporter were arrested under the Internal Security Act for alleged involvement in an Islamic militant group known as Kumpulan Mujahidin Malaysia, bringing to 10 the number arrested over a few days. Federal police said they were Nik Adli Datuk Nik Abdul Aziz, 34, and Md Lothfi Ariffin, 33.

Nik Adli, a teacher and hostel warden at Sekolah Menengah Arab Darul Anwar in Pulau Melaka, made news two years earlier for allegedly assaulting a student at the school. Sekolah Menengah Arab Darul Anwar was a religious school administered by the State Government through the Kelantan Islamic Foundation. Police also revealed that eight people, including two Pas Youth chiefs were detained in Terengganu, Perak, Kedah and Johor for their alleged involvement in an Islamic militant cell.

Malaysian Muslims 'can learn from China'

28 July Kuala Lumpur

Malaysians, particularly Muslim Malays, should learn more about Islam in China as the religion had been accepted and widely practised in the country before it arrived here, Dato' Seri Dr Mahathir Mohamad said. The Malays should also 'open their eyes', he added, and carefully study the basis of Prophet Muhammad's advice when he said: 'Seek knowledge, even if you have to go to China.'

The Prime Minister was speaking at the opening ceremony of the Six Centuries of Islamic Art in China exhibition at the Islamic Arts Museum here, 'I'm quite sure if the Muslims had made an injunction of what the Prophet had said [about China], they would be much better off than at present,' Dr Mahathir said, adding that even during the Prophet's time, China had advanced tremendously and acquired the skills to make paper and explosives long before other races on the globe.

Puteri Umno launched

3 August Kuala Lumpur

Dato' Seri Dr Mahathir Mohamad launched Puteri Umno with a call to its members and everyone else in the party to look after and nurture the new movement together. Although Puteri was still in its infancy, it had already attracted 84,372 members.

Dr Mahathir said: 'Women's role in Umno should be noted and enhanced, and they should also be given more roles in our struggle. They have proved to be a force to be reckoned with in the party.'

He said it was Puteri's responsibility to help nurture the younger generation of women into leaders who could cope with future challenges, both socially and politically. 'Women are very courageous and cannot be easily swayed,' he said.

Happy families

9 August Kuala Lumpur

Deputy Prime Minister Dato' Seri Abdullah Ahmad Badawi, Datin Paduka Seri Endon Mahmood and Women and Family Development Minister Datuk Shahrizat Abdul Jalil leading a group of children to the stage for the launch of the Happy Family campaign.

25 sauce products withdrawn

13 August Kuala Lumpur

The Health Ministry has withdrawn 25 sauce products containing 3-MCPD, a cancer-causing agent, from the market. The products—16 locally-made and nine imported—were among 385 tested at Universiti Sains Malaysia's Doping Centre.

The Ministry's Food Quality Control Division said the contaminated products would be withdrawn immediately and destroyed. Earlier, Health Minister Datuk Chua Jui Meng had said the Ministry had recalled 22 brands of soya sauce.

Giant Jalur Gemilang

24 August Ipoh

Perak Menteri Besar Dato' Seri Tajol Rosli Ghazali led a parade of 2,000 students and teachers from SM Seri Ampang to carry the world's largest Jalur Gemilang from the school to nearby Sekolah Tuanku Abdul Rahman.

Completed in just 19 days, the flag, measuring 159 metres by 105 metres, beat the current record as stated in the *Malaysian Book of Records* and held by Universiti Putra Malaysia undergraduates. It was also expected to surpass the world record, which stood at 77 metres by 154 metres. The flag was unfurled on STAR's main field in an hour amid cheers and applause from those who attended the event. The SM Seri Ampang students, with the help of their teachers and parents, had been working since 5 August, using some 40 sewing machines piecing together large segments of cloth. The flag cost RM65,000.

100 airmen on rampage

12 August Labuan

About 100 airforce personnel ran amok armed with steel pipes, golf clubs and hockey sticks, attacking nine nightspots and entertainment outlets, damaging four cars and injuring two people. Police believed the incident was in revenge for the death of an air force member a week earlier.

Drumming with one heart

31 August Kuala Lumpur

The 1,200-strong Malaysian Folk Drum Symphony set the tempo for the 44th National Day celebrations at Dataran Merdeka with a harmonious beat drawn from traditional multi-ethnic drums. The ensemble comprised the Malay rebana ubi, and Chinese, Indian and Siamese drums.

Witnessing the event were the Yang di-Pertuan Agong Sultan Salahuddin Abdul Aziz Shah, Prime Minister Dato' Seri Dr Mahathir Mohamad and Cabinet Ministers.

2001

11 September
Two hijacked airliners crash into the World Trade Centre, New York.

18 September
Letters containing anthrax spores are mailed to media offices and two US senators. Five die and 17 others are infected.

7 October
US and British forces invade Afghanistan.

11 October
Trinidad-born writer V.S. Naipaul wins the Nobel Prize for Literature.

7 December
News magazine *Asiaweek* publishes its final issue and ceases publication due to a downturn in advertising.

10 December
Secretary-General Kofi Annan accepts the Nobel Peace Prize on behalf of the UN.

13 December
The Parliament of India is attacked by five gunmen and a suicide bomber. They are stopped by police who lose half a dozen men.

Landslide win for BN in Sarawak State election

27 September | **Kuching**

Barisan Nasional clinched 60 seats in the 62-seat Sarawak State Assembly. The two other seats went to the DAP and independent candidate Wong Judat. The landslide victory was a blow to the opposition Pas and Parti Keadilan Nasional which were spreading their wings to the East Malaysian State.

Death of a patriot

22 November | **Kuala Lumpur**

National Laureate Datuk Dr Usman Awang died aged 72 at the Pantai Medical Centre here. Literary figures, politicians and theatre personalities were among the hundreds who paid their last respects.

Usman was seen as the 'voice of humanity' and father of modern Malay literature. He was survived by four children and seven grandchildren.

NY Twin Towers horror

11 September | **Kuala Lumpur**

The twin towers of the World Trade Centre in New York were razed to the ground after two hijacked airliners crashed into them. Another plane crashed into the US military headquarters, the Pentagon.

As the world reeled in shock at the news, Prime Minister Dato' Seri Dr Mahathir Mohamad cancelled a scheduled trip to Britain and said he was saddened by the attacks.

Three Malaysians were among the 3,000 dead. One was Vijayashanker Paramsothy, who was working in the South Tower and died trying to save his manager. There were fears that the toll of Malaysians might be higher as the Consulate-General was nearby but according to Wisma Putra, all staff were safe. Malaysia Airlines suspended 12 flights to Los Angeles and New York. Many local travel agencies cancelled or deferred US tours.

In a message to US President George W. Bush, Dr Mahathir said he was deeply saddened and horrified by the devastating attacks in New York and Washington. He urged the US Government not to seek revenge, which he said could only lead to more deaths.

On 10 November the United States placed new requirements on visa applications by Muslim men from Malaysia and other predominantly Muslim nations as part of a tightening of US visa policies after the attacks.

The Twin Towers ablaze after the airliners crashed into them. Inset: Vijayashanker Paramsothy, one of the three Malaysian victims of the 9/11 tragedy.

The King dies

21 November | **Kuala Lumpur**

The 11th Yang di-Pertuan Agong Sultan Salahuddin Abdul Aziz Shah Alhaj Ibni Al-marhum Sultan Hisamuddin Alam Shah Alhaj died at the Gleneagles Intan Medical Centre in Jalan Ampang. He was 75.

Prime Minister Dato' Seri Dr Mahathir Mohamad announced the death over radio and television and declared a seven-day period of national mourning.

19 guilty of treason

28 December | **Kuala Lumpur**

Nineteen Al-Ma'unah members, including its leader Mohd Amin Mohd Razali, were convicted of waging war against the Yang di-Pertuan Agong in July 2000.

Amin and his two right-hand men, Zahit Muslim and Jamaludin Darus, were sentenced to death while 16 others were jailed for life.

High Court judge Datuk Zulkefli Ahmad Makinudin said Amin was the main planner of a mission to topple the Government by force in the name of jihad (*see 26 June 2003*).

Golden start to SEA Games

8–17 September | **Kuala Lumpur**

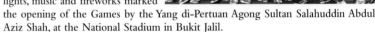

The men's gymnastic team won the first gold of the 21st SEA Games for Malaysia. Loke Yik Siang, Ng Shu Wan, Wooi Wei Siang, Mohamed Irwan Miskob, Heng Wah Jing and Onn Kwang Tung turned on an inspired performance to pip Thailand by 0.25 points to the delight of Sports Minister Datuk Hishammuddin Hussein.

A colourful mix of costumes, lights, music and fireworks marked the opening of the Games by the Yang di-Pertuan Agong Sultan Salahuddin Abdul Aziz Shah, at the National Stadium in Bukit Jalil.

It was the fifth time Malaysia had hosted the Games, which were the first of the new millennium. The first SEA Games were held in 1959.

As the Games progressed, Roslin Hashim ended Malaysia's 28-year wait to win the men's singles badminton gold medal. The joint third-seeded Malaysian overpowered Boonsak Polsana of Thailand 17–14, 15–3 in the final in 46 minutes to send 5,000 supporters into a frenzy. Datuk Punch Gunalan was the last Malaysian to win the singles gold in the 1973 Singapore SEAP Games.

At the end of the Games the 'Malaysia Boleh' spirit was given credit when Malaysia was crowned SEA Games champions for the first time in history. Malaysia achieved an unprecedented haul of 111 gold, 75 silver and 85 bronze medals to topple defending champions Thailand, who finished second with 103 gold, 86 silver and 89 bronze medals.

The unprecedented gold harvest ranked Malaysia among the sporting elite of the region. Thailand, Indonesia and Myanmar were the other countries to have won the overall title since the Games started in 1959.

Malaysia wins Asian rally title

3 December | **Petaling Jaya**

Flying Sikh Karamjit Singh and Allen Oh beat the odds to become the first Malaysians to win the overall title in the seven-round Asia Pacific Rally Championship in Thailand on Sunday. The duo, in Petronas EON Racing Team colours, also made it a grand double by clinching the overall Group N title in the final round of the championship in Pattaya.

2002

Upheavals and closures. The nation was sent into shock when Dato' Seri Dr Mahathir Mohamad announced his resignation from all Umno and Barisan Nasional posts. After 21 years at the helm, he felt it was time to quit. However, at the urging of his Umno colleagues, he agreed to stay on until October 2003. A few months later, he called for the building of a 'truly Malaysian race'. Police arrested more suspected hardcore members of Militan Malaysia, bringing to partial closure the Malaysian connection to the 11 September World Trade Centre attacks. Malaysia sought closure to the untold story of *Black Hawk Down*, the US-made movie that failed to credit Malaysian troops for their role in the rescue of US forces in Somalia in 1993.

JANUARY
Hollywood chided for inaccurate portrayal of Malaysian soldiers in the film *Black Hawk Down*.

FEBRUARY
Statewide operation to arrest illegal immigrants and remove their squatter colonies launched in Sabah.

APRIL
Police arrest members of the hardcore Kumpulan Militan Malaysia suspected of abetting the terrorists of the 11 September World Trade Centre attacks.

AUGUST
Dr Mahathir urges Malaysians to focus on building a truly Malaysian race.

April: The Raja of Perlis is installed as Malaysia's 12th King.

'The kind of globalisation promoted by the rich Western countries has not convinced Asia that this is the answer to economic ills.'

Dato' Seri Dr Mahathir Mohamad, 2002.

2002

5 January
Singapore announces the arrest of 15 militants suspected of plotting to attack targets in Singapore, including the US Embassy.

11 January
The first prisoners from Afghanistan arrive at Guantanamo Bay, Cuba.

12 February
The trial of former Serbian President Slobodan Milosevic begins at the UN War Crimes tribunal in The Hague.

17 February
A Saudi Arabian man is sentenced to six years and 4,750 lashes for having sex with his sister-in-law. The woman, who was raped, gets six months' prison and 65 lashes.

19 February
A gas canister catches fire on a train from Cairo to Luxor, Egypt, killing 361.

22 February
The Sri Lankan Government and Tamil Tiger separatist rebels sign a Norwegian brokered ceasefire plan.

Nurseries teaching songs of hate

1 January Butterworth

Instead of nursery rhymes, several religious kindergartens in Penang were teaching the children to sing politically-laced songs promoting hatred of national leaders and the Government, said Deputy Chief Minister Datuk Dr Hilmi Yahaya.

He said the State Islamic Religious Department made the discovery recently following complaints by parents. He said the religious department would now appoint board of governors at religious schools to monitor their activities.

Workers clear up after the landslide disaster.

Landslide strikes sleeping longhouse folk

28 January Kuching

Sixteen villagers from several families were feared buried alive in a landside that hit an Iban longhouse at Kampung Ruan Changkul, about 40km from Simunjan town. Five others were injured, four of them seriously. The landslide occurred following recent heavy rain that hit parts of Sarawak.

Millions collected in donation scam

11 February Kuala Lumpur

Racketeers claiming to collect donations for Afghan refugees had taken millions of ringgit from well-wishers all over the region, including Malaysia, Foreign Ministry and police officials said. Members of the 30- to 40-strong syndicate operated from budget hotels in areas near Chow Kit and the Masjid Pakistan and Masjid India here.

Dr Mahathir welcomes PBS leader Datuk Joseph Pairin Kitingan as the party rejoins the Barisan Nasional.

PBS rejoins Barisan

24 January Kuala Lumpur

Parti Bersatu Sabah returned to the Barisan Nasional as its 14th member. Applications from the Indian Progressive Front, Punjabi Party of Malaysia and Malaysian Indian Muslim Congress were rejected.

Barisan chairman Dato' Seri Dr Mahathir Mohamad said the Supreme Council had accepted the PBS application without reservations or conditions. The 200,000-strong PBS, which had been out of Barisan for 11 years, cited its aspiration to create better understanding as the main reason for rejoining.

120 Africans escape on way to detention centre

2 February Bahau

Roadblocks set up after the Africans' escape.

More than 120 African illegal immigrants escaped on the road from Kuala Lumpur to the Kemayan detention camp in Pahang, triggering a massive manhunt.

The convoy of 10 vehicles had left Kuala Lumpur with 215 Africans detained by city police. On the road some jumped off and at Air Hitam police station, where the convoy stopped to secure the locks on the lorries, about 120 more fled. One policeman said he did not dare arrest the Africans because they were not only bigger physically but 'very fierce'. By nightfall police had re-arrested most of the Africans at roadblocks.

Untold story of 'Black Hawk'

24 January Kuala Lumpur

In the Hollywood action film *Black Hawk Down*, there are only fleeting shots of Asians helping to rescue 75 US soldiers pinned down by militia fire in Mogadishu, Somalia. And that is not good enough for Brig-Jen (Rtd) Datuk Abdul Latif Ahmad, commander of the Malaysian contingent of the UN peacekeeping force there. He saw 114 of his men go into battle along with US forces on 3 October 1993 and emerged six hours later with one man killed, nine injured and four armed personnel carriers destroyed.

Forgotten heroes? Malaysian peacekeepers in Somalia.

'We were there in the thick of the battle. It is only right to set the record straight for Malaysian moviegoers who will get the wrong impression that the battle was fought by the Americans alone, while we were mere bus drivers, to ferry them out,' said the 59-year-old former officer.

In fact the US made four unsuccessful attempts to rescue its soldiers. Only after considerable discussion and delay did Malaysian troops and US Ranger teams move into action. Eighteen US soldiers died and 70 were wounded. Private Mat Aznau Awang was the sole Malaysian casualty. He received the highest gallantry award from the Yang di-Pertuan Agong. Other members of the team were also decorated.

More satisfying was the praise the Malaysian soldiers received. Brig-Gen Greg Gile, commander of the US Ranger Force, wrote on 14 October 1993: 'Your forces proved essential to accomplish the mission. The Rangers were saved, thanks to your soldiers.' On 19 March Malaysian Permanent Representative to the United Nations Datuk Hassmy Agam received, on behalf of their next-of-kin, Dag Hammarskjold Medals awarded to 23 Malaysians killed on UN peacekeeping duty, three of them in Somalia.

Avian sex life hots up

22 February Seberang Jaya

The heat wave seemed to have brought a sizzle into the sex life of the big birds. Ostriches and emus at the Penang Bird Park are mating more often and females are laying twice the usual number of eggs. The ostriches are also pecking off their feathers, leaving their backs naked, but this is merely to cool the body temperature, said park director Dr Gino Ooi.

He added that the four female ostriches had laid 50 eggs since December 2001, an average of one every three days, compared with one a week previously.

But the heat had taken its toll on the fertility of the eggs, with only 60 per cent able to hatch, compared to more than 80 per cent under normal weather conditions. The three female emus at the bird park were also producing twice the number of eggs they did in 2001, said Dr Ooi.

Dr Ooi collecting ostrich and emu eggs at the Penang Bird Park.

Sabah crackdown nets 2,500 illegals

27 February Kota Kinabalu

More than 2,500 illegal immigrants were arrested and 227 squatter houses destroyed in a massive operation launched in Sabah at dawn. The largest-ever crackdown in the State on illegals and their squatter colonies, the operation was also aimed at weeding out armed militant groups, especially from the Philippines. As the operation got under way simultaneously in 12 districts and Labuan, hundreds of Filipino and Indonesian immigrants were packed off to detention centres to be deported immediately.

Immigration officers give instructions to detainees before their documents are checked.

Singapore reclamation 'a threat to shipping'

12 March Kuala Lumpur

Singapore's Pulau Tekong reclamation project could pose a serious threat to shipping and the future development of southern Johor, according to an independent consultant who conducted a study on the tidal effect and impact of land reclamation in the area. Datuk Nik Mohd Kamel Nik Hassan, principal consultant of Dr Nik & Associates Sdn Bhd, is of the opinion that the result of the island expansion would choke the Johor Straits and change tidal and seabed profiles.

One effect, he said, would be to increase the current by twice its existing speed of 0.7 metres per second, posing navigational risks to ships entering and leaving Pasir Gudang Port. Due to the narrow channel and faster flow of water, ships might run aground.

He said the land expansion, if not done properly, would also destroy marine ecology and reduce water quality.

'Not ready for inter-faith association'

27 February London

Prime Minister Dato' Seri Dr Mahathir Mohamad called for patience in the setting up of an inter-faith association in Malaysia because Muslim religious leaders feel 'uncomfortable' about it, he said in reply to a question at an afternoon tea hosted by Baroness Uddin of Bethnal Green and attended by about 80 guests at the House of Lords.

He said some conservative Muslims were fearful of being 'infected' by other thoughts, though he had no problems meeting leaders of other religious faiths. He also explained that the Malaysian Government was cautious in its approach to translations of Christian texts into Bahasa Malaysia because the use of the same terms as in Islam would cause confusion among Muslims.

Earlier Dr Mahathir said Islam was greatly misunderstood in the West, which equated religious extremism with fundamentalism when, in fact, the fundamentals of Islam preached peace and tolerance. 'If we follow the fundamental tenets of Islam, we are moderates, accepting and respecting religious differences and trying to accommodate people of other faiths.' Islam abhors turmoil, the Prime Minister said.

Dr Mahathir accused Pas of misinterpreting Islam and criticised the party for its narrow stand on the role of Muslim women in society, in sharp contrast to Umno's encouragement of to women to participate fully in the country's development.

Dr Mahathir is greeted by British Prime Minister Tony Blair at 10 Downing Street. Their discussion included issues relating to Sept 11.

12th King installed

26 April Kuala Lumpur ▶ The Raja of Perlis, Tuanku Syed Sirajuddin Syed Putra Jamalullail, 58, was installed as the 12th Yang di-Pertuan Agong at Istana Negara.

The trumpet was sounded and the nobat or the royal ensemble from Istana Kedah struck up the *Raja Berangkat* (*The King Goes Forth*) to announce the arrival of the Yang di-Pertuan Agong and the Raja Permaisuri Agong Tuanku Fauziah Tengku Abdul Rashid at the Balairong Seri (throne room).

The ceremony was attended by the Malay Rulers, members of the royal household, the Yang di-Pertuas Negeri and Prime Minister Dato' Seri Dr Mahathir Mohamad. Also present were Cabinet Ministers, Chief Ministers, Menteris Besar, members of the diplomatic corps and local and foreign guests.

Greed 'hampering NEP targets'

30 March Shah Alam

People who wanted to get rich quickly had hampered the achievements of the New Economic Policy (NEP), said Prime Minister Dato' Seri Dr Mahathir Mohamad.

It would take some time before equal distribution of the nation's wealth, as outlined in the NEP, could be achieved, he said.

Dr Mahathir said the original target of 20 years to meet the objectives of the NEP could not be met because certain Bumiputras given Government assistance wanted to get rich quickly. 'We give something to them and they sell it to others,' he said after opening the Selangor Barisan Nasional convention. 'We give them shares and they sell them to others.'

Sparkling success

8 March Sepang

Second-placed BMW Williams driver Juan Pablo Montoya of Colombia (left) sprays champagne on his teammate and race winner Ralf Schumacher of Germany on the podium after the Petronas Malaysian F1 Grand Prix.

2002

---

world news

27 February
A train carrying Hindu activists is set on fire in Gujarat State, India, killing 58.

13 March
The Governor of the central bank of Indonesia is jailed for three years for corruption.

2 April
More than 100 Palestinian gunmen force their way into the Church of Nativity in Bethlehem, birthplace of Jesus, sparking a 39-day siege.

16 April
The Dutch Government resigns after a report on the 1995 massacre of more than 7,000 Bosnian Muslim men in Srebenica, while supposedly under the protection of Dutch troops.

17 April
The UN declares former guerrilla leader Xanana Gusmao the winner of East Timor's presidential election.

22 April
Argentina closes all banks and foreign exchange markets to stop the outflow of money.

Death sentence for Suzaily's killer

27 April Shah Alam

Bus driver Hanafi Mat Hassan, 34, who raped and murdered 24-year-old computer engineer Noor Suzaily Mukhtar two years ago, was sentenced to death, jailed for 20 years and ordered to receive 12 strokes of the rotan. High Court judge Datuk Hishamudin Mohd Yunus, who found Hanafi guilty of the crimes, ordered him to be hanged for the murder and to receive the maximum jail term and whipping for the rape. The punishments were to run concurrently, with priority to the death sentence since it is the ultimate penalty.

Dr M and Pope share views on Middle East

8 June Vatican City

After a historic meeting between Prime Minister Dato' Seri Dr Mahathir Mohamad and Pope John Paul II, Malaysia and the Holy See called for international intervention in the Middle-East conflict through the involvement of a third party to separate the Palestinians and the Israelis.

Dr Mahathir said: 'We must try to put an end to this violence through negotiations.' The joint stand was considered significant in view of the growing world consensus for third party involvement.

Dr Mahathir told the press after the meeting with the Pope and talks with Vatican officials including Secretary of State Cardinal Angelo Sodano that the two sides shared similar views on terrorism and the Middle-East issue.

14 KMM members arrested

19 April Kuala Lumpur

Police in Kuala Lumpur arrested 14 more suspected hardcore Kumpulan Militan Malaysia members, including a woman, under the Internal Security Act, bringing to 62 the number of KMM members held since May 2001.

The woman, Sejahratul Dursina @ Chomel Mohammad, was the wife of Yazid Sufaat, the man alleged to have met two of the terrorists who hijacked and crashed passenger planes into the World Trade Center and the Pentagon on 11 September 2001.

Inspector General of Police Tan Sri Norian Mai said the authorities had also identified more than 100 KMM members still at large. Police also seized training manuals for guerrilla warfare, maps, receipts and other documents during a two-day operation. Five of the arrested were Government servants. Twelve were Malaysian and two Indonesian permanent residents in Malaysia. Investigations revealed that several were graduates of US universities. Tan Sri Norian said three of those still at large had been identified.

Soh (centre) was fined RM6 million in 2007.

Wanted businessman back and charged

14 May Shah Alam

Businessman Datuk Soh Chee Wen, 43, sought by the authorities for four years, returned from abroad to face two fraud charges. At the Sessions Court here, the former chief executive officer of Promet Bhd pleaded not guilty and was released on RM2-million bail. On 14 May 2007 Soh was fined RM6 million after admitting to two alternative charges of conspiring to provide false statements to the KLSE.

Eight drown in river

28 May Grik

Eight participants in a motivation course organised by a cosmetics company drowned when the boat to their campsite capsized near Pulau Peladang, in Tasik Banding, about 50km from here.

University merit system will be retained

20 May Shah Alam

The merit system for admission to local public universities was likely to be retained in 2003 even though it had been questioned by some quarters in Government, said Prime Minister Dato' Seri Dr Mahathir Mohamad.

'We have made a promise to use the merit system for admission to local universities. If we change the system, we will not be credible any more,' he said at the opening of the MIC's 56th AGM.

Women's Minister protests at State law

29 May Kuala Lumpur

Women and Family Development Minister Datuk Shahrizat Abdul Jalil urged women leaders to join in pressuring the Terengganu State Government to  withdraw its proposed Syariah Criminal Enactment which, she said, encouraged discrimination against women.

Former A-G new Suhakam head

23 April Petaling Jaya

Former Attorney-General Tan Sri Abu Talib Othman was appointed chairman of the Human Rights Commission (Suhakam), taking over from Tan Sri Musa Hitam.

Tan Sri Abu Talib's appointment and that of 12 other commission members was for two years.

Tan Sri Abu Talib was the Attorney-General for 13 years before retiring in 1994 and was the special investigator in the inquiry into the complaint of police brutality lodged by Dato' Seri Anwar Ibrahim in 1999 as well as the chairman and board member of several publicly-listed companies.

Suhakam was set up in April 2000 with the objective of promoting and protecting human rights and to investigate complaints of human rights violations in the country.

Ahmad Daud dies at 70

11 June Kuala Lumpur

One of Malaysia's most prominent entertainers, Datuk Ahmad Daud, died aged 70. The veteran singer was laid to rest at the Klang Gate cemetery near Taman Melawati.

Born Ahmad Daud Mohd Hashim on 12 March 1932 in Penang, he recorded the song *Pengantin Bersanding* in 1958 in Singapore. Other popular songs were *Aksi Kucing*, *Manis 17* and *Pontianak*.

He was also in the films *Siapa Besar* (1962), *Aksi Kucing*, (1963), *Pusaka Pontianak* (1964) and *Jungle Boy* (1967) as well as *Permintaan Terakhir* and *Kau Sumber Ilhamku* in the 1970s.

RM19m gem of a dress

5 July Kuala Lumpur

This is probably the world's most expensive gown, valued at RM19 million. The gown, encrusted with almost 2,500 of the world's most perfectly cut diamonds, was created by Anne Bowen who had designed outfits for pop group Destiny's Child, film star Catherine Zeta Jones and model Cindy Crawford.

The silk-and-cotton tulle dress was modelled by former Malaysian beauty queen Kavita Kaur Sidhu. In total, the diamonds on the gown, which was brought to Malaysia by a local jewellery company, weighed 625.25 carats. After Malaysia, the gown was taken on a world tour then auctioned for a children's charity.

Science and Maths in English from next year

21 July Seremban

Science and Mathematics were to be taught in English. This would be introduced in phases from 2003 to give teachers and students time to adjust to the change. At first only Year One, Form One and Lower Six students in national schools would be involved.

However, whether Chinese and Tamil schools would follow suit would have to wait for 'a political decision'. Announcing the outcome of a special Cabinet meeting, Education Minister Tan Sri Musa Mohamad said: 'this matter concerning national-type schools has to be discussed at a political level among the Barisan Nasional component parties.'

Shock as Dr M says 'I quit'

22 June Kuala Lumpur

The nation was sent into shock when Dato' Seri Dr Mahathir Mohamad announced his resignation from all Umno and Barisan Nasional posts. The announcement came out of the blue as he was winding up the debate at the 56th Umno general assembly. No one, not even his aides, had any inkling that he had any intention to quit.

Dr Mahathir's announcement came after he had been talking about Malaysia's success, more than an hour into his winding-up address. Without any indication whatsoever, Dr Mahathir, who had been at Umno's helm for 21 years, paused, took a sip of water and said: 'I would like to take this opportunity to make an announcement. I would like to announce that I am resigning as Umno president and all my posts in the party and as Barisan Nasional chairman and all other posts in Barisan Nasional.'

As he spoke several Umno leaders surged forward and urged him to retract and on 26 June it was announced that his resignation would take effect only after the Organisation of the Islamic Conference summit in Kuala Lumpur in October 2003. The delay was to allow a smooth transition of power to his deputy Dato' Seri Abdullah Ahmad Badawi.

Diva Rafeah Buang dies

24 July Kuala Lumpur

Datin Rafeah Buang, singing diva of the 1960s and 1970s, died at the Kuala Lumpur Hospital. Rafeah, who was married to Pahang prince Tengku Asmawi Tengku Datuk Hussain, was to have celebrated her 55th birthday and 31st wedding anniversary the following day. She leaves three children, Tengku Ahmad Ashraf, 30, Tengku Khairul Ashraf, 29, and Tengku Nurimah Soleha, 6.

Think-tank charts path to excellence in education

25 July Petaling Jaya

A National Brains Trust on Education proposed changes in the education system to create a world-class workforce capable of meeting the challenges of globalisation. The trust, a think-tank of the National Economic Action Council (NEAC) set up two months earlier with 68 notable members of the education sector, submitted its report to the council's executive committee.

Its chairman, Tan Sri Dr Noordin Sopiee, said the report outlined seven fundamental reforms in the existing education system. He said Malaysia was intent on making a massive quantum leap to become a First World economy.

Saidin found guilty of corruption

25 July Shah Alam

Former Selangor State Executive Councillor Datuk Saidin Tamby was found guilty by the Sessions Court here of corruptly receiving RM1 million from a private company in 1995. Judge Suraya Othman said the prosecution had proved beyond reasonable doubt that Saidin received the money.

Penang's first CM dies

31 August Penang

Penang's first Chief Minister Tan Sri Wong Pow Nee, who read out the proclamation of independence 45 years ago today at the Esplanade here, died in his family home in MacAlister Road aged 91. He was survived by his wife Elizabeth Law, 10 children and 17 grandchildren.

Dubbed the reluctant politician, the MCA veteran and former teacher was Chief Minister from 1957 at the age of 46 until 1969.

Tan Sri Wong's funeral procession in Penang.

Dr M: Build a truly Malaysian race

29 August Putrajaya ▶ As the nation made final preparations to celebrate its 45th National Day, Malaysians from all walks of life were urged by Dato' Seri Dr Mahathir Mohamad to put aside their differences and focus on building a truly Malaysian race. This was the best time for Malaysians to reaffirm their cooperation and friendship, he said. 'At the time when we celebrate the anniversary of our independence, let's forget that we are made up of different races and religions. Let us focus on our patriotic spirit, our commitment and our responsibility towards building a truly Malaysian race,' he told a pre-Merdeka gathering at Dataran Perdana. It was attended by about 2,000 representatives of organisations including student groups, Malaysians of Siamese descent and various ethnic groups from Sabah and Sarawak.

2002

world news

Rare sawfish caught

15 September | Petaling Jaya

A group of fishermen from Kuala Sungai Baru in Malacca caught a rare sawfish weighing 1,500kg in the Straits of Malacca. The fish got entangled in the net and died soon after the boat reached shore.

'Mat Komando' killed

12 September | Alor Star

Gang leader Ahmad Mohd Arshad, known as 'Mat Komando', was killed in a dawn shoot-out with police at a kampong in Pendang near here. When police surrounded his hideout, the 37-year-old leader of the 'Gang 13' group tried to shoot his way out with guns blazing in both hands. Ten members of the Special Operations Force who had surrounded the hut responded with rapid fire, bringing him down.

Bizarre haul of animals in anti-smuggling check

20 November | Kangar

A routine anti-smuggling check on a lorry turned up more than 2,000 animals and insects under a stack of old boxes. The bizarre haul—20 puppies, 990 lizards, 30 snakes, 1,000 spiders, 100 centipedes and 200 scorpions—was believed to be the first of its kind by the Anti-Smuggling Unit (UPP) in Perlis.

The puppies were kept in six wire-mesh cages, the scorpions, spiders and centipedes were found in five gunny sacks and the snakes and lizards in seven

plastic bags. A UPP patrol crew detained the lorry driver after stumbling upon the animals while checking the lorry near the Malaysian–Thai border. It was thought that the animals were smuggled in from Thailand and were meant for the export market.

Musharraf heaps praise on Mahathir

19 October | Islamabad

Pakistani President General Pervez Musharraf fondly recalled as 'my most fruitful visit' a trip to Malaysia in 2000, a few months after he came to power, as he sang the praises of visiting Prime Minister Dato' Seri Dr Mahathir Mohamad.

He spoke of Dr Mahathir's wise, determined and dynamic leadership that had brought tremendous economic and social progress.

Banker's landslide tragedy

21 November | Kuala Lumpur

Affin Bank chairman Tan Sri Ismail Omar was rescued alive five hours after a landslide at 4.30am flattened his double-storey bungalow at Taman Hillview in Ampang but six of his family died. His grandchildren Ilya Syamira, 8, and Shamir Izat, 6, were also rescued as were his daughter Intan Jasmin and her son Mohamad Shazwan, 9 months old.

Conjoined twins successfully separated

25 November | Kuala Lumpur

Conjoined twins Azama and Azami Kamarul Zaman spent their first day as individuals recuperating in the intensive care unit of Kuala Lumpur Hospital's Paediatric Institute after a successful 19-hour operation to separate them.

Queen launches Endon's book

3 November | Kuala Lumpur

A book on the evolution of different styles of the Nyonya kebaya written by Datin Seri Endon Mahmood, wife of Deputy Prime Minister Dato' Seri Abdullah Ahmad Badawi, *The Nyonya Kebaya: A Showcase of Nyonya Kebaya from Endon's Collection*, was launched by the Raja Permaisuri Agong Tuanku Fauziah Tengku Abdul Rashid. The Queen also launched a Nyonya kebaya stamp series by Pos Malaysia Bhd.

Datin Seri Endon, who had been collecting Nyonya kebaya for 20 years, said she hoped the book would inspire Malaysians to preserve traditional arts and culture.

The Queen with Endon (left).

'I have admired the Nyonya kebaya since I was young. Although my mother is not a Nyonya, she used to wear the Nyonya kebaya in and around the house. By just looking at a kebaya, I am reminded of her,' she said at the launch.

She said she was amazed by the artistic passion of the creators, but that much information about the Nyonya kebaya had been lost.

Sipadan and Ligitan awarded to Malaysia

18 December | The Hague

The International Court of Justice decided by a 16–1 majority that Malaysia has a rightful claim to Sipadan and Ligitan islands off Indonesia based on its effective control of both islands. The judgment is final, without appeal and binding. Indonesian delegation head Abdul Irsan said his country accepted the judgment.

RM1m in tithes collected illegally

24 December | Kuala Lumpur

Selangor religious authorities raided an illegal zakat collection centre in Taman Melawati here following a tip-off and detained an employee. The centre, operated by a company, is believed to have illegally collected some RM1 million in zakat since March. Computers and documents were seized, and the premises sealed.

Brutal M16 robbers shot dead

29 December | Kuala Lumpur ▸ The three-year reign of the brutal M16 gang, which made off with more than RM21 million, ended when three gang members, including its leader Sum Wing Chang @ Sunny Chai @ Fei Chai, were shot dead in separate shootouts in Mantin, Negeri Sembilan and Johor Bahru. The two others were Hew Yan, 48, and Chang Kew Yin @ Loh Kui, 49. Police also captured two other members alive. The gang had terrorised their victims, mostly goldsmiths, with their daring robberies armed with M16 rifles.

Federal CID director Commissioner Datuk Salleh Mat Som (with seized weapons) described the gang, which had connections in Malaysia, Thailand and Singapore, as 'multi-talented'. He said Sum put on a front as a businessman, attending high-profile official functions after committing crimes. Police had identified all nine members of the gang, he said, and were searching for the remaining four.

2003

The year of individual and corporate achievements: Shalin Zulkifli won the Aviva Asian Bowling Grand Slam final; the men's and women's bowling teams won the world team titles in Denmark; and Datuk Dr Jemilah Mahmood was awarded the East Asia Women Peace Award along with Myanmar's Aung San Suu Kyi and the Philippines' Corazon Aquino. In the corporate world, Petronas completed in Bintulu the world's largest liquefied natural gas facility in a single location. At the Bukit Jalil Stadium, 200,000 Malaysians of all races turned up in a show of unity and support for the Prime Minister's call to 'give peace a chance'. Dato' Seri Dr Mahathir Mohamad stepped down as Prime Minister, Dato' Seri Abdullah Ahmad Badawi took over.

FEBRUARY
Malaysians turn up in droves to witness the presentation of 2.8 million signatures collected during the Malaysians for Peace campaign.

MAY
Abdul Malik Mydin becomes the first Malaysian to swim across the English Channel.

AUGUST
Datuk Dr Jemilah Mahmood (centre), president of Mercy Malaysia, becomes the first Malaysian woman to receive the East Asia Women Peace Award.

OCTOBER
Dato' Seri Abdullah Ahmad Badawi is sworn in as Malaysia's fifth Prime Minister.

April: The month-long National Water Festival in Lumut gets under way.

'Work with me, not for me.'
Dato' Seri Abdullah Ahmad Badawi, addressing officers of the Prime Minister's Department after taking over as Prime Minister, 29 December 2003.

2003

world news

1 February
Space shuttle *Columbia* disintegrates over Texas on re-entry, killing all seven astronauts aboard.

7 February
Chess champion Gary Kasparov plays to a 3–3 draw against the 'Deep Junior' computer program.

14 February
Dolly, 6, a ewe, the first mammal to be cloned from a cell, dies in Britain from a lung infection.

18 February
A man intending suicide sets fire to a subway train in South Korea. The blaze spreads to another train. He survives; 198 other passengers don't.

26 February
An American businessman is admitted to a hospital in Hanoi with what will later be classified as the first known case of SARS (Severe Acute Respiratory Syndrome). Patient and doctor die. By July 2003, when the epidemic has largely expended itself, the WHO has registered more than 8,000 cases worldwide and 774 deaths.

Shalin's No. 1

5 January Singapore

Malaysia's leading woman bowler Shalin Zulkifli walked away with US$10,000 (RM38,000) after winning the Aviva Asian Bowling Grand Slam final at the Cathay Bowl here. She beat team-mate Lai Kin Ngoh for the title in a final that saw Shalin's consistency pulling her through. To cap a memorable week for Shalin there was the additional US$1,000 prize money for her 299 in the preliminary round, the highest in the women's competition.

Missing air force commando found

6 January Mersing

RMAF commando Sarjan Saad Che Omar, 34, of Jitra, Kedah, who was missing at sea after the boat carrying him and five others capsized off Pulau Sibu two days ago, has been found alive after a 57-hour ordeal in rough seas. He was rescued by a police aerial unit about 2km from Tanjung Siang in Kota Tinggi, some seven hours after a navy patrol unit spotted the bodies of his companions Korporal Hasrul Abdul Rahman and Korporal Ayub Sidek. Three others were missing.

'No' to quit offer

8 January Putrajaya

Prime Minister Dato' Seri Dr Mahathir Mohamad confirmed that he had received a resignation letter from Transport Minister Dato' Seri Dr Ling Liong Sik, but had not yet accepted it. He received the undated resignation letter 'a long time ago', he said, but did not agree with Dr Ling's intention to retire. Asked if Dr Ling's second announcement of his intention to resign had undermined the Cabinet, Dr Mahathir replied that this was not the case.

Dr Ling announced the previous day that he had submitted his letter to Dr Mahathir on 15 August 2002. It was to take effect on a date to be fixed by Dr Mahathir if the resignation was accepted by him (*see 28 May 2003*).

No more toll in Jalan Kuching

7 January Kuala Lumpur

Thousands of people gathered at the Jalan Kuching toll plaza (below) to celebrate its closure after 16 years of operation. At midnight on 6 January, the toll lights went off after Minister in the Prime Minister's Department Datuk Tengku Adnan Tengku Mansor became the last motorist to pay the toll at 11.59pm. There was also a 10-minute fireworks display and mandarin oranges were handed out to motorists by the Federal Territory MCA liaison committee. In October 2002, Deputy Works Minister Datuk Khaled Nordin said toll collection at Jalan Kuching had begun on 28 December 1987 and that up to 31 August 2002, a total of RM327,557,000 had been collected.

Datuk Tengku Adnan said that over the years the toll road had eased traffic heading to the city 'but the time has arrived to open it free to the public'.

Ponggal record

15 January Kuala Lumpur

A Ponggal cook-in at the Sri Veerakathy Vinayagar Temple here entered the *Malaysian Book of Records* after 400 people attended the two-hour mass-cooking event organised by the temple and local residents.

Sweetened rice was cooked in more than 300 claypots in the temple grounds. *Malaysia Book of Records* representative Sujatha Nair certified the event as the largest culinary event in the country.

Power sharing the key to success, says DPM

10 February Kuala Lumpur

Deputy Prime Minister Dato' Seri Abdullah Ahmad Badawi said power sharing among the races as practised in Malaysia would remain the strength of the country. 'This is the most important trait that has made Malaysia successful and peaceful'.

Speaking after launching a seminar titled "Father of Independence and Founder of Racial Unity' in memory of the Tunku's 100th birthday, he said that Bapa Malaysia and first Prime Minister Tunku Abdul Rahman Putra propagated this trait when the nation gained its sovereignty in 1957.

He said: 'The Tunku started this brand of brotherhood and peace which in turn became the basis for racial unity and harmony between religion and race, making it the strength of the independent country that we are now. '

'He created a politically stable and economically vibrant country.'

Bali bomb funder arrested

3 February Jakarta

Indonesian police said they had arrested a Malaysian believed to have been involved in the planning and funding of the 12 October Bali bombing. Noordin Mohammad Top was arrested in the East Java town of Gresik early today, deputy national police spokesman Chief Commissioner Didi Rohayadi said. Noordin was being questioned by police at their Java headquarters in Surabaya. He was also one of eight wanted in Malaysia as key members of Kumpulan Militan Malaysia.

Nordin, 33, was a BSc holder from Universiti Teknologi Malaysia. He was a former senior supervisor of Sekolah Islam Luqmanul Hakiem, Johor Bahru, and was married with two children.

Police named three other Malaysians as being involved in the Bali blasts, which killed more than 190 people and has been blamed on the Jemaah Islamiyah (JI) regional terror network.

Wan Min Wan Mat was in custody and police were hunting for Zulkifli Marzuki and a man known as Dr Azahari. All three were said to have attended a meeting called by JI in Bangkok last February at which bombing targets were discussed.

Train derailed after flood

3 February Gemas

Some 400 passengers on the Tumpat-bound Express Timuran had a rude shock and a narrow escape when their train hit a flood-weakened stretch of track that caused six of its 11 coaches and a locomotive to jump the rails.

Two of the coaches plunged into the swollen Sungai Anak Air Besi in the 5.45am incident which disrupted train services between KL and Singapore. At least seven people were treated for minor injuries.

200,000 say no to war

23 February Kuala Lumpur

Malaysians rallied behind the call for peace when about 200,000 people of all races and walks of life turned up at the Bukit Jalil Stadium in a show of unity and support for the PM's call to 'give peace a chance to solve problems'. Even a downpour did not dampen the spirit and enthusiasm of the people. The slogan 'Malaysians for Peace' was seen on T-shirts, banners, placards and flags and also heard on everyone's lips.

Prime Minister Dato' Seri Mahathir Mohamed said he feared the superpowers would not stop even after going to war with Iraq and would go after North Korea, Iran and other countries. Dr Mahathir arrived at 8.30pm for the event highlight—the presentation of 2.8 million signatures collected during the Malaysians for Peace campaign.

Peace Malaysia patron Datuk Hishammuddin Hussein said: 'Tonight we are gathered regardless of race and religion and demand for peace.' He later handed Dr Mahathir the 'Memorandum from the Citizens of Malaysia to the People of the World' to be delivered to the Non-Aligned Movement Summit in Kuala Lumpur.

Opening the NAM Summit the following day, Dr Mahathir called for the world community, through the United Nations, to outlaw war and create a new world order with power shared by all nations.

Security fleet for heads of 114 NAM nations

12 February Kuala Lumpur

More than 1,000 security vehicles would be used to escort foreign Heads of State and Government from 114 countries at the 13th Non-Aligned Movement Summit here, it was announced. About 2,500 police officers would be responsible for the leaders' safety on the road.

Ahmad Nor dies

12 February Kuala Lumpur

DAP vice-chairman and former Cuepacs president Ahmad Nor died at the Kuala Lumpur Hospital today. He was 60.

Ahmad, who was also a former Malaysian Trades Union Congress vice-president, had been in a coma caused by a brain haemorrhage. He was taken off life support at the request of the family.

He was survived by wife Mariam Beebi Ibrahim, sons Khairul Anwar, Addri and Amran, and daughters Suhaila and Mazlina, as well as four grandchildren.

The Malaysian men's and women's bowling teams pose after their double victory.

Simply bowled over

23 February Petaling Jaya

Malaysian men and women bowlers turned in an awesome performance to sweep both titles at the Fifth World Tenpin Team Cup tournament at Odense Bowling Hall in Denmark. The double victory ended a 23-year barren run for the national team on the world stage.

Malay classics banned

12 April Kuala Lumpur

Four Malay classics were on a list of 22 films banned by the Film Censorship Board. Considered gems in their time, with repeated screenings over RTM, they were *Anak Buluh Betung, Gergasi, Sumpah Wanita* and *Semusim di Neraka*. Censorship Board vice-chairman Datuk Ismail Mohd Jah said the films were deemed unsuitable for public screening because of their irreligious content. In February the board banned *Daredevil* for being 'too violent'.

One up for rally

24 March Kula Lumpur

Rally champions Karamjit Singh and Allen Oh won recognition for themselves and the sport when they were named the winners of the 2002 Sportsman of the Year award at a ceremony here.

The Yang di-Pertuan Agong presented them with the award which carried a cash prize of RM10,000.

First SARS death

5 April Sepang

The Health Ministry confirmed that a 64-year-old man from Jerantut died of Severe Acute Respiratory Syndrome (SARS) at the Kuala Lumpur Hospital on 30 March. Health director-general Tan Sri Dr Mohamad Taha Arif said a post-mortem showed he had congested lungs, signs of pneumonia and an enlarged heart.

The man's family were under 'home quarantine' and the Ministry directed the authorities to trace passengers who flew with him to the Kuala Lumpur International Airport on 16 March. The cabin crew would also be screened. Five suspected SARS cases reported the previous day brought the total in the country to 75.

Special treat by top designers at fashion gala

23 April Kuala Lumpur

A fashion gala dinner, themed 'Style and Sensuality', in conjunction with KL Fashion Week was held at the Mandarin Oriental Hotel, featuring top models from Dalian, China (above, in rehearsal) showing creations by Malaysian designers, who included international figures Zang Toi, Sarimah Adzrina and Justin Oh. The finale of the show was a qi pao collection by Dalian-based designer Wu Guo Bin.

2003

world news

1 March
Pakistan captures Khalid Shaikh Mohammad, the mastermind behind the 1993 and 2001 World Trade Centre and 2002 Bali attacks, among others.

20 March
Troops from the US, the UK, Australia and Poland invade Iraq.

22 July
Uday and Qusay Hussein, sons of Saddam Hussein, are killed in a shootout.

5 August
A car bomb outside the Marriott Hotel in Jakarta kills 10.

11 August
Riduan Isamuddin aka Hambali, leader of Jemaah Islamiyah, an affiliate of Al-Qaeda, and head of terrorist activities in the region, is captured in Ayutthaya, Thailand.

19 August
A car bomb in front of UN headquarters in Baghdad kills the UN Special Representative to Iraq, Brazilian Viera de Mello, and 22 others.

Water festival begins

12 April Lumut

Thousands of people braved the rain to watch as mythical creatures and colourful underwater 'life' signalled the start of the National Water Festival.

The month-long festival was launched by the Yang di-Pertuan Agong Tuanku Syed Sirajuddin.

Lumut was abuzz with the increased number of visitors who came to watch the fireworks, listen to singer Siti Nurhaliza and comedy group Senario, and watch cultural troupes perform on a floating stage.

The theme, 'Keharmonian Malaysia: Air Dicincang Tak Kan Putus', used an allegory of running water to emphasise continuing peace and harmony in the country.

Milestone for Petronas

22 April Kuala Lumpur

Petronas marked another milestone with last month's completion of its third liquefied natural gas plant in Tanjung Kidurong, Bintulu. With three LNG plants within its Bintulu LNG complex, Petronas is now the world's largest LNG producer in a single location with a combined output of 23 million tonnes a year.

Jailed for 20 years

25 April Taiping

The High Court sentenced four men to a maximum of 20 years' jail each on a reduced charge of culpable homicide not amounting to murder for causing the death of Hasleza Ishak, 26, the second wife of the Raja di-Hilir Perak, Datuk Seri Raja Jaafar Raja Muda Musa, in 2002.

They were carpenter Sabarudin Non, 34, fisherman J. Manimaran, 26, bomoh Rahim Ismail, 47, and palace aide Tengku Aristonsjah Tengku Mohamed Ansary, 40.

Their appeals to the Court of Appeal were dismissed on 30 October 2004.

However, Tengku Aristonsjah and Rahim were freed on 18 August 2006 after the Federal Court absolved them of any involvement in the death of Hasleza.

Sabarudin and Manimaran also appealed against their conviction but their appeals were rejected. However, the Federal Court reduced their jail term to 14 years.

Mercy doctors ambushed

13 April Baghdad

Five Malaysian Medical Relief Society (Mercy) volunteers and three Malaysian journalists were attacked by a group of armed militiamen in this war-torn city on 12 April. An Iraqi associate and their Syrian driver were killed. Mercy president Datuk Dr Jemilah Mahmood and Dr Baba Deni suffered gunshot wounds.

The other three, Mejar (B) Don Cheang, Dr Taufiq Hidayah and Anita Ahmad, escaped unhurt while the newsmen—*New Straits Times* photographer Mohd Anuar Hashim, RTM cameraman Omar Salleh and *The Sun* chief reporter Terence Fernandez—escaped unhurt despite being held captive for more than three hours.

Dr Jemilah and Dr Baba were taken to Al Qadasyah for treatment and transferred to the Saddam Hospital for further treatment and surgery.

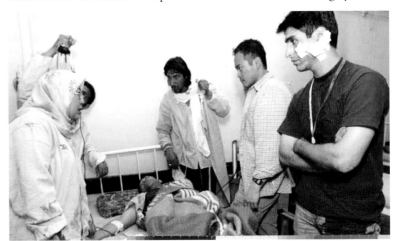

Despite her own injury, Dr Jemilah (left) tended to Dr Baba (in bed) in a Baghdad hospital.

Delayed BioValley project launched

20 May Dengkil

After much delay, the BioValley project was launched. Prime Minister Dato' Seri Dr Mahathir Mohamad performed the ground-breaking ceremony. BioValley Malaysia is located on a 200ha site south of Cyberjaya. Phase I was the development of an 80ha site housing a wide spectrum of biotechnology-related activities such as drug research and bio-processes operating on different platforms of technology.

The project aimed to consolidate all ongoing biotechnology initiatives using the country's rich natural resources and flora and fauna. It would also assist, coordinate and promote commercialisation of research findings and products of the stakeholders. In his speech, Dr Mahathir said Malaysia, with its lush tropical forests, had enormous resources to be tapped.

Swimmer beats two channels

24 May Langkawi

Abdul Malik Mydin, 28, was the first Malaysian to swim from Kuala Perlis to Kuah, a distance of 48km. He then went on to conquer the English Channel.

On his Langkawi Channel swim, the 1994 Malaysia Games cycling gold medallist clocked 14 hours, three minutes and 13 seconds, about four hours faster than expected. Prime Minister Dato' Seri Dr Mahathir Mohamad flagged him off.

His next challenge was to swim 34km across the English Channel, a feat he achieved on 2 August.

He completed the feat in just under 18 hours and would have made it hours earlier if not for strong winds.

MCA president resigns

28 May Putrajaya

Prime Minister Dato' Seri Dr Mahathir Mohamad accepted Dato' Seri Dr Ling Liong Sik's resignation as Transport Minister. Dato' Seri Dr Ling also resigned as MCA party president, a post he has held since 1986, and Dato' Seri Lim Ah Lek resigned as deputy president. Dato' Seri Ong Kah Ting and Datuk Chan Kong Choy were elected to replace them.

Dato' Seri Ong said the next few months would be 'crucial' for the party which must close ranks ahead of the general election, scheduled to be held next year.

On 24 June, MCA deputy president Datuk Chan was appointed Transport Minister, replacing Dato' Seri Dr Ling.

Anniversary of Laila Taib Welfare Complex

25 July Kuching

The Laila Taib Welfare Complex in Semariang near Kuching was set up in 1993 with the aim of helping needy members of society. At its 10th anniversary celebration, Sarawak Chief Minister Tan Sri Abdul Taib Mahmud said that looking after and caring for orphans were the responsibility of all and that the spirit of wanting to make sacrifices for others was important. His wife, Puan Sri Laila Taib, was the patron of the complex.

Raja Tun Mohar dies

8 June Kuala Lumpur

Perusahaan Otomobil Kedua Sdn Bhd (Perodua) chairman and former Special Economic Adviser to the Prime Minister Raja Tun Mohar Raja Badiozaman, 81, died of broncho-pneumonia at the Pantai Medical Centre at 3.19am.

He leaves his wife Toh Puan Norella Talib, 67, three children and nine grandchildren. Prime Minister Dato' Seri Dr Mahathir Mohamad described Raja Tun Mohar as a man who had served his country until his last breath. 'He was not only my Economic Adviser. He had also served under Tun Abdul Razak and Tun Hussein (Onn).'

Historical find in Malacca fort

`23 June` **Malacca**

Archaeologists discovered the base of a tower once part of the Porto de Santiago built by the Portuguese 500 years ago, near Padang Pahlawan, where workers were preparing for the building of a shopping complex. A Bastardo coin from the Portuguese era, skeletal remains and broken pottery from the Ming and Ching dynasties were also found. Museums and Antiquities Department officials said they hoped the State Government would review development plans.

Umno permanent chairman dies

`5 July` **Kuala Lumpur**

Umno's longest-serving permanent chairman Tun Sulaiman Ninam Shah, 83, died at the Pantai Medical Centre here.

The Umno permanent chairman for 28 years, Tun Sulaiman left a wife Toh Puan Rose Othman, nine children, 15 grandchildren and two great-grandchildren.

Lawyer cleared of murder

`23 July` **Kuala Lumpur**

Lawyer Datuk Balwant Singh (below), who shot dead a despatch rider last year, was today acquitted of murder by the High Court. Judge Datuk S. Augustine Paul held that Balwant, 82, had proven on a balance of probabilities that he was exercising his right of self-defence when he shot R. Gobala Krishnan, 33, in Jalan Maarof at 4.30pm on June 7.

Paul said the fact that Balwant was armed with a pistol and Gobala with a stick did not make any difference in law when it came to exercising the right of self-defence.

Death for Al-Ma'unah man who killed soldier

`26 June` **Kuala Lumpur**

The Federal Court confirmed a High Court decision and sentenced to death Jemari Jusoh, the Al-Ma'unah member who shot and killed army commando Corporal Mathew ak Medan.

The court also upheld the death sentences of the group leader, Mohd Amin Mohd Razali, and his right-hand men, Zahit Muslim and Jamaludin Darus. In addition it unanimously upheld the life imprisonment of 15 other members of the group.

Water dispute: the facts

`27 July` **Kuala Lumpur**

The Government published two advertisements by the National Economic Action Council (NEAC) about the dispute over the price of water supplied to Singapore. This was in response to an advertisement placed by the republic in the *Asian Wall Street Journal*.

The NEAC said it had 'no choice but to respond yet again to the island republic's claims and misrepresentations.' The NEAC advertisements broke down Singapore's claims and tackled them point by point. Thousands of copies of an NEAC booklet on the issue were snapped up within hours.

. The 20-page booklet entitled *Water: The Singapore–Malaysia Dispute—The Facts* was sold at three sen, the same price Singapore pays for every 1,000 gallons of water it is getting from Malaysia

Gold in the pay packet

`27 July` **Kuala Lumpur**

The Royal Mint of Malaysia rolled out its first batch of gold dinar for public use. Royal Mint employees were given an option to receive a portion of their monthly salaries, mainly that allotted for savings purposes, in the form of a quarter dinar or one dinar, equivalent to RM52.50 and RM181 respectively. The gold dinar is minted in accordance with the standard of Caliph Umar Al-Khatab who set the weight of one gold dinar at 4.25g of gold of 91.7 per cent purity.

Apart from the quarter dinar and one dinar, the Royal Mint will also be producing half-dinar, two-dinar and four-dinar denominations soon.

Mahathir's farewell

Last message as President

`21 June` **Kuala Lumpur**

Prime Minister Dato' Seri Dr Mahathir Mohamad's goodbye to the nation started with his final address as president to the Umno general assembly when he asked members to give his successor, Deputy Prime Minister Dato' Seri Abdullah Ahmad Badawi, the same kind of support that they had showed him. Looking relaxed and upbeat, he said he was satisfied he was leaving a strong Umno to his successor.

On 21 September, Dato' Seri Abdullah launched a 10-volume collection of speeches by Dr Mahathir, saying that the Prime Minister's ideas and visions would continue to inspire the people.

'A statesman and friend'

`7 October` **Bali**

Delegates from all Asean nations at the summit in Bali paid tribute to Dato' Seri Dr Mahathir Mohamad.

Indonesian President Megawati Sukarnoputri, the chairperson, wept as she bade farewell to Dr Mahathir, describing him as a 'statesman and steadfast friend'.

Tears flow at final Cabinet meeting

`29 October` **Putrajaya**

Emotions ran high when Dato' Seri Dr Mahathir Mohamad chaired his last Cabinet meeting. At 12.30pm, he signed the minutes of the meeting in the presence of his deputy Dato' Seri Abdullah Ahmad Badawi and other Ministers who were trying hard to stay in control. Three women Ministers were in tears.

What the foreign press said

In its 3 November issue, *Newsweek* magazine carried a cover story on Dr Mahathir and his successor Dato' Seri Abdullah. Excerpts: 'Abdullah is expected to concentrate his efforts on improving education and tackling corruption, which he has denounced publicly, calling it 'a terrible disease that can hurt our image and competitiveness'. 'Many wonder if he (Abdullah) has the right stuff to end the cronyism and graft that is endemic in Malaysia'. The article quoted author M. Bakri Musa as saying that Abdullah's 'only redeeming quality, apart from his legendary honesty, is his humility'.

Aerobatic tribute to Dr Mahathir from the RAF on 27 September.

Abdullah takes over

`31 October` **Kuala Lumpur**

Dato' Seri Abdullah Ahmad Badawi was sworn in as the country's fifth Prime Minister before the Yang di-Pertuan Agong at Istana Negara. Later in the day in Putrajaya, Dr Mahathir officially handed over the desk file to Dato' Seri Abdullah, to signify the transfer to him of responsibilities of the high office, in the presence of the Chief Secretary to the Government. 'Work with me and not for me,' Dato' Seri Abdullah said, in a call to the Ministers, Deputy Ministers and staff who work in the Prime Minister's Department. The call extends to all civil servants, whom he encouraged to work together for 'the sake of our race, religion and this beloved nation'.

Honour for Dr M

`22 December` **Putrajaya**

The Yang di-Pertuan Agong Tuanku Syed Sirajuddin Syed Putra Jamalullail and the Raja Permaisuri Agong Tuanku Fauziah Tengku Abdul Rashid stood up at the VIP table on arrival at a dinner to honour former Prime Minister Dato' Seri Dr Mahathir Mohamad. The dinner, at the Putrajaya Convention Centre, was hosted by Prime Minister Dato' Seri Abdullah Ahmad Badawi.

2003

world news

15 September
More than 100 South Korean tourists fly to North Korea on the first commercial flight since the countries were divided six decades earlier.

15 October
China becomes the third country to launch a man, 'taikonaut' Yang Liwei, 38, into space orbit.

24 October
The last commercial flight of the Concorde ends an era of supersonic passenger service.

20 November
Michael Jackson is arrested on charges of child molestation.

12 December
A dishevelled Saddam Hussein is captured in a hidden bunker in Tikrit.

26 December
An earthquake levels more than half the Iranian city of Bam, killing over 35,000.

30 December
In Cambodia, former Khmer Rouge Head of State Khieu Samphan acknowledges that his regime had committed genocide.

Award for Mercy chief

12 August Petaling Jaya

Malaysian Medical Relief Society president Datuk Dr Jemilah Mahmood was the first Malaysian woman to receive the East Asia Women Peace Award, sharing the honour with fellow recipients Aung San Suu Kyi and Corazon Aquino. Dr Jemilah, one of the seven recipients, received her award with both current and past Philippine Presidents Gloria Arroyo and Corazon Aquino present at a ceremony in Manila.

Landslide at expressway

26 November Kuala Lumpur

A massive rockfall on the New Klang Valley Expressway (NKVE) caused 20,000 tonnes of boulders and soil to crash on to the expressway. No lives were lost or vehicles damaged but the road was closed between the Bukit Lanjan and Kota Damansara interchanges.

Authorities said there might have been casualties had the usually busy road not been quiet because it was a public holiday.

Projek Lebuhraya Utara-Selatan (PLUS) said its officials were working closely with UEM Construction, the Malaysian Highway Authority and rescue and services departments to clear the rocks blocking the highway. Work was expected to be completed in two weeks.

Of queens and princesses

24 August Kuala Lumpur

A book, *101 Princesses of the Malay World*, was among attractions on display for the 40th anniversary of the National Museum. The work of authors Nisriwani Yahya and Syed Zulfida S.M. Noor, it highlights stories of strong royal women from Queen Adruja Wijamala of Langkasuka, who ruled from 1317 to 1345, to Che Manjalara, the mother of Tunku Abdul Rahman.

Pygmy elephant a new sub-species

3 September Kuala Lumpur

The pygmy elephants found in Borneo have been identified by DNA testing to be a distinct sub-species from those found in mainland Asia and Sumatra, World Wide Fund for Nature Malaysia chairman Tengku Zainal Adlin said.

Monorail a huge success

31 August Kuala Lumpur

The opening of Kuala Lumpur's RM1.18-billion monorail service in conjunction with National Day saw Malaysians taking advantage of the free ride on its elevated tracks. They packed the station in the Bukit Bintang area after the line was launched by Prime Minister Dato' Seri Dr Mahathir Mohamad.

Former Supreme Court judge dies

30 September Kuala Lumpur

Human Rights Commission of Malaysia (Suhakam) deputy chairman and former Supreme Court judge Tan Sri Harun Hashim died at the Damansara Specialist Hospital after a heart attack. He was 74.

Bowlers strike gold

17 September Petaling Jaya

Malaysia's women bowlers won the country's first-ever women's gold medal in the World Bowling Championships in Bandar Sunway. Anchored by Asian champion Shalin Zulkifli, the team, comprising Choy Poh Lai, Sharon Chai, Wendy Chai and Sarah Yap, knocked down a total 6,208 pins to beat overnight leaders Sweden by 97 pins for the title.

Toxic drums dumped

4 December Petaling Jaya

Fifty drums of toxic paint thinner and other chemical wastes have been found dumped near a residential area and golf course in Kelana Jaya. Petaling Jaya Municipal Council (MPPJ) enforcement officers stumbled on the dumpsite during a routine check. The drums were found at an isolated piece of land in Kampung Seri Dangang, a former squatter area.

Former Selangor MB dies

19 October Kuala Lumpur

Selangor's longest-serving Menteri Besar Datuk Harun Idris died hours after he suffered a heart attack at his home in Taman Duta yesterday. He was 79.

First batch for National Service

8 December Kuala Lumpur

Some 85,000 teenagers born in 1986 have been selected for the inaugural National Service programme. They were chosen at random from a list of 480,000 names in a computer ballot.

Meanwhile, NS Department director-general Kamaruzaman Mohd Nor said candidates who wish to be exempted on health grounds must undergo a medical examination at Government or military hospitals, the list of which was expected to be released soon.

First gold for archery

4 December Petaling Jaya

Archer Mohd Marbawi Sulaiman bagged the country's first gold at the Vietnam SEA Games in Hanoi.

The chubby Marbawi, 20, defeated Singapore's Loh Wen Liang 104–102.

Hospital turns 122

29 December Kuala Lumpur

Tung Shin Hospital, which celebrated its 122th anniversary recently, started as a community hospital built and meant for the people. In the late 1890s bullock carts served as ambulances to carry patients to the hospital during what were difficult days for the thousands of Chinese immigrants who worked in the tin mines that surrounded Kuala Lumpur. Many did not have money for treatment.

2004

A tsunami killed 66 people in Malaysia following a massive earthquake off the west coast of Sumatra. Penang, Langkawi and the northwest coastal regions were the worst hit. Damage to life and property was estimated at billions of ringgit. Prime Minister Dato' Seri Abdullah Ahmad Badawi, who had earlier led the Barisan Nasional to one of its best election victories, offered aid to Indonesia's Aceh province where villages and fishing boats were swallowed by waves up to five metres high. Anwar Ibrahim was cleared of the sodomy charge for which he was earlier jailed but lost his appeal over his conviction on corruption charges. Two more women—one 25 years old, and the other 8,000 years old—made headline news. Read on…

JULY
All seven onboard are killed in a helicopter crash in the Sarawak jungle.

OCTOBER
Singer Jaclyn Victor becomes the first Malaysian Idol.

NOVEMBER
Datin Paduka Sharifah Mazlina Syed Abdul Kadir becomes the first Asian woman to ski-sail across Antartica.

DECEMBER
Killer tsunami kills more than 125,000 throughout Asia, including Malaysia.

March: Barisan Nasional gains a clear mandate in the general election.

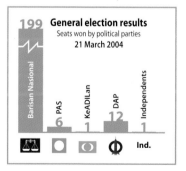

General election results
Seats won by political parties
21 March 2004

199 — Barisan Nasional
6 — PAS
1 — KeADILan
12 — DAP
1 — Independents (Ind.)

'Spring will always be around if there is harmony among people.'

Dato' Seri Abdullah Ahmad Badawi and Datin Paduka Seri Endon's Chinese New Year message, 14 January 2004.

2004

world news

13 January
A US soldier reports US abuse of Iraqi prisoners in Abu Ghraib prison.

2 February
Pakistan says Abdul Qadeer Khan, founder of its nuclear programme, passed on sensitive technology to Iran, Libya and North Korea to aid their nuclear programmes.

3 February
The CIA admits there was no imminent threat from weapons of mass destruction before the 2003 invasion of Iraq.

11 March
Bombs kill 190 on rush-hour trains in Madrid.

15 March
The new socialist Spanish Government says it will withdraw the 1,300 Spanish troops in Iraq.

20 March
Taiwan President Chen Shui-bian wins elections with a margin of only 0.2%.

22 March
In Palestine, an Israeli missile kills Sheik Ahmad Yassin, co-founder and leader of Hamas.

Dato' Sri Najib seeks blessings from his mother Tun Rahah Noah. Looking on is his wife Datin Seri Rosmah Mansor.

Najib is DPM

8 January   Kuala Lumpur

Dato' Sri Najib Tun Razak was made Deputy Prime Minister in a Cabinet reshuffle that saw the appointment of a new Minister and three portfolios swapped. Dato' Sri Najib remained Defence Minister.

The new face was Tan Sri Nor Mohamed Yakcop, Second Finance Minister; Tan Sri Muhyiddin Yassin was appointed Agriculture Minister; Datuk Jamaludin Jarjis Domestic Trade and Consumer Affairs Minister; and Dato' Seri Effendi Norwawi Special Functions Minister in the Prime Minister's Department.

Dato' Seri Abdullah Ahmad Badawi (left) is greeted by his deputy Dato' Sri Najib after his appointment.

CID 'needs more men'

2 January   Kuala Lumpur

The police aims to solve high-profile cases within 14 days and to more than double manpower in its criminal investigation department in a revamp involving five problematic sections of the CID. Its director, Dato' Seri Salleh Mat Som, said a study conducted by the Public Service Department showed that the CID needs a 120 per cent increase in manpower.

1,000 made homeless

16 January   Kuala Perlis

Fire destroyed nearly 100 wooden homes in two fishing villages here, leaving 1,000 people homeless. Losses were estimated at millions of ringgit. Fanned by strong winds, the fire swept through the villages in less than an hour.

Harmony is message of PM's CNY cards

14 January   Petaling Jaya

Prime Minister Dato' Seri Abdullah Ahmad Badawi and Datin Paduka Seri Endon Mahmood sent out 3,000 Chinese New Year cards, reading in bold calligraphy: 'Spring will always be around if there is harmony among people; the world will be peaceful if there is political stability in the country'.

政穩世乃安
人和春長在

Rape and death of girl, 10, sparks calls for action

21 January   Kuala Lumpur

There were demands for chemical castration, the death sentence or life imprisonment for child rapists and a register of offenders following the case of a 10-year-old girl in Johor Bahru who died after she was raped.

On 27 January, the Sessions Court imposed the maximum sentence of 20 years' imprisonment and 24 strokes of the rotan on security guard Mohd Abbas Danus Baksan who admitted raping the girl on 17 January.

On 27 August, the High Court sentenced Mohd Abbas to death for the girl's murder. Judicial Commissioner K.P. Gengaharan Nair told him: 'You have snuffed out the life of a young, innocent girl just to satisfy your lust.' The only sentence he was allowed to pass, he added, 'is the sentence of death' (see 16 October 2008).

Speed limit stays

16 January   Kuala Lumpur

The Cabinet decided not to increase the speed limit on highways to 120kph from the current 110kph, said Works Minister Dato' Seri S. Samy Vellu. The decision was in view of the high accident rate, he said.

Walking in step

16 January   Bangkok

Prime Minister Dato' Seri Abdullah Ahmad Badawi and Thai Prime Minister Thaksin Shinawatra pictured at Government House in Bangkok during the official ceremony to welcome Dato' Seri Abdullah, who was on a one-day visit to discuss trade and joint security with his Thai counterpart.

IGP welcomes Royal Commission on force

4 February   Kuala Lumpur

Inspector General of Police Dato' Seri Bakri Omar welcomed the Special Commission on the Police Force whose members were announced by the Prime Minister's Department. He said this would mean that the role and burdens of the police would be thoroughly studied. 'It is our hope, and I believe the hope of everyone, to see improvements in the workings and management of the police force.'

Prime Minister Dato' Seri Abdullah Ahmad Badawi said he hoped the Royal Commission on Police would draw up a comprehensive report for the future benefit and effectiveness of the force.

Ex-Perwaja MD held

9 February **Kuala Lumpur**

Former Perwaja Steel Sdn Bhd managing director Tan Sri Eric Chia Eng Hock, 71, was arrested by Anti-Corruption Agency officers. He was in a wheelchair as he was taken to the ACA headquarters. After questioning, he was taken to the Putrajaya Hospital where he was detained until the following day when he was charged in the Kuala Lumpur Sessions Court. He pleaded not guilty to criminal breach of trust involving RM76.4 million, and was remanded on bail of RM2 million.

Tan Sri Eric talks to the press after his arrest.

Tan Sri Eric's arrest came after one of the most long-drawn-out inquiries ever conducted by the ACA. Perwaja was established in 1982 as a joint venture between the Heavy Industries Corporation of Malaysia (HICOM) and Nippon Steel of Japan. The company became saddled with RM10 billion in debts and losses, including current liabilities of RM926 million, long-term liabilities totalling RM6.013 billion, and losses amounting to RM2.985 billion. In 2007, Chia was acquitted after the court said the prosecution had failed to establish a prima facie case against him (*see 26 June 2007*).

Landslide victory for BN in Sarawak

21 March **Kuching**

In the Sarawak State election, Barisan Nasional won all Parliamentary seats with the exception of Bandar Kuching which went to DAP's Chong Chieng Jen. Chief Minister Tan Sri Abdul Taib Mahmud's seat was uncontested. Prime Minister Dato' Seri Abdullah Ahmad Badawi said the victory proved the acceptance and support of the people for BN.

Sports stars honoured

29 March **Subang Jaya**

Sprinter Nazmizan Mohamed, who ended Malaysia's 36-year wait for a SEA Games sprint double, and Nicol David, the first Malaysian and Asian squash player to qualify for the semi-finals of the World Championships, were crowned 2003 Sportsman and Sportswoman of the Year respectively. The awards came with prize money of RM10,000 each. It capped a memorable year for them as they defied the odds to shine in their respective events.

Harley-Davidson store opens in PJ

21 February **Petaling Jaya**

Sultan Sharafuddin Idris Shah of Selangor, who rides a Harley himself, launched the Harley Davidson flagship store in a ceremony punctuated by the revving of 600 Harley Davidson motorcycles and the thunderous beat of the kompang. The shop showcased Harley models, parts and accessories, apparel and memorabilia such as T-shirts, leather jackets and bags. Harley bikers, both local and from Singapore, Thailand, Brunei, Indonesia and Hong Kong, watched a lion dance and a fashion show.

Travel fair success

15 February **Kuala Lumpur**

Congestion hit several parts of the city for the second day running with the blame once again falling on the Le Tour de Langkawi and the Malaysia Airlines Travel Fair at the MidValley Megamall. The two events reduced traffic in most parts of the city to a virtual standstill.

The travel fair saw ticket sales of RM14 million recorded so far for the two-day event and the national carrier was planning to turn it into an annual event.

The most popular domestic destinations were Langkawi, Kuching, Kota Kinabalu and Redang Island in Terengganu.

Teething problems for NS

15 February **Kuala Lumpur**

Confusion reigned on the first morning of National Service for the first group of 26,000 teenage trainees as many pick-up points nationwide were in disarray.

The exercise brings together 18-year-old youngsters of different ethnic and religious backgrounds from all over the country for a three-month patriotic stint.

While the problems were sorted out by nightfall, with all the youngsters safely at their designated camps, exasperated trainees and their relatives had few nice things to say earlier in the day.

Describing these as 'teething problems', Prime Minister Dato' Seri Abdullah Ahmad Badawi said what was important was that the problem was identified and action taken immediately to rectify the situation. On 6 March the induction was staggered to avoid a repeat of the problem.

Dream comes true

15 March **Kuala Lumpur**

The first *Akademi Fantasia* winner Vincent Chong was holding on to his dreams. The 24-year-old's debut album contains seven songs that he penned himself.

'They are my ideas, yes, and my music,' he said at the launch of his album. One of the two English numbers on the album, *Hold on to Your Dreams*, is his favourite song.

Passenger trains collide

2 March **Seremban** ▶ Two KTM Komuter trains carrying more than 500 passengers collided at a level crossing in Bukit Tembok near here, leaving eight seriously injured. Rescuers freed one of the drivers trapped in the wreckage. The other driver was not injured. Most of the passengers were heading home after work when the 6.15pm collision took place.

The crash affected inter-city train services heading to Singapore and the east coast. This was the first major crash involving commuter trains since they started running in 1995.

The next day, investigations showed that a breakdown in communications between the trains and the Seremban KTM station could have caused the collision which occurred 10 minutes after a lightning strike caused a blackout at the station.

Rescuers work to free the trapped driver.

Islam Hadhari praised at Buddhist meeting

10 April **Seri Kembangan**

Non-Muslims have been very receptive to Islam Hadhari, or progressive Islam, a concept advocated by Prime Minister Dato' Seri Abdullah Ahmad Badawi, said MCA president Dato' Seri Ong Ka Ting.

'It is important for Malaysians to live in religious harmony. We want to stick to the original concept of the Constitution, drafted in 1957.'

At the opening of an International Buddhist Forum organised by the Young Buddhist Association of Malaysia and attended by 800 participants from Malaysia and other countries around the region, he said: 'The Government ensures freedom of worship and religion.'

He said freedom of religion was enshrined in the Constitution, and that Malaysians wanted religious tolerance.

2004

---

world news

---

11 April
An Indian steel tycoon pays US$128 million for a mansion in London.

23 April
In Thailand's restive south, 50 public buildings in all 13 districts of Narathiwat province are torched. An army officer is killed.

24 April
Three boats explode off Iraq's port of Umm Qasir when approached by US sailors. This Al-Qaeda operation was targeting oil terminals.

28 April
Thai police gun down 112 men who were stoning military outposts.

10 May
Philippine President Gloria Macapagal-Arroyo wins re-election, beating actor Fernando Poe by a million votes.

12 August
Singapore PM Goh Chok Tong hands over the reins of the country to Lee Hsien Loong, the son of the country's first PM.

13–29 August
The Summer Olympics are held in its ancient homeland, Greece.

BN landslide win

21 March Kuala Lumpur

Prime Minister Dato' Seri Abdullah Ahmad Badawi delivered the Barisan Nasional one of its best-ever victories in a general election, demolishing Pas and Keadilan, winning back control of Terengganu from PAS and coming within a hair's breadth of doing so in Kelantan. All Keadilan candidates lost their seats apart from its president Datin Seri Dr Wan Azizah Wan Ismail. The DAP, however, bettered its 1999 election performance.

Immediately after BN's official two-thirds majority was declared, Dato' Seri Abdullah re-affirmed his promise that all BN elected representatives would be tasked with giving the best possible service to their constituents.

There was little doubt that it was the feel-good sentiment surrounding his first four months in office and the widespread acceptance of his brand of Islam Hadhari, or progressive Islam, that propelled the BN to victory.

Dato' Seri Abdullah said he was happy that voters had turned out in large numbers, exceeding the number who voted in the 1999 general election.

He said the mandate they gave was for Barisan to continue its agenda of 'excellence, distinction and glory' to develop the nation and ensure continuous peace and prosperity. The next day, the Kuala Lumpur Stock Exchange Composite Index (KLCI) stayed well above the 905-mark as the market reacted positively to the BN victory.

Schumacher raises the trophy on high to celebrate his win.

A stroll for Schumacher

21 March Sepang

Ferrari's Michael Schumacher led from start to finish to win the Petronas Formula One Malaysian Grand Prix at the Sepang Circuit, his third win in six years.

History was written in many ways as Schumacher recorded the 72nd win of his career and he maintained his 100 per cent record of wins from pole position this year.

Population now 25.1 million

10 June Kuala Lumpur

Malaysia's population has grown to 25.1 million, having grown 2.2% since 2000, but there has been a decline in the fertility rate of 0.2% between 1990 and 2002, said Women, Family and Community Development Minister Dato' Seri Shahrizat Abdul Jalil.

The drop in the fertility rate could be due to an increasing number of people placing their careers first or because people were marrying late or staying single, she said after launching the fourth Malaysian Population and Family Census. The census would be conducted to assess population movement, family development and reproductive health. This would help to formulate the Ninth Malaysia Plan due to be launched in 2006.

Integrity Plan aims to create moral society

23 April Putrajaya

The National Integrity Plan was launched, aimed at promoting a values-based society with a clear sense of morals. Prime Minister Dato' Seri Abdullah Ahmad Badawi said the plan had five targets for the first five years, from 2004 to 2008.

These were to effectively reduce corruption and abuse of power; enhance efficiency in the public service delivery system and overcome bureaucracy; enhance corporate governance; strengthen the family as an institution; and improve quality of life of Malaysians.

To meet the targets, Dato' Seri Abdullah said a National Integrity Institute would be set up to monitor and coordinate the programmes. It would be independent and have its own office and staff.

Cheers and tears

30 April Kuala Lumpur

Their smiles say it all. This group of National Service trainees based in Universiti Malaya can't wait to go home at the end of their three-month stint which ends today. But there was also sadness as they said goodbye to newfound friends. Many said they had a good time and some even felt the programme should be longer.

No Selangor deputy MB

26 March Shah Alam

Selangor will not have a deputy menteri besar, said Menteri Besar Dato' Seri Dr Mohamed Khir Toyo. He was speaking at a Press conference after being sworn in as Menteri Besar before Sultan Sharafuddin at Istana Bukit Kayangan.

The Sultan, he added, had consented to his request not to appoint a deputy menteri besar.

Richness of marine life

24 June South China Sea

With the blessings of the Yang di-Pertuan Agong, the 1,700-ton vessel *Allied Commander* set off with many of Malaysia's marine scientists aboard on a 7,000km voyage funded by the new Science, Technology and Innovation Ministry.

Its objective was to find out more about the South China Sea and perhaps answer some questions about its biodiversity. The expedition had taken a year to plan.

Four confess to being in terrorists' network

2 April Kuala Lumpur

Four Malaysians detained in Indonesia confessed to being part of an international network of terrorists involved in several bomb attacks, including those in Bali and Manila. The four—Mohamad Nasir Abbas, Amran Mansor, Jaafar Anwarul and Shamsul Bahri Husein—made their confession in an interview. They admitted to being members of Jemaah Islamiyah (JI) and having links with Al-Qaeda. Nasir said he trained several top JI leaders in military warfare, including Bali bombers Ali Imron and Imam Samudera. JI members believed that they were acting on the orders of Osama bin Laden. Nasir said Osama's call to kill Americans was passed on to JI members in the region by Hambali and Abu Bakar Bashir, two of the JI senior leaders. Hambali was in US custody after being arrested in Thailand in 2003 while Abu Bakar Bashir was serving a prison term for immigration offences.

New face of terror

22 June Kuala Lumpur

Hambali, once dubbed the face of terror in Southeast Asia, was providing vital information to security agencies on Osama bin Laden's al-Qaeda operations in the region, it was reported.

Hambali, or Riduan Isamuddin (right), was the brains behind the fanatical JI, accused of carrying out a series of church bombings in Indonesia and the Bali blasts in 2002 that killed more than 200 people.

Meanwhile, JI bomb expert Dr Azhari Husin, the alleged mastermind of the Bali bomb blasts, remains elusive. He and fellow Malaysian Noordin Mohd Top, both on the run, are said to have taken over the leadership of the terrorist organisation (*See 9 November 2005*).

Abuse of Indonesian maid shocks nation

19 May Kuala Lumpur

A severely-bruised and scalded Indonesian maid was given shelter at the Indonesian Embassy here and her employer's wife was remanded to help police investigate the matter. Police described it as the worse abuse case they had seen.

Three days later, housewife Yim Pek Ha, 35, was charged in the Sessions Court and Attorney-General Tan Sri Abdul Gani Patail promised to push for the maximum sentence which could result in a 67-year jail term. Yim was charged with four counts of causing grievous hurt. Victim Nirmala Bonet claimed that for the last five months, Yim had abused her daily, burning her with a hot iron, pouring boiling water on her and using other objects to hit her (*see 27 November 2008*).

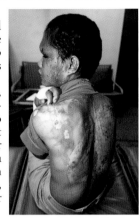

Honoured educators

6 May Kuala Lumpur

The 2004 Tokoh Guru award recipients (from left) Ali Suhaili, Md Ismail Zam Zam, Krishnasamy Tambusamy, Alice Wee Siew Eng and Wan Safinah Saleh look at a programme booklet held by former Education director-general Tan Sri Dr Murad Mohd Noor during the Teachers' Day celebrations at Stadium Malawati in Shah Alam. On the same day a 'super teachers' plan was announced enabling teachers to gain promotion without moving into administrative positions.

Kris recovered from 400-year-old wreck

3 July Dungun

A long kris was recovered from a 400-year-old wrecked ship laden with Ming-era porcelain in waters off Dungun. The wreck was discovered in June 2003.

'The kris is a mysterious find,' said Culture, Arts and Heritage Minister Dato' Seri Dr Rais Yatim, who visited the site of the wreck today. It could have belonged to a Malay hired by the ship owner to help navigate the South China Sea or it could have been a gift from a Malay dignitary.

The ship was believed to be Portuguese, and was heading to either Johor, Malacca or Batavia (present-day Jakarta) according to information provided by Sten Sjostrand, the principal researcher of the company excavating the shipwreck with the Department of Museums and Antiquities.

Some of the porcelain recovered showed the reign marks of Chinese Emperors Chenghua (r. 1465–1487) and Chia-ching (r. 1522–1566).

Cross-channel swimmer

15 July London

Cambridge University medical student Lennard Lee successfully swam across the 33.6km-wide English Channel in 9 hours 45 minutes. Lee, 20, said he was inspired by Abdul Malik Mydin, who made it in 17 hours 35 minutes on 3 August 2003.

Lee's attempt was also meant to help raise funds for Christie Hospital, a cancer hospital in Manchester, and to build a new swimming pool for his university. His feat also helped to raise RM134,773.50 for the Seck Kia Eenh Cancer Fund in Malacca.

1,300-year-old tree a boost for eco-tourism

8 June Kuala Terengganu

Terengganu Menteri Besar Datuk Idris Jusoh declared a 1,300-year-old chengal tree in Hulu Dungun a State treasure. He said it would boost eco-tourism like the Jomon Sugi in Yakushima, Japan, and the Giant Sequoia at the Yosemite National Park in California.

The State Forestry Department would be keeping a vigilant watch to safeguard what is believed to be the biggest chengal tree in the world. The tree is 65m tall with a circumference of 16.75m that requires 13 people to hug its trunk.

Murder accused freed

1 July Kuala Lumpur

Engineer Hanif Basree Abdul Rahman, accused of murdering part-time guest relations officer Noritta Samsudin, walked out of court a free man without his defence being called. When High Court judge Mr Justice Abdull Hamid Embong ruled that the prosecution had not made a prima facie case against Hanif, the gallery erupted in loud cheers and applause. Hanif collapsed in tears as family members and friends surged forward to embrace him.

Walk for peace

18 July Kuala Lumpur

Some of the 3,000 devotees of Mel Maruvathur Aathi Parasakthi Sittar Peedam made their way to Batu Caves to attend prayers for spiritual upliftment, world peace and national prosperity today.

The devotees, carrying pots of milk and porridge, prayed to cleanse negative feelings.

Abdullah unopposed as Umno president

18 July Kuala Lumpur

Dato' Seri Abdullah Ahmad Badawi and Dato' Seri Najib Razak have won the top two posts in Umno.

Dato' Seri Abdullah won unopposed after his only conceivable challenger, Tengku Razaleigh Hamzah, was knocked out. Dato' Sri Najib received 174 nominations for deputy president. The results were not unexpected following the overwhelming victory by the Abdullah-led Barisan Nasional in the March general election.

Nations show sea power

20 July Straits of Malacca

Warships from Indonesia, Singapore and Malaysia at sea during a ceremony to launch a coordinated patrol by navies of the three nations in the Straits of Malacca. The joint patrols were aimed at countering rising piracy in one of the world's most important shipping lanes.

2004

world news

27 August
Two Chechen women suicide bombers bring down two Russian airliners almost simultaneously.

29 August
Michael Schumacher wins a record 7th Formula One championship.

1 September
Chechen rebels take 1,000–1,500 hostages, many of them children, in a school in Beslan, North Ossetia. Russian forces storm the school and kill 32 Chechens. Also killed are 334 hostages, including 186 children.

9 September
A car bomb outside the Australian Embassy in Jakarta kills 11.

14 October
Norodom Sihamoni becomes King of Cambodia on the abdication of his father Norodom Sihanouk.

20 October
Susilo Bambang Yudhoyono becomes the first directly-elected President of Indonesia.

Blair greets the PM at Downing Street.

Blair praises Malaysia

22 July | **Kuala Lumpur**

British Prime Minister Tony Blair became the latest leader to endorse the country's brand of progressive Islam and said it should be replicated in other parts of the Muslim world. He said this during a one-hour meeting with Dato' Seri Abdullah Ahmad Badawi at 10 Downing Street.

Helicopter crash in jungle kills seven

30 July | **Miri**

All seven people aboard a Bell Long Ranger helicopter that crashed in the jungles of Sarawak on 12 July were confirmed dead. Search-and-rescue personnel remained at the site to complete their investigations.

The victims were Assistant State Minister in the Chief Minister's Department Dr Judson Sakai Tagal, Sarawak Electricity Supply Corporation CEO Roger Wong, Padawan Municipal Council chairman Lawrence Th'ng, Sesco engineers Jason Eng and Ling Tian Ho, contractor Datuk Marcus Raja and pilot Capt Samsudin Hashim. The helicopter went missing while en route to inspect a hydro-electric facility.

The wreckage of the helicopter.

21,000 letters undelivered

5 August | **Kuala Lumpur**

After a guard informed Pos Malaysia he had found 200 undelivered letters in a vacant apartment in Kepong, postal authorities investigated and found 21,455 letters in a room in Jinjang rented by a former postman.

Among them were bank statements, telephone bills, magazines, four registered letters and one PosEkspress letter, dated as far back as 2000. Some had been damaged. Sentul police were to meet Pos Malaysia Bhd officials to decide the fate of the ex-postman, who was sacked on 19 March because he was often absent from work.

Honorary doctorate for Endon

14 August | **Johor Bahru**

Sultanah Zanariah Tunku Ahmad of Johor, Dato' Seri Abdullah Ahmad Badawi and Datin Seri Endon Mahmood (right) after the convocation ceremony at Universiti Teknologi Malaysia in Johor Bahru. The Sultanah, who is UTM Chancellor, presented an honorary doctorate to Endon.

Fireflies fading due to pollution

21 August | **Kuala Selangor**

The fireflies of Kampung Kuantan here were in danger of becoming extinct, Malaysian Nature Society honorary secretary Associate Prof Dr Mustafa Kamal Abdul Aziz said.

The MNS had submitted 13 research papers and three proposals to the State Government in the past two years warning about this.

He added that fireflies were used as indicators of water health in Japan and as an early warning system.

It was believed that the fireflies' habitat was threatened by pollution caused by indiscriminate discharge of effluents from upstream industries, oil palm plantations and mills and sand mining. Meanwhile, the Sultan of Selangor, Sultan Sharafuddin Idris Shah, ordered the State Government to save the firefly colony.

Anwar cleared of sodomy charge...

2 September | **Putrajaya**

Dato' Seri Anwar Ibrahim left the Palace of Justice a free man after the Federal Court acquitted him of a charge of sodomising his former driver for which he had been sentenced to nine years' jail.

Mr Justice Abdul Hamid Mohamad held that from the record of appeal, he found evidence that the appellants were involved in homosexual activities and was inclined to believe that the alleged incident at Tivoli Villa did occur. However, he said the Federal Court could only convict Anwar if the prosecution had successfully proved beyond reasonable doubt the alleged offences stated in the charges.

Supporters greet Datuk Seri Anwar Ibrahim as he is released.

...but loses appeal over corruption

15 September | **Putrajaya**

The Federal Court upheld Dato' Seri Anwar Ibrahim's corruption conviction, ending his bid to erase his criminal record and get back immediately into active politics. The three-member Federal Court panel of Datuk Abdul Malek Ahmad, Datuk Siti Norma Yaakob and Datuk Alauddin Mohd Sheriff unanimously ruled that there was no merit in reviewing the case.

Doctors and nurses to be redeployed

14 August | **Kuala Lumpur**

A nationwide redeployment exercise of doctors and nurses was underway, according to Health Minister Datuk Dr Chua Soi Lek.

The move stemmed from the problem of manpower distribution, resulting in government hospitals being underused or staff being overloaded with work. The exercise will involve 117 hospitals.

Archaeologists find 8,000-year-old skeleton

23 August | **Penang**

The skeletal remains of a woman who lived 8,000 years ago have been found at Gua Teluk Kelawar in Lenggong, Perak. In May, Universiti Sains Malaysia archaeologists, led by Datuk Prof Zuraina Majid, found her buried in a foetal position, together with food and stones.

The 148cm-tall woman was believed to have been in her 40s when she died. In 1991, Prof Zuraina and researchers found Perak Man, a complete skeleton dating back between 10,000 and 11,000 years.

Target of 30% women

25 August | **Kuala Lumpur**

The Government wanted 30 per cent of those involved in decision-making in the public sector to be women and hoped the private sector would follow suit, Prime Minister Dato' Seri Abdullah Badawi said. The Cabinet decision was announced at Women's Day celebrations.

However, no deadline was fixed for the achievement of the target.

Abdullah points way for Malays to succeed

23 September Kuala Lumpur

In his first presidential address to the 55th Umno general assembly, Dato' Seri Abdullah Ahmad Badawi spoke of his innermost thoughts on the future of the Malays and his role as leader of the country.

Dato' Seri Abdullah also elaborated for the first time on the concept of progressive Islam which he believed would help Malays change their mindset and build them up to be a strong, confident people.

'Malays must develop a vision of a global civilisation in order to be more successful global players,' he said. 'Malays must embrace knowledge, skills and expertise in order to build capacity. Islam makes it compulsory for Muslims to embrace knowledge in all fields.'

A giant TV screen gives delegates a view of proceedings.

Guan Eng (left) announces the new DAP line-up.

Karpal Singh heads DAP as Kit Siang steps down

4 September Ipoh

Karpal Singh became the first non-Chinese chairman of the DAP after Lim Kit Siang, who led the party for more than 35 years, stepped down. Lim Guan Eng was appointed DAP secretary-general.

The appointments were unanimously made by the newly-elected central executive committee of the party after only 20 minutes.

Guan Eng, Kit Siang's son, said: 'I will work hard to serve the party because of my 19 colleagues and the members. Although he [Kit Siang] is my father, the support comes from the members.'

Karpal said it would not be easy for him to equal Kit Siang.

On whether he would now be a full-time politician (he is also a well-known lawyer), Karpal said: 'I have to make every effort to reconcile the irreconcilable.'

Sungai Pinang Assemblyman Teng Chang Khim said Karpal and Guan Eng were 'natural choices' to take over their respective posts in the party.

Don't link Islam to terrorism, says PM

27 September New York

Prime Minister Dato' Seri Abdullah Ahmad Badawi, current chair of the 57-member Organisation of the Islamic Conference, warned that the 'war on terror' was being tainted by anti-Muslim bigotry.

'There is an urgent need to stop tarnishing the Muslim world by unfair stereotypes,' he told the UN General Assembly in New York.

'Most damaging of all is the increasing tendency to attribute linkages between international terrorism and Islam.'

Condemning the 'prejudices and bigotry' triggered by the 9/11 attacks on the United States, Dato' Seri Abdullah said Islam was all too often being associated with violence.

He urged the UN to assume its proper role in combating international terrorism and said Malaysia was convinced that the fight could not be won by arms alone.

Chefs get bronze in Culinary Olympics

20 October Erfurt, Germany

Although it was assembled only 100 days before the prestigious Culinary Olympics here, the 11-member Malaysian team managed to clinch four bronze medals for hot cooking, cold food presented cold, hot food presented cold and patisserie. Some 1,500 chefs from 32 countries took part in the event, held every four years and the oldest such event in the world.

Royal premiere for 'Gunung Ledang'

25 August Kuala Lumpur

Billed as the most expensive local film, the RM16-million *Puteri Gunung Ledang* was given a royal premiere. The event at Suria KLCC's Tanjong Golden Village was attended by the Yang di-Pertuan Agong Tuanku Syed Sirajuddin Syed Putra Jamalullail and Raja Permaisuri Agong Tengku Fauziah Tuanku Abdul Rashid and 800 guests. The star of the show, Tiara Jacquelina, wore a pink gown resembling that worn in the film.

Dewan Rakyat Speaker for 22 years dies

14 October Kuala Lumpur

The longest-serving Dewan Rakyat Speaker, Tun Dr Mohamed Zahir Ismail, died aged 80. He had served as Speaker for more than 22 years since June 1982.

First Malaysian Idol

29 October Genting Highlands

Jaclyn Victor became the first Malaysian Idol. After three months of competition, the 25-year-old club singer's dream of becoming a superstar came true after she was chosen above fellow finalist Faradina Mohd Nazir in front of a 6,000-strong audience in the final of the television talent competition.

She won a recording contract from record label BMG and the opportunity to share the stage with winners of other 'Idol' contests worldwide.

Datuks suspended

19 October Shah Alam

In an unprecedented move, the Sultan of Selangor suspended the Datukship of six people, five of whom had been charged in court while the other had been convicted. They could no longer use the 'Datuk' title until and unless found innocent.

They were former Perwaja managing director Tan Sri Datuk Diraja Eric Chia Eng Hock, former Selangor Speaker Datuk Saidin Tamby, former Universiti Teknologi Mara dean Datuk Mohd Saberi Mohd Salleh, former Tabung Haji senior executive Datuk Mohamad Shafie, former State Executive Councillor Datuk Mohd Sharif Jajang and Indonesian businessman Datuk Kenneth Chow @ Wira Tjakrawinata. The next day, the Sultan of Pahang revoked the titles of two businessmen, Dato' Seri Koh Kim Teck and Datuk Tee Yam, for similar reasons.

Acquitted, Datuk Seri on murder charge

28 September Kuala Lumpur

Dato' Seri Koh Kim Teck (right), 50, and his bodyguard Resty Agpalo were jointly charged with murdering Chinese national 14-year-old Xu Jian Huang on 26 September. Koh faced an alternative charge of abetting Agpalo in committing the murder. Agpalo was alternatively charged with committing the murder.

One of Koh's bodyguards was said to have found the boy's body in the swimming pool of the businessman's house.

On 20 September 2005 Koh, Resty and another bodyguard Mohamad Najib Zulkifli were acquitted by the High Court, which ruled that the prosecution had failed to clear many unresolved and unanswered doubts. The prosecution filed an appeal against the decision (*see 2 September 2010*).

Highway landslide

12 October Kuala Lumpur

A motorcyclist was hurt and at least six vehicles damaged when boulders and earth crashed down on the North–South Expressway near Gua Tempurung. The expressway was closed and traffic diverted to the Federal trunk road via Tapah and Gopeng. Heavy rain was blamed for the landslide.

Repair work was expected to take three months to complete.

2004

world news

25 October
At least 78 men suffocate or are crushed to death after they and hundreds of others are crammed into police trucks in southern Thailand.

25 October
Hamid Karzai becomes the first elected President of Afghanistan.

11 November
Yasser Arafat, founder of Fatah in 1957, chairman of the PLO and President of the Palestinian National Authority, dies.

26 December
A 9.0-magnitude earthquake just off the west coast of Sumatra generates tsunami waves that swamp Indonesia and other countries. The toll is nearly 187,000 dead with more than 40,000 missing.

31 December
In Taiwan, Taipei 101 raises the bar for tallest building in the world, peaking at a height of 509 metres.

Childhood friends relive family history

12 November Kuching

Childhood friends Celia Margaret Captier Brooke (below, left) and Melissa North fulfilled a dream when they arrived for a two-week visit to Sarawak, a land with a special place in their family history. Their great-great-great uncles were James Brooke, the first White Rajah of Sarawak, and Admiral Keppel, commander of the British Royal Navy in the South China Sea in the 19th century.

Antarctic trekker leaves

21 November Santiago

Dato' Seri Abdullah Ahmad Badawi flagged off Datin Paduka Sharifah Mazlina Syed Abdul Kadir who was attempting to become the first Asian woman to ski-sail across Antarctica. She completed the 1,100km trip on 30 November, eight days ahead of schedule.

Cuban award for PM

25 November Havana

President Fidel Castro of Cuba conferred the Jose Marti Order, Cuba's highest honour, on Prime Minister Dato' Seri Abdullah Ahmad Badawi at the Palace of the Revolution for his 'exemplary career in serving his country for more than two decades'.

Syed Mokhtar wins

1 December Kuala Lumpur

Businessman Tan Sri Syed Mokhtar Al-Bukhary won a 15.8 per cent stake in DRB-Hicom after a last-minute move by Prime Minister Dato' Seri Abdullah Ahmad Badawi to reverse a Government decision in favour of a consortium led by Tan Sri S.M. Nasimuddin S.M. Amin.

Sharifah Aini charged

1 December Kuala Lumpur

Datuk Sharifah Aini Syed Jaafar pleaded not guilty to a charge of defaming pop princess Siti Nurhaliza. Datuk Muhammad Shafee Abdullah, defending, called the charge a 'very silly one' and suggested the case was a waste of public funds. He said if everyone who received an SMS and forwarded it to their friends was hauled to court, 'half the population would be going to jail'. Datuk Sharifah was said to have alleged that the younger singing star had demanded appearance fees for performing, and made other disparaging comments (see 23 January 2006).

Tan Sri Ling Beng Siew passes away

3 December California

Timber tycoon and banker Tan Sri Datuk Amar Ling Beng Siew passed away aged 77. A former member of the Sarawak Legislative Council and Sarawak Supreme Council, as President of the Sarawak Chinese Association he played an important role in the formation of Malaysia.

Tuah tunnel milestone

11 December Kuala Lumpur

Tuah, the first tunnel-boring machine for the Stormwater Management and Road Tunnel (SMART) flood diversion project, completed the first phase of drilling work along a 734-metre stretch of the north junction box in Jalan Cochrane.

Tuah, which is 70m in diameter and weighs 2,500 tonnes, began work in July. SMART was a project to alleviate the flood problem in the city as well as to ease traffic congestion.

Killer tsunami after quake

26 December Kuala Lumpur

A massive earthquake of 9.0 magnitude centred off the west coast of Sumatra resulted in a tidal wave that killed over 125,000 people in Malaysia, Indonesia, India, Sri Lanka, Maldives, Thailand, Myanmar and Bangladesh. Thousands more were still missing. In Malaysia, 66 people were reported dead with hundreds injured and missing in the aftermath of the tsunami.

Langkawi, Penang and northwest coastal regions were among the worst hit. Damage to life and property was estimated to amount to billions of ringgit. Communication links were affected with ports and airports closed in some of the affected areas. From 1.15pm, tidal waves three storeys high flattened coastal villages and destroyed homes and infrastructure in the northern coastal states, tossing boats and cars about like toys.

Prime Minister Dato' Seri Abdullah Ahmad Badawi offered aid to Indonesia's Aceh province where villages and fishing boats were swallowed by tidal waves up to five metres high.

PM offers aid

30 December Langkawi

Malaysia would use Royal Malaysian Air Force (RMAF) helicopters and planes to send aid to the earthquake victims in Sumatra. Dato' Seri Abdullah Ahmad Badawi made the offer to Indonesian President Susilo Bambang Yodhoyono. Malaysia would send a CN 235 aircraft and a Nuri helicopter with a team of four armed forces doctors to Aceh.

The Prime Minister also announced that all celebrations to usher in the New Year would be cancelled in view of the tragedy. He called on everyone to hold prayers for the victims instead.

The day before, a team from Malaysian Medical Relief Society (Mercy Malaysia) left for Aceh for its emergency earthquake relief mission. Mercy Malaysia was sending another team to Sri Lanka.

Cameron bus tragedy

23 December Ipoh

Five people were killed and many more seriously injured when their bus plunged into a ravine, about 18km from here. The bus was on its way to Penang on the Simpang Pulai–Kampung Raja road, the new alternative route between Ipoh and Cameron Highlands. The impact tore the roof off the bus.

2005

Money talks: the Malaysian ringgit was released from its peg to the US dollar imposed in 1998; the RM1 coin was withdrawn from circulation; and government coffers raked in RM7 million in three days as traffic offenders settled their summonses. Illegal immigration checked: a nationwide operation to catch illegal immigrants netted 438 people. The next day, three Myanmar illegal immigrants, trying to cross into Thailand were caught, hiding in a car. The Home Affairs Ministry estimated that some 800,000 illegals were in the country. An international magazine explored the reasons why interracial marriages blossom in Sarawak. A foreigner attributed this phenomena to, among others, the selfless generosity of the Kelabit people.

AUGUST
Haze emergency declared in Klang and Kuala Selangor as the Air Pollutant Index breaches 500.

OCTOBER
Popular singer Mawi has an audience with Kelantan Menteri Besar Datuk Nik Abdul Aziz Nik Mat.

NOVEMBER
Dr Azahari Husin, the master bomb-maker and one of Asia's top terrorists, kills himself in South Surabaya.

DECEMBER
Squash queen Nicol David is the youngest and the first Asian to win the squash World Open.

July: The commune area of the 'Sky Kingdom'.

26.1 million	Population	
RM574.7 billion	Gross Domestic Product	
RM20,885	Gross National Income (per capita)	
18.5	Crude Birth Rate (per 1,000 persons)	
6.6	Infant Mortality (per 1,000 live births)	
71.4 / 76.2	Life Expectancy (male / female)	
87.7	Consumer Price Index (base 2010=100)	

Malaysia Facts

'Lack of respect for the environment ... must be stopped.'
Dato' Seri Abdullah Ahmad Badawi, 3 March 2005.

2005

world news

17 January
Zhao Ziyang, PM of China for the period 1980–1987, dies at 86.

2 April
Pope John Paul II dies.

9 April
Charles, Prince of Wales, weds Camilla Parker Bowles.

26 April
Lien Chan, head of Taiwan's Nationalist Party, arrives in China for the first meeting between the Kuomintang and the Communist Party since they split and fought each other six decades ago.

26 April
Syria pulls out the last of its 14,000-strong garrison in Lebanon, ending 29 years of presence in Lebanese politics.

1 May
A Thai fisherman nets a 646lb catfish, the largest freshwater fish ever eaten.

13 June
Michael Jackson is acquitted of all charges relating to child molestation.

30 June
China overtakes Japan as the world's largest holder of foreign reserves—equivalent to US$711 billion.

'Miracle' tsunami rescues

3 January | Penang

An Acehnese woman swept into the sea by the 26 December tsunami survived for five days on the fruit of a sago palm tree that she had clung to. Four-months-pregnant Melawati Wakidaud, 25 (pictured), who was washing clothes in her home when a 15-metre-high wave struck, was picked up by a tuna-fishing boat 100 nautical miles off Aceh in the Indian Ocean on New Year's Eve and brought ashore here today.

On 6 January another survivor, Rizal Shah Putra, 20, who had stayed afloat for eight days on a raft of intertwined branches, was brought ashore at Port Klang. He was rescued by a Malaysian vessel, also about 100 nautical miles off Aceh. Rizal was clearing the grounds of a mosque when the tsunami struck, sweeping about 30 people into the sea. 'I saw others float by, holding on to logs and other objects,' he said. 'On the second day, some tried to swim ashore after spotting land in the distance… I don't know what has happened to anyone. I'm just thankful to be alive.' Rizal said he survived on anything edible among the debris floating around him.

Free-for-all seafood after slump in sales

12 January | Penang

After a slump in sales of seafood since the 26 December tsunami, the Cecil Street Fish Wholesalers Association here organised a free lunch promotion to show that their catches were safe to eat.

More than 3,000 Penangites were treated to a meal of rice and seafood—400kg of fresh fish, prawns, squid and clams—prepared in a variety of ways.

The association said seafood sales had dropped by about 70 per cent since the tsunami. Association chairman Tan Eng Wai said its 40 members spent about RM10,000 on the event.

Turtles return to Penang beach

16 February | Penang

Residents of Tanjung Bungah here were surprised to see turtle hatchlings along the beach. The last time this occurred was six years earlier. The 31 baby green sea turtles are believed to be been hatched from the eggs of an adult washed ashore after the December tsunami last year.

Prominent businessman found shot dead

31 January | Kuala Lumpur

Businessman Datuk Syed Ibrahim Syed Mohamed, 55, was found dead with two gunshot wounds at his double-storey bungalow in the wealthy enclave of Bukit Tunku. His .38-calibre revolver was found at the scene. Police classified the case as sudden death.

Datuk Syed Ibrahim's flagship company—Sisma Group—had interest in the automotive industry, stockbroking and water projects. It is the local franchise holder for Jaguar cars.

Sources said Datuk Syed Ibrahim was shot in the abdomen and pelvis. He was alone in his room when a maid heard gunshots. She went to his aid but he ordered her to leave. She then called his son, who alerted police.

RM7 million in traffic fines collected in three days

19 January | Kuala Lumpur

Traffic offenders have settled more than 70,000 summonses amounting to about RM7 million in the first three days of a crackdown codenamed Ops Warta IV o dodgers. Federal traffic police chief SAC II Datuk Ginkoi Saman Pancras said 3,156 arrest warrants had been served in the first two days of the operation on those who had failed to pay their fines.

Film stars (from left) Gong Li of China, Datuk Michelle Yeoh of Malaysia and Kaori Momoi of Japan meet at a film premiere in Tokyo.

Interracial marriages blossom in Sarawak

8 February | Kuching ▶ Intermarriage between Sarawak's 25 ethnic groups, especially those with similar backgrounds, has been common for generations—but now mixed marriages have expanded to encompass unions with Chinese, Malays and even Westerners, according to a feature in the *Christian Science Monitor*.

'In those days,' said former chieftain Taman Saging, 90, 'it must be between Kelabit and Kelabit', adding that his only son was married to an Englishwoman. In some cases, almost all of a family's members had spouses from overseas.

Lilla Raja, a Kelabit, married oil industry worker Tony Hodder from Devon, England, 12 years ago. Her four sisters also married Europeans—two Englishmen, a Scot and a Dutchman. Her eldest brother married a Canadian. Only her younger brother chose a spouse closer to home—a Malay.

'The Kelabit community is very small,' said Lilla, 'and we are closely related. So you don't really think of getting married to them.' Many of the indigenous children too were receiving better education in hostels, away from their villages.

'Nowadays, people with good education are bound to meet people of all races… from somewhere,' said Jaman Riboh, who owns a guest lodge. Australian pilot David Bennett, who met his Kelabit wife in Bario, believed history had a part to play in East-West marriages here. Much good, such as development of the area, by Westerners, was appreciated by the locals, while the Westerners liked the good principles, sharing and progressive thinking of the native groups. 'I had absolutely nothing when I met my wife, and that didn't matter,' said Hodder. 'Kelabit people just give, give, give,' added Bennett. 'You give them something, they give three back!'

First woman Chief Judge

8 February | Kuala Lumpur

Justice Datuk Siti Norma Yaakob, the country's first Malay woman barrister and the first woman to hold an executive post in the Government legal service, made history once again when she was appointed the Chief Judge of Malaya. Again, she was the first woman to hold the position. She succeeded Tan Sri Haidar Mohd Noor.

Legal Year procession

29 January | Kuching

For the first time, more than 800 judges and lawyers, led by Chief Judge of the High Court in Sabah and Sarawak Tan Sri Steve Shim Lip Kiong and all wearing official legal attire, took part in a procession to mark the start of the Legal Year 2005.

The procession, headed by the Royal Malaysian Police Bagpipers band, started at the State Legislative Assembly building and ended at the Court Complex.

Death sentence for rapist-murderer

23 February **Kuala Lumpur**

Aircraft cabin cleaner Ahmad Najib Aris, 29, was sentenced to death for the murder of IT analyst Canny Ong, 28, in June 2003. Ahmad Najib (pictured) was also given the maximum sentence of 20 years in jail and ordered to be given 10 strokes of the cane (rotan) for raping her.

In his 66-page decision, the judge said that Ahmad Najib's decision to keep silent at the close of the prosecution's case had given him little choice but to convict him.

Canny Ong's mother Mrs Pearly Viswanathan, 58, said that even though the death sentence had been imposed, it would not bring her daughter back. 'In truth I'm angry with God. I feel He has not been fair to me', she said. 'Sometimes the pain is so unbearable that I want to scream. I miss my darling daughter so much.'

Ahmad Najib said: 'I consider all this a test. I don't feel scared. I feel normal.' (*see 5 March 2007*).

Book on Petronas' Young Turks launched

27 February **Kuala Lumpur**

A book on the pioneering seven-member management task force which led Petronas in its early days was launched today. Entitled *The Young Turks of Petronas*, the book was written by former Petronas vice-president and task force head Datuk Ismail Hashim. The team was dubbed 'the Young Turks' by Shell and Exxon then. The book was launched by Deputy Prime Minister Dato' Sri Najib Tun Razak who worked with Petronas from 1974 to 1976.

Myanmar nationals found 'stuffed' in car

2 March **Bukit Kayu Hitam**

Three Myanmar illegal immigrants, trying to cross from this border town into Thailand, were caught— two women in the boot of a car and a man hiding among boxes in the back seat. The driver of the Thai-registered vehicle was detained.

The immigrants crammed in the boot of the car.

Illegal immigrants rush to board a bus taking them to a ship to beat the amnesty deadline.

Immigration crackdown nets more than 500

1 March **Johor Bahru**

A nationwide operation to catch illegal immigrants, Ops Tegas, began with 438 people detained for not having valid documents. They comprised 219 Indonesians, 216 Filipinos and three Bangladeshis. As many as 31,000 Immigration officers, police, Rela and National Registration Department personnel checked 1,795 immigrants.

The Home Ministry estimated that some 800,000 illegals were in the country, as only 400,000 had left voluntarily when an amnesty ended in February.

Trapped crane driver rescued in high drama

14 March **Subang Jaya**

Fireman rescued an injured crane driver trapped in the cabin of a mobile crane that had overturned. The crane was being used to hoist pre-fabricated slabs for a flyover project when it tipped over and landed in a monsoon drain. The 30-year-old driver was lifted to safety by six firemen.

Student scores record 17 A1s in SPM

9 March **Johor Bahru**

A record 17 A1s were achieved by Nur Amalina Che Bakri of Sekolah Menengah Ulu Tiram in the Sijil Pelajaran Malaysia (SPM) exam in 2004, results of which were announced today. Nur Amalina sat for seven extra subjects not offered by her school—and without the aid of extra tuition.

She said: 'I was inspired by Mahatma Gandhi who said, 'The measure of success is not the result but the effort.' I also remember reading about a girl who scored 15 A1s in her SPM and thought if she could do it, why couldn't I?' She won a Bank Negara Malaysia scholarship to read medicine in the United Kingdom.

Danny Chia's slice of golf history

7 April **Petaling Jaya**

Malaysia's top golfer Danny Chia, 32, made history at the Asian qualifying tourney at Saujana by becoming the country's first golfer to earn a place in the oldest major in the world—the British Open at the fabled St Andrew's in July. After carding a brilliant 67 in the first round, Chia—ranked 674 in the world—picked up steam to birdie the last two holes in the second round to finish with a par-72. In July at St Andrew's, amid hundreds of SMS-ed words of encouragement from Malaysian supporters, Chia shot a respectable one-over 73. However, his two-day total of 147 was agonisingly short of the qualifying cut by two strokes. 'I'll be back,' Chia vowed.

Not a pretty sight, says the PM

3 March **Shah Alam**

Shocked by what he saw in an aerial inspection of the development bordering the Bukit Cahaya Agricultural Park, Prime Minister Dato' Seri Abdullah Ahmad Badawi lambasted 'selfish' developers and ordered a string of measures to be taken immediately to prevent further ecological damage.

The PM looks down on the devastation.

These include the submission of Environmental Impact Assessment (EIA) reports for land developments of 20 hectares and above (reduced from the current 50 hectares) and the enforcement of regulations preventing developers from chopping down trees with trunks that are more than six inches in diameter.

Stating the scarred land 'wasn't pretty', he said that 'such lack of respect for the environment and attitude must be stopped'.

On 26 April, four developers were fined a total RM132,000 for degrading the environment and for a variety of non-compliance offences relating to the Bukit Cahaya projects.

MPs say they turn to TV for problem solving

31 March **Kuala Lumpur**

Why was it that when MPs complain of environmental issues nobody took notice, but when TV raises concerns, action is taken? This was the question asked by several MPs in the Dewan Rakyat.

The MPs said they had to turn to TV3 journalist Karam Singh Walia to solve environmental problems in their constituencies. The Barisan Nasional MP for Kalabakan, Datuk Abdul Ghapur Salleh, complaining that no action had been taken over air pollution by a quarry in his constituency despite his highlighting the matter in the House as well as with local authorities, asked whether he had to resort to getting Karam Singh to broadcast the issue to attract the authorities' attention.

Olympic medallists to get allowances for life

31 March **Putrajaya**

Winners of gold, silver and bronze medals at the Olympic Games would each receive a monthly allowance for life of RM3,000, RM2,000 and RM1,000 respectively, Deputy Prime Minister Datuk Najib Tun Razak said. Five national badminton players who had won medals at previous Olympic meets were eligible for the fixed allowances which would begin in January 2006, he added.

2005

world news

7 July
Three suicide-bombers in three London Underground trains and one on a bus kill 52 commuters.

14 July
The southern Thai town of Yala is plunged into darkness after transformers are destroyed. Muslim rebels roam the streets with bombs.

24 July
American cyclist Lance Armstrong wins his 7th and last Tour de France.

26 July
Myanmar agrees to forgo its chairmanship of Asean in 2006 so that Western nations will not boycott its meetings.

23 August
Israel clears the last two of 25 Israeli settlements in the Gaza Strip and the West Bank.

31 August
In Baghdad, rumours of a suicide bomber spread panic in a Shi'ite religious procession. A stampede kills more than 960.

Oldest woman dies short of 114th birthday

15 April Taiping

Three months short of her 114th birthday, Malaysia's oldest woman Lim Khoo Chai died in her sleep at the Government hospital. She had been admitted six days earlier following complaints of stomach discomfort. Born on 5 July 1891, Lim was endorsed as the nation's oldest woman by the *Malaysian Book of Records* in July 2003.

Borders opens its largest book store

19 April Kuala Lumpur

The Michigan-based book store chain Borders opened its largest store in the world here, saying the multiracial country was chosen because of its diverse culture. Datin Paduka Seri Endon Mahmood, wife of Prime Minister Dato' Seri Abdullah Ahmad Badawi, inaugurated the store.

Last survivor of Bukit Kepong incident dies

14 April Malacca

Sergeant Yusoff Rono, the last surviving member of a group that put up a heroic stand against an assault by 200 Communist terrorists on the Bukit Kepong police station 55 years ago, died at the Malacca Hospital. He was 83.

Yusoff was one of four policemen who survived the incident in 1950. Nineteen others were killed defending the station in Muar. Deputy Internal Security Minister Datuk Noh Omar visited the family to offer his condolences and mentioned the possibility of conferring on Yusoff a posthumous medal for bravery, the Pingat Gagah Berani.

Police form bicycle patrol

24 May Kuching

Sarawak police formed the first mobile bicycle unit in the country to patrol busy areas and tourist spots in the city. Deputy Police Commissioner SAC2 Abang Abdul Wahap bin Abang Julai handed over the bicycles to the contingent at the Jalan Badruddin headquarters. He said that a bicycle brigade was nothing new as in the 1970s police were patrolling on bicycles but that the bikes back then were slower.

Theatre director-critic Krishen Jit dies at 65

28 April Kuala Lumpur

Leading theatre director-critic Krishen Jit, 65, died at the Universiti Malaya Medical Centre of heart complications.

In 2003, Krishen, who co-founded the Five Arts Centre with his wife Marion D'Cruz, won the inaugural Cameronian Award for Lifetime Achievement.

His works were highly acclaimed because of their experimental style and his commitment to using both traditional and contemporary forms of the arts from different cultures.

In a fitting tribute, music at his funeral service included Balinese gamelan, P Ramlee's *Lagu-lagu Cinta* and Vivaldi's *Four Seasons*.

Krishen was highly regarded by arts enthusiasts.

Tourist spots to stay open after midnight

25 May Kuala Lumpur

Shopping complexes and other tourist haunts were encouraged to stay open until 2am in a new move to lure thousands of rich Arab holidaymakers.

The number of Arab tourists visiting Malaysia doubled in 2004 to about 126,000. Deputy Tourism Minister Datuk Ahmad Zahid Hamidi said about 200,000 Arab tourists were expected to spend their summer holidays here from 15 June until September.

Child detainee freed in Australia

23 May Sydney

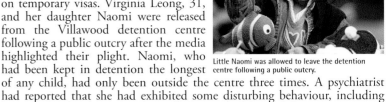

Little Naomi was allowed to leave the detention centre following a public outcry.

A three-year-old Stateless girl, who has lived as a virtual prisoner since she was born in a Sydney detention centre, was freed tonight with her Malaysian mother on temporary visas. Virginia Leong, 31, and her daughter Naomi were released from the Villawood detention centre following a public outcry after the media highlighted their plight. Naomi, who had been kept in detention the longest of any child, had only been outside the centre three times. A psychiatrist had reported that she had exhibited some disturbing behaviour, including banging her head against the wall. Leong had been fighting attempts to deport her since she was caught trying to leave the country with a false passport when she was two months' pregnant.

Naomi was born at Villawood in May 2002, but was not granted Australian citizenship. Leong did not want to leave Australia as she did not want to be separated from her seven-year-old son, who lives in Sydney.

Five-day week for Government workers

1 July Kuala Lumpur

Malaysia's one million civil servants got what they had been seeking for years—a five-day working week. Previously, civil servants got the first and third Saturdays of the month off and worked half-day on other Saturdays.

In May, Prime Minister Dato' Seri Abdullah Ahmad Badawi announced the move, saying it would bolster family ties and promote domestic tourism. He also said the cost of living allowance paid to civil servants in the 1970s would be reinstated.

Ringgit peg lifted

22 July Kuala Lumpur

Malaysia ended the ringgit peg to the US dollar imposed in September 1998. Bank Negara Malaysia announced that the exchange rate would 'be allowed to operate on a managed float.'

35,000 gather for education pilgrimage

7 August Penang

Some 35,000 Hindu students and parents gathered for a special educational pilgrimage where participants pray for help in their studies and success in the examinations. The annual half-day event known as Kalvi Yathirai was normally held at the Batu Caves in Kuala Lumpur, but owing to renovations at the cave temples, it was held at the Waterfall hilltop temple here.

Student fitted with mechanical heart

2 August Kuala Lumpur

Student Muhammad Fikri Nor Azmi, 15, became the country's first recipient of an Implantable Ventricular Assist Device (IVAD) or mechanical heart. The life-extending procedure was the first in Asia and Australasia. The surgery was performed by a team at the National Heart Institute headed by chief cardiothoracic surgeon Datuk Dr Mohamad Azhari Yakub.

Fikri was diagnosed with dilated cardiomyopathy, which could lead to heart failure, when he was an infant but he started showing signs of deterioration only early this year. He was put on the waiting list in March. On 17 December, Fikri successfully underwent a 10-hour heart transplant.

Cheaper cosmetic surgery lures visitors

28 August London

Britons were travelling to Malaysia for low-price cosmetic surgery. More than 10,000 Britons a year were being tempted abroad by plastic surgery firms for tummy tucks, breast enlargements and facelifts—with a recuperation beach holiday thrown in.

While a tummy tuck could cost as much as £6,500 (RM44,200) in Britain, it would be about £1,500 in Malaysia, with the holiday included. A 35-year-old woman from Cheltenham in southwest England said: 'The hospital was like a five-star hotel and the surgeon was trained in the UK.'

Esther Cheah wins World Championship

12 August Aalborg

Esther Cheah (centre), 19, delivered Malaysia's first-ever individual gold medal at the bowling World Championships here. Making her debut in the tournament,  Esther was bowling in the final of the five squads event with top bowler Shalin Zulkifli when, against all odds, she pipped China's Zhang Yuhong to the gold with her 1,296 effort over six games.

Cabinet nod for new university in Terengganu

24 August Putrajaya

The Cabinet has approved the setting up of Universiti Darul Iman Malaysia, the country's 18th public university, in Terengganu. Higher Education Minister Datuk Dr Shafie Salleh said the university would boost the east coast economy and balance the socio-economic situation in Terengganu.

Congratulations, it's a boy, eh, a girl

28 August Sungai Petani

Factory worker Azman Hassan, 31, was told by the General Hospital here that his wife had delivered a baby boy. But when he went to the nursery the next day, the nurse showed him a baby girl. When he and his wife queried the hospital, a DNA test was conducted. The test proved that the 3.5kg baby girl was indeed his—and hers.

AirAsia scores with Manchester United

17 September Manchester

Budget airline AirAsia has clinched a 'junior' sponsorship deal with Manchester United, stating its ultimate objective was to attract more non-Asians to visit Asia at a fraction of the normal cost. The tie-up, believed to have cost AirAsia about RM14 million, gives the airline the right to use United's name for promotional, advertising and merchandising activities. United chief executive officer David Gill, speaking to a Malaysian delegation headed by Datuk Azalina Othman at Old Trafford, said the team had more than 40 million fans in Asia.

Haze emergency

11 August Putrajaya

A haze emergency was declared in Kuala Selangor and Klang when the Air Pollutant Index (API) breached the hazardous 500 mark. Prime Minister Dato' Seri Abdullah Ahmad Badawi said the National Security Division would also declare emergencies in other towns if they were similarly affected. All schools in Kuala Lumpur, Klang and Kuala Selangor were ordered closed. The previous day the Sultan Abdul Aziz Shah Airport in Subang was closed at 12.30pm after visibility fell to 200 metres.

The Cabinet announced after its weekly meeting that it was lifting an eight-year ban on publishing API readings. Natural Resources and Environment Minister Dato' Seri Adenan Satem said the Prime Minister 'wanted transparency in the matter' and the public also wanted to know the API readings.

The haze had been progressively worsening for a week due to open burning at plantations in Sumatra and local fires in Peninsular Malaysia and Sabah and Sarawak.

Quick-witted driver traps pickpockets

19 September Kuala Lumpur

A bus driver, getting wind of the presence of pickpockets on his bus, locked the doors of the vehicle and drove with its full load of passengers into the Brickfields police station. The move by the quick-witted driver resulted in two men being nabbed on the spot. It was later learnt that the duo could have been responsible for at least 30 such cases.

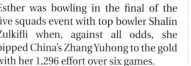

21 members of religious deviationist sect arrested

3 July Kuala Terengganu

Twenty-one suspected followers of a deviationist sect known as 'Sky Kingdom' headed by Ariffin Mohamad, popularly known as Ayah Pin, were detained at the commune's compound in an operation in Kampung Batu 13, Hulu Besut. Those detained included a police inspector from Perak and a member of a popular local rock group. Ayah Pin, 65, however, evaded arrest.

The seven-hour operation, which began at 5.30pm, was conducted by the State Religious Affairs Department, assisted by police and the Immigration Department. The detainees, including nine women, were aged between 30 and 60.

Giant structures found in the sect's commune.

Search on for Malaysia's first astronaut

23 August Kuala Lumpur

Malaysia's first astronaut will be chosen from a list of 894 candidates who will be required to prove their physical fitness by running 3.5km within 20 minutes. National Space Agency director-general Datuk Dr Mazlan Othman said those who completed the first hurdle will be subjected to a series of rigorous medical and psychological tests. Five to 10 people will be shortlisted. Successful candidates will be sent to Russia in January 2006 for the final test to pick two astronauts, one will be sent into space.

Couples tie the knot on auspicious 'double nine'

9 September Penang

Forty-five couples took part in a mass wedding ceremony at the Penang Chinese Town Hall. Two of the grooms, Lim Eng Siong and Lim Kooi Hong, whose birthdays also fall on 9 September, said it was an auspicious day because in Mandarin 'double nine' denoted 'eternity'.

Twenty-two couples were married at the Che Hoon Khor Moral Uplifting Society here. In Ipoh, 19 couples wed at the Ipoh Chin Woo Association.

5,000 exhibits in Kuala Lumpur aquarium

8 September Kuala Lumpur

The newly-opened aquarium in Kuala Lumpur, the Aquaria KLCC, is set to be the nation's latest tourist attraction. It expects to have one million visitors this year. Its underwater tunnel is the longest in Asia and it boasts more than 5,000 aquatic creatures.

2005

world news

Rights champion wins 'alternative Nobel Prize'

30 September Stockholm

For her work in stopping violence against women and abuse of migrant workers, Irene Fernandez, who headed the non-governmental organisation Tenaganita, was named one of four winners of the Right Livelihood Awards.

She shared the honour and two- million kronor (about RM1 million) prize money with two Canadians and a man from Botswana. The awards, known as the 'alternative Nobels', were presented by King Carl XVI Gustaf of Sweden at the Swedish Parliament on 9 December, one day before the Nobel Prizes were presented.

'Godfather of soul' gives thrilling performance

19 September Kuala Lumpur

James Brown, the 'Godfather of Soul', brought down the house at a charity show at the Hilton Kuala Lumpur. Brown, 72, thrilled the 1,000-odd audience, including local celebrities and VIPs. He was accompanied by an 11-piece band, three back-up singers and dancers.

James Brown in action.

First Muslim woman doctor dies at 94

11 October Taiping

The country's first Muslim woman doctor, Dr Latifah Ghows, died here aged 94. Dr Latifah studied medicine at the University of Hong Kong and received her MBBS degree in January 1942, during World War II. In 1956 she was the senior medical officer in Penang. Dr Latifah, who was single, was in private practice here before her retirement.

Gaur-breeding plan to prevent extinction

9 October Jenderak Selatan

A Government programme was launched to breed the endangered seladang or Malayan gaur by artificial insemination. It could be extended to other threatened species but the seladang was the first choice because of its high economic value. The programme would enable conservation of the species by re-introducing captive-bred animals into the wild while exploring the potential of commercial breeding.

ISIS head Noordin dies

29 December Kuala Lumpur

Tan Sri Dr Noordin Sopiee, chairman and chief executive officer of the Institute of Strategic and International Studies (ISIS), died at the Gleneagles Intan Medical Centre after fighting thyroid cancer for several months. He was 61. Noordin, a former newsman, was the director-general of ISIS for 10 years from 1984 before his appointment as its chairman. A scholar, intellectual and thinker, Noordin's views and advice on strategic and economic matters were keenly sought at home and abroad.

Kota Bharu an 'Islamic' city

1 October Kota Bharu

The Kelantan Pas Government declared the State capital an 'Islamic' city, assuring residents that the new status would not result in rigid legislation that could curtail their daily activities. The declaration was made by the Sultan of Kelantan, Sultan Ismail Petra, before a capacity crowd at the Stadium Mohamed IV. Afterwards there was a concert starring reality show *Akademi Fantasia* winner Asmawi Ani, better known as Mawi.

'Demolition man' dies in blast

9 November Batu

Master bomb-maker Dr Azahari Husin, 48, one of Asia's top terrorist suspects and most wanted men, blew himself up after being cornered by Indonesian police. Azahari, a Malaysian national belonging to the Al-Qaeda-linked Jemaah Islamiyah militant network, and known as the 'Demolition Man', reportedly set off explosives after a shootout with police in his remote South Surabaya hideaway.

Fingerprint tests concluded that Azahari was one of three men killed in the gun battle with Indonesian security forces. Azahari had eluded capture for three years after allegedly supplying explosives to the Jemaah Islamiyah for suicide attacks in Bali and Jakarta, including the 2002 Kuta nightclub bombings, the 2003 JW Marriott Hotel blast in Jakarta and last September's attack on the Australian Embassy in Jakarta.

Squash queen Nicol wins World Open

4 December Hong Kong

Third-seeded Nicol David became the youngest and first Asian to win the squash World Open after beating former world number one Rachael Grinham of Australia in four sets. On 18 October, she won the British Open, becoming the first Asian to do so. The Government rewarded the Penang lass with a cash award of RM200,000. She was greeted with a hero's welcome by fans upon touchdown at the KLIA the next day.

Corporate hotshot dies

30 December Kuala Lumpur

One of the country's brightest and youngest corporate figures, Dr Liew Boon-Horng, 35, was killed when an iron mould weighing almost two tonnes fell on his car from a condominium block under construction in Jalan Sri Hartamas.

Prime Minister's wife succumbs to cancer

20 October Putrajaya

Datin Paduka Seri Endon Mahmood, 64, the wife of Prime Minister Dato' Seri Abdullah Ahmad Badawi, succumbed to breast cancer at her residence, Sri Perdana. Her family were with her.

Kak Endon, as she was fondly known, was publicly loved for her strength and courage, her advocacy of breast cancer awareness and for spearheading the resurgence of batik and the kebaya form of dress. In 2004 she was given the Tun Fatimah Award for her service to the community.

Thousands lined the road to Sri Perdana to pay their last respects.

RM1 coins are dropped

7 December Kuala Lumpur

The RM1 coin ceased to be legal tender after being in circulation since 1989. The public was given three months to exchange their RM1 coins at commercial banks or Bank Negara Malaysia.

Over the years, there had been many cases of syndicates that had minted fake RM1 coins.

2006

Women to the fore, part II. Four women were appointed to key positions—Datuk Zarinah Anwar was appointed chairman of the Securities Commission (SC); Datuk Rafiah Salim was appointed Vice-Chancellor of University of Malaya; SAC II Zaleha Abdul Rahman was made Deputy Chief Police Officer; and Datuk Dr Sharifah Hapsah Syed Shahbuddin was appointed vice-chancellor of Universiti Kebangsaan Malaysia. April was an auspicious month for Malaysians who thronged temples and churches throughout the country to pray for peace and prosperity as part of the celebrations of the Tamil New Year, Malayalee New Year, Sinhalese New Year, Thai New Year, Vaisakhi and Good Friday, all of which fell on the same day.

JANUARY
Malaysian Tash Aw wins the First Novel award in Britain's Whitbread Book Awards.

MARCH
The region's first low-cost carrier terminal opens.

AUGUST
Pop princess Siti Nurhaliza in a fairy-tale wedding.

DECEMBER
Massive floods in Johor force 73,000 people to abandon their homes.

December: Before and after—heritage landmark Bok House demolished despite protests.

'The job of a good leader is to take people to heights that they didn't know they could get to.'

Prof Datuk Dr Sharifah Hapsah, speaking about her appointment as UKM vice-chancellor, 27 August 2006.

2006

world news

25 January
Hamas wins a huge majority in Palestinian parliamentary elections, prompting Western financial sanctions against the Palestinian State.

11 March
Slobodan Milosevic is found dead in his cell after a heart attack.

3 April
Thai PM Thaksin claims victory, his party winning more than half the popular vote in snap elections called following weeks of protests against his Government.

19 April
Han Myeong-Sook becomes the first woman PM of South Korea.

5 June
Montenegro decides to break from Serbia. The former Yugoslavia welded together by Tito has now reverted to its original separate States.

9 June
Thailand celebrates the 60th anniversary of the accession of His Majesty Bhumiphol Adulyadej to the throne.

Malaysian writer wins Whitbread Award

3 January   London

Tash Aw, 33, won the First Novel award—and £5,000 (about RM32,800)—for *The Harmony Silk Factory* in Britain's Whitbread Book Awards. It is the first Malaysian book to have won an international literary award. Aw (above) grew up in Kuala Lumpur before attending Cambridge University. He was a lawyer until taking a master's degree in creative writing at the University of East Anglia.

'Bigfoot' may boost tourism

4 January   Johor Bahru

The Johor tourism industry was eager to cash in on the Bigfoot craze. Citing recent reports that an Orang Asli man had seen 'Bigfoot' in the jungle on the outskirts of Kota Tinggi, Johor Tourist Guides Association chairman Jimmy Leong said: 'This is a boon for Johor. The news has put the State on the international tourism radar.' Mohamed Hashim, the director of the Johor National Parks, said television stations and journalists from around the world were coming to Johor to record the sightings. In April, the Johor Government announced total protection for the Bigfoot if its existence was confirmed. This won the praise of the American-based Bigfoot Research Organisation, which said this disproved the assumption that no Government would declare the species protected until a specimen was obtained.

Jungle rafflesia flower may be new species

4 January   Dungun

Forestry officers were excited over what appears to be a new species of the rafflesia, the biggest flower on earth. Spotting the flower itself is rare but finding one that does not meet conventional descriptions is even rarer. This specimen, found at the Pasir Raja jungle here, resembled a *Rafflesia cantlii* but its internal form is that of the *Rafflesia azlanii*, said South Terengganu forestry official Roslee Jamaludin. 'We have checked all known rafflesia species and so far, we have not found anything similar,' he said. The location of the rafflesia, which was flowering as a climber on a big tree, was kept secret.

Ex-bank officer jailed for CBT

6 January   Kuala Lumpur

Former senior bank officer Roslin Abdul Malik, 44, was sentenced by the Sessions Court to five years' jail and ordered to receive two strokes of the rotan (cane) for criminal breach of trust involving RM498,500 belonging to account holders.

Roslin, who worked for the Hock Hua Bank here, was found guilty of directing another officer to prepare huge sums of money purportedly for a cash withdrawal by a company, which would issue a cheque later to cover the amount withdrawn. Roslin then pocketed the money. Judge Nursinah Adzmi said: 'He abused his position.'

Police ordered to stop 'nude squat' searches

16 January   Kuala Lumpur

The Independent Inquiry Commission investigating the incident of a woman suspect in police custody who was forced to do a 'nude squat' while holding her ears has condemned this form of strip search. The commission called for legislation on police codes of practice on such matters. It said properly-conducted body searches were acceptable but recommended that police be given instruction on human rights principles. The five-member commission was appointed by the Yang di-Pertuan Agong to look into the incident, which was recorded by video-phone and distributed publicly via multimedia messaging.

Rare migratory birds flock to ash ponds

15 January   Klang

Globally endangered migratory shorebirds are being increasingly found at the ash ponds of the Kapar power station.

Species such as the Nordmann's Greenshank and Spoonbilled Sandpiper have come to rely on the ponds for sanctuary as they can feed in the nearby mangrove forests.

Over the years, some 60 species of birds have been spotted at the ponds. The ash ponds were created to store heavy ash, a non-toxic by-product of the power plant.

RM18.8m medical aid not utilised

16 January   Putrajaya

'It's a pity,' is how Health Minister Datuk Dr Chua Soi Lek described the non-utilisation of millions of ringgit made available for helping people in need of long-term medical treatment for chronic diseases.

Only RM6.1 million of the RM25-million Medical Assistance Fund launched in 2005 was disbursed to 398 recipients. 'We want the people to benefit,' Dr Chua said.

Tallest Lord Muruga statue unveiled

29 January   Kuala Lumpur

Hundreds of Hindu devotees thronged the Batu Caves temple to witness the unveiling by MIC leader Dato' Seri S. Samy Vellu of the world's tallest statue of the Hindu deity Lord Muruga.

The golden, 42.7-metre-tall statue, costing RM2 million, is situated at the foot of the 272 steps leading to the Sri Subramaniar Swamy temple inside the magnificent limestone caves. It is expected to double the number of tourists that visit the Batu Caves.

The temple hired 15 sculptors from India and 15 general workers to construct the statue which took more than three years to complete. Earthworks commnced after a ground-breaking ceremony in March 2002. A total of 1,550 cubic metres of concrete, 250 tonnes of steel bars and 300 litres of gold paint were used.

Senator fined RM550 for SMS divorce

19 January   Kuala Lumpur

In 2001 Senator Datuk Kamaruddin Ambok divorced his wife—via SMS and by leaving a voice-mail message.

Today, he was fined RM550 by the Syariah Court after pleading guilty to violating the Islamic Family Law (Federal Territory) Act 1984 by attempting to divorce his wife Mahani Hussain, 50, on 1 October 2001 in such a manner.

Kamaruddin, 52, the Segambut Umno division chief and Federal Territory information chief, was given a stern lecture on the sanctity of marriage by the Syariah Court judge Zainor Rashid Hassin, who said the law clearly stated that a declaration of divorce must be uttered in court.

Defamation suit verdict

23 January   Kuala Lumpur

Datuk Sharifah Aini, known as Malaysia's 'Queen of Song', beamed as she walked out of court after being granted a discharge not amounting to an acquittal on charges of defaming pop princess Siti Nurhaliza Tarudin in e-mails sent to her adopted brother Ahmad Shaharil Jamaludin.

Arrested friends shaved bald by police

30 January Kajang

As is their tradition every year, 11 friends met up on the second day of the Chinese New Year for supper, drinks and mahjong at a coffee shop in Balakong here. However, they were shocked when a police team arrived and arrested them. They were taken to the Kajang police district headquarters where they had a bigger shock—several policemen came into the cell and shaved their heads. The men, aged between 31 and 69, were released the next evening. On 3 February, the men claimed trial in a Kajang magistrate's court to a charge of illegal gambling. The incident was met with widespread public indignation. Kajang OCPD Asst Comm Mohd Noor Hakim defended his men's action, saying police could shave a detainee's head.

Tribune's newspaper permit revoked

9 February Kuching

The permit of the Sarawak Press Sdn Bhd, publisher of *Sarawak Tribune*, was suspended indefinitely after it published caricatures of Prophet Muhammad.

Prime Minister Dato' Seri Abdullah Ahmad Badawi, who is also the Internal Security Minister, announced the decision today—a day after the Cabinet discussed the daily's reproduction of the caricatures, which had been published by several newspapers in Europe. The Cabinet felt that the action of the newspaper, which has a 48,000 circulation, was a serious matter.

Record swim by youngsters

26 February Lumut

Salman Ali Shariati Abdul Halim, 8, and his sister Zahra Ma'soumah, 14, became the youngest pair in the country to swim across the 8.9km Dinding Straits from Pulau Pangkor to here. Their gruelling 3 hour 40 min swim earned them a place in the *Malaysian Book of Records*. 'It started to get very difficult to move forward,' said Zahra, of the strong winds that blew against them after they passed the 4km mark after more than an hour.

A police helicopter rescues a man who jumped into the sea after being taken hostage when pirates hijacked a tugboat on 17 March.

Low-cost carrier terminal opened

23 March Sepang

The region's first low-cost carrier terminal opened for business, receiving its first flight just minutes after Prime Minister Dato' Seri Abdullah Ahmad Badawi officially launched it. Transport Minister Dato' Seri Chan Kong Choy said the 35,290-sq m terminal was equipped with 72 check-in counters and had parking bays for 30 aircraft.

Lightning strikes fuel storage tanks at depot

28 April Pasir Gudang

Lightning caused an inferno at the Johor Port in Pasir Gudang that could be seen 10km away and from across the straits in Singapore. The bolt struck a tank at the Petronas

Dagangan Bhd fuel depot that held nearly 90,000 litres of petrol. Two bigger tanks—with a total capacity of about 700,000 litres—also then went up in flames. No casualties were reported.

The first tank was razed as more than 100 firefighters attempted to stop the blaze from reaching a fourth tank.

Two of the tanks were holding petrol for Petronas service stations in the southern region and the third stored jet fuel for the Sultan Ismail International Airport in Senai.

Bank Negara to help people in debt

30 March Kuala Lumpur

Bank Negara stepped in to help 200,000 Malaysians heavily in debt because of non-performing loans or household debts arising from credit card, hire-purchase and housing loans by setting up the Credit Counselling and Debt Management Agency. The agency would assess the financial situation of a client and propose a repayment plan to the creditors.

Bank Negara assistant governor Datuk Mohd Razif Abdul Kadir said the agency was an avenue enabling individual borrowers to seek advice and assistance in managing their credit.

Some of the devotees who flocked to a temple on the rare holy day for several faiths.

Big day for thousands

14 April Kuala Lumpur

Thousands of Malaysians thronged temples and churches throughout the country to pray for peace and prosperity.

It was a rare occasion as the Tamil New Year, Malayalee New Year, Sinhalese New Year, Vaisakhi, Good Friday and Songkran, the Thai New Year, were observed on the same day.

Women appointed to key positions

2 March Kuala Lumpur

Datuk Zarinah Anwar has been appointed chairman of the Securities Commission (SC) from April 1. The SC's deputy chief executive since 2001, Zarinah, a lawyer by training, was with Shell Malaysia for 22 years.

22 April Kuala Lumpur

Datuk Rafiah Salim made history when she was appointed the first woman to the highest academic position in a university. She was appointed Vice-Chancellor of Universiti Malaya (UM), effective from 1 May. The executive director of the International Centre for Leadership in Finance, Rafiah was lecturer, deputy dean and UM Law Faculty dean from 1974 to 1988. She had also worked with the United Nations and Bank Negara.

22 April Kuala Lumpur

SAC II Zaleha Abdul Rahman was made Deputy Chief Police Officer. Having served with the force for 30 years, Zaleha, the principal assistant director of the logistics department (IT division), becomes the second-highest ranking officer in Malacca.

27 August Kuala Lumpur

Datuk Dr Sharifah Hapsah Syed Shahbuddin was appointed the Vice-Chancellor of Universiti Kebangsaan Malaysia. Formerly chief executive of the National Accreditation Board, she was a lecturer at UKM's Medical Faculty from 1975 until 1996 when she headed the department. From 1996 to 2000, she was UKM's international relations director before moving to the Education Ministry as deputy director of the Higher Education Department.

2006

world news

26 June
Warren Buffett, the world's second richest man, donates more than 80% of his fortune, US$37 billion, to foundations run by Bill Gates and the Buffett family.

26 June
A new survey shows Moscow has supplanted Tokyo as the most expensive city in the world.

17 July
A 7.7-magnitude earthquake generates a 2m tsunami that swamps Java, killing 531 and with over 270 missing.

4 September
Steve Irwin aka the Crocodile Hunter, 44, a famous environmentalist, dies after a stingray's tail pierces his heart.

14 September
In Washington, two people demonstrate prosthetic arms that move in response to their thoughts.

19 September
A military coup removes Thai PM Thaksin from power.

Girl performs classical dance on bed of nails

23 April Ipoh

Her parents were on tenterhooks during Thibashini Palani's six-minute Indian classical dance performance at a temple here—and rightly so because the 12-year-old was dancing on 10,000 nails set on a 0.6m by 2.4m platform. Thibashini, who began learning Indian classical dance at the age of five, said she was happy with her achievement. 'I am now training to dance non-stop for an hour on a platform of nails. I hope to stamp my mark in the *Malaysian Book of Records*,' she said.

Passing of two patriots

22 April Kuala Lumpur

Former Deputy Prime Minister Tun Abdul Ghafar Baba died at the Gleneagles Intan Medical Centre in Jalan Ampang due to heart, lung and kidney complications. He was 81.

19 November Kuala Lumpur

One of the founding fathers of the nation, former Minister Tan Sri Khir Johari died after a heart attack at his apartment in Jalan Tun Sambanthan, Brickfields. He was 83 years old.

Organ donor gives new lease of life to 35

17 May Kota Bharu

A college student's pledge to donate his tissue and organs two years ago gave 35 people a new lease of life. Teoh Chit Hwa, 19, who had been suffering from a brain tumour, was declared brain dead at the Universiti Sains Malaysia Hospital in Kubang Kerian on 11 May, and his family said it wanted to fulfil his wish.

Chit Hwa's liver, heart and kidneys were immediately transplanted into waiting recipients while his bones and skin were being kept at the hospital's tissue bank, awaiting transplant. The bones will be used to treat between 20 and 25 patients suffering from bone cancer or other bone disease, and also accident victims suffering loss of bone. His skin can benefit either two to three adults or up to six children needing treatment for burns.

His mother Yew Shot Foon, 55, a seamstress, said Chit Hwa told the family two years ago that he wanted to donate his organs after being inspired by a Korean television series.

Mental disorders afflict 21 per cent of Malaysians

21 May Kuala Lumpur

Twenty-one per cent of Malaysians have mental disorders as a result of the pressures of life, and the figure is rising. According to Health Ministry clinical psychologist Mahadir Mohamad, based on a survey from 1995 to 2000, depression topped the list, followed by psychosis, and drug- and alcohol-related mental disorders.

20m use mobile phones

25 May Kuala Lumpur

Malaysia's mobile subscriber base hit the 20-million mark as the penetration level reached 80 per cent in March 2006, it was announced. Experts predicted that this could rise to 85 per cent by year-end despite a saturating market.

A mobile subscriber base of 20 million indicates that four in five people in the country are mobile subscribers but in fact, one person may own two or three SIM cards.

The richest Malaysians

25 May Kuala Lumpur

Malaysia's 40 richest business people had a combined wealth of US$26 billion (RM94.4 billion), with the top nine accounting for 82 per cent of this amount, according to *Forbes Asia*. The top 10 were:

1. Robert Kuok ('Sugar King') — RM20.3b
2. Ananda Krishnan (property, gaming, oil trading) — RM16.7b
3. Tan Sri Teh Hong Piow (Public Bank) — RM7.6b
4. Tan Sri Lee Shin Cheng (IOI Group) — RM7.4b
5. Tan Sri Quek Leng Chan (Hong Leong Bank) — RM7.25b
6. Tan Sri Lim Goh Tong (Genting Group) — RM5.44b
7. Tan Sri Yeoh Tiong Lay (YTL Corp) — RM3.99b
8. Tan Sri Tiong Hiew King (timber and media) — RM3.81b
9. Tan Sri Syed Mokhtar Al-Bukhary (MMC Corp) — RM3.62b
10. Tan Sri Lim Kok Thay (Genting) — RM1.59b

Four killed as landslide flattens longhouses

31 May Kuala Lumpur

Four members of a family were killed when a retaining wall being built on a slope in Kampung Pasir, Hulu Kelang, collapsed in rain, bringing down tonnes of mud on three longhouses. The victims were Fatimah Suri, 73, granddaughter Hayati Yunus, 24, and two great-granddaughters, aged three and four, whom she was babysitting. The landslide also caused an electrical short circuit that set one of the longhouses ablaze. More than 160 people were left homeless.

The devastation caused by the landslide that left more than 160 people homeless.

Mahathir accuses PM of 'betraying his trust'

7 June Kuala Lumpur

Tun Dr Mahathir Mohamad levelled his harshest criticism yet against Dato' Seri Abdullah Ahmad Badawi, saying the Prime Minister had dismantled many of his initiatives and betrayed his trust. 'I would be failing in my duty as an ordinary citizen and an ex-Prime Minister if I don't direct attention to the wrong things being done,' he said.

The former Prime Minister, who retired in 2003, said Dato' Seri Abdullah was not his first choice as successor but second after the current Deputy Prime Minister Dato' Sri Najib Tun Razak. Cabinet Ministers rallied around Dato' Seri Abdullah. Minister in the Prime Minister's Department Dato' Seri Mohd Nazri Abdul Aziz said Tun Dr Mahathir should not forget that when he was Prime Minister the Cabinet had stood by him.

Petaling Jaya now a city

20 June Petaling Jaya

Once a satellite township on the outskirts of Kuala Lumpur, Petaling Jaya was officially declared a city by Selangor Sultan Sharafuddin Idris Shah. A statement from the State Secretary's office said Petaling Jaya had fulfilled all the criteria for a city, including having a population of more than 700,000 (well above the required 300,000) and financial independence, with an annual income of RM190 million (compared with the required RM80 million).

Tioman declared a 'biological goldmine'

15 July **Kuala Lumpur**

Since 2000, 14 new species of reptile and amphibian have been found on Tioman Island—and five more were in the process of being officially recognised, said Dr Lee Grismer, a scientist with 40 years' research experience. Tioman was proving to be a biological goldmine. It and its islands had a rich bio-diversity which was reflective of its rich evolutionary history, he said, and 'on that basis, many countries such as those in Central America and China cannot hold a candle to Tioman.' For example, in 2003, the only gecko in the world known to live in an inter-tidal zone (in close proximity to beaches) was found there. Dr Grismer, who is a visiting research professor at Universiti Kebangsaan Malaysia, said the biological diversity in Tioman was far greater than any of the other places he had worked.

Top songstress Siti Nurhaliza marries

21 August **Kuala Lumpur**

Pop princess Siti Nurhaliza Tarudin was married to Datuk Khalid Mohamad Jiwa in a ceremony rich in Malay tradition and witnessed by thousands on live television. The akad nikah ceremony was held at the Federal Territory Central Mosque during which Khalid, popularly known as Datuk K, offered a mas kahwin (marriage gift) of RM22,222. On 29 August, the couple held a lavish bersanding ceremony attended by 2,000 guests, including royalty.

Pahang princess slashed to death

24 July **Kuantan**

Tengku Puteri Kamariah Sultan Abu Bakar, 64, younger sister of the Sultan of Pahang, was killed and her partially-paralysed husband seriously injured when their son, under the influence of drugs, attacked them. The son, Tunku Rizal Shahzan, 21, died of an apparent drug overdose a few hours later. Tengku Puteri Kamariah was stabbed in the back while trying to protect her husband Tunku Datuk Ismail Tunku Sulaiman, 74, after Tunku Rizal slashed him in the abdomen with a hunting knife for no apparent reason.

The incident occurred in their family home, Villa Ismaputri, at Lorong Kubang Buaya here. About six hours later, Tunku Rizal, the youngest of the couple's eight children, died at the Tengku Ampuan Afzan Hospital. Police had earlier arrested him at the villa. Tunku Ismail, who is a member of the Negeri Sembilan royalty, was reported to be in stable condition after undergoing an operation at the hospital.

RM15b construction projects up for tender

19 July **Kuala Lumpur**

The building of 450 schools forms the bulk of 880 construction projects worth a total of RM15 billion that are to be put out for tender soon.

A preliminary list of projects under the Ninth Malaysia Plan was issued by the Prime Minister. Other projects to be implemented through tenders include water supply projects in Terengganu, the Integrated Transportation Terminal in Gombak, Selangor, and the building of roads.

Botox fix forbidden for Muslims

27 July **Kota Kinabalu**

Muslim men and women are forbidden from using Botox to slow the ageing process, keep their skin wrinkle-free or other cosmetic purposes, the National Fatwa Council ruled. However, Botox is allowed in the treatment of medical conditions such as cerebral palsy.

The council said Botox injections—a growing fad among the well-to-do in Malaysia—contained prohibited substances, including those from pigs, adding that the treatment could also result in negative side-effects. The fatwa does not carry the force of law but those who ignore it are committing a sin. 'The council arrived at the decision after studying reports from abroad, local specialists and fatwas made in Middle-Eastern countries,' said its chairman Prof Datuk Shukor Husin. Even in medical cases, he said, Botox must be used only when the patient is in a dire situation, there are no alternatives and the treatment is provided by a specialist.

Director Ang Lee filming in Malaysia

6 September **Ipoh**

A touch of Hollywood was brought here when shooting for award-winning Taiwanese director Ang Lee's latest film *Lust, Caution* began.

Lee, who recently won an Oscar for best director for *Brokeback Mountain,* arrived at Jalan Bandar Timah here for a last-minute inspection at 11.45am before the cameras started rolling.

Five days later, shooting for the spy thriller, based on a short story by the Chinese writer Zhang Ailin or Eileen Chang, shifted to Penang, where traffic came to a standstill near Wisma Yeap Chor Ee in China Street Ghaut which had been transformed into a shopping boutique in Shanghai.

After 130 years, two sons of Perak come home

7 September **Singapore**

After more than a century of being buried in foreign soil, the remains of two Perak heroes, Tengku Menteri Ngah Ibrahim of Larut and Laksamana Mohd Amin Alang of Hilir Perak, were exhumed at two Muslim cemeteries here and shipped to Lumut, Perak.

Ngah Ibrahim and Laksamana Mohd Amin were implicated in the murder of Perak's first British resident J.W.W. Birch in 1875 and, together with Sultan Abdullah of Perak, exiled.

Sultan Abdullah was allowed to return after 16 years, and is buried at the Kuala Kangsar Royal Mausoleum. Laksamana Mohd Amin's grave was found in the 1980s while Ngah Ibrahim's grave was finally found in August 2004.

17 June: Record squeeze—21 people inside a Mini.

Natural rubber expert B.C. Sekhar dies

6 September **Chennai**

Tan Sri Dr B.C. Sekhar, who revolutionised and modernised Malaysia's rubber industry, died of a heart attack here. He was 77.

Known as Mr Natural Rubber, he was visiting his cousin in Chennai when he died.

Tan Sri Sekhar was the first Asian director of the Rubber Research Institute of Malaysia in 1966 and later became the first Asian Controller of Rubber Research and chairman of the Malaysian Rubber Research and Development Board.

Under his leadership, the Rubber Research Institute of Malaysia, the Tun Razak Rubber Research Centre in Britain, and the Malaysian Rubber Board won international recognition for excellence in research and modernisation of the rubber industry.

Fuming mad over haze

6 October **Kuala Lumpur**

There was widespread protest from Malaysians having to bear with a blanket of haze. Environmentalists and Government officials criticised the Indonesian authorities for the haze originating from forest fires in Sumatra, Kalimantan, Riau province and other parts of the republic. Deputy Prime Minister Dato' Sri Najib Tun Razak said there was only so much the Malaysian Government could do to combat the haze.

2006

world news

13 October
Bangladeshi
economist
Muhammad Yunus
and the Grameen
Bank he founded
are awarded the
Nobel Peace Prize for
extending micro-
credit to the poor.

5 November
Saddam Hussein and
two of his senior aides
are sentenced to death
by hanging.

30 December
Saddam Hussein
is executed, the
unruly last moments
captured by a cell-
phone camera.

30 December
A 67-year-old Spanish
woman becomes the
world's oldest mother,
giving birth to twins in
Barcelona after in- vitro
fertilisation in the US.

31 December
New Year celebrations
are called off in
Bangkok after the
setting off of nine
bombs. Three people
are killed.

New life for country's longest-serving prisoner

2 October | **Taiping**

Mohd Salleh (right) and his brother at their mother's grave.

After serving a total of 30 years, 11 months and nine days in jail here, 57-year-old Mohd Salleh Talib, the country's longest-serving prisoner, was freed. His release was the result of a royal pardon by the Pardons Board, which is chaired by the Sultan of Kedah, Sultan Abdul Halim Mu'adzam Shah. 'I am finally reunited with my family,' said the bachelor, who planned to find work and possibly raise a family.

As he emerged from the prison gates, Mohd Salleh hugged his wheelchair-bound father Talib Arabullah, 76, and youngest brother Abdul Wahab, 37. The former railway porter was jailed 'for the duration of his natural life, for armed robbery in Baling, Kedah, in 1976.

While in prison, Mohd Salleh said he had learnt various skills and believed he would be able to eke out a living by being a cobbler.

Zam wins Tokoh Wartawan award

19 November | **Kuala Lumpur**

Information Minister Dato' Seri Zainuddin Maidin won the Tokoh Wartawan Negara award for 2006.

An author of several books in Bahasa Malaysia, Dato' Seri Zainuddin started his journalistic career as a stringer for *Utusan Melayu* in 1957 at the age of 18.

He became Utusan Melayu group editor before entering politics in 2001.

He was appointed Information Minister in February 2006.

Ancient wall halts tower project

29 November | **Malacca**

A piece of history has somehow managed to do what local residents failed to do—stop the construction of a 110-metre revolving tower in the middle of this historic town.

Work on the tower, near the Stadhuys building, was suspended after an ancient wall, believed to date back to the era of Portuguese rule in Malacca, was discovered four days ago.

The two-week stop-work order was to allow workers from the Museums Department to dig deeper.

Goodbye Bok House

16 December | **Kuala Lumpur**

The heritage landmark Bok House, located a stone's throw from the Petronas Twin Towers on Japan Ampang, was torn down today. Built 77 years ago by tycoon Chua Cheng Bok, the house boasted a good mix of Asian and Western architectural influences, particularly in the broad verandas and neo-classical columns. The land on which the house sat commands prime rates, with luxury condominiums nearby selling for more than RM1,000 a square foot. Chua began his business mending bicycles and carriages.

During the Japanese Occupation, Yokohama Specie Bank occupied the house. After the war, British Air Force women used the house as a boarding house. In 1958, the house was turned into a French fine-dining restaurant Le Coq d'Or (The Golden Cockerel), which closed in 2001.

An aerial view of the bridge connecting Panchor to Grisek, inaccessible after the river burst its banks.

Floods claim 11 lives

19 December | **Johor Bahru**

Unusually heavy rains in Johor caused massive flooding in the State, forcing more than 10,000 people to abandon their homes. The figure jumped to 54,000 the next day, rising to 63,000 on 22 December and peaking at 73,000 on the 23rd. All but one of the State's eight districts—Johor Bahru, Pontian, Batu Pahat, Muar, Segamat, Kluang and Kota Tinggi—were affected by the monsoon havoc which claimed 11 lives. Based on Drainage and Irrigation Department records, this phenomenon of heavy rains in central Johor occurs only once every 100 years, when the monsoon rain comes from the northeast instead of east. On 24 December, Tenaga Nasional Berhad said a total of 791 substations supplying power to some 75,000 houses had been shut down.

An LRT train hangs precariously over the railway gantry after it overshot the track at Sentul Timur terminus in Kuala Lumpur on 10 October.

2007

Visit Malaysia Year 2007 was also the 50th anniversary of the country's independence, the celebration of which culminated in a patriotic re-enactment of the raising of the national flag at Dataran Merdeka in 1957. A new Yang di-Pertuan Agong was installed, and Malaysia's first astronaut spent 10 days on a space station. It was not all smooth sailing though as demonstrations were held in Kuala Lumpur by Bersih and Hindraf. Nonetheless, the economy performed strongly, with the ringgit hitting a high against the US dollar and ambitious regional development plans launched. Meanwhile, in court, the Altantuya murder trial began and Lina Joy lost her appeal to remove the word 'Islam' from her identity card.

APRIL
Tuanku Mizan Zainal Abidin installed as the 13th Yang di-Pertuan Agong.

JUNE
Prime Minister Dato' Seri Abdullah Ahmad Badawi launches the Northern Corridor Economic Region.

JULY
Datuk Michelle Yeoh appointed Chevalier in the French Legion of Honour for services to charity.

NOVEMBER
245 protesters arrested at the Bersih rally in Kuala Lumpur.

March: A police special forces unit performs a battle dance during the 200th Police Day celebrations.

'...there is no full stop to success and there is no time for us to relax.'

Dato' Seri Abdullah Ahmad Badawi, at the Youth Patriotism Congress, Putrajaya, 18 August 2007.

2007

world news

1 January
South Korea's Ban Ki-Moon becomes Secretary-General of the UN.

5 January
Momofuko Ando, 97, inventor of instant noodles in 1958, dies.

24 January
Israeli President Moshe Katsav will be charged with rape, announces Israeli Justice Ministry.

27 February
A suicide bomber attacks Bagram Air Base in Afghanistan while US Vice-President Dick Cheney is visiting. Twenty-three people are killed.

16 April
Thirty-two students and staff of Virginia Polytechnic Institute and State University, USA are killed by Cho Seung-Hai before he turns a gun on himself.

25 April
The Dow Jones Industrial Average index hits 13,000 for the first time in history, closing at 13,089.89.

27 June
Tony Blair formally tenders his resignation as Prime Minister of the United Kingdom. Gordon Brown is his successor.

VMY off to sparkling start

6 January   Kuala Lumpur

In a spectacular ceremony that included a firework display, Prime Minister Dato' Seri Abdullah Ahmad Badawi launched Visit Malaysia Year 2007 and the 60-metre-high ferris wheel, named Eye on Malaysia, at Taman Tasik Titiwangsa. He said Visit Malaysia Year, the country's biggest tourism event, would bring the best of Malaysia to millions of visitors.

Dato' Seri Abdullah at the launch of Visit Malaysia Year.

Malaysians must keep the country clean to ensure it remained attractive to foreign tourists as an impressed tourist might also be a businessman who could invest in Malaysia, he added.

'The year is special as it marks the golden jubilee of our nation. We are not only inviting the world to come and enjoy the country's beauty but also to feel the significance of our golden jubilee celebration.'

National Education Blueprint unveiled

16 January   Kuala Lumpur

Prime Minister Dato' Seri Abdullah Ahmad Badawi unveiled the National Education Blueprint 2006–2010 outlining improvements including better racial integration in schools, better-trained teachers and, most importantly, better implementation of education strategies.

The Education Ministry aimed to provide 300 selected schools with autonomy to help them boost standards.

Dato' Seri Abdullah signs the visitors' book at the unveiling of the blueprint.

Major gas find

1 February   Kuala Lumpur

US-based Murphy Oil Corp. announced a significant gas discovery in Block H off the coast of Sabah, its first such discovery in deepwater fields in Malaysia. Its president and chief executive officer, Claiborne P. Deming, said the results were very positive and provided a strong beginning for the company in 2007.

Ringgit at nine-year high against US dollar

6 February   Kuala Lumpur

The ringgit jumped to a nine-year high of 3.496 against the US dollar on the back of strong foreign fund flows into the stock market. Many traders had anticipated that Bank Negara might intervene to prevent the ringgit from strengthening further in case it affected Malaysia's export competitiveness, but Bank Negara governor Tan Sri Dr Zeti Akhtar Aziz said the stronger currency was not hurting exporters. 'What is important in the foreign exchange market is that we don't see sudden and disruptive changes,' she said.

In a further sign of the strengthening economy, ECA International, which surveys salary trends in 45 countries, said Malaysia had moved up nine spots to eighth place in relation to salary increases.

Turtles found dead

28 March   Kota Kinabalu

An international turtle-poaching group was broken up and nearly 260 protected turtles recovered after a Chinese trawler was seized in Malaysian waters. Attempts were being made to save 20 turtles found alive. The rest were dead. Three sharks were also among the catch. This was the second time in 48 hours that the marine police had waylaid trawlers from Hainan province poaching valuable hawksbill and green turtles in Malaysian waters.

In the earlier case, 19 crew members were arrested off Mantanani Kecil Island and 78 turtles recovered. Only five were still alive.

Giant leap in trade

8 February   Kuala Lumpur

Malaysia took a giant leap as a trading nation when its trade registered an unprecedented RM1 trillion for 2006. Prime Minister Dato' Seri Abdullah Ahmad Badawi, who also holds the Finance portfolio, said Malaysia's trade totalled RM1.069 trillion, an increase of 10.5 per cent from the previous year. This surpassed by 50 per cent the estimated seven per cent global growth projected by the World Trade Organisation. The other significant profile change was in Malaysia's trading partners, he said.

Duo claim All England doubles title

10 March   Birmingham

Koo Kien Keat (right) and Tan Boon Heong gave a devastating performance to end the country's 25-year wait for the All England men's badminton doubles title at the National

Indoor Arena here. They blew away world champions and top seeds Cai Yun–Fu Haifeng of China in the final, winning 21–15, 21–18 in 38 minutes. They were the first Malaysian pair to win the title since the Sidek brothers, Razif and Jalani, in 1982. In claiming the All England title, the duo set a record for not dropping a single game in the tournament.

The King inspecting the guard of honour at the parade.

King joins 10,000 at police parade

25 March   Kuala Lumpur

More than 10,000 people watched a colourful show at Dataran Merdeka to mark the 200th Police Day celebrations. The parade began with the arrival of Yang di-Pertuan Agong Tuanku Mizan Zainal. Prime Minister Dato' Seri Abdullah Ahmad Badawi, who was also the Internal Security Minister, and Inspector General of Police Tan Sri Musa Hassan were also present.

'Floating' mosque

15 March   Penang

Prime Minister Dato' Seri Abdullah Ahmad Badawi called on religious authorities to use mosques as a venue for intellectual discourse. After opening a RM15-million mosque at Tanjung Bungah, he said Muslims must enhance their knowledge to appreciate the beauty of Islam.

The mosque, which at high tide looks as though it is floating, can accommodate 1,500 people. It is a blend of local and Middle-Eastern architecture. It boasts a seven-storey minaret and an open space for people to enjoy the view of the sea.

Gerakan president steps down

8 April   Kuala Lumpur

Dato' Seri Dr Lim Keng Yaik ended his 26-year term as Gerakan president. He officially passed the baton to acting president Tan Sri Dr Koh Tsu Koon.

13th King installed

26 April Kuala Lumpur ▶ The Sultan of Terengganu, Tuanku Mizan Zainal Abidin, 45, was installed as the 13th Yang di-Pertuan Agong in a ceremony steeped in the customs and traditions of the Malay Rulers at the Balairong Seri of Istana Negara.

Soon after the King read out his pledge as the head of State, the VIPs and guests, led by Datuk Maharaja Lela Tengku Farouk Tengku Jalil, hailed 'Daulat Tuanku' three times. The King, in his pledge inscribed in Jawi on a goat hide, vowed to govern the nation with fairness in accordance with the provisions of the Federal Constitution.

Biggest drug bust

9 April Klang

Barely 24 hours after police struck at what they believed was the country's biggest *syabu* laboratory in Johor, they uncovered the 'mother' of all drug-processing centres, a nondescript double-storey house in Taman Botanical here. During the midnight raid, several people were busy processing ice, the street name for *syabu*.

The previous day, more than 30 people were arrested in simultaneous raids co-ordinated by the Narcotics Crime Investigations Department in Johor, Negeri Sembilan and Penang.

Everest conqueror

21 May Kathmandu

Marina Ahmad, 25, became the first Malaysian woman to reach the summit of Mount Everest at 8,848m above sea level. She was the sole woman in the seven-member 'Merdeka de Everest' 2007 expedition. Six of the seven team members made it to the peak.

Young 'grandmaster'

28 May Bukit Jalil

Unlike other five-year-olds, Puteri Munajjah Az-Zahra Azhar leaves baby stuff to babies. The name of her game is chess. Puteri, from Kuala Langat, Selangor, was the youngest participant in a competition held in conjunction with the Second National Women's Games at Bukit Jalil. She was even spotted keeping notes of the moves made on the board.

'No-frills' hotel opens

22 May Kuala Lumpur

Tune Hotels.com, the first no-frills hotel owned by AirAsia, opened in Jalan Tuanku Abdul Rahman in Kuala Lumpur.

AirAsia's no-frills hotel in Kuala Lumpur.

PM irked by building defects

30 April Putrajaya

Outraged at the discovery of embarrassing defects in new Government offices, the Prime Minister instructed the Public Works Department to inspect all buildings immediately.

An angry Dato' Seri Abdullah Ahmad Badawi issued the directive in the wake of the recent collapse of the ceiling at the Entrepreneur and Co-operative Development Ministry's multi-purpose hall in Putrajaya due to a faulty sprinkler system and another incident in which ceiling panels at the Jalan Duta court complex fell to the floor from the weight of improperly installed light fixtures. On 11 April, the Immigration Department headquarters in Putrajaya were closed after water flooded the building, also from a failure in the plumbing. 'I feel ashamed. These are new buildings and there are problems.'

Workers repairing the damage caused by the faulty sprinkler system.

Lina Joy loses appeal

30 May Putrajaya

The Federal Court rejected Lina Joy's appeal to get the National Registration Department to remove the word 'Islam' from her identity card. The court held that the issue of conversion should be dealt with by the syariah court.

The three-judge panel, comprising Chief Justice Tun Ahmad Fairuz Sheikh Abdul Halim, Chief Judge of Sabah and Sarawak Datuk Richard Malanjum and Datuk Alauddin Mohd Sheriff, ruled 2–1 against Lina, who has been trying to effect the change for nine years.

Lina, 43, born Azlina Jailani, had managed to change her name on her identity card, but her religion remained listed as Islam. She made several applications between 1998 and 2000 to remove the word, but these were rejected. Tun Ahmad Fairuz said the court felt that the determination of whether a person had renounced Islam was within the realm of Islamic law, and that the right authority was thus the syariah court.

Lina received the failure of her Federal Court appeal with 'great sorrow'. Her counsel Benjamin Dawson issued a brief statement on her behalf in which she said: 'Only God knows what is in my heart and I hope everyone will respect my conviction.'

Proton posts RM591m loss

31 May Petaling Jaya

Proton Holdings Bhd failed to meet its key performance indicators (KPIs) for the fiscal year ended 31 March (FY07) as revenue dropped 37 per cent to RM4.9 billion from RM7.8 billion in FY06.

The company posted a net loss of RM591.4 million against a profit of RM46.7 million previously. Proton only managed to sell 110,358 cars in FY07, a 40 per cent drop from 183,824 units sold in FY06.

The weak performance was attributed to a challenging operating environment, with intense competition compounded by lower used-car values.

Geopark status for Langkawi

8 June Langkawi

Langkawi was the first location in Southeast Asia to become a Unesco National Geopark. 'The island was accorded geopark status on 1 June because it fulfilled three key criteria set by Unesco,' said Kedah Menteri Besar Dato' Seri Mahdzir Khalid. These included having a large mangrove park and natural resources such as beaches and islands.

Former Steel company executive acquitted

26 June Kuala Lumpur

Tan Sri Eric Chia Eng Hock (picture) was acquitted of a criminal breach of trust charge involving RM76.4 million without his defence being called.

After a three-year court battle, the former managing director of Perwaja Steel Sdn Bhd emerged smiling, declaring that 'the truth had prevailed'.

Sessions Court judge Akhtar Tahir said the charge against Tan Sri Chia was 'weak' and questioned why the prosecution had failed to produce two vital witnesses despite plenty of opportunities to do so.

Is this the Taming Sari? In May it was announced that evidence had emerged that the kris at the Istana Iskandariah, Bukit Chandan, Kuala Kangsar, was indeed the fabled Taming Sari of legendary Malay hero Hang Tuah. A manuscript, dating back more than 300 years, was found that describes the kris in detail. It has a diagram of a kris, labelled the Taming Sari, which resembles the one in the possession of the Perak royal family.

2007

17 July
Plane crashes upon landing during rain in São Paulo, Brazil, killing 199.

23 July
Mohammed Zahir Shah, the last King of Afghanistan who abdicated in 1973, dies, aged 92.

25 July
Pratibha Patil, 72, is sworn in as India's first woman president

15 August
An 8.0-magnitude earthquake off the Pacific coast devastates the city of Ica and various regions of Peru; over 500 are dead and 1,500 injured.

25 August
Forty-three people are killed in two bomb blasts in Hyderabad, India.

6 September
Tenor Luciano Pavarotti, 71, dies of pancreatic cancer.

12 September
Former Philippines President Joseph Estrada is found guilty of taking more than US$85 million in bribes and sentenced to life imprisonment. He is pardoned by President Gloria Macapagal Arroyo.

Altantuya murder trial begins

18 June Shah Alam

A murder trial began with the prosecution out to prove that political analyst Abdul Razak Baginda conspired with police officers Azilah Hadri and Sirul Azhar Umar to get rid of his former lover Altantuya Shaariibuu by killing her because she was pestering him for money. The two

Razak with his wife Mazlinda Makhzan at one court hearing.

policemen were charged with the murder of the Mongolian model in Mukim Bukit Raja, Selangor, on 19 October 2006. Altantuya was apparently shot and her body blown up with explosives. Her remains, just bone fragments, were found in Puncak Alam, Shah Alam, on 7 November (*see 9 April 2009*).

Bloggers beware

24 July Kuala Lumpur

Minister in the Prime Minister's Department Dato' Seri Nazri Aziz said the Government would be taking legal action against bloggers who flagrantly belittled Islam or the Yang di-Pertuan Agong, using the Internal Security Act, Sedition Act and Section 121b of the Penal Code.

Deputy Prime Minister Dato' Sri Najib Razak said the Government was deeply troubled by the growth of 'irresponsible' alternative media. 'In the name of freedom, these websites allow the broadcast of slander, lies and swearing, the use of harsh, degrading language and racial slurs without regard for the reader or those concerned,' he said.

Our national treasures

6 July Kuala Lumpur

Parliament House, Batu Caves, St George's Church in Penang, the Selangor Chinese Assembly Hall building and the lion dance on a pole have now something in common—they are all considered national heritage and protected by legislation. They are among the 50 entries (18 buildings, 20 objects and 12 cultural practices), selected from 500 entries, that were granted such status in conjunction with the country's 50th Merdeka celebrations.

Ambitious economic plans for the north

30 July Alor Star

Prime Minister Dato' Seri Abdullah Ahmad Badawi launched the ambitious RM177-billion Northern Corridor Economic Region (NCER) development plan aimed at transforming the mainly agricultural north into a logistics, food-processing and tourism powerhouse by 2025.

The plan, covering Penang, Perak, Kedah and Perlis, was drawn up to create 500,000 jobs by 2012, rising to one million by 2018, besides increasing the region's GDP from RM52.7 billion in 2005 to a targeted RM214 billion by 2025.

Abdullah looks at a scale model of the Penang Sentral Project. With him is Penang Chief Minister Tan Sri Dr Koh Tsu Koon.

Swimmer qualifies for Olympics

21 August Petaling Jaya

A childhood dream came true for young swimmer Daniel Bego, 17. He qualified for the Olympics in the Japan international championships in China. He smashed Anthony Ang's six-year-old 200m butterfly national record of 2:00.12, set at the 2000 Sydney Olympics, to earn his ticket to the Beijing Games in 2008 under Category B. The qualifying mark was 2:01.79. He clocked 1:59.40 and was the 14th fastest finisher in the heats.

Explain delay, judge told

21 August Petaling Jaya

Chief Justice Tun Ahmad Fairuz Sheikh Abdul Halim (picture) is waiting for an explanation from a senior judge who is alleged to have failed to write the grounds of judgments in more than 30 cases. This emerged when he commented on Prime Minister Dato' Seri Abdullah Ahmad Badawi's demand for an explanation over a report alleging that Federal Court judge Datuk Hashim Yusoff had accumulated 35 unwritten judgments for civil and criminal cases.

Datuk Hashim was identified as the judge by DAP chairman and Gelugor MP Karpal Singh in the Dewan Rakyat. Dato' Seri Abdullah said it was disappointing that there might be judges who had not performed their duties adequately in the pursuit of justice.

One-legged man swims for Merdeka

25 August Kuching

Junaidi Pauzan, 55, did the country proud when he swam 13km from Satang Island to Santubong beach here—which was an exceptional feat as he has only one leg.

Dedicating his gruelling marathon swim to the country in its 50th Merdeka year, he said he was determined to succeed despite the rough seas and strong winds, the age factor and his physical disability.

Junaidi, who lost his leg in an accident four years earlier, was greeted by his wife, his five children and friends when he landed on the beach after his exhausting swim.

Express bus crash

13 August Taiping

Twenty people were killed and 10 injured, three of them critically, in what was probably the country's worst express bus crash, at kilometre 229 of the North–South Expressway at Bukit Gantang. The death toll eventually reached 22 following the deaths of three-year-old Abdul Karim Abu Bakar and a Vietnamese factory worker.

Charges against Klang Assemblyman dropped

21 August Klang

All 37 charges relating to contravention of the Companies Act that had been brought against Port Klang Assemblyman Datuk Zakaria Md Deros and five of his business partners were dropped. They had been charged, by virtue of their positions as directors of two companies, with failing to notify a change of address, failing to hold annual general meetings, failing to submit financial statements and failing to submit profit-and-loss accounts.

Zakaria had attracted much media attention the previous year for building a palatial home in Pandamaran without local authority approval and for defaulting on assessment payments for more than a decade.

50 years of independence

31 August Kuala Lumpur

The whole country was in a festive mood as the people came out in droves to celebrate the 50th anniversary of independence. Various activities were held in the State capitals and cities while firework displays added to the happy atmosphere.

Prime Minister Dato' Seri Abdullah Ahmad Badawi led the celebrations at Dataran Merdeka in Kuala Lumpur on Merdeka eve. People came in their patriotic best, waving the national flag and carrying banners proclaiming their joy and pride in the nation. Dataran Merdeka was bathed in colour and lights. The giant 'Merdeka' emblazoned on the Sultan Abdul Samad Building, emulating that displayed in 1957, served as a reminder of the importance of the occasion.

After the clock struck 12, a symbolic lowering of the Union Jack took place. The national flag was then raised to the singing of the national anthem *Negaraku*. Against the background of a 1957 image of Tunku Abdul Rahman shouting 'Merdeka', Dato' Seri Abdullah cried 'Merdeka' seven times, drawing a resounding response from the thousands there to witness the occasion.

What the foreign press said

Palm oil: Malaysia refutes charge

31 August London

The Times of London said that Malaysia's drive for pre-eminence in palm oil-based biodiesel had come under attack from environmentalists and importing countries who questioned the sustainability of its production. The paper quoted Minister of Plantation Industries Peter Chin as denying that the country was destroying rainforests for palm oil production. 'We have not cleared rainforest for oil palm for 10 years,' he said. 'We are focusing on increasing production of palm oil by replanting old palms with new high yielding varieties.'

The development of biofuel in Malaysia gained momentum after the price of crude oil soared in 2006. The demand for biodiesel in the EU was set to reach 10 million tonnes by 2010. Asian palm oil producers have a planned capacity of 8.7 million tonnes, of which Malaysia would account for three million tonnes.

Civil service mums get 5 years off work

4 September Kuala Lumpur

The Cabinet has approved extended maternity leave of up to five years for women in the civil service so they can raise their children.

Deputy Prime Minister Dato' Sri Najib Razak said if the women decide to return to work after that, they would be given up to three notional increments. The five years could be split according to the number of children they have.

Just dial 999

2 October Putrajaya

If you have an emergency, call 999. The common number for all emergency services was launched yesterday with the motto "One Nation, One Number".

Energy, Water and Communications Deputy Minister Datuk Shaziman Abu Mansor said the Government decided on a single, coordinated emergency number after many 'worrying incidents'.

Michelle Yeoh gets French award

3 October Kuala Lumpur

Datuk Michelle Yeoh has been made a 'Knight' of the Legion of Honour by the French Government. On behalf of President Nicolas Sarkozy, the French Ambassador to Malaysia Alain du Boispean presented Yeoh with the Chevalier award for her involvement in various charity organisations throughout the world.

She is the 12th Malaysian to have been accorded the Legion of Honour since 1998. Yeoh is actively involved in AIDS Concern Hong Kong, American Foundation for AIDS Research and the Brain Centre Foundation among others.

Yeoh (centre) with partner Dato' Seri Jean Todt (right) and French Ambassador Alain du Boispean.

Blast off...into space

10 October Baikonur, Kazakhstan

Dr Sheikh Muszaphar Shukor became the first Malaysian to blast off into space aboard Soyuz TMA-11 at 9.12pm (Malaysian time). Prime Minister Dato' Seri Abdullah Ahmad Badawi joined a huge crowd who gathered to watch the launch, shown live on Astro, on nine big screens at the KL Convention Centre in Kuala Lumpur. Ten days later, the Soyuz landed safely at Arkylk, Kazakhstan.

Earlier, a computer glitch sent the spacecraft 340km off target but was quickly located by rescue teams.

She is Nurin

21 September Kuala Lumpur

The parents of Nurin Jazlin Jazimin have finally accepted her death, five days after her body was found in a gym bag. The eight-year-old was buried this afternoon at the Danau Kota Muslim cemetery.

The day before, taxi driver Jazimin Abdul Jalil, 33, was adamant that the body was not his daughter's despite the police saying that DNA tests results confirmed that it was Nurin.

Nurin went missing on 20 August after a trip to the pasar malam near her home in Wangsa Maju. Inspector General of Police Tan Sri Musa Hassan said the police had new leads on the killer and expected to make an arrest soon.

East Coast boom

29 October Kuala Terengganu

Prime Minister Dato' Seri Abdullah Ahmad Badawi launched the East Coast Economic Region (ECER) master plan today, with an initial allocation of RM6 billion from the Government for high-impact projects. An ECER Council would be established to oversee its implementation.

ECER is a joint effort between the Federal and State Governments, based on a master plan drawn up by the private sector led by Petronas with the cooperation of the Economic Planning Unit.

2007

23 October
In London, a Qur'an written in 1203, believed to be the oldest known complete copy, sells for more than US$2.3 million in auction.

20 December
Spain bans parents from using corporal punishment on children.

23 December
Nepal's political parties agree to end the world's last Hindu monarchy, 240 years old, as part of a deal to bring former communist rebels back into the government.

23 December
Allies of deposed Thai PM Thaksin are the biggest winners in the post-coup elections, but their 233 seats are eight short of a majority.

24 December
Authorities close the mausoleum of Taiwan's late leader Chiang Kai-Shek as part of a campaign to diminish his legacy.

27 December
Pakistan's opposition leader Benazir Bhutto is assassinated in a suicide attack in Rawalpindi.

Drop in ranking for varsities

9 November Kuala Lumpur

For the first time, not a single Malaysian university made it to the top 200 placing in the Times Higher Education Supplement (THES)–Quacquarelli Symonds (QS) World University Rankings this year.

The vice-chancellors of Universiti Malaya (UM) and Universiti Kebangsaan Malaysia (UKM) blamed this on the change in methodology for the categories of peer review and citation per faculty which comprised 40 per cent and 20 per cent respectively of the overall score.

On the other hand, Universiti Teknologi Malaysia (UTM) celebrated its debut on the list of the best 500. It was ranked 415. UM was ranked 246, Universiti Sains Malaysia (USM) at 307, UKM at 309 and Universiti Putra Malaysia (UPM) at 364.

Bersih gathering in city causes chaos

10 November Kuala Lumpur

An illegal march organised by the Coalition For Clean And Fair Elections or Bersih, a grouping of opposition parties and non-governmental organisations, caused massive traffic jams in the city.

Demonstrators converged on Masjid Jamek and the National Mosque to march towards Dataran Merdeka but failed when police cordoned off the area. Police used tear gas and water cannon to disperse the crowd. They arrested 245 people who were later released after their statements had been taken. A month later, 17 demonstrators including Pas vice-president Mohamad Sabu and Parti Keadilan Rakyat information chief Tian Chua were charged with taking part in an illegal assembly.

Chronicle launched

5 November Kuala Lumpur

Housing and Local Government Minister Dato' Seri Ong Ka Ting, representing Prime Minister Dato' Seri Abdullah Ahmad Badawi, launched the book *Chronicle of Malaysia* published by Editions Didier Millet. The launch, attended by more than 500 invited guests, was held at the Mandarin Oriental hotel.

Gold in world exams

10 November Kuala Lumpur

Isaac Tay Shao An, 16, was the first Malaysian to bag three gold medals in the International Competitions and Assessments for Schools (ICAS) exams. The SMK Methodist Boys School student clinched gold medals in Mathematics, Science and Computer Skills. The secret of his succeess: concentrating during lessons and not letting his mind wander.

ICAS is an assessment programme which enables schools and students to assess their capabilities.

Rounding up makes sen-se

13 November Kuala Lumpur

The odd sen in over-the-counter payments would be rounded off to the nearest five sen from 1 April 2008. Bank Negara Malaysia's assistant governor Datuk Mohd Nor Mashor said the move was aimed at reducing the demand for one-sen coins, with a view to stopping production altogether.

Lingam video inquiry

16 November Putrajaya

On 16 November, Prime Minister Dato' Seri Abdullah Ahmad Badawi announced that a Royal Commission of Inquiry (RCI) would be set up to investigate the Lingam video clip. The video, allegedly showing lawyer Datuk V.K. Lingam brokering the appointment of judges with a senior judge, had been released by Dato' Seri Anwar Ibrahim on 19 September.

On 12 December, the Cabinet appointed Tan Sri Haidar Mohamed Noor to chair the RCI which was held from 14 January to 15 February 2008 to investigate if there was misconduct by the persons in the video. In its report, which was submitted to the Yang di-Pertuan Agong on 9 May 2008, the RCI concluded that the video clip was authentic, that Lingam was the person in conversation and that appropriate action be taken against six individuals, including Lingam, for misconduct (*see 21 October 2009*).

A protester throws back a tear gas canister at Malaysian riot police during the demonstration by ethnic Indians in Kuala Lumpur on 25 November. The protesters were rallying in support of a four trillion dollar lawsuit that blamed Britain for their economic problems and pushed their way towards the British High Commission despite a heavy security presence.

Protestors charged

4 December Shah Alam

A week after they were charged with illegal assembly and rioting at the Selayang Court, 25 Hindu Rights Action Force (Hindraf) supporters were charged at the Shah Alam Sessions Court with the attempted murder of policeman Dedi Abd Rani and with causing disturbances by damaging seven vehicles. Another six individuals were charged later.

On 25 November, several thousand Hindraf protesters had taken to the streets of Kuala Lumpur, in defiance of a court injunction, to protest the marginalisation of Indians. More than 240 protesters were arrested. The protest started outside the Sri Subramaniam Temple at Batu Caves.

Five held under ISA

13 December Kuala Lumpur

Five men associated with the Hindu Rights Action Force (Hindraf) were detained under the Internal Security Act (ISA). The five, Hindraf legal adviser P. Uthayakumar, organising secretary K. Vasantha Kumar and lawyers M. Manoharan, R. Kenghadharan and V. Ganabatirau, were sent to Kamunting detention centre in Taiping where they will be held for 2 years.

Heart girl Hui Yi leaves IJN

23 December Kuala Lumpur

After spending over a year in hospital, Tee Hui Yee, 14, was finally discharged from Institut Jantung Negara (IJN), having received her second heart transplant on 5 October. Her body had rejected the first transplant carried out a day earlier. Chief cardiac surgeon Datuk Dr Mohd Azhari Yakub said it was a miracle that they managed to get two hearts in two days. Tee was diagnosed with end-stage heart failure when she was only 2.

2008

While the world economy suffered setbacks as the great recession that had begun in late 2007 deepened, in Malaysia the big news was political. Democracy was the winner when the country's 12th general election resulted in a Barisan Nasional victory but with a reduced majority in Parliament. At State level, the elections resulted in the opposition coalition gaining control of five states, up from just one previously. It was also a time for reconciliation, with Prime Minister Dato' Seri Abdullah Ahmad Badawi acknowledging the 'pain and loss' suffered by Tun Salleh Abas and other former senior judges as a result of the 1988 judicial crisis. Raja Petra Kamarudin was frequently in the news—and in court—as a result of charges brought against him.

MARCH
Voters go to the polls in Malaysia's 12th general election. The Barisan Nasional wins, but with a greatly reduced majority.

APRIL
Tun Salleh Abas and five other former senior judges receive an apology and compensation from Prime Minister Dato' Seri Abdullah Ahmad Badawi's Government for their suspension and sacking in the 1988 judicial crisis.

SEPTEMBER
Blogger Raja Petra Kamarudin is detained under the Internal Security Act and charged with sedition among other things.

DECEMBER
A landslide at Bukit Antarabangsa in Kuala Lumpur kills four and sweeps away 14 bungalows. Some 2,000 residents are trapped as their access road is cut off.

June: Demonstrators march along Jalan Tuanku Abdul Rahman, Kuala Lumpur, carrying a banner reading 'Reduce the Price of Petrol' after Friday prayers to protest the government's decision to dramatically raise fuel prices.

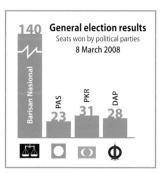

General election results
Seats won by political parties
8 March 2008

Barisan Nasional	PAS	PKR	DAP
140	23	31	28

'I had hoped Malaysians could accept my apology ... some Malaysians have a holier-than-thou attitude.'

Dato' Seri Dr Chua Soi Lek on his resignation as Health Minister and MCA vice-president, 3 January 2008.

2008

27 January
Death of Suharto, former Indonesian President for 32 years.

1 February
Scientists in Finland replace 65-year-old man's upper jaw with bone transplant cultivated from his stem cells and grown in his abdomen.

11 February
Rebel soldiers seriously wound East Timor President Jose Ramos-Horta in a failed coup attempt in the newly independent nation.

19 February
An ailing Fidel Castro, 81, resigns after leading Cuba as president for nearly half a century.

27 February
In Singapore Mas Selamat Kastari, leader of the Jemaah Islamiyah militant group, escapes from detention. He was accused of planning to hijack a plane and crash it into Changi Airport.

28 February
Former Thai PM Thaksin flies home to a rapturous welcome from thousands of supporters.

MCA minister in sex tape

2 January Johor Bahru

Health Minister and MCA vice-president Dato' Seri Chua Soi Lek resigned from all government and party posts today, including as Labis MP, Johor MCA liaison committee chairman and Batu Pahat division chairman.

Just a day earlier, he apologised and confessed that he was the person caught on video having sex with a 'personal friend' but refused to relinquish cabinet and party posts.

Chua's wife and family said they accepted his apology and stood by him.

The Indonesian President and the Prime Minister at their joint press conference in Putrajaya.

On common ground

11 January Putrajaya

Malaysia and Indonesia agreed to set up a group to address issues affecting bilateral ties such as migrant labour, culture, border disputes, religion and economy.

Indonesian President Susilo Bambang Yudhoyono proposed this to Prime Minister Dato' Seri Abdullah Ahmad Badawi who assured the president that Malaysia does not discriminate against Indonesian workers.

Both leaders agreed that there should be an inter-media dialogue mechanism to discuss these issues. Indonesia also wanted acknowledgement when dances or 'shared songs' such as 'Rasa Sayang' were used in Malaysia for commercial purposes including Tourism Malaysia campaigns.

Trainees get more allowance

19 January Pekan

Deputy Prime Minister Dato' Sri Najib Tun Razak announced that the monthly training allowance for National Service trainees would be increased from RM100 to RM150, with immediate effect. The insurance payout for death was increased from RM30,000 to RM40,000, with coverage extended to injuries sustained during training.

Thaipusam cheer

20 January Kuala Lumpur

Prime Minister Dato' Seri Abdullah Ahmad Badawi announced that Thaipusam would be declared a public holiday in the Federal Territories of Kuala Lumpur and Putrajaya from this year. The Indian community had long awaited the declaration. The festival was already a State holiday in Johor, Negeri Sembilan, Penang, Perak and Selangor.

Score to empower Sarawak

11 February Bintulu, Sarawak ▶ Prime Minister Dato' Seri Abdullah Ahmad Badawi announced a RM5-billion allocation for high-impact projects identified under the Ninth Malaysia Plan for the development of the Sarawak Corridor of Renewable Energy (Score). The corridor would be developed in the central region of the State, encompassing 70,700 sq km in the Bintulu, Kapit, Sibu, Mukah and Sarikei divisions. Spillover benefits would be seen in other parts of Sarawak as well.

The Prime Minister said that Score would transform the State by the year 2030. He also directed that a 'green development framework' study be undertaken to ensure the development is friendly.

Prime Minister Dato' Seri Abdullah Ahmad Badawi, Sarawak Chief Minister Tan Sri Abdul Taib Mahmud and Cahya Mata Sarawak Bhd (CMS) CEO Dato' Richard Curtis learn about the proposed US$2 billion world–class aluminium smelter project to be owned by Salco, a joint venture between Rio Tinto Alcan and CMS.

Markets meltdown

22 January Kuala Lumpur

World stock markets plunged into turbulence today amid near-panic selling, affected by growing concerns over an impending recession in the United States. Asian stocks fell on fears of recession in the UK and markets in Europe took a dip.

Prime Minister Dato' Seri Abdullah Ahmad Badawi pointed out that the fluctuation in the Malaysian markets was not as severe as that in other regional and global markets.

Travel survey gives Malaysia thumbs up

9 February Kuala Lumpur

Malaysia has emerged as the second most price-competitive country in the world in the travel and tourism (T&T) industry after Indonesia, according to the Geneva-based World Economic Forum (WEF).

The new police uniforms incorporate communication devices, handcuffs, baton and pepper spray.

New look for police

25 March Kuala Lumpur

The 201-year-old police force got a fresh look, with uniforms made of lightweight, flame-resistant cloth as well as gadget belt, baton, pepper spray, handcuffs, walkie-talkie and semi-automatic gun.

Inspector-General of Police Tan Sri Musa Hassan unveiled the new uniform at the national-level Police Day celebration and urged the 100,000-strong force to embrace the qualities of the force's new motto: *Tegas, Adil dan Berhemah* (Firm, Fair and Courteous).

Simultaneous divorce

1 April Kuala Terengganu

A 44-year-old businessman divorced both his wives in what may be a first in syariah court history. Roslan Ngah's wives Norhayati Ismail, 46, and Mastura Ahmad, 35, had sent him a notice of *fasakh* (divorce) several days earlier. He claimed they had engineered it for April Fool's Day "to get at me". That both women live next to each other only served to strengthen his claim.

Child prodigy turns prostitute

5 April London

Ten years ago, Sufiah Yusof, 13, became the youngest undergraduate admitted to Oxford University to study maths. Now there are graphic newspaper pictures of her selling sex from the dingy basement of a Salford flat. As Shilpa Lee, Sufiah, 23, was advertising her services on the internet as a £130-a-time prostitute. Her Malaysian mother, Halimahton, was devastated. Sufiah first ran away at age 15, accusing her father Farooq of making her childhood a 'living hell'.

BN rocked!

8 March Penang

Barisan Nasional won the 12th general election with 140 Parliamentary seats out of 222 while the opposition coalition of PKR, DAP and Pas held on to Kelantan and wrested four more States—Penang, Perak, Kedah and Selangor—from the Barisan.

The big winners of the day were Lim Guan Eng, Khalid Ibrahim, Nurul Izzah Anwar, Hannah Yeoh, Tian Chua, Gobind Singh Deo and Teresa Kok. BN casualties included Tan Sri Dr Koh Tsu Koon, Dato' Seri Shahrizat Abdul Jalil, Datuk Tan Chai Ho, Dato' Seri S. Samy Vellu and Datuk M. Kayveas. Meanwhile, BN leaders rallied behind PM Dato' Seri Abdullah Ahmad Badawi, saying there was no need for him to resign despite the poor results.

Dato' Seri Abdullah was sworn in as Prime Minister on 10 March. In the week that followed, Lim Guan Eng was sworn in as Penang Chief Minister, Tan Sri Khalid Ibrahim as Selangor Menteri Besar and Datuk Dr Md Isa Sabu and Mohammad Nizar Jamaluddin as Menteris Besar in Perlis and Perak respectively.

On 18 March, the PM announced a smaller Cabinet comprising 32 Ministers and 37 Deputy Ministers. New Ministers included Malayan Banking chief executive officer Datuk Amirsham A. Aziz, lawyer Datuk Zaid Ibrahim and Johor Bahru MP Datuk Shahrir Samad.

Prime Minister Dato' Seri Abdullah Ahmad Badawi and Deputy Prime Minister Dato' Sri Najib Tun Razak celebrate the Barisan Nasional's victory in the 12th general election.

5 hurt in KLIA shootout

9 April Sepang

Four gunmen opened fire on two moneychangers and two security guards as soon as they got out of their vehicles outside Gate 7 of the departure area at the Kuala Lumpur International Airport (KLIA) at 7.50pm before escaping with S$1.5 million (RM3.5 million).

The shoot-out, which lasted for about five minutes, left five injured. Roadblocks were set up around KLIA within 15 minutes of the incident but no suspects were detained.

Day of firsts at Parliament

27 April Kuala Lumpur

As the 12th Parliament began its session, Barisan Nasional was, for only the second time in its history, without a two-thirds majority. It was also a day of historic firsts including the commencement of a daily 30-minute live telecast of the question hour, a record 99 first-time MPs, 24 women MPs and Datin Seri Dr Wan Azizah Wan Ismail as the first woman opposition leader.

Members of the Royal Malay Regiment First Battalion parade in front of Buckingham Palace.

Buckingham Palace, here we come

6 April Kuala Lumpur

A British Army instructor was training men from the Royal Malay Regiment First Battalion at the Sungei Besi Camp in Kuala Lumpur. The soldiers were part of 122 personnel chosen to undertake the prestigious 'London Public Duties' in England from 18 April to 12 June.

Najib: 'I've never met Altantuya'

14 May Kuala Lumpur

Deputy Prime Minister Dato' Sri Najib Razak reiterated that he had never known or met murdered Mongolian model Altantuya Shaariibuu. 'I will say again that I have never known or even met this woman before,' he said. Several opposition MPs had linked Dato' Sri Najib to the late model. The allegations triggered heated exchanges between Government backbenchers and the opposition.

Beaufort train derails: two killed

9 April Tenom

A train heading for Beaufort derailed about 2km from the old township and plunged 20m into Sungai Padas at about 3.15pm. A man and a woman were killed and 39 others injured.

District police chief Deputy Superintendent Mazlan Lazim said that rain over the past week could have affected the stability of the soil and, as a result, it was unable to withstand the weight of the train.

The Sabah Railway Department is the only railway service in Borneo and has been managing the trains in the State since 1963. The railway itself dates back to 1896.

New look ACA

21 April Kuala Lumpur

Prime Minister Dato' Seri Abdullah Ahmad Badawi unveiled a comprehensive reform of the country's graft-busting effort, including restructuring the Anti-Corruption Agency. The proposed revamp of the ACA into the Malaysian Commission on Anti-Corruption (MACC) was part of a four-pronged strategy covering institutions, enforcement, laws and public procurement to start a new era of transparency and public accountability. An independent Corruption Prevention Advisory Board and a Parliamentary Committee on the Prevention of Corruption would be established to oversee the Commission.

The 'new' ACA would also increase its staff strength from 2,000 to 7,000 and get a better wage structure. In addition, legislation would be introduced to protect whistleblowers and improve the public procurement process.

Goodwill payment to ex-judges

17 April Kuala Lumpur

The Malaysian Bar gave Prime Minister Dato' Seri Abdullah Ahmad Badawi a standing ovation when he acknowledged 'the pain and loss' suffered by former judges Tun Salleh Abas, the late Tan Sri Eusoffe Abdoolcader, the late Tan Sri Wan Suleiman Pawanteh, Tan Sri Azmi Kamaruddin, Tan Sri Wan Hamzah Mohamed Salleh and Datuk George Seah. All six had been either suspended or sacked in the 1988 judicial crisis. The PM, speaking at a Bar Council dinner, said the Government would make goodwill ex gratia payments to them and that a Judicial Appointments Commission would be appointed to nominate, appoint and promote judges in a transparent and representative manner.

On 5 June, de facto Law Minister Datuk Zaid Ibrahim presented the ex gratia payment to Datuk George Seah, Tan Sri Wan Hamzah and the late Tan Sri Wan Suleiman's family at their homes. On 13 June, Tan Sri Eusoffe's daughter received the payment on behalf of her late father. A week later, Tan Sri Azmi accepted the payment, saying justice had been served.

On 29 August, a six-man panel of prominent names in the judiciary, both local and foreign, absolved the senior judges involved in the 1988 judicial crisis. The total sum awarded was later revealed to be RM10.5 million.

Tun Salleh (right) being greeted by Chief Justice Datuk Abdul Hamid Mohamad at the Bar Council dinner in Kuala Lumpur.

2008

world news

The Red Kebaya goes to Cannes

14 May Kuala Lumpur

When *The Red Kebaya* was screened in Malaysia two years ago, response was lukewarm. But the tale of an orphaned photographer and his journey of self-discovery was well received internationally.

And now it was to be screened at the Marché Du Film in Cannes for two days starting 19 May. The 10-day Marché Du Film is an important gathering featuring film stalwarts and international distributors of the prestigious Cannes Film Festival.

Directed by Olivier Knott and produced at a cost of RM2.5 million, the bilingual *The Red Kebaya* starred Ramli Hassan, Vanidah Imran, Samantha Schubert, Fauziah Nawi, Zahim Albakri, Sabera Shaik and British actor Bob Mercer.

'I only wished that the film had fared better in Malaysia. I'm so glad that my hard work has paid off and I'm happy that the film is welcomed internationally,' said Ramli Hassan of L'Agenda Production, who doubled as the producer as well as playing the lead role, Latiff. He hoped the screening in Cannes would open more doors for *The Red Kebaya*.

A GIFT OF PASSION.
A SHOCKING TRUTH.
AN EXTRAORDINARY JOURNEY.
The Red Kebaya
RAMLI HASSAN VANIDAH IMRAN
BOB MERCER SAMANTHA SCHUBERT
COMING SOON 2006

UMNO MPs stand by PM

20 May Kuala Lumpur

Umno MPs threw their support behind Prime Minister Dato' Seri Abdullah Ahmad Badawi and assured him none of them would be leaving the party. The PM said he would not bow to pressure from former Prime Minister Tun Dr Mahathir Mohamad, 83, who announced that he was quitting Umno until Dato' Seri Abdullah resigned as party president and Prime Minister.

Cuts from the top

9 June Kuala Lumpur

The Government is going on an austerity drive after the fuel price hike. It is hoping to save RM2 billion to expand the social safety net for the poor and lower-income group and for food subsidies such as rice.

Measures include a 10% cut in entertainment allowance for Ministers, and a partial freeze on hiring in the civil service.

Malaysia loses Pulau Batu Puteh

23 May Kuala Lumpur

The International Court of Justice awarded the disputed Middle Rocks to Malaysia while Pulau Batu Puteh (picture) went to Singapore. Sovereignty over a third disputed cluster of rocks, South Ledge, was to be determined later.

Malaysia had disputed Singapore's rule of the 0.8-hectare island listed on most maps as Pedra Branca, on which a lighthouse stands.

However, on 22 July, Singapore wanted to claim a territorial sea and exclusive economic zone around Pulau Batu Puteh, going back on its word to discuss with Malaysia territorial issues and activities around the island.

Blogger in court

17 July Kuala Lumpur

Blogger Raja Petra Kamarudin was charged with criminally defaming Datin Sri Rosmah Mansor, wife of Deputy Prime Minister Dato' Sri Najib Razak, bomb expert Acting Colonel Abdul Aziz Buyong and his wife Colonel Norhayati Hassan in his statutory declaration filed at the Kuala Lumpur High Court on 18 June. He was freed after his wife Marina Lee Abdullah posted bail.

Earlier, on 6 May, Raja Petra had been charged under the Sedition Act 1948 for posting the article 'Let's send the Altantuya murderers to hell' on the website www. malaysia-today.net on 25 April, implicating individuals in the murder of Mongolian Altantunya Shaariibuu. He posted bail the following day.

Six-vehicle pile-up

1 August Kuala Lumpur

Two people died when a lorry carrying boulders crashed into six vehicles at the East–West Link Highway, in Taman Connaught, Cheras. Six others were seriously injured.

Sultan of Brunei at Sarawak Regatta

3 August Kuching

Despite the tight schedule of his two-day visit to Sarawak, Sultan Hassanal Bolkiah of Brunei headed straight for the Kuching Waterfront to witness the Sarawak Regatta. On arrival at Kuching International Airport earlier, he was greeted by Head of State Tun Datuk Patinggi Abang Haji Muhammad Salahuddin and his wife as well as Chief Minister Tan Sri Haji Abdul Taib Mahmud and his wife.

Manhunt for policeman

5 August Johor Bahru

At least three policemen were identified as culprits behind the theft of *syabu* worth RM1 million from the Johor police headquarters last week. Two are in custody while a manhunt is on for the third suspect who is believed to be in possession of the drugs. The drugs were part of a RM48 million haul on 30 March by police who also seized RM1.1 million in cash in three raids in Johor Bahru.

Bar forum on conversions halted

9 August Kuala Lumpur

The Bar Council's public forum on conversion to Islam at its premises in Lebuh Pasar Besar was stopped after one hour. Hundreds of representatives and members of 29 Muslim non-governmental organisations and political parties had gathered outside from 8.00am, carrying banners written with words such as *Jangan Cabar Islam* (Don't Challenge Islam), and demanded a stop to the forum. Police found two bottles of unknown substances on the steps in front of the building. These were taken away by a bomb disposal unit for examination. Police said they had issued the Bar Council a warning not to hold such a public forum again.

School with only one pupil

11 August Taiping

At SJK (C) Padang Gajah in Trong, V. Sivasanthiran had the full attention of his teachers in class. The 12-year-old was the only pupil of the Chinese school which opened in 1953 and was possibly the only school in the country where the teachers outnumbered the students.

This had been going on for the last two years, following a drop in the school's enrolment in the late 1980s when more people migrated to the cities.

Sivasanthiran was personally tutored by headmaster Ooi Ah Bee, 55, and teacher Lim Shu Miin, 28—the school's only teachers. Asked why he remained at the school instead of asking for a transfer, Sivasanthiran said in halting Mandarin: 'My father wants me to learn Mandarin so that it will be easy for me to get a job....'

His parents, who were estate workers, had enrolled him in the nearby SMK Tat Beng for his secondary education. However, SJK (C) Padang Gajah would close at the end of the year and be relocated to Bandar Seri Botani at Simpang Pulai, near Ipoh.

V. Sivasanthiran raises the national flag at SJK (C) Padang Gajah watched by his headmaster and teacher.

It's Datuk Lee Chong Wei

28 August Georgetown

Olympic silver medallist Lee Chong Wei, 25, was conferred the Darjah Setia Pangkuan Negeri (DSPN), which carries the title Datuk, by Penang Yang di-Pertua Negeri Tun Abdul Rahman Abbas today at the latter's official residence, Seri Mutiara, here.

Petrol price floats

1 August Putrajaya

Effective 1 September, the retail price of petrol would be based on the average monthly market price of world crude oil with the government maintaining the subsidy rate at 30 sen per litre. However, Prime Minister Dato' Seri Abdullah Ahmad Badawi assured that the price would not exceed RM2.70 a litre in 2008.

On 13 June, several thousand people walked from the Kampung Baru Mosque to the Pas headquarters in Jalan Raja Laut to protest a recent fuel price hike. The following day, Pos Malaysia Bhd paid RM116.734 million in rebates to 239,414 motor vehicle owners at 683 post offices. The rebate was for those who bought new vehicles or renewed their road tax between 1 April and 31 May this year.

Malaysians shout slogans and carry posters condemning the rise in petrol prices as they leave the Kampung Baru Mosque after Friday prayers on 13 June.

The rail Prime Minister

21 August Kuala Lumpur

Setting aside protocol, Dato' Seri Abdullah Ahmad Badawi took a morning rush hour ride on the KTM Komuter and LRT from Serdang to the city centre to experience transport problems faced by the public.

He waited and waited as packed trains flashed by and when he finally managed to board one, he found out how KL folk had to push, shove and hang on to dear life to get to work every day.

After disembarking at the Masjid Jamek LRT station, he said he was not satisfied with the rail services and wanted immediate improvements to be made.

The Prime Minister chatting with commuters.

Inaugural Merdeka Award

21 August Kuala Lumpur

Royal Professor Ungku Aziz and the Malaysian Nature Society were among the recipients of the inaugural Merdeka Award. Recipients of each category received RM500,000, a trophy and certificate. The award, jointly initiated by Petronas, ExxonMobil and Shell, was announced by Prime Minister Dato' Seri Abdullah Badawi on 21 August 2007.

Anwar wins Permatang Pauh

26 August Butterworth

Dato' Seri Anwar Ibrahim won the Permatang Pauh by-election. He polled 31,195 votes compared with 15,524 obtained by Barisan Nasional's Datuk Arif Shah Omar Shah.

With the win, Anwar took back the seat he held from 1982 to 1999. His wife Dr Wan Azizah won the seat in the 1999 and held it until 31 July 2008 when she resigned to force a by-election so that Anwar could return to Parliament.

Hindraf outlawed

15 October Kuala Lumpur

The Hindu Rights Action Force (Hindraf) was banned by the Government and declared illegal. Home Minister Dato' Seri Syed Hamid Albar said the decision covered all activities it had been involved in since it was formed.

The movement, which has been advocating Indian rights since late 2007, began to register on the police radar in July last year after some of the leaders held talks and gatherings in some States.

Zaki is new Chief Justice

16 October Kuala Lumpur

Court of Appeal president Tan Sri Zaki Azmi, 63, was appointed Chief Justice of the Federal Court. He would be succeeded by Chief Judge of Malaya Tan Sri Alauddin Mohd Sheriff, 62. The Conference of Rulers has consented to the appointments.

ISA blitz

12 September Bukit Mertajam

Sin Chew Daily reporter Tan Hoon Cheng was arrested under the Internal Security Act (ISA) over a report on alleged racist remarks by Datuk Ahmad Ismail. She was released after police verified that she was no threat to public order and national security.

From left: Raja Petra, Tan Hoon Cheng and Teresa Kok.

Seputeh MP Teresa Kok was also detained under the ISA for allegedly telling mosque officials in Kota Damansara, Sri Serdang and Puchong Jaya to tone down the call to prayer. She has denied the allegations. She was also released after police were satisfied that she was not a threat to public order and security.

Blogger Raja Petra Kamarudin was detained under the ISA for writing articles considered to have maligned Islam, and being malicious and seditious. He was sentenced to two years' detention in the Kamunting detention centre. On 7 November, the High Court ordered his release, after allowing his habeas corpus application.

2008

world news

28 September
Haile Gebrselassie of Ethiopia is the first man to run the marathon under two hours and four minutes. In the Berlin Marathon he set the new world record of 2:03.59.

30 October
South Korea's Constitutional Court upholds a 55-year-old law banning adultery, rejecting arguments that the law was an invasion of privacy.

4 November
Barack Obama wins the US presidential elections.

6 November
Bhutan crowns a new king, Oxford-educated Jigme Khesar Namgyel Wangchuck, at the age of 28.

26 November
Ten Islamic militants from Pakistan attack 10 sites in Mumbai, killing 173 and wounding over 300.

2 December
Thai PM Somchai Wongsawat resigns after weeks of protests against his government, and a week-long shutdown of Bangkok's two airports leaves 300,000 travellers stranded.

Nurul Huda rapist spared gallows

16 October Putrajaya

Citing incomplete investigations and insufficient evidence, the Federal Court set aside the murder conviction and death sentence on a former security guard accused of murdering a 10-year-old girl four years earlier. Mohd Abbas Danus Baksan, 52, was spared the gallows but would serve a 20-year jail sentence after pleading guilty at the Johor Bahru Sessions Court in 2004 to raping Nurul Huda Abdul Ghani.

The 24 strokes imposed on Mohd Abbas by the court for the rape were also set aside due to his age as the law states that those aged 50 and above would be spared the rotan.

Nurul Huda was raped, sodomised and strangled at a Tenaga Nasional Berhad guardhouse in Kampung Pekajang, Johor, on 17 January 2004.

Massive landslide at Bukit Antarabangsa

6 December Kuala Lumpur

Four people were killed in a landslide that hit two housing estates in Bukit Antarabangsa at 4.00am and swept away 14 bungalows. This was the 12th major landslide to hit the area since the Highland Towers tragedy in 1993.

It took two days to open an alternative route for 2,000 nearby residents trapped after the access road to their homes was cut off.

Rescuers are seen around damaged houses hit by the landslide.

Zaid quits!

31 October Putrajaya

Former Minister in the Prime Minister's Department Datuk Zaid Ibrahim resigned as senator. He quit the Cabinet in mid-September in protest against at the arrest of a journalist, an opposition politician and a blogger under the Internal Security Act. He said he was disillusioned by the resistance he faced in the Cabinet when pushing for reforms to the judiciary.

RM7b stimulus package

4 November Kuala Lumpur

The Government unveiled a RM7 billion stimulus package to stimulate the economy. The money is to come from savings derived from cuts in the fuel subsidy. Deputy Prime Minister and Finance Minister Dato' Sri Najib Razak said the package was aimed at alleviating hardship and encouraging spending and includes RM1.2 billion to build 25,000 low- and medium-cost houses.

Aye for MACC Bill

16 December Kuala Lumpur

The Dewan Rakyat passed the Malaysian Anti-Corruption Commission Bill 2008 which would see the Anti-Corruption Agency evolve into the more powerful Malaysian Anti-Corruption Commission (MACC) in 2009.

The next day, MPs gave a resounding 'aye' to the Judicial Appointments Commission (JAC) Bill. Prime Minister Dato' Seri Abdullah Ahmad Badawi said that both bills were important as they underlined the Government's commitment to tackle corruption and to fight the public's negative perception of the judiciary following the disclosure of the Datuk V.K. Lingam video clip allegedly showing the prominent lawyer brokering judicial appointments.

Yim and her husband at the courthouse.

Guilty of harming maid

27 November Kuala Lumpur

Former air stewardess Yim Pek Ha, 40, was found guilty of causing grievous hurt to her maid, Nirmala Bonat, and sentenced to 18 years in prison. The sentences would run concurrently. Judge Akhtar Tahir found her guilty of scorching Nirmala with a hot electric iron and scalding her with hot water in January, March and April 2004.

On 3 December 2009, Yim's 18-year jail sentence was reduced by the High Court to 12. This decision was upheld by the Court of Appeal on 1 October 2012.

1948 massacre witness seeks justice

20 December Batang Kali

Tham Yong, 77, was old and sickly. The sole living survivor of the Batang Kali massacre said she still remembered 'the day the British killed our men'. With tears streaming down her cheeks, she recounted the slaying of 24 unarmed villagers by Scots Guards troops. The former rubber tapper had spent decades fighting for compensation over the massacre on 11 and 12 December 1948.

On 20 August, a group known as the Action Committee Condemning the Batang Kali Massacre asked the UK government to hold a public inquiry. It began a signature campaign to be submitted to Queen Elizabeth II, seeking an apology, compensation and a memorial.

Tham Yong died on 2 April 2010. On 4 September 2012, the High Court in London upheld the UK government's decision not to hold a public hearing.

Obituaries

25 Jan **Tan Sri Megat Junid Megat Ayub**, 65, former Domestic Trade and Consumer Affairs Minister.

28 April **Chen Voon Fee**, 77, architect, heritage conservationist and founder member of Badan Warisan Malaysia.

30 April **Tan Sri M.G. Pandithan**, 68, former Indian Progressive Front (IPF) president.

1 May **Tan Sri S.M. Nasimuddin S.M. Amin**, 54, founder of the Naza Group of Companies.

20 Aug **Tunku Abdullah Tuanku Abdul Rahman**, 83, Negeri Sembilan royalty.

4 Sept **Tan Sri A. Samad Ismail (Pak Samad)**, 84, journalist and former managing editor of the New Straits Times Press Group.

27 Dec **Tuanku Ja'afar Tuanku Abdul Rahman**, 86, Yang di-Pertuan Besar of Negeri Sembilan.

2009

This was the year that the 1Malaysia concept was launched in June, just two months after Dato' Sri Najib Tun Razak took over from Dato' Seri Abdullah Ahmad Badawi as Prime Minister. It was also announced in July that the teaching of Science and Mathematics would revert to Bahasa Malaysia and vernacular languages from English which had been the medium of instruction since 2003. Teoh Beng Hock was found dead next to the MACC offices at which he had been questioned and A. Kugan was killed while in police custody. Construction and engineering standards were called into question when the roof of a stadium in Kuala Terengganu collapsed and the old Jaya Supermarket in Petaling Jaya crumbled on top of Indonesian workers.

FEBRUARY
Dato' Seri Mohammad Nizar Jamaluddin is ousted as Menteri Besar of Perak when the Barisan Nasional took over the State Government.

APRIL
Dato' Sri Najib Tun Razak becomes Malaysia's sixth Prime Minister, replacing Dato' Seri Abdullah Ahmad Badawi.

SEPTEMBER
The KD *Tunku Abdul Rahman*, the first submarine in the Royal Malaysian Navy fleet, arrives in Malaysia from France.

NOVEMBER
Landslide on the Rawang–Kuala Lumpur trunk road affects more than 80,000 motorists.

November: Numerous vehicles and cattle were stranded on an 'island' created by floodwaters at a village in Rantau Panjang, Kelantan. The water subsided four hours after this photograph was taken.

'I urge us to rise to the challenge of building a One Malaysia. People First. Performance Now.'

Dato' Sri Najib Tun Razak's maiden speech after being appointed sixth Prime Minister of Malaysia, 3 April 2009.

2009

1 January
Bank of America purchases Merrill Lynch to save it from bankruptcy. It is later revealed that just before the acquisition the company paid out US$43.8 billion in bonuses to over 39,000 employees.

16 January
Frenchman Lluis Colet breaks the world record for the longest speech after rambling nonstop for 124 hours about Spanish painter Salvador Dali, Catalan culture, etc.

20 January
The inauguration of President Barack Obama, the 44th and first black president of the USA.

22 February
The film *Slumdog Millionaire* wins eight Oscars.

26 February
The Royal Bank of Scotland posts a 2008 loss of £24.1 billion, the largest in British corporate history.

11 April
Thailand cancels the Asean summit and airlifts the leaders out by helicopter after anti-government protesters storm a convention centre in Pattaya.

No to Race Relations Act

20 January Kuala Lumpur

The Cabinet has turned down a proposal for a Race Relations Act after a study revealed that Malaysians were generally not in favour of legislating for better racial ties. Unity, Culture, Arts and Heritage Minister Dato' Seri Mohd Shafie Apdal said the decision came after exhaustive discussions within the Cabinet and with representatives of all communities.

'Based on the conclusions drawn from the study, the Cabinet decided there was no need for such an act,' said Shafie who added that 'unity should be nurtured and not forced on people.'

Family members mourn over the body of Ananthan Kugan at his funeral on 28 January.

Kugan's death is murder

23 January Putrajaya

The death of A. Kugan on 20 January while in police custody was classified as murder. Kugan, 22, collapsed and died at the Subang Taipan police lock-up during questioning over vehicle thefts in the Klang Valley. Selangor police chief Datuk Khalid Abu Bakar said 11 policemen were being investigated (*see 26 June 2013*).

RM10b stimulus

5 March Kuala Lumpur

The Government unveiled plans to inject RM10 billion to stimulate the sagging economy, with more to come. This was in addition to the RM7 billion announced in December 2008.

Deputy Finance Minister Datuk Kong Cho Ha tabled the allocation as part of the proposed second economic stimulus package.

Chief Justice heads JAC

9 February Kuala Lumpur

Chief Justice Tan Sri Zaki Azmi was appointed chairman of the Judicial Appointments Commission (JAC).

The other eight members were Court of Appeal President Tan Sri Alauddin Mohd Sheriff, Chief Judge of Malaya Datuk Arifin Zakaria, Sabah and Sarawak High Court Chief Judge Tan Sri Richard Malanjum, Federal Court judge Datuk Zulkefli Ahmad Makinudin, former Chief Justice Tun Abdul Hamid Mohamad, former Sabah and Sarawak High Court Chief Judge Tan Sri Steve Shim Lip Kiong, ex-High Court judge Tan Sri L.C. Vohrah and former Attorney-General Dato' Seri Ainum Mohd Saaid.

The JAC was established on 2 February 2009 with its main role being to uphold the continuous independence of the judiciary through the selection of superior court judges.

Perak political crisis

18 February Ipoh

Perak legislative assembly speaker V. Sivakumar suspended Menteri Besar Datuk Dr Zambry Abdul Kadir for 18 months and his six exco members for 12 months, with immediate effect.

He said they had failed to provide any explanation to the Committee of Privileges on the charge of having committed contempt of the State Legislative Assembly when they declared themselves as Menteri Besar and State excos.

The drama began on 1 February when Prime Minister Dato' Seri Abdullah Ahmad Badawi said Pakatan Rakyat State assemblymen from Perak would be crossing over to Barisan Nasional. Two days later, BN said it had enough votes to form the State Government when Behrang assemblyman Jamaluddin Mohd Radzi, Changkat Jering assemblyman Mohd Osman Mohd Jailu and Hee Yit Foong of DAP—left the State government to be 'friendly independents' to BN (*see 9 February 2010*).

Perak Menteri Besar Datuk Seri Mohammad Nizar Jamaluddin (centre) addresses his supporters gathered at the Menteri Besar's residence in Perak on 5 February.

Heritage status for VI

13 February Kuala Lumpur

Victoria Institution (VI), which celebrated 116 years in 2008, was the first day-school in the country to be awarded national heritage status. Unity, Culture, Arts and Heritage Minister Dato' Seri Shafie Apdal presented the award to VI.

Founded by Selangor's Sultan Abdul Samad, Resident of Selangor William Hood Treacher, businessman Loke Yew, Thamboosamy Pillai and Kapitan Cina Yap Kwan Seng on 14 August 1893, VI has produced many leaders and luminaries over the years. Those who passed through its hallowed halls included Sultan Hassanal Bolkiah of Brunei, former and current ministers such as Tan Sri Rafidah Aziz, Dato' Seri Zulhasnan Rafique, Dao' Seri Shafie Apdal himself, Dato' Seri Dr Ng Yen Yen and former judge Datuk Mahadev Shankar.

US Secretary of State Hillary Clinton and First Lady Michelle Obama present the award to Datuk Ambiga.

Woman of Courage

11 March Washington ▶ Malaysian Bar Council president Datuk Ambiga Sreenevasan said she was honoured to be presented with the US State Department's award for International Women Of Courage.

Other recipients were female activists including from Afghanistan, Guatemala, and Uzbekistan who had fought to end discrimination and inequality. Ambiga was honoured for championing the rule of law and advancing human rights, the status of women and religious tolerance in Malaysia. She had 'emerged as a strong voice for tolerance and justice, and ... had a direct impact on judicial reform ... contributing to strengthening of the role of women in civil society.'

Limbang officially part of Malaysia

17 March Bandar Seri Begawan

Prime Minister Dato' Seri Abdullah Ahmad Badawi announced that Brunei had officially dropped its long-standing claim over the Limbang district in Sarawak. A joint press statement issued the same day mentioned that the demarcation of the land boundaries between the two countries would be resolved on the basis of historical agreements and, as appropriate, the watershed principle. Letters of Exchange were signed by the Prime Minister and Brunei's Sultan Hassanal Bolkiah at Istana Nurul Iman to mark the successful conclusion of negotiations.

The following day Brunei announced that, in the discussions that led to the Letters of Exchange, the Limbang claim had not been discussed.

Najib's Umno team

26 March Kuala Lumpur

In the new Umno line-up, president Dato' Sri Najib Tun Razak would be backed by his deputy, Tan Sri Muhyiddin Yassin and vice-presidents Datuk Ahmad Zahid Hamidi, Dato' Seri Hishammuddin Hussein and Dato' Seri Mohd Shafie Apdal.

The day before, outgoing president Dato' Seri Abdullah Ahmad Badawi came up with two radical proposals for Umno to adopt in its agenda for change: limiting the number of terms of its office-bearers and a one-man-one-vote system in the election process.

Hindraf leaders freed

3 April Kuala Lumpur

Two Hindu Rights Action Force (Hindraf) leaders, V. Ganabatirau and R. Kengadharan, both 40, were among 13 Internal Security Act detainees released immediately. They were arrested with M. Manoharan, 46, P. Uthayakumar, 46, and Hindraf coordinator K. Vasantha Kumar, 34, on 13 December 2007 for taking part in an illegal rally on 25 November that year against alleged racial discrimination.

About a month later, on 9 May, the three remaining Hindraf leaders at the Kamunting detention centre were also released, about a month after their two fellow leaders were freed. Kota Alam Shah assemblyman M. Manoharan and K. Vasantha Kumar, were freed at 2.30pm. Hindraf legal adviser P. Uthayakumar was the last to leave at 2.55pm. He said the police wanted him to agree to a conditional release but he refused.

Earlier, seven men, believed to be ISA detainees from Indonesia and the Philippines, were released at 12.40pm, followed by three other local ISA detainees at 1.20pm.

Freed Hindraf leaders K. Vasantha Kumar (left) and Hindraf legal adviser P. Uthayakumar (right) upon their release.

Farewell, Abdullah. Welcome, Najib

New Prime Minister Najib Tun Razak receiving official documents from former premier Abdullah Ahmad Badawi at the Prime Minister's office in Putrajaya on 3 April 2009.

1–3 April Putrajaya

Prime Minister Dato' Seri Abdullah Ahmad Badawi chaired his last Cabinet meeting on 1 April. His last piece of advice to his colleagues: pursue the national missions and policies put in place to ensure the country's strength in facing challenges of the future.

Dato' Sri Najib Razak, 55, was sworn in as the country's sixth Prime Minister before Yang di-Pertuan Agong Tuanku Mizan Zainal Abidin on 3 April at Istana Negara. At 4.50pm that afternoon, Tun Abdullah Ahmad Badawi officially handed over the duties of Prime Minister to Dato' Sri Najib at the Prime Minister's Department in the Perdana Putra building in Putrajaya.

On 10 April, Deputy Prime Minister Tan Sri Muhyiddin Yassin led the newly appointed Ministers and Deputy Ministers in taking their oath of office before the King. A day earlier, Dato' Sri Najib warned that he would be involved personally in reviewing their performance every six months.

Economic liberalisation

22 April Putrajaya

The Government has removed the 30 per cent Bumiputera quota on equity ownership in 27 services sub-sectors including health and social services, computer and related services, tourism services, transport, business services, rental/leasing services without operators and other supporting and auxiliary transport services.

Civil solutions on conversions

23 April Putrajaya

In the event of a spouse converting to Islam, the Cabinet decided that civil courts were the right place to dissolve a marriage and that the children should follow the faith that the parents had agreed on at the time of marriage, or implied by their common religion. The attorney-general had been ordered to review and propose changes to the law to prevent any future complications to the family unit when a spouse converted to Islam.

Datuk Seri Nazri Aziz, Minister in the Prime Minister's Department, said: 'The marriage followed civil law, so it should be dissolved in a manner provided for by civil courts. Conversion to another religion is not a ground for automatic dissolution of a civil marriage.'

Foreign equity to spur growth

27 April Putrajaya

In a major move to open up the financial services sector and make Malaysia more competitive amid the economic downturn, up to seven new foreign banks—including two mega-Islamic ones—would be allowed to operate here by 2012. Foreign ownership rules were also eased to allow foreigners controlling stakes in non-commercial banks. The new measures would be implemented between this year and 2012. There are currently 13 financial institutions which are fully foreign owned, with a combined market share of 25 per cent.

Three new Federal Court judges

13 April Putrajaya

Datuk Gopal Sri Ram, Datuk Wira Ghazali Mohd Yusof and Datuk James Foong would be receiving their appointment letters as Federal Court judges from the Yang di-Pertuan Agong at Istana Negara on 15 April.

Datuk Gopal, 65, was the first lawyer to have been appointed straight to the Court of Appeal. He had never served as a judicial commissioner nor a High Court judge.

Five High Court judges would also be appointed to the Court Of Appeal.

Azilah, Sirul to hang

9 April Shah Alam ▶ High Court judge Datuk Mohd Zaki Md Yasin sent chief inspector Azilah Hadri and corporal Sirul Azhar Umar to the gallows for the murder of Mongolian translator Altantuya Shaariibuu.

After 159 days of hearings, he simply found that the defence presented by both accused were only 'denials and blaming each other'. He said: 'I hereby convict both accused for murder and sentence them to death. The both of you will hang by your necks until you are dead.'

Azilah and Sirul showed no emotion. After the proceedings, Azilah's fiancee, Norazila Baharuddin, said the duo seemed resigned to the fact that they would be found guilty.

Azilah and Sirul, both commandos with the elite Special Action Squad, were found guilty of the murder of Altantuya at Mukim Bukit Raja between 9.54pm on 18 October 2006, and 9.45pm the next day.

Azilah testified that he had handed Altantuya to Sirul to send her back to Hotel Malaya, where she was staying, and that he was not at the scene at the time of the murder. But Sirul denied that Azilah handed Altantuya to him. He said he was at Devi's Corner in Sri Hartamas having tea and had later gone to Kampung Baru in Kuala Lumpur for *sahur* on the night of the murder.

Political analyst Abdul Razak Baginda was charged with abetting the duo in Altantuya's murder but was freed by the High Court on 31 October 2008 without his defence being called (*see 23 August 2013*).

Policemen Azilah Hadri and Sirul Azhar Umar arrive at court on 15 January.

Three killed in shopping centre collapse

28 May Petaling Jaya

A section of the old Jaya Shopping Centre in Section 14, Petaling Jaya, crumbled, killing three and injuring two others, with four more trapped in the rubble. All were Indonesians. The building, which was being demolished, crumbled as nine workers were unloading scaffolding at 4.45pm. A week later, the Government established a committee to investigate whether there was any element of negligence in the collapse.

Much of the old Jaya Supermarket building, once a landmark in Petaling Jaya, turned to rubble.

2009

17 May
Tamil Tigers admit defeat after their 25-year-old war against Sri Lanka's government.

28 May
A 16-year-old Iraqi immigrant in Sweden cracks a mathematics puzzle that had stumped mathematicians for more than 300 years.

25 June
Michael Jackson, 50, dies from drug-related causes. His 1982 album *Thriller* is the best-selling album ever with an estimated 50 million copies sold.

15 July
Suicide attacks on the Marriot and Ritz-Carlton hotels in Jakarta result in nine deaths, including the two suspected bombers. Fifty-three are wounded.

8 August
Unveiled: two piano pieces identified as compositions of Mozart when he was seven years old.

17 September
Indonesian police kill Noordin Mohammad Top, the Southeast-Asian leader of Al-Qaeda in Java.

Onlookers assess the damage at the Sultan Mizan Zainal Abidin Stadium, Kuala Terengganu.

Stadium roof collapse

2 June Kuala Terengganu

It was sheer luck. If the roof of the RM292 million Sultan Mizan Zainal Abidin Stadium had collapsed a day later, thousands would have been killed as the stadium hosted the Public Institutions of Higher Learning Games. About 80 metres of the roof collapsed at about 9.30am.

Works Minister Datuk Shaziman Abu Mansor lashed out at contractors for not building a proper structure.

1Malaysia idea for all

15 June Putrajaya

Dato' Sri Najib Razak made his 1Malaysia concept the highlight of his first day in Parliament as Prime Minister. He said 1Malaysia emphasised 'acceptance' among the various races, where each race accepted the uniqueness of the others and all lived in mutual respect as the people of one nation. He added that 1Malaysia was a continuation of the country's nation-building. 'When unity is achieved, the process of national development will be smoother,' he said.

Jakarta suspends maid service

25 June Jakarta

Indonesia has temporarily halted sending domestic helpers to Malaysia pending review of a memorandum of understanding (MoU) on migrant workers. This applied only to domestic workers. The move followed widespread public outrage over the alleged abuse of Indonesian maid Siti Hajar by her Malaysian employer.

First DAP senator

6 July Kuala Lumpur

The DAP made its entrance in the Senate yesterday when its vice-chairman, Tunku Abdul Aziz Tunku Ibrahim, was sworn in as a senator for Penang. Tunku Abdul Aziz, who had carved a name for himself with Transparency International, said it was a great moment for him as he would be his party's first representative in the Senate.

Seats for the Upper House are not contested and members are appointed by the Federal Government or the State legislative assemblies. Each State legislature can nominate two senators.

New deal for education

8 July Putrajaya

Deputy Prime Minister Tan Sri Muhyiddin Yassin announced that Science and Mathematics would be taught in Bahasa Malaysia and vernacular languages in stages, from 2012. Measures would also be taken to strengthen the teaching of English. The policy would be implemented in stages for Year One, Year Four and Form One but would not involve Form Six and matriculation. Former Prime Minister Tun Dr Mahathir Mohamad, who introduced the teaching and learning of Science and Mathematics in English in 2003, expressed dismay.

PM opens KIA runway

17 June Kuching

Prime Minister Dato' Sri Najib Tun Razak declared open the newly completed extended runway of the Kuching International Airport. The runway, extended from 2,454m previously to 3,780m, is the longest in Borneo and the fourth-longest in Southeast Asia after the KL International Airport, Singapore's Changi Airport and Bangkok's airport. It can now accommodate the Airbus 380.

DPM seeks Unesco's help

29 June Putrajaya

The United Nations Educational, Scientific and Cultural Organization (Unesco) would help review our education system. Deputy Prime Minister and Education Minister Tan Sri Muhyiddin Yassin said a team consisting of local educationists and Unesco representatives would be formed for the purpose. 'There is a need to get the views of outsiders and Unesco is the best body to conduct the review,' he said.

New Sarawak landmark

27 July Kuching

Yang di-Pertuan Agong Tuanku Mizan Zainal Abidin opened the new State assembly building in Petra Jaya today. Sarawak Chief Minister Tan Sri Abdul Taib Mahmud said the RM300 million nine-storey building was a new landmark for the city.

The new building was needed to meet the expected increase in the number of State Assembly members. It could accommodate up to 108 members; there were 71 at the time of its opening. The building design reflects the various ethnic groups in Sarawak. It is equipped with state-of-the-art and multimedia communication facilities.

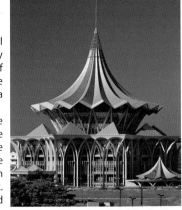

The new Sarawak State Assembly Building, Kuching.

World's best school band

9 July Sepang

Victoria Institution's cadet corps band proved that it was the best in the world when it clinched the grand prize at the World Band Challenge 2009 in Modena, Italy. The band beat the defending champion from Holland on 6 July to win. The band was welcomed home by some 50 VI Supporters Club members and parents.

Political aide found dead

16 July Shah Alam

Teoh Beng Hock, 30, the political aide to DAP Seri Kembangan assemblyman Ean Yong Hian Wah, was found dead at 1.30pm on the roof of the fifth floor of Plaza Masalam, next to the offices of the Malaysian Anti-Corruption Commission. Teoh had been called in for questioning by the MACC at about 5pm the previous day as part of investigations into alleged misuse of state allocations by assemblymen (*see 12 October 2009*).

Heroes shabbily treated

19 July Kuching

They were invited to Kuala Lumpur to attend the Warriors Day celebration in an all-expenses paid trip but most of the 14 surviving recipients of the Pingat Gagah Berani would not be going because the Veterans Department had told them to pay for their own airfares and accommodation.

Malaysian YouTube sensation

8 August | Kuala Lumpur

Many people dream of being a star but Zee Avi, 23, is living her dream ... and more. Not only is she a singing sensation but she is also on a two-month US tour with singer-songwriter Pete Yorn.

Miri-born, Kuala Lumpur-raised Zee, whose real name is Izyan Alirahman, rose to fame after posting her songs on YouTube for a friend. To her surprise, she started to get comments from strangers and almost overnight, she became a worldwide web sensation. She was offered a recording deal with Monotone Records and flew to Los Angeles to record her debut and the single 'No Christmas For Me' was featured on a holiday charity album *This Warm December, A Brushfire Holiday, Vol. 1*.

Residents and supporters attempt to prevent workers and contractors entering Kampung Buah Pala, Penang.

High Chaparral no more

21 August | Putrajaya

The residents of Kampung Lorong Buah Pala would have to vacate their homes, allowing the land owner and developer to move in their bulldozers, after the Federal Court struck out their leave application today. The 45 families had earlier failed to convince the court that they had a right over the property, dubbed Penang's High Chaparral and said to be the only Indian village on urban land in Penang.

Above: Mask-wearing anti-ISA protester marching to the Istana Negara.

Left: Protesters march against the ISA.

Hundreds arrested in illegal demo

1 August | Kuala Lumpur

More than 5,000 demonstrators took to the streets calling for the repeal of the Internal Security Act, bringing traffic in many parts of the city to a standstill. LRT commuters at Masjid Jamek and Bandaraya stations were also left stranded.

Various Pakatan Rakyat leaders, including Pas secretary-general Datuk Mustafa Ali, Batu Member of Parliament Tian Chua, Pas president Dato' Seri Abdul Hadi Awang and opposition leader Dato' Seri Anwar Ibrahim addressed the crowd. City police chief Datuk Muhammad Sabtu Osman said police arrested 589 people, including 44 juveniles. Federal Reserve Unit personnel fired tear gas and used water cannon to disperse the crowds. Two days later, 29 people were charged with taking part in an illegal assembly.

Tuanku Muhriz installed as Negeri Ruler

26 October | Kuala Pilah

Tuanku Muhriz Tuanku Munawir was installed the 11th Yang di-Pertuan Besar of Negeri Sembilan in a ceremony steeped in the *perpatih* tradition unique to the State, at Balairong Seri, Istana Besar Seri Menanti.

The ceremony last took place four decades ago when Tuanku Ja'afar Tuanku Abdul Rahman was installed as the 10th Yang di-Pertuan Besar after the demise of his brother, Tuanku Munawir Tuanku Abdul Rahman.

Tuanku Muhriz inspecting the guard of honour before his installation.

Not Malaysia's fault!

11 September | Jakarta

Simmering anger in Indonesia over Malaysia's alleged 'theft' of a traditional dance spurred calls for war. Word spread in August that Malaysia had screened tourism advertisements featuring Bali's traditional *pendet* dance. It turned out to be a promotion for a Discovery Channel programme to promote its *Enigmatic Malaysia* series. Discovery Networks Asia-Pacific removed the clip as soon as the problem was identified and reiterated that Malaysia was not responsible for the clip.

Protesters vowing to 'crush Malaysia' burned Malaysian flags and threw eggs at the country's embassy. Local media ignored an admission of guilt and apology from Discovery and ran a steady stream of reports of Malaysia's outrages, most of them recycled.

McDonald's loses the Mc-fight for good

8 September | Putrajaya

Fast-food chain McDonald's failed to stop McCurry Indian restaurant from using the prefix 'Mc'. The Federal Court dismissed McDonald's application for leave to appeal against the Court of Appeal's finding over the use of the prefix on the grounds that the questions posed by McDonald's in the application were not properly framed. McDonald's was ordered to pay RM10,000 costs to McCurry, which operates in Jalan Ipoh, Kuala Lumpur. McCurry director A.M.S.P. Suppiah, 55, said he was relieved that the dispute had been settled.

First Scorpene submarine arrives

3 September | Port Klang

Malaysia's first submarine, KD *Tunku Abdul Rahman*, sailed into Port Klang and docked at the National Hydrography Centre in Pulau Indah today.

The second submarine, KD *Tun Razak*, is expected next year. The two Scorpene vessels, the country's single biggest defence procurement to date, were acquired in 2002 under a RM3.4 billion package that includes a second-hand Agosta training vessel.

The *Tunku Abdul Rahman*, with a crew of 32 and commanded by Cdr Zulhelmy Ithnain, left Toulon in France on 11 July. She sailed to the Lumut naval base on 4 September for a three-day stopover before proceeding to its home base at Teluk Sepanggar in Sabah.

The KD *Tunku Abdul Rahman* docks at Port Klang.

Fantastic Four!

27 September | Amsterdam

Nicol David won her fourth World Open title in Amsterdam and joined the world squash legends. She sealed her place in the pantheon of squash greats by winning her fourth World Open title after an engrossing battle with Natalie Grinham in the final in Amsterdam yesterday. Nicol, still apparently dazed from her stunning achievement, said: 'I don't know what I'm saying. In fact, I can't believe it still ... four titles!'

The triumph put Nicol on par with New Zealand great Susan Devoy on four world titles and just one behind her mentor, Sarah Fitz-Gerald of Australia. The world title is Nicol's sixth title on the Wispa Tour this year.

2009

world news

1 October
The 19th Ig Noble Prizes are awarded at Harvard. The physics prize went to a study of why pregnant women don't tip over. The veterinary medicine prize was given for a finding that cows given names gave more milk than anonymous ones.

18 October
Jessica Watson, 16, leaves Sydney Harbour in her 10-metre yacht to try and become the youngest person to sail round the world unassisted. She completes her voyage on 15 May 2010.

4 November
Thailand is upset that Cambodia appointed former Thai PM Thaksin as economic adviser to Premier Hun Sen and recalls its ambassador.

11 November
Andy Warhol's painting '200 One Dollar Bills' sells for a whole lot more than that in auction—a record US$43,800,000.

26 December
China launches the world's fastest train, average speed 350km per hour, on the Guangzhou–Wuhan line.

Flown home to safety

30 September Kuala Lumpur

A 7.6-magnitude earthquake rocked Padang, Sumatra, killing 1,120 people. Early the following morning, 128 Malaysian students in Padang were evacuated and brought home in three Royal Malaysian Air Force C130H transport planes. Another 102 were expected to be brought back later in the day.

Meanwhile, Malaysian armed forces personnel were on standby to go to Padang for relief work, while a Mercy Malaysia team had already gone in to assess the needs in the earthquake-hit area.

Teoh Beng Hock inquest

21 October Shah Alam

A stir was caused at the inquest into the death of 30-year-old political aide Teoh Beng Hock when Thai forensic expert Dr Pornthip Rojanasunan suggested his death could be homicide and offered to carry out a second post-mortem to prove her findings. Teoh was found dead on the rooftop of a building adjacent to the MACC offices on 16 July having been brought in for questioning there the previous day (see 5 January 2011).

Thai forensic expert Dr Pornthip Rojanasunan arrives at the Shah Alam court beside a photo of Teoh Beng Hock.

Lingam case closed

21 October Putrajaya

Legal action would not be taken against lawyer Datuk V.K. Lingam for lack of evidence and testimony in the findings of the Royal Commission of Inquiry into the Lingam tapes. Prime Minister Dato' Sri Najib Razak said the findings were not substantial enough to initiate legal proceedings. He said no evidence was found to prove abuse of power in judicial appointments as presented in the then Anti-Corruption Agency's investigation report on the issue.

Ship on fire

8 October Port Dickson

Fire broke out aboard the KD *Sri Inderapura*, the Royal Malaysian Navy's largest logistics ship, causing it severe damage. The ship was off the coast of Lumut at the time while on its way to the Teluk Sepanggar base. The fire was put out at about 2.00pm but the 159m-long ship was in danger of sinking. There were no casualties. The ship was first commissioned into the US Navy in 1971 and then into the RMN in 1995.

Malaysia Day joy

19 October Kuala Lumpur

Malaysia Day on 16 September will be a public holiday from next year. Dato' Sri Najib Razak said Malaysia will now have two National Day celebrations—Merdeka Day on 31 August when Malaya gained independence from the United Kingdom in 1957 and 16 September when Malaya, Sabah and Sarawak became Malaysia in 1963. (Singapore joined the federation but left in 1965.) He said Merdeka Day would continue to commemorate the struggle to win independence with official functions such as parades, while Malaysia Day would focus on unity.

Petronas in giant oil deal

11 December Baghdad

Petronas won rights to develop two huge oil fields in Iraq under a second auction of oil contracts since the 2003 US invasion.

Petronas and Royal Dutch Shell were awarded the Majnoon field in southern Iraq, with 12.6 billion barrels of reserves, one of the largest untapped oil fields left on earth. The project would be split 60 per cent for Shell and 40 per cent for Petronas.

In a second deal, Petronas and partners CNPC and Total won the rights to develop Halfaya, which had estimated reserves of 4.1 billion barrels.

Plan for 50 1Malaysia clinics

16 December Kuala Lumpur

Fifty 1Malaysia clinics will be opened simultaneously nationwide on 7 January to provide quick access to medical treatment. Costing RM10 million, the clinics, to be staffed by a medical assistant and a nurse, will be situated in densely populated areas in town centres and housing estates with more than 20,000 residents. Health Minister Dato' Seri Liow Tiong Lai said the clinics will mostly be within walking distance from where people live. They can seek treatment for minor ailments such as fever, cough, cold, headaches, wounds and cuts.

Landslide on Rawang road

3 November Rawang

Tonnes of earth in a 2.45am landslide at Km12 of the Rawang–Kuala Lumpur trunk road covered two lanes leading towards Rawang and affected over 80,000 motorists on their way to work. The landslide covered an area estimated at 100m long, 70m wide and 4.5m high.

The landslide occurred after a downpour. Search-and-rescue teams from the Civil Defence Department, police, Fire and Rescue Department and Special Malaysian Rescue Team arrived at the scene within minutes and police and Public Works Department officials diverted traffic towards Selayang Heights and searched for likely victims.

Aerial view of the landslide along the old trunk road.

Manohara told to return RM1m

13 December Kota Bharu

Indonesian actress Manohara Odelia Pinot, 17, was ordered to return to her husband, Tengku Temenggong Kelantan Tengku Muhammad Fakhry Petra Sultan Ismail Petra within 14 days. The Syariah High Court also ruled that she must repay her husband a debt of more than RM1 million within 30 days. The two judgments would take effect once Tengku Muhammad Fakhry Petra takes the *yamin istizhar syariah* oath on 3 January. If she failed to return, she would lose all her rights as a wife to the prince.

Meanwhile, Manohara's mother said the teenager would not be returning to her husband as she was still traumatised by his mistreatment of her.

RMAF jet engines stolen

21 December Kuala Lumpur

Two jet-fighter engines, each worth RM50 million, were stolen from the Royal Malaysian Air Force (RMAF) base at Sungai Besi. Attorney-General Tan Sri Abdul Gani Patail said the engines, which served as powerplants to the F-5E Tiger II fighter and RF-5E Tigereye reconnaissance jets, were discovered stolen in May 2008 and a police report was made. A brigadier general and 40 other armed forces personnel had been sacked in late 2008 over their alleged involvement in the case.

Meanwhile, Defence Minister Dato' Seri Dr Ahmad Zahid Hamidi said parts of the F-5E Tiger II and RF-5E Tigereye aircraft were also discovered missing.

Obituaries

18 Feb Ibrahim Hussein, 72, artist.

9 July Maria 'Nadrah' Hertogh, 72, who, as a child, was at the centre of a legal tussle between her Dutch parents and Malay foster mother.

26 July Yasmin Ahmad, 51, film-maker.

27 Aug Prof Datuk Dr Ismail Md Salleh, 61, economist senator.

1 Sept Tun Abdul Hamid Omar, 80, former Lord President.

2010

The year ended on a high note with the Prime Minister declaring a special public holiday to celebrate the national football team's success winning the AFF Suzuki Cup. The year had started on a much more sombre note with attacks on places of worship, primarily churches. Pudu Jail was demolished and the Greater Kuala Lumpur area was announced as part of the Government's Economic Transformation Plan, for which a second batch of development and entry-point projects were announced later in the year. The Federal Court confirmed Dato' Seri Dr Zambry Abdul Kadir as Menteri Besar of Perak. Meanwhile, long-serving Malaysian Indian Congress (MIC) President Dato' Seri S. Samy Vellu passed the baton to his successor Datuk G. Palanivel.

APRIL
Prime Minister Dato' Sri Najib Razak meets US President Barack Obama for bilateral talks in Washington.

MAY
The country's first baby hatch is opened, enabling those unable to take care of their babies to drop them off anonymously.

JUNE
A long stretch of Pudu Jail's mural-bedecked wall is demolished to make way for a road-widening project.

JULY
The Population and Housing Census gets underway. It is the fifth decennial census to be conducted since the formation of Malaysia in 1963.

December: Jubilant members of the Harimau Malaya celebrate their 4–2 aggregate victory over Indonesia in the AFF Suzuki Cup final in Jakarta.

Malaysia Facts		
28.3 million	Population	
RM766.0 billion	Gross Domestic Product	
RM26,175	Gross National Income (per capita)	
17.9	Crude Birth Rate (per 1,000 persons)	
6.8	Infant Mortality (per 1,000 live births)	
71.7 / 76.6	Life Expectancy (male / female)	
100	Consumer Price Index (base 2010=100)	

'For me, it was love at second sight.'
Comedian Harith Iskandar on falling in love with his wife-to-be, Dr Jezamine Lim, whom he married on 13 June 2010.

2010

world news

16 February
The Taliban's No. 2 leader and military commander Mullah Abdul Ghani Baradar is captured in Karachi.

25 February
A 1939 copy of *Detective Comics No. 37*, in which Batman made his debut, is sold in auction for more than US$1 million.

19 May
Downtown Bangkok burns as the Thai army moves to end a 10-week long protest by Red Shirt protesters. Final death toll for two-and-a-half months of confrontation: 91.

22 May
In Poland, Nicolaus Copernicus (1473–1543), the astronomer whose findings were condemned by the Roman Catholic Church as heretical, is removed from his unmarked grave and reburied as a hero.

28 May
A South Korean couple is convicted of abandoning their newborn daughter, who starved to death while they addictively played an online game—raising a virtual child.

Aid convoy in port clash

6 January Gaza

Malaysian student Ibrahim Mohd Azmi and six others were arrested when the Viva Palestina aid convoy clashed with Egyptian riot police at the Egyptian port of El-Arish. All seven were released later.

Riots broke out after Gaza's Hamas rulers called for a protest over the clash. Four activists were seriously injured. Viva Palestina was on a mission to send food, medicine and school equipment to Palestinians in Gaza. But the Egyptian government refused to allow the convoy use of the port of Nuweiba for entry to Rafah before arriving in Gaza.

Perdana Global Peace Organisation members Juana Jaafar and Ram Kartigasu were driving an ambulance donated by the organisation to the people of Gaza.

Aid for Haitians

16 January Kuala Lumpur

Malaysians rallied to help victims of the 12 January earthquake in Haiti which killed about 200,000. In line with the fund set up by the International Federation of Red Cross and Red Crescent Societies which had appealed for US$10 million (RM33.4 million) in aid, the Malaysian Red Crescent Society set up a fund two days after the catastrophe and hoped to raise RM500,000.

Mercy Malaysia president Dr Ahmad Faizal Perdaus said it was monitoring the situation and would launch an appeal for funds if the Medical Emergency Relief International (Merlin) needed it desperately.

Multipurpose MyKad

18 January Putrajaya

With the new MyKad, Malaysians need only give their MyKad numbers for 760 government applications, including transactions with the Employees Provident Fund and the Inland Revenue Board. Deputy Prime Minister Tan Sri Muhyiddin Yassin, who launched the MyID initiative, said people could also use their MyKad numbers to access and conduct searches on the websites of government agencies.

The '1 Number For All Transactions' initiative, inspired by the Prime Minister's People First concept, was also applicable in dealings at the State Government level.

A rousing send-off

9 February Kuala Lumpur

Petroliam Nasional Bhd (Petronas) president and CEO Tan Sri Mohd Hassan Marican was given a rousing send-off at the company headquarters in Kuala Lumpur. Under his direction, Petronas grew to become one of the industry's most respected and profitable organisations, with operations in more than 32 countries.

As the clock ticked closer to 5.00pm, the crowd at the lobby of Petronas Twin Towers swelled and all cheered when Tan Sri Hassan emerged from the elevator.

Call for calm after church arson

9 January Kuala Lumpur

Malaysians came out to condemn arson attempts after Metro Tabernacle Church in Desa Melawati, Wangsa Maju, Assumption Church in Petaling Jaya and Life Chapel in Section 17/21E were attacked on 8 January. That same day, Prime Minister Dato' Sri Najib Razak announced an allocation of RM500,000 to rebuild Metro Tabernacle Church and directed the police to beef up security at all places of worship.

On 2 January, Pakatan Rakyat MP Zulkifli Nordin had wanted the National Fatwa Council to decide on the use of the word 'Allah' after the High Court ruled on 31 December 2009 that Catholic weekly *The Herald*, could use the word in its articles. The Home Ministry filed a notice of appeal at the Court of Appeal. Shah Alam MP Khalid Samad felt that to say 'Allah is only for Muslims' limited the greatness of Allah to Muslims only, but Selangor opposition leader Dato' Seri Dr Mohamad Khir Toyo said the word was exclusive to Muslims. Minister of Information, Communications and Culture Dato' Seri Dr Rais Yatim warned that overzealous opinions would be detrimental to peace in the country.

On 15 January, the Government announced that 'Allah' was not allowed to be used in churches in the peninsula although it had no issue with it being used by Christians in Sabah and Sarawak because the people there had traditionally used the word in religious services.

Malaysian forensic experts and security officials investigate at the gutted administrative block of a church following an attack in Kuala Lumpur in the early hours of 8 January.

Stronger ties with the US

12 April Washington ▶ At the Nuclear Security Summit, Prime Minister Dato' Sri Najib Razak met US President Barack Obama for bilateral talks at the Walter E. Washington Convention Center.

The meeting set the tone for new US–Malaysia relations. Both leaders touched on issues relating to Malaysia's role in the Islamic world, Asean regional security and the country's new laws regulating international trade and business.

Prime Minister Najib Razak meets US President Barack Obama at the Nuclear Security Summit in Washington.

The White House said Obama and Dato' Sri Najib agreed on the need to send a clear signal to Iran that while it has the right to develop peaceful uses of nuclear energy, it should not use this right to develop nuclear weapons.

Forty-seven world leaders took part in the summit.

Zambry confirmed as Perak Menteri Besar

9 February Kuala Lumpur

A five-member Federal Court ruled that the Sultan of Perak was right in appointing Dato' Seri Dr Zambry Abdul Kadir as Menteri Besar as Dato' Seri Mohammad Nizar Jamaluddin had lost the majority support of the assemblymen.

Chief Judge of Malaya Tan Sri Arifin Zakaria said there was no requirement in the State constitution for a vote of no-confidence to be taken in the State assembly. 'There was no doubt that Zambry had the support of 31 of the 59 members of the ... assembly,' he said.

Dato' Seri Zambry, who is the BN assemblyman for Pangkor, expressed hope that all quarters, regardless of political affiliation, would set aside their differences to work together for the people of Perak.

Better deal for police

25 March Kuala Lumpur

For the first time in the history of the police force, 33,000 officers and personnel performing general duties would receive a monthly allowance of RM200, while 52,000 would benefit from a time-based promotion scheme. The exercise would cost RM84 million a year. Inspector-General of Police Tan Sri Musa Hassan said the exercise would make his personnel more committed and dedicated in carrying out their duties.

UKMMC bypass history

12 April Kuala Lumpur

Consultant cardiothoracic surgeon, associate professor Dr Mohd Ramzisham Abdul Rahman (left) carried out the country's first heart bypass using an innovative vein harvesting technology at Universiti Kebangsaan Malaysia Medical Centre.

Invented by Dr Peter Hjc. Sporen of Holland (right), the Vascular-Micro-Milling-System cut vein-harvesting time from about an hour to merely 10 minutes. The recuperation period was also reduced greatly as the patient could start walking faster which helped in the heart recovery process.

The technology was initially developed as a means to remove varicose veins. It enabled tracking of the vein down to the bottom of the leg and then cutting it out without having to cut open the entire stretch of the leg.

Star attraction

3 April Genting Highlands

Press and public alike rushed to photograph Kinabatangan MP and his 31-year-old second wife, actress Zizie Ezette, at the Anugerah Bintang Popular 2009 awards at the Arena of Stars, Genting Highlands. The two had married secretly a few months earlier.

The hot couple at the awards night.

Melaka sultanate said to have begun in 1278

17 April Melaka

According to researchers headed by Prof Dr Abdullah Zakaria Ghazali from the Department of History, Universiti Malaya, the Malacca Malay Sultanate began in 1278 and not in the 1400s.

Chief Minister Dato' Seri Mohd Ali Rustam said the year 1278 was chosen based on the Raja Bongsu version of the *Malay Annals* or the *Sulalatus al-Salatin* (Raffles 18).

'Ladies Only' coaches

28 April Kuala Lumpur

With the introduction of special 'Ladies Only' coaches, women on board Keretapi Tanah Melayu Bhd Komuter trains (Sentul–Port Klang route) needn't worry about pickpockets, sex fiends and thieves anymore. The coaches would be indicated by large pink stickers with the message, 'Ladies only at all times'.

Malaysia's first baby hatch

29 May Petaling Jaya Non-governmental organisation OrphanCARE has set up the country's first baby hatch. Those unable to take care of their babies can drop them off at the hatch anonymously and the babies will be put up for adoption.

The baby hatch had provoked a debate, with some people saying it encouraged premarital sex and reckless behaviour while others lauded the move which would prevent cases of unwanted babies dumped in garbage bins. Women, Family and Community Development Minister Dato' Seri Shahrizat Abdul Jalil said the initiative was part of the solution to provide desperate mothers with a place to go to instead of taking the life of their child.

BABY HATCH
PELINDUNG BAYI

Legendary wedding

8 May Langkawi

Even Mahsuri would have approved to see over 1,000 guests at the wedding reception of her seventh generation descendant, Wan Aisyah Nawawi, and Alee Tongyon, in Kota Mahsuri Complex in Kampung Mawat.

Clad in a modern white kebaya, Wan Aisyah, 23, and Alee, 27, arrived accompanied by her parents and grandfather. The entourage spent 20 minutes at the Mahsuri mausoleum before the feast started. According to legend, Mahsuri cursed Langkawi island for seven generations after she was executed for alleged adultery.

Chua, three others stripped of titles

11 June Johor Bahru

Four people were stripped of their Johor State titles effective 4 June. They were former minister Dato' Seri Chua Jui Meng, South Pole adventurer Sharifah Mazlina Syed Abdul Kadir, who had been bestowed the First Class Order of the Crown of Johor, Dato' Seri Paduka Mahkota Johor (SPMJ) and the Second Class Datuk Paduka Mahkota Johor (DPMJ), naval Commander Shaftdean Lufty Rusland (SPMJ, DPMJ) and lawyer Hassan Yunos (DPMJ).

Datuk Abdul Rahim Ramli, secretary of the Johor Council of Royal Court, said it had nothing to do with politics and that the Sultan had the unquestionable right to bestow or revoke any title awarded to his subjects.

10th Malaysia Plan towards 2020

10 June Kuala Lumpur

The 10th Malaysia Plan would turn the country into a high-income economy by 2020 with an allocation of RM230 billion. Prime Minister Dato' Sri Najib Razak said the Government had drawn up a new approach which emphasised quality human capital, innovation and creativity.

The allocation included RM126b for the economic sector, RM69b for the social sector, RM23b for security and RM20b to promote private sector investment in infrastructure, education and healthcare.

The house in Gombak where lectures were held to recruit members for al-Qaeda and Jemaah Islamiah.

Terror plot foiled!

16 June Kuala Lumpur

Police thwarted a plot to blow up two places of worship in Penang and Selangor when they arrested a group of students, mostly from two local universities, in Gombak. The 10 key members were detained under the Internal Security Act.

The group felt Malaysia was losing its identity as an Islamic country and that the Government was not doing anything to uphold Islam here. Its leader, 45-year-old Syrian Aiman Al Dakak, came here in 2004 on a student visa to recruit members for al-Qaeda and Jemaah Islamiah. The financier, Malaysian religious teacher Azzahari Murad, 39, had received military training in Afghanistan in the 1990s and was a member of the terror group Lashkar-e-Toiba.

Harith gets hitched

12 June Kuala Lumpur

Harith Iskander Musa finally ended his bachelor days when he married Dr Jezamine Lim. The solemnisation ceremony was attended by family members. Harith and Jezamine would be throwing a wedding reception later for friends. The bride is also a model and an actress. Harith said it was love at second sight. 'When I met her the second time, I knew that I had fallen in love with her and everything just fell into place,' said Harith.

Students of St John's Institution rejoiced upon hearing that their school dated 1904 had been declared a heritage site, 21 May 2010.

2010

world news

Pudu Jail demolished

21 June Kuala Lumpur

A 394m stretch of Pudu Jail wall which once set a record for the longest mural in the world (384m), was demolished at 10.00pm for a road-widening project.

Deputy Finance Minister Datuk Dr Awang Adek Hussin said although Pudu Prison was more than 100 years old, it would not be turned into a heritage site as the government did not think it was something to be proud of. Pudu Prison, formerly known as Pudu Gaol, was built in stages in 1891 on a 10ha site and was completed in 1895. The prison was officially closed in 1996 when the new prison in Sungai Buloh was completed.

National census starts

6 July Putrajaya

The national census starts today. Some 26,000 officers, on duty until 22 August, would be armed with forms consisting of 51 questions ranging from demographics, migration, income range, gender, race, religion, level of education, employment status, deaths and fertility.

Statistics Department director-general Datuk Wan Ramlah Wan Abd Raof said there were five new questions that included whether any house owner or tenant were engaged in agriculture, where they were staying last year, mode of transport and how old they were on their first marriage.

Justice for maid

19 July Shah Alam

Judge Mohd Yazid Mustafa sent night-market trader A. Murugan to the gallows for the murder in 2009 of Indonesian maid Muntik Bani. She was starved and beaten until she was paralysed before she died.

Murugan, 36, looked calm when sentence was passed. Witnesses testified that they saw Murugan beating, kicking and slapping Muntik. One neighbour said she saw Muntik crawling on the floor of the house asking for help just before she was locked in the toilet for two days.

Police found her on 20 October 2009 and she died in hospital six days later.

KL to Ipoh in 2 hours

12 August Kuala Lumpur

The new Ipoh–Kuala Lumpur electric train service (ETS) had reduced travelling time from three hours to two, though the introductory one-way fare of RM30 (to be raised to RM45.40 after six months) might not persuade people to commute daily to work in Kuala Lumpur or Ipoh.

The ETS has six coaches and can carry 350 passengers at one time.

High aims for Greater Kuala Lumpur

15 August Kuala Lumpur

Greater KL, a new term to many, is the area administered by the 10 municipalities covering and surrounding Kuala Lumpur and is targeted to be in the top 20 list for world economic growth and most liveable metropolises by 2020. It will be a sprawling city and economic hub with more open space, improved waterfronts and a superior public transportation system, said Minister in the Prime Minister's Department Tan Sri Nor Mohamed Yakcop.

The 10 municipalities included are Kuala Lumpur, Putrajaya, Selayang, Ampang Jaya, Petaling Jaya, Subang Jaya, Shah Alam, Klang, Kajang and Sepang. At 279,327ha, Greater KL will be about four times the size of Singapore.

Prime Minister Dato' Sri Najib Razak (centre) looks at a model of the future development of Kuala Lumpur City during a public open day for the Economic Transformation Programme.

Malaysia is 37th best country

23 August Kuala Lumpur

In a survey by *Newsweek* magazine apportioning marks for quality of life, economic dynamism and education, Malaysia ranked 37th in the 'Best Countries In The World' list.

Newsweek said that overall, the top three countries in the world were Finland, Switzerland and Sweden. Other Asian countries in the list included Singapore (20th), Thailand (58th), China (59th), the Philippines (63rd), Sri Lanka (66th), Indonesia (73rd) and India (78th).

Cosmetics queen missing

6 September Kuala Lumpur

Cosmetics millionaire Datuk Sosilawati Lawiya, 47, was reported missing for a week together with three others. Her disappearance was deemed mysterious as there was no known motive nor had the family been contacted for ransom.

It was subsequently discovered that she and the three others had been murdered (*see 4 July 2011*).

Makeover for immigration centres

24 August Putrajaya

The Home Ministry admitted that none of the country's 13 immigration depots met international standards in security measures and living conditions required of restricted areas.

But its Secretary-General Dato' Seri Mahmood Adam said that a major revamp is being planned which would also look at the segregation of detainees, including separate camps for men and women and for those who flout immigration laws and hardcore criminals.

However, human rights activists said the changes should be about humanitarian concerns, and not security issues. Tenaganita director Dr Irene Fernandez said basic rights like bedding had become a privilege in detention centres.

Villagers refuse to move for dam

29 August Kuching

About 1,600 people from four villages, affected by the construction of the RM310 million Bengoh Dam, have refused to move out until the government gives them 'full compensation'.

The Bidayuhs from Kampung Taba Sait, Kampung Rejoi, Kampung Semban and Kampung Bojong were supposed to relocate to a new area in Kampung Semadang.

A 43-year-old villager said they did not want to move because they were happy there. She added that the amount offered was paltry as they would lose their houses, native land and cash crops.

Fugitive Soosai taken

31 August Chennai

Fugitive Michael Soosai, who faked his death and fled the country, was arrested in Tamil Nadu, India, after allegedly conning several people there with offers of high-paying jobs before escaping with their jewellery.

Coimbatore Police Commissioner Dr C. Sylendra Babu said Soosai, who used the name Rajasekhar, and his Indian wife, Rajeswari, were arrested in a hotel in Chennai.

Ismail is new IGP

1 September Putrajaya

Home Minister Dato' Seri Hishammuddin Hussein announced that Tan Sri Ismail Omar (picture), 57, would be appointed the new inspector-general of police when Tan Sri Musa Hassan retired. Ismail, in his third year as Musa's deputy, had been working closely with the IGP since his days in the Criminal Investigation Department more than a decade ago.

On 12 September, Musa, 58, was given a farewell parade at the Police Training Centre in Kuala Lumpur 41 years after he first joined the force.

He joined the force as an inspector in 1969. In 2004, he was appointed Criminal Investigation Department director, then Deputy Inspector General of Police in 2006 and later, as IGP.

Absentee accused freed

2 September Putrajaya

Businessman Koh Kim Teck, accused of the murder of his nephew in 2004, is now a free man because the prosecution could not serve him with a warrant of arrest. The Court of Appeal threw out the prosecution's appeal over Koh's acquittal by the High Court in 2005 and revoked the warrant of arrest issued against the businessman, who had failed to attend court since 2007.

Koh, 56, Resty Agpalo, 38, and Mohamad Najib Zulkifli, 30, were acquitted of murdering Koh's nephew, Xu Jian Huang, 14, at a bungalow in Jalan Mengkuang, Kuala Lumpur in 2004.

Youngest F1 test driver

2 September London

Malaysian Nabil Jeffri became Formula One's youngest test driver at the age of 16 on Wednesday, after being driven to the track by his proud father.

Nabil, still too young to take a driving test in Britain or drive on public roads, conducted a day of straight line aerodynamic testing for F1 newcomers Lotus on an airfield runway in Duxford, eastern England.

The Malaysian-owned team's regular race driver Heikki Kovalainen and Malaysian reserve driver Fairuz Fauzy were also present to advise the teenager. 'I have had an incredible day, one of the best days of my life,' said Nabil.

Cartoonist arrested

24 September Kuala Lumpur

Police arrested *Malaysiakini* cartoonist Zulkiflee Anwar Ulhaque, popularly known as Zunar, under the Sedition Act. They raided his office in Kuala Lumpur and seized copies of his new book *Cartoon-o-phobia* that was supposed to be launched later in the day. The cartoonist had previously used cartoons to highlight contentious issues such as police shootings.

Lizard King nabbed

6 September Kuala Lumpur

Reptile smuggler Anson Wong Keng Liang, 52, (picture) was sentenced to six months' jail and fined RM190,000 for illegally exporting 95 boa constrictors in a suitcase at the Kuala Lumpur International Airport on 26 August. He was on his way to Jakarta. He pleaded guilty.

Wong was notorious in the 1980s for smuggling wildlife. He was arrested in 1998 in the United States and sentenced to six years in a federal prison there for his smuggling activities.

Action against online abuse

5 September Kuala Lumpur

The Malaysian Communications and Multimedia Commission (MCMC) has identified 13 Internet crimes which the Attorney-General's Chambers can prosecute. These cover offences such as abuse of religion, pornography, phishing and sedition.

Information Minister Dato' Seri Dr Rais Yatim said the MCMC had worked hard in the past 1½ years investigating websites and social networking pages containing offensive articles. He said MCMC need not wait for the public to lodge reports or complaints for it to start acting.

Business potential in BIMP-EAGA

28 September Sarawak

Member countries of the Brunei, Indonesia, Malaysia and Philippines–East ASEAN Growth Area (BIMP–EAGA) must take full advantage of the area's strategic location at the centre of the booming China–India region, said Sarawak Chief Minister Tan Sri Abdul Taib Mahmud. The Chief Minister was speaking at the official opening of the BIMP–EAGA Expo 2010 at the Borneo Convention Centre Kuching.

Marina lodges report against imposter

15 October Kuala Lumpur

Datin Paduka Marina Mahathir lodged a police report today against a woman whom she claimed had been impersonating her and using her name for the past 10 years. She said that in late 1999 or 2000, the woman turned up uninvited at the official opening of the Malaysian AIDS Council office in Sentul and told the staff there that she was related to her.

In another incident, she received a call in 2003 from the then mayor of KL who told her that someone claiming to be her called and asked him not to demolish a stall with a temporary operating licence. He named the person who operated the stall. Datin Paduka Marina lodged her report against that person.

Malaysia a thought leader

2 November Putrajaya

US Secretary of State Hillary Clinton (left) shakes hands with Malaysian Foreign Minister Anifah Aman in Putrajaya.

Washington hailed Malaysia's promotion of religious moderation and pledged its endorsement of Prime Minister Dato' Sri Najib Razak's call for a Global Movement Of Moderates (GMM) at the United Nations general assembly in September. GMM aimed to rally Muslim leaders and intellectuals to state their stand against extremism.

Secretary of State Hillary Rodham Clinton, who was in Malaysia on a three-day visit, said the United States stood behind Malaysia in its stand that moderates should not lose out to extremism as it was not the path to building sustainability and stability, as well as peace and democracy. Clinton said the recognition of Malaysia as a global 'thought leader' and a 'model nation to the world' made the US enthusiastic about building on its ties with the country.

Sex education from Year 1

13 November Kuala Lumpur

Sex education would be part of the primary school curriculum from Year One next year. Deputy Education Minister Datuk Dr Wee Ka Siong said it would be part of Physical and Health Education lessons and would focus on family values and not merely on sex.

He said sex education was first introduced four years ago in secondary schools as part of co-curricular activities in a module called 'I'm In Control'. The module would continue to be used, with focus on high-risk groups, HIV and other social issues. Pupils would learn about the reproductive system, sexually transmitted diseases, precautions and learning to say no.

1 October: The people of Sabah voted the rare Sumazau slipper orchid as the State's official orchid. The *Paphiopedilum rothschildianum* is unique to Sabah's rainforests.

The world's smallest frog, *Microhyla nepenthicola*, was discovered in the jungles of Sarawak. It measured between 1cm and 1.28cm.

2010

4 November
In India, Irom Sharmila, 38, dubbed 'the Iron Lady,' marks 10 years of a hunger strike started to protest an anti-terror law that granted soldiers sweeping powers to act against rebels. She had her last meal on 4 November 2000, was arrested three days later and force-fed through her nose ever since.

7 November
Myanmar holds its first election in 20 years. The military-backed party wins by a landslide.

13 November
Myanmar's military government frees Aung San Suu Kyi after her latest term of detention expired.

15 November
In Indonesia, nine wardens are charged with accepting US$40,000 from former tax official Gayus Tambunan and letting him out of jail at least 60 times since his incarceration in April.

23 November
North and South Korea trade artillery fire after North Korea shelled an island, killing two marines and two civilians.

National talent blueprint

2 December Kuala Lumpur

Talent Corporation will develop a national talent blueprint and an expert workforce database to reach out and woo 700,000 Malaysians working overseas to return home.

In his 1Malaysia blog at www.1malaysia.com, Prime Minister Dato' Sri Najib Razak said a different approach would be to create more business opportunities and offer remunerations in line with global wages.

Meanwhile, the Higher Education Ministry was also working to retain foreign students to work in Malaysia after completing their studies here.

Dato' Sri Najib had announced the establishment of Talent Corporation when tabling the 10th Malaysia Plan in Parliament in June. It was set up under the Prime Minister's Department to identify shortages in key sectors and attract and retain skilled human capital.

Nod for ETP projects

30 December Kuala Lumpur

Prime Minister Dato' Sri Najib Razak unveiled a second batch of nine development and entry-point projects under the Economic Transformation Programme, involving investments of over RM8.2 billion. Three promoted growth in the oil, gas and energy industries, two bolstered electronic and electrical services, three focused on tourism and one on education.

In November, Najib had said that nine projects worth over RM30 billion were approved which would create 13,000 new jobs. These included the construction of five wafer fabrication plants in Kulim Hi-Tech Park, Kedah by German firm LFoundry and a RM1 billion commitment from retailer Mydin to build 14 new branches.

Samy Vellu quits

6 December Kuala Lumpur

MIC leaders yesterday bade an emotional farewell to the man who had been their rambunctious leader for the past 31 years.

Dato' Seri S. Samy Vellu, 74, passed the baton to Deputy Plantation Industries and Commodities Minister Datuk G. Palanivel. Dato' Seri Samy Vellu said he would like to be remembered for changing the mindset of the community with regard to the importance of and need for an education.

27 die in bus crash

20 December Ipoh

An express bus overturned and crashed into a rocky slope along the Simpang Pulai–Kampung Raja road, killing three Malaysians and 24 Thais, and seriously injuring 10.

This was the country's worst road accident. The roof of the bus was partially torn from its body with the upper deck floor pressing down on passengers in the lower deck. A rescue team of 100 personnel took three hours to retrieve the dead and injured.

Sime Darby probe

23 December Kuala Lumpur

Sime Darby Berhad filed a suit today against former group CEO Dato' Seri Ahmad Zubir Murshid and four senior executives over their alleged roles in the RM1.7 billion losses suffered by its energy and utilities division in 2010. It claimed at least RM338 million and damages for losses caused by them in three projects—the Bulhanine and Maydan Mahzam project, the Maersk Oil Qatar project and the building of marine vessels for the Maersk Oil Qatar project.

The next day, it filed a second suit seeking RM92.2 million in relation to the Bakun Dam project.

Harimau Malaya triumphs

29 December Kuala Lumpur

The national football team won the AFF Suzuki Cup in Jakarta and Prime Minister Dato' Sri Najib Razak declared 30 December a public holiday. 'Well done, Malaysian Tigers!' he said in his Twitter account after the second leg of the final.

Malaysia went down to Indonesia 1–2 in that nail-biting match but walked away winners on a 4–2 aggregate after winning the first leg 3–0 at the Bukit Jalil National Stadium on Sunday.

The country came to a standstill as Malaysians were glued to their television sets and at Dataran Merdeka, a giant screen telecast the match live.

Malaysia's captain Safiq Rahim lifts the AFF Suzuki Cup trophy in Jakarta.

Obituaries

1 Jan	**Tan Sri Mohamed Rahmat**, 71, former Information Minister.
2 Jan	**Dato' Seri S. Augustine Paul**, 66, judge who shot to prominence after presiding over Dato' Seri Anwar Ibrahim's corruption case in 1998.
9 Jan	**Tun Fatimah Hashim**, 85, first woman minister.
22 Jan	**Sultan Iskandar ibni Al-marhum Sultan Ismail**, 77, Sultan of Johor.
24 Jan	**Tun Mohd Ghazali Shafie**, 88, former Home Minister, Information Minister and Foreign Minister.
23 March	**Tan Sri Dr Sulaiman Daud**, 77, former Education Minister, Culture, Youth and Sports Minister, Land and Regional Development Minister, Minister in the Prime Minister's Department, Domestic Trade and Consumer Affairs Minister, and Agriculture Minister.
2 April	**Mior Ahmad Fuad Mior Badri (Din Beramboi)**, 43, comedian and radio presenter.
6 April	**Nurfaradhini Zakaria**, 27, Sea Games cycling silver medallist.
13 May	**Ashaari Muhammad**, 73, founder of the Al Arqam movement.
2 July	**Toh Puan Norashikin Mohd Seth**, 80, widow of former Deputy Prime Minister, Tun Dr Ismail Abdul Rahman.
28 Aug	**Isa Bakar**, 58, former international football striker.
15 Oct	**Yalal Abu Chin (Yalal Chin)**, 67, actor.
28 Nov	**Tun Dr Lim Chong Eu**, 91, former Penang Chief Minister.
23 Dec	**Gen. (R) Tun Ibrahim Ismail**, 88, former armed forces chief.

2011

International events had a direct impact this year: Malaysian commandos rescued the crew of a ship hijacked by pirates in the Gulf of Aden, thousands of Malaysians were evacuated from Egypt as a result of the revolution there and Mara student Mohd Asyraf Haziq was injured and robbed in the London riots. In June the art-deco Tanjong Pagar railway station in Singapore was vacated by Keretapi Tanah Melayu (KTM) following an agreement made by the Malaysian and Singapore governments in 2010. Passengers would subsequently have to board KTM trains at the much blander-looking Woodlands Checkpoint. The following month, business in Kuala Lumpur came to a standstill for a day due to the Bersih 2.0 demonstration.

JANUARY
In Shah Alam, a coroner records an open verdict for the death of political aide Teoh Beng Hock.

MAY
Landslide in Hulu Langat kills 16 and injures nine in the grounds of an orphanage.

NOVEMBER
A passenger train crashes into an oil tanker at a level crossing near Kota Kinabalu International Airport, injuring nine.

DECEMBER
The 14th Yang di-Pertuan Agong, Tuanku Abdul Halim Mu'adzam Shah, takes the oath of office.

July: Anti-riot police stand forming a cordon in front of the Petronas Twin Towers during the Bersih 2.0 rally calling for electoral reform.

'Today, I apologise to the Prime Minister ... he has done something meaningful and big in repealing the ISA.'

Former Law Minister Datuk Zaid Ibrahim on the repeal of the Internal Security Act, 16 September 2011.

2011

world news

Teoh Beng Hock: Coroner returns open verdict

5 January Shah Alam

The coroner investigating the death of political aide Teoh Beng Hock returned an open verdict, ruling out suicide but saying there was insufficient evidence to prove homicide.

Teoh, 30, was found dead on 16 July 2009 on the fifth floor corridor of Plaza Masalam just hours after he was questioned by the Malaysian Anti-Corruption Commission (MACC) over the alleged misappropriation of Selangor Government funds. The MACC occupied the 14th and 15th floors of the building.

On 22 July 2011, a Royal Commission of Inquiry (RCI) set up to investigate the circumstances leading to Teoh's death found that he was driven to suicide. The panel, led by Federal Court judge Tan Sri James Foong Cheng Yuen, said continuous and aggressive sessions by three MACC officers had driven Teoh to end his life.

On 20 June 2012, the Attorney-General's Chambers cleared the MACC trio implicated by the RCI in causing the death of Teoh. On 7 February 2013, Teoh's family filed a civil suit against the MACC and the Government.

Sarawak CM weds

16 January Kuching

The glittering wedding reception of Sarawak Chief Minister Tan Sri Abdul Taib Mahmud and his Syrian wife, 29-year-old Puan Sri Ragad Waleed Alkurdi was held at the new State legislative assembly complex. The couple had married in Petra Jaya on 18 December 2010.

Next, the Olympics

13 January Putrajaya

The Malaysian Tigers had created history by winning the AFF Suzuki Cup for the first time in the tournament's 14-year history. Dato' Sri Najib Tun Razak wanted the national football team to use their win as a stepping stone to the 2012 London Olympics. To ensure a greater chance of success, the Prime Minister announced that the government would sponsor players who wanted to train with top clubs worldwide. He also said that the Youth and Sports Ministry would allocate RM500,000 to the Football Association of Malaysia (FAM) to upgrade facilities at Wisma FAM in Kelana Jaya.

Middle-income Felda

19 January Labis

The Felda community has become part of the country's middle-income group, 54 years after the first scheme began at Lurah Bilut in Pahang. The Prime Minister said this was based on their average income of RM3,000 per month.

Coin craze!

18 January Rembau

Road users risked life and limb as they rushed to collect coins strewn all over the highway after a four-wheel-drive vehicle, which was transporting RM70,000, overturned near Rembau.

The incident occurred at Km244 of the North–South Expressway. The money, all in coins, was stored in a large metal container in the vehicle.

Zairulhisham Mansor, 28, lost control of the vehicle when he was suddenly hit from behind. The four-wheel-drive vehicle overturned on the road shoulder. The driver and his friend escaped with minor injuries but the accident caused the coins to be strewn all over the road. The coins were being distributed by a company in Shah Alam to several shopping outlets in Malacca.

Malaysians evacuated in midst of Egypt protests

7 February Kuala Lumpur

More than 10,000 Malaysians had been evacuated following the heightened turmoil in Egypt. They were being evacuated by air, land and sea in stages. The rest had either left the country or opted to stay on.

There were 11,700 students registered with the Malaysian embassy in Cairo. Those who returned home on commercial flights told stories of living in fear and staying out of the way of protesters.

IJN scores a first

12 February Kuala Lumpur

The National Heart Institute (IJN) became the first centre in Southeast Asia to successfully implant a new stent device, the Bioresorbable Vascular Scaffold (BVS), in a 62-year-old man. A cardiology team led by IJN managing director and chief executive officer Tan Sri Dr Robaayah Zambahari and consultant cardiologist Datuk Dr K. Balachandran performed the operation.

High-seas rescue

22 January Kuala Lumpur

Malaysian commandos rescued 23 Filipino crew members of an oil tanker which was hijacked by Somali pirates in the Gulf of Aden. Seven pirates were detained after a fierce gunfight on board the hijacked tanker, MT *Bunga Laurel*. Three pirates were injured while there were no casualties among the Malaysian commandos or tanker crew.

The *Bunga Laurel*, hired by the Malaysian International Shipping Corporation, was on its way from the Gulf to Singapore when it was attacked by pirates armed with AK-47 assault rifles, light machine guns and pistols.

Court strikes out former Ruler's petition

11 February Putrajaya

The Federal Court struck out a final legal challenge to contest the proclamation of Sultan Muhammad V (Tengku Muhammad Faris Petra) as ruler of Kelantan by his father. Sultan Muhammad was proclaimed ruler on 13 September 2010 following his tenure as regent after Tuanku Ismail Petra Sultan Yahya Petra was incapacitated from May 2009.

Tuanku Ismail had earlier filed two petitions challenging Sultan Muhammad in his capacity as regent on grounds that he had acted beyond the powers as stated in the State constitution.

On 26 November 2010, the Federal Court dismissed the petitions and gave its opinion that a regent once appointed enjoyed and assumed the powers of a sultan.

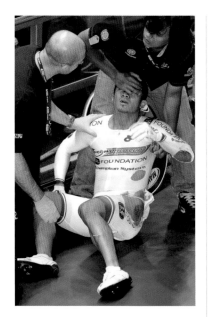

Courageous cyclist

21 February Manchester, UK

National cyclist Azizul Hasni Awang courageously jumped back onto his bicycle following a four-rider crash to cross the finish line at the Track Cycling World Cup here. He won the bronze medal in the keirin event but was unable to make the podium. Instead, after the race, he was rushed to hospital where medics removed a 20cm wooden splinter from his calf.

First female Armed Forces Brigadier-General

17 February Kuala Lumpur

Colonel Norhuda Ahmad created history when she was promoted as the first woman brigadier-general in the Malaysian armed forces (general duty).

Norhuda, 54, who was previously the head of the Asean Branch, Integrated Intelligence Centre (IIC), Strategic Directorate, Defence Intelligence Staff Division, was promoted as head of the Directorate's Training Division.

She was among 27 senior officers from the army to be promoted to various ranks, including from Major to Lt-Colonel and from Brigadier-General to Major-General.

Two women in the Royal Medical Corps had been promoted to Brigadier-Generals previously, namely Brig-Gen Datuk Dr Roshidah Ishak and Brig-Gen Dr T. Thavachelvi Thangaraja.

Team Lotus can keep its name

28 February London

Britain's High Court ruled that Team Lotus can continue to race under that name.

Group Lotus, owned by car company Proton, had lodged the court case in an attempt to prevent Team Lotus owner Tony Fernandes from using the Team Lotus name in Formula 1 (F1). Fernandes had initially entered F1 in 2010 using the name Lotus Racing, under licence from Group Lotus. But the two parties fell out. Lotus Cars agreed to a sponsorship deal with the Renault team for 2011 and terminated its licensing agreement with Fernandes. The latter bought the rights to the Team Lotus name from businessman David Hunt—brother of 1976 F1 world champion James Hunt—in 2010.

In 2012, Team Lotus became known as Caterham F1 Team and Lotus Renault was rebranded as Lotus.

Taib sworn in as CM

17 April Kuching

Barisan Nasional (BN) retained its two-thirds majority in the 71-seat Sarawak State Assembly. Parti Pesaka Bumiputera Bersatu (PBB), a Malay–Melanau–Dayak component party of BN headed by Chief Minister Tan Sri Abdul Taib Mahmud, won all 35 seats it contested. The Sarawak United Peoples' Party (SUPP), the second largest BN component, did well in mixed constituencies. It won six out of 19 seats, losing to DAP in all Chinese-majority seats except in Bawang Assan.

Kemala is 11th National Laureate

4 May Putrajaya

Datuk Dr Kemala Abdullah, 70, or Kemala, was announced as the 11th National Laureate. Deputy Prime Minister Tan Sri Muhyiddin Yassin said the title was awarded to Kemala for his contributions to literature and creative thinking. Kemala, a visiting scholar at University Putra Malaysia, was picked by a panel of judges ahead of 13 nominees. He won RM60,000 and publication of 50,000 copies of his works.

Kemala, who was born in Gombak, Selangor, began writing in primary school and has authored 11 books on poetry, 25 anthologies of poems, 10 books on literary research, four short stories, eight anthologies of short stories, four plays, three children's story books and more than 50 essays and literary critiques.

Inspiring Malaysians

3 March Kuala Lumpur

Two Malaysian women made it into a New York-based advocacy group's list of 100 most inspiring people around the world in advocating the rights of women and girls.

Zainah Anwar, who founded Sisters In Islam (SIS) and is project director of Musawah (an international group for equality and justice in the Muslim family), and blogger, women's rights and HIV/AIDS awareness activist Datin Paduka Marina Mahathir were named in the list by Women Deliver.

Zainah and Marina joined the ranks of other personalities, including former United States First Lady Laura Bush, ABC news anchor and television personality Christiane Amanpour, US Secretary of State Hillary Clinton and talk show host Oprah Winfrey.

Freeze on medical courses

6 May Kuala Lumpur

A freeze of five years on new medical courses was imposed on institutions of higher learning in the country.

Higher Education Minister Dato' Seri Mohamed Khaled Nordin said the freeze, effective 1 May 2013, would end on 30 April 2016.

The Cabinet decided on the moratorium based on the increase in the number of medical graduates and the competency of housemen, teaching staff and teaching hospitals.

Landslide horror

22 May Kajang

A devastating landslide in Kampung Gahal, Hulu Langat, Selangor claimed 16 lives with nine people injured. Three adults, said to be a warden and religious authorities, were among the dead. The rest were children between the ages of 8 and 14.

All the victims were in a tent on the grounds of an orphanage, rehearsing a *nasyid* performance for a function. The orphanage grounds also included a motivational camp and a resort. Survivors claimed there was a sudden gust of wind and a thunderous sound before tonnes of earth and huge boulders came crashing down at 1.30pm from a hill behind the buildings. Almost 300 workers from the Fire and Rescue department, Police, Civil Defence department and the Malaysia Disaster Assistance and Rescue team dug through the rubble looking for missing children.

The dead were sent to Kajang Hospital for a post-mortem while the injured were being treated at Ampang Hospital.

There were 44 children between the ages of seven and 18 as well as five caretakers staying at the orphanage when the killer landslide struck.

Serve husbands like first-class prostitutes

5 June Kuala Lumpur

Obedient Wives Club (OWC) international vice-president Dr Rohaya Mohamed.

The newly formed Obedient Wives Club is calling for wives to obey and serve their husbands like 'first-class prostitutes' to keep them from straying and to prevent greater social ills. The Malaysian branch of the club was formed as an answer to social problems such as infidelity, prostitution, domestic violence and abandoned babies. The club is open to women of all faiths and races. and offers counselling sessions and sex advice.

Women's groups have charged the club for perpetuating a culture of women-blaming and male chauvinism and encouraging husbands to treat wives as sex slaves.

The OWC, formed by Global Ikhwan Sdn Bhd, an offshoot of the defunct Islamic religious movement Al-Arqam, has 1,000 members worldwide with 800 in Malaysia.

2011

11 April
In France a law goes into effect banning women from wearing full-face veils in public places.

11 April
An Indonesian MP, who is also a strong advocate of anti-pornography laws, is caught watching blue movies on his computer in Parliament. He resigns.

2 May
Osama Bin Laden is killed in Abbotabad, Pakistan by US troops. Osama's body is buried at sea in an undisclosed location.

14 May
Dominique Strauss-Kahn, head of the International Monetary Fund and a possible candidate for president of France, is arrested in the US for an alleged sexual assault on a hotel maid.

22 July
Norwegian Anders Behring Breivik guns down 69 people, mainly teenagers, on an island. Earlier, motivated by his anti-Muslim, anti-immigrant beliefs, he set off a bomb in Oslo killing eight and seriously damaging several buildings.

Farewell, Tanjong Pagar

30 June Singapore

Thousands thronged Keretapi Tanah Melayu (KTM) Bhd's Tanjong Pagar station to bid farewell and to have a final view of the station that had served both Malaysia and Singapore for 79 years. The last Kuala Lumpur–Singapore train, Ekspres Sinaran, which left KL Sentral at 9.00am, reached Tanjong Pagar at 6.00pm. The last north-bound passenger train, Ekspres Senandung Sutera, departed Tanjong Pagar at 10.00pm with the Sultan of Johor, Sultan Ibrahim Sultan Iskandar in the driver's seat.

The train service to Tanjong Pagar in Keppel Road, Singapore, was introduced in 1932 as a trade link between vegetable and agricultural producers on the mainland and Singapore. The handing over of the Tanjong Pagar station follows an agreement made between Singapore and Malaysia in 2010 which includes Singapore taking possession of KTM land.

The Singaporean government promised to conserve the station building after taking possession of it.

Trial of the year begins

4 July Shah Alam

A former lawyer and his three workers were to stand trial in a case that has gripped the nation. N. Pathmanabhan, 41, T. Thilaiyalagan, 19, R. Matan, 20 and R. Kathavarayan, 30, are accused of the murders of cosmetics queen Sosilawati Lawiya, her driver Kamaruddin Shansuddin, CIMB bank officer Noorhisham Mohamad and lawyer Ahmad Kamil Abdul Karim in Banting on 30 August 2010.

Sosilawati and the three other victims had been reported missing after going to meet Pathmanabhan over a land deal. Police said they were murdered and burnt, and their ashes thrown into a river near a farm owned by Pathmanabhan (*see 23 May 2013*).

Pope Benedict XVI and Prime Minister Dato' Sri Najib Razak exchanging presents during the private audience.

KL–Vatican ties

19 July Rome

Malaysia and the Vatican have agreed to establish formal diplomatic ties to promote bonds of mutual friendship and strengthen co-operation.

The announcement followed Prime Minister Dato' Sri Najib Razak's audience with Pope Benedict XVI at the papal summer residence outside Rome. It was the second meeting between a Malaysian prime minister and the Pope, after Tun Dr Mahathir 's audience in June 2002.

Trouble at Bersih 2.0 demo

9 July Kuala Lumpur

The Bersih 2.0 demonstration was held in the city, organised by the Coalition for Clean and Fair Elections (Bersih) and supported by the Pakatan Rakyat. Protesters, many of them dressed in yellow, clashed with anti-riot police leading to the arrest of 1,667 people while scores of others were reported injured. One protester died.

Police used water cannon and tear gas to disperse demonstrators who police said numbered 'about 5,000 to 6,000'. However, the organisers claimed that some 50,000 took part in the event.

Those arrested included Pas president Dato' Seri Hadi Awang, opposition Members of Parliament Azmin Ali, R. Sivarasa, Tian Chua and Bersih 2.0 steering committee chairman Datuk S. Ambiga.

Protesters rallying near the Puduraya bus station in central Kuala Lumpur.

KL–Canberra refugee swap plan in limbo

9 August Kuala Lumpur

Australia's highest court ruled that a refugee swap deal with Malaysia was unlawful. It said Malaysia, which was not a signatory to the UN Convention Relating to the Status of Refugees, offered inadequate legal protection for asylum seekers. Malaysia had agreed to take 800 boat people who had arrived in Australia illegally. In return, Australia would resettle 4,000 registered refugees currently living in Malaysia.

Thousands of asylum seekers from Sri Lanka, Afghanistan and Iraq flock to Australia each year, leading to overcrowded immigration centres and prompting violent unrest at the remote units.

In October, however, Prime Minister Julia Gillard announced she was abandoning her government's controversial plan and that the refugees would be processed on Australian soil.

'Mai Pulai' begins for gallant fighters

27 July Sarawak

Traditional rites were performed at the graves of 21 Iban trackers and Sarawak Rangers at six different locations in the country and in Singapore over five days. The remains of these servicemen who died in action fighting the communists were exhumed and placed in urns for an official reburial ceremony codenamed 'Ops Mai Pulai' (Iban for 'bringing home').

Church raid 'legitimate'

6 August Shah Alam

The Sultan of Selangor ruled that the State religious authority's raid on Damansara Utama Methodist Church (DUMC) on 3 August was legitimate.

But Sultan Sharafuddin Idris Shah said that although the Selangor Islamic Religious Department (Jais) had found evidence of attempts to subvert Muslims, it was 'insufficient' for further legal action and therefore, no one would be prosecuted.

Jais disrupted a charity dinner at DUMC after acting on a complaint that participants at the dinner were trying to convert the 12 Muslims present to Christianity. The organiser of the dinner, NGO Harapan Komuniti, which helps AIDS patients and impoverished single mothers, denied it was proselytising.

Air Asia–MAS deal

10 August Kuala Lumpur

Government investment arm Khazanah Nasional Bhd and the founders of AirAsia Bhd inked a deal that will see Malaysia Airlines exit the low-cost segment as well as greater collaboration in aircraft purchasing, engineering and training between the two airlines. MAS's low-cost arm, Firefly, will become a regional premium full-service carrier.

Mara student hurt in London riots

10 August London

A Mara-sponsored student suffered a broken jaw after he was attacked while making his way home from college in east London. Mohd Asyraf Haziq, 20, an accountancy student at Kaplan Financial College, was also robbed.

The attack, which was filmed and appeared on YouTube and Sky News, showed Asyraf first being helped and then robbed of his wallet and mobile phone.

Green efforts start at 24°C

10 August Putrajaya

A directive was sent to all Government agencies that air-conditioners in all Government buildings be set at no lower than 24°C. Energy, Green Technology and Water Minister Dato' Seri Peter Chin Fah Kui explained that by increasing the temperature from 16°C to 24°C, energy consumption in these buildings would be reduced by 32 to 56 per cent.

RM2b biotech venture

13 August Putrajaya

The world's first bio-methionine plant and its related facilities will be built in Malaysia for RM2 billion, marking the country's largest industrial biotechnology investment so far.

Prime Minister Dato' Sri Najib Tun Razak said the plant, which will produce chemicals used in animal feed, was set to generate RM20 billion sales by 2020.

Fernandes buys QPR

19 August Kuala Lumpur

AirAsia owner Tony Fernandes is the new majority owner of Queens Park Rangers, having bought Bernie Ecclestone's 66 per cent stake in the club for around £35m.

No more ISA

16 September Kuala Lumpur

Prime Minister Dato' Sri Najib Razak announced the Government would repeal the Internal Security and Banishment Acts. He also added that he would amend the Printing Presses and Publications Act so that publishers would no longer need to renew their licences annually. The Government would also review Section 27 of the Police Act 1967, which dealt with freedom of assembly, which was guaranteed by Article 10 of the Federal Constitution. He also added that no individuals would be detained solely for their political ideologies.

To prevent subversive acts, planned acts of violence and terrorism, Dato' Sri Najib said two new laws would be drafted to preserve public peace and order. The new laws would have shorter detention periods by the police and further detentions could only be done by a court order.

On 6 October, Dato' Sri Najib announced all 125 people detained under the Restricted Residence Act would be freed immediately. He described the move as a 'reasonable decision because the Act was outdated and no longer relevant.' The Restricted Residence Act was mainly used against individuals involved in gambling and illegal numbers forecasting.

Nicol is world champ again

6 November Kuala Lumpur

Nicol David won the World Open crown for a record-breaking sixth time when she outclassed England's Jenny Duncalf 11–2, 11–5, 11–0 in the women's final in Rotterdam, the Netherlands. This makes the 28-year-old the most successful woman player in the history of the game. She had earlier shared the honour, five titles apiece, with her mentor Sarah Fitz-Gerald of Australia.

Gold for men's 4x400m

14 November Palembang

The men's 4x400m relay quartet ran the race of their lives to win a gold for Malaysia at the Sea Games in Palembang, Indonesia. S. Kannathasan, P. Yuvaraaj, Schzuan Ahmad Rosely and Muhammad Yunus Lasaleh stunned favourites Thailand to secure the gold in 3:10.47.

Elton John rocks Genting

23 November Genting Highlands

Rock singer, songwriter, composer and pianist Sir Elton John thrilled legions of fans here last night.

In a mesmerising three-hour concert held at the Arena of Stars, Resorts World Genting, the flamboyant singer belted out some of his best-known numbers which made him a household name in a career spanning four decades.

The singer performed 25 songs, including all-time favourites like 'Candle in the Wind', 'Rocketman', 'Sacrifice', 'Circle of Life' and 'Crocodile Rock'.

NFC fights back

18 November Gemas

National Feedlot Corporation (NFC) countered allegations levelled at the nation's biggest cattle farming company. NFC executive chairman Dato' Seri Dr Mohamad Salleh Ismail revealed that the company bought two condominiums for RM6.9 million each in Bangsar, a move he considered as a 'good business decision' as it gave better investment returns than keeping NFC funds in fixed deposits.

Dato' Seri Salleh said the company had secured the project in a selective tender.

Electric proton car

15 September Putrajaya

Proton Holdings Bhd's global compact electric and hybrid car, Emas, could enter the market in two or three years, said its chairman Dato' Seri Mohd Nadzmi Mohd Salleh. The electric vehicle, designed by Italdesign Giugiaro and developed by Proton, was first unveiled at the Geneva International Motor Show in 2010.

Emas, short for Eco Mobility Advance Solution, is a plug-in electric vehicle or hybrid Range Extender Electric Vehicle and includes a turbo-charged engine of 1.2-litre capacity or lower. Proton is currently fleet-testing the Exora REEV and Saga EV to assess their potential. Dato' Seri Nadzmi said 250 electric-powered cars would be handed to the Government in phases for fleet-testing by year-end.

Train–tanker mishap

1 November Kota Kinabalu

Nine people, including a pregnant woman, were injured when a Sabah Railway passenger train crashed into an oil tanker at a level crossing near the Kota Kinabalu International Airport yesterday.

The 5.30pm collision at Jalan Kota Kinabalu–Petagas caused a loud explosion and a huge ball of fire which damaged the first carriage of the train. The three-carriage train, carrying 200 passengers, was transporting fuel to a petrol station located across the railway track.

2011

world news

24 August
Steve Jobs resigns as chief executive of Apple Inc. He dies on 5 October.

26 August
Japan's nuclear agency says the amount of radioactive caesium that escaped from the tsunami-damaged Fukushima nuclear plant was equal to 168 times that released when the atomic bomb was dropped on Hiroshima in 1945.

20 October
Libya's National Transition Council says its men found Moammar Gadhafi in a convoy that had been attacked by NATO planes, and killed him with a shot to the head.

4 November
In Moscow, a team of international researchers complete 520 days in a windowless module as a simulation of a flight to Mars.

13 December
The Palestinian flag is raised for the first time at UN agency UNESCO's headquarters in Paris, in a diplomatic victory despite resistance from the US and Israel.

Doctors leaving Government service

22 November Kuala Lumpur

A total of 1,441 Government doctors have quit the service between 2008 and August this year. Among the reasons they cited were continuing their studies, serving as lecturers at public or private institutions of higher learning, or because of personal problems.

Statistics showed that 452 doctors left in 2008, 338 in 2009, 386 last year and 265 in the first eight months of the year.

Unsung heroes honoured

22 November Kota Kinabalu

Scaling up and down the summit trail of Mount Kinabalu to transport essential goods is not an easy task. Since there are no roads, the supplies for the Laban Rata Resthouse at 3,270 metres high are carried by porters.

They transport up to 30kg of supplies such as food items, equipment and cooking gas cylinders on their backs. Many of these porters are Kadazan Dusun from Ranau and Kundasang, about 90km from here. In recognition of their dedication, Sabah Tourism, Culture and Environment Minister Datuk Masidi Manjun presented the Minister's Special Award to the porters of Mount Kinabalu at the Sabah Tourism Awards 2011.

'Taxis for Women' launched

27 November Kuala Lumpur

Public transport became safer for women with the launch of 'Taxis for Women' by the Women, Family and Community Development Ministry.

Daulat Tuanku!

14 December Kuala Lumpur

Tuanku Abdul Halim Mu'adzam Shah took the oath of office as the 14th Yang di-Pertuan Agong in a ceremony steeped in royal tradition at the new Istana Negara.

At 84, the oldest monarch in Malaysia is the first head of state to become king twice. He began his first five-year tenure aged 43 in 1970. Tuanku Abdul Halim replaces the Sultan of Terengganu Sultan Mizan Zainal who ended his term as the 13th Yang di-Pertuan Agong yesterday. Tuanku Mizan and his consort Tuanku Nur Zahirah were given a grand send-off before leaving for Terengganu.

The five-year rotation system for the post of Yang di-Pertuan Agong among the nine Malay hereditary rulers began after the country's independence on 31 August 1957.

Business set up in a day with MyCoID

2 December Kuala Lumpur

The Malaysian Corporate Identity (MyCoID) system would boost Malaysia's competitiveness at the global level, said Prime Minister Dato' Sri Najib Razak.

With the implementation of the second phase of MyCoID, those who want to set up businesses could now complete the process within a day instead of 11 days previously. The MyCoID system would also reduce the number of processes from nine to one. This would improve Malaysia's ranking with the World Bank's 'Doing Business' category from the current 23rd spot from 183 countries to 17th by next year.

1 Malaysia TV reaches out to youths

19 December Kuala Lumpur

Politicians who do not use technology to engage with the young will soon become redundant, said Prime Minister Dato' Sri Najib Razak. He said this was because youths relied on alternative media and social networks to get real-time information.

'If we don't engage with them, they get their real-time news somewhere else and it's not necessarily correct,' he added.

The Prime Minister was speaking at the launch of the first Internet protocol television—1MalaysiaTV—which provides information, movies, news and music for free and is run by 1Media IPTV.

Former Selangor MB found guilty

24 December Shah Alam

Former Selangor Menteri Besar Dr Mohamad Khir Toyo was sentenced to 12 months' jail on a corruption charge. He had purchased two pieces of land and a bungalow at a much lower price than its original value from Ditamas Sdn Bhd director Shamsuddin Hayroni in 2007. High Court judge Datuk Wira Mohtarudin Baki ordered his land and bungalow forfeited. However, the judge later granted Khir a stay pending appeal after his lawyer M. Athimulan made the request. The properties involved were purchased at RM3.5 million although Ditamas had bought them for RM6.5 million.

'Konserto Terakhir' replaces 'Interlok'

22 December Kuala Lumpur

The controversy surrounding *Interlok*, the literature textbook for secondary schools, has been resolved. Education Director-General Dato' Seri Abdul Ghafar Mahmud, said another of Datuk Abdullah Hussain's novel's, *Konserto Terakhir*, will replace *Interlok*.

The move to adopt Abdullah's book *Interlok*, written in 1971, as a literature text for Form Five students early in the year had sparked a heated debate over its suitability.

Malaysian crowned Miss Tourism International

31 December Petaling Jaya

Malaysia's Aileen Gabriella Robinson (centre) defeated 53 competitors to win the Miss Tourism International 2011 crown. The 22-year-old dance instructor of Chinese, Indian and English heritage did the country proud by being the first Malaysian to win in the pageant's 15-year history.

Obituaries

18 July **Datuk Amar James Wong Kim Min**, 89, Sarawak's longest-serving State assemblyman, first Deputy Chief Minister and first President of the Sarawak National Party (Snap).

11 Aug **Datuk Syed Ahmad Syed Jamal**, 82, National Art Laureate 1995.

11 Aug **Lorrain Esme Osman**, 81, businessman and lawyer involved in the BMF scandal in the 1980s.

2012

At the London Olympic Games, Datuk Lee Chong Wei won a silver medal in badminton and Pandelela Rinong Pamg a bronze medal in the 10m individual platform diving event, becoming Malaysia's first woman medallist and first-ever medallist in a sport other than badminton. Dato' Seri Anwar Ibrahim was cleared of a sodomy charge and Dato' Seri Shahrizat Abdul Jalil absolved of involvement in the award of a RM250m loan to the National Feedlot Corporation (NFC). The Bersih 3.0 demonstration held in Kuala Lumpur in April resulted in police taking action to disperse the crowd. In October gold investment firm Genneva Malaysia Sdn Bhd was raided by the authorities, leading to a suit being brought against the company by investors.

JANUARY
Datuk Seri Anwar Ibrahim is acquitted of a sodomy charge. Three explosive devices detonate close to the court an hour later.

APRIL
The peaceful Bersih 3.0 demonstration for free and fair elections descends into violence.

SEPTEMBER
The Duke and Duchess of Cambridge make a four-day visit to Malaysia.

DECEMBER
Investors file a suit against gold investment company Genneva Malaysia Sdn Bhd, whose offices were raided by authorities in October.

August: Olympic diving bronze-medallist Pandalela Rinong with Sarawakian Olympic teammates Traisy Vivien Tukiet and Bryan Nickson Lomas celebrate as they travel in a cavalcade from Kuching International Airport to Kuching city centre and the Astana there to receive an award from Sarawak Yang di-Pertua Negeri Tun Abang Muhammad Salahuddin.

'My grandmother told me that Malaysia would provide us with some wonderful experiences and unforgettable memories, and so indeed, it has proved….'

Prince WIlliam at the British Malaysia Chamber of Commerce luncheon at the Kuala Lumpur Convention Centre, 14 September 2012.

2012

world news

5 January
In Japan a restaurant pays a record US$750,000 for a bluefin tuna.

20 January
The FBI closes down megaupload.com, one of the world's largest file-sharing sites, and its founder Kim Dotcom aka Kim Schmitz is arrested in New Zealand.

28 February
A Thai court sentences media mogul Sondhi Limthongkul, 64, to 20 years in prison for corporate fraud. Sondhi is the founder of the royalist 'Yellow Shirt' protest movement.

1 April
Myanmar holds elections to fill 45 seats in the 664-seat Parliment. Aung San Suu Kyi wins a seat and her National League for Democracy wins in 43 of the 44 constituencies it contested.

2 April
A Pakistani court convicts Osama bin Laden's three widows and two of his daughters of illegally entering and living in Pakistan and sentences them to 45 days in prison, with credit for time served.

Diana Tong (right) and her artist husband Leong during the ceremony.

Ancient Chinese wedding

1 January   Malacca

Malaysian couple Leong Jiun Wee and Diana Tong Huey Li, both 33, were married according to ancient rituals dating back to the Zhou Dynasty (1046–256 BC). The couple travelled to Beijing last year to source their elaborate red wedding costumes.

Two new Rafflesia species discovered

1 January   Raub

Two new Rafflesia species may have been discovered in the Lata Jarum forests in Ulu Dong. Fraser's Hill Research Centre head Professor Dr Jumaat Adam said he was still studying the discovery and cross-checking against the criteria of other species in the world to confirm it. One species has a 14cm diaphragm and more anthers than other Rafflesia found in the Peninsula. The diaphragm is the hole where insects enter and collect pollen.

The Universiti Kebangsaan Malaysia researcher, a pioneer in Rafflesia research, had yet to come up with names for the new species.

Three-day Kaul Festival

5 January   Dalat

In Sarawak, Kampung Medong's annual Kaul Festival is not only rich in tradition but also a fascinating sight to behold. Many villages in the district have their own celebrations.

The Melanaus believe in the Ipouh guardian of the sea and the festival is to ask the Ipouh for a bountiful harvest and protection from diseases and other dangers. Every ritual is followed closely. 'Serarang', made with leaves, are placed on the main boat for the ceremony, together with other offerings such as popcorn.

Royal policeman

7 January   Kuala Lumpur

For nine months, Tunku Abdul Jalil Iskandar Ibrahim Ismail left the comfort and luxury of the palace to stay in a police academy barrack. The 21-year-old prince graduated together with 959 other probationary inspectors at the Police Training Centre here. Tunku Abdul Jalil is the first member of the Johor royal family to join the police force. His three siblings joined the army.

Bomb blast follows Anwar's acquittal

9 January   Putrajaya

Dato' Seri Anwar Ibrahim was acquitted by the High Court on a charge of sodomising his former personal aide Mohd Saiful Bukhari Azlan. Justice Mohd Zabidin Mohd Diah said the court could not rely on the DNA evidence.

An hour after the verdict, a lawyer and four others were injured when explosions rocked three locations close to the court complex. Police said this was the work of a person with a background in explosives.

Police had earlier advised organisers of the planned 'Free Anwar 901' rally to hold it at a suitable location to avoid disrupting public order. It was planned for outside the Kuala Lumpur Court Complex in Jalan Duta.

Supporters of Dato' Seri Anwar Ibrahim outside the Kuala Lumpur High Court.

Dying breed of dead 'whisperers'

15 January   Malacca

A small Gujerati community fears that funeral rites involving talking to the dead are dying because the young are not interested.

Nishrint Chimanlal Ravichand, 48, who had performed the last rites at more than 20 funerals, learnt the rites from his father and grandfather.

Animated feature on Sabah to hit China

9 January   Kuala Lumpur

Borneo Head Hunter, an animated feature on Sabah tribal leader Limping Payau, would be shown in China in October. Jointly produced by local TV channel Jia Yu and China's Daley Entertainment, it tells the true story of Limping, whose death at the hands of his adversaries caused an inter-tribal conflict lasting two generations. The feud was eventually ended by his descendants, some of whom became prominent nation-builders.

Navy vessel on fire

13 January   Johor Bahru

A fire which broke out on board the Royal Malaysian Navy ship KD *Mutiara* probably started from sparks during welding works in the central part of the vessel. Shipyard workers tried to put out the blaze but called the Fire Department when the fire started spreading.

The ship, docked at a shipyard in Pasir Gudang, was built in Penang in 1977.

Illiterate NS trainees

9 January   Rawang

About 8 per cent of 6,667 National Service (NS) trainees from 30 selected camps were found to be illiterate, the Defence Ministry revealed. The findings were based on a pilot project using a module called I-Smart conducted on the third batch of NS trainees in August last year. The Education Ministry had been alerted to this matter.

AES to be implemented

18 January   Kuala Lumpur

The Automated Enforcement System (AES) would be implemented nationwide to catch traffic offenders and detect expired road tax. There would be 566 speed cameras, 265 traffic light cameras and 250 mobile cameras installed.

The system commenced on 24 September in Perak, Selangor, Putrajaya and Kuala Lumpur. Within two days, 809 drivers were caught for speeding and 2,143 for beating red lights.

On 18 December, the Attorney-General's Chambers froze all court proceedings related to summonses issued under the AES to study legal concerns raised.

Autonomy for five varsities

26 January   Putrajaya

Universiti Malaya, Universiti Kebangsaan Malaysia, Universiti Sains Malaysia, Universiti Putra Malaysia and Universiti Teknologi Malaysia have been given autonomous status. They will now manage their own academic, administrative and financial matters.

Petronas ink RM37b deal

16 January Putrajaya

Petroliam Nasional Bhd (Petronas) and Shell Malaysia signed a deal worth RM37.3 billion that would see the implementation of the world's largest enhanced oil recovery (EOR) projects off the shores of Sabah and Sarawak over 30 years.

Prime Minister Dato' Sri Najib Tun Razak said the project was expected to increase oil production and extend the lifespan of the oil fields beyond 2040. 'The project will include the building of local capabilities in a niche technology area as well as increasing the average recovery factor in Baram Delta and North Sabah fields from 36% to about 50%,' he said.

He said the Government had identified the rejuvenation of existing fields through EOR as one of the 19 Entry Point Projects in order to provide additional supplies for the country's power and industrial needs.

'The team will also undertake joint research and development in the area of EOR technology. This is a radical shift in our development strategy and serves as an opportunity for Malaysia to be at par with other high-performing Asean countries,' he said.

Centuries-old temple restored

28 January Kuala Terengganu

Razed in a fire two years ago, the more-than-200-year-old Ho Ann Kiong temple in Kampung Cina was fully restored. The temple was built by the Hokkien community in 1801. It is the oldest structure in the Kuala Terengganu's Chinatown tourist belt and is a major historical and tourism site. The RM1.3 million restoration work was carried out with public funds.

Full access to assets declaration

28 January Putrajaya

The Malaysian Anti-Corruption Commission (MACC) will have full access to the declaration of assets of all members of the Federal administration, including ministers and their families.

Expert lauds Malaysian Hokkiens

5 February Malacca

The Hokkien culture and dialect in Malaysia is more vibrant than in China. French anthropologist Fiorella Allio noted that the Hokkiens here had preserved the culture and language better and that they were similar to that in ancient China. 'There is not much distortion in the way the culture is preserved and the dialect spoken here is authentic. In China, the Hokkien tradition is somewhat skewed,' she said. Allio was in Malacca for research on the age-old Wangkang festival practised by the Chinese Peranakan.

Housewife finds artefact in baby shark

21 February Malacca

Housewife Suseela Menon from Klebang was gutting a baby shark when she found an ancient artefact in the fish.

The medallion, 7.4cm long, 6cm wide and weighing 10g, was believed to have been worn by Portuguese soldiers in the 16th century for divine protection. One side of it bore the profile of a woman's head with a crown and encircled by a halo and an unclear inscription. The other bore a crucifix with the inscription ANTONII.

Flying with Bluebirds

18 February Kuala Lumpur

He claimed he didn't even know about the offside rule until about two years ago when he took over Cardiff City but Berjaya chairman Tan Sri Vincent Tan had become a passionate Bluebird (Cardiff) fan. Tan Sri Vincent and his business partner Datuk Chan Tien Ghee own 49% of Cardiff City.

'The fans appreciate what we have done for their football team. And because of the branding (Malaysia is emblazoned on all the team's jerseys), they are also very pleased to meet Malaysians,' he said.

Taking Lent to the peak

24 February Kota Kinabalu

Some 24 devotees from the St John parish in Tuaran climbed Mount Kinabalu to attend mass performed by two priests near Low's Peak (4,101m) a week before Ash Wednesday and the beginning of Lent, a period of fasting and penance.

Having the service on the mountain made observing Lent more significant, said Father Rayner Bisius.

Federal focus on Sarawak

24 February Selangau

The Federal Government will continue to give full support to Sarawak's development and aspirations, said Deputy Prime Minister Tan Sri Muhyiddin Yassin. He said most of the 312 projects promised during the last general election had been implemented at a cost of RM213.67 million. He also promised to build more vocational schools in the State.

Diving into history

28 February Sepang

With eight quota spots already in the bag, Malaysia was sending its biggest diving squad ever for an Olympic Games. Head coach Yang Zhuliang felt that Malaysia stood a better chance of striking a first-ever medal at the Olympics in the synchro disciplines. He vowed to guide his charges to make Olympic history when they returned to London's Aquatic Park in July.

On 23 February, Leong Mun Yee partnered Pandelela Rinong to secure a coveted Olympic spot in the women's 10m platform synchro final.

Nostalgic ride back on track

3 February Kota Kinabalu

After a six-year hiatus, Sabah's colonial-style steam locomotive pulled out of Tanjung Aru station to mark the relaunch of the State's tourist rail service.

Dubbed the North Borneo Railway, the joint venture project between Sabah Railways Department and Sutera Harbour Resort would allow tourists to experience the bygone era of British North Borneo (now Sabah). The train runs from Tanjung Aru through the small towns of Kinarut, Kawang and Papar on a three-hour return trip. The refurbished locomotives had plied Sabah's railway lines since the 1880s.

City culture

25 February Kuala Lumpur ▶ Inspired by the 'No Pants Subway' in New York, about 500 people, each dressed in a sarong, took part in the *Keretapi Sarong* flash mob in an LRT train at KL Sentral.

27 February Kuala Lumpur ▶ Graffiti artists hard at work on the wall of the Klang River bank near Central Market during the KUL Sign Festival 2012. The festival, which attracted 200 foreign graffiti artists, was to promote better ties with graffiti artists and to promote and ensure the maintenance of public property.

2012

6 April
Authorities in China indict five people for involvement in illegal organ trading after a teenager sells one of his kidneys to buy an iPhone and an iPad.

2 May
Edvard Munch's pastel 'The Scream' (1895) sells for a record US$119,922,500 in New York City.

18 May
Saudi Arabia bans the use of the Gregorian calendar in all official dealings.

23 May
Pakistani doctor Shakil Afridi, who helped the US track down Osama bin Laden, is convicted of treason and sentenced to 33 years in prison and fined US$3,500.

26 May
Miami police shoot dead a naked man chewing on the face of another naked man on a highway ramp.

30 June
Two days after UNESCO names Timbuktu in northern Mali a world heritage site, Islamic militants go on a rampage destroying its ancient tombs of Muslim saints.

Billions pouring into ECER

Datuk Jebasingam (left) with Pahang Menteri Besar Datuk Seri Adnan Yaakob (centre) at the ECER exhibition booth at the Pahang Economic Convention 2012.

28 February Putrajaya

Over RM9 billion in 12 projects were pledged in the first two months of this year and were expected to create some 20,000 jobs in the East Coast Economic Region (ECER) that comprises Johor, Pahang, Terengganu and Kelantan.

ECER Development Council Chief Executive Officer Datuk Jebasingam Issace John said the new projects included a RM4.2 billion hotel and resort enclave and a RM1 billion integrated resort and township development, both in Mersing, Johor. Another major project was a RM1.3 billion golf and resort project at Cherating in Pahang.

Is Marwan dead?

29 February Petaling Jaya

Early this month, Philippines regional military commander Maj. Gen. Noel Coballes said Jemaah Islamiyah (JI) leader Zulkifli Abdul Hir, also known as Marwan, a Malaysian militant high on the FBI's Most Wanted Terrorists list, was killed in an air raid on a military stronghold in Jolo island, Mindanao, on 2 February.

Fifteen militants were also killed, including JI militant Mohammad Ali (Muawiyah) and Abu Sayyaf leader Abu Pula. However, a month later, Marwan's body had still not been found. Muar-born Marwan was believed to be head of the Kumpulan Mujahidin Malaysia terrorist organisation and a leader of JI.

Three new entrants to wealthiest list

1 March Petaling Jaya

Malaysia's wealthiest welcomed three newcomers. First was doctor-turned-retail magnate and MBF Holdings CEO Tan Sri Dr Ninian Mogan Lourdenadin, who shot to 22nd place with a net worth of RM1.5 billion.

Crescendo Corp. Bhd chairman and managing director Gooi Seong Lim was in 34th place with a net worth of RM660 million and Pacific Andes International Holdings' Ng Joo Siang, who took over the family business from his father, was at 37th place with a net worth of RM555 million.

Disharmony in orchestra

2 March Petaling Jaya

The Malaysian Philharmonic Orchestra (MPO) gave several musicians notice to leave at the end of this season, including key expatriate members who had been with the MPO since it was set up in 1998.

There were allegations that those asked to leave had wanted MPO music director Claus Peter Flor out. There was also speculation that the expatriates were removed to bring in locals to give MPO a Malaysian identity.

Minimum wage fixed

4 March Putrajaya

The minimum monthly wage for private sector employees has been set at between RM800 (Sarawak, Sabah and Labuan) and RM900 (Peninsula). It covers employees in all economic sectors except those in the domestic service sector such as maids and gardeners.

The different minimum wages for the Peninsula and Sarawak, Sabah and Labuan were due to the variation in wage structures and cost of living.

'We have delivered'

2 April Putrajaya

The Government Transformation Programme (GTP) has exceeded some of its targets for 2011. Prime Minister Dato' Sri Najib Tun Razak said all seven National Key Result Areas had stayed true to the ideals of 1Malaysia.

New paradise for birdwatchers

10 March Malacca

The Malacca Government wants to promote Kampung Pengkalan in Machap as a destination for bird-watching. 'I am sure birdwatchers and nature enthusiasts are willing to make the trip just to catch a glimpse of these birds here,' said Chief Minister Dato' Seri Mohd Ali Rustam.

Commuting by horse

10 April Alor Setar

Electrical contractor Mohd Sabri Salleh, 51, rides a horse to work for convenience. He leaves his horse in a stable at the Taman Jubli Emas field, Alor Setar and walks to his office nearby.

Topsy-turvy house

10 March Kota Kinabalu

Malaysia's first and only upside-down house is a tourist attraction in Sabah, recording over 3,000 visitors in the six weeks since it opened.

The RM500,000 house at Kampung Bantayan–Telibong, about 40km from the city and on the foothills of Mount Kinabalu, was built by entrepreneur Alexander Yee who said the house was a reminder to protect the environment or the world would become upside down.

Everything from its roof to its floor, including a car parked in the garage, is upside down. It is furnished with various native arts and crafts as well as refrigerator and sofa sets and all are upside down.

Peaceful demo turns unruly

28 April Kuala Lumpur

What started as a peaceful assembly turned chaotic at 2.50pm when Bersih 3.0 demonstrators breached police barricades at Dataran Merdeka. Police fired water cannons and tear gas to disperse the crowd.

The previous day, a court order declaring Dataran Merdeka out of bounds until noon on Sunday, 29 April was handed to Bersih co-chairman Datuk S. Ambiga. Bersih 3.0 organisers said they would abide by the order but that the rally would continue.

Bersih 3.0 protesters blocked by a razor wire barricade and police near Dataran Merdeka. Thousands of people gathered to seek changes to polling regulations to curb fears of electoral fraud.

Archaelogical find in Mansuli Valley

9 April **Kota Kinabalu**

The Mansuli Valley in Sabah's east coast district of Lahad Datu has yielded evidence of the oldest human settlement in east Malaysia, said archaeologists.

In 2003, researchers from Universiti Sains Malaysia and the Sabah Museum stumbled upon a treasure trove of more than 1,000 stone tools believed to date back 235,000 years, 27,000 years earlier than previously thought.

On 23 May, an excavation team in interior Keningau unearthed a 200,000-year-old settlement which researchers believe was one of the earliest human settlements in the country. Sabah Museum would propose to the State Government that the site be conserved as an archaeological-tourism area.

PM's MASwings move hailed

29 April **Kuching**

Prime Minister Dato' Sri Najib Razak had assured that the Federal Government would review the present structure of MASwings so that the State Governments of Sabah and Sarawak could have a part in the airline and more connectivity. The Federal Government also agreed for Kuching and Kota Kinabalu to be the secondary hubs for Sarawak and Sabah. This would enable both States to access routes to areas involved in the Sarawak Corridor of Renewable Energy (Score) and Sabah Corridor. Better air connectivity would have a huge impact on the economies of both States.

Malaysian Lamborghini

3 May **Kuala Lumpur**

The new Lamborghini Gallardo MLE (Malaysia Limited Edition) made its debut in a glitzy ceremony here. The V10 powered Gallardo MLE is the result of a year-long collaboration between Lamborghini Kuala Lumpur and the principal company in Italy, Automobili Lamborghini S.p.A.

Awang Batil honoured

6 May **Kangar**

Romli Mahmud, 55, the last Awang Batil storyteller, was named Perlis' arts personality of the year.

Romli, who inherited the mantle from his late father, Mahmud Wahid, was the only one in the State keeping the art alive. He received RM1,000 and a certificate.

Awang Batil is a form of storytelling accompanied by the batil or brass pot to bring alive long tales peppered with humour and sadness. Awang was the protagonist in most of these tales.

Shahrizat cleared

31 May **Kuala Lumpur**

Wanita Umno chief Dato' Seri Shahrizat Abdul Jalil was cleared of any involvement in the awarding of a RM250 million loan to the National Feedlot Corporation (NFC).

The Malaysian Anti-Corruption Commission investigation ruled that she did not have a hand in the company selection process and the awarding of the loan, and the Attorney-General decided to close the case.

NFC was owned by Dato' Seri Shahrizat's husband, Dato' Seri Dr Mohamad Salleh Ismail, who was also the company chairman, and her children, who were the company directors.

The company first came into focus following the Auditor-General's 2010 Report highlighting its failure to meet the annual beef production target set by the Government.

Lenggong is Unesco World Heritage Site

1 July **Bukit Mertajam**

The Lenggong Valley in Perak is now a Unesco World Heritage Site.

This was where the earliest human skeletal remains in the Peninsula, the Perak Man, was found in 1991. There is also evidence of human settlement from the Palaeolithic age at the site.

Lenggong joins the list of other World Heritage Sites in Malaysia, including George Town, Malacca and the Mulu and Kinabalu National Parks.

On 10 November 2011, the Federal Government agreed to return Perak Man to its 'home'.

Sedition Act to go

11 July **Putrajaya**

The Sedition Act 1948 would be replaced by the National Harmony Act.

Prime Minister Dato' Sri Najib Razak said the decision was made as the government wanted to find a mechanism that could best balance the need for freedom of speech with the provisions stipulated in the Federal Constitution.

He also said that recent amendments to laws as well as new ones relating to civil liberties would be implemented immediately. They were the Security Offences Act (Special Measures), the Printing Presses and Publications Act involving newspapers' annual permits as well as the Universities and University Colleges Act that allowed students to be involved in politics.

Gov't to take over EDL

30 August **Putrajaya**

The Government decided to take over the Eastern Dispersal Link (EDL) from Malaysian Resources Corp. Bhd to settle issues related to policy and toll charges for the highway.

The six-lane EDL, which opened on 1 April, became a hot topic as motorists felt that the toll rate to and from Singapore was too high at RM15.30.

The 8.1km expressway connects the end of the North–South Expressway's Southern Route at Pandan to the new Sultan Iskandar Building's CIQ Complex in Johor Bahru city centre.

Royal visit to Malaysia

13 September **Kuala Lumpur**

The Duke and Duchess of Cambridge, Prince William and Catherine Middleton, visited Hospis Malaysia in Kuala Lumpur while on an official visit to Malaysia.

Catherine, Duchess of Cambridge and Prince William, Duke of Cambridge visit the Assyakirin Mosque in Kuala Lumpur.

Breast cancer patient Chin Kim Thye was very surprised to meet the royal couple in, of all places, Malaysia. She described them as 'very nice' and 'caring'.

Catherine also spent 15 minutes chatting with a boy suffering from leukaemia and signed his birthday card.

On the eve of Malaysia Day, the Duke and Duchess ended their four-day visit of the country by taking in the beauty of Sabah's tropical rainforest.

London 2012 Olympic Games

The elusive gold

5 August **London** ▶ The gold medal proved elusive as Datuk Lee Chong Wei lost in a nail-biting 21–15, 10–21, 19–21 finish to China's Lin Dan in the men's badminton singles final at the London Olympics. But he remained the country's hero and said he is game for another shot at it during the Olympics in Rio in 2016. In Petaling Jaya, people queued up for a free dinner at Original Penang Kayu Nasi Kandar that restaurateur Burhan Mohamed promised for Chong Wei's success, while in Sarawak, a man collapsed and died while watching the match. Kota Alam Shah State assemblyman M. Manoharan, who came under heavy criticism for his tweets criticising Chong Wei's performance, apologised.

Our diving queen

10 August **London** ▶ Malaysians were ecstatic when diver Pandelela Rinong Pamg wrested a bronze medal in the 10m individual platform event. Pandelela, 19, finished third behind China's Chen Ruolin and Australia's Brittany Broben. She pipped Melissa Wu of Australia by 1.1 points to take the bronze.

Malaysians from all walks of life took to Twitter to congratulate the petite Bidayuh diver from Sarawak for making history as Malaysia's first woman Olympic medallist and the first to win one outside of badminton.

A Facebook user, Johari Pain, said in a status update that he would cut off his genitals if Pandelela won. After netizens urged him on, he deleted the Facebook post before tweeting an apology.

world news

15 August
An 8.0-magnitude earthquake off the Pacific coast devastates the city of Ica and various regions of Peru; over 500 are dead and 1,500 injured.

11 September
In Libya US ambassador Chris Stevens dies of asphyxiation in the US Consulate in Benghazi when it is attacked by a mob.

11 October
Guan Moye, better known as Mo Yan, becomes the first Chinese to win the Nobel Prize for Literature.

14 October
Austrian Felix Baumgartner drops into the record books for the highest sky-dive when he leaps out of a hot-air balloon more than 24 miles above New Mexico and goes supersonic at Mach 1.24 (833.9 mph).

21 December
On this day the Mesoamerican Long Count calendar (Mayan Calendar) reaches the date 13.0.0.0.0, disproving the various doomsday myths associated with it.

Genneva gold raid

20 December   Kuala Lumpur

Nine people, including housewives, businessmen and professionals filed a suit against gold investment firm Genneva Malaysia Sdn Bhd and its four directors, asking for the return of their investments totalling over RM2 million. They claimed that the defendants had falsely represented to them that the scheme was based on *syariah* principles.

Gold buyers and traders gathered in front of Genneva Malaysia's premises at Kuchai Lama, Kuala Lumpur, during the investigatory raid on 1 October.

Shocked investors and agents crowded Genneva offices in KL and Penang after an investigative raid on the company by Bank Negara Malaysia and the Ministry of Domestic Trade, Co-operatives and Consumerism on 1 October. Singapore's Commercial Affairs Department conducted a similar swoop on Genneva Pte Ltd's Orchard Towers offices there (*see 16 May 2013*).

M'sia's singing champ

21 September   Petaling Jaya

Three songs in three languages belted out with virtuosity, confidence and style won Nur Shahila Amir Amzah, 22, the top prize in Asia's first reality singing contest in Shanghai. Speechless, the host said, 'Wow. Oh my God.'

Also known as Shila Amzah, she emerged as Asian Wave 2012 champion, beating contestants from China, South Korea, Singapore, Thailand and India. She sang a cover version of Jaclyn Victor's *Gemilang*, followed by her rendition of Bruno Mars' *Grenade*. But it was her third song, *Zheng Fu*, a Mandarin number by Chinese star Na Ying, that clinched her the title.

Legoland Malaysia opens

15 September   Nusajaya

The first Legoland theme park in Asia officially opened its doors to the public. The RM700-million park, which occupies 30ha in Iskandar Malaysia, was the sixth in the world after Denmark, the UK, California in the US, Germany and Florida also in the US. The park had sold 35,000 annual passes in advance of its opening, 60 percent of them to locals.

Passport to Jerusalem

19 December   Putrajaya

Malaysia has relaxed restrictions for religious visits to Israel, lifting the quota on the number of pilgrims and allowing anyone to travel for up to 21 days at a time.

Previously, pilgrimages to Israel were limited to 700 Malaysians each year, with only 40 from one church and a stay of only up to 10 days at a time.

There are now no more quotas.

Rape of Cameron Highlands

11 December   Cameron Highlands

Once famed for its cool temperatures and verdant growth, Cameron Highlands is now battling land clearing by farmers who either do not have a permit or are flouting regulations. On 11 December several residents obtained an injunction to stop a developer from carrying out soil movement works near their homes. High Court judge Mariana Yahya also set aside the plaintiff LTT Development's ex parte and inter parte injunctions to stop residents from encroaching or dwelling on the land in Ulu Telom.

Two months earlier, the Malaysian Anti-Corruption Commission started a probe following district officer Datuk Ahmad Daud's admission that the authorities found it hard to catch those clearing land illegally because its personnel were in cahoots with the culprits.

Land clearing at Sg Menson has caused tonnes of soil to be eroded.

Majestic Hotel reopens

8 December   Kuala Lumpur

More than 1,000 guests dined at the newly reopened Majestic Hotel at its grand opening. The hotel, which closed in 1984 and was later home to the national art gallery, had originally opened for business in 1932. Following extensive renovations, the hotel now had 47 suites in the old building and more than 200 suites and deluxe rooms in the new Tower Wing.

Forbidden hair cut

12 December   Kota Bharu

Following widespread criticism, the Kelantan Pas-led Government temporarily exempted non-Muslims from bylaws forbidding women to wash and cut the hair of men and vice versa but stressed that workers were prohibited from attending to Muslims of the opposite sex. Gender segregation was also observed at supermarket check-outs in the State.

In November, salon operators had complained that they had been fined for letting female workers cut the hair of non-Muslim male patrons. The fines were imposed under Section 107(2) of the Local Council Act bylaws which prohibited a woman from cutting the hair of a man and vice versa regardless of religion.

Mega catch

18 December   George Town

A giant grouper weighing 195kg and measuring 1.8m is believed to be the largest catch in Malaysian waters.

Orang Asli rightful owners of land

19 December   Temerloh

The High Court ordered portions of Malay reserve land encroaching into more than 2,000ha of Orang Asli customary land in the Bera district to be degazetted. Justice Akhtar Tahir also directed the Pahang land and mines office to gazette the whole area as Orang Asli customary land within a year. He ruled that the reserve land was subservient to Orang Asli rights as they were the earliest inhabitants.

Obituaries

9 July   **Azah Aziz**, 84, Malay culture icon; wife of Royal Professor Ungku Aziz and mother of Bank Negara Governor Dr Zeti Akhtar Aziz.

15 Aug   Datuk Gunalan Panchacharan (**Punch Gunalan**), 68, former badminton player, coach and administrator.

22 Dec   **Tun Dr Lim Keng Yaik**, 73, former Gerakan president.

2013

After much speculation over the date of the general election, GE13 was held on 5 May, resulting in another win for Barisan Nasional, albeit with a slightly reduced majority. There was also speculation regarding the origins and purpose of the attempted Sulu invasion of Sabah. Another story grabbing the headlines was the verdict in the case of the murders of Sosilawati and three others. A spate of violent crimes, including gangland turf wars, sent Malaysians scurrying for cover and causing restaurants, clinics and other establishments to close earlier than usual. And even before its official launch, a book on the years of Tun Abdullah Ahmad Badawi as Prime Minister created a furore ahead of the Umno party elections slated for later in the year.

MARCH
Malaysian security forces clash with Sulu militants at Lahad Datu, Sabah.

MAY
Captain James Anthony Tan is the youngest pilot to circle the globe solo.

JUNE
Citrawarna 1Malaysia (Colours of 1Malaysia) attracted more than 100,000 people to Dataran Merdeka.

JULY
In the run-up to Malaysia Day, Sarawak celebrates the 50th anniversary of its independence by re-enacting the departure of the last British Governor to Sarawak.

July: The Battersea Power Station redevelopment—Dato' Sri Najib Razak (far right), British Premier David Cameron (second right) and Mayor of London Boris Johnson (centre) are shown the plans for the redevelopment of Battersea Power Station. Decommissioned in 1983, the power station has been purchased by a consortium of Malaysian companies and is to be converted into apartments, offices, shops and a cinema.

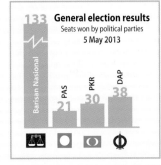

General election results
Seats won by political parties
5 May 2013

Barisan Nasional	PAS	PKR	DAP
133	21	30	38

29.3 million	Population	
RM881.1 billion	Gross Domestic Product[1]	
RM29,661	Gross National Income (per capita)[2]	
17.1	Crude Birth Rate (per 1,000 persons)[3]	
6.8	Infant Mortality (per 1,000 live births)[4]	
72.3 / 77.3	Life Expectancy (male / female)[5]	
106.4	Consumer Price Index (base 2010=100)[6]	

Malaysia Facts

[1] 2011 [2] 2011 [3] 2011 [4] 2010 [5] 2012 estimate [6] July 2013

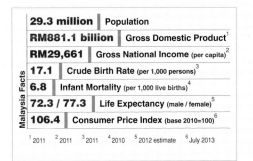

'National reconciliation lies in all of us accepting the results of the 13th general elections.'

Dato' Sri Najib Razak urging the opposition to accept the general election result post GE13, 26 June 2013.

2013

world news

13 January
Air quality in Beijing breaches the air pollution index (which has a maximum of 500), reaching 755.

16 January
In Algeria, gunmen attack the gas complex at Ain Amenas in retaliation for France's military intervention against Al-Quaeda-linked rebels in Mali. The attack leaves 49 hostages and 32 militants dead.

14 February
South African double-amputee Olympic 'blade runner' Oscar Pistorius is arrested on the charge of murdering his girlfriend Reeva Steenkamp.

8 April
Baroness Margaret Thatcher (b. 1925) dies. The longest serving British Prime Minister of the 20th century (1979–1990) did not have a promising start when, fresh out of university, she applied for a job at ICI and was rejected by the personnel department because she was 'headstrong, obstinate and dangerously self-opinionated.'

Yuna signs with US label

5 January Petaling Jaya

Los Angeles-based Malaysian singer-songwriter Yuna, 26, has inked a major label record deal with Verve Music Group in the United States, joining its stable of artistes which includes Diana Krall, Jamie Cullum, Herbie Hancock and Rod Stewart. Her debut album for the Verve Music imprint is due out in the later half of this year. She is also contributing music to the soundtrack of the upcoming movie, *The Croods*, a 3D film produced by DreamWorks Animation.

Yuna performing in Malaysia later in the year.

Peaceful gathering

13 January Kuala Lumpur

The Himpunan Kebangkitan Rakyat rally went on smoothly and peacefully with police maintaining a minimal but effective presence to ensure safety and order.

The police deployed only 200 personnel and did not mount any roadblock in the city. People gathered at various meeting points as early as 7.00am and walked to Merdeka Stadium. The orderly situation contrasted with the scenes during Bersih 2.0 and 3.0. The organisers considered the gathering a milestone towards political changes despite falling short of achieving its targeted attendance of one million.

Oil find after 24 years

18 January Miri

Rich deposits of crude oil and gas have been discovered near Miri City in northern Sarawak, the first time in 24 years that 'black gold' has been found in such a sizeable volume in the inland areas of Malaysia.

The discovery was at Block SK 333 onshore of Sarawak, via the Adong Kecil West 1 well, 20km northeast of Miri. Petronas said the last time such an onshore discovery was made was in 1989, in the Asam Paya oil field.

First Apostolic Nuncio soon

19 January Putrajaya

Pope Benedict XVI has appointed American Archbishop Joseph Marino as the first Apostolic Nuncio (diplomatic representative), with the rank of ambassador, to Malaysia.

Prime Minister Dato' Sri Najib Razak said the appointment was testament to a commitment that he and Pope Benedict had pledged during a meeting two years earlier.

'Having established diplomatic ties in 2011, Pope Benedict and I vowed to work together to increase understanding between Christians and Muslims,' said Najib who visited Rome in July 2011 to meet Pope Benedict at the papal summer residence in Castel Gandolfo.

A Vatican embassy was set up in Kuala Lumpur, known as the Apostolic Nunciature Malaysia. It was officially recognised in May last year.

Deviant sect raided

5 January Malacca

Police who raided the house of a reclusive 'spiritual leader' of a deviant sect in Kampung Chabau, Jasin, found a cache of weapons. The 46-year-old man, whom villagers described as having 'supernatural powers', was arrested. Members of the Panji Langit sect claim to be 'warriors of righteousness and crusaders of truth' to uplift moral values among mankind.

The State Islamic Religious Department (Jaim) said Panji Langit was similar to the Sky Kingdom sect led by Ayah Pin.

A cache of weapons, including swords, kris, axes, machetes, bows and arrows, spears, 23 canisters of gunpowder and several fake guns were found in a store at the back of the bungalow. Police said the weapons were part of the sect's doomsday preparations as the members had believed in the Mayan prophecy that the world would end on 21 December last year.

Police also seized a laptop, medicine and antiseptic lotion used to treat injuries, gas masks, camping equipment used by soldiers during operations, vests, gloves, ropes and military hats.

Dato' Sri Najib shown Gaza's destruction by Palestinian National Authority Prime Minister, Ismail Haniyeh.

Unity plan for Gaza

22 January Gaza City

Malaysia has offered to help unite rival Palestinian groups Fatah and Hamas. Visiting Palestine, Dato' Sri Najib Tun Razak expressed support for a reconciliation plan to end the division between the two Palestinian movements.

He said that peace and prosperity could only be achieved through unity. A split between the two groups in 2007 led to the West Bank being governed by Fatah and the Gaza Strip by Hamas.

First Chinese overseas campus

21 January Sepang

Top Chinese varsity Xiamen University will set up its first overseas campus at Salak Tinggi.

'This is the first time that the Chinese government has allowed one of its universities to set up a campus abroad,' Prime Minister Dato' Sri Najib Razak said after meeting university president Prof. Zhu Chongshi in Kuala Lumpur.

Five faculties would be set up: Electrical bio-engineering and chemical engineering, medicine, information and communications technology, business and economics, and Chinese language and literature. Zhu said the campus would cost RM600 million.

Malaysians in Algerian hostage crisis flown home

23 January Algiers

The bodies of two Malaysians killed in the 16 January Algerian hostage crisis arrived at Kuala Lumpur on Monday.

The deceased, Chong Chung Ngen and Tan Ping Wee, together with three Malaysian survivors Patrick Purait Awang, K. Ravi and Lau Seek Ching, were among 130 Amenas Oil and Gas Production Complex staff of various nationalities held hostage by a militant group.

The incident was one of the biggest international hostage crises in decades. Out of 800 hostages, 39 foreign hostages were killed.

Cancer cases on the rise

3 February Kuala Lumpur

More than RM2 million had to be raised every month to provide treatment for cancer patients. The National Cancer Registry recorded 17,763 cases in 2008, of whom 9,936 were females.

National Cancer Council president Datuk Mohd Farid Ariffin said the rising cases were mostly contributed by smokers. He added that Malaysians have also become careless about their eating habits and adopted unhealthy lifestyles which do not help to keep cancer at bay.

Borneo pygmy elephants found dead

30 January Kota Kinabalu

Thirteen endangered Borneo pygmy elephants were found dead in the Gunung Rara Forest Reserve.

Wildlife officials feared more might be found as they believed the dead elephants and a rescued calf were part of a single herd which was believed to have consumed some form of natural or pesticide poison.

Malaysia–China Kuantan Industrial Park launched

5 February Kuantan

Prime Minister Dato' Sri Najib Razak and the National Committee of the Chinese People's Political Consultative Conference chairman Jia Qinglin today launched the Malaysia–China Kuantan Industrial Park (MCKIP).

The MCKIP in Gebeng is the first industrial park to be accorded national status and was expected to bring relations between the two countries to greater heights as it would play a synergistic role with its sister park, the China–Malaysia Qinzhou Industrial Park in Qinzhou.

The MCKIP had already attracted investment commitments worth RM10.5 billion, creating 8,500 jobs. Dato' Sri Najib said the true impact of MCKIP would be in the developer's commitment to provide training for all levels of workforce and work with local training institutions for skills development.

Psy show in Penang

12 February Sepang

South Korean K-pop sensation Psy summed up his sentiments over the rousing response to his performance at the Penang Barisan Nasional Chinese New Year open house the previous day with a tweet: 'U were hotter than the weather, hotter than ever!! One Malaysia!!'

The 80,000 crowd at Han Chiang College roared as Psy broke into the 'Gangnam Style' dance, accompanied by dancers all decked in white. After his first performance, the crowd shouted 'Encore! Encore!' and Psy did not disappoint.

Sulu 'army' enters Sabah

12 February Lahad Datu

They sneaked into Lahad Datu by boat but the 235 armed men in army fatigues were spotted in Kampung Tanduo by local fishermen who made a police report.

Two days later, the nation was shocked to learn that the intruders had been identified as Filipinos with links to self-styled Sulu Sultan Jamalul Kiram. They had entered Sabah to reassert the Sultanate's centuries-old claim to the area and had holed up in Kampung Tanduo.

Meanwhile, Home Minister Dato' Seri Hishammuddin Tun Hussein said the situation was under control and Prime Minister Dato' Sri Najib said the Government would start negotiations to resolve the intrusion without bloodshed.

Babies-for-sale ring busted

21 February George Town

Police launched operations in Penang, Selangor, Johor, Perak, Kuala Lumpur, Pahang and Negeri Sembilan and rescued 10 boys and 11 girls between the ages of one month and nine years.

They also arrested 43 people, including couples who had adopted the children, a doctor and a National Registration Department employee. Last month, 10 children, mostly babies, were rescued and 36 people arrested. Their biological parents had sold them for between RM2,500 and RM4,500 each. The babies were then resold to childless couples for more than 10 times the amount.

The attack begins

1 March Lahad Datu

Two policemen were slain in a shootout with armed intruders holed up in Kampung Tanduo today. Twelve intruders linked to the Sulu Sultanate were shot dead.

On 4 March, after a three-week stand-off that saw eight policemen killed, some 2,000-strong security forces successfully launched an offensive using F-18 and Hawk fighter jets, by army and police follow-up operations and searches in the village area to flush out the terrorists holed up in a coastal village. Three boats were also intercepted and 27 people on board detained. As the conflict entered its 28th day, 53 Sulu militants were killed.

On 26 March, security forces patrolling the waters off Sungai Bilis were involved in a gunfight with three Sulu intruders at 7.30am. No one was wounded but a pistol, ammunition and a machete were recovered.

Sabah police commissioner Datuk Hamza Taib said: 'Sweeping and mopping up operations are still continuing and after we have cleared the area, we will move to nearby villages such as Tanjung Labian, Kampung Tanagian and Sungai Bilis,' adding that although Kampung Tanduo had been declared free of intruders, its villagers would be relocated.

The Government had also set up the Eastern Sabah Safety Zone under the Eastern Sabah Security Command (Esscom) to protect 10 districts on the eastern seaboard (see 15 July 2013).

Above: Filipinos protest alleged human rights abuse at a rally outside the Malaysian Embassy in Makati City, the Philippines on 13 March.

Top: Malaysian soldiers fire towards Kampung Tanduo, 8 March.

Tampin railway station demolished

6 February Tampin

The 108-year-old Tampin Railway Station in Malacca was demolished to make way for Keretapi Tanah Melayu Berhad's electrified double-tracking Seremban–Gemas line. Laid in 1903, the 32km railway line from Tampin to Malacca was scrapped to build the Death Railway in Burma (Myanmar) during the Japanese Occupation. It was never rebuilt but the station served as a link for tourists, especially from Singapore. The station was the location for the 1955 P. Ramlee movie *Sarjan Hassan*.

English a compulsory passing subject

7 March Port Dickson

English Language will be made a compulsory subject to pass in the Sijil Pelajaran Malaysia (SPM) as early as 2016.

Deputy Prime Minister Tan Sri Muhyiddin Yassin said the Government was retraining about 61,000 English primary and secondary teachers for this.

RM60.6 billion from 5m tourists in 2012

3 February Kuala Lumpur

Malaysia saw 25,032,708 tourist arrivals in 2012 which yielded RM60.6 billion compared with RM58.3 billion in the previous year. The double-digit growth was largely contributed by Iraq, Nepal, the Philippines, China, Japan, Vietnam, Saudi Arabia and Kazakhstan, besides competitive travel offers and tourism products such as Johor Premium Outlet. CNN Travel has rated Kuala Lumpur as the world's fourth best shopping city.

Malaysian pianist wins BBC award

9 April London

Malaysian concert pianist Foo Mei Yi, winner of the Maria Callas Grand Prix 2008 in Athens, was named 'Best Newcomer' at the prestigious BBC Music Magazine Awards 2013. She received her award at King's Place in central London where she performed three pieces from her album, *Musical Toys*.

The Seremban-born Foo was shortlisted from more than 1,300 entrants whose recordings on discs and DVDs were heard by a jury panel, and *Musical Toys*, on new label Odradek Records, was named the winner.

The album featured Sofia Gubaidulina's *Musical Toys* as well as György Ligeti's *Musica Ricercata* and the world premiere recording of Unsuk Chin's *Six Piano Etudes*.

2013

10 April

The death of Robert Edwards, 87, the father of thousands of 'test-tube babies'. The Nobel Prize for Physiology or Medicine had been awarded him in 2010 in recognition of his work in in-vitro fertilisation.

16 April

EU officials say that nearly five per cent of food products labelled as beef tested throughout the Union had horse meat.

24 April

In Dhaka, Bangladesh, an eight-storey building housing five garment factories collapses. The toll: 1,129 dead. A 19-year-old seamstress is rescued from the ruins after 17 days.

2 May

China's Ministry of Public Security says police busted a criminal gang that had sold more than US$1 million of mutton that was actually rat meat.

13 May

Belize authorities say a construction company destroyed one of the country's largest Mayan pyramids, 2,300 years old, turning it into crushed rock for a road-building project.

Above: Election Commission officials (left) verify voter identification.

Right: A Malaysian voter shows her inked finger.

Dato' Sri Najib Razak and BN party leaders celebrate after winning the election.

Barisan Nasional returned to power

5 May   **Kuala Lumpur**

Barisan Nasional was returned to power in a hotly contested general election that saw a record voter turnout of 80 per cent. Dato' Sri Najib Razak called for national reconciliation after BN won 133 seats out of 222. BN recorded a slightly reduced performance compared to 2008.

'The people's decision showed polarising trends. If they are not addressed, they will cause conflicts in the nation,' Dato' Sri Najib said.

One of the biggest upsets was former Johor Menteri Besar Datuk Abdul Ghani Othman who lost to DAP stalwart Lim Kit Siang in Gelang Patah. In Melaka, former Chief Minister Dato' Seri Mohd Ali Mohd Rustam lost to PKR's Shamsul Iskandar @ Yusre Mohd Akin and in Lembah Pantai, former Federal Territories and Urban Wellbeing Minister Datuk Raja Nong Chik Raja Zainal Abidin lost to Nurul Izzah Anwar.

On 25 June, the Election Commission admitted in Parliament that the indelible ink used to identify those who had voted was in fact food colouring.

Thousands at Kelana Jaya Pakatan rally

8 May   **Petaling Jaya**

Neither the rain nor the traffic congestion deterred the crowd from attending the Pakatan Rakyat rally in Kelana Jaya. They parked their cars elsewhere or were dropped off at the Kelana Jaya LRT station and walked to the stadium near the Subang Airport road to listen to opposition leader Dato' Seri Anwar Ibrahim (inset) and DAP strongman Lim Kit Siang.

Anwar arrived after 10.00pm on a scooter and was greeted with loud roars by the crowd who chanted 'Kami Anak Malaysia'. An estimated 64,000 to 69,000 people, most dressed in black, packed the stands and the football pitch in the stadium. In Marang, Terengganu, thousands crowded Masjid Rusila for another rally.

Najib sworn in as PM

6 May   **Kuala Lumpur**

Dato' Sri Najib Tun Razak took the oath of office as Prime Minister before the Yang di-Pertuan Agong Tuanku Abdul Halim Mu'adzam Shah at Balai Rong Seri, Istana Negara at 4.07pm today. This would be his second term as Prime Minister.

21-year-old flies solo around the world

14 May   **Subang Jaya**

Captain James Anthony Tan, 21, completed a 48-day solo flight around the world and earned himself a place in both the *Guinness Book Of Records* and *Malaysia Book Of Records*.

He is the youngest solo pilot to have circled the globe solo on his Cessna P210 Eagle plane, named 'Spirit Of Malaysia'. He started his 21,103 nautical mile-journey from Langkawi on 28 March as part of the '1Malaysia Around The World' programme.

The son of Tan On Chin and Olive Beverley Tan admitted to some dangerous situations on his journey. He said part of his engine froze when he flew over Alaska and he had difficulty when flying through a storm from Taiwan to Japan.

Coach Harun Rasheed banned for 10 years

24 May   **Kuala Lumpur**

Former national chief coach Harun Rasheed has been banned for 10 years by the Swiss-based Court of Arbitration for Sports (CAS) while six national sprinters who skipped doping tests in 2011 were given suspensions ranging from 18 months to two years.

The decision by CAS overturned the one-year ban handed out by the Malaysian Athletics Federation (MAF) to Harun for telling the athletes to skip the out-of-competition dope tests at the National Sports Institute on 24 May 2011.

Athletes Norjannah Hafiszah Jamaluddin, Nurul Sarah Kadir, Siti Zubaidah Adabi, Yee Yi Leng and Noor Imran Hadi were banned for two years and Siti Fatima Mohamed for 18 months.

Manila–KK route boosts Sabah tourism

11 May   **Kota Kinabalu**

The newly launched Zest Airways' Manila–Kota Kinabalu route will boost tourist arrivals in Malaysia.

Tourism Malaysia Manila director Fazdila Mansor said the initiative was to attract more tourists from the Philippines. 'It comes at a perfect time since we will be celebrating the fourth Visit Malaysia Year in 2014,' she said.

Last year, Malaysia welcomed 508,744 Filipino tourists, 40.5 per cent more than the 362,101 tourists in 2011. Passengers on the inaugural flight included celebrity singer and songwriter Jim Paredes. Zest, the sister airline of AirAsia Philippines, flies to Kota Kinabalu four times a week on Tuesday, Wednesday, Friday and Sunday.

Genneva directors cleared of charges

16 May   **Kuala Lumpur**

The Sessions Court acquitted three directors and a former director of gold investment company Genneva Sdn Bhd of 224 counts of money laundering involving about RM141 million, allegedly committed between July 2008 and June 2009.

Liew Chee Wah, 58, Datuk Ng Poh Weng, 62, Datuk Marcus Yee Yuen Seng, 60, and Datuk Chin Wai Leong, 36, were also acquitted of illegal deposit-taking charges.

Sessions Court judge Datuk Rozana Ali Yusoff ruled that the company's 'buy-back guarantee concept' was not illegal deposit-taking and that the gold trading was genuine.

Bank Negara Malaysia said the Attorney-General's Chambers and Bank Negara were not satisfied with the court decision and would be filing a notice of appeal.

Four to hang for Sosilawati murder

Shah Alam

The High Court found guilty all four accused in the murder of cosmetics millionairess Datuk Sosilawati Lawiya (left) and three others and sentenced them to death by hanging.

Judge Datuk Akhtar Tahir found former lawyer N. Pathmanabhan (picture below, centre) and his three farm hands—T. Thilaiyalagan, 22, R. Matan, 23, and R. Kathavarayan, 33—guilty of murdering Datuk Sosilawati, 47, bank officer Noorhisham Mohamad, 38, lawyer Ahmad Kamil Abdul Karim, 32, and driver Kamaruddin Shansuddin, 44, at Ladang Gadong, Lot 2001 in Jalan Tanjong Layang, Tanjung Sepat, Banting, between 8.30pm and 9.45pm on 30 August 2010.

He found that Pathmanabhan's unethical decision in acting for two opposing sides in a land deal, as well as acquiring interests in the transactions, had led to him being caught in a web of deceit. He said Pathmanabhan had appeared for Datuk Sosilawati as the seller in a land deal, and had also acted for the buyer, Datuk Abdul Rahman Palil, a former assemblyman for Sementa.

A total of 108 prosecution and 30 defence witnesses took the stand and 742 exhibits were tendered as evidence during the course of the two-year-long trial that started on 4 July 2011.

Football clash

29 May **Kuantan**

It was a night of shame for Malaysian football when unruly fans caused the FA Cup semi-final second-leg between Pahang and Johor at the Darul Makmur Stadium in Kuantan to be stopped.

After the 8.45pm kick-off was delayed by several tense incidents and the match declared postponed at 10.30pm, the fans invaded the pitch and clashed with police. They hurled stones and mineral water bottles at Johor fans gathered in the middle of the pitch. The fans also threw firecrackers on the tracks. Forty-two thousand people turned up at the stadium which could only accommodate 35,000.

First woman Speaker

30 May **Klang**

Subang Jaya assemblywoman Hannah Yeoh of DAP was named Speaker of the Selangor State Assembly when the Selangor Government unveiled its new Exco line-up. She made history as the first woman Speaker in the country. Her deputy is Seri Setia assemblyman Nik Nazmi Nik Ahmad from PKR.

Cadets get scholarships to top military academies

5 June **Port Klang**

Three National Defence University cadets were awarded a RM1 million scholarship each for study at prestigious military academies in the US.

Mohamad Aidil Shafiq Abd Aziz, Muzaffar Abdul Halim and Santos J. Jayagopal were accepted to attend degree programmes at the US Military Academy (USMA) in West Point, New York, the US Naval Academy (USNA) in Annapolis, Maryland and the US Air Force Academy (USAFA) in Colorado Springs, Colorado, respectively.

They received their acceptance letters from US Pacific Command chief Admiral Samuel J. Locklear III on board the visiting *USS Blue Ridge*.

Putrajaya worker dies on Everest

5 June **Putrajaya**

Mount Everest claimed its first Malaysian climber. Mohamad Shahrulnizam Ahmad Nazari, an employee of Perbadanan Putrajaya (PPj) died while heading for the Everest base camp. He died from Acute Mountain Sickness (AMS). Mohamad Shahrulnizam was a part of a Sports Club's expedition to Kalapathar and the Everest base camp, along with 13 other employees.

Rescue team members bringing accident victim Tujok Lah's body to the Belaga bazaar jetty.

Boat capsizes in Belaga

28 May **Sarawak**

An overloaded express boat capsized near Tanjong Giam Bungan, about an hour's boat ride from Belaga, claiming one life so far. Police said 12 passengers were still missing.

In the 9.00am incident, 204 passengers boarded express boat *Kawan Mas*, which could carry only 74 passengers. Many passengers were seen sitting on its roof. The boat was heading for Kapit when it struck a boulder and capsized.

Kapit District Council member Daniel Levoh said the passengers could have been workers from Bakun, Murum or Sungai Asap heading back for the Gawai Dayak celebrations this weekend.

Malaysian author wins Scott prize

14 June **Scotland**

Penang-born author Tan Twan Eng won the Walter Scott Prize, which honours historical fiction writers, for his post-World War Two novel, *The Garden Of Evening Mists*.

Tan lives in South Africa. He was the first writer from outside the United Kingdom to win the award, established four years ago.

The Garden Of Evening Mists, set in the Malaysian jungle, is Tan's second novel.

Haze claims two victims

26 June **Muar**

Yu Sheng Ye, 62, is believed to be the second person to die of haze-related complications in two days. The first was asthmatic housewife Li Cai Lin, 51, who died at the Muar Hospital on Monday, after a stroke which a doctor said could have been caused by an asthma attack triggered by the haze.

On 24 June, Indonesian President Susilo Bambang Yudhoyono apologised to Singapore and Malaysia over the haze caused by forest fires in Sumatra. Muar's air pollutant index (API) hit 750 and two towns in the State of Malacca recorded levels higher than 300.

Putrajaya warned Malaysian-owned companies in Indonesia to ensure they did not contribute to the haze. Senior Indonesian Minister Agung Laksono claimed Malaysian palm oil investors might be responsible for the forest fires.

Colours of 1Malaysia

2 June **Kuala Lumpur**

More than 100,000 locals and foreigners swarmed Dataran Merdeka for the annual Citrawarna 1Malaysia (Colours of 1Malaysia) festivities.

This year's event, themed 'Visit Malaysia Year 2014—Celebrating 1Malaysia Truly Asia', started with a colourful parade where participants marched from Jalan Raja through Jalan Raja Laut and Jalan Isfahan to Jalan Tuanku Abdul Rahman.

There were 15 segments featuring dazzling floats and multicultural dances, all highlighting eco-tourism, sports tourism and the diverse communities. A total of 500 drummers captivated the audience during the Gegaran Gendang Citrawarna 1Malaysia with their energetic performance. The event ended with a fireworks display and a *joget lambak* dance participated by everyone, including the tourists.

2013

6 June

The *Washington Post* reports that the National Security Agency and the FBI, running a classified anti-terrorism programme codenamed PRISM, tapped into the central servers of Microsoft, Yahoo, Google, Facebook, Skype, YouTube and Apple, mining e-mails, photos and documents.

16 July

Two weeks after the Egyptian army seized power from President Mohamad Morsi, Egypt has an interim cabinet without a single representative from either of the two main Islamist groups, the Muslim Brotherhood and Nour. These two parties had, since 2011, won two parliamentary elections, a presidential vote and two constitutional referendums.

16 August

Both sides in the two-year civil war in Syria have accused each other of being responsible for the use of sarin gas from which more than 1,400 people died.

Double mishaps

Four killed in Second Penang Bridge collapse

6 June Georgetown ▶ An uncompleted flyover connecting to the still-under-construction Second Penang Bridge at Batu Maung collapsed at 7.00pm, burying at least one car and a motorcycle. Four people were feared dead.

State Fire and Rescue Department confirmed that a motorcyclist trapped under the debris had been pulled out. At 11.30pm, there were three injuries reported, comprising two foreign workers and a woman who injured her hand after debris flew and crashed on her car.

The Department of Safety and Health (DOSH) said the collapse could be due to procedural and technical negligence by the contractor.

Freak storm wreaks havoc

13 June Georgetown ▶ A storm at 7.00pm blew off a lightning arrester and a chunk of concrete from the Umno building in Macalister Road, and sent it crashing to the street below. It crashed onto some vehicles and injured several motorists who were sent to hospital for treatment. The co-driver of a lorry, an Indian national, died of head injuries.

Meanwhile, hawker Lim Chin Aik, 44, was believed to be buried with his car in the incident when the excavation team recovered parts of a Honda City with a chassis number that matched Lim's car. The search for Lim was called off after four days and his family conducted a simple funeral ceremony for him on 24 June.

Blackout in Sarawak

27 June Kuching

Most of Sarawak experienced a power blackout this evening because of tripped circuits at the Kemena–Bintulu transmission line at 5.40pm.

The blackout caused traffic congestion stretching more than two kilometres at the Jalan Satok flyover, Jalan Tun Abang Openg junction and other roads because the traffic lights were affected.

Sarawak Energy Berhad (SEB) activated its Blackout Restoration Plan to start up all the power generation plants and its engineers and technicians worked to restore power.

Electricity was restored in certain areas of Kuching, including Poh Kwong Park and Matang, by 6.30pm. The state grid was re-established at 11.30pm.

92-year-old ex-cop gets hero's parade

2 July Sungai Siput

Former police Sgt Arthur Albert Walter, 92, was given a hero's parade and honoured in the presence of the Regent of Perak Raja Dr Nazrin Shah and Inspector General of Police Tan Sri Khalid Abu Bakar.

Wearing an old police uniform, he was driven in a vintage car accompanied by policemen to meet Raja Nazrin on stage.

Walter served at the Sungai Siput Police Station in 1948, and killed communists during the Emergency. He later became a rubber planter and settled here.

Walter died less than two months after the parade, on 28 August.

Nicol wins third World Games gold

4 August Cali, Columbia

World No. 1 Nicol David dispatched Holland's Natalie Grinham to win her third consecutive World Games gold medal at Cali, Colombia. The Penangite was too good for the 35-year-old Grinham, winning 11–6, 11–9, 11–8.

In a rematch of the 2009 final in Kaohsiung, Taiwan, Nicol and Grinham were evenly matched in the first set tied at 4–4 before the former as usual stepped it up to take the set. The seven-time world champion then demonstrated her superior fitness to pick up everything Grinham threw at her before romping home for the gold.

Malaysian squash queen Nicol David celebrates after winning the gold medal in the World Games at Cali, Colombia.

Battersea project on

4 July London

Work has begun on the £8 billion (RM39 billion) Battersea Power Station redevelopment, marking the involvement of Malaysian companies in the single largest property project by value in Europe. Sime Darby Bhd, SP Setia Bhd and the Employees Provident Fund set up a consortium, called Battersea Power Station Holding Co., to undertake the project which will change the area's landscape.

Mayor of London Boris Johnson, British Prime Minister David Cameron and Dato' Sri Najib Razak discuss the project against the backdrop of Battersea Power Station.

IGP 'responsible for Kugan's death'

26 June Kuala Lumpur

The Kuala Lumpur High Court ruled that Inspector General of Police Tan Sri Khalid Abu Bakar was responsible for the death of detainee A. Kugan who was tortured during interrogation by police four years ago. Tan Sri Khalid was then the Selangor police chief. Judge Datuk V.T. Singham awarded RM801,700 to Kugan's mother, N. Indra.

Sulu intruders charged in court

15 July Tawau

Thirty people were charged in the High Court in Tawau with various offences in connection with the intrusion incident in Lahad Datu in February which had escalated into an all-out military operation by Malaysian security forces. The accused include a nephew of Jamalul Kiram III, the self-styled Sulu Sultan. The charges are waging war against the King and being members of a terrorist group.

No to Shia, shisha and beauty contests

20 July Alor Star

The Kedah Government gazetted the National Fatwa Council's ruling in 1996 that Shia teachings are deviant. This means State religious authorities will be empowered to act against anyone or any organisation preaching Shia teachings.

Meanwhile, the National Council for Islamic Affairs issued an edict that shisha or water-pipe smoking is haram (forbidden) as it is detrimental to health. Malacca and Kelantan were the first to ban the sale of shisha in 2011.

In Kuala Lumpur, four Muslim women selected for the Miss Malaysia/World 2013 finals were disqualified from competing. Official pageant licensee Datuk Anna Lim said this was in line with Federal Territory mufti Datuk Wan Zahidi Wan Teh's instructions that Muslim women were prohibited from beauty pageants.

RM65m spent to bring back talent

18 July Kuala Lumpur

The Government spent RM65 million to persuade Malaysians abroad to return and work via its Talent Corporation programmes, including the Returning Expert Programme (REP), said Minister in the Prime Minister's Department Dato' Seri Abdul Wahid Omar.

He said 2,105 applications had been approved up to June. Most of the applicants were aged 30 and above, with 75 percent being males. Chinese made up 60 percent of the applicants, followed by Bumiputeras (30 percent).

Court nullifies conversion of three minors by father

25 July Ipoh

In a landmark decision, the High Court yesterday nullified the conversion of three minors by their Muslim convert father. Judicial commissioner Lee Swee Seng said the conversions of Tevi Darsiny, 16, Karan Dinish, 15, and Prasana Diksa, 5, were unlawful.

Mohd Ridzuan Abdullah (previously K. Patmanathan) converted them in April 2009. Their mother, M. Indira Gandhi, then filed an application the same year to seek the nullification of the conversion on the basis that the conversions contravened the Administration of the Religion of Islam (Perak) Enactment 2004 and other laws.

Palace stormed

5 August Kuala Lumpur

Ten members of cult group Kumpulan Panji Hitam (Black Flag Group) tried to storm Istana Negara at 4.10am but were apprehended, including the 40-year-old group leader from Kedah, his wife and their daughter. It was learnt that they had gone to the palace to 'replace' the Yang di-Pertuan Agong as they claimed their leader was the rightful heir to the throne.

City CID chief Datuk Ku Chin Wah said: 'The claim is ridiculous. Documents seized showed that they belonged to a kingdom in the Philippines.' The group were to be charged with waging or attempting to wage war or abetting the waging of war against the Yang di-Pertuan Agong.

Former bank MD shot dead

29 July Kuala Lumpur

Hussain Ahmad Najadi, the first managing director and CEO of Arab-Malaysian Development Bank, was shot dead in Lorong Ceylon, near the bank's headquarters. Hussain, 75, who held an Iranian passport, and his wife, Cheong Mei Kuen, 49, were walking out of the Ceylon Kuan Tin Chinese temple when a man walked up to Hussain and fired multiple shots at him. He died on the spot. Cheong was injured.

Resort surau used for Buddhist chanting

12 August Kota Tinggi

The operator of Tanjung Sutera Resort was arrested for allowing a group of Singaporean Buddhists to use its surau for religious chants. Two police reports were lodged after a video showed a group of 14 Buddhist devotees and a monk chanting. On 27 August, the surau was demolished (picture).

37 die in bus crash

21 August Genting Highlands

Thirty-seven people died when a bus plunged 20m into a ravine while travelling from Genting Highlands to Kuala Lumpur in one of the country's worst bus crashes in recent years.

Bentong OCPD Supt Mohd Mansor Mohd Nor said 160 police personnel combed the site for missing victims and their belongings. Investigations by Puspakom, chemists and forensics teams were ongoing at the site.

Of the 16 injured, six were in critical condition at Kuala Lumpur Hospital. Survivors said the driver was negotiating a sharp bend at Km3.5 Jalan Genting when he lost control of the bus.

Emergency services attend the scene of the accident.

Launch of Suprima hatchback

31 August Kuala Lumpur

Former prime minister Tun Dr Mahathir Mohamad launched Proton's latest model, the Suprima S hatchback. The car is available in two variants, Executive and Premium. Both models share the same engine derived from the Preve Premium variant, which is a turbocharged 1.6-litre CamPro engine.

Power is transmitted to the road via a seven-speed Punch VT3 CVT transmission. Balancing power and performance, the powertrain package enables the Suprima S to sprint from zero to 100km/h in just 9.9 seconds, with a combined fuel consumption rate of 9.1 litres/100km.

Azilah, Sirul acquitted of murder

23 August Putrajaya

The two policemen who were earlier found guilty of murdering Mongolian national Altantuya Shaariibuu at Mukim Bukit Raja in Shah Alam in 2006 and sentenced to death, were freed after the Court of Appeal overturned the High Court's decision. Azilah, 37, and Sirul, 42, were accordingly acquitted and discharged.

The three-member bench, led by Dato' Seri Mohamed Apandi Ali, unanimously allowed Chief Inspector Azilah Hadri and Corporal Sirul Azhar Umar's appeal against the conviction by the High Court.

Attorney-General Tan Sri Abdul Gani Patail said that while he respected the Court of Appeal, the prosecution was dissatisfied with the decision and would file an appeal with the Federal Court.

Cinemas to play Negaraku

28 August Kuala Lumpur

The national anthem *Negaraku* would be played in 123 cinemas nationwide before the start of all movies for one week. Communications and Multimedia Minister Dato' Seri Ahmad Shabery Cheek said the move was to promote patriotism in the run-up to the country's 56th National Day.

Two promotional video clips on Merdeka, *Pesanan Terakhir* and *Tanah Tumpahnya Darahku*, would be screened, along with the national anthem, by five cinema operators, namely GSC, MBO Cinemas TGV Cinemas, Lotus Five Star and Cathay Cineplexes.

Obituaries

29 Jan	**Datuk Eddy Choong**, 82, badminton superstar.
4 Feb	**Wilfred Gomez Malong**, 64, Sarawak wartime hero and youngest recipient of the Pingat Gagah Berani.
25 March	**Alan Zachariah**, 71, legendary RTM radio announcer.
8 May	Tan Sri Lim Phaik Gan (**P.G. Lim**), 96, pioneer woman ambassador and early female lawyer.
5 June	**S. Shamsuddin**, 84, veteran comedian and film star.
10 June	**Latifah Omar**, 74, veteran actress.
2 July	**Professor Tan Sri Awang Had Salleh**, 79, academician.
25 July	**Datin Umi Kalthum**, 80, veteran actress.
1 Aug	**Chua Boon Huat**, 33, national hockey player.
7 Sept	**Maimon Mutalib**, 55, film and drama actress.
16 Sept	**Chin Peng** (Ong Boon Hua), 88, former leader of the Malayan Communist Party.

Celebrating Malaysia

Clockwise from above: Soldiers of the 13th Battalion of the Royal Malay Regiment carrying the Malaysian flag march past assembled dignitaries in Kuching; the Yang di-Pertuan Agong accompanied by the Chief Minister of Sarawak in Kuching; in Sabah, the Prime Minister, Deputy Prime Minister and Chief Minister of Sabah are welcomed by large crowds in Kota Kinabalu.

Nighttime revelry

Fireworks illuminate the Sarawak State Assembly Building during the river pageant on the eve of Malaysia Day. Below: the flotilla passes the Astana.

15 September Kuching

The Sarawak State capital hosted a river pageant on the eve of Malaysia Day. The Yang di-Pertuan Agong joined thousands of people along the popular waterfront on the banks of the Sarawak River to witness the spectacle. Falling rain failed to dampen the crowd's spirit.

50 years of solidarity

16 September Kuching and Kota Kinabalu

This year the official national-level celebration of Malaysia Day took place in Kuching and Kota Kinabalu. Prime Minister Dato' Sri Najib Razak attended both events on the same day.

Harmony in Sarawak, prosperity for all

More than 20,000 people attended the parade held in conjunction with the 50th anniversary of Malaysia Day in Kuching. The event capped a series of Golden Jubilee events in Sarawak with the theme *Sarawak Harmoni, Kemakmuran Dinikmati* (Harmony in Sarawak, Prosperity for all).

At 8am six cannons at the historic city's Padang Merdeka were fired to mark the start of the parade. The Yang di-Pertuan Agong, Tuanku Abdul Halim Mu'adzam Shah, accompanied by Raja Permaisuri Agong Tuanku Hajah Haminah formally launched the ceremony and inspected the guard of honour mounted

> *That decision made 50 years ago was very apt and that is why we are witnessing this joyous and meaningful celebration today.*
>
> Prime Minister Dato' Sri Najib Tun Razak, Kuching, 16 September 2013.

by the 13th Battalion of the Royal Malay Regiment. Also present were Prime Minister Dato' Sri Najib Razak, his deputy Tan Sri Muhyiddin Yassin and Sarawak Chief Minister Tan Sri Abdul Taib Mahmud.

Dato' Sri Najib and Tan Sri Taib gave speeches and a special video, which included archival footage of the proclamation of Malaysia that took place on the same padang 50 years before, was shown on a huge LED screen. This was followed by the parade itself involving 10,000 people including students, civil servants, car enthusiast clubs and uniformed bodies. A highlight of the nearly three-hour parade was the low-altitude flypast by Sukhoi SU-30 and BAE Hawk jet fighters.

Joining in the festivities in Kota Kinabalu were (clockwise from top left) Bajau horse riders from Kota Belud dressed in traditional outfits, flag-waving children, members of the Orang Ulu community, Unduk Ngadau beauty queens from the Kadazandusun and Murut communities, and members of the Rungus community.

Sabah: 50 years of development in Malaysia

Later in the day, Dato' Sri Najib launched Sabah's 50th Independence in Malaysia celebration at the Prince Philip Park at Tanjung Aru. The event was also attended by Tan Sri Muhyiddin and Sabah Chief Minister Dato' Seri Musa Aman.

Addressing the crowd at the coastal location, he said that Sabah had enjoyed tremendous progress over the past 50 years as could be seen from the construction of roads in the State from just 1,500 kilometres to more than 21,000 kilometres in 2013. The crowd, which began gathering as early as 4pm, sang patriotic songs and was entertained with traditional performances and a showcase of five traditional houses which reflected the State's various communities.

During the event, Dato' Sri Najib launched the Tanjung Aru Eco Development project which will give the once iconic beach a major facelift.

Meanwhile in Kuala Lumpur

While the nation's official Malaysia Day celebrations took place in Sabah and Sarawak, Kuala Lumpur played host to a two-hour Asia Harley Days parade in conjunction with motorcycle company Harley-Davdison Inc.'s 110th anniversary celebrations. The parade was part of a week-long event organised by Tourism Malaysia, the Malaysian Convention & Exhibition Bureau (MyCEB) and Harley-Davidson. It was the first of its kind in Southeast Asia and hundreds of 'buddies' joined in.

Bill Davidson (centre), great-grandson of Harley-Davidson co-founder William A. Davidson, poses with fans during the bike parade in the heart of the city.

Lest we forget

On 16 September 1963, Tunku Abdul Rahman spoke the following words:

Now finally, the peoples of Malaysia are celebrating the establishment of Malaysia. This is the time to think earnestly and hopefully on the future of Malaysia as the whole country resounds with joy.

So I pray that God may bless the nation of Malaysia with eternal peace and happiness for our people.

The Federation of Malaya now passes into history. Let us always remember that the Malayan Nation was formed after many difficulties during a long period of national Emergency, yet its multi-racial society emerged, endured and survived as a successful and progressive nation, a true democracy and an example to the world of harmony and tolerance.

As it was with Malaya, so it can be with Malaysia. With trust in Almighty God, unity of purpose and faith in ourselves, we can make Malaysia a land of prosperity and peace.

In doing so, let every Malaysian in all the States of Malaya, Singapore, Sarawak and Sabah ensure that our Malaysia is truly worthy of the aims and hopes we have shared, the trials and stress we have endured, in working together to achieve our common destiny.

MERDEKA! MALAYSIA!

MALAYSIA BY NUMBERS 1963–2013

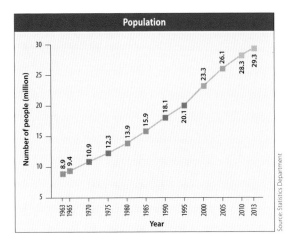

Population

Number of people (million) vs Year

8.9, 9.4, 10.9, 12.3, 13.9, 15.9, 18.1, 20.1, 23.3, 26.1, 28.3, 29.3

Years: 1963, 1965, 1970, 1975, 1980, 1985, 1990, 1995, 2000, 2005, 2010, 2013

Source: Statistics Department

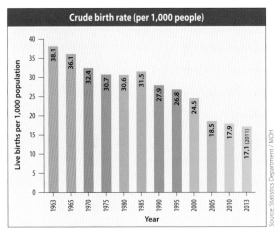

Crude birth rate (per 1,000 people)

Live births per 1,000 population vs Year

38.1, 36.1, 32.4, 30.7, 30.6, 31.5, 27.9, 26.8, 24.5, 18.5, 17.9, 17.1 (2011)

Years: 1963, 1965, 1970, 1975, 1980, 1985, 1990, 1995, 2000, 2005, 2010, 2013

Source: Statistics Department / MOH

Health Indicators

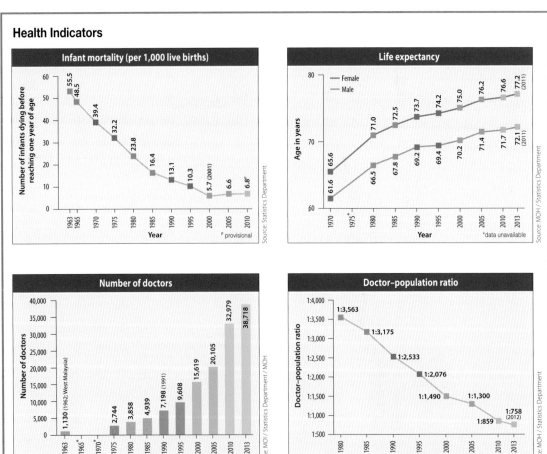

Infant mortality (per 1,000 live births)

Number of infants dying before reaching one year of age

55.5, 48.5, 39.4, 32.2, 23.8, 16.4, 13.1, 10.3, 5.7 (2001), 6.6, 6.8ᵖ

ᵖ provisional

Source: Statistics Department

Life expectancy (Age in years)

Female: 65.6, 71.0, 72.5, 73.7, 74.2, 75.0, 76.2, 76.6, 77.2 (2011)
Male: 61.6, 66.5, 67.8, 69.2, 69.4, 70.2, 71.4, 71.7, 72.1 (2011)

*data unavailable

Source: MOH / Statistics Department

Number of doctors

1,130 (1962: West Malaysia), *, *, 2,744, 3,858, 4,939, 7,198 (1991), 9,608, 15,619, 20,105, 32,979, 38,718

*data unavailable

Source: MOH / Statistics Department / MOH

Doctor–population ratio

1:3,563, 1:3,175, 1:2,533, 1:2,076, 1:1,490, 1:1,300, 1:859, 1:758 (2012)

Source: MOH / Statistics Department

Economic Indicators

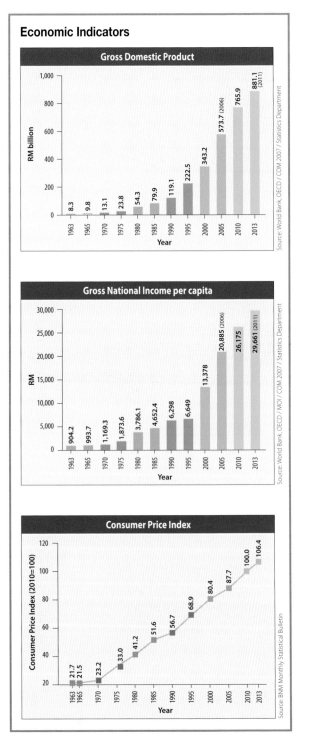

Gross Domestic Product (RM billion)

8.3, 9.8, 13.1, 23.8, 54.3, 79.9, 119.1, 222.5, 343.2, 573.7 (2006), 765.9, 881.1 (2011)

Source: World Bank, OECD / COM 2007 / Statistics Department

Gross National Income per capita (RM)

904.2, 993.7, 1,169.3, 1,873.6, 3,786.1, 4,652.4, 6,298, 6,649, 13,378, 20,885 (2006), 26,175, 29,661 (2011)

Source: World Bank, OECD / MOH / COM 2007 / Statistics Department

Consumer Price Index (2010=100)

21.7, 21.5, 23.2, 33.0, 41.2, 51.6, 56.7, 68.9, 80.4, 87.7, 100.0, 106.4

Source: BNM Monthly Statistical Bulletin

Transport Indicators

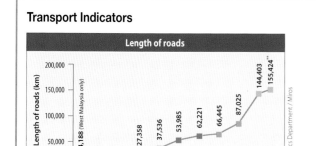

Length of roads

Length of roads (km) — Year

14,188 (West Malaysia only), 27,358, 37,536, 53,985, 62,221, 66,445, 87,025, 144,403, 155,424**

Years: 1965, 1970*, 1975*, 1980, 1985, 1990, 1995, 2000, 2005, 2010, 2013

*data unavailable **2012 estimate

Source: MOI / Statistics Department / Miros

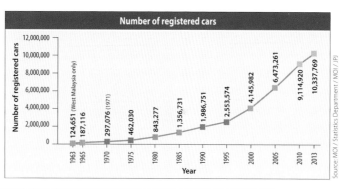

Number of registered cars

Number of registered cars — Year

124,651 (West Malaysia only), 187,116, 297,076 (1971), 462,030, 843,277, 1,356,731, 1,986,751, 2,553,574, 4,145,982, 6,473,261, 9,114,920, 10,337,769

Years: 1963, 1965, 1970, 1975, 1980, 1985, 1990, 1995, 2000, 2005, 2010, 2013

Source: MOI / Statistics Department / MOI / JPJ

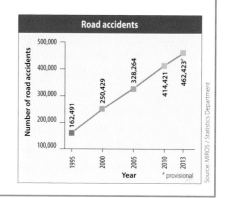

Road accidents

Number of road accidents — Year

162,491, 250,429, 328,264, 414,421, 462,423ᴾ

Years: 1995, 2000, 2005, 2010, 2013

ᴾ provisional

Source: MIROS / Statistics Department

Education Indicators

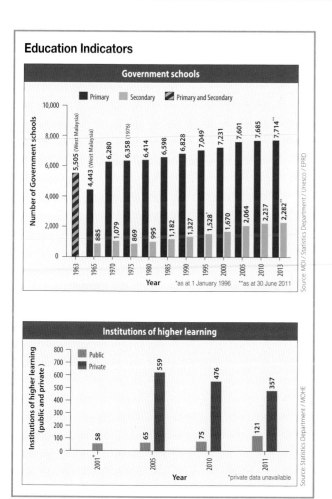

Government schools

Legend: ■ Primary ■ Secondary ▨ Primary and Secondary

Number of Government schools — Year

Year	Primary	Secondary
1963	5,505 (West Malaysia) Primary and Secondary	
1965	4,443 (West Malaysia)	885
1970	6,280	1,079
1975	6,358 (1976)	869
1980	6,414	995
1985	6,598	1,182
1990	6,828	1,327
1995	7,049*	1,528*
2000	7,231	1,670
2005	7,601	2,064
2010	7,685	2,237
2013	7,714**	2,282*

*as at 1 January 1996 **as at 30 June 2011

Source: MOI / Statistics Department / Unesco / EPRD

Institutions of higher learning

Legend: ■ Public ■ Private

Institutions of higher learning (public and private) — Year

Year	Public	Private
2001*	58	—
2005	65	559
2010	75	476
2011	121	357

*private data unavailable

Source: Statistics Department / MOHE

Technology Indicators

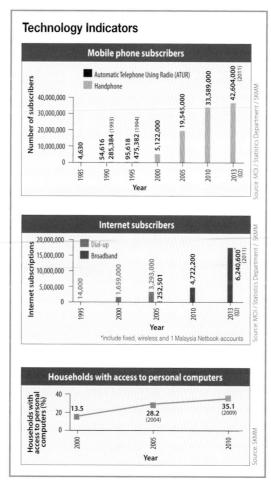

Mobile phone subscribers

Legend: ■ Automatic Telephone Using Radio (ATUR) ■ Handphone

Number of subscribers — Year

4,630, 54,616 (1993), 285,384 (1993), 95,618 (1994), 475,382 (1994), 5,122,000, 19,545,000, 33,589,000, 42,604,000 (2011)

Years: 1985, 1990, 1995, 2000, 2005, 2010, 2013 (Q2)

Source: MOI / Statistics Department / SKMM

Internet subscribers

Legend: ■ Dial-up ■ Broadband

Internet subscriptions — Year

14,000, 1,659,000, 3,293,000, 252,501, 4,722,200, 6,240,600* (2011)

Years: 1995, 2000, 2005, 2010, 2013 (Q2)

*include fixed, wireless and 1 Malaysia Netbook accounts

Source: MOI / Statistics Department / SKMM

Households with access to personal computers

Households with access to personal computers (%) — Year

13.5, 28.2 (2004), 35.1 (2009)

Years: 2000, 2005, 2010

Source: SKMM

Tourists

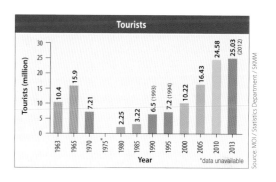

Tourists (million) — Year

10.4, 15.9, 7.21, 2.25, 3.22, 6.5 (1993), 7.2 (1994), 10.22, 16.43, 24.58, 25.03 (2012)

Years: 1963, 1965, 1970, 1975*, 1980, 1985, 1990, 1995, 2000, 2005, 2010, 2013

*data unavailable

Source: MOI / Statistics Department / SKMM

Top 3 exports

	No.1 export	No. 2 export	No. 3 export
1962	Rubber ($1,374m)	Tin and tin ore ($642m)	Iron ore ($176m)
1964	Rubber ($1,303m)	Tin and tin ore ($728m)	Iron ore ($163m)
1970ᴾ	Rubber ($1,663m)	Tin and tin ore ($1,013m)	Iron ore ($246m)
1980	Rubber ($4,618m)	Timber ($2,616.2m)	Palm oil ($2,515.3m)
1985	Petroleum crude ($8,823m)	Manufactures ($4,505.7m)	Rubber ($2,871.4m)
1990	Manufactures (RM46,654m)	Crude petroleum (RM10,190m)	Palm oil (RM4,312m)
1995	Manufactures (RM143,466m)	Sawlogs and sawn timber (RM7,400m)	Palm oil (RM7,205m)
2001	Electrical and electronic products (RM189.49b)	Palm oil and palm-oil based products (RM15.08b)	Timber and timber-based products (RM14.53b)
2006	Electrical and electronic products (RM281.02b)	Palm oil and palm-oil based products (RM32.17b)	Crude petroleum (RM14.53b)
2010	Electrical and electronic products (RM249.8b)	Palm oil and palm-oil based products (RM65.85b)	Liquefied natural gases (RM38.1b)
2011	Electrical and electronic products (RM236.54b)	Palm oil and palm-oil based products (RM83.40b)	Liquefied natural gases (RM49.96b)

ᴾ provisional

Source: MOI / Statistics Department

A MULTITUDE OF SOVEREIGNTIES

By Rehman Rashid

THE NAME will probably remain the same. Fifty years from now, there ought to be no reason why the Federation of Malaysia shouldn't still be our prime identifier at the United Nations. Just as there's no reason not to expect the United Nations still to exist by then. However, for both entities—as for the entire world—the reasons for existence will have changed.

The 20th century dawned with half-a-dozen imperial powers defining the world; the 21st with 200 nations defining themselves. (Tot up all the secessionist, separatist and independence movements extant today and there are some 2,000 more waiting their turn, with varying degrees of impatience.) Malaysia was and remains part of this grand explosion of sovereignties, at once spreading to encompass the globe while contracting to the smallest tribe. Such has been the empowerment of three generations of democracy and the technology-driven global sociopolitics it has enabled, which in turn nurtured it into the expansive Overmind it has become.

Perhaps it is natural for viral globalisation to catalyse a return to tribalism among those suffering corrosive effects on their identities. Equalities of opportunity reveal inequalities of ability; meritocracies alienate the mediocre; level playing fields don't work for the unequally endowed. Democracy, in all its brutish, brawling honesty, reveals truths about our societies that give the lie to our most cherished myths.

So be it. Indeed, so must it be. Nationalism was a cradle; an incubator in the intensive care unit of a shattered world. In just 50 years, mankind has so far assembled (or reassembled) 200 nations out of the rubble of empires; one of them this one. It helped the world get going again. Now, three generations on, the world wants to get somewhere, and so do we.

The wonderful irony is that what exercises our populations today is what our fledgling nations agreed were the inviolable principles of their founding and cooperation half-a-century ago: independence, sovereignty, self-determination, and 'non-interference in each other's internal affairs'. The difference is, the Bandung Conference of 1955 was a convivial and hopeful event. Today, those same principles, no longer constrained within national constructs administered by professional diplomats and their technocracies, are convulsing the planet. Conflict, whether or not amounting to war, has become Clausewitz's 'continuation of politics by other means'.

There will still be an Asean in 50 years, just as there will still be a Malaysia. Asean will probably still be a consortium of ten nations (perhaps 11, with Timor Leste), and Malaysia still a federation of 13 States, plus Federal Territories. But the internal sociocultural landscapes of the region will have shifted—and, as always, Malaysia will be the very pivot of that shift, and the fulcrum of whatever new balance emerges thereafter. This is perceptible now; in another three generations it will be an obvious fact of life for the billion or more human beings by then inhabiting archipelagic and continental Southeast Asia.

Our 'shadow nations' have always existed, of course, tacitly known, understood and accepted as an unspoken element within our various national unities. Long hidden beneath the maps drawn by empires, they are ancient, rooted, and real. Their populations, too, have grown to critical mass. In the north of Peninsular Malaysia, it is possible to see an 'Islamic' polity stretching from the South China Sea across the Straits of Malacca to northern Sumatra and up to the southern provinces of Thailand—the region discreetly administered for the past 20 years as the 'Indonesia–Malaysia–Thailand Growth Triangle'.

Sabah and Sarawak, on their part, are establishing their own third-generation identities—both of them as different from each other as from the peninsula. If history's wry eye for irony doesn't blink, it may be that by 2063 the implementation of the '20 Points' (or thereabouts) of our two Bornean states' federation agreements will not be an issue.

Whether from those original blueprints or with entirely new drafts, both of Malaysia's Bornean states will have the ability, as well as the obligation, to address their unique needs. Their first half-century under Malaysia has not been without challenges, as the priorities of federalism supplanted the socioeconomic autonomy both states had expected on merger with the peninsula. There's little doubt now, as their federation turns 50, that both states have reached the turning point enabling the self-awareness critical for self-assertion.

Meanwhile, the former Straits Settlements of Penang and Malacca, along with the former colonial capitals of the peninsula, are also returning to less overtly 'Malay' and more multiracial administrations, in accordance with their demographics. The principle of never measuring nations by their commercial capitals will grow ever more obvious, as Malaysia's rural heartland becomes more of a familiar sanctuary for those alienated by the freewheeling modern liberalism of the urban centres.

In the first 50 years of nationhood, the shadows at the edge of town offered refuge to the immobile. In the second, those shadows will recede to vanishingly distant peripheries. The 80:20 rural/urban ratio at the time of Malaysia's birth had reversed to 20:80 by the advent of the third generation—with one cardinal difference. Where the first decades of nationhood had galvanised the phenomenon of 'urban drift', with the cities expanding exponentially on the influx of human capital from the hinterland, now the trend has slowed, even reversed, as those first movers retire to their hometowns to live out their dotage.

In the process, those hometowns are transformed as much as those people themselves were by their lives in the city. Today, rural villages boast satellite dishes, multi-vehicle households and a mature political consciousness, along with the expansive modern communications and transport infrastructure to maintain their vital connections with the wider world. The countryside offers the solace of Malaysia's equable climate and quality of life, but the huddled ignorance and isolation of yore is gone. In another 50 years, it will hardly be remembered.

The heartland is also being vitalised by the lower rungs of the nation's economic ladder now being occupied almost entirely by foreign workers from Indonesia, Bangladesh, Myanmar, Vietnam, Cambodia and the Philippines. Indeed, this will likely be the most significant demographic change in the next 50 years—dynamic, driven and ambitious communities powering the nation's agricultural base, transforming that sector from the 'green rut of poverty' it used to be into a launchpad for upward socioeconomic mobility.

Immigrant workers in 2013 constitute more than a tenth of Malaysia's resident population and are here as much for the long term as their predecessors were a century ago, auguring within 50 years as vital a bond with their countries of origin as our earlier immigrant communities ensured with China and India.

Many view with foreboding this infiltration of energetic and determined new generations of immigrants, and indeed major adjustments will be needed. But this nation was built partly on immigrants and their communities, they were founding partners in our national contract, and they offer now as they did then a broad, stable and (for now) apolitical base for our economy's human capital resources.

What's more, their prospects as future Malaysians must be enfolded into the grand sweep of geopolitical change already well upon our world. With the emergence of China and India as great powers and the repercussions of that on Asean's regional dynamics, fears of the impending changes to Malaysia's own populace will need to be ameliorated by a greater political maturity and economic cohesion among the 10 (or 11) nations of Asean. As with Europe before it, the region may find that such maturation will offer both a measure of political security and the economic integrity to enable it. Despite the vast expansion of commingled demographics that will surely characterise the next 50 years, Asean's founding ethos of 'consultation, compromise and consensus' will still be applicable.

These trends are ineluctable. Some form of Malaysia's party-political system will almost certainly survive, for survival is the greatest challenge for politicians. It will have to accommodate these changes, though. For a new day to dawn over our Parliament, perhaps some parties will have to call it a night. It need not matter, notwithstanding whatever ruckus they may kick up on exit. Having abided by our communal identities for so long—having accepted and accommodated our different languages, educational conventions, cultural norms and religious imperatives for three generations—we may now have to live with them forever.

Which isn't that awful a prospect. It's the way we've always been, after all. We've become reasonably adept at conflict management. Harmony is a cherished myth, too noble to disdain. But there is dynamism in conflict—in 'equalities of inequity'—and it can be harnessed. After tripling our population and increasing gross domestic product a hundredfold in 50 years through ten Five-Year Plans and 13 general elections, if we know nothing else, we know how to do Malaysia.

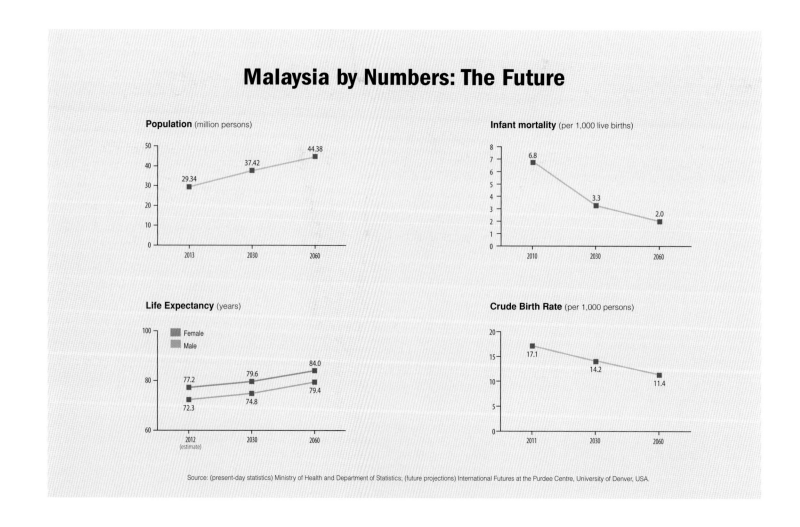

Malaysia by Numbers: The Future

Population (million persons)

50
40 — 44.38
30 — 37.42
29.34
2013   2030   2060

Infant mortality (per 1,000 live births)

8
7 — 6.8
6
5
4 — 3.3
3
2 — 2.0
2010   2030   2060

Life Expectancy (years)

■ Female
■ Male

100
84.0
80 — 77.2   79.6   79.4
72.3   74.8
60
2012   2030   2060
(estimate)

Crude Birth Rate (per 1,000 persons)

20
17.1
15 — 14.2
11.4
10
5
0
2011   2030   2060

Source: (present-day statistics) Ministry of Health and Department of Statistics; (future projections) International Futures at the Purdee Centre, University of Denver, USA.

MAP OF MALAYSIA

Locations marked are those referred to in news stories in *Chronicle of Malaysia*.

Klang Valley

Selangor

Key
Highways

Kuching

Key
Roads

Key

- ■ Federal Territories
- ■ State capitals
- ● Towns/suburbs
- International borders
- State borders

- North–South Expressway
- Pan Borneo Expressway
- Highways
- Rivers
- Lakes

0   300 km

Central Kuala Lumpur

Kuala Lumpur Hospital

Jalan Tun Razak
(*Jalan Pekeliling/Circular Road*)

Putra World Trade Centre (PWTC)

Gombak River

Kampung Baru

Jalan Sultan Ismail
(*Jalan Treacher*)

Jalan Dang Wangi
(*Jalan Campbell*)

Jalan Ampang

Tabung Haji

Dataran Merdeka

AIA building

Parliament House

Selangor Club

Bangunan Sultan Abdul Samad
(*Secretariat building*)

Petronas Twin Towers

National Monument

Central Market

Maybank

Jalan Raja Chulan
(*Weld Road*)

National Mosque

Dayabumi

Jalan Tun Perak
(*Jalan Mounbatten*)

Stadium Negara

National Museum

Merdeka Stadium

Bangsar

Jalan Tun Tan Cheng Lock
(*Jalan Foch*)

Key

■ Buildings

Roads

Jalan Travers
(*Travers Road*)

Klang River

KL Sentral

Brickfields

Istana Negara (2011)

Sulu Sea

Kota Belud

Erb West oil field

Tuaran

Gulisan Island

Bakkungan Island

Selingan Island

Kota Kinabalu
(*Jesselton*)

Kinarut

Ranau

Sandakan

Beluran

Sabah

Kinabatangan River

LABUAN ■

Keningau

Kampung Tanduo

Spitang

Tenom

Lahad Datu

Gunung Rara Forest Reserve

Kunak

Semporna

Maliau Village

Pandanan Island

BRUNEI

Tawau

Sipadan Island

Tanjong Giam Bungan

Limbang

Ligatan Island

Miri

Mulu

Bakelalan

Sulawesi Sea

Baram River

Gunung Murud

South China Sea

Bario

Niah

Bintulu

Belaga

Bakun

Mukah

Dalat

Selangau

Sarawak

Sibu

Kapit

Balui River

Sarikei

Rajang River

Saratok

Simanggang

Kalimantan
INDONESIA

Satellite image

Glossary

A

ACP: Assistant Commissioner of Police.

Akad nikah: The Muslim formal contract, or solemnisation, of marriage. It is normally presided over by a kadi, although in the past it was customary for the bride's biological father to perform this function.

Alliance: Coalition of political parties which began as an ad hoc alliance between the MCA and Umno in 1952, and was formalised in 1953. In 1954, the MIC joined; other Peninsula-based parties joined in the early 1970s. It was officially registered as a political party, known as the Alliance Party, in 1957, and secured parliamentary majorities at each general election until it was superseded by the Barisan Nasional in 1974.

Angkatan Sasterawan 50: 1950 Generation of Writers. Literary organisation founded by 19 young Malay poets and fiction writers in 1950. It championed several aims including to foster Malay nationalism, and to refine and promote the Malay language as the lingua franca of Malaya. It is still a registered organisation.

API: Angkatan Pemuda Insaf (Generation of Conscious Youth). The youth wing of the Malay Nationalist Party (MNP).

Asar: The third of the five daily Muslim prayer times, in the afternoon.

Asean: The Association of Southeast Asian Nations. A geopolitical and economic organisation of 10 countries located in Southeast Asia. It was formed in 1967 by Indonesia, Malaysia, the Philippines, Singapore and Thailand. Its other five present members are Brunei, Vietnam, Laos, Myanmar and Cambodia. Its aims include the promotion of economic growth, social progress, cultural development and peace in the region.

B

Bahasa Malaysia: The official name for the Malay language. Also referred to by the initialism BM.

Bajau: One of the indigenous communities of Sabah.

Baju kurung: A woman's outfit comprising a long-sleeved, loose-fitting, long blouse worn over a matching sarong.

Baju Melayu: Literally 'Malay shirt'. A traditional Malay outfit for men consisting of a long-sleeved shirt and trousers. The two parts are made out of the same type of fabric, usually cotton or a mixture of polyester and cotton.

Balairong Seri: The throne room in the palaces of the Malay Rulers. It is used for installation ceremonies, State banquets and investiture ceremonies.

Bank Negara: The Central Bank of Malaysia.

Bapa: The Malay term for father.

Barisan Nasional/BN: Political party that is itself a coalition of political parties. It superseded the Alliance in 1974 and has secured a majority of parliamentary seats at the general elections of 1974, 1978, 1982, 1986, 1990, 1995, 1999, 2004, 2008 and 2013.

Barisan Sosialis: Socialist Front. A left-wing Singaporean political party that split from the People's Action Party (PAP) in 1961. It was dissolved in 1988.

Belacan: Shrimp paste that is made from ground shrimp, fermented and sun dried. It is an essential ingredient in many Malay curries and sauces.

Berhad: Literally 'Limited'. The appellation used to denote public limited companies. Often shortened to Bhd.

Bernama: The national news agency of Malaysia which provides real-time news on subjects including politics, business, the economy, commodities and sports.

Bersanding: After the akad nikah, the Muslim couple are seated on a decorated dais to receive the blessings of family and close friends. The event is held during a wedding reception.

Bersih: Coalition for Clean and Fair Elections. It is a coalition of non-governmental organisations seeking electoral reforms in Malaysia. Since its inception in 2006, Bersih has organised three mass rallies in 2007, 2011 and 2012.

Bomoh: Malay traditional medicine man, healer or shaman. Also commonly known as a pawang.

BonusLink card: A consumer reward card which offers points that are redeemable for a range of gifts or cash vouchers.

Bubur pulut hitam: Black glutinous rice porridge.

Bumiputra: Literally 'sons of the soil'. Official ethnic definition that includes Malays as well as other indigenous ethnic groups.

Bumiputra Malaysia Finance/BMF: A deposit-taking company set up in Hong Kong. It was embroiled in a loan scandal involving the Carrian Group.

C

CBT: Criminal breach of trust.

Che: The Malay appellation for Miss, now more commonly written as Cik.

Chief Justice of Malaya: The judge who headed the High Courts in Malaya. In 1994, the position was renamed Chief Judge of the High Court in Malaya.

Chief Minister/CM: Head of the executive branch of the State Government in the States of Penang, Malacca, Sabah and Sarawak.

CID: Criminal Investigation Department, a branch of the police.

Colombo Plan: A regional organisation that embodies the concept of a collective intergovernmental effort toward the economic and social development of member countries in the Asia-Pacific region. The primary focus of Colombo Plan activities is human resources development in the Asia-Pacific region. The organisation was created following the Commonwealth Conference of Foreign Ministers held in Colombo, Sri Lanka in 1950.

Conference of Rulers: Council comprising the nine Rulers of the Malay States and the four Yang di-Pertua Negeri (formerly called Governors), a major function of which is the election of the Yang di-Pertuan Agong and his Timbalan (deputy).

Confrontation: Indonesian President Sukarno's policy of Konfrontasi from 1963 to 1966 when Indonesia attempted to crush the newly formed nation of Malaysia.

CPO: Chief Police Officer, the top-ranking policeman in a State.

Cuepacs: Congress of Unions of Employees in the Public and Civil Service. The umbrella body of unions representing employees in the government service.

D

Dacing: Weighing scales widely used in the past.

DAP: Democratic Action Party. Formed in 1965 as an offshoot of the People's Action Party after Singapore's separation from Malaysia.

Dato' Seri, Datuk: Federal and State titles granted by the Yang di-Pertuan Agong, Malay Rulers and Yang di-Pertua Negeri.

Datuk Bandar: The Malay term for mayor.

Dayak: A loose term for over 200 riverine and hill-dwelling ethnic subgroups, indigenous to and principally located in Borneo, each with its own dialect, customs, laws, territory and culture.

Dewan Bahasa dan Pustaka: Institute of Language and Literature. This Government body was established in 1956 and is responsible for coordinating the use of the Malay language in Malaysia.

Dewan Rakyat: House of Representatives, the lower House of Parliament.

DPM: Deputy Prime Minister.

DSP: Deputy Superintendent of Police.

Deposit-taking Cooperative/DTC: A company which accepts cash deposits from members who, in return, receive dividends for their money saved.

Durbar: Meeting of Malay Rulers of the Federated Malay States and their British Residents with the Resident-General and the High Commissioner. Twelve Durbars were held from 1897 to 1939.

E

Elite Highway: A 63km highway that connects the New Klang Valley Expressway to the North–South Expressway.

Emergency: The British declared a state of Emergency in June 1948. The British colonial administration and, later, the Malayan Government fought successfully against the Malayan Communist Party and its guerrilla army. The Emergency ended in 1960.

Employees Provident Fund/EPF: A Government-administered compulsory savings scheme. The EPF is intended to help employees from both private and non-pensionable public sectors save a fraction of their salary to be used if the employee is temporarily or permanently unfit to work or has reached the mandatory retirement age. Partial contributions can also be withdrawn to meet medical, education and housing needs.

Encik: The Malay appellation for Mr (see Inche).

F

Fatwa: A religious edict or ruling issued by a mufti (scholar) on syariah (Islamic law).

Federal Court: From 1963 to 1984, this was the highest judicial authority in Malaysia. In 1985, it was renamed the Supreme Court of Malaysia, with the abolition of final appeals to the Privy Council in the United Kingdom. It was once again renamed the Federal Court in 1994.

Felda/FLDA: Federal Land Development Authority. The foremost land development agency in Malaysia, it was established in 1956 to help the Government carry out rural land development schemes and to uplift the economic status and living standard of the rural community. It later became more commonly known as Felda.

Force 136: Cover name used to refer to a division of the Special Operations Executive, a secret British organisation active in World War II. Between 1941 and 1945, Force 136 operated in the areas of Southeast Asia which were occupied by the Japanese. It was led by British officers, who trained and employed indigenous agents to provide resistance by carrying out acts of sabotage and espionage.

G

Ganja: Cannabis (also known as marijuana).

Gawai: Festival celebrated at the end of harvesting season and the start of a new farming season by the Dayak community in Sarawak.

Godown: A warehouse, especially one at a dockside.

H

Hang Tuah: Legendary Malay hero who lived during the reign of Sultan Mansur Shah of the Sultanate of Malacca in the 15th century CE. He was the greatest of the laksamana, or admirals, and was known to be a ferocious fighter. Hang Tuah is held in the highest regard in present-day Malay culture, and is arguably the most well-known and illustrious figure in Malay history and literature.

Hartal: A mass protest often involving a total shutdown of workplaces, offices, shops, schools and courts of law as a form of civil disobedience.

I

Ikan duri: The Malay term for catfish.

Inche: The Malay appellation for Mr (now spelt 'Encik').

Intan: Institut Tadbiran Awam Negara or National Institute of Public Administration; a training centre for Malaysian civil servants.

Internal Security Act/ISA: A law enacted in 1960 under which, among other things, any person may be detained by the police for up to 60 days without trial for an act which allegedly threatens the security of the country. After 60 days, the detention period may be extended for periods of two years, subject to periodic reviews of the cases. The law was repealed in 2012 and replaced with the Security Offences (Special Measures) Act 2012.

Islam Hadhari: Civilisational and comprehensive Islam. In 2005, Prime Minister Dato' Seri Abdullah Ahmad Badawi formally launched a guidebook on Islam Hadhari in which he listed 10 general principles.

J

Jais: Jabatan Agama Islam Selangor or the Selangor Islamic Religious Department.

JAL: Japan Airlines.

K

Kadi: A Muslim religious officer.

Kapitan Cina: The title given to the headman of the Chinese community in early Malaya. His primary duty was to keep the peace, administer civil and criminal law, and, occasionally, collect tax when required. The position was abolished in 1902.

Kaul Festival: An annual purification and thanksgiving festival celebrated by the Melanau community in Sarawak. During the festival, unclean things such as uninvited spirits and bad influences are escorted out of the village by boats, and ceremonial offerings are placed on a decorated pole (Serahang) at the river mouth. The highlight of this festival is the 'tibau', a 20-foot high swing.

Kebaya: A traditional blouse worn by women, usually made from sheer material, batik or traditionally knitted songket fabric and worn with a sarong.

Kesas Highway: A 34.5km six-lane expressway connecting the major industrial and residential areas of the Klang Valley, namely, Kuala Lumpur, Petaling Jaya, Subang Jaya, Shah Alam and Klang, terminating at the access road to Port Klang.

Khalwat: The Malay term for close proximity. An offence under Islamic law committed by unmarried couples in situations where intimate contact is possible.

Khat: Islamic calligraphy.

KLSE: Kuala Lumpur Stock Exchange. It changed its name to Bursa Malaysia in 2004.

Kompang: A popular Malay traditional instrument. Resembling and played in a manner similar to the tambourine, the kompang is approximately 40cm in diameter, with a narrow circular frame made out of the dried wood of the balau tree that is covered with a goat hide skin on one side.

KTM: Keretapi Tanah Melayu Berhad or Malayan Railway.

Kuah pecal: A chilli-based sauce used for salad dishes.

Kuah satay: The peanut-based sauce that is served with satay (seasoned and barbecued meat).

Kuay teow, fried: Literally 'fried flat noodles'. A popular noodle dish made from flat rice noodles fried over a very high heat together with light and dark soy sauce, chilli, prawns, cockles, egg, bean sprouts and chives.

L

Laksa assam: Noodles served in sour fish soup flavoured with tamarind.

Land Dayak: Term previously used to describe the Bidayuh, one of the indigenous peoples of Sarawak.

LCE examination: Lower Certificate of Education examination for secondary school students in Year Nine.

Lebuhraya Damansara–Puchong: The Damansara–Puchong Expressway which stretches 40km from Sri Damansara in the north, connecting Petaling Jaya and Puchong and Putrajaya in the south.

LNG: Liquefied natural gas.

Loh shee fun: A variety of Chinese noodles.

Lord President: The title of the head of the judiciary in Malaysia from 1963 until 1994. The title is now known as the Chief Justice of Malaysia.

M

MACC: Acronym for Malaysian Anti-Corruption Commission. Its predecessor was the Anti-Corruption Agency. In 2008, Prime Minister Abdullah Ahmad Badawi's government approved the formation of the MACC which was supposed to be independent of government interference.

Magsaysay Award: The award created in 1957 to commemorate Ramon Magsaysay, the late president of the Philippines (1907–1957). Prizes are given to Asian individuals and organisations for achieving excellence in six categories: Government Service; Public Service; Community Leadership; Journalism, Literature and Creative Communication Arts; Peace and International Understanding; and Emergent Leadership.

Malayan Nationalist Party/MNP: A left-wing political party.

Malaysia Boleh: A slogan which loosely translated means 'Malaysia Can Do It!' It was adopted by the Government under Prime Minister Dato' Seri Dr Mahathir Mohamad in the 1980s.

Malaysia Plans: Five-year plans to promote the welfare of all citizens, and improve the living conditions in rural areas, particularly among low-income groups.

Mara: Majlis Amanah Rakyat or Council of Trust for the Indigenous Peoples. The council was incorporated as a statutory body in 1966 under an Act of Parliament and entrusted with the responsibility to promote, stimulate, facilitate and undertake the economic and social development of Bumiputras particularly in rural areas.

Mardi: Malaysian Agricultural Research and Development Institute. The institute was set up with the primary aim of developing and promoting new and improved technologies in agriculture. These technologies are intended to increase productivity and efficiency, thereby modernising the agricultural sector as well as maximising farming income.

MAS: Malaysian Airline System, now Malaysia Airlines.

MCA: Malaysian Chinese Association, originally the Malayan Chinese Association. The major ethnic Chinese-based political party.

Mee rebus: Literally 'boiled noodles'. A Malay-inspired noodle dish made of yellow egg noodles, with a spicy, slightly sweet, curry-like gravy.

Mejar (B): A retired major in the armed forces. The 'B' stands for 'bersara' or 'retired' in English.

Mej-Jen: A major-general in the armed forces.

Melayu baru: Literally 'new Malays'. It refers to the emerging middle-class Malays.

Melayu lama: The older generation of Malays.

Menteri Besar/MB: The head of the executive branch of the State Government in each of the nine States ruled by a Malay Ruler. The office is elective, with the leader of the largest party in the State legislative assemblies assuming the post.

Mercy Malaysia: Volunteer relief organisation providing medical and humanitarian services locally and abroad.

MIC: Malaysian Indian Congress, originally the Malayan Indian Congress. The major ethnic Indian-based political party.

MSAB: Maktab Sultan Abu Bakar, which is also known as English College, a premier school located in Johor Bahru.

MTUC: Malaysian Trades Union Congress. The umbrella organisation of unions in the private sector.

Mukim: A subdivision of a daerah (district).

N

NAAFI: Navy, Army and Air Force Institute. It was created by the British Government in 1921 to run recreational establishments for the Armed Forces, and to sell duty-free goods to servicemen and their families.

Nasi lemak: A traditional Malay breakfast dish of rice cooked in coconut milk and pandanus (screwpine) leaves served with fried anchovies, toasted peanuts, sambal and sambal prawns or fish.

National school: A government school where the medium of instruction is Bahasa Malaysia.

National-type school: A government-aided school that uses Mandarin or Tamil as the medium of instruction.

New Economic Policy/NEP: The socioeconomic restructuring, affirmative action programme launched by the Government in 1971 under then Prime Minister Tun Abdul Razak. The NEP ended in 1990, and was succeeded by the National Development Policy in 1991.

Non-Aligned Movement/NAM: Formed in 1961, this organisation originally comprised nations aiming to form a Third World force through a policy of non-alignment with the United States and the Soviet Union. Its focus has now shifted away from essentially political issues to the advocacy of solutions to global economic and other problems.

Nyonya: Women of the Baba-Nyonya community in Malaysia. Also known as Peranakan or Straits Chinese (named after the Straits Settlements), they are the descendants of the very early Chinese immigrants to the region who have partially adopted the Malay language and customs.

O

OCM: Olympic Council of Malaysia.

OCPD: Officer in charge of police district.

OPP3: Third Outline Perspective Plan. The long-term plan in which the Government outlines the policies and direction of Malaysia's development for 2001 till 2010.

Orang Asli: The indigenous minority peoples of Peninsular Malaysia. The name, a Malay term which transliterates as 'original people' or 'first people', is a collective term introduced by anthropologists and administrators for the 18 ethnic subgroups generally classified for official purposes as Negrito, Senoi and Proto-Malay.

P

PABX: A semi-automated telephone exchange system serving a particular business or office.

Padang: The Malay term for field.

Pakatan Rakyat: Opposition coalition meaning 'People's Pact', it consists of Parti Keadilan Rakyat, DAP and PAS.

Parang: The Malay term for machete.

Parti Bansa Dayak Sarawak/PBDS: Sarawak Native People's Party, a Sarawak-based political party, now deregistered. It was a member of the BN coalition.

Parti Keadilan Rakyat: People's Justice Party; formed in 2003 as a result of a merger between Parti Keadilan and Parti Rakyat Malaysia. Parti Keadilan was formed in 1999 following the sacking and arrest of former Deputy Prime Minister Dato' Seri Anwar Ibrahim.

Parti Rakyat/Socialist Party: One of the oldest political parties in Malaysia, founded in 1955.

Pas: Parti Islam SeMalaysia, formerly known as Pan-Malaysian Islamic Party (PMIP).

Pata: Pacific Asia Travel Association.

PBS: Parti Bersatu Sabah (United Sabah Party).

Pekemas: Parti Keadilan Masyarakat Malaysia or Social Justice Party of Malaysia. This political party was founded by Dr Tan Chee Khoon after he left Gerakan in 1972 following its decision to join the Barisan Nasional. Upon his retirement from politics in 1978, most of Pekemas' supporters defected to the DAP.

Permodalan Nasional Berhad/PNB: The Government's investment corporation with extensive investments in every major component of the Malaysian economy including substantial holdings in companies involved in sectors such as finance, plantations, manufacturing and property.

Pesta: The Malay term for festival.

Petronas: Acronym for Petroliam Nasional Berhad, an oil and gas company wholly owned by the Malaysian Government. Petronas is vested with all of the oil and gas resources in Malaysia and is entrusted with the responsibility of developing and adding value to these resources. It has grown to be an integrated international oil and gas company with business interests in 31 countries.

PLO: Palestine Liberation Organisation.

PPP: People's Progressive Party. It was formed in 1953 by the Seenivasagam brothers mainly as an opposition party to the Alliance. In 1974, PPP became one of the founding members of the Barisan Nasional.

Privy Council: During the British colonial era, decisions of the Malayan courts could be taken on appeal to the Privy Council in London. The Privy Council continued to function as the highest court in Malaya even after Independence. Privy Council appeals on criminal and constitutional matters were abolished on 1 January 1978. Civil appeals were abolished on 1 January 1985, whereupon the Federal Court, then renamed the Supreme Court, became the final court of appeal.

Prof Madya: Malay for associate professor.

PSRM: Parti Sosialis Rakyat Malaysia (Malaysian People's Socialist Party).

Puteri Umno: An Umno wing whose membership is open to young women.

R

RAAF: Royal Australian Air Force.

RAF: The British Royal Air Force.

Raja Permaisuri Agong: The consort of the Yang di-Pertuan Agong, who takes precedence immediately after him.

Red Crescent Society: The Malaysian equivalent of the Red Cross.

Rela: Ikatan Relawan Rakyat Malaysia (People's Volunteer Corps). It consists of volunteers who supplement the duties of the police and other Government enforcement agencies.

Remove Classes: Students from national-type primary schools spend one year in Remove Classes for extra lessons to equip them to enter the national secondary school system.

RMAF: Royal Malaysian Air Force.

Roti canai: A type of flatbread that is usually eaten with lentil curry. It is a favourite snack food in Malaysia, and is served 24 hours—for breakfast, lunch, dinner and as a midnight snack.

RTM: Radio Televisyen Malaysia, the Government-owned public broadcaster which operates a number of radio and television stations.

S

SAC II: Senior Assistant Commissioner II, a police rank.

Samsu: A locally distilled potent and cheap spirit. It typically contains between 37 and 70 per cent alcohol.

Sarong kebaya: (See Kebaya).

Sdn Bhd: Private limited. The appellation used to denote private limited companies.

SDP: Social Democratic Party.

SEA Games: Southeast Asian Games. A biennial multi-sport event involving participants from the 11 countries of Southeast Asia. It started as the SEAP Games in 1959, and changed its name to the SEA Games in 1977 with the inclusion of more participating nations.

Secretariat/Secretariat Building: The building now known as Bangunan Sultan Abdul Samad was Dataran Merdeka (Merdeka Square) in Kuala Lumpur.

Sepak raga: A traditional game in which players position themselves in a circle and attempt to keep a rattan ball in the air using their feet and various parts of the body except the hands.

Sesco: Sarawak Electricity Supply Corporation.

Sessions Court: Subordinate court that stands above the magistrates' courts in the Malaysian judicial system.

Shia: The second largest Islamic sect in the world, after Sunni Islam. Malaysia is largely Sunni Muslim.

Silat: The Malay art of self-defence, which has many forms, styles or branches.

SIM card: Subscriber Identity Module card. A removable smart card for mobile phones.

SMJK: Sekolah Menengah Jenis Kebangsaan. See national-type school.

SMS: Short Message Service, often called text messaging, a means of sending short messages to and from mobile phones.

Snap: Sarawak National Action Party.

Socso: Social Security Organisation. A compulsory scheme to provide benefits for workers who meet with accidents in the course of their employment.

Southeast Asia Treaty Organisation/SEATO: Alliance of Australia, France, Britain, New Zealand, Pakistan, the Philippines, Thailand and the United States organised in 1954 to oppose further Communist gains in Southeast Asia.

Sprint Highway: Three highway links totalling 26.5km in Kuala Lumpur.

Suhakam: The acronym for the Human Rights Commission of Malaysia. Its inaugural meeting was held on 24 April 2000.

SUPP: Sarawak United People's Party.

Supreme Court: (See Federal Court).

T

Tan Sri: The second most senior federal title used to denote recipients of the PMN (Panglima Mangku Negara) and the PSM (Panglima Setia Mahkota).

Thaipusam: An annual Hindu festival.

Thomas Cup: An international badminton competition contested by men's national teams. Only Malaysia, Indonesia and China have won the tournament since its inception in 1948.

Tun: The most senior federal title awarded to recipients of either the SMN (Seri Maharaja Mangku Negara) or SSM (Seri Setia Mahkota).

U

Ujian Pencapaian Sekolah Rendah/UPSR: The Primary School Assessment Examination which Year Six students must take before entering secondary school.

Umno: United Malays National Organisation. The main ethnic Malay political party.

Usno: United Sabah National Organisation.

W

Wayang: Literally 'a show'. Wayang kulit means 'puppet show' while wayang gambar means 'film show'.

White Rajahs: Rulers of Sarawak from 1841 to 1941. The White Rajahs were James Brooke, his nephew Charles Brooke and Charles's son Vyner Brooke.

Y

Yang di-Pertuan Agong: The Head of State of Malaysia.

Yang di-Pertua Negeri: The State Governor.

Index

Index

Picture Credits

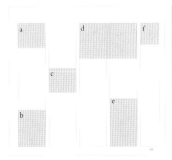

The list below gives the page numbers on which images appear. The letter after the page number identifies which image on that page is being referred to. As demonstrated in the diagram (above), the images on each page are identified by *a*, *b*, *c*, etc.; the sequence runs down from top to bottom in each column in turn, starting with the column furthest to the left. Where an image spans two columns, the column to the left is the one that matters. Pictures within special features are identified by their page number plus a description or number.

Every effort has been made to trace copyright holders. In the event of errors or omissions, appropriate credit will be made in future printings of the *Chronicle of Malaysia*.

Agence France-Presse (AFP) 222a; 229b; 261d; 263b; 279c; 282d; 292f; 299c; 316c; 317c; 318a–b; 321d; 323c; 324a–b; 327d; 330b; 334d; 335b; 335d–e; 336c; 337a; 338a–b; 344b; 349a; 350d; 352c; 355d

Ahmad Sarji 57d; 95b

Arkib Negara Malaysia 21; 26a; 31; 39e; 41d; 45b; 50b; 51b; 51d; 59b; 60b–c; 61a; 69e; 72b; 75d; 78e; 82d; 83a; 84d; 84f; 87a; 88a; 90a–c; 93a; 105a; 109d; 118c; 119a

Asiaweek 256d–e

Associated Press (AP) 118a; 258d; 262c; 264c; 271d; 294c; 306a; 317c; 320c; 322b; 323a; 327b; 329a; 329c; 329e; 334a; 340b; 344d; 345d; 345f; 349d

Badan Warisan Malaysia 165e–h

Morton Beebe/Corbis 112d

Bernama 5; 172b; 175b; 181b; 182a; 193d; 223b; 224d; 275a; 279e; 282a–b; 284d; 285b–c; 286d; 287b–c; 288a; 288c; 289c; 290e; 292a; 293b; 293d; 294a; 295a–b; 296a–b; 296e; 297b; 298b; 298d; 299b; 300a–b; 300d; 301a; 301c–e; 302a; 303a; 304a; 304d; 307c–d; 308b; 309c; 312a–b; 312d; 313c; 314d; 319b; 321c; 323b; 325c; 334c; 347a; 347d; 351c; 354a–b; 354d

© Bettmann/Corbis 62a; 75e; 78c; 94b; 112c; 115a

Eddi Boehnke/zefa/Corbis 304b

BOH Plantations Sdn Bhd 100a

Bukit Merah Laketown Resort 270b

© Bureau L.A. Collection/Sygma/ Corbis 261a

Chan Looi Tat 259e

Cheah Jin Seng 14

Crown Copyright © 289d

Richard Curtis 318c

Robert Dowling/Corbis 173b

EDM Archives 41c; 63b; 64b; 262g; 316b; 326c; 339b

John Falconer 15

Ronald Fauvel@hbl Network 352d

© Najlah Feanny/Corbis Saba 249d

Federal Information Department, Sabah 41e

Federal Information Department, Sarawak 24a; 40b–c

P.K. Fong 16

Paul Gadd/Corbis 262c

Getty Images 35a; 45c; 107d; 117a; 122b; 144b; 161a; 206c; 254a–b; 257a; 262b; 265c; 266d; 273c; 275b; 277a; 298e; 300c; 301b; 302c; 303d; 304e; 311a; 313a–b; 314a; 317a; 319a; 324c; 326b; 341c; 345e; 347e; 350c; 351d

David Alan Harvey 127e; 129a–c; 129e

Heng Kim Song 256c

Hijjas Kasturi Sendirian/Azrul K. Abdullah 214a

Institut Kefahaman Islam Malaysia (IKIM) 231b

Isma Yusoof/L'Agenda Productions 320b

Jabatan Penerangan Malaysia 17; 22a; 47d; 49c; 56c; 57b; 59a; 80b; 89c; 93b; 97b; 107a; 123a; 141a; 149b; 174b; 196b; 206b; 235b; 278c

Jabatan Perdana Menteri 292d

Johor Heritage Foundation 262f

C.W. Kee 174a

Lat 32–33; 44c; 101d; 111b; 125c; 126b; 151d; 155c; 156b; 159e; 160b; 161d; 165a; 168a; 171a; 177b; 179a; 194c; 205e; 208a; 215d; 220c; 228b; 239c; 240b; 245b; 250c; 253c; 361

James Lee Peek Kuan 235a

Dr Lee Siow Ming 295c

C.Y. Leow 161e; 230d; 261e

Danny Lim 315a

Dato' Seri Lim Chong Keat 275d

Tan Sri Dato' Dr Lim Kok Wing 158c; 176a

M. Magendran 253a

Majlis Sukan Negara Malaysia 115e

Malaysia Tenpin Bowling Congress 287d

Malaysian Remote Sensing Agency (satellite image) 363

Measat Satellite Systems Sdn Bhd 243e

Ministry of Information, Communications and the Arts (courtesy of National Archives of Singapore) 25a; 53e

Muzium Negara 39a–b

Muzium Polis Diraja Malaysia 112a

Muzium Sejarah Nasional 41a

Nanyang Siang Pau 297a

National Geographic/Getty Images 2

National Geographic Society 42a–d; 43a–h

New Straits Times Press (Malaysia) Bhd 8; 10; 18–19; 20; 22b–c; 23a–g; 24b; 35b–e; 36a; 37a–c; 39c–d; 40a; 44a–b; 45a; 45d–e; 46a–b; 47a–c; 48a–b; 49a–b; 50d; 51a; 51c; 51e; 52a–c; 53a; 53c–d; 53f; 54a; 54c–d; 55c; 56a–b; 57a; 57c; 57e; 61a–c; 62c; 63a; 63c–e; 64a; 64d; 65a–b; 65d; 66a; 69a; 69c–d; 70b–c; 71; 72a; 72c–d; 74a–d; 75a–b; 76a–c; 77a–d; 78a–b; 79b–d; 80a; 81a–b; 82b–c; 83b; 83d–e; 84a–b; 84e; 85a–b; 87c; 88c; 91a–b; 91d; 92a–b; 94a; 95a; 95f; 96a–c; 97a; 97c; 98a; 99a; 99c; 101a; 103a–e; 104a; 106c–d; 107b–c; 107e; 108a; 108d; 108f; 109a–b; 109e; 110a–b; 112b; 113a–c; 114a–b; 115b–d; 118b; 119b–d; 120a–c; 121a–b; 121d–e; 122c; 123c–d; 124a–c; 126c; 127a–b; 128b; 129d; 130a–b; 131a; 132a; 132c; 133a; 133c; 134a–b; 135a; 136a; 137a–b; 139a; 139c; 142b–c; 143b–c; 145b; 145d–e; 149a; 151a; 152a; 152c; 153c; 154e; 155d; 157c; 158a; 158d; 159a; 159c; 160a; 160c; 162a–b; 163a–b; 163d; 175a; 178b; 181a; 181d; 185b–c; 187d–e; 189b–c; 191a; 193b; 194a; 194d; 199c; 200a; 201a–b; 201e; 202a; 207b; 207e; 213b; 213d; 217b; 218d; 219a–b; 219d–e; 220b; 220d; 221a; 223d; 224c; 225b–d; 226b; 230c; 231a; 231c; 232c–d; 236a; 237a; 237e; 243b; 244a; 247a; 247d; 248b; 249a–c; 249e; 250d; 251a–b; 252b; 255a; 255c–d; 260d; 260f; 261c; 262a; 263a; 266a; 267b; 268e; 282g; 283b–c; 285d; 291e; 299d; 306b; 307g; 308d; 313c; 321a; 323e; 326a; 329d; 330a; 331a–d; 331f; 331h; 332a; 332c;

333e–f; 335a; 335c; 336b; 337b; 337d; 338c; 339c–d; 339f; 340a; 340c; 341b; 341e; 342b–d; 343d; 344a; 344e; 346a–b; 347b–c; 348a–c; 349b; 350f; 351a–b; 351e; 352b; 353a–d; 354 (bar); 354c; 354e; 355a–c; 355e–f

Dr Nobuyoshi Ohba, Malaysian Nature Society 296d

Nurshafenath Shaharuddin 89d

S. Paramsothy 278a

Parti Rakyat Malaysia 46c

Jacques Pavlovsky/Sygma/Corbis 139b

Pelanduk Publications (M) Sdn Bhd 89b

Private collection 37d; 38b–c; 50a; 50c; 53b; 54b; 55b; 58a–b; 58d; 60a; 61d; 62b; 67b; 68a–c; 70a; 73a; 73c; 79a; 85c; 86a; 87b; 87d–e; 88b; 89a; 91c; 94c; 95c–e; 97d–e; 98c; 98e; 99b; 101b–c; 102a–b; 105b–c; 106a; 108e; 111a; 114c; 116c; 117b; 119e; 123b; 130c; 136b; 140a–c; 141c; 144a; 147c; 155e; 156a; 160d–e; 161b; 171d–h; 176c; 178d; 182c; 183c–d; 186c; 187c; 188b; 190a–b; 191c–f; 192b; 209e; 211d; 220a; 227d; 230b; 232b; 250a; 257b; 259b

Reuters 230a; 260e; 267e; 269a; 271c; 274a; 278b; 279b; 281b–d; 295e; 302d; 303c; 311e; 312c; 312e; 313d; 314c; 315c; 321b; 325e; 327f; 330c; 333d; 339a; 341a; 349c; 350a–b; 350e

Patrick Robert/Sygma/Corbis 280e

Photograph courtesy of Sabah State Library 22d

Sarawak Tribune 41b; 61e; 83c; 228c; 268c

Datin Paduka Sharifah Mazlina 291c

Sin Chew Daily 243a; 243c; 259d; 274b; 297d; 307a

Singapore Press Holdings Ltd ('SPH')/The Straits Times. Permission required for reproduction. 65c; 78d

Ravi John Smith 248a; 267a

STR/AFP/Getty Images 311d; 316a

Samsul Said/AFP/Getty Images 317d

Star Publications (Malaysia) Bhd 104b–c; 125a; 126a; 127c–d; 128a; 132b; 133b; 133d–e; 138b; 139d–e; 141b; 145a; 145c; 146; 147a–b; 148a–b; 150a–b; 151b–c; 151e; 152b; 153a–b; 154a–d; 155a; 155f; 156c; 157b; 157c; 158b; 158e; 159d; 161c; 163c; 163e; 164a–e; 165b–d; 166a–c; 167a–f; 168b–d; 169a–b; 169d–e; 170a–c; 172a; 173a; 173c; 174c; 175c–e; 176b; 177a; 177c–d; 178a; 178c; 178e; 179b; 180a–g; 181c; 181e; 182d–e; 183a–b; 183e; 184a–d;

185a; 186a; 187a–b; 190c; 191b; 192c; 193a; 193c; 193e; 194b; 195a–b; 196a; 196c; 197a; 197c; 198b–e; 199a–b; 199e; 200b–c; 200e; 201c–d; 202b–c; 203a–b; 204a–d; 205a–d; 205f; 206a; 207a; 207c; 208b; 209a–d; 210a–b; 211b–c; 212a–b; 213a; 213c; 213e; 214b; 215a–c; 216a; 217a; 217c–d; 218a–c; 218e; 219c; 221b–d; 222b; 223a; 223c; 224a–b; 225a; 225e; 226a; 226c; 227a–c; 228a; 229a; 229c–d; 231d–e; 232a; 233a–b; 234a–d; 237b–d; 238a–c; 239a–b; 240a; 240c; 241a; 241c–d; 242b–d; 243d; 245c; 246b–c; 247b–c; 248c–d; 250b; 251c–e; 252a; 253b; 255b; 255e; 256a; 258a–c; 259a; 259c; 260a–c; 262d; 264a–b; 265a–b; 265d; 266b–c; 266e; 267c–d; 268a–b; 268d; 269b; 270a; 270c–d; 271a–b; 272a–e; 273a; 273d–e; 275c; 275e; 276a–c; 277b–d; 278d; 279d; 280a–d; 281a; 282c; 282e–f; 283a; 283d; 284a; 284c; 285a; 285e; 286a–c; 287a; 287e; 288b; 289a–b; 290a–b; 290d; 290f; 291a–b; 291d; 292e; 293a; 293c; 294b; 295d; 295f; 296c; 297c; 298a; 298c; 298f; 299a; 299e; 302b; 303b; 304c; 305a–e; 306c; 307b; 307e–f; 307h; 308c; 309a–b; 310a–e; 311b; 312f; 314b; 317b; 319c; 320a; 321e–f; 322c; 323d; 325a–b; 325d; 327a; 327c; 327e; 328a; 329b; 331e; 332b; 333a–c; 334b; 336a; 337c; 339e; 340d; 341d; 342a; 343a–c; 343e; 344c; 345a–c; 346c–d; 352a

Tenaga Nasional Berhad 135b

Tengku Bahar/AFP/Getty Images 311c; 315b

The Picture Desk (AFP) 279a

The Star/Bernama 155b; 157a; 157d; 158f; 159b; 159f; 171c; 182b; 186b; 188a; 189d; 192a; 197b; 197d; 198a; 199d; 200d; 203c; 211a; 212c; 216d; 220e; 236b; 241b; 242a; 244b–c; 245a; 246a; 246d; 261b; 262h

The Star/Guang Ming Daily 284b

The Star/Tamil Nesan 308a

Time 36b; 256b

Tun Hussein Onn Memorial 125b; 136c; 142a

Tunku Abdul Rahman Memorial 6; 55a; 64c; 69b; 73b; 82a; 84c

UN Photo 29a

UPI 26b; 28; 29b; 38a; 75c; 116b

Utusan Borneo 338d

Utusan Melayu (Malaysia) Berhad 58c; 66b; 67a; 86b; 90b; 91e; 93c; 98b; 98d; 100b; 106b; 107f; 108b–c; 109c; 116a; 121c; 122a; 131b; 135c; 138a; 143a; 169c; 207d; 216b–c; 229e; 273b; 292b–c; 318d; 322a; 328b–c; 331g

Nik Wheeler/Corbis 189a

WWF–Malaysia 290c

1963 1964 1965 1966 1967 1968 1969 1970 1971 1972 1973 1974 1975 1976 1977 1978 1979 1980 1981 1982 1983 1984 1985 1986